CORPORATE GOVERNANCE

ICSA STUDY TEXT

CORPORATE GOVERNANCE

SIXTH EDITION

BRIAN COYLE AND TRINA HILL

icsa

The Governance
Institute

First published as Corporate Governance by Brian Coyle (ICSA Publishing Limited, 2010)

Published by
ICSA Publishing Limited
Saffron House,
6–10 Kirby Street,
London EC1N 8TS

Designed and typeset by Paul Barrett Book Production, Cambridge
Printed in Great Britain by Hobbs the Printers Ltd, Totton, Hampshire

British Cataloguing in Publication Data
A catalogue record for this book is available from the British Library.

ISBN 978 1 86072 7023

Contents

How to use this study text

ICSA study texts developed to support ICSA's Chartered Secretaries Qualifying Scheme (CSQS) follow a standard format and include a range of navigational, self-testing and illustrative features to help you get the most out of the support materials.

Each text is divided into three main sections:

- introductory material;
- the text itself, divided into Parts and Chapters; and
- additional reference information.

The sections below show you how to find your way around the text and make the most of its features.

Introductory material

The introductory section of each text includes a full contents list and the module syllabus which reiterates the module aims, learning outcomes and syllabus content for the module in question.

Where relevant, the introductory section will also include a list of acronyms and abbreviations or a list of legal cases for reference.

The text itself

Each **part** opens with a list of the chapters to follow, an overview of what will be covered and learning outcomes for the part. Some part openings also include a case study, which introduces a real-world scenario related to the topics covered in that part. Questions based on this case and designed to test the application of theory in practice appear in the chapters and at part endings (see below).

Every **chapter** opens with a list of the topics covered and an introduction specific to that chapter. Chapters are structured to allow students to break the content down into manageable sections for study. Each chapter ends with a summary of key content to reinforce understanding.

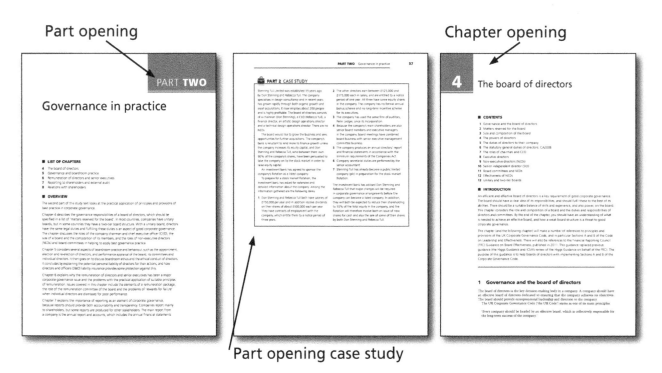

Part opening

Chapter opening

Part opening case study

Features

The text is enhanced by a range of illustrative and self-testing features to assist understanding and to help you prepare for the examination. Each feature is presented in a standard format, so that you will become familiar with how to use them in your study.

The texts also include tables, figures and checklists and, where relevant, sample documents and forms.

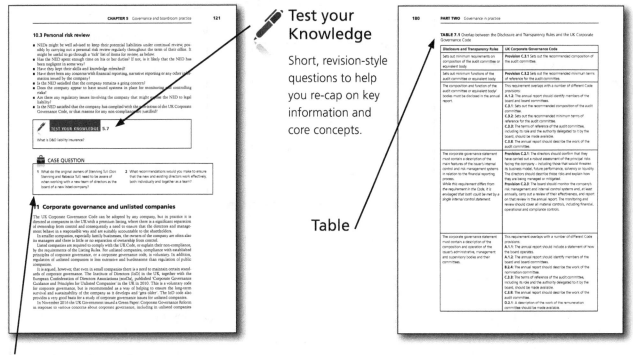

Test your Knowledge

Short, revision-style questions to help you re-cap on key information and core concepts.

Table

Case Questions

Case questions relate to the part opening case study, encouraging you to apply the theory you're learning to a real-world business scenario.

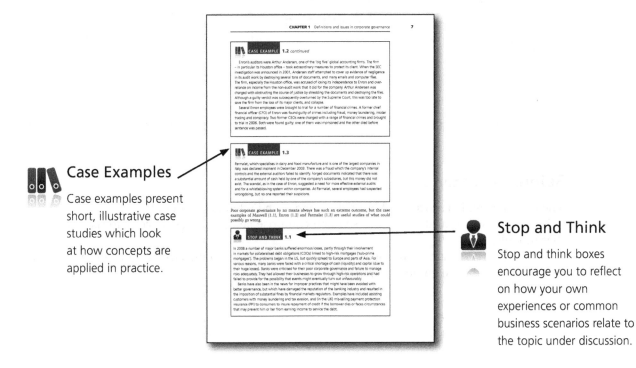

Case Examples

Case examples present short, illustrative case studies which look at how concepts are applied in practice.

Stop and Think

Stop and think boxes encourage you to reflect on how your own experiences or common business scenarios relate to the topic under discussion.

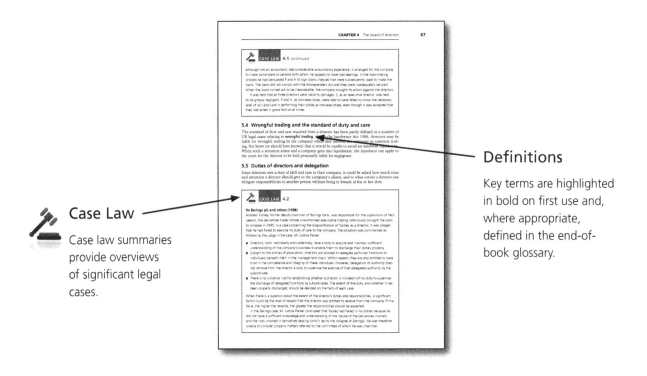

Case Law

Case law summaries provide overviews of significant legal cases.

Definitions

Key terms are highlighted in bold on first use and, where appropriate, defined in the end-of-book glossary.

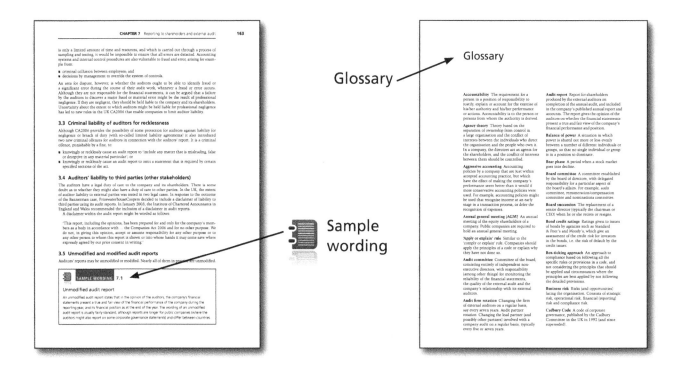

Glossary

Sample wording

Reference material

The text ends with a range of additional guidance and reference material.

Most texts will include appendices which comprise additional reference material specific to that module.

Other reference material includes a glossary of key terms, a directory of further reading and web resources and a comprehensive index.

Corporate Governance syllabus

Module outline and aims

The aim of the Corporate Governance module is to equip the Chartered Secretary with the knowledge and key skills necessary to act as adviser to governing authorities across the private, public and voluntary sectors. The advice of the Chartered Secretary will include all aspects of the governance obligations of organisations, covering not only legal duties, but also applicable and recommended standards of best practice.

The module will enable the development of a sound understanding of corporate governance law and practice in a national and international context. It will also enable you to support the development of good governance and stakeholder dialogue throughout the organisation, irrespective of sector, being aware of legal obligations and best practice.

Learning outcomes

On successful completion of this module, you will be able to:

- Appraise the frameworks underlying governance law and practice in a national and international context.
- Advise on governance issues across all sectors, ensuring that the pursuit of strategic objectives is in line with regulatory developments and developments in best practice.
- Analyse and evaluate situations in which governance problems arise and provide recommendations for solutions.
- Demonstrate how general concepts of governance apply in a given situation or given circumstances.
- From the perspective of a Chartered Secretary, provide authoritative and professional advice on matters of corporate governance.
- Assess the relationship between governance and performance within organisations.
- Apply the principles of risk management and appraise the significance of risk management for good governance.
- Compare the responsibilities of organisations to different stakeholder groups, and advise on issues of ethical conduct and the application of principles of sustainability and corporate responsibility.

Syllabus content

Candidates will be required to discuss in detail statutory rules and the principles or provisions of governance codes, and apply them to specific situations or case studies. Candidates will also be expected to understand the role of the company secretary in providing support and advice regarding the application of best governance practice. Although the syllabus presents governance issues mainly from the perspective of companies, candidates may be required to apply similar principles to non-corporate entities, such as those in the public and voluntary sectors.

Governance is a continually developing subject, and good candidates will be aware of any major developments that have occurred at the time they take their examination.

The detailed syllabus set out here has a strong UK emphasis, and it is expected that UK corporate governance will be the focus of study for most candidates. A good knowledge of the principles and provisions of the UK Corporate Governance Code will therefore be required, together with any supporting Guidance on the Code published from time to time by the Financial Reporting Council. However, a good knowledge and understanding of the code of corporate governance in another country will be acceptable in answers, provided that candidates indicate which code they are referring to in their answer.

The UK Corporate Governance Code ('the Code'; formerly 'the UK Combined Code') is subject to frequent review and amendment by the Financial Reporting Council. You are advised to check the student newsletter and student news area of the ICSA website to find out when revisions to the Code will first be examined.

Candidates will not be required to learn in detail codes of governance in countries other than the UK, although they will be given credit for referring to the code in their own country outside the UK. Similarly they will not be required to learn in detail codes of governance for unquoted companies, public sector bodies or not-for-profit organisations. However, they must be prepared to discuss governance issues in these organisations, and be aware of how these issues differ from corporate governance in listed companies.

General principles of corporate governance – weighting 10%

The nature of corporate governance and purpose of good corporate governance:

- Separation of ownership and control.
- Agency theory and corporate governance.
- Stakeholder theory and corporate governance.

Key issues in corporate governance:

- Leadership and effectiveness of the board; accountability; risk management and internal control; remuneration of directors and senior executives; relations with shareholders and other stakeholders; and sustainability.

Principles of good corporate governance:

- G20/OECD Principles of Corporate Governance.

Framework of corporate governance:

- Legal framework.
- Rules-based and principles-based approaches.
- Codes of corporate governance and their application: UK Corporate Governance Code.
- Concept of 'comply or explain'.

Governance and ethics:

- Potential consequences of poor corporate governance.

The board of directors and leadership – weighting 10%

- Role of the board.
- Division of responsibilities on the board.
- Matters reserved for the board.
- Role and responsibilities of the board chairman.
- Role and responsibilities of the chief executive officer.
- Role and responsibilities of non-executive directors.
- Independence and non-executive directors.
- Role of the Senior Independent Director.
- Statutory duties of directors.
- Rules on dealing in shares by directors: insider dealing.
- Liability of directors: directors' and officers' liability insurance.
- Unitary and two-tier boards.

Effectiveness of the board of directors – weighting 15%

- Role of the company secretary in governance.
- Size, structure and composition of the board: board balance.
- Board committees.
- Appointments to the board: role of the Nomination Committee; succession and board refreshment.

- Induction and development of directors.
- Information and support for board members.
- Performance evaluation of the board, its committees and individual directors.
- Re-election of board members.

Governance and accountability – weighting 10%

- Financial and business reporting and corporate governance.
- The need for accountability and transparency.
- The need for reliable financial reporting: true and fair view, going concern statement.
- Responsibility for the financial statements and discovery of fraud.
- Role of the external auditors.
- Auditor independence; threats to auditor independence; auditors and non-audit work.
- The Audit Committee: roles, responsibilities, composition; FRC Guidance.
- Reporting on non-financial issues: narrative reporting; strategic report.

Remuneration of directors and senior executives – weighting 10%

- Principles of remuneration structure: elements of remuneration.
- Remuneration policy.
- Elements of a remuneration package and the design of performance-related remuneration.
  - Candidates will not be required to discuss performance targets in detail, but need to be aware of short-term incentives (e.g. cash bonuses) and longer-term bonuses (share grants, share options). They also need to be able to discuss the difficulties in designing a suitable remuneration structure.
- Role of the Remuneration Committee.
- Compensation for loss of office.
- Disclosures of directors' remuneration – candidates will be expected to show an awareness of issues relating to the disclosure of directors' remuneration in the annual report and accounts, but not the detail (e.g. not the detail of the directors' remuneration report).
- Shareholder approval of incentive schemes and voting rights with regard to remuneration.
- The recommendations or guidelines of institutional investor groups on matters relating to directors' remuneration.

Relations with shareholders – weighting 10%

- The equitable treatment of shareholders; protection for minority shareholders.
- Rights and powers of shareholders.
- Dialogue and communications with institutional shareholders (companies) or major stakeholders.
- Role of institutional investor organisations (or major stakeholders):
  - in the UK, the role of the Association of British Insurers (ABI) and Pensions and Lifetime Savings Association (PLSA) and the relevance for corporate governance;
  - UK Stewardship Code.
- Constructive use of the annual general meeting.
- Shareholder activism.
- Candidates will be required to have an awareness of the benefits of electronic communications between companies and their shareholders, but will not be required to know the detailed law and regulations on electronic communications.

Risk management and internal control – weighting 15%

The nature of risks facing companies and other organisations: categories of risk:

- The difference between 'business risk' and 'governance risk' (internal control risk).
- Internal control risks: financial, operational and compliance risks.
- Elements in an internal control system: Turnbull Guidance.

Risk and return; identifying, monitoring and reporting key risk areas; risk appetite and risk tolerance; responsibility of the board of directors.

Responsibilities for risk management and internal control: board of directors, executive management, audit committee, internal and external auditors:

- Risk Committees of the board.
- Risk management committees.
- Role of internal audit within an internal control system.

Disaster recovery plans.

Whistle-blowing policy and procedures:

- ICSA best practice on whistle-blowing procedures.

Reviewing and reporting on the effectiveness of the risk management and internal control systems.

Corporate social responsibility and sustainability – weighting 10%

The nature of sustainability.
The nature of corporate responsibility and corporate citizenship.

Corporate responsibility and stakeholders:

- Internal and external stakeholders.

Elements of corporate social responsibility: employees, the environment, human rights, communities and social welfare, social investment, ethical conduct.
Reputation risk: placing a value on reputation.
Formulating and implementing a policy for corporate social responsibility.
Reporting to stakeholders on sustainability and corporate social responsibility issues:

- Voluntary social and environmental reporting.
- Sustainability reporting: triple bottom line; Global Reporting Initiative (GRI) Guidelines.
- Integrated reporting.

Other governance issues – weighting 10%

- International aspects of corporate governance.
- Governance problems for large global groups of companies.
- Corporate governance: unquoted companies and small quoted companies.
- Governance in the public sector.
- Governance in the not-for-profit sector.

Acronyms and abbreviations

ABI	Association of British Insurers
AC	Audit Committee
ACCA	Association of Chartered Certified Accountants
ACEVO	Association of Chief Executives of Voluntary Associations
AGM	annual general meeting
AIM	Alternative Investment Market
AIRMIC	Association of Insurance and Risk Managers
AO	accounting officer
AQF	Audit Quality Forum
BIS	Department for Business, Innovation & Skills
BSI	British Standards Institution
CA	Companies Act
CACG	Commonwealth Association of Corporate Governance
CCAB	Consultative Committee of Accountancy Bodies
CDO	collateralized debt obligation
CEO	chief executive officer
CFO	chief financial officer
CIMA	Chartered Institute of Management Accountants
CIPFA	Chartered Institute of Public Finance and Accountability
CMA	Competition and Markets Authority
COSO	Committee of Sponsoring Organizations of the Treadway Commission (COSO)
CR	corporate responsibility
CRO	chief risk officer
CSR	corporate social responsibility
CTN	Charity Trustee Network
D&O	directors and officers
Defra	Department for the Environment, Food and Rural Affairs
DTR	Disclosure and Transparency Rules
EBITDA	earnings before interest, taxation, depreciation and amortisation
ECGI	European Corporate Governance Institute
ecoDa	European Confederation of Directors Associations
EGM	extraordinary general meeting
EHRC	Equality and Human Rights Commission
EPS	earnings per share
ERM	Enterprise Risk Management
ESB	Ethical Standards Board
ESG	environmental, social and governance
EU	European Union
EY	Ernst & Young
FCA	Financial Conduct Authority
FRC	Financial Reporting Council
FSA	Financial Services Authority
FSMA	Financial Services and Markets Act 2000
GC100	Association of General Counsel and Company Secretaries working in FTSE 100 companies
GRI	Global Reporting Initiative
G20	Group of Twenty
HAZOPS	hazard and operability studies
IA	Internal audit
IASB	International Accounting Standards Board

IBE	Institute of Business Ethics
ICAEW	Institute of Chartered Accountants in England and Wales
ICGN	International Corporate Governance Network
IFAC	International Federation of Accountants
IFRS	International Financial Reporting Standard
IIRC	International Integrated Reporting Council
IMA	Investment Management Association
IoD	Institute of Directors
IOSCO	International Organisation of Securities Commissions
IPC	Investor Protection Committee
IPPR	Institute for Public Policy Research
IRM	Institute of Risk Management
ISC	Institutional Shareholders Committee
ISO	International Organization for Standardization
ISS	Institutional Shareholder Services Inc
KPI	key performance indicators
LLA	liability limitation agreement
LLP	limited liability partnership
LPDT	Listing, Prospectus and Disclosure and Transparency Rules
LR	Listing Rules
MAR	Market Abuse Regulation
NCVO	National Council for Voluntary Organisations
NDPB	non-departmental public body
NED	non-executive director
NRSRO	nationally recognised statistical ratings organisation
NYSE	New York Stock Exchange
OECD	Organisation for Economic Co-operation and Development
OFR	Operating and Financial Review
OPM	Office for Public Management
PBIT	profit before interest and tax
PDMR	person discharging managerial responsibilities
PIE	Public Interest Entity
PCAOB	Public Company Accounting Oversight Board
PIRC	Pensions & Investment Research Consultants Ltd
PLSA	Pensions and Lifetime Savings Association (formerly National Association of Pension Funds (NAPF))
PPI	payment protection insurance
PR	public relations
PRA	Prudential Regulation Authority
QCA	Quoted Companies Alliance
RIS	Regulated Information Service
RREV	Research Recommendations and Electronic Voting
SE	social and environmental
SEC	Securities and Exchange Commission
SEE	social, environmental and ethical
SFO	Serious Fraud Office
SID	senior independent director
SMEs	small and medium-sized enterprises
Solace	Society of Local Authority Chief Executives and Senior Managers
SOX	Sarbanes-Oxley Act 2002
SRI	socially responsible investment
STOR	suspicious transaction and order reports
Transpub	Transparency and Publicity Act
TSR	total shareholder return
UKSA	UK Shareholders Association
VaR	Value at Risk
VFM	value for money

Acknowledgements

The publisher and author acknowledge the following organisations for the permission to reproduce extracts of content in this edition.

Extracts
CCAB Developing and implementing a code of ethical conduct. A guide for businesses and other organisations. January 2014 pages 7–11.

Prudential Regulation Authority Supervisory Statement SS5/16 Corporate governance: Board responsibilities. March 2016 pages 7–8.

This study text contains public sector information licensed under the Open Government Licence v3.0.

Appendices

Appendix 1: The UK Corporate Governance Code (2016) © Financial Reporting Council (FRC). Adapted and reproduced with the kind permission of the Financial Reporting Council. All rights reserved. For further information, please visit www.frc.org.uk or call +44 (0)20 7492 2300.

Appendix 2: The G20/OECD Principles of Corporate Governance 2015 (OECD Publishing), www.oecd.org/daf/ca/Corporate-Governance-Principles-ENG.pdf, are ©OECD (2015) and reproduced with permission.

Appendix 4: FRC Guidance on Board Effectiveness (2011)

Appendix 5: FRC Guidance on Audit Committees (2016)

Appendix 6: FRC Guidance on Risk Management, Internal Control and Related Financial and Business Reporting 2014

Appendix 7: FRC UK Stewardship Code (2012)

Appendix 8: FRC Corporate Culture and the Role of Boards. Report of Observations 2016

Appendix 9: The King Code of Governance principles (King IV) November 2016 "The King IV Report on Corporate Governance for South Africa 2016, Institute of Directors Southern Africa" and the IoDSA website link is: www.iodsa.co.za/?page=AboutKingIV

Every effort has been made to locate and acknowledge sources and holders of copyright material in this study text. In the event that any have been inadvertently overlooked, please contact the publisher.

General principles of corporate governance

■ **LIST OF CHAPTERS**

1 Definitions and issues in corporate governance
2 Legal and regulatory aspects of governance
3 Voluntary codes of corporate governance: the role of the company secretary

■ **OVERVIEW**

The first part of this study text introduces **corporate governance**, its significance for the contemporary business world and the role of the company secretary in corporate governance awareness and compliance.

The term 'corporate governance' is commonly used, but it is often hard to define exactly what it means and what its objectives should be. Chapter 1 begins by providing a definition and explaining the possible consequences of poor governance. Different theoretical frameworks for an approach to best practice in governance are explained, and the close connection between governance and business ethics is explored. The chapter also highlights some of the key issues in corporate governance, including the structure and balance of the board of directors, boardroom practice, the remuneration of senior executives, financial reporting and auditing, shareholder communications, risk management systems and **internal control** systems. To put these in context, Chapter 1 includes a brief history of the development of corporate governance both in the UK and globally, and compares a voluntary approach to the practice of corporate governance with a regulatory approach. The chapter ends with a discussion of the similarities and differences in governance issues between companies and organisations in the public sector (including government itself) and the voluntary sector.

Chapter 2 looks briefly at how certain requirements relating to corporate governance are included in laws and regulations.

Chapter 3 looks at the voluntary frameworks for best practice in corporate governance, with particular focus on the corporate governance code in the UK, corporate governance principles issued by the **G20/Organisation for Economic Co-operation and Development (OECD)** and the ground-breaking code of governance in the King Code in South Africa. The chapter also explains the role of **institutional investors** in the promotion of best practice in corporate governance, and concludes by considering the role of the company secretary in corporate governance.

■ LEARNING OUTCOMES

Part One should enable you to:

- appraise the frameworks underlying governance law and practice in a national and international context;

- distinguish between and compare the legal obligations for governance and recommended best practice; and

- discuss the role of the Chartered Secretary in providing authoritative, credible and professional advice on governance.

Definitions and issues in corporate governance

1

■ CONTENTS

■ INTRODUCTION

This chapter explains the nature and scope of corporate governance, the theoretical frameworks for corporate governance, and the voluntary and regulatory approaches that are used to apply best practice (i.e. the generally accepted best way of doing something) in corporate governance. Corporate governance is compared with governance in the public and voluntary sectors of the economy, for which codes of best practice have also been developed.

1   Defining corporate governance

'Governance' refers to the way in which something is governed and to the function of governing. The governance of a country, for example, refers to the powers and actions of the legislative assembly, the executive government and the judiciary.

Corporate governance refers to the way in which companies are governed and to what purpose. It is concerned with practices and procedures for trying to ensure that a company is run in such a way that it achieves its mission and goals. This could be to maximise the wealth of its owners (the shareholders), subject to various guidelines and constraints and with regard to other groups or individuals with an interest in what the company does. Guidelines and constraints include behaving in an ethical way and in compliance with laws and regulations. From a shareholder's perspective, corporate governance can be defined as a process for monitoring and control to ensure that management runs the company in the interests of the shareholders.

Other groups with an interest in how the company acts include employees, customers, suppliers, the communities in which the company operates and the general public. Individuals, organisations or groups with an interest in how a company operates are called **stakeholders**. It can be argued that companies should be governed in the interests of all its major stakeholders, not just its owners. This argument is particularly relevant to large companies whose activities have a big impact on the economy and society.

1.1 Alternative definitions of corporate governance

There are several useful definitions of corporate governance that might help to convey an impression of what it is.

The **G20/Organisation for Economic Co-operation and Development (OECD)** has suggested that a corporate governance framework involves a set of relationships between a company's management, its board, its shareholders and other stakeholders. Corporate governance also provides the structure through which the objectives of the company are set, and the means of attaining those objectives and monitoring performance are determined.

The Cadbury Commission, which produced the first corporate governance code in the UK in 1992, provided the following definition:

'Corporate governance is the system by which companies are directed and controlled. Boards of directors are responsible for the governance of their companies. The shareholders' role in governance is to appoint the directors and the auditors and to satisfy themselves that an appropriate governance structure is in place. The responsibilities of the board include setting the company's strategic aims, providing the leadership to put them into effect, supervising the management of the business and reporting to shareholders on their stewardship. The board's actions are subject to laws, regulations and the shareholders in **general meeting**.'

The **UK Corporate Governance Code** comments:

'The purpose of corporate governance is to facilitate effective, entrepreneurial and prudent management that can deliver the long-term success of the company.... Corporate governance is therefore about what the board of a company does and how it sets the values of the company, and it is to be distinguished from the day to day operational management of the company by full-time executives.'

For large companies, the main issue with corporate governance is the relationship between the board of directors and the shareholders, and the way in which the board exercises its powers. The relationship between the shareholders and the board can be described as a 'principal–agent' relationship. In some companies, other stakeholders may have significant influence.

Principles of corporate governance are based on the view that a company should be governed in the interests of the shareholders, and possibly also in the interests of other stakeholder groups. The board ought to use its powers in an appropriate and responsible way, and should be accountable in some ways to the shareholders (and other stakeholders, perhaps).

1.2 Why is corporate governance important?

A company should have a purpose, goals and objectives. Some of these, such as the reasons for its existence, may be set out in its written constitution. Others may be implied or assumed, rather than clearly documented objectives. A company should be governed in a way that moves it towards the achievement of its goals.

However, although a company exists as a legal person, in reality it is the organised, collective effort of many different individuals. It is controlled by a board of directors in the interests of its owners, the shareholders. The interests of the board and the shareholders ought to coincide, but in practice they may be in conflict with each other. The challenge of good corporate governance is to find a way in which the interests of shareholders, directors and other interest groups can all be sufficiently satisfied.

1.3 Governance and management

It is important to recognise the difference between the governance of a company and its management.

Powers to manage the affairs of a company are given to the board of directors, but most of these powers are delegated to a **chief executive officer (CEO)** or managing director, and are delegated further to **executive directors** and executive managers. The board of directors should retain some powers and responsibilities, and certain matters should be reserved for board decision-making rather than delegated to the management team (see Chapter 4).

The board of directors should also be responsible for monitoring the performance of the management team. However, the board of directors is not responsible for day-to-day management. It is responsible for governing the company.

Responsibilities for governance go beyond management, and governance should not be confused with management. Even so, it is probably true to say that when a senior executive manager is 'promoted' to the board, she or he may consider the position of an executive director to be recognition of their senior executive position. However, the promotion of an executive manager to the board creates new responsibilities for governance that are not related to management. Executive directors ought to think as members of the board, rather than as senior executives, in performing their duties as directors.

2 Consequences of poor corporate governance

Corporate governance is a matter of much greater importance for large public companies, where the separation of ownership from management is much wider than for small private companies. Public companies raise capital on the stock markets, and **institutional investors** (see Chapter 3) hold vast portfolios of shares and other investments. Investors need to know that their money is reasonably safe. Should there be any doubts about the integrity or intentions of the individuals in charge of a company, the value of the company's shares will be affected and the company will have difficulty raising new capital should it wish to do so. If there is weak corporate governance in a country generally, the country will struggle to attract foreign investment.

Commenting on the numerous corporate scandals in the US in 2001 and 2002, Arthur Levitt, a former **chairman** of the Securities and Exchange Commission (SEC), said in a speech:

> 'If a country does not have a reputation for strong corporate governance practice, capital will flow elsewhere. If investors are not confident with the level of disclosure, capital will flow elsewhere. If a country opts for lax accounting and reporting standards, capital will flow elsewhere. All enterprises in that country, regardless of how steadfast a particular company's practices, may suffer the consequences. Markets exist by the grace of investors. And it is today's more empowered investors who will determine which companies and which markets stand the test of time ... .'

It might seem self-evident that good (or adequate) corporate governance supports capital markets. In some countries, the impetus for high standards of corporate governance has come from wanting to attract foreign investors and investment, to strengthen their financial markets and the economy generally. However, the initial demand for codes of best governance practice and stricter regulatory regimes came largely from scandals and setbacks, where evidence of bad corporate governance emerged, and company share prices and the stock market generally suffered as a consequence.

 TEST YOUR KNOWLEDGE 1.1

a   Why is corporate governance more significant for large companies than for small private companies?

b   What is the difference between governance and management?

c   What is meant by 'separation of ownership from control'?

 **CASE EXAMPLE 1.1**

Maxwell Corporation consisted mainly of Maxwell Communication Corporation and Mirror Group Newspapers. As its chairman and CEO, Robert Maxwell had a position of dominant power on the board of directors. He was also a domineering personality, who was able to run his companies in whatever way he liked. He apparently made no clear distinction between his privately-owned companies and the public Maxwell Corporation. In the early 1990s, his companies got into serious financial difficulties. Maxwell drowned falling off his yacht in 1991; after his death it emerged that his companies had accumulated debts of £4 billion, and an unauthorised 'hole' of more than £400 million existed in the pension fund of Mirror Group Newspapers. Maxwell's ability to accumulate unsustainable debts and to raid the pension fund was attributed to a combination of his domineering personality and position of power, a weak board of directors and questionable accounting practices. The Maxwell 'empire' collapsed.

Bad corporate governance is a problem for any country with large companies and capital markets. Events over the past few decades have shown that it often takes a scandal to focus the attention of the regulators. In recent years, a number of corporate scandals have raised questions about governance in companies in the UK (e.g. Mirror Group Newspapers and Polly Peck International in the early 1990s, Kids Company in 2015 and BHS and Sports Direct in 2016), in the US (e.g. Enron and WorldCom in 2001/2002 and more recently – and for different reasons – Lehman Brothers in 2008), in mainland Europe (e.g. Ahold in the Netherlands, Parmalat in Italy and Siemens in Germany) and in Japan (e.g. Olympus in 2011). The problems and challenges of corporate governance are worldwide, and laws and regulations about corporate governance are now applied in many countries across the world.

The US was much slower than the UK to recognise problems of bad corporate governance, but in 2001 and 2002 there were a number of major corporate collapses that could be attributable partly to governance issues and fraud. The most well-known case is probably Enron Corporation.

 **CASE EXAMPLE 1.2**

Enron was founded in 1985 with the merger of two US natural gas pipelines. In the 1990s it diversified into selling electricity and other activities; by 2000 it was one of the world's largest companies when measured by reported annual revenue. It appeared to have a highly competent board of directors and **audit committee** (see Chapter 7). However, although investors and regulators were not aware of it at the time, the rapid growth in the reported assets and profits of Enron was attributable largely to misleading accounting practices. It inflated the value of its reported assets (sometimes recording expenses as assets) and it kept liabilities off its balance sheet by means of establishing 'special purpose entities'. It also anticipated profits by becoming the first non-financial services company to adopt 'mark to market' accounting techniques. This enabled it to earn profits on long-term contracts 'up front' as soon as the contract started. In one case it claimed a large profit on a 20-year contract agreed with Blockbuster Video in 2000, and continued to claim the profit even after the project failed to work successfully and Blockbuster Video pulled out of the deal.

Senior management were rewarded on the basis of annual earnings and were highly motivated to continue reporting large increases in profits, regardless of the longer-term consequences. Investors began to have doubts about the reliability of Enron's reported profits in 2001. A 'whistleblower' (see Chapter 10) reported her concerns to the CEO, but her allegations of dubious accounting practices were ignored. However, in October 2001 Enron was eventually forced to announce that it would be re-stating its accounts for 1997–2000 to correct accounting violations. The SEC announced an investigation into the company, and the stock price collapsed. There were also doubts about whether Enron had sufficient liquidity (cash) to remain in business for long. Its debt was downgraded to junk bond status and in December 2001 the company filed for bankruptcy.

CASE EXAMPLE 1.2 *continued*

Enron's auditors were Arthur Andersen, one of the 'big five' global accounting firms. The firm – in particular its Houston office – took extraordinary measures to protect its client. When the SEC investigation was announced in 2001, Andersen staff attempted to cover up evidence of negligence in its audit work by destroying several tons of documents, and many emails and computer files. The firm, especially the Houston office, was accused of losing its independence to Enron and over-reliance on income from the non-audit work that it did for the company. Arthur Andersen was charged with obstructing the course of justice by shredding the documents and destroying the files. Although a guilty verdict was subsequently overturned by the Supreme Court, this was too late to save the firm from the loss of its major clients, and collapse.

Several Enron employees were brought to trial for a number of financial crimes. A former chief financial officer (CFO) of Enron was found guilty of crimes including fraud, money laundering, insider trading and conspiracy. Two former CEOs were charged with a range of financial crimes and brought to trial in 2006. Both were found guilty: one of them was imprisoned and the other died before sentence was passed.

 CASE EXAMPLE 1.3

Parmalat, which specialises in dairy and food manufacture and is one of the largest companies in Italy, was declared insolvent in December 2003. There was a fraud which the company's internal controls and the external auditors failed to identify. Forged documents indicated that there was a substantial amount of cash held by one of the company's subsidiaries, but this money did not exist. The scandal, as in the case of Enron, suggested a need for more effective external audits and for a whistleblowing system within companies. At Parmalat, several employees had suspected wrongdoing, but no one reported their suspicions.

Poor corporate governance by no means always has such an extreme outcome, but the case examples of Maxwell (1.1), Enron (1.2) and Parmalat (1.3) are useful studies of what could possibly go wrong.

 STOP AND THINK 1.1

In 2008 a number of major banks suffered enormous losses, partly through their involvement in markets for collateralised debt obligations (CDOs) linked to high-risk mortgages ('sub-prime mortgages'). The problems began in the US, but quickly spread to Europe and parts of Asia. For various reasons, many banks were faced with a critical shortage of cash (liquidity) and capital (due to their huge losses). Banks were criticised for their poor corporate governance and failure to manage risks adequately. They had allowed their businesses to grow through high-risk operations and had failed to provide for the possibility that events might eventually turn out unfavourably.

Banks have also been in the news for improper practices that might have been avoided with better governance, but which have damaged the reputation of the banking industry and resulted in the imposition of substantial fines by financial markets regulators. Examples have included assisting customers with money laundering and tax evasion, and (in the UK) mis-selling payment protection insurance (PPI) to consumers to insure repayment of credit if the borrower dies or faces circumstances that may prevent him or her from earning income to service the debt.

2.1 What do we mean by bad corporate governance?

The issues involved in governance are described in more detail throughout this text. Briefly, however, aspects of poor corporate governance include:

- a board of directors that fails to perform its duties properly, perhaps because it is dominated by one or more individuals, or because it fails to carry out the tasks that it is supposed to;
- misleading financial reporting to shareholders and other investors, and perhaps inadequate auditing of the **financial statements**;
- a poor relationship between the board and the main shareholders;
- ineffective systems of risk management, and exposure to errors and fraud due to inadequate internal control systems;
- inappropriate remuneration and reward systems for directors and senior executives; and
- unethical business practices.

A key issue in corporate governance is the relationship between the board of directors, the shareholders and other important stakeholders.

 STOP AND THINK 1.2

Poor standards of corporate governance can deter investors from buying shares of companies, and may even bring a stock exchange into disrepute. This is why stock markets in many countries seek to maintain high standards of governance through a code of corporate governance and a **'comply or explain'** approach.

An extreme example of how bad corporate governance creates a risk to the reputation of a stock market is the experience of Naibu, a Chinese sportswear maker whose shares were listed in 2012 on London's junior market for fast-growing companies, the Alternative Investment Market (AIM). In January 2015, its UK non-executive directors admitted that they had lost contact with their chairman and CEO, who were thought to be somewhere in China. The non-executive directors (NEDs) reported to the market that as they had been unable to obtain a response from these individuals to their enquiries, they were not in a position to assess their company's financial performance. Following this announcement, the company's shares were suspended from trading on AIM, having fallen in value from £1.24 to £0.115.

Previously, in October 2014, the company had re-stated details in its 2013 financial statements, revising the reported profits down due to a 'typographical error' in which an expense item for office decoration and factory machinery had been stated as 2.6 million renminbi when the cost should have been 26 million renminbi.

The events in this company raise serious questions about corporate governance standards – not just the behaviour of the chairman and CEO, but also possible failings by the NEDs and the company's auditors.

When the 'disappearance' of the chairman and CEO were reported, questions were raised about the reputation of the AIM market and whether it might deter investors from investing in companies with an AIM listing.

 TEST YOUR KNOWLEDGE 1.2

Give six examples of bad corporate governance practice.

3 Stakeholders

A stakeholder in a company is someone who has an interest or 'stake' in it, and is affected by what the company does. A stakeholder, in turn, has an influence on what companies do. Each stakeholder or stakeholder group may expect the company to behave or act in a particular way with regard to the stakeholders' interests. A stakeholder can also expect to have some say in some of the decisions a company makes and some of the actions it takes. The **balance of power** (see Chapter 4) between different stakeholder groups, and the way in which that power is exercised, are key issues in corporate governance.

A public company has a number of different stakeholder groups, which can be divided into different categories. One method of categorisation is to divide stakeholders into internal stakeholders (stakeholders inside the organisation: executive directors, management and other employees); **connected stakeholders** (who have close connections with the company without being inside it, such as shareholders, lenders, customers, suppliers and non-executive directors); and **external stakeholders**, such as government, the general public and pressure groups.

Another method of categorisation is to divide stakeholders into:

- financial stakeholders; and
- other stakeholders.

3.1 Financial stakeholders

Financial stakeholders are stakeholders with a financial interest in the company. These consist mainly of shareholders and lenders. Lenders may be banks or investors in bonds.

A company's members or equity shareholders are the owners. In a small company, the owners may also be directors. In a large public company, the directors may own some shares, but are not usually the largest shareholders. The interests of the shareholders are likely to be focused on the value of their shares and dividend payments. However, the powers of shareholders in large public companies are usually fairly restricted and shareholders have to rely on the board to act in their best interests.

- A different situation arises when there is a **majority shareholder** or a significant shareholder. A shareholder with a controlling interest is able to influence decisions of the company through an ability to control the composition of the board of directors.
- A distinction can also be made between long-term and short-term institutional investors. Short-term investors buy shares with the expectation of making a short-term profit from an increase in the price before selling the shares in the market. This includes, for example, hedge funds which buy shares in what they consider to be an undervalued and badly managed company with potential for a significant increase in value if the management problems can be resolved (or if the company becomes a takeover bid target). Long-term investors are more interested in the longer-term returns from a company than short-term profit.
- Lenders and bondholders provide debt capital to a company but are not owners. Even so, they have a financial interest in the company, and expect payment of interest and repayment of capital on schedule. Excessive borrowing by a company might put lenders as well as shareholders at risk financially; therefore, lenders have an interest in preventing the financial gearing or leverage of the company from getting too high. Loan covenants might set limits on borrowing by the company.

In recent years, due largely to the relatively low cost of debt capital, many listed companies have borrowed extensively by issuing corporate bonds. A consequence of this development is that in many companies, providers of long-term debt capital are significant investors. At the same time, many companies have reduced their equity share capital by buying back shares and cancelling them. Not surprisingly, bond investors have become more interested in the corporate governance practices of the companies in which they invest, because they want assurance that their investment will be protected.

This is recognised in the UK Corporate Governance Code, which includes the following comment in its Preface:

'While in law the company is primarily accountable to its shareholders, and the relationship between the company and its shareholders is also the main focus of the Code, companies are encouraged to recognise the contribution made by other providers of capital and to confirm the board's interest in listening to the views of such providers insofar as these are relevant to the company's overall approach to governance.'

STOP AND THINK 1.3

It may be tempting to think of 'major shareholders' in a listed company as shareholders who have such a large number of shares that they are able to exercise substantial influence over decision-making by the board of directors, or use their votes to significant effect at general meetings of the company.

In reality, although some UK listed companies have a very large and influential shareholder, most do not. A 'major' shareholder in a listed company is likely to hold less than 5% of the shares. Individually, they can meet with the company to express their views; but to have significant influence, major shareholders must usually act collectively and express their shared views to the company's board.

However, in some other countries, majority shareholders in listed companies are not uncommon.

3.2 Other stakeholders

Other stakeholders in a company could also have significant influence. They include the board of directors, although some directors might also be large shareholders.

The board has the **responsibility** for giving direction to the company. It delegates most executive powers to the executive management, but reserves some decision-making powers to itself, such as decisions about raising finance, paying dividends and making major investments. Executive management is also held accountable to the board for the company's operational performance.

- A board of directors is made up of both executive directors and NEDs. Executive directors are individuals who combine their role as director with their position within the executive management of the company. NEDs perform the functions of director only, without any executive responsibilities. Executive directors combine their stake in the company as a director with their stake as a fully paid employee, and their interests are therefore likely to differ from those of the non-executives.

- The board may take decisions collectively, but it is also a collection of individuals, each with personal interests and ambitions. Some individuals may try to dominate the decisions by a board and to exert strong influence over their colleagues. In particular, the most influential individuals are likely to be the chairman, who is usually a non-executive but may occasionally have executive powers and responsibilities, and the CEO. The chairman is responsible for the functioning of the board. The CEO is the senior executive director, and is accountable to the board for the executive management of the company. The term CEO derives from the US, but is now widely used in the UK (where the term 'managing director' is also used). The main interests of individual executive directors are likely to be power and authority, a high remuneration package and a wealthy lifestyle.

- Management is responsible for running the business operations and is accountable to the board of directors (and more particularly to the CEO). Individual managers, like executive directors, may want power, status and high remuneration. As employees, they may see their stake in the company in terms of the need for a career and an income.

- Employees have a stake in their company because it provides them with a job and an income. They too have expectations about what their company should offer them, e.g. security of employment, good pay and suitable working conditions. Some employee rights are protected by employment law, but the powers of employees are generally limited.

- Major suppliers have an indirect interest in a company, because they expect to be paid what they are owed. If they deal with the company regularly or over a long time, they will expect the company to do business with them in accordance with their contractual agreements. If the company becomes insolvent, unpaid creditors will take a more significant role in its governance, depending on the insolvency laws in the country, e.g. by taking legal action to take control of the business or its assets.

- A number of representative bodies act in the interests of members of the investment community and can influence public companies whose shares are traded on a stock market. Representative bodies include the Association of British Insurers (ABI) and the Pensions and

Lifetime Savings Association (PLSA) in the UK, and the **International Corporate Governance Network** (ICGN; see Chapter 3), an association of activist institutional investors around the world (insurance companies and pension funds are major investors in securities). These bodies may coordinate the activities of their members, e.g. by encouraging them to vote in a particular way on resolutions at the **annual general meetings** (AGMs) of companies in which they are shareholders. These bodies represent the opinions of the investment community generally.

- The general public are also stakeholders in large companies, often because they rely on the goods or services provided by a company to carry on their life. For example, households expect gas, electricity and water companies to provide an uninterrupted supply to their homes. Commuters expect a rail company to be under an obligation to provide a convenient and reliable transport service to and from work, and at a reliable price. Pressure groups, such as environment protection groups, sometimes try to influence the decisions of companies in the interests of society in general.
- As discussed later in this chapter, in November 2016 the UK Government issued for consultation a Green Paper on Corporate Governance Reform. This Green Paper seeks views on three areas where the Government want to consider options for updating our corporate governance framework including on whether there are measures that could increase the connection between boards of directors and other groups with an interest in corporate performance such as employees and small suppliers.

STOP AND THINK 1.4

People who work in large organisations are usually more familiar with management than with the board of directors, and it is tempting to assume that corporate governance is about management of the company at the most senior level. However, this is not what corporate governance is about.

In the UK, corporate governance is concerned largely with the role and responsibilities of the board of directors to lead the company in a way that is expected of it, by shareholders, employees, lenders, customers and other stakeholders, including society in general.

The board should monitor the performance of management, decide major policies and strategic objectives and even make some major decisions, such as decisions about takeovers or major capital investments. But the board does not manage the business: this role is delegated to executive managers, and corporate governance is not about management.

TEST YOUR KNOWLEDGE 1.3

a   List the major stakeholders in a school that is run by a non-profit-making charity organisation.

b   Do you agree with the view that a board of directors should give more consideration to the interests of its longer-term shareholders than to those of short-term shareholders such as hedge funds? Give your reasons.

4   Theoretical frameworks

It is useful to consider the theoretical justification for a system of rules or guidelines on corporate governance. Two different frameworks are described here.

1   Agency theory.
2   Stakeholder theory.

Agency theory can be used to justify a 'shareholder approach' to corporate governance. **Stakeholder theory** can be used to justify a 'stakeholder' approach. These alternative approaches are explained later.

4.1 Agency theory

Agency theory was developed by US economists Michael Jensen and William Meckling (1976). The theory is based on the separation of ownership and control in a company – the ownership of a company by its shareholders and control over the company's actions by its directors and senior executives. Jensen and Meckling defined the agency relationship as a form of contract between a company's owners and its managers, where the owners (as principal) appoint an agent (the managers) to manage the company on their behalf. As part of this arrangement, the owners must delegate decision-making authority to the management.

Jensen and Meckling suggested that the nature of governance in a company reflects the conflicts of interest between the company's owners and managers.

- The shareholders want to increase their income and wealth over the long term. The value of their shares depends on the long-term financial prospects for the company. Shareholders are therefore concerned not only about short-term profits and dividends; they are even more concerned about long-term profitability.
- The managers run the company on behalf of the shareholders. If they do not own shares in the company, managers have no direct interest in future returns for shareholders or in the value of the shares. They have an employment contract and earn a salary. Unless they own shares, or unless their remuneration is linked to profits or share values, their main interests are likely to be the size of their remuneration package and their status within the company.

Ideally, the 'agency contract' between the owners and the managers of a company should ensure that the managers always act in the best interests of the owners. However, it is impossible to arrange the 'perfect' contract because any decisions managers make affect their personal welfare as well as the interests of the owners.

Agency conflict

Agency conflicts are differences in the interests of owners and managers. They arise in several ways.

- **Moral hazard.** A manager has an interest in receiving benefits from his or her position in the company. These include all the benefits that come from status, such as a company car, use of a company plane, a company house or flat, attendance at sponsored sporting events, and so on. Jensen and Meckling suggested that a manager's incentive to obtain these benefits is higher when they have no shares, or only a few shares, in the company. For example, senior managers may pursue a strategy of growth through acquisitions, in order to gain more power and 'earn' higher remuneration, even though takeovers might not be in the best interests of the company and its shareholders.
- **Level of effort.** Managers may work less hard than they would if they were the owners of the company. The effect of this lack of effort could be smaller profits and a lower share price.
- **Earnings retention.** The remuneration of directors and senior managers is often related to the size of the company (measured by annual sales revenue and value of assets) rather than its profits. This gives managers an incentive to increase the size of the company, rather than to increase the returns to the company's shareholders. Management are more likely to want to reinvest profits in order to expand the company, rather than pay out the profits as dividends. When this happens, companies might invest in capital investment projects where the expected profitability is quite small, or propose high-priced takeover bids for other companies in order to build a bigger corporate empire.
- **Time horizon.** Shareholders are concerned about the long-term financial prospects of their company, because the value of their shares depends on expectations for the long-term future. In contrast, managers might only be interested in the short term. This is partly because they might receive annual bonuses based on short-term performance, and partly because they might not expect to be with the company for more than a few years.

Agency costs

Agency costs are the costs of having an agent make decisions on behalf of a principal. Applying this to corporate governance, agency costs are the costs that the shareholders incur by having managers run the company on their behalf, instead of running the company themselves. Agency costs are potentially very high in large companies, where there are many different shareholders and a large professional management.

Agency costs consist of three elements:

1 **Costs of monitoring.** Shareholders need to establish systems for monitoring the actions and performance of management, to try to ensure that management is acting in their best interests. An example of monitoring is the requirement for the directors to present an annual report and accounts to the shareholders, setting out the financial performance and financial position of the company. These accounts are audited, and the auditors present a report to the shareholders. Preparing accounts and having them audited has a cost.

2 **Bonding costs.** Costs may be incurred in providing incentives to managers to act in the best interests of the shareholders. The remuneration packages for directors and senior managers are therefore an important element of agency costs, since they include both long- and short-term incentives.

3 **Residual loss.** Residual loss is the cost to the shareholder which occurs when the managers take decisions that are not in the best interests of the shareholders (but are in the interests of the managers themselves). Residual loss occurs, for example, when managers pay too much for a large acquisition. The managers would gain personally from the enhanced status of managing a larger group of companies. The cost to the shareholders comes from the fall in share price that results from paying too much for the acquisition.

The key elements of agency theory

Agency theory is based on the view that the system of corporate governance should be designed to minimise the agency problem and reduce agency costs. One approach to reducing the agency problem is to make the board of directors more effective at monitoring the decisions of the executive management. Another approach is to design schemes of remuneration for directors and senior managers that bring their interests more into line with those of the shareholders.

Agents should also be accountable to their principals for their decisions and actions. **Accountability** means reporting back to the principals and giving an account of what has been achieved, and the principal having power to reward or punish an agent for good or bad performance. Greater accountability should reduce the agency problem, because it provides management with a greater incentive (obtaining rewards/avoiding punishments) to achieve performance levels that are in the best interests of the shareholders.

Agency theory may therefore be summarised as follows.

- In large companies there is a separation of ownership from control. Professional managers are appointed to act as agents for the owners of the company.
- Individuals are driven by self-interest.
- Conflicts of self-interest arise between shareholders and managers.
- Managers, because they are driven by self-interest, cannot be relied on to act in the best interests of the shareholders. This creates problems in the agency relationship between shareholders and management.
- These agency problems create costs for the shareholders.

The aim should be to minimise these costs by improving the monitoring of management and/or providing management with incentives to bring their interests closer to those of the shareholders.

4.2 Stakeholder theory

Agency theory is based on the assumption that the main objective of a company should be to maximise shareholder wealth. Stakeholder theory takes a different view. The stakeholder view is that the purpose of corporate governance should be to satisfy, as far as possible, the objectives of all key stakeholders – employees, investors, major suppliers and creditors, customers, the government, local communities and the general public. A company's directors should therefore consider the interests of all the major stakeholders. However, some stakeholders are more important than others, so that management should give priority to their interests above the interests of other stakeholder groups.

Stakeholder theory states that a company's managers should make decisions that take into consideration the interests of all the stakeholders. This means trying to achieve a range of different objectives, not just the aim of maximising the value of the company for its shareholders. This is because different stakeholders each have their own (different) expectations of the company, which the company's management should attempt to satisfy.

Stakeholder theory also considers the role of companies in society, and the responsibility that they should have towards society as a whole. It could be argued that some companies are so large, and their influence on society so strong, that they should be accountable to the public for what they do. The general public are taxpayers and as such they provide the economic and social infrastructure within which companies are allowed to operate. In return, companies should be expected to act as corporate citizens and in ways that benefit society as a whole. This aspect of stakeholder theory is consistent with the arguments in favour of **corporate social responsibility (CSR)**.

 TEST YOUR KNOWLEDGE 1.4

a   In agency theory, what are agency costs and what are the three main elements of agency cost?
b   In agency theory, how is moral hazard an aspect of agency cost?
c   How are agency costs minimised?

---

5   Approaches to corporate governance

There has been considerable debate about what the objectives of sound corporate governance should be. The different views can be divided into four broad approaches that can be related to the agency theory or the stakeholder theory of governance:

1   The **shareholder value approach**.
2   The **stakeholder approach**, also called the stakeholder-inclusive approach or pluralist approach.
3   The enlightened shareholder approach.
4   An integrated approach, as recommended by the King Report (a report on recommended corporate governance practice for South Africa).

5.1 The shareholder value approach

The shareholder value approach is the well-established view, supported by company law in advanced economies, that the board of directors should govern their company in the best interests of its owners, the shareholders. This could mean that the main objective of a company should be to maximise the wealth of its shareholders, in the form of share price growth and dividend payments, subject to conforming to the rules of society as embodied in laws and customs. The directors should be accountable to their shareholders, who should have the power to remove them from office if their performance is inadequate.

The strength of this approach to corporate governance is its general acceptance. Many people hold the view that public companies are in business to earn profits for the benefit of their shareholders. Successful companies are perceived as those paying dividends to shareholders and whose share price goes up. However, within the broad objective of maximising shareholder values, the board of directors will also act fairly in the interests of employees, customers, suppliers and others with an interest in the company's affairs.

5.2 The stakeholder approach (pluralist approach)

An alternative approach to the requirements of good corporate governance is based on stakeholder theory. This argues that the aim of sound corporate governance is not just to meet the objectives of shareholders, but also to have regard for the interests of other individuals and groups with a stake in the company, including the public at large.

From a 'stakeholder view', corporate governance is concerned with achieving a balance between economic and social goals and between individual and communal goals. Sound corporate governance should recognise the economic imperatives companies face in competitive markets and should encourage the efficient use of resources through sound investment. It should also require accountability from the board of directors to the shareholders for the stewardship of those resources. Within this framework, the aim should be to recognise the interests of other individuals, companies and society at large in the decisions and activities of the company.

A problem with the stakeholder approach is that company law gives certain rights to shareholders, and there are some legal duties on the board of directors towards their company. However, the interests of other stakeholders are not reinforced to any great extent by company law.

A stakeholder or pluralist approach is that co-operative and productive relationships will be optimised only if the directors are permitted or required to balance shareholder interests with the interests of other stakeholders who are committed to the company. Changes in company law would be required to introduce such an approach in practice.

It is important to remember that although stakeholder interests are not well protected by company law, extensive protection is provided by other aspects of law such as employment law, health and safety legislation, and environmental law.

5.3 The enlightened shareholder approach

The **enlightened shareholder approach** to corporate governance is that the directors of a company should pursue the interests of their shareholders, but in an enlightened and inclusive way. It is a form of compromise between the agency view and the stakeholder view. The directors should look to the long term, not just the short term, and they should also have regard to the interests of other stakeholders in the company, not just the shareholders. Managers should be aware of the need to create and maintain productive relationships with a range of stakeholders having an interest in their company.

A UK Company Law Review Steering Group issued a consultative document in 1998, in which it commented that UK company law did not embrace the enlightened shareholder approach, and if this approach was desirable, suitable changes in the law would be needed. Enlightened change, it felt, would not come voluntarily, but (like a pluralist approach) would need the backing of the law.

A criticism of the enlightened shareholder view is that most shareholders do not fit the image of enlightened investors. Most shares in public companies are owned by institutional investors, who themselves may be relatively unaccountable to their beneficiaries. When companies become a target for a takeover bid, speculative investors such as hedge funds may acquire large but short-term shareholdings, with a view to making a quick profit from their investment.

5.4 The King Report: a 'stakeholder-inclusive' approach to corporate governance

The **King Code** or King Report (see Chapter 3), developed by the Institute of Directors (IoD) in South Africa, was first introduced in 1994. Revised Codes were published in 2004 (King II) and in 2009 (King III). A further revision (King IV) was published in 2016. King IV (and King II and III before it) advocates an inclusive, stakeholder-centric approach which stands in contrast with a shareholder-centric approach.

King IV (like its predecessors) advocates a stakeholder-inclusive approach, in which the governing body takes account of the legitimate and reasonable needs, interests and expectations of all material stakeholders in the execution of its duties in the best interests of the organisation over time. By following this approach, instead of prioritising the interests of the providers of financial capital, the governing body gives parity to all sources of value creation, including among others, social and relationship capital as embodied by stakeholders.

Stakeholder inclusivity involves the balancing of interests over time by way of prioritising and, in some instances, trading of interests. A decision on how to achieve this balance is made on a case-by-case basis as current circumstances and exigencies require, but should always be done in the best interests of the organisation over the longer term. Balancing the needs, interests and expectations of stakeholders is a dynamic and ongoing process. The quality of stakeholder relationships indicates how effectively an organisation is able to strike this balance in making its decisions.

Part 5.5 in the King IV Code contains the principles and practices that deal with relationships in accordance with the stakeholder-inclusive approach.

TEST YOUR KNOWLEDGE 1.5

a   What are the limitations of the influence on corporate governance practice of national organisations (such as the ABI and PLSA) representing the interests of their institutional investor members?

b   What are the main differences between the shareholder and pluralist approaches to corporate governance?

c   According to King IV Code, why should governing bodies adopt a stakeholder-inclusive approach to corporate governance?

---

6   Principles of good corporate governance

Several concepts apply to sound corporate governance in all countries where international investors invest their money. Many of these are ethical in nature and the original King Code described them as the 'overarching corporate governance principles':

- **fairness**
- accountability;
- responsibility;
- transparency.

6.1 Fairness

Fairness is a concept that is linked to ethical behaviour and integrity (honesty). For example:

- There should also be fairness in the treatment of minority shareholders when there is a majority shareholder or dominant shareholder. This concept might seem fairly straightforward in the UK, where the rights of minority shareholders are protected to a large extent by company law. In some countries, however, minority shareholder rights are often disregarded by the larger shareholders and the board of directors.
- Other stakeholders should also be treated in a fair and ethical way.

6.2 Accountability

Decision-makers who act on behalf of a company should be accountable for the decisions they make and the actions they take. In a company, the board of directors should be accountable to the shareholders, the company's owners. Shareholders should be able to assess the actions of their board of directors and the committees of the board, and have the opportunity to query them and challenge them.

A problem with accountability is deciding how the directors should be accountable, and in particular over what period of time. According to financial theory, if the objective of a company is to maximise the wealth of its shareholders, this will be achieved by maximising the financial returns to shareholders through increases in profits, dividends, prospects for profit growth and a rising share price. It might therefore follow that directors should be held accountable to shareholders on the basis of the returns on shareholder capital that the company has achieved.

However, there is no consensus about the period over which returns to shareholders and increases in share value should be measured. Performance can be measured over a short term of one year at a time, or over a long term of (say) five or ten years – or even longer. In practice, it is usual to measure returns over the short term and assess performance in terms of profitability over a 12-month period. In the short term, however, a company's share price may be affected by influences unrelated to the company's underlying performance, such as excessive optimism or pessimism in the stock markets generally. In the short term, it is also easier to soothe investors with promises for the future, even though current performance is not good. It is only when a company fails consistently to deliver on its promises that investor confidence ebbs away.

If company performance were to be judged by the return to shareholders over a 12-month period, the directors would focus on short-term results and short-term movements in the stock market price. Short-termism is easy to criticise, but difficult to disregard in practice if performance targets ignore the long term. They should really be looking after the underlying business of the company and its profitability over the longer term.

Writing in the *Financial Times* (29 January 2002), John Kay, reflecting on the reasons given by the former finance director of Marconi for the company's financial collapse in 2000, commented:

'[A director's] job is to run a business that adds value by means of the services it provides to customers. If he succeeds, it will generate returns to investors in the long term. And this is the only mechanism that can generate returns to investors. The problem is that the equivalence between value added in operations and stock market returns holds in the long run but not the short. Share prices may, for a time, become divorced from the fundamental value of a business. This has been true of most share prices in recent years... . In these conditions, attention to **total shareholder returns** [TSR; see Chapter 6] distracts executives from their real function of managing businesses.'

The problem of accountability remains, however. Even if it is accepted that company performance should not be judged by short-term financial results and share price movements, how can the board be made accountable for its contribution to longer-term success?

6.3 Responsibility

The board of directors is given authority to act on behalf of the company, and a further principle of corporate governance is that it should accept full responsibility for the powers that it is given and the authority that it exercises. A board of directors should understand what its responsibilities are, and should carry them out to the best of its abilities.

Accountability goes hand in hand with responsibility. The board of directors should be made accountable to the shareholders for the way in which it has carried out its responsibilities. Similarly, executive management should be responsible for the exercise of powers delegated to them by the board of directors, and should be made accountable to the board for their achievements and performance.

6.4 Transparency

Transparency means openness. In the context of corporate governance, this is a willingness by the company to provide clear information to shareholders and other stakeholders about what the company has done and hopes to achieve, without giving away commercially sensitive information. It might be useful to think of openness in terms of its opposite, which is to be a 'closed book' and refuse to divulge any information whatsoever.

Transparency should not be confused with 'understandability'. Information should be communicated in a way that is understandable, but transparency is concerned more with the content of the information that is communicated. A principle of good governance is that stakeholders should be informed about what a company is doing and plans to do in the future, and about the risks involved in its business strategies.

6.5 The relevance of these principles to corporate governance

The relevance of these basic principles to corporate governance can be summarised briefly as follows:

Principle	
Fairness	Companies should act in an ethical manner. Ethical conduct underpins good corporate governance.
Accountability and responsibility	Management should be accountable to the board of directors for the way in which they have exercised their responsibilities. Similarly, the board of directors should be accountable to the shareholders (and other stakeholders).
Transparency	Companies should be open about what they are doing, in matters that are of interest or concern to shareholders and other stakeholders. Reporting is an important element of governance. Shareholders (and other stakeholders) have a right to be told.

7 Ethics and corporate governance

Ethics are the rules or codes of behaviour that individuals and organisations apply in their decision-making and actions. Personal ethics and business ethics underlie the regulations and codification in corporate governance. The owners and leaders of companies should establish the standards of ethical behaviour that they expect all their employees to follow, and this behaviour (and the attitudes associated with it) should be consistent with the way in which the company is governed.

7.1 Personal ethics

Personal ethics are closely associated with morality and a view of what is right and what is wrong. Unethical behaviour by an individual is regarded as unacceptable. To some extent, the law can establish rules about what is 'wrong'. A breach of the criminal law is illegal. Other aspects of law, such as contract law and employment law, can also establish standards of behaviour that are required, and legal action can be taken against anyone in breach of the law.

However, standards of behaviour are determined by social attitudes of morality and good conduct, much more than by legal rules, even though the attitudes of individuals often differ about whether a particular action is 'wrong' and unethical. Ethical personal behaviour helps to build trust. In the context of corporate governance, ethical personal behaviour is commonly associated with integrity (honesty) and transparency.

Unethical personal behaviour may be associated with selfishness, seeking personal satisfaction and the fulfilment of personal objectives. Company leaders are sometimes accused of this.

7.2 Corporate ethics

Corporate ethics are standards of business behaviour by companies. The way in which employees act can be influenced strongly by the way in which the employer expects them to act, and each company has its own ethical (or unethical) standards. This can affect the company's dealings with its employees, customers, suppliers and agents, as well as the government, local communities and society as a whole.

There is a connection between corporate ethics (or business ethics) and the different approaches to corporate governance. If a company has a shareholder approach to corporate governance, it puts the interests of shareholders ahead of the interests of anyone else. If it adopts a stakeholder approach to governance, it will act in a way that takes into consideration the needs and concerns of other stakeholders. The concerns of an ethical company that adopts a stakeholder approach are described briefly in the following section on corporate codes of ethics.

7.3 Professional ethics

The professions, such as medicine, law and accountancy, are governed by professional bodies that require all members to comply with standards of professional ethics. Members of the accountancy profession, for example, are required to act with integrity, to be independent in their opinion and judgement, to be objective (avoid bias), and to comply with all relevant laws and regulations. In addition, they are required in most circumstances to maintain client confidentiality. These broad principles apply to all accountants, including employees of companies as well as accountants acting as company auditors. In the UK, ethical standards have been issued by the Institute of Chartered Accountants in England and Wales.

In the context of corporate governance, it is essential that auditors should retain their independence, objectivity and integrity, because shareholders rely on the opinion they provide about the company's annual financial statements. Unfortunately, a number of corporate scandals in the past, notably the collapse of Enron (see Case example 1.2), have raised questions about the integrity of the information in financial statements and the independence and judgement of the company's auditors.

The measures that should be taken to protect auditor independence are described more fully in Chapter 7.

8 A corporate code of ethics

A large number of large companies have developed, adopted and disclosed a formal code of ethics that employees are required to apply. In the US, one of the requirements for a listing on the New York Stock Exchange (NYSE) is that the company must adopt and disclose a code of business conduct and ethics for its directors and employees. Key features of a corporate code of ethics are that:

- it is a formal document;
- it is adopted by the board of directors;
- it is disclosed to employees and to the public, including other stakeholders who have direct dealings with the company;
- it is made clear to employees that they should comply with the code; and
- its application in practice should be monitored, and breaches of ethical conduct should be dealt with according to established rules and procedures.

The effectiveness of a code of ethics depends on the leadership of the company – its directors and senior managers. These individuals must be seen to comply with the ethical code, otherwise employees will see no purpose in complying with the code themselves. The culture of a company drives its ethical behaviour, and a code of ethics provides useful guidance.

It has been suggested that there are three reasons why companies might develop a formal code of ethics. These are progressive, which means that companies might begin by having a code of ethics for the first reason, but then progress to the second and third reasons as they gain experience with implementing the code and appreciating its potential benefits.

- **Compliance and customer service.** The company wants to ensure that all its employees comply with relevant laws and regulations, and conduct themselves in a way that the public expects. Compliance with a code of ethics is necessary for both legal and commercial reasons. For example, companies providing a service to the general public need to ensure that their employees are courteous in their dealings with customers; otherwise they will lose customers.
- **Managing stakeholder relations.** A code of ethics can help to improve and develop the relations between the company and its shareholders, by improving the trust that shareholders have in the company. The code might therefore include the ethical stance of the company on the disclosure of information to shareholders and the investing public (openness and transparency) and respect for the rights of stakeholders.
- **Creating a value-based organisation.** It might be argued that an ethical company, like a well-governed company, is more likely to be successful in business in the long term. A company might therefore recognise the long-term benefits of creating an ethical culture, and encouraging employees to act and think in a way that is consistent with the values in its code of ethics.

8.1 Contents of a code of corporate ethics

There are no rules about what a code of corporate ethics should contain. The Consultative Committee of Accountancy Bodies (CCAB) is developing and implementing a code of ethical conduct.

The CCAB Guide states that the following elements of a code of ethical conduct may be relevant, although smaller organisations with clear, uncomplicated reporting lines may not require all elements:

- mission statement;
- high-level values;
- clear ethical principles;
- internal policies (linked to values and ethical principles where appropriate); and
- implications of breaches of the code.

It might also be appropriate for the code to refer to guidance and support (produced by the organisation or available externally), which will aid understanding and compliance.

Mission statement

A mission statement is a statement of the purpose of the organisation and, in effect, asserts the organisation's reason for existing. It may be expected to serve as a foundation upon which all the organisation's activities are based. It can be a strong motivator for staff, and an inspiration for those leading the organisation. In order to integrate ethical conduct into the operations of the organisation, it is advisable to incorporate a reference to the organisation's ethical values into its mission statement. This will help to embed strong ethical principles into the activities and decision-making of individuals. An inspirational mission statement will be succinct and memorable. It will, therefore, resonate throughout the code.

High-level values

One's values form the basis for one's ethical action. They are acquired over time, and tend to influence attitudes and behaviour. It benefits an organisation if the values of individuals within it are consistent. This will, to a great extent, depend upon the organisation's recruitment policies and processes, and also its own values as clearly expressed within its code of ethical conduct.

Examples of commonly held personal and business values, which an organisation may strive to mirror within its code include:

- respect;
- equality;
- integrity;
- recognition of excellence.

Ethical principles

In support of the organisation's high-level values, ethical principles set out expected standards of behaviour, while remaining broad and fundamental in nature. All those to whom the code relates will be expected to understand and comply with these principles.

The more detailed content of the code must be consistent with these overarching ethical principles.

In different types of organisation, it will be appropriate to emphasise different ethical principles. By way of example, the following set of principles would be appropriate for a public sector organisation, as they are based on the seven principles of public life (see Chapter 13): selflessness, integrity, objectivity, accountability, openness, honesty and leadership.

The example set of principles above may only need to be tailored slightly to be appropriate for a public interest organisation such as a charity. However, for a commercial organisation, it might be necessary to adopt a different emphasis (bearing in mind its fiduciary obligation to investors), resulting in a slightly different set of ethical principles. If developing a code of ethical conduct for a professional practice, the code of ethics of the practice's professional body would almost certainly form the starting point.

The ethical principles underpinning an organisation's code of ethical conduct should be formulated with input from those within the organisation itself. However, a professional accountant leading on such a project may also refer to the fundamental ethical principles within their own professional code.

Specific behaviours

Having established the organisation's values and delineated agreed ethical principles, the code of ethical conduct may then cover a range of more detailed matters. These specific behaviours must, of course, be consistent with the organisation's values and ethical principles. Excessive detail should be avoided, and specific behaviours should only be included if they add clarity, as the code should not be perceived as overly prescriptive. The specific behaviours are organisational policies that need to be stated, and the following may be relevant to a particular organisation:

- Standard of work and behaviour.
- Compliance with legislative and regulatory requirements.
- Personal interests.
- Disclosure of personal information.
- Health and safety.
- Harassment.
- Serious misconduct.
- Gifts and hospitality.
- Use of resources.
- Appointments and other employment matters.
- Outside commitments.
- Complaints.
- Raising concerns – employees might be advised of external organisations that support whistle-blowers by providing confidential advice, for example, in the UK, *Public Concern at Work*, www.pcaw.org.uk.
- Seeking advice.

TEST YOUR KNOWLEDGE 1.6

a   What is accountability? What is transparency in corporate governance, and why is it a feature of good governance practice?

b   In what ways do personal ethics differ from corporate ethics?

c   What are the typical contents of a code of corporate ethics?

9   Key issues in corporate governance

Good corporate governance should promote the best long-term interests of the company. It requires an effective board of directors, with an appropriate balance of skills and experience, and well-motivated individuals as directors. The composition of the board, its functions and responsibilities, and its effectiveness, are therefore core issues in corporate governance.

At the heart of the debate about corporate governance lie the conflicts of interest, or potential conflicts of interest, between shareholders, the board of directors as a whole and individual board members, and possibly also a number of other stakeholder groups. The directors may be tempted to take risks and make decisions aimed at boosting short-term performance. Many shareholders are more concerned about the longer term, the continuing survival of their company and the value of their investment. If a company gets into financial difficulties, professional managers can move on to another company to start again, whereas shareholders suffer a financial loss.

Issues in corporate governance where a conflict of interests might be apparent are:

- **Financial reporting and auditing.** The directors should be honest and transparent in reporting on the company's performance to shareholders, and the external auditors should give an independent opinion of the financial statements.

- **Remuneration of directors and senior executives.** Remuneration policy should be fair and consistent with good governance practice.
- **Company–stakeholder relations.**
- **Risk-taking and the management of risk.** There should be effective systems for the management of business risk.
- **Effective communication between the directors and shareholders.** Issues in governance are what information should be reported to stakeholders, and the transparency of reporting.
- Ethical conduct and CSR.

These issues will be considered in more detail in the chapters that follow.

9.1 Financial reporting and auditing

The directors may try to disguise the true financial performance of their company by 'dressing up' the published accounts and giving less than honest statements. 'Window-dressed' accounts make it difficult for investors to reach a reasoned judgement about the financial position of the company. Concerns about misleading published accounts provided an early impetus in the 1980s and early 1990s to the movement for better corporate governance in the UK. Accounting irregularities in a number of companies led to a tightening of accounting standards, although the problems of window dressing are unlikely ever to disappear completely.

Concerns about financial reporting in the US emerged with the collapse of Enron in 2001 (see Case example 1.2), which filed for bankruptcy after 'adjusting' its accounts. This was followed by similar problems at other US companies, such as telecommunications group WorldCom (which admitted to fraud in its accounting), Global Crossing and Rank Xerox. Problems then emerged in some European companies, most notably at the Italian group Parmalat at the end of 2003 (see Case example 1.3). It was also suggested that incomprehensible or misleading accounts contributed to the global banking crisis in 2007–2009, with banks such as Lehman Brothers (which collapsed in 2008) possibly using questionable accounting practices to disguise the true state of their financial position.

A corporate governance issue is the question of the extent to which the directors were aware in each case of the impending collapse of their company, and if they knew the problems, why shareholders were not informed much sooner. It is now widely accepted that the directors of a company should be responsible for giving an assurance to their shareholders that they consider their company to be a going concern that will not collapse within the next 12 months.

When the annual financial statements of a company prove to have been misleading, questions are inevitably raised about the effectiveness of the external auditors. There are two main issues relating to the external audit of a company:

- whether it should be the job of the auditors to discover financial fraud and material errors; and
- the problem of the relationship between a client company and its auditors, and the extent to which the auditors are independent and free from the influence of the company's management.

If auditors are subject to influence, they might be persuaded to agree with a controversial method of accounting for particular transactions, which shows the company's performance or financial position in a better light.

 **CASE EXAMPLE 1.4**

In 2011 Hewlett-Packard (HP) paid $11 billion to acquire UK software company Autonomy, but after the acquisition, HP wrote down the value of the acquisition by half to $5.5 billion. HP management claimed misleading reporting by Autonomy in its 2010 financial statements as the reason for the write-down, an accusation denied by Autonomy's former directors.

In 2014, with the help of its US auditors, HP filed re-stated financial results for Autonomy for 2010, and cut the reported profits of the company by 81 %, to £19.6 million. Autonomy's former UK auditors denied that there was anything wrong with the original figures in the 2010 accounts.

CASE EXAMPLE 1.4 *continued*

The arguments between HP and the former directors of Autonomy raised questions that are fundamental to good governance. Were the Autonomy financial statements true and fair, and transparent? And were the auditors independent or effective?

 CASE EXAMPLE 1.5

In 2014, Tesco admitted that it had over-stated its half-year profits and questions were raised about the composition of the company's board of directors and the use of inappropriate accounting policies.

Tesco's board had no non-executive directors with retail experience, until the appointment of two new non-executive directors in October 2014. It was suggested that this weakness in retail sector knowledge meant that the board lacked the necessary expertise to raise appropriate questions with the executives.

Tesco's first-half figures for 2014 prematurely recognised income and anticipated cost savings. The issue came to light following an employee questioning the accounting treatment used. The company estimated the overstatement at £250 million.

Tesco then reported that profits had been overstated by £263 million and that this was the result of incorrect recognition of income, which had happening over a number of years. The announcement that the Chairman of the Board would be stepping down was also made.

At the end of October 2014 the UK's Serious Fraud Office (SFO) announced the launch of a criminal investigation into the alleged accounting irregularities at Tesco, which is continuing.

In 2016, three former Tesco executives were charged by the SFO with Fraud and False Accounting. The case is before Southwark Crown Court.

9.2 Directors' remuneration

Directors may reward themselves with huge salaries and other rewards, such as bonuses, a generous pension scheme, **share options** (see Chapter 6) and other benefits. Institutional shareholders do not object to high remuneration for directors. However, they take the view that rewards should depend largely on the performance of the company and the benefits obtained for the shareholders. The main complaint about 'fat cat' directors' remuneration is that when the company does well, the directors are rewarded well, which is fair enough, but when the company does badly, the directors continue to be paid just as generously.

Interest in arguments about directors' pay has varied between different countries. In the UK, concerns led to the establishment of the Greenbury Committee in the 1990s and the production of the **Greenbury Report**. Directors' remuneration has remained a contentious issue ever since.

- In 2002 UK company law was changed by the Directors' Remuneration Report Regulations, requiring listed companies to produce a directors' remuneration report annually and to invite shareholders to vote on the report at the company's AGM.
- In 2013 the law was changed again to allow shareholders in quoted companies a binding vote every three years on their company's remuneration policy and an annual advisory vote on their company's implementation report.

9.3 Company–stakeholder relations

Most decision-making powers in a company are held by the board of directors. The corporate governance debate has been about the extent to which professional managers, acting as board directors, exercise those powers in the interests of their shareholders and other stakeholders in the company, and whether the powers of directors should be restricted. This aspect of corporate governance is about:

- the structure of the board of directors and the role of independent NEDs;
- the responsibilities of the board of directors;
- the duties of directors;
- the powers of shareholders under company law and whether these should be extended by corporate law reform, e.g. by giving shareholders the right to approve the company's remuneration policy or its remuneration packages for board members (see Chapter 6); and
- whether shareholders actually make full use of the powers they already have: for example, by voting not to re-elect directors.

9.4 Corporate governance and risk management

As a general rule, investors expect higher rewards to compensate them for taking higher **business risks** (see Chapter 9). If a company makes decisions that increase the scale of the risks it faces, profits and dividends should be expected to go up. Another issue in corporate governance is that the directors might take decisions intended to increase profits without giving due regard to the risks. In some cases, companies may continue to operate without regard to the changing risk profile of their existing businesses.

When investors buy shares in a company, they have an idea of the type of company they are buying into, the nature of its business, the probable returns it will provide for shareholders and the nature of its business and **financial risks** (see Chapter 10). To shareholders, investment risk is important, as well as high returns. Directors, on the other hand, are rewarded on the basis of the returns the company achieves, linked to profits or dividend growth, and their remuneration is not linked in any direct way to the risk aspects of their business. Risk management is now recognised as an ingredient of sound corporate governance.

Some companies are also guilty of poor procedures and systems, so that the risk of breakdowns, errors and fraud can be high. In addition to controlling 'business risk', companies should also have effective internal controls for managing **operational risks** (see Chapter 10).

9.5 Information and communication

Another issue in corporate governance is communication between the board of directors and the company's shareholders. Shareholders, particularly those with a large financial investment in the company, should be able to voice their concerns to the directors and expect to have their opinions heard. Small shareholders should at least be informed about the company, its financial position and its plans for the future, even if their opinions carry comparatively little weight.

The responsibility for improving communications rests with the companies themselves and their main institutional shareholders. Companies can make better use of the annual report and accounts to report to shareholders on a range of issues and the policies of the company for dealing with them. The annual report and accounts should not be simply a brief **directors' report** (see also Chapter 7) and a set of financial statements. The company should explain its operations and financial position in a strategic review and report on a range of governance issues, such as directors' remuneration, internal controls and risk management and policies on health, safety and the environment. Many companies now use their website to report on such matters.

A company can also try to encourage greater shareholder attendance and participation at AGMs as a method of improving communications and dialogue. Electronic communications, including electronic voting, should also be considered. For their part, institutional investors should develop voting policies and apply these in general meetings. Where necessary, they can vote against the board to alert the directors to the strength of their views.

Requirements for greater disclosures – and transparent disclosures – are an important way in which company boards of directors are obliged to give greater consideration to governance issues. A guiding principle is if companies have to make public disclosures about something, they will give it more serious attention than if disclosures are not required.

9.6 Ethical conduct and CSR

The relevance of ethical conduct to corporate governance has already been described. There is also a growing recognition that many companies need to consider social and environmental issues, for commercial reasons and governance reasons, as well as ethical reasons. Many shareholders (including institutional shareholders) and many customers expect companies to have regard to social issues and environmental issues; furthermore, the financial risks from government regulation to protect the environment continue to grow. Social and environmental issues can therefore affect reputation, sales, profits and the share price.

9.7 Corporate culture

It has been recognised that there needs to be a concerted effort to improve trust in the motivations and integrity of business. Rules and sanctions clearly have their place, but will not on their own deliver productive behaviours over the long term. The FRC issued a report in 2016, *Corporate Culture and the Role of Boards: Report of Observations*, which looks at the increasing importance which corporate culture plays in delivering long-term business and economic success. This is discussed in Chapter 5.

TEST YOUR KNOWLEDGE 1.7

List six key issues in corporate governance.

10   A brief history of corporate governance

10.1 Corporate governance in the UK

Concerns about corporate governance have grown over time. The main impetus for better practices in corporate governance began in the UK in the late 1980s and early 1990s. The Report of the Committee on the Financial Aspects of Corporate Governance (the 'Cadbury Report') was published in 1992, and was later described as 'a landmark in thinking on corporate governance'. The Report included a Code of Best Practice (the **Cadbury Code**), and UK listed companies came under pressure from City institutions to comply with the requirements of the Code.

In 1995, a working group was set up to look into the relationship between companies and institutional investors. It produced the **Myners Report**, which made a number of recommendations about how the relationship between institutional investors and company management should be conducted. The Report included suggestions for improving the communications between companies and institutional investors and for the conduct of AGMs. The significance of the Myners Report is that it urged institutional investors to reassess their role as shareholders, their responsibilities for ensuring good corporate governance and the success of the companies in which they invest. When a company is performing badly, institutional investors should try to do something to put matters right, instead of selling their shares and washing their hands of the company. Representative bodies of the institutional investor organisations, such as the ABI and the PLSA, responded by issuing guidelines for their members on corporate governance issues and principles of corporate governance.

On the recommendation of the Cadbury Committee, another committee was set up to review progress on corporate governance in UK listed companies. This committee issued the Greenbury Report in 1995, which focused mainly on directors' remuneration. At the time, the UK press was condemning 'fat cat' directors, particularly those in newly privatised companies. The Greenbury Report issued a Code of Best Practice on establishing **remuneration committees**, for disclosures of much more information about the remuneration of directors and remuneration policy, and for more control over notice periods in directors' service contracts and compensation payments in the event of early termination of contracts.

A Committee on Corporate Governance, chaired by Sir Ronald Hampel, was set up in 1995 to review the recommendations of the Cadbury and Greenbury Committees. The final report of the **Hampel Committee** was published in 1998. This covered a number of governance issues, such as the composition of the board and role of directors, directors' remuneration, the role of shareholders (particularly institutional shareholders), communications between the company and its shareholders, and financial reporting, auditing and internal controls. The Hampel Report also suggested that its recommendations should be combined with those of the Cadbury and Greenbury Committees into a single code of corporate governance. This suggestion led to the publication of the original 1998 **Combined Code** on Corporate Governance (Combined Code), which applied to all UK listed companies.

Corporate governance issues remained in the spotlight in the UK, and two influential reports were produced in January 2003. The **Higgs Report**, commissioned by the government, considered the role and effectiveness of NEDs. The Smith Report, commissioned by the Financial Reporting Council (FRC), provided guidance for audit committees. The responsibility for the Combined Code was transferred to the FRC and in 2003 a revised Combined Code was issued, incorporating many of the Higgs and Smith recommendations.

Although the Combined Code has been voluntary, the **UK Listing Rules** included an obligation on listed companies to disclose the extent of their compliance with it. Listed companies were required to state that they have complied in full with the provisions of the Code, or must explain any non-compliance. This '**comply or explain rule**' for listed companies applies to all provisions of the Code.

The UK Code and related guidelines are now the responsibility of the FRC. The FRC reviews and amends the Code regularly. In June 2010 it issued a revised version of the Code, under the new name of the **UK Corporate Governance Code**. The most recent revision of this Code was in 2016.

The global financial markets and world economy were badly damaged by a banking crisis that emerged in 2007 and 2008. In the US, Lehman Brothers collapsed and other banks and brokerage firms were taken over to prevent their collapse. In the UK, Northern Rock bank collapsed in 2007 and in 2008 Royal Bank of Scotland was virtually nationalised, and the government acquired a major stake in Lloyds TSB Bank after Lloyds had agreed to take over another ailing bank, HBOS. Recognition of governance problems in UK banks led to a review by Sir David Walker and the **Walker Report** (2009). Some recommendations of the Walker Report were included by the FRC in the UK Corporate Governance Code.

A **UK Stewardship Code** was published in 2010 and is reviewed regularly. Whereas the UK Corporate Governance Code is concerned with governance by companies, the Stewardship Code is for institutional investors that are share owners or that manage shareholdings for other financial institutions such as pension funds. The Stewardship Code is the responsibility of the FRC and it aims to enhance the quality of engagement between institutional investors and companies, so that institutional shareholders contribute positively to the governance of the companies in which they invest.

The UK Corporate Governance Code is concerned mainly with corporate governance in listed companies. The governance problems facing unlisted companies are different and a corporate governance code and guidance for unlisted companies was issued by the Institute of Directors (IoD) in 2010. This is described in Chapter 5.

In November 2016, following concerns about poor corporate governance at BHS and Sports Direct, the government issued for consultation a Green Paper Corporate Governance Reform. This Green Paper seeks views on three areas where the government want to consider options for updating our corporate governance framework:

- first, on shareholder influence on executive pay, which has grown much faster over the last two decades than pay generally and than typical corporate performance;
- second, on whether there are measures that could increase the connection between boards of directors and other groups with an interest in corporate performance such as employees and small suppliers; and
- third, whether some of the features of corporate governance that have served us well in our listed companies should be extended to the largest privately-held companies at a time in which different types of ownership are more common.

Some aspects of corporate governance have been brought into UK law, with much of the initiative coming from the EU and EU Directives and EU legislation (see Chapter 2). New regulations in 2002 were introduced for greater disclosures of directors' remuneration by listed companies, replacing similar regulations that had been included in the Listing Rules (see Chapter 6 for more details). The Companies Act (CA) 2006 introduced **statutory duties** of directors (similar to the duties that existed previously in common law and equity), and contains a requirement for companies to be more accountable to shareholders by publishing a strategic review (until 2013 a business review) in narrative form each year.

Corporate governance in the UK is subject to influence from the European Commission (EC).

Amendments to the Fourth and Seventh EU Company Law Directives approved in 2006 included a requirement for quoted companies to include a corporate governance statement in their annual reports, and amendments to the Eighth Company Law Directive in 2008 require 'public interest entities' (which include listed companies) to have an audit committee consisting of independent NEDs and to publish an annual corporate governance statement.

The **European Commission** continues to promote improvements in corporate governance and the harmonisation of corporate governance within the European Union.

Following the UK referendum in June 2016 resulting in a majority vote for the UK to leave the EU, there are likely to be some changes in the level of influence that the EU may have on corporate governance in the UK.

 STOP AND THINK 1.5

From what you have read or heard in news reports, identify a recent example of pressures for better corporate governance that is bringing about changes in a company's management, policies or practices.

10.2 Corporate governance in other countries

Although the UK is seen as a leading country in the development of a corporate governance framework, there have been similar developments in many other countries. For many countries, particularly developing countries, good corporate governance is seen as an essential basic requirement for attracting foreign investment capital.

In South Africa, a code of corporate governance was developed by the King Committee. This was revised and strengthened in 2002, 2009 and again in 2016. On an international basis, recommended principles on corporate governance have been published by the G20/OECD.

The US appeared to show little concern for better corporate governance throughout the 1990s, although there were some activist institutional shareholders such as CalPERS. The situation changed dramatically with the collapse of Enron in 2001 and some other major companies. The major auditing and accountancy firm Arthur Andersen, caught up in the Enron scandal and prosecuted for obstructing the course of justice, collapsed and was broken up in 2002 (see Case example 1.2). Recommendations for change were proposed by the NYSE, and statutory provisions on corporate governance were introduced in 2002 with the **Sarbanes-Oxley Act** (SOX). However, the adequacy of corporate governance provisions in the US (and the UK) was questioned following the banking crisis in 2007–2009.

Many other countries have corporate governance codes and legislation covering aspects of corporate governance practice. The regulations and guidelines vary between countries, but many countries have adopted a **voluntary code of governance** for listed companies based on the UK model. It is also usual for stock market regulations to have a 'comply or explain' or **'apply or explain' rule**: listed companies must apply the provisions of the code or explain any non-compliance.

A summary of the laws and guidelines in each country can be found on the website of the European Corporate Governance Institute, at www.ecgi.org/codes/all_codes.php.

10.3 National variations in corporate governance

As stated earlier, the need for good corporate governance is a matter of international concern. However, it is important to be aware that although corporate governance has become a matter of some interest in many countries, the pace of change and the nature of corporate governance vary substantially between countries.

Much of the pressure for change has come from institutional investors, particularly in the US, who have invested fairly heavily in companies in other countries. As shareholders in foreign companies, US investors expect to be allowed to exercise their right to vote and to be treated on an equal footing with other equity shareholders. In countries where minority shareholder rights are not always well respected, US investor influence has probably been influential in the corporate governance changes that have been introduced. The International Corporate Governance

Network (ICGN) is a voluntary organisation established to promote good governance practice worldwide; this has issued a corporate governance code, based largely on the UK model.

In many developing countries, there have been substantial investments in recent years by multinational companies. It might be expected that US and UK multinationals would establish a system of corporate governance within their subsidiaries along similar lines to the parent company, e.g. with NEDs on the board representing interest groups in the local country. Many multinationals are aware of their reputation in overseas markets, and alert to the demands of pressure groups as well as governments in the countries where they have operating subsidiaries.

TEST YOUR KNOWLEDGE 1.8

What is the 'comply or explain rule' in corporate governance for listed companies?

11 Arguments for and against corporate governance regimes

There are differences of opinion about the benefits of corporate governance, and whether these justify the costs of compliance with corporate governance regulations. It is therefore useful to consider just what the benefits of good corporate governance might be for public companies, and what the arguments may be against having laws or codes of corporate governance practice.

The main arguments in favour of having a strong corporate governance regime for listed companies are as follows.

- Good governance will eliminate the risk of misleading or false financial reporting, and will prevent companies from being dominated by self-seeking CEOs or chairmen. By reducing the risks of corporate scandals, and promoting fairness, accountability, responsibility and transparency in companies, investors will be better protected. This should add generally to confidence in the capital markets, and help to sustain share prices.
- In a well-governed company, there is a keen awareness of significant risks and the importance of effective risk management. Risks need to be kept within acceptable levels; otherwise companies may fail to respond adequately to adverse risk events and developments, and profitability may be damaged as a result.
- It has been argued that companies that comply with best practice in corporate governance are also more likely to achieve commercial success. Good governance and good leadership and management often go hand-in-hand. Badly governed companies may be very successful, and well-governed companies may fail. However, the probability is greater that badly governed companies will be less successful and more likely to fail than well-governed ones.
- Well-governed companies will often develop a strong reputation and so will be less exposed to reputation risk than companies that are not so well governed. Reputation risk can have an adverse impact on investors and customers.
- Good governance encourages investors to hold shares in companies for the longer term, instead of treating shares as short-term investments to be sold for a quick profit. Companies benefit from having shareholders who have an interest in their longer-term prospects.

The main arguments against having a strong corporate governance regime for listed companies focus on costs, benefits and value and are as follows:

- It is argued that, for many companies and institutional investors, compliance with a code of corporate governance is a box-ticking exercise (see Chapter 3). Companies adopt the required procedures and systems without considering what the potential benefits might be. The only requirement is to comply with the 'rules' and put a tick in a box when this is done. Corporate governance requirements therefore create a time and resource-consuming bureaucracy, with compliance officers, and divert the attention of the board of directors from more important matters.

- Good corporate governance is likely to reduce the risk of scandals and unexpected corporate failures. However, it could be argued that the current regulations or best practice guidelines are far too extensive and burdensome.
- When regulations and recommended practice become burdensome, there is an inevitable cost, in terms of both time and money, in achieving compliance. It could be argued that less regulation is better regulation. However there has not yet been an authoritative assessment of the costs of corporate governance compliance with the benefits of better corporate governance systems.
- Companies that are obliged to comply with corporate governance regulations or best practice are at a competitive disadvantage to rival companies from countries where corporate governance regulation is weaker. As corporate governance regimes have extended to more countries, however, this argument is weaker than it used to be. There is no evidence, for example, that UK companies have lost competitiveness because of the relatively strong governance regime in the UK.
- The connection between good corporate governance and good financial results (due to good leadership and management) has not been proved or demonstrated.

TEST YOUR KNOWLEDGE 1.9

What are the arguments in favour and against the application of corporate governance codes of practice to large companies?

12 Governance in other organisations

Corporate governance applies to companies, and codes of corporate governance apply only to listed companies. However, principles of good governance should not be ignored in other organisations, such as:

- companies that are not listed, especially large private companies and non-listed public companies whose shares are traded on a stock market (such as the second-tier AIM market in the UK);
- central government departments;
- local government authorities; and
- not-for-profit organisations, such as charities.

In the UK (and some other countries), governance codes have been issued for each of these different types of organisation. They are described later in this text, after the main governance issues for listed companies have been explained in the following chapters.

CHAPTER SUMMARY

- Corporate governance refers to the way in which a company is led, mainly by its directors. It is not concerned with executive management or business operations.
- Experience has shown that when companies collapse, poor corporate governance has usually contributed to the collapse. It is also widely believed that best practice in corporate governance results in good company performance over the long term.
- Companies (and all organisations) have stakeholders. These are individuals or groups with an interest in what the company does. Stakeholders in companies include financial stakeholders (such as shareholders and lenders) and non-financial stakeholders (such as senior management, other employees, suppliers, customers and the general public). Some stakeholders are more influential than others.

- Agency theory examines the conflicts of interest between the owners of a company and their agents, the company directors. These conflicts give rise to costs, such as the costs of monitoring the activities of agents and costs of incentivising them. Ideally, the aim should be to minimise these agency costs.
- There are different approaches to corporate governance, which vary according to the extent to which the interests of stakeholders other than the company shareholders are recognised. The differing approaches may be referred to as a shareholder approach, an enlightened shareholder or inclusive approach, and a stakeholder or pluralist approach. The approach taken by the directors of an organisation affects decision-making at a strategic level.
- Principles of good governance are fairness, accountability, responsibility and transparency.
- There is a close connection between best practice in governance and ethical behaviour. Individuals have personal ethics and professional bodies require professional ethical behaviour from their members. Corporate ethics refer to the way in which a company conducts its business: companies may have a corporate code of ethics that employees are expected to comply with.
- The main issue in corporate governance is the effectiveness of the board of directors in promoting the long-term success of the company. Other key issues in corporate governance are financial reporting and auditing, the remuneration of senior executives, relationships between a company and its stakeholder groups, risk management and internal control, communication between a company and its shareholders, ethics and CSR.
- The UK has a history of mainly voluntary corporate governance practice. Its first governance code was the Cadbury Code (1992). The Combined Code (1998) was revised and renamed the UK Corporate Governance Code in 2010. The UK Code and related guidelines are the responsibility of the FRC. Other countries have developed their own corporate governance regimes, mainly based on voluntary codes of practice for listed companies. The US relies more on a regulatory system of corporate governance.
- Although there are some differences, concepts of good governance in non-commercial organisations are similar to concepts of best practice in corporate governance.

Legal and regulatory aspects of governance

2

■ INTRODUCTION

This brief chapter considers the extent to which best practice in corporate governance is imposed on companies by the law or other regulations. There are two different approaches to establishing a system of best practice in corporate governance. One approach is to establish voluntary principles and guidelines, and invite (or expect) companies to comply with them. A second approach is to establish laws and other regulations for corporate governance that companies must obey. In practice, many countries combine legal and regulatory requirements with voluntary principles and codes of conduct. After reading and understanding the contents of this chapter and working through the 'Test your knowledge' questions, you should be able to:

■ identify aspects of corporate governance practice that may be regulated by law or regulations; and

■ appreciate that laws and regulations on corporate governance vary in their scope between countries, so that some countries adopt a 'rules-based' approach to governance and other countries rely more on a **'principles-based'** approach.

1 Governance and the law

Governance is concerned with the way in which companies are led. The directors of a company should be responsible for safeguarding the assets of the company and for protecting the rights and interests of the shareholders and other stakeholders, and they should also be accountable to the shareholders. It is inevitable that some aspects of governance practice should be regulated by law and that companies should be required to comply with 'best practice'. Regulations on corporate governance may be found in:

■ company law;
■ laws regulating financial markets and financial services;
■ insolvency law; and
■ laws on money laundering and insider dealing.

The law and corporate governance should not be seen as separate issues. Governance occurs within a framework of the law. This point is made in the King IV Report (the South Africa corporate governance code).

As in King III, the King IV Code recommends that those charged with governance should ensure that compliance is understood, not only as an obligation, but also as a source of rights and protection. A holistic view is needed on how applicable laws and non-binding rules, codes and standards relate to one another. This includes how corporate governance codes relate to applicable legislation.

1.1 UK company law and governance

In the UK, the main item of company legislation is the Companies Act (CA 2006). This includes regulations relating to:

- the preparation and auditing of annual financial statements, for approval by the shareholders;
- the powers and duties of directors;
- other disclosures to shareholders, such as the requirement for companies to publish a strategic report in their annual report and accounts;
- the disclosure of information about directors' remuneration;
- general meetings of companies, and shareholder rights to call a general meeting; and
- shareholder voting rights at general meetings, including the right to re-elect directors and have a binding vote on the company's remuneration policy.

Similar regulations are included in the company legislation of other countries; however, this study text will concentrate mainly on UK company law. Each of the aspects of governance listed earlier will be described in the relevant chapters that follow.

There have been a number of EU Directives relating to company law. A proposal for a new or amended EU Directive is initiated by the European Commission in Brussels. Legislation is then agreed by the European Council and the European Parliament in a process known as the 'co-decision procedure'. When a Directive has been agreed, its contents must be implemented by all EU member states within a stated time frame, either in a law or other regulation, if suitable legislation does not already exist. EU Directives on company law have included a requirement for companies to publish an annual business review and, for companies whose shares are traded on a regulated exchange, there have been:

- a Shareholder Rights Directive;
- requirements to publish an annual corporate governance statement;
- requirements to have an audit committee;
- requirements to introduce measures that provide for the independence and ethical conduct of their external auditors; and
- requirements in respect of auditing, including a 70% non-audit service fee cap.

The EU has therefore been responsible for the extension of legislation for aspects of corporate governance, and in doing so it has been influenced by the rules-based approach adopted in the US (see later in section 3, 'The US and the Sarbanes-Oxley Act 2002 (SOX)').

1.2 Governance, the law and financial services

Countries with regulated stock markets and markets for other financial products and services need legislation to regulate the conduct of participants in the markets. Financial markets should be regulated in order to give investors confidence to invest. Customers are important stakeholders in banks, and some elements of financial services legislation are intended to provide consumer protection. In the UK, following the crisis in the banking industry in 2007–2009, the UK financial markets regulator recognised serious weaknesses in corporate governance in banks, particularly inadequate risk management systems, and its responsibility for enforcing improvements.

1.3 Insolvency law and governance

Companies become insolvent for reasons unconnected with corporate governance. Occasionally, however, the directors of a company may allow it to continue in business when they are aware that it is insolvent and will be unable to pay its creditors or employees. In the UK, CA2006 includes provisions that make fraudulent trading a criminal offence and the Insolvency Act 1986 makes wrongful trading a civil offence. Fraudulent trading and wrongful trading are explained in Chapter 5.

1.4 Criminal law and governance

Some aspects of 'bad' corporate governance practice are illegal.

- Directors and other individuals may possess price-sensitive 'inside' knowledge about a company to buy or sell shares in the company with the intention of making a profit (or avoiding a loss). **Insider dealing** is related to corporate governance because it is often carried out by a director or professional adviser of a company. It is also a criminal offence. In the UK, insider dealing is a criminal offence under Part V of the Criminal Justice Act 1993.

■ **Money laundering** is the process of disguising the source of money that has been obtained from serious crime or terrorism, so that it appears to come from a legitimate source. Companies are often used for the purpose of money laundering, which is a criminal offence in most countries, and the owners or directors of the companies concerned are often involved in the money laundering activity themselves.

There is no Corporate Governance Law in any country: rather, some aspects of corporate governance are regulated by sections of different laws. Other aspects of governance are not regulated by law at all, or are regulated only partially. Even in the US, where there is greater emphasis on regulation of corporate governance, many elements of 'best practice' in corporate governance are voluntary.

A point to note about legislation on aspects of corporate governance and a code of corporate governance is that:

■ a code of corporate governance usually applies to listed companies only (although there are codes for non-listed companies too); and

■ legislation can apply to all companies, not just listed companies; however legislation may exclude some types of company, such as small companies, from aspects of legislation relating to corporate governance.

 TEST YOUR KNOWLEDGE 2.1

a What is the relevance of the law on insider dealing to corporate governance?
b What is the relevance of money laundering to good corporate governance practice?

---

2 The UK Listing Regime and corporate governance

In every country where there is a regulated stock market, companies whose shares are traded on the market are required to comply with certain rules of conduct. In the UK, these are contained in the Financial Conduct Authority (FCA) Handbook. This includes the UK Listing Rules and also **Disclosure Guidance and Transparency Rules (DTR)**. These Rules are the responsibility of the Financial Conduct Authority (FCA), one of the UK financial services regulatory bodies. All companies that have a listing for their shares on the main UK stock market (the main market of the London Stock Exchange) must comply with these Rules.

A few of the UK Listing Rules are concerned with corporate governance. These will be explained in some detail in later chapters. Briefly, however, all companies with a **premium listing** in the UK must comply with all aspects of the UK Corporate Governance Code or explain their non-compliance in their annual report and accounts. This rule applies to non-UK companies as well as to UK companies with a premium listing. This is the so-called 'comply or explain' rule.

Public companies that are listed on the Alternative Investment Market (AIM), the London Stock Exchange's international market for smaller growing companies, are not subject to the Code but are required to state which governance standards they apply. The majority choose to follow the Corporate Governance Code for Small and Mid-Size Quoted Companies published by the Quoted Companies Alliance. This adopts key elements of the Code but applies these to the needs and particular circumstances of smaller companies.

A section of the DTR sets out regulations relating to audit committees and corporate governance statements by listed companies.

The **Market Abuse Regulation (MAR)** came into effect on 3 July 2016 across the EU. It aims to increase market integrity and investor protection, enhancing the attractiveness of securities markets for raising capital. MAR contains prohibitions of insider dealing and market manipulation, and provisions to prevent and detect these. MAR is explained further in Chapter 5.

TEST YOUR KNOWLEDGE 2.2

How are the UK Listing Rules enforceable?

3   The US and the Sarbanes-Oxley Act 2002 (SOX)

A different approach to the regulation of corporate governance was taken in the US, following a number of financial scandals and corporate collapses in 2001–2002 involving major corporations such as Enron, WorldCom and Tyco. Previously, corporate governance issues had not been considered a matter of any significance. As a result of Enron and the other corporate scandals, there was an immediate recognition of a need to protect investors, mainly by improving the accuracy and reliability of financial reporting and other disclosures by companies.

The US took a regulatory approach to dealing with the problems that were recognised at the time, and a number of corporate governance measures were included in the Sarbanes-Oxley Act 2002 (sometimes referred to as SOX). The law applied to all public companies in the US and also to all non-US companies that had shares or debt securities registered with the Securities and Exchange Commission (SEC). Chief executive officers (CEOs) and chief financial officers (CFOs) were made personally liable for the accuracy of the financial statements of their company, and new rules on financial reporting were introduced including a requirement to publish an internal audit report with the annual financial statements. Several other corporate governance measures were included in the Act, such as a requirement for legal protection for whistleblowers (explained in Chapter 10).

With the enactment of SOX, the US was considered to have adopted a rules-based approach to corporate governance, different from the 'principles-based' approach in most other countries (described in Chapter 3). However, SOX is not a comprehensive law on corporate governance, and many aspects of corporate governance are not covered by the Act. For example, SOX does not contain any rules about the composition of the board of directors, remuneration of senior executives or dialogue between companies and their shareholders.

TEST YOUR KNOWLEDGE 2.3

Identify two of the main requirements of the SOX 2002 in relation to corporate governance practice in corporations (companies) registered with the SEC in the US.

4   Compulsory regulation and voluntary best practice

This chapter has identified aspects of corporate governance where laws or regulations might apply. In many countries there are voluntary codes of corporate governance, based mainly on principles of good governance rather than detailed and specific rules. Each of these approaches to governance – compulsory regulation and voluntary best practice – has limitations and advantages.

There are several advantages with compulsory regulation of corporate governance issues.

■ There are areas of business where laws are essential to protect the interests of shareholders, employees and other stakeholders in companies. For example, employment laws are needed to give protection to employees against unfair treatment by employers. There should be a legal requirement for companies to prepare annual financial statements and have them audited, and the duties of directors should be subject to the law, in order to protect shareholders. There may be different views about the extent of regulation that is required. However, the need for some regulation seems unquestionable.

■ Best practice in corporate governance has some connection with ethical business practice. Some aspects of corporate behaviour may be considered unethical but legal. Laws are needed to prevent or punish activities that are considered so unethical that they should be illegal.

Bribery is an example of corporate behaviour that has been tolerated in the past but which is now accepted as illegal in some countries, although anti-bribery laws do not appear to be rigorously enforced in practice, even in the UK.

■ Regulation may be needed to address public concerns and maintain public confidence in the capitalist system. This has probably been most evident in the US. The SOX was a response to public outrage against the many corporate scandals that emerged after the collapse of Enron. Public fury against the banks following the financial crisis in 2007–2008 prompted demands for legislative action that would affect the governance of banks.

■ There are arguments in favour of voluntary corporate governance systems.

■ It is difficult to devise a set of rules that should apply to all companies in all circumstances. Rules that are appropriate for one company might not be appropriate for another company whose circumstances are very different. Although a voluntary system of corporate governance (such as the system in the UK) places an expectation on listed companies to comply with the guidelines, it also allows them to breach the guidelines if it seems appropriate and sensible to do so.

■ The biggest concerns about corporate governance practice apply to large stock market companies with large numbers of shareholders. Governance is less of a problem in small companies.

■ As a general rule, governance issues become greater as a company gets bigger. A voluntary code of best practice in governance can be targeted at the largest companies (listed companies), and smaller companies are able to choose whether they want to model their own governance systems on parts of the code for listed companies. Governance practices can therefore be adapted to the circumstances of the company.

■ There may be a risk that if different countries have their own corporate governance regulations, companies will migrate to those countries where the rules are less onerous. Governments may therefore compete to offer a corporate governance regime that is more attractive in their country than in other countries, in order to attract foreign companies.

■ Excessive regulations may deter companies from becoming a listed company, particularly if the rules for listed companies are stricter than the rules for private companies.

In practice, corporate governance is a combination of regulation and voluntary best practice. In some countries there is more emphasis on regulation and in others there is greater reliance on voluntary codes of practice for large companies. However, unless corporate governance is regulated by law, it is probable that standards of governance will vary substantially between companies, especially in small- and medium-sized enterprises (SMEs).

Voluntary best practice is explained more fully in Chapter 3.

 TEST YOUR KNOWLEDGE **2.4**

Explain the disadvantages of a rules-based approach to corporate governance, compared with a principles-based approach.

CHAPTER SUMMARY

■ Corporate governance practices are guided partly by laws and regulations, and partly by voluntary adoption of codes of practice.

■ In many countries, including the UK, certain aspects of corporate governance are covered by the law. These include parts of companies' legislation and laws on corporate insolvency, insider dealing and money laundering.

■ The UK has a voluntary system of corporate governance, but this voluntary system is enforced in UK listed companies (including foreign companies with a premium listing in the UK) by regulations in the UK Listing Rules, the DTR and MAR.

■ The US has a system of corporate governance based more on compliance with regulations, originating with SOX in 2002.

3

Voluntary codes of corporate governance: the role of the company secretary

■ CONTENTS

1 Voluntary codes of best governance practice
2 Corporate governance codes and guidelines in the UK
3 G20/OECD Principles of Corporate Governance
4 Role of the company secretary in corporate governance

■ INTRODUCTION

This chapter describes the nature and purpose of voluntary codes of corporate governance, and compares a 'principles-based' approach to governance with a 'rules-based' approach. It describes the general principles of governance set out in the G20/OECD Principles of Corporate Governance, which were written as a guide to standards of corporate governance that should be applied worldwide. The chapter concludes with an explanation of the role of the company secretary in applying best practice in corporate governance, including complying with governance principles and provisions.

1 Voluntary codes of best governance practice

1.1 The nature and purpose of a voluntary code

A **voluntary code of (corporate) governance** is issued by an authoritative national or international body and contains principles or best practice in corporate governance that major companies (listed companies) are encouraged to adopt and apply. The principles may consist of main principles with associated supporting principles, and for each principle, there may also be provisions or recommendations about how the principle should be applied in practice. Voluntary codes have been adopted in many countries, e.g. in all the countries of the Commonwealth and all the countries of the EU.

There is no statutory requirement for companies to apply the principles or provisions of a voluntary code. However, a well-established code should attract the support of major companies and investors, and this develops an expectation that companies should adopt the code unless their circumstances are such that non-compliance with some of the code's provisions is a more sensible option.

1.2 Principles and provisions

The UK Corporate Governance Code (and the corporate governance codes in many other countries) consists of a number of:

■ principles; and
■ supporting provisions, with one or more provisions for each principle.

In the UK Code, most of the principles are 'main' principles, but for some main principles there are also supporting principles. Provisions indicate how a principle should usually be applied in practice.

The Listing Rules in the UK require listed companies with a premium listing to apply all the main principles of the UK Code, without exception and to report to shareholders (in the annual report) how they have done so.

1.3 'Comply or explain'

Although voluntary, companies whose shares are traded on a major stock market may be required by their Listing Rules to adopt the country's code of governance or to explain in their annual report and accounts their non-compliance with any aspect of the code and their reasons for non-compliance.

In the UK, the Listing Rules require listed companies that are incorporated in the UK to include in their annual report and accounts:

- a statement of how it has applied the main principles of the UK Corporate Governance Code; and
- a statement of whether it has complied throughout the period with all the relevant provisions of the Code; if it has not complied with any of the provisions, it must explain the nature of the non-compliance and the reasons for it.

This requirement, common in many countries, is known as 'comply or explain'. This 'comply or explain' rule applies to the detailed provisions of the UK Code. Any non-compliance by a company with any provision of the Code must not involve any breach of any main principle.

Foreign companies with a primary listing in the UK are required to disclose in their annual report and accounts whether they comply with the corporate governance code of their country of incorporation, and the significant ways in which their corporate governance practices differ from the provisions in the UK Corporate Governance Code.

It is important to be clear that the 'comply or explain' rule in the Listing Rules applies to the provisions of the UK Code, not to the principles.

- Listed companies must apply the main principles of governance as set out in the Code.
- Listed companies are not required to comply with the provisions, but if they do not they must explain their non-compliance. The non-compliance should be for the reason that the company is applying the principles of good governance more effectively than if it did comply with the Code provision.

The UK Corporate Governance Code includes a requirement that when a company explains its non-compliance with a provision of the Code, it should aim to illustrate how its actual governance practices:

- are consistent with the principle to which the particular provision relates;
- contribute to good governance; and
- promote delivery of business objectives.

  'It should set out the background, provide a clear rationale for the action it is taking, and describe any mitigating actions taken to address any additional risk and maintain conformity with the relevant principle.'

1.4 Reasons for the 'comply or explain' rule

The purpose of a voluntary code is to raise standards of corporate governance in major companies (although other companies are also encouraged to comply with relevant provisions). It is principles-based, because there is a recognition that the same set of rules is not necessarily appropriate in every way for all companies, and that there will be situations where:

- non-compliance with provisions in the Code is desirable, given the circumstances that the company faces; and
- implementing a principle of best practice is not always best achieved by following the detailed provisions or recommendations in the Code, and some flexibility should be allowed.

The 'comply or explain' approach recognises that a Code cannot provide detailed guidelines for every situation, and a single rule cannot necessarily apply to all companies in all circumstances. The preface to the 2016 version of the UK Corporate Governance Code includes the following comment:

'It is recognised that an alternative to following a provision may be justified in particular circumstances if good governance can be achieved by other means. A condition of doing so is that the reasons for it should be explained clearly and carefully to shareholders ... In providing an explanation, the company should aim to illustrate how its actual practices are consistent with the principle to which the particular provision relates, contribute to good governance and promote delivery of business objectives.'

1.5 'Apply or explain'

In the UK, the Listing Rules require listed companies to comply with the UK Corporate Governance Code or explain any non-compliance. In other countries there is a view that the word 'comply' will encourage companies to follow the provisions of a code in all its details, without giving proper consideration to the principles that underpin the code. This encourages a **box-ticking approach**, and a view that the detailed provisions must be followed without considering whether the provisions might actually be appropriate or a suitable way of applying the governance principles in the actual circumstances.

For this reason, some countries have adopted what they call an 'apply or explain' rule (or approach), not a 'comply or explain' approach. The King Code IV (the governance code for South Africa has moved from a 'apply or explain' rule in King III to an 'apply and explain' rule) gives its reasons for doing this:

'The required explanation allows stakeholders to make an informed decision as to whether or not the organisation is achieving the ... good governance outcomes required by King IV. Explanation also helps to encourage organisations to see corporate governance not as an act of mindless compliance, but something that will yield results only if it is approached mindfully, with due consideration of the organisation's circumstances.'

Thus King IV considers the application of all the principles is assumed and companies should explain the practices that have been implemented to give effect to each principle.

1.6 Shareholder response to non-compliance

The UK Code provides some guidance on how shareholders should respond to any non-compliance with a provision of the Code by their company. Since the Code allows non-compliance, it recommends that shareholders should consider carefully the reason that the company gives for non-compliance. It suggests that shareholders should:

- give due regard to the particular circumstances of the company; and
- bear in mind the size and complexity of the company and the nature of the risks and challenges that it faces.

'Whilst shareholders have every right to challenge companies' explanations if they are unconvincing, they should not be evaluated in a mechanistic way and departures from the Code should not be automatically treated as breaches.'

The Code recognises that some if its provisions may not be the most suitable approach to good governance for smaller listed companies, especially those that are new to listing. Even so, it encourages all listed companies to comply with the Code's provisions.

The Code does not give any further guidance to shareholders. However, shareholder displeasure with a company's governance practices may be discussed with the company, or possibly expressed at a general meeting of the company by voting against a particular proposal from the board.

- The Stewardship Code provides guidance on how institutional shareholders should discuss issues with board representatives.
- The Pensions and Lifetime Savings Association (PLSA) has issued voting guidelines, indicating how shareholders should vote on particular proposals at a general meeting if they wish to express their opposition to the board on particular issues.

TEST YOUR KNOWLEDGE 3.1

a What is the difference between principles and provisions in a code of corporate governance?
b In the UK, how does the 'comply or explain' rule apply to foreign companies with a premium listing?
c What is the difference between 'comply or explain' and 'apply or explain'?
d What is a box-ticking approach to compliance with corporate governance requirements and how might such an approach be harmful for companies?

2 Corporate governance codes and guidelines in the UK

2.1 The UK Corporate Governance Code

It is useful to look at the main sections of the UK Code of Corporate Governance, to see what the main areas of corporate governance are. The Code has five sections.

1 **Leadership.** This contains principles and provisions relating to the responsibilities of the board as a whole, its chairman and its non-executive directors (NEDs).
2 **Effectiveness.** This section is concerned with the effectiveness of the board of directors. It deals with issues such as the composition of the board of directors, the appointment and re-election of directors, induction and training for directors, and annual performance reviews for the board, its committees and individual directors.
3 **Accountability.** This section deals with the accountability of the board of directors, and also its responsibility for risk and risk management, including **internal control risk** (see also Chapter 10).
4 **Remuneration.** The fourth section of the Code contains principles and provisions relating to the remuneration of directors and senior executives.
5 **Relations with shareholders.** The final section of the Code sets out the responsibilities of the board for establishing a dialogue with shareholders, and using the AGM to communicate with shareholders and encourage their participation.

2.2 Additional guidance

When the Combined Code was first published in the UK in 2003, there was some uncertainty about how some aspects of the Code should be applied. This led to the development of three additional guidelines, which are all now the responsibility of the Financial Reporting Council (FRC).

A report was produced on the role of the chairman and independent NEDs, known as the Higgs Report (or the Higgs Guidance). This was updated following a review on behalf of the FRC by ICSA, and amended guidance was issued as the **FRC Guidance on Board Effectiveness** in 2011.

Another report was published providing more detailed guidance on the role of the audit committee. It was originally called the Smith Report (after the name of the committee chairman) but is now called the **FRC Guidance on Audit Committees (2016)**.

A third report, known as the Turnbull Report or **Turnbull Guidance**, was published giving additional guidance on the responsibilities of the board for the systems of risk management and internal control in the company. This has now been replaced by the FRC's **Guidance on Risk Management, Internal Control and Related Financial and Business Reporting** (2014).

Relevant sections of the UK Code and the additional guidance will be described in subsequent chapters.

TEST YOUR KNOWLEDGE 3.2

a   Which body is responsible for the UK Code of Corporate Governance?
b   What are the five sections of the UK Corporate Governance Code?

3   G20/OECD Principles of Corporate Governance

Before going on to study the UK Code in more detail, it is useful to look at the corporate governance principles issued by the OECD in 1999, and revised in 2004. The OECD Corporate Governance Committee conducted a further review of the OECD Principles of Corporate Governance. The review process started in 2014 and concluded in 2015. The 2015 edition, the G20/OECD Principles of Corporate Governance, has been adopted as one of the Financial Stability Board's Key Standards for Sound Financial Systems and endorsed by the G20.

The G20/OECD Principles set out broad principles of good corporate governance that should apply worldwide, in developed and developing economies alike. Although they were written after the first UK codes, they nevertheless help to show what voluntary codes of corporate governance should be trying to achieve.

The G20/OECD Principles are intended to serve as a reference point for countries to use when evaluating their legal, institutional and regulatory provisions for corporate governance. They also offer guidance and suggestions for stock exchanges, investors, companies and other bodies involved in developing good corporate governance practices.

Unlike national codes of corporate governance, such as the UK Code, the G20/OECD Principles do not contain any detailed provisions about how the principles should be applied in practice. They are simply a set of main principles and supporting principles, with some additional explanations or 'annotations'. The principles deal with six aspects of governance, as follows.

1   Ensuring the basis for an effective corporate governance framework.
2   The rights and equitable treatment of shareholders and key ownership functions.
3   Institutional investors, stock markets and other intermediaries.
4   The role of stakeholders in corporate governance.
5   Disclosure and transparency.
6   The responsibilities of the board.

3.1   Ensuring the basis for an effective corporate governance framework

The G20/OECD Principles begin with a statement that the corporate governance framework should:

- promote transparent, fair markets, and the efficient allocation of resources;
- be consistent with the rule of law; and
- support effective supervision and enforcement.

In the UK these basics are probably accepted as 'normal' for public companies, but it is a useful reminder that this is not necessarily the case at all times or in all countries.

3.2   The rights and equitable treatment of shareholders and key ownership functions

The framework of principles provided by the G20/OECD is notable because of the emphasis they give to shareholder rights. It states: *'The corporate governance framework should protect and facilitate the exercise of shareholders' rights and ensure the equitable treatment of all shareholders, including minority and foreign shareholders. All shareholders should have the opportunity to obtain effective redress for violation of their rights.'*

These are basic rights that all equity shareholders should be permitted by their company's constitution. It should be remembered that the principles are intended to apply to all countries with public companies, not just to countries with advanced economies or only with an Anglo-Saxon corporate culture.

An initial principle is that equity shareholders have certain property rights that should be protected. These are the rights to:

- secure methods of ownership registration;
- transfer shares, for example by selling them;
- obtain relevant information about the company on a timely and regular basis;
- participate and vote in general meetings of the company;
- elect and remove directors; and
- share in the profits of the company.

These may seem basic rights, but they have not been respected at all times in all countries.

The principles also state that shareholders should have the right to be informed about matters that would fundamentally change the company and to participate in decisions about them. Examples of such matters are:

- amendments to the constitution of the company;
- authorising the issue of additional shares; and
- extraordinary transactions, such as the transfer of all or most of the assets of the company (which would effectively mean the sale of the company, or substantially all of it).

Shareholders should have the opportunity to participate effectively and vote in general shareholder meetings and should be informed of the rules, including voting procedures, which govern general shareholder meetings:

1 Shareholders should be furnished with sufficient and timely information concerning the date, location and agenda of general meetings, as well as full and timely information regarding the issues to be decided at the meeting.
2 Processes and procedures for general shareholder meetings should allow for equitable treatment of all shareholders. Company procedures should not make it unduly difficult or expensive to cast votes.

Shareholders should have the opportunity to ask questions to the board, including questions relating to the annual external audit, to place items on the agenda of general meetings, and to propose resolutions, subject to reasonable limitations.

Effective shareholder participation in key corporate governance decisions, such as the nomination and election of board members, should be facilitated. Shareholders should be able to make their views known, including through votes at shareholder meetings, on the remuneration of board members and/or key executives, as applicable. The equity component of compensation schemes for board members and employees should be subject to shareholder approval.

Shareholders should be able to vote in person or in absentia, and equal effect should be given to votes whether cast in person or in absentia.

Impediments to cross-border voting should be eliminated.

Ability to consult

Shareholders, including institutional shareholders, should be allowed to consult with each other on issues concerning their basic shareholder rights as defined in the Principles, subject to exceptions to prevent abuse.

Equal treatment

All shareholders of the same series of a class should be treated equally. Capital structures and arrangements that enable certain shareholders to obtain a degree of influence or control disproportionate to their equity ownership should be disclosed.

Related-party transactions

Related-party transactions should be approved and conducted in a manner that ensures proper management of conflict of interest and protects the interest of the company and its shareholders.

Minority shareholders

Minority shareholders should be protected from abusive actions by, or in the interest of, controlling shareholders acting either directly or indirectly, and should have effective means of redress. Abusive self-dealing should be prohibited.

Capital markets

Markets for corporate control should be allowed to function in an efficient and transparent manner.

 **CASE EXAMPLE** 3.1

Luxury goods company LVMH had a large shareholding in fashion company Gucci, a Dutch-registered company. However, in March 1999, the Pinault-Printemps-Redoute group (PPR) acquired a 42% stake in the company. The PPR share purchase was arranged through a $3 billion increase in Gucci's capital, diluting LVMH's stake from 34% to 20%. LVMH applied to the Enterprise Chamber of the Amsterdam Court of Appeals, in an attempt to get the capital increase annulled. Meanwhile, Gucci instigated criminal proceedings against LVMH for alleged defamation, backed by PPR.

In a counter-move, LVMH said it would ask the US SEC to examine the disclosure of a stock option plan of Gucci (Gucci shares were listed in New York as well as in Amsterdam). LVMH believed it had discovered an unlawful move to cover up the true nature of the share options offered at the time of the PPR share acquisition in Gucci, and believed it had sufficient evidence to force PPR to make a full takeover bid. Under Dutch company law, PPR did not have to make a full takeover bid for Gucci even though it had control of the company.

In November 2000, LVMH had already asked the Dutch court to establish whether two employees in Gucci, the chief executive and the chief designer, had received 8 million undisclosed share options in return for their supporting the PPR bid in 1999. Gucci counter-argued that the share options were granted later, and only about 6 million (not 8 million) were granted. The two managers disclosed that their stock options were equal to 5% of Gucci's equity. The SEC was now being asked to examine whether Gucci had violated rules for stock options in terms of disclosure and audit under US accounting rules, rather than under the less rigorous Dutch laws.

The crux of the argument was still the validity of the capital increase, but the stock option argument had opened up a second route of investigation.

LVMH wanted to be bought out by PPR, but a sticking point was the share price. Gucci shares were trading below the price that LVMH wanted. The shareholders' meeting at which the stock option plan had been agreed in June 2000 was held just two days after PPR and LVMH announced that they had failed to find a settlement to their dispute, and LVMH abstained from the vote. LVMH said later that it did not vote against the stock options because it had been misled about who would benefit from them.

In January 2001, Gucci made a complaint to the European Commission, alleging that LMVH was abusing its dominant market position and using its 20% stake in Gucci to frustrate Gucci's business plans. It called on the Commission to force LMVH to divest itself of the shareholding. Gucci was complaining that another lawsuit filed by LMVH in the Netherlands disputing Gucci's takeover of the fashion house Yves St Laurent was not in the interests of shareholders.

3.3 Institutional investors, stock markets, and other intermediaries

The notes to the G20/OECD Principles acknowledge that a corporate governance framework should provide sound incentives throughout the investment chain and provide for stock markets to function in a way that contributes to good corporate governance. It is also highlighted that the share of equity investments held by institutional investors such as mutual funds, pension funds, insurance companies and hedge funds has increased significantly, and many of their assets are managed by specialised asset managers.

The G20/OECD Principles recommend that institutional investors disclose their policies with respect to corporate governance. They note, however, that voting at shareholder meetings is only one channel for **shareholder engagement**; and that direct contact and dialogue with the board and management, represent other forms of shareholder engagement that are frequently used. The Principles acknowledge that, in recent years, some countries have begun to consider adoption of codes on shareholder engagement ('stewardship codes') that institutional investors are invited to sign up to on a voluntary basis.

The G20/OECD Principles state that:

- institutional investors should disclose their corporate governance and voting policies with respect to their investments, including the procedures that they have in place for deciding on the use of their voting rights;
- votes should be cast by custodians or nominees in line with the directions of the beneficial owner of the shares;
- institutional investors should disclose how they manage material conflicts of interest that may affect the exercise of key ownership rights regarding their investments;
- the corporate governance framework should require that **proxy** advisors and analysts disclose and minimise conflicts of interest that might compromise the integrity of their analysis or advice;
- insider trading and market manipulation should be prohibited and the applicable rules enforced;
- for companies who are listed in a jurisdiction other than their jurisdiction of incorporation, the applicable corporate governance laws and regulations should be clearly disclosed; and
- stock markets should provide fair and efficient price discovery as a means to help promote effective corporate governance.

3.4 The role of stakeholders in corporate governance

The G20/OECD Principles also recognise that companies should recognise the rights and role of stakeholders other than shareholders. The emphasis is mainly on the recognition of legal rights. The corporate governance framework should 'recognise the rights of stakeholders established by law or through mutual agreements', and should 'encourage active co-operation between corporations and stakeholders in creating wealth, jobs and the sustainability of financially sound enterprises'.

- Stakeholder rights established by law or by mutual agreements should be respected. Where stakeholder interests are protected by law, stakeholders should have the opportunity to obtain effective redress for violation of their rights.
- Mechanisms for employee participation should be allowed to develop. Where stakeholders participate in the corporate governance process, they should have access to relevant, sufficient and reliable information on a timely and regular basis.
- Employees and other stakeholders should be able to 'freely communicate their concerns about illegal or unethical practices to the board and to the competent public authorities and their rights should not be compromised for doing this'.
- Corporate governance should be complemented by an effective, efficient insolvency framework and the effective enforcement of creditors' rights.

3.5 Disclosure and transparency

Another aspect of the G20/OECD Principles is a requirement for 'timely and accurate' disclosure of information by a company (the importance of transparency for good corporate governance was explained earlier). The information provided by companies should include material information about their financial and operating results, corporate objectives, major share ownership, details of members of the board and their remuneration, related party transactions, material risk factors, material issues affecting employees and other stakeholders, and governance structures and policies.

Information should be prepared and disclosed in accordance with high quality standards of accounting and financial and non-financial reporting.

Channels for disseminating information should provide equal, timely and cost-efficient access to relevant information by users.

An annual audit should be conducted by an independent, competent and qualified auditor. External auditors should be accountable to shareholders and owe a duty of professional care to the company in the conduct of the audit. The audit provides external and objective assurance that the financial statements give a fair representation of the financial position and performance of the company.

In notes to the Principles, the G20/OECD comments:

'A strong disclosure regime that promotes real transparency is a pivotal feature of market-based monitoring of companies and is central to shareholders' ability to exercise their shareholder rights on an informed basis. Experience shows that disclosure can also be a powerful tool for influencing the behaviour of companies and for protecting investors. A strong disclosure regime can help to attract capital and maintain confidence in the capital markets … Insufficient or unclear information may hamper the ability of the markets to function, increase the cost of capital and result in a poor allocation of resources.'

In the case of multinational companies operating in other countries, disclosure also helps to improve the understanding of the local populations about the company, its activities and its policies, with respect to environmental and ethical standards and the relationships between the companies, and the communities in which they are operating.

3.6 The responsibilities of the board

The G20/OECD Principles end with a section on the responsibilities of the board of directors:

'The corporate governance framework should ensure the strategic guidance of the company, the effective monitoring of management by the board and the board's accountability to the company and the shareholders.'

Board members should act on a fully informed basis, in good faith, with due diligence and care, and in the best interest of the company and the shareholders. Where board decisions may affect different shareholder groups differently, the board should treat all shareholders fairly. The board should apply high ethical standards. It should take into account the interests of stakeholders.

The board should fulfil certain key functions, including:

- reviewing and guiding corporate strategy, risk policy, annual budgets and business plans, major capital expenditures and acquisitions and divestments;
- monitoring the effectiveness of corporate governance;
- the recruitment and compensation of key executives;
- the remuneration of key executives, which should be aligned with the long-term interests of the company and its shareholders;
- ensuring a formal and transparent board nomination and election process; monitoring and managing potential conflicts of interest of management, board members and shareholders, including misuse of corporate assets and abuse in related party transactions;
- ensuring the integrity of the company's accounting and financial reporting systems, including the external audit, and the effectiveness of systems of control and risk management; and
- overseeing the process of disclosure and communication.

 TEST YOUR KNOWLEDGE 3.3

a   What are the six aspects of corporate governance covered by the G20/OECD Principles?
b   List six rights of shareholders in the G20/OECD Principles.
c   Why might there be impediments to cross-border voting by foreign shareholders?
d   Identify three ways in which the treatment of shareholders might be made more equitable, according to the G20/OECD Principles.
e   What approach and framework do the G20/OECD principles set out for institutional investors?
f   What do the G20/OECD Principles state about the role of stakeholders in corporate governance?
g   According to the G20/OECD Principles, what are the benefits of a strong disclosure regime?

4 Role of the company secretary in corporate governance

4.1 General responsibilities

The King IV Code includes as one of its principles that the board should ensure it has access to professional and independent guidance on corporate governance and its legal duties, and also that it has support to coordinate the functioning of the governing body and its committees.

For some companies, the appointment of a company secretary is a statutory requirement. In respect of those companies, the company secretary provides professional corporate governance services. The governing body of an organisation not so obliged should, as a matter of leading practice, consider appointing a company secretary or other professional, as is appropriate for the organisation, to provide professional corporate governance services to the governing body. As recommended practice, it specifies what the governance-related responsibilities of the company secretary should be.

In the UK, Companies Act 2006 (CA 2006) (s. 271) states that public companies must have a company secretary.

Company secretaries are in a unique position to fulfil an important role in corporate governance. They are not members of the board of directors, and so do not have direct responsibility for corporate governance and accountability to shareholders. Without being a director, they know about what is going on at board level in the company and can give advice and administrative assistance, to:

- the chairman;
- the board as a whole;
- board committees; and
- other individual directors.

Company secretaries have a range of different responsibilities, including company administration matters and providing support for board meetings. Many of these responsibilities are not related (or only indirectly related) to corporate governance. Some responsibilities, however, are specifically related to corporate governance matters, and one of the functions of the company secretary should be to promote high standards of governance in the company.

- The UK Code states that 'Under the direction of the chairman[person], the company secretary's responsibilities include: ensuring good information flows:
  - within the board and its committees; and
  - between senior managers and NEDs.'
- Good corporate governance relies on communication and the exchange of information, and the company secretary is in a position to help ensure that this happens. By attending board meetings and committee meetings, they should ensure that relevant information is passed from board to committee or from one committee to the board or another committee. By acting as a point of communication and contact for NEDs, the company secretary should also be able to contribute to the flows of information between NEDs and senior executive managers in the company.
- 'All directors should have access to the advice and services of the company secretary, who is responsible to the board for ensuring that board procedures are complied with.'
- 'The company secretary should be responsible for advising the board through the chairman on all governance matters.' The company secretary should have a full understanding of corporate governance requirements, and should be able to identify governance issues that arise and advise the board accordingly.

4.2 FRC Guidance on Board Effectiveness: board support and the role of the company secretary

The FRC Guidance on Board Effectiveness (2011) states that the company secretary should support the chairman of the board of directors and report to the chairman on all governance matters (the company secretary may report to the chief executive officer (CEO) on other administrative matters, but should report to the chairman on governance issues).

- The appointment and removal of a company secretary should be a matter for the board as a whole to decide.
- The company secretary should be responsible for ensuring that the board committees function effectively (and ICSA recommends as a matter of good governance practice that the company secretary should act as secretary to the main board committees). This responsibility includes ensuring that the board and its committees are provided with high quality information.
- The company secretary should also assist the chairman with the induction and development of directors (explained in Chapter 5).
- With the chairman, the company secretary should periodically review corporate governance arrangements, and whether they are fit for purpose or whether improvements should be considered.

4.3 ICSA Guidance on Corporate Governance Role of the Company Secretary

The specific responsibilities of a company secretary for corporate governance matters should be decided by the company. The 'ICSA guidance on the corporate governance role of the company secretary' (2013) suggests a list of responsibilities relating to corporate governance. These are divided into three main areas.

1 Specific responsibilities derived from the UK Code.
2 Responsibilities relating to statutory and regulatory compliance.
3 Corporate responsibility.

The responsibilities in the ICSA guidance are listed below in section 4.4 (although the list is not comprehensive). They are detailed, and you may find it useful to return to this section when you have finished reading this text.

4.4 Specific responsibilities derived from the Code

Summarised below are the main responsibilities, which should be assumed by the company secretary in assisting the chairman to implement the Code principles and comply with its provisions. The company secretary should report to the chairman on all board governance matters. This issue is covered in more detail in the guidance note Duties and Reporting Lines of the Company Secretary.

Board composition and procedures

- Establishing a formal schedule of matters reserved for decision by the Board and a formal division of responsibilities between the chairman and CEO.
- Scheduling board meetings, assisting with the preparation of agendas, providing guidance on board paper content, ensuring good and timely information flows within the board and its committees and between senior management and NEDs; recording board decisions clearly and accurately, pursuing follow-up actions and reporting on matters arising.
- Ensuring that appropriate insurance cover is arranged in respect of any potential legal action against directors.
- Ensuring board committees are constituted in compliance with the Code and that the committees have the appropriate balance of skills, experience, independence and knowledge of the company.
- Supporting the board and nominations committee on **board succession** planning and on the process for the appointment of new directors to the board.

Board information, development and relationships

- Planning and organising director induction programmes which provide a full, formal and tailored introduction to the board and the business. There is a separate ICSA guidance note on the induction of directors.
- Planning and organising director professional development programmes to refresh the directors' skills and knowledge.

- Arranging for major shareholders to be offered the opportunity to meet new directors.
- Facilitating good information flows between board members, the committees and senior management as well as and fostering effective working between executive directors and NEDs.
- Establishing and communicating procedures for directors to take independent professional advice at the company's expense if required.
- Developing a proactive relationship with board members, providing a source of information and advice, and acting as the primary point of contact with NEDs.
- Supporting the process for the board to undertake formal annual evaluation of its own performance and that of its committees and individual directors.

Accountability

Financial and business reporting:

- Having a detailed knowledge of, and advising on, the board's responsibility to present a fair, balanced and understandable assessment of the company's position and prospects in annual and interim reports plus other price sensitive public reports and reports to regulators and that information required under statute. The company secretary should also ensure that the requirements of the FCA's Listing, Prospectus, and Disclosure and Transparency Rules (LPDT Rules) are met and be aware of the guidance available on these areas.

Risk management and internal control:

- Assisting the board in an annual review of the effectiveness of the company's risk management and internal control systems including financial, operational and **compliance controls**. Audit committee and auditors.
- Ensuring that the audit committee is fully conversant with the Code principles around corporate reporting, risk management and internal control principles. This should include the relationship with the external auditors, in particular as regards audit quality, provisions of non-audit services, recommendations for appointment and renewal of auditors and putting the audit contract out to tender.
- Ensuring the implementation of and monitoring the effectiveness of the procedure for staff to raise concerns about possible improprieties in matters of financial reporting or other matters.

Remuneration:

- Ensuring that the remuneration committee is familiar with the Code principles and provisions on remuneration, including the provisions on the design of performance related remuneration for executive directors set out in Schedule A of the Code.
- Ensuring that grants of share options and other long term incentive awards do not contravene the Code.
- Ensuring that the provisions in the directors' term of appointment in relation to early termination are in accordance with the Code.
- Ensuring that non-executive remuneration is determined in line with Code provisions and within the limits set by the articles of association.
- Ensuring that all new long-term incentive schemes and significant changes to existing schemes are submitted to shareholders for approval, in accordance with the Listing Rules.
- Ensuring compliance with the legal requirements in relation to directors' remuneration, including any necessary shareholder approvals, contributing to the drafting of the directors' remuneration report and ensuring its compliance with the full range of disclosure requirements.

Relationship with shareholders:

- Ensuring the board keeps in touch with shareholder opinion on a continuing basis.
- Managing relations with institutional investors on corporate governance issues and board procedures in accordance with the principles established in the UK.

Stewardship Code:

- Managing the convening and conduct of the annual general meeting (AGM) in line with statutory and regulatory requirements and the Code, and using it as an opportunity to communicate with retail investors.

Disclosure and reporting:

■ Ensuring that the necessary disclosures on corporate governance and the workings of the board and its committees are included in the annual report.

All companies with a premium listing of equity shares in the UK are required under the Listing Rules to report how they have applied the Code in the annual report and accounts:

■ Ensuring that the requisite types of governance information are made available, as required, for example on the company's website.

4.5 Statutory and regulatory compliance

As well as the corporate governance role, the company secretary normally has full responsibility for Companies Act compliance and, where the company is listed, carries much of the responsibility for compliance with the FCA's LPDT Rules. For listed companies, there is also the need to make the board aware of the market abuse provisions of the Financial Services and Markets Act 2000 (FSMA) including, in particular, the responsibility not to release misleading information about the company's financial performance or trading condition, or to mislead the market by the failure to disclose relevant information.

Set out below are the areas of action required to discharge those governance responsibilities which are normally managed or shared by the company secretary.

Directors' duties:

■ Implementing procedures to help directors discharge their statutory duties as codified under ss. 171 to 177 of the CA2006, in particular their specific duties to promote the success of the company taking account of a wide range of stakeholder interests and to avoid conflicts of interest. Guidance on these particular duties is available in the ICSA guidance note *Directors' General Duties*.

Share dealing:

■ Communicating and implementing procedures for listed company directors and any other 'person discharging managerial responsibilities', as defined in s. 96B of FSMA (PDMR) to comply with the Model Code on share dealing annexed to the Listing Rules.
■ Establishing and operating procedures for disclosure of dealings in shares by major shareholders and PDMRs.

Protection of inside information:

■ Implementing procedures to comply with the provisions of the Disclosure Rules on the protection of 'inside information' as defined in s. 118C of FSMA and on the maintenance of **'insider' lists**.

Verification of published information:

■ implementing a 'verification and approval' process to review and confirm the accuracy of all company statements prior to publication and to authorise their release to the market.

Responsible release of market information:

■ Developing a formal policy and established procedures to make the announcements required under the Listing Rules and the Disclosure and Transparency Rules and, particularly, on the disclosure of inside information so that the company's shareholders and the market generally are kept fully informed.
■ Ensuring that there is appropriate and timely consultation with the company's brokers and other advisers on the release of significant information about corporate performance and developments whenever the company is in any doubt.

Compliance with continuing obligations under the LPDT Rules:

■ Developing and implementing policies and procedures for compliance by the company and its directors of all other aspects of continuing obligations under the LPDT Rules, including the restrictions in relation to class and related party transactions, requirements in relation to notifications of particular events, restrictions and requirements in relation to share issues and share buy-backs, and requirements in relation to the issue and contents of circulars to shareholders.

4.6 Corporate responsibility

In 2010 the FRC published the first version of the Stewardship Code based largely on the **Institutional Shareholders Committee's** (ISC's) Statement of Principles for Institutional Shareholders and Agents that had been in existence since 2002. The UK Stewardship Code is aimed mainly, but not exclusively, at institutional investors and is designed to assist institutional investors in exercising their stewardship responsibilities in relation to the companies they invest in. Companies have an equal role to play in improving engagement and purposeful dialogue between investors and companies and the company secretary will be in the frontline of those areas of engagement. As part of the growing awareness and debate on corporate responsibility in recent years, some institutional investors, and their agents, have issued guidelines and disclosure principles to highlight those issues on which shareholders place particular importance such as environmental and social issues and directors' remuneration, as well as clarifying their particular policy and standpoint on corporate governance matters.

The company secretary should share responsibility with relevant specialist functions for ensuring that the board is aware of current guidelines in these areas and that it identifies and takes account of the significance of corporate responsibility issues in its stewardship and oversight of the company.

The role of the company secretary should be kept in mind as you read the following chapters on the various major issues in corporate governance.

The following case example (3.1) is an illustration of the involvement of the company secretary in corporate governance matters, in this case where concerns were raised about illicit or improper share dealings by a director, and poor communications between the company and its shareholders. Issues of corporate governance are rarely clear-cut, as this case suggests. As a useful exercise, you should consider the role of the company secretary in these events and what the company should have done differently, if anything, from what it actually did do.

 CASE EXAMPLE 3.2

In March 2000, the Anglo-French IT services company Sema acquired LHS, an Atlanta-based software company that sold mobile phone billing software. It was bought for £3 billion in March 2000, at a 75% premium to its current share price. Herr L, the founder of LHS and a major shareholder, became a NED of Sema. The acquisition by Sema was seen as a strategic move by the company into the US market.

Investors started to become uneasy when Sema's interim results were announced in September 2000. These had very little to say about either the acquisition or Sema's expansion plans in the US. Analysts were also annoyed by what they regarded as window dressing in the company's interim financial results. The company included in its profits a £14.3 million refund from its Swedish pension fund. Stripping out this one-off non-operational item would have left operating profits much lower. The share price fell by about 17% in the week the interim results were announced.

Unbeknown to Sema's board, in the week leading up to its interim results, Herr L had started selling shares in large quantities. He sold 1.8 million Sema shares for £24 million in the run-up to the Sema interim results, making three separate sales through a German bank. Each of these sale transactions was in breach of the Model Code requirement for UK listed companies that directors should not deal in shares of their company in a 'closed period', i.e. in the two months before the announcement of the company's results. Herr L sold a further 800,000 shares for £9 million on the day the results were announced. The average sale price for these transactions was about £12.70.

Sema's company secretary was reported as saying that he learned of the improper sales on 11 October, when he was contacted by an investment bank. It appears that when Sema purchased LHS, an arrangement in the transaction (intended to avoid German tax penalties) was that Herr L would hold on to his LHS shares after the acquisition, but with an option to exchange them for Sema shares

from January 2002. From the investment bank, the Sema company secretary learned in October that Herr L had exercised his option over part of his stake, ahead of schedule and without notifying anyone at Sema.

The company secretary tried to obtain details of the share deals by Herr L, in order to make an announcement to the stock market. However, he needed the transaction dates, number of shares sold and price received for Sema in order to make a statement. He found Herr L obstructive and unhelpful and it took two weeks to get the information. Sema then informed the UK Financial Services Authority (FSA).

Herr L apparently stated that he made the share transactions in all honesty, misunderstanding the stock exchange rules. Investors, however, were sceptical, since LHS had been quoted on the **Nasdaq** stock market in the US, and so its directors would have been familiar with the restrictions in the US on director share dealings.

A further problem for Sema was the poor trading performance of LHS after the acquisition. Far from growing, as the market had been led to expect when the acquisition was made in March, sales slumped from £42 million in the first quarter to £36 million in the second quarter and £24 million in the third. Profits were consequently well below expectations, and the company issued a profits warning on 25 November. The market suspected that Sema had known about the problem long before it issued the warning. The share price fell 44% on the day of the profits warning, and a further 10% (to 329p) on the following Monday. This was a long way below the level at which Herr L had sold his shares in September.

On 28 November, the *Financial Times* carried a report that the company was going to ask him to resign 'after concluding that he was damaging the company's standing with investors'. On 29 November, Sema announced that Herr L had resigned. The story of the share dealings by Herr L was given in the financial press, and it was reported that Herr L had apparently not followed Sema's formal compliance procedures and that an investigation was started by the FSA. Investors were said to be angry about the delay in informing the FSA, with questions asked about the company's compliance procedures. How could the company have remained ignorant for so long about the share dealings by Herr L? With the profits warning as an additional problem, and the lack of adequate information from the company, the credibility of the company's senior management was at risk.

The *Daily Telegraph* commented on 3 December 2000:

'A botched acquisition, a profits warning and a share dealing scandal have shredded management credibility. After years of growth, the shares ended last week at a sixth of their February peak, threatening Sema's place in the FTSE 100 index.'

A stockbroker was reported to have said:

'The issue for everyone, and the reason the shares have been so weak since the profits warning, is that the market believes it has been misled for most of this year.'

The financial press identified a major problem as poor communications with investors by Sema's chief executive and finance director, caused to some extent by language difficulties. The report ended with a comment that the board needed strengthening, with someone who will 'fight the corner' of British investors, given the dominance of French directors at the moment.

On 4 December, the Sema share price fell to 271p and the company subsequently dropped out of the FTSE 100. This followed a decision by the company to postpone until January a scheduled meeting with analysts on 6 December. The company stated the postponement was 'appropriate' and that it had set up a board committee to investigate why the company did not warn earlier of the problems at LHS, and to examine the share dealings of Herr L. The board committee would consist of the company's CEO, the board chairman, one other NED and the company secretary, and would be advised by solicitors Clifford Chance.

CASE EXAMPLE 3.2 *continued*

This immediately raised another corporate governance concern. One institutional investor, holding 2% of Sema shares, was reported to have said that an independent committee would have been more appropriate.

'We would prefer the involvement of independent accountants other than their auditors. This would give added credibility to the outcome of the process, and seems particularly necessary given the constitution of the committee … . Clearly the co-operation of Sema's executives is important. But it would have been quite possible for the board to have set up a committee with the power to co-opt the views of the executives from time to time.'

The company's difficulties were not yet over. On 23 January 2001, it made another profits warning. The share price fell by 47.5p. Its pre-tax profit forecast for the year was reduced to £90 million from £95 million, having been cut the previous November from £130 million to £100 million. Sema also announced that it had started the search for a new chief executive to replace 'in due course' the current CEO. The low level of Sema's share price was thought to make it vulnerable to a bid. France Telecom, the largest investor in Sema with a shareholding of 18%, stated that it did not regard its holding in Sema as 'core'.

4.7 The company secretary as the conscience of the company

In the context of business ethics and corporate governance, the company secretary can be described as the 'conscience of the company'. Acting in accordance with conscience means acting in a way that seems ethical.

There will often be situations where it is in the best short-term interests of a company to ignore best governance practice or even act in an unethical way. For example, the board of directors may want to 'window dress' the financial statements and make the financial performance of the company appear better than it really is. Or a company may wish to bribe a government official in order to win a major contract. The company secretary should speak out against bad governance and unethical practice, and remind the board and senior executives of the appropriate course of conduct and the principles of good governance that they should apply.

In order to act in this way, as a 'conscience' for the directors and senior executives, the company secretary must be independent-minded, and should not be under the influence of any other individual, such as the company chairman or CEO.

4.8 Independence of the company secretary: appointment and removal

The role of the company secretary in corporate governance is such that it is essential to ensure their independence from undue influence and pressure from a senior board member. An ICSA guidance note on 'Reporting lines of the company secretary' (2013) has commented:

'Boards of directors have a right to expect the company secretary to give impartial advice and to act in the best interests of the company. However, it is incumbent on boards of directors to ensure that company secretaries are in a position to do so, for example, by ensuring that they are not subject to undue influence of one or more of the board of directors. If the board fails to protect the integrity of the company secretary's position, one of the most effective inbuilt internal controls available to the company is likely to be seriously undermined. The establishment of appropriate reporting lines for the company secretary will normally be a crucial factor in establishing that protection.'

The guidance recommends that:

- in matters relating to their duties as an officer of the company, the company secretary should, through the chairman, be accountable to the board as a whole;

- if the company secretary has additional executive responsibilities to their core role, they should report to the CEO or appropriate executive director on such matters;
- the company secretary's remuneration should be set (or at least noted) by the board as a whole, or by the remuneration committee of the board on the recommendation of the chairman or CEO.

The UK Code also makes a specific provision about the appointment and removal of the company secretary. It states that: 'Both the appointment and removal of the company secretary should be a matter for the board as a whole.' In this way, the company secretary is not dependent on one individual, or a small group of board members, for their job.

Similar recommended practice is included in King IV, which states that the board should appoint and remove the company secretary and empower the individual to enable them to fulfil their duties properly. It also recommends that the company secretary should have an 'arm's length relationship' with the board, emphasising the requirement for independence.

4.9 The company secretary and the in-house lawyer

Many of the corporate governance duties of a company secretary have a legal aspect or involve compliance with regulations or a voluntary code of governance practice. It could be argued that many of these tasks could be performed better by an in-house lawyer working for the company, since corporate lawyers are specialists in company law and regulations.

However, as stated previously, independence is a critical aspect of the corporate governance role of the company secretary. To perform the task effectively, the company secretary needs to be as independent as it is possible for a full-time employee to be.

In their legal work, an in-house lawyer must at times consider the specific interests of the company and individual directors, and may be required to advise them on the most appropriate way of dealing with legal issues that arise. In performing this role, the lawyer will often have to 'take sides' to represent a particular interest. This would be inconsistent with the requirement to be independent when advising on governance issues.

It would therefore be inappropriate for the company's in-house lawyers to take on the responsibilities for corporate governance that are usually given to the company secretary in a listed company. An individual who has trained and qualified as a professional lawyer could be a suitable candidate to act as company secretary or take on corporate governance responsibilities within the company, but only if two key conditions are applied:

- the qualified lawyer does no legal work for the company; and also
- the independence of the individual can be protected in the same way as for a company secretary, with the board as a whole responsible for appointing and dismissing them and deciding their remuneration.

 STOP AND THINK **3.1**

It is tempting for students of corporate governance to assume that a company secretary has authority to enforce good governance practice in a company, but this is an unrealistic view.

A company secretary provides administrative support to the board chairman and other board members (for example, by organising meetings, distributing information in advance of meetings and taking minutes, making statutory returns, and so on). The company secretary can also provide information and advice on certain matters to the chairman and other directors, such as advice on governance or legal requirements.

The company secretary does not have the authority to tell board members what to do, or to assume responsibilities that properly rest with the board.

The influence of a company secretary on board members depends on his or her knowledge, ability and personality – and the respect that these qualities earn with colleagues.

4.10 ICSA *The Company Secretary: Building trust through governance*

In 2014 ICSA, in conjunction with Henley Business School, published *The Company Secretary: Building trust through governance* focusing on the role of the company secretary in governance. Its key findings were as follows:

- The role of the company secretary is much more than just administrative. At its best, it delivers strategic leadership, acting as a vital bridge between the executive management and the board and facilitating the delivery of organisational objectives.
- Company secretaries are ideally placed to align the interests of different parties around a boardroom table, facilitate dialogue, gather and assimilate relevant information, and enable effective decision-making. They are often the only people to know first-hand how the decisions made have been reached.
- The skills and attributes of the best company secretaries are closest to those of the chairman: humanity, humility, high intelligence, understanding of agendas, negotiation and resilience.
- It is vital that company secretaries have both direct and informal access to board members – executive and NEDs, CEOs and chairmen.
- Maximising effectiveness requires that the company secretary's direct reporting line should be to the chairman, and there should be parity of esteem and good team-working between the 'triumvirate at the top' – the chairman, the company secretary and the CEO.
- The role is changing: it is increasingly outward-focused (incorporating investor engagement and corporate communications), and not just about internal administration.
- ICSA-qualified company secretaries deliver a more rounded governance and board member service than those who have come to the role via other professional routes.
- There is a conflict of interest in the combined 'Head of Legal (or General Counsel) and Company Secretary' role. The roles should be separate, as they can be incompatible.
- Board members often have a lack of awareness of the ways in which the company secretary supports an organisation in its decision-making. Boards may miss out on making full use of the skills, knowledge and experience at their disposal.
- Company secretaries are often the longest-serving members present at board meetings, and so are a vital repository of company history and culture, and a guarantor of continuity.
- Company secretaries are embedded in the process of making boards more effective; they contribute by observing boards in action and advising on any skills gaps that need filling.
- The breadth of the company secretarial role includes additional responsibilities such as being an officer of the company, chief of staff to the chairman and adviser to the board on governance. Consequently, the secretariat needs to retain independence to rebalance power as required and demonstrate accountability.

 TEST YOUR KNOWLEDGE 3.4

a List 15 corporate governance responsibilities that could be given to a company secretary.

b What is the meaning of 'conscience of the company'?

c Why is it important that a company secretary should be independent, and how can this independence be protected?

d Why is it inappropriate to give corporate governance responsibilities to an individual who acts as the company's in-house lawyer?

CHAPTER SUMMARY

- A voluntary code of corporate governance is a code issued by a well-established body that sets out principles and provisions of best practice in corporate governance. Most codes are issued nationally, but some are issued internationally.

■ National codes of corporate governance are effectively 'enforced' on listed companies in practice, because of a 'comply or explain' or 'apply or explain' requirement in the rules for companies whose shares are traded on the main national stock market(s).

■ Voluntary codes of governance are principles-based, and consist of general principles supported by some practical provisions. They are not 'rules-based' (i.e. consisting of many detailed rules for application).

■ The code of corporate governance in the UK is the UK Corporate Governance Code (most recently revised in 2016). This is the responsibility of the FRC, which also has responsibility for other supporting guidance on the application of the Code in practice.

■ The G20/OECD has issued general principles of good corporate governance, with the intention of encouraging countries worldwide to improve their standards of corporate governance.

■ The company secretary is in a unique position to ensure that best practice in corporate governance is implemented by the company, and that the board is kept aware of governance issues.

■ To fulfil this role effectively, the company secretary should be independent from pressure or influence from any board members.

Governance in practice

■ **OVERVIEW**

The second part of this study text looks at the practical application of principles and provisions of best practice in corporate governance.

Chapter 4 describes the governance responsibilities of a board of directors, which should be specified in a list of 'matters reserved for the board'. In most countries, companies have unitary boards, but in some countries they have a two-tier board structure. With a unitary board, directors have the same legal duties and fulfilling these duties is an aspect of good corporate governance. The chapter discusses the roles of the company chairman and chief executive officer (CEO), the size of a board and the composition of its members, and the roles of non-executive directors (NEDs) and board committees in helping to apply best governance practice.

Chapter 5 considers several aspects of boardroom practice and behaviour, such as the appointment, election and re-election of directors, and performance appraisal of the board, its committees and individual directors. It then goes on to discuss boardroom ethics and the ethical conduct of directors. It concludes by explaining the potential personal liability of directors for their actions, and how directors and officers (D&O) liability insurance provides some protection against this.

Chapter 6 explains why the remuneration of directors and senior executives has been a major corporate governance issue and the problems with the practical application of suitable principles of remuneration. Issues covered in this chapter include the elements of a remuneration package, the role of the remuneration committee of the board and the problems of 'rewards for failure' when individual directors are dismissed for poor performance.

Chapter 7 explains the importance of reporting as an element of corporate governance, because reports should provide both accountability and transparency. Companies report mainly to shareholders, but some reports are produced for other stakeholders. The main report from a company is the annual report and accounts, which includes the annual financial statements of the company and also a variety of mainly narrative reports. The annual report and accounts are required to give a 'true and fair view', and the external auditors are expected to give an independent professional opinion to shareholders about whether they do so. The chapter discusses the relationship between a company and its external auditors, the independence and competence of the auditors, the role of the audit committee, and the relevance and importance of these for good governance.

Agency theory in corporate governance is based on a conflict of interests between shareholders and the directors. Chapter 8 explains how the interests of shareholders can be protected, and the objectives of the company promoted, through a constructive two-way relationship between institutional shareholders and the board ('shareholder engagement' and 'dialogue') and constructive use of the annual general meeting (AGM). Institutional shareholders should be prepared where necessary to use their influence and exercise their rights, and the chapter explains shareholder activism and also the responsible use of voting.

■ LEARNING OUTCOMES

Part Two should enable you to:

- advise on governance issues across all sectors, ensuring that the pursuit of strategic objectives is in line with regulatory developments and developments in best practice;

- assess the relationship between governance and performance within organisations;

- advise on the structure and composition of the board to maximise effectiveness and meet regulatory requirements;

- understand, interpret and apply the principles of the UK Corporate Governance Code in relation to boardroom practice and behaviour;

- understand the role and responsibilities of the key board committees;

- understand, interpret and apply the principles of the UK Corporate Governance Code in relation to audit and disclosure; and

- understand the powers and rights of shareholders and the responsibility of both the board and institutional investors to develop constructive dialogue between each other with a view to improving corporate governance.

PART 2 CASE STUDY

Stenning Tull Limited was established 15 years ago by Don Stenning and Rebecca Tull. The company specialises in design consultancy and in recent years has grown rapidly through both organic growth and small acquisitions. It now employs about 200 people and is highly profitable. The board of directors consists of a chairman (Don Stenning), a CEO (Rebecca Tull), a finance director, an artistic design operations director and a technical design operations director. There are no NEDs.

The board would like to grow the business and sees opportunities for further acquisitions. The company's bank is reluctant to lend more to finance growth unless the company increases its equity capital, and Don Stenning and Rebecca Tull, who between them own 90% of the company's shares, have been persuaded to take the company on to the stock market in order to raise equity capital.

An investment bank has agreed to sponsor the company's flotation as a listed company.

To prepare for a stock market flotation, the investment bank has asked for extensive and detailed information about the company. Among the information gathered are the following items.

1 Don Stenning and Rebecca Tull both have salaries of £750,000 per year and in addition receive dividends on their shares of about £500,000 each per year. They have contracts of employment with the company, which entitle them to a notice period of three years.

2 The other directors earn between £125,000 and £175,000 each in salary, and are entitled to a notice period of one year. All three have some equity shares in the company. The company has no formal annual bonus scheme and no long-term incentive scheme for its executives.

3 The company has used the same firm of auditors, Penn Ledger, since its incorporation.

4 Because the company's main shareholders are also senior board members and executive managers in the company, board meetings have combined board business with senior executive management committee business.

5 The company produces an annual directors' report and financial statements in accordance with the minimum requirements of the Companies Act.

6 Company secretarial duties are performed by the senior accountant.

7 Stenning Tull has already become a public limited company (plc) in preparation for the stock market flotation.

The investment bank has advised Don Stenning and Rebecca Tull that major changes will be required in corporate governance arrangements before the company can become a listed company. In addition, they will both be expected to reduce their shareholding to 10% of the total equity in the company, and the flotation will therefore involve both an issue of new shares for cash and also the sale of some of their shares by both Don Stenning and Rebecca Tull.

4 The board of directors

CONTENTS

INTRODUCTION

An efficient and effective board of directors is a key requirement of good corporate governance. The board should have a clear idea of its responsibilities, and should fulfil these to the best of its abilities. There should be a suitable balance of skills and experience, and also power, on the board. This chapter considers the role and composition of a board and the duties and responsibilities of directors and committees. By the end of the chapter, you should have an understanding of what is needed to achieve an effective board, and how a weak board structure is a threat to good corporate governance.

This chapter (and the following chapter) will make a number of references to principles and provisions of the UK Corporate Governance Code, and in particular Sections A and B of the Code on Leadership and Effectiveness. There will also be references to the Financial Reporting Council (FRC) Guidance on Board Effectiveness, published in 2011. This guidance replaced previous guidance (the Higgs Guidance and ICSA's review of the Higgs Guidance on behalf of the FRC). The purpose of this guidance is to help boards of directors with implementing Sections A and B of the Corporate Governance Code.

1 Governance and the board of directors

The board of directors is the key decision-making body in a company. A company should have an effective board of directors dedicated to ensuring that the company achieves its objectives. The board should provide entrepreneurial leadership and direction to the company.

The UK Corporate Governance Code ('the UK Code') states as one of its main principles:

> 'Every company should be headed by an effective board, which is collectively responsible for the long-term success of the company.'

This principle recognises that the board should not focus on short-term achievements, if these are inconsistent with longer-term success.

1.1 Governance role of the board

The UK Code states that the **role of the board** should be to:

- provide entrepreneurial leadership for the company within a framework of prudent and effective risk management;
- set the company's strategic aims;
- make sure that the necessary financial and human resources are in place for the company to meet its objectives;
- review management performance;
- set the company's values and standards; and
- make sure that the company's obligations to its shareholders are understood and met.

The FRC Guidance on Board Effectiveness states that **an effective board** is one that:

- provides direction for management;
- demonstrates ethical leadership, displaying (and promoting throughout the company) behaviour that is consistent with the culture and values it has defined for the organisation;
- creates a performance culture that drives value creation without exposing the company to excessive risk of value destruction;
- makes well-informed and high-quality decisions based on a clear line of sight into the business;
- creates the right framework for helping directors meet their statutory duties under the Companies Act 2006 (CA2006), and other relevant statutory and regulatory regimes;
- is accountable, particularly to the providers of the company's capital (shareholders); and
- thinks carefully about its governance arrangements and embraces evaluation of their effectiveness.

The Guidance comments: 'An effective board should not necessarily be a comfortable place. Challenge, as well as teamwork, is an essential feature.' A board that demonstrates that it has suitable governance policies and systems in place is much more likely to generate trust and support among its shareholders and other stakeholders.

Except for its monitoring role, the board should not get involved with operational matters, for which the responsibility is delegated to executive management. The Code also states that all directors must act in what they consider to be the best interests of the company, without specifying what those 'best interests' are or might be.

The King IV Report identifies other responsibilities for the board, including responsibility for:

- ethical conduct and sustainability of the business;
- compliance with laws, regulations and codes; and
- governing the relationships between the company and its stakeholders.

1.2 Decision-making by the board

Decision-making is an important board activity. The board should have clear policies about what matters need a board decision or approval, and the processes required for each type of decision. Good decision-making can be improved by giving directors sufficient time to prepare for meetings, allowing sufficient time for issues to be discussed at board meetings, and making clear to executives what action they must take to implement board decisions.

The **FRC Guidance on Board Effectiveness** recognises that there is always a risk of poor decision-making by a board, but states that this risk can be minimised by investing time in the design of decision-making policies and processes.

The Guidance suggests that good decision-making may be facilitated by:

- high-quality documentation for the board;
- where appropriate, obtaining the views of an expert;
- allowing time for debate and challenge about proposals for board decisions;
- achieving 'timely closure' so that issues do not remain unresolved for too long; and
- when decisions are made, making it clear what actions are required, within what timescales, and who is responsible for carrying them out.

The Guidance also provides a warning about factors that may limit the quality and effectiveness of decision-making:

- the effect of a dominant personality on the board or a dominant group;
- giving insufficient attention to risk and a lack of awareness of significant risks in the decision;
- a reluctance by executive directors to involve the non-executive directors (NEDs) in certain matters;
- a weak organisational culture, including inadequate information;
- failure to recognise the implications for value of decisions that are motivated by self-interest;
- weak ethical standards;
- complacent attitudes;
- intransigent attitudes;
- emotional attachments;
- conflicts of interest;
- inappropriate reliance on previous experience; and
- inadequate information about the issue or analysis.

 STOP AND THINK **4.1**

The chairman of the board should allow sufficient time for issues to be discussed thoroughly, as this will improve the quality of decision-making by the board, and prevent hasty and ill-considered decisions.

On the other hand, meetings can drag on interminably if individuals are given a free hand to talk about issues. The aim should be thorough discussion of issues, but not excessive discussion. A board therefore needs a chairman who can control a meeting, but without in any way trying to dominate it.

The FRC Guidance also suggests that:

- The decision-making process by a board in reaching a particular decision should be documented in board papers (for example, the minutes of the board meeting(s) where the decision was discussed and reached).
- Where appropriate, the chairman should consider:
  - commissioning an independent report or advice from an expert;
  - introducing a 'devil's advocate' into a discussion in order to test proposals thoroughly;
  - establishing a temporary sole-purpose committee of the board to look into a matter in greater detail;
  - reaching a decision through a series of meetings.

 TEST YOUR KNOWLEDGE **4.1**

a According to the UK Code of Corporate Governance, what are the governance responsibilities of a board of directors?

b What additional governance responsibilities of the board are identified in the King IV Code?

c According to the guidance 'Improving Board Effectiveness', what are the characteristics of an effective board?

2   Matters reserved for the board

The main decision-making powers belong to the board of directors. Although the board delegates many of the operational decision-making responsibilities to executive management, it should:

- retain the most significant decisions to itself; and
- monitor the performance of the executive management.

An aspect of corporate governance is therefore the nature of the decisions the board reserves to itself (rather than delegating them to executive management). The UK Corporate Governance Code does not specify which matters should be reserved by the board for its own decision-making, but states simply in a provision that: 'There should be formal schedule of matters reserved for its decision.'

It then goes on to state that the annual report should include a statement of how the board operates, and a high-level statement of the types of decision that it reserves for its own decisions and the types of decision that it delegates to executive management.

ICSA has produced a guidance note, 'ICSA guidance on matters reserved for the board' (2013), on the matters that should be reserved for the board's own decision-making, which is consistent with the provisions of the UK Code. The list of items in the guidance note is extensive, and includes decisions relating to matters such as:

- approval of overall strategy and strategic objectives;
- approval of annual operating and capital expenditure budgets;
- oversight of operations (including accounting, planning and internal control systems);
- compliance with legal and regulatory requirements;
- management/operational performance review;
- changes in corporate or capital structure;
- approving the risk appetite of the company (annual review);
- approving the annual report and accounts;
- declaring an interim dividend and recommending a final dividend;
- approval of formal communications with shareholders;
- approval of major contracts and investments; and
- approval of policies on matters such as health and safety, corporate social responsibility (CSR) and the environment.

You may notice that this list of matters reserved for the board involves monitoring management performance and approving important management proposals (such as proposed budgets and proposed major capital expenditure projects). The board does not, however, have a management function or management responsibilities.

The company secretary may be given the task of preparing and maintaining the list of matters to be reserved for the board (for board approval), and reminding the board whenever necessary that certain decisions should not be delegated.

2.1 The dividing line between board decision-making responsibilities and management responsibilities

There are some areas of decision-making where the board should clearly take the decisions, and should not delegate decision-making to management. Overall strategic policy decisions, dividend decisions, and approving the group budget are examples.

It also seems appropriate as a guiding principle that all major transactions should be approved by the board. A problem, however, is deciding what transactions are 'major' and which can be delegated to management. For example, should IT strategy be decided by the board at group level, or should IT investment decisions be made by management at divisional level? In a group of companies with several operating subsidiary companies, what decisions should be taken by the group board and what decision should be taken by the boards of the subsidiary companies?

A code of corporate governance cannot be specific about these matters. This is why, to achieve clarity about decision-making responsibilities, the matters reserved for the board should be set out in a formal document.

TEST YOUR KNOWLEDGE 4.2

List ten matters that should be reserved for decision-making by the board of directors.

3 Size and composition of the board

The effectiveness of a board of directors depends on its size and composition.

3.1 The size of the board

The typical size of a board of directors varies with the size of the company and possibly also the industry or business sector in which it operates. In addition, the average size of boards in listed companies varies between different countries.

- A board should not be larger than it needs to be. Large boards are more difficult to manage, because there are more individuals involved, and board meetings can be very long and waste time.
- On the other hand, boards should be sufficiently large so that their members collectively have the knowledge, skills and experience to make effective decisions. In addition, if a board is very small, the loss of one or possibly two members due to resignation or retirement could make it difficult for the board to function effectively until new board appointments have been made and the new directors have started to become familiar with their role and responsibilities.

The UK Code also suggests that the board should be sufficiently large to avoid a situation in which it becomes over-reliant on one or two individuals, for example, as chairmen of board committees (nominations, remuneration, audit and risk committees). It states:

'The board should be of sufficient size that the requirements of the business can be met and that changes to the board's composition and that of its committees can be managed without undue disruption, and should not be so large as to be unwieldy.'

 STOP AND THINK 4.2

Select any listed company that you know. Given the size and complexity of its business, make an estimate of how large its board of directors might be. Next, find the company's website and check the size and composition of its board. If you have difficulty in finding this information, it should be contained in the directors' report in its report and accounts. See how close your estimate was to being correct.

Do you consider a board of 11 directors, including the chairman, to be a good size for a medium-to-large listed company? Or do you think a board should be larger – or smaller – than this?

3.2 The composition of the board

The composition of a board of directors depends partly on its size. In the UK, the board of a large public company commonly consists of:

- a chairman;
- possibly a deputy chairman;
- a chief executive officer (CEO);
- a **senior independent director** (SID) (who may also be the deputy chairman);
- executive directors; and
- NEDs.

Collectively, the members of the board should have sufficient skills and experience to provide effective leadership for the company. This suggests that they should have a variety of different backgrounds and expertise.

There should also be a suitable balance of power on the board, so that one individual or a small group of individuals is unable to dominate the board and its decision-making. In countries such as the UK, it is therefore considered appropriate to appoint independent NEDs to a board, because:

- they act as a counter-balance to executive directors, who may give priority to their own interests above those of the shareholders (and other stakeholders); and
- they have skills and experience that executive directors do not have, because they come from a different background and so are able to contribute different ideas and views to board discussions and decision-making.

Because they do not have a strong personal financial interest in the company, NEDs are more easily able to represent the interests of shareholders and to act (where required) as a restraint on executive management.

These principles relating to board composition are set out in the UK Code as follows:

- 'The board and its committees should have the appropriate balance of skills, experience, independence and knowledge of the company to enable them to discharge their respective duties and responsibilities effectively.'
- 'The board should include an appropriate combination of executives and NEDs (and in particular independent NEDs) such that no individual or small group of individuals can dominate the board's decision-taking.'

In the UK, a key principle of good corporate governance is that there should be a sufficient number of independent NEDs on the board of directors to create a suitable balance of power and prevent the dominance of the board by one individual or a small number of individuals. The UK Code sets out different requirements for large listed companies and for smaller companies (smaller companies are defined as companies outside the FTSE 350 for the whole of the year immediately prior to the reporting year).

- Except for smaller companies, at least one half of the board, excluding the chairman, should be independent NEDs.
- For smaller companies, there should be at least two independent NEDs.

Guidelines about the composition of the board differ between countries. The King IV Code, for example, recommends that the majority of directors should be NEDs and the majority of NEDs should be independent, but also adds that there should be at least two executive directors on the board – the CEO and another designated executive which may be the chief finance officer (finance director) (CFO).

TEST YOUR KNOWLEDGE 4.3

a What would be the disadvantages of a large listed company in the UK restricting the total size of its board to six members?

b What are the provisions in the UK Code for the size and composition of the board of directors of a listed company in the FTSE 350?

STOP AND THINK 4.3

The board of ABC plc, a FTSE 350 company, consists of a chairman, three executive directors, three independent NEDs and another NED who is not independent. The board of DEF plc, another FTSE 350 company, consists of a chairman, six independent NEDs and one executive director.

Do these boards comply with the UK Code provision about board composition?

Answer: The board of ABC plc does not comply with the UK Code, because (excluding the chairman) the number of independent directors (three) is less than half the size of the board. The board of DEF plc does comply, since more than half of the board consists of independent NEDs.

4 The powers of directors

4.1 The general powers of directors

The powers of the board of directors are set out in a company's constitution. In the UK, this means the articles of association. UK company legislation provides a standard form of articles of association (known as **model articles of association**). For companies formed under the Companies Act (CA) 1985, this means the 1985 Table A articles, which most companies have used as a model for their own articles. CA2006 revised the model articles and introduced different model articles for public and private companies. The revised model articles apply to all new companies incorporated under CA2006 on or after 1 October 2009. The powers of directors are broadly comparable, however, in all the model articles.

Article 3 of the model articles for public companies states: 'Subject to the articles, the directors are responsible for the management of the company's business, for which purpose they may exercise all the powers of the company.' The shareholders may instruct the directors what they should do (or should not do) but only by passing a special resolution in a general meeting, and a special resolution of the shareholders cannot invalidate what the directors have already done.

Article 5 of the model articles for public companies states that the directors may delegate any of the powers conferred on them under the articles to any person (e.g. the CEO) or committee (e.g. to an audit committee), by such means (including by power of attorney), to such an extent, in relation to such matters or territories, and on such terms and conditions as they think fit. If the directors so specify, any such delegation may authorise further delegation of the directors' powers by any person to whom they are delegated. For example, the CEO may delegate some of his or her powers to other executive managers.

Standard articles of association in the UK, therefore, provide for the board collectively to be the main power centre in the company, but with delegation of powers to **board committees** and executive directors.

A distinction should be made between the powers and duties of executive directors as members of the board, and their responsibilities as managers of the company. Under the articles of association, managers have neither powers nor duties. The relationship they have with the company (including their authority and responsibilities) is established by their contract of employment and by the law of agency.

4.2 Borrowing powers of directors

In the UK, there is no restriction in law on how much the directors can borrow on behalf of their company unless the constitution (articles of association) includes a specific restriction. As far as the law is concerned, the borrowing powers of companies are limited only by what lenders are prepared to make available to them. Conceivably, the directors could therefore put the investment of their shareholders at risk by borrowing more than the company can safely afford.

5 The duties of directors to their company

The directors act as agents of their company. They have certain duties, which are to the company itself, but not to its shareholders, its employees or any person external to the company, such as the general public. Although a company is a legal person in law, it is not human. Since the relationship between directors and the company is by its very nature impersonal, it might be wondered just what 'duty' means.

The concept of duty is not easy to understand, and it is helpful to make a comparison with the duties owed by other individuals or groups.

Examples of individuals owing a duty to something inanimate are not common, although personnel in the armed forces have a duty to their country. It is more usual to show loyalty to something inanimate than to have a duty. For example, individuals might be expected to show loyalty to their country, and they might voluntarily show loyalty to their sports team or group of friends or work colleagues. Arguably, solicitors have a duty to their profession to act ethically, although the solicitors' practice rules in the UK specify that solicitors owe a duty of care to their clients. Similarly, doctors have a duty to act ethically, but their duty is to their patients. Duty is normally owed to individuals or a group of people. It might therefore be supposed that directors should owe a duty to their shareholders and possibly to the company's employees, but this is not the case.

- Accountability and responsibility should not be confused with duty.
- Directors have a responsibility to use their powers in ways that seem best for the company and its shareholders.
- They should be accountable to the owners of the company, the shareholders, for the ways in which they have exercised their powers and/or the performance of the company.
- They have duties to the company.

If a person is guilty of a breach of duty, there should be a process for calling him to account. There might be an established disciplinary procedure: for example, in a court or before a judicial panel, with a recognised set of punishments for misbehaviour. With companies, however, disciplinary mechanisms are difficult to apply in practice, except perhaps in extreme cases of misbehaviour. Where measures are taken, they are likely to be initiated by shareholders seeking legal remedies on behalf of the company.

5.1 Common law duties and statutory duties of directors

Before CA2006, the main legal duties of directors to their company were duties in common law – a **fiduciary duty** and **duty of skill and care** to the company. These are duties to the company, not its shareholders. CA2006 has now written the common law duties of directors into statute law. It states that these general duties 'are based on certain common law rules and equitable principles as they apply to directors, and have effect in place of those rules and principles as regards the duties owed to a company by a director' (CA2006, s. 170). The Act goes on to state that the statutory general duties should be interpreted in the same way as the common law rules and equitable principles.

It is therefore useful to begin by looking at the nature of the common law duties, and what they have meant.

5.2 Fiduciary duty of directors

'Fiduciary' means given in trust, and the concept of a trustee (as established in US and UK law) is applicable. The directors hold a position of trust because they make contracts on behalf of the company and also control the company's property. Since this is similar to being a trustee of the company, a director has a fiduciary duty to the company (not its shareholders).

If a director were to act in breach of his or her fiduciary duty, legal action could be brought against him by the company. In such a situation, 'the company' might be represented by a majority of the board of directors, or a majority of the shareholders, or a single controlling shareholder.

A director would be in breach of their fiduciary duty in carrying out a particular transaction or series of transactions in any of the following circumstances.

1   The transaction is not in any way incidental to the business of the company. For example, the CEO of a building construction company might decide to trade in diamonds and lose large amounts of money in these diamond trading transactions.
2   The transaction is not carried out *bona fide*, which means in good faith, with honesty and sincerity.
3   The transaction has not been made for the benefit of the company but for the personal benefit of the director or an associate. A director has a fiduciary duty to avoid a conflict of interest between him or her personally and the company, and must not obtain any personal benefit or profit from a transaction without the consent of the company. In other words, it would be a breach of fiduciary duty for a director to make a **secret profit** from a transaction by the company in which he or she has a personal interest.

CASE EXAMPLE 4.1

A company wishes to buy some land and has identified a property for which it would be prepared to pay a large sum of money. The CEO secretly sets up a private company of his own to buy the property, and then sells this on to the company of which he is CEO, making a large profit in the process. The actions of the CEO are a breach of fiduciary duty, because his actions have not been bona fide and he has made a secret profit at the expense of the company. Under CA2006 these actions of the CEO would now be a breach of statutory duty.

5.3 A director's duty of skill and care

Directors are also subject to a duty of skill and care to the company. This was a common law duty that became a statutory duty with CA2006. A director should not act negligently in carrying out his or her duties, and could be personally liable for losses suffered by the company as a consequence of such negligence.

A director is expected to show the technical skills that would reasonably be expected from someone of his or her experience and expertise. If the finance director of a scientific research company is a qualified accountant, they would not be expected to possess the technical skills of a scientist, but would be expected to possess some technical skill as an accountant.

The duty of skill and care does not extend to spending time in the company. A director should attend board meetings if possible, but at other times is not required to be concerned with the affairs of the company. This requirement is perhaps best understood with NEDs, who might visit the company only for board or committee meetings. The duties of a director are intermittent in nature and arise from time to time only, such as when the board meets. If a director holds an executive position in the company, a different situation arises, because they are an employee of the company with a contract of service. This contract might call for full-time attendance at the company or on its business. However, this requirement arises out of their job as a manager, not out of their position as a director.

It is also not a part of the duty of skill and care to watch closely over the activities of the company's management. Unless there are particular grounds for suspecting dishonesty or incompetence, a director is entitled to leave the routine conduct of the company's affairs to the management. If the management appears honest, the directors may rely on the information they provide. It is not part of their duty of skill and care to question whether the information is reliable, or whether important information is being withheld.

A board of directors might make a decision that appears ill-judged or careless. However, the courts in the UK are generally reluctant to condemn business decisions made by the board that appear, in hindsight, to show errors of judgement. Directors can exercise reasonable skill and care, but still make bad decisions.

For a legal action against a director to succeed, a company would have to prove that serious negligence had occurred. It would not be enough to demonstrate that some loss could have been avoided if the director had been a bit more careful. For this reason, legal actions in the UK against company directors for breach of duty are rare.

CASE LAW 4.1

***Dorchester Finance Co. Ltd v Stebbing* [1989]**
In the UK legal case *Dorchester Finance Co. Ltd v Stebbing* [1989], a company brought an action against its three directors for alleged negligence and misappropriation of the company's property. The company (Dorchester Finance) was in the money-lending business and it had three directors, S, H and P. Only S was involved full-time with the company; H and P were non-executives who made only rare appearances. There were no board meetings. S and P were qualified accountants and H,

CASE LAW **4.1** *continued*

although not an accountant, had considerable accountancy experience. S arranged for the company to make some loans to persons with whom he appears to have had dealings. In the loan-making process he had persuaded P and H to sign blank cheques that were subsequently used to make the loans. The loans did not comply with the Moneylenders Act and they were inadequately secured. When the loans turned out to be irrecoverable, the company brought its action against the directors.

It was held that all three directors were liable to damages. S, as an executive director, was held to be grossly negligent. P and H, as non-executives, were held to have failed to show the necessary level of skill and care in performing their duties as non-executives, even though it was accepted that they had acted in good faith at all times.

5.4 Wrongful trading and the standard of duty and care

The standard of duty and care required from a director has been partly defined in a number of UK legal cases relating to **wrongful trading**. Under the Insolvency Act 1986, directors may be liable for wrongful trading by the company when they allowed the company to continue trading, but knew (or should have known) that it would be unable to avoid an insolvent liquidation. When such a situation arises and a company goes into liquidation, the liquidator can apply to the court for the director to be held personally liable for negligence.

5.5 Duties of directors and delegation

Since directors owe a duty of skill and care to their company, it could be asked how much time and attention a director should give to the company's affairs, and to what extent a director can delegate responsibilities to another person without being in breach of his or her duty.

CASE LAW **4.2**

Re Barings plc and others (1998)
Andrew Tuckey, former deputy chairman of Barings bank, was responsible for the supervision of Nick Leeson, the derivatives trader whose unauthorised speculative trading notoriously brought the bank to collapse in 1995. In a case concerning the disqualification of Tuckey as a director, it was alleged that he had failed to exercise his duty of care to the company. The situation was summarised as follows by the judge in the case, Mr Justice Parker.

- Directors, both individually and collectively, have a duty to acquire and maintain sufficient understanding of the company's business to enable them to discharge their duties properly.
- Subject to the articles of association, directors are allowed to delegate particular functions to individuals beneath them in the management chain. Within reason, they are also entitled to have trust in the competence and integrity of these individuals. However, delegation of authority does not remove from the director a duty to supervise the exercise of that delegated authority by the subordinate.
- There is no universal rule for establishing whether a director is in breach of his duty to supervise the discharge of delegated functions by subordinates. The extent of the duty, and whether it has been properly discharged, should be decided on the facts of each case.

When there is a question about the extent of the director's duties and responsibilities, a significant factor could be the level of reward that the director was entitled to receive from the company. Prima facie, the higher the rewards, the greater the responsibilities should be expected.

In the Barings case, Mr Justice Parker concluded that Tuckey had failed in his duties because he did not have a sufficient knowledge and understanding of the nature of the derivatives markets and the risks involved in derivatives dealing (which led to the collapse of Barings). He was therefore unable to consider properly matters referred to the committee of which he was chairman.

6 The statutory general duties of directors: CA2006

The duties of directors in common law and equity to their company were introduced into UK statute law by CA2006 (ss. 171–177). These consist of a duty to:

- act within powers;
- promote the success of the company;
- exercise independent judgement;
- exercise reasonable care, skill and diligence;
- avoid conflicts of interest;
- not accept benefits from third parties; and
- declare any interest in a proposed transaction or arrangement.

It is worth remembering that these duties (as in common law) apply to non-executive as well as to executive directors. The UK Corporate Governance Code includes a supporting principle that: 'All directors must act in what they consider to be the best interests of the company, consistent with their statutory duties.'

The consequences for breach of these duties are most likely to be legal action taken in the name of the company (perhaps by shareholders). However, failure to declare an interest could result in a criminal prosecution of the director concerned.

6.1 Duty to act within powers

A director must act within their powers in accordance with the company's constitution, and should only exercise these powers for the purpose for which they were granted. However, if a director acts outside his or her powers to make a contractual agreement with a third party, the company is still liable for any obligation to the third party, provided that the third party has acted in good faith.

ICSA's guidance note, 'Directors' general duties' (2015), suggests that directors must ensure that they comply with the company's constitution. For example, when a group of directors meets, it must be clear whether the meeting is a board meeting, or a formal constituted committee of the board and other meetings involving directors. Unless the meeting is a formal board meeting, the directors would be acting outside their powers if they took a decision on a matter that is reserved for decision-making by the board.

6.2 Duty to promote the success of the company

A director, in good faith, must act in the way he or she considers would be most likely to 'promote the success of the company for the benefit of its members as a whole'. The Act does not define 'success', but the term is likely to be interpreted as meaning 'increasing value for shareholders'. However ICSA's guidance note 'Directors' general duties' states, in doing so, a director must also have regard, among other matters, to the:

- likely long-term consequences of any decision;
- interests of the company's employees;
- need to foster the company's relationships with its customers, suppliers and others;
- impact of the company's operations on the community and the environment;
- desirability of the company maintaining its reputation for high standards of business conduct; and
- need to act fairly as between members of the company.

The Act does not create a duty of directors to any stakeholders other than the shareholders (members), but it requires directors to give consideration to the interests of other stakeholders in reaching their decisions. The Act specifically mentions employees, customers, suppliers and the community. It therefore appears, in a small way perhaps, to promote a form of enlightened shareholder approach to corporate governance.

This aspect of directors' duties has given rise to some concerns that directors will need to create a 'paper trail' to provide evidence if required in a court of law to show that they have given due consideration to the interests of other stakeholders in their decision-making, although the government has denied that this is intended by the Act.

6.3 Duty to exercise independent judgement

A director must exercise independent judgement. This duty to exercise independent judgement applies to all directors, executive and non-executive and whether or not they are considered 'independent' for the purpose of the UK Corporate Governance Code.

However, this requirement does not prevent a director from acting in a way authorised by the company's constitution (e.g. accepting resolutions passed by the shareholders in a general meeting) or from acting in accordance with an agreement already entered into by the company that prevents the director from using discretion. The requirement for independent judgement does not prevent a director from taking advice and acting on it.

The ICSA guidance note on 'Directors' general duties' comments as follows on this duty.

■ A director must not allow personal interests to affect his or her independent judgement. This means that if the board is considering a contract in which a director has a personal interest, ideally he or she should leave the meeting while the matter is being discussed. This is also relevant to the duty of directors to avoid any conflict of interest with the company.

■ An executive director should not attend a board meeting to 'promote a collective executive line'. He or she should attend the board meeting in his own right and give the board the benefit of his or her independent opinion.

■ Similarly, directors representing a particular interest should 'set any representative function aside and make final decisions on their own merits'. For example, a director who is a representative of a family interest in the company 'may consult his family but be clear that he will make the final decision'.

6.4 Duty to exercise reasonable care, skill and diligence

This is similar to the common law duty of care.

6.5 Duty to avoid conflicts of interest

A director has a duty to avoid conflicts of interest with the interests of the company. However, this duty is not breached if the director declares to the board their interest in a transaction and the interest is authorised/approved by the board.

In the commercial world, it is inevitable that many directors will have a potential conflict of interest, whether direct or indirect, with their company. For example, a company might be planning to trade with another company in which one of its directors is a shareholder. In such a situation, the director concerned is required to declare that interest in the proposed contract to the other directors and must not make a secret profit.

A director or a connected person might have a material interest in a transaction undertaken by the company. For example, the company might award a contract to a firm of building contractors to rebuild or develop a property owned by the company, and the director or his or her spouse might own the building company.

A director might also have a direct or indirect interest in a contract (or proposed contract) with the company. For example, the director might be a member of another organisation with which the company is planning to sign a business contract. Such a contract is not illegal, although the company can choose to rescind it should it wish to do so.

If a director has an interest in a contract with the company and has failed to disclose it, and has received a payment under the contract, he or she will be regarded as holding the money in the capacity of constructive trustee for the company (and so are bound to repay the money).

The 2006 Act recognises three situations in which an actual or potential conflict of interests may arise.

1   A conflict of interest may arise in a situation where the company is not a party to an arrangement or transaction, but where the director might be able to gain personally from 'the exploitation of any property, information or opportunity'. For example, a director might pursue an opportunity for his or her personal benefit that the company might have pursued itself.

2   A conflict of interest may arise in connection with a proposed transaction or arrangement to which the company will be a party. If a director has a direct or indirect personal interest in any such transaction or arrangement, he or she must disclose the interest to the board of directors before it is entered into by the company. An example would be a proposal to acquire a target company in which a director owns shares.

3   A third type of conflict of interest arises in relation to existing transactions or arrangements in which the company is already a party. It can be a criminal offence for a director not to make or update his or her declaration of interest in an arrangement or transaction to which the company is a party.

6.6 Duty not to accept benefits from third parties

A director must not accept benefits from a third party unless they have been authorised by the shareholders or cannot reasonably be regarded as giving rise to a potential conflict of interest. Clearly, accepting a bribe from a supplier in return for awarding a supply contract would be a breach of this duty. It would also be illegal to accept lunch or dinner from the same supplier or customer every week, accepting an all-expenses paid holiday or accepting frequent invitations to 'hospitality' events. On the other hand, it should be within the law to accept an invitation to a day out to tennis at Wimbledon, or an invitation to dinner to celebrate the successful completion of a project.

In practice, many listed companies already have strict internal policies on the acceptance of gifts and corporate hospitality, especially from other companies that are or might be about to tender for business with the company. An internal policy might include a requirement for a director to obtain clearance from another director before accepting any such benefits, and for all instances of gifts or hospitality to be recorded in a register.

6.7 Duty to declare interests in proposed transactions with the company

This duty is linked to the duty relating to conflicts of interest. A director must declare the nature and extent of his or her interest to the other directors, who may then authorise it.

A director may have a personal interest in a proposed transaction with the company. For example, a director may own a building that the company wants to buy or rent; or a director may be a major shareholder in another company that is hoping to become a supplier or customer.

Proposed transactions do not necessarily create a conflict of interests, but they must nevertheless be declared, and subject to approval by the rest of the board. If a conflict of interest would arise from the proposed transaction, the director must take measures to ensure that the conflict is avoided, because directors have a statutory duty to avoid a conflict of interest.

This duty applies to a director's proposed transactions with the company. It does not apply to intentions by a director to buy or sell shares in the company. Share transactions are with other investors, not the company. However, strict rules apply to share dealing by directors, and these are explained in Chapter 5.

6.8 Consequences of a breach of the statutory general duties: derivative actions by shareholders

A director owes his or her duties to the company, so if the director is in breach of these duties, only the company can bring a legal claim against that director. In practice, this has usually meant that the rest of the board might bring an action against a fellow director in the name of the company.

The 2006 Act states that the consequences of a breach of a director's general duties are the same as if the corresponding common law rule or equitable principle applied, but it does not set out in detail what these consequences should be.

In addition, the Act also introduces a procedure whereby individual members of the company can bring a legal action for a derivative claim against a director. A **derivative action** may be brought in respect of 'an actual or proposed act or mission involving negligence, default, breach of duty or breach of trust by a director of the company'. A shareholder would have to bring the action against a director in the name of the company. If the action is successful, the company and not the individual shareholder would benefit.

The procedures for bringing a derivative action are set out in ss. 260–264 of the 2006 Act. They include safeguards designed to prevent individual shareholders from bringing actions that are not reasonable on the basis of the prima facie evidence. Even so, there is a possibility that future legal actions against directors might be brought by shareholders under the derivatives claims procedure for breach of their general duties.

In practice, shareholders are unlikely to bring a derivative action against a company director. Legal action is expensive and time-consuming, and the outcome may be uncertain. It makes more sense for shareholders to discuss their grievances with the company and to persuade the rest of the board to take measures to deal with the 'offending' director.

6.9 Directors' responsibilities to company outsiders

Although the duty of directors is to their company, a breach of that duty could also affect outsiders. When the directors make a contract with an outsider, the contract is binding on the company when it is in accordance with its constitution (articles of association). However, the directors might exceed their powers in making the contract; for example, because they should have obtained shareholder approval first, but failed to do so. Contracts entered into without proper authority are known as 'irregular contracts', and might seem to be void.

An outsider making a contract in good faith with the directors, when the contract is irregular, would be unable to enforce the contract if it is void. On the other hand, if an irregular contract is not void and is enforceable, a company has no protection against the consequences of unauthorised actions by its directors. So should irregular contracts be void or should they be enforceable by an outsider?

The main provision of UK company law is that an irregular contract is binding on a company when an outsider, acting in good faith, enters into the contract and the contract has been approved by the board of directors. The directors will be liable to the company for any loss suffered. This rule means that irregular contracts do not affect third parties (outsiders). Instead, when they occur, they would be a corporate governance problem.

6.10 Related party transactions and the UK DTR for listed companies

For listed companies, the requirements of UK law are reinforced by the UK's Disclosure and Transparency Rules (DTR) for listed companies, which include a section on **related party transactions**. In broad terms, a related party means a substantial shareholder of the company, a director of the company, a member of a director's family or a company in which a director or family member holds 30% or more of the shares. A related party transaction is a transaction between a company and a related party, other than in the normal course of business.

For most related party transactions above a minimum size, a listed company is required to:

- make an announcement to the stock market giving details of the transaction;
- send a circular to shareholders giving more details;
- obtain the prior approval of the shareholders for the transaction; and
- ensure that the related party does not vote on the relevant resolution and take all reasonable steps to ensure that the related party's associates do not vote on the relevant resolution.

The effect of the Rules should be to prevent directors or major shareholders of UK listed companies from obtaining a personal benefit from any non-business transaction with their company, unless the shareholders have given their approval.

TEST YOUR KNOWLEDGE 4.5

a   What are the seven statutory duties of directors under the provisions of the UK CA2006?

b   In what circumstances is it acceptable for a director to have an interest in a third party transaction with the company?

c   What is a derivative action for breach of a statutory duty by a director of a UK company?

d   What are the provisions of the UK DTR for listed companies with regard to related party transactions with the company?

7   The roles of chairman and CEO

7.1 The CEO

The CEO leads the executive team and is responsible for the executive management of the company's operations. As the title suggests, they are the senior executive in charge of the management team and to whom all other executive managers report. Other executive managers might also be directors of the company, but the CEO is answerable to the board for the way the business is run and its performance. The CEO:

- proposes strategy to the board; and
- implements strategy as decided by the board.

In order to improve the standard of boardroom discussion, the CEO should also act as a spokesperson for the executive directors in board discussions and:

- explain the views of the executive directors to the rest of the board; and
- explain in a balanced way any differences of opinion within the executive team.

They have the primary responsibility for:

- communicating to employees the expectations of the board with regard to the company's culture and values; and
- ensuring that appropriate standards of governance are applied at all levels within the organisation.

7.2 The chairman

Whereas the CEO is responsible for the executive management, the chairman's responsibilities relate primarily to managing the board of directors, and ensuring that the board functions effectively. To do this, he or she needs to ensure that the board discusses relevant issues in sufficient depth, with all the information needed to reach a decision, and with all the directors contributing to the discussions and decision-making. Key roles of a chairman are therefore to:

- set an appropriate agenda for board meetings;
- ensure that relevant information is provided to the directors, in advance of the meeting;
- encourage open discussions to board meetings, with constructive debate and discussion; and
- encourage all directors to contribute to discussions and decision making.

The UK Corporate Governance Code includes the following comments about the role of the chairman:

- 'The chairman is responsible for leadership of the board and ensuring its effectiveness on all aspects of its role.'
- 'The chairman is responsible for setting the board's agenda and ensuring that adequate time is available for discussion of all agenda items, in particular strategic issues.'
- 'The chairman should also promote a culture of openness and debate by facilitating the effective contribution of non-executives in particular and ensuring constructive relations between executives and NEDs.'
- 'The chairman is responsible for ensuring that the directors receive accurate, timely and clear information.'

- 'The chairman should ensure that communications with shareholders are "effective".'

These principles emphasise the role of the chairman in trying to ensure that all directors, and in particular NEDs, contribute effectively to board discussions. There is always a risk that individuals who do not work full time for the company may have difficulty in challenging the views of full-time executive directors. The chairman should make sure that this does not happen.

The role of the chairman is pivotal in creating conditions for an effective board and individual director effectiveness. The FRC Guidance on Board Effectiveness provides a list of matters for which the chairman is responsible. The chairman should:

- demonstrate ethical leadership;
- set the board agenda, which should focus mainly on strategy, performance, value creation and accountability;
- ensure that decisions relating to relevant issues are reserved for decision-making by the board;
- make sure that there is a timely flow of high-quality information to board members, so that an effective decision-making process operates at board level;
- make certain that the board determines the nature and extent of the risks that it is willing to tolerate in the implementation of its strategy;
- regularly consider succession planning and the composition of the board;
- ensure that the board committees are properly constituted and have appropriate terms of reference;
- encourage active engagement by all board members in board and committee meetings;
- build effective relationships both within and outside the boardroom, built on mutual respect and open communication, between the NEDs and the executive management team;
- develop a constructive working relationship with the executive directors and in particular the CEO: the chairman should provide support and advice but should also respect executive responsibilities;
- consult the SID when appropriate;
- take the lead on matters relating to director development, including induction for new directors, and act on the results of formal reviews of board and director performance (discussed in the next chapter); and
- ensure effective communication with shareholders and other stakeholders, and that all directors are made aware of the views of major investors.

An effective chairman is therefore a team-builder. They should develop a board whose members communicate effectively and enjoy good relationships with each other. They should develop a close relationship of trust with the CEO, giving support and advice whilst still respecting the CEO's responsibilities for executive matters. They should also ensure the effective implementation of board decisions, provide coherent leadership for the company and understand the views of the shareholders.

The Preface to the UK Corporate Governance Code recommends that the chairman's statement to the shareholders in the company's annual report should make some comment about board effectiveness:

'Chairmen are encouraged to report personally in their annual statements how the principles relating to the role and effectiveness of the board ... have been applied. Not only will this give investors a clearer picture of the steps taken by boards to operate effectively but also, by providing fuller context, it may make investors more willing to accept explanations when a company chooses to explain rather than to comply with one or more provisions.'

 STOP AND THINK 4.4

On paper, the role of the chairman may seem quite straightforward. He or she needs to build a 'team' of directors who collaborate in the best interests of the company and reach collective decisions through vigorous and constructive discussion.

In practice it is not nearly so easy. Directors are often strong-minded individuals, and this often means that they know they are right and other people must be wrong. The UK Code comments on the challenge of providing effective leadership to the board:

STOP AND THINK 4.4 *continued*

'To run a corporate board successfully should not be underrated. Constraints on time and knowledge combine with the need to maintain mutual respect and openness between a cast of strong, able and busy directors dealing with each other across the different demands of executive and non-executive roles. To achieve good governance requires continuing and high-quality effort.'

7.3 Independence of the chairman

As a general rule, the chairman of a listed company should be independent when first appointed. This is a provision of the UK Code.

In addition the UK Code states that the CEO of a company should not subsequently become the chairman. This is consistent with the view that the chairman should be independent when he or she is first appointed: a former CEO will not be independent. The King IV Code, however, states that a former CEO should not become chairman for at least three years after ceasing to be CEO, taking the view that this is sufficient time in which to become independent.

A governance problem with 'promoting' the CEO to become the company chairman is that the incoming CEO may find it difficult to run the company as they wish because the former CEO is still on the board, monitoring what they are doing.

Even so, there have been several cases where a CEO has gone on to become chairman without any serious protest from shareholders or investor groups. For example, in 2014 the CEO of Experian plc, Don Robert, was appointed as the new chairman of the company.

7.4 Separating the roles of chairman and CEO

As leader of the management team and leader of the board of directors, the CEO and chairman are the most powerful positions on the board of directors.

It is important for the proper functioning of the company that the chairman and CEO should be able to work well together. Acting in alliance, the chairman and CEO can dominate the board and its decision-making, particularly if the chairman also has executive responsibilities in the company's management.

When the same person holds the position of both chairman and CEO, there is a possibility that they could become a dominant influence in decision-making in the company. As leader of the executive management team, a chairman-cum-CEO may be reluctant to encourage challenges from NEDs about the company's performance or to question management proposals about future business strategy.

In some countries (including the US), it is common to find company leaders who are both chairman and CEO, although separation of the roles has become more common there. The UK Code states as a principle that the roles should be separated:

'There should be a clear division of responsibilities at the head of the company between the running of the board and the executive responsibility for the running of the company's business. No one individual should have unfettered powers of decision.'

The UK Code therefore states that the roles of chairman and CEO should not be performed by the same individual. In addition, the division of responsibilities between the chairman and CEO should be established, clearly set out in writing and agreed by the board, to prevent one of them from encroaching on the area of responsibility of the other.

When an individual holds the positions of chairman and CEO, they could exercise dominant power on the board, unless there are strong individuals on the board, such as a deputy chairman or a SID, to act as a counterweight. If the individual also has a domineering or bullying personality, the situation will be even worse, because a chairman-cum-CEO who acts in a bullying manner will not listen to advice from any board colleagues, and the board would not function as an effective body.

There is even a risk that the individual will run the company for his or her own personal benefit rather than in the interests of the shareholders and other stakeholders. The only way to prevent a chairman-cum-CEO from dominating a company is to have an influential group of directors capable of making their opinions heard. However, it is important to distinguish between:

- the position of 'unfettered power' that is created when the roles of chairman and CEO are combined and given to one individual; and
- acting in a dominant or tyrannical way, possibly out of self-interest.

Combining the two roles increases the risk that the company and its board will be dominated by a tyrannical individual, but this does not happen every time.

However, there might occasionally be situations where it is appropriate for the same person to be both chairman and CEO. When a company gets into business or financial difficulties, for example, there is an argument in favour of appointing a single, all-powerful individual to run the company until its fortune has been reversed. The combination of the roles of chairman and CEO might have been necessary in the short term to give a company strong leadership to get it through its difficulties.

7.5 Non-compliance with the UK Code on separation of the roles

In spite of the principle and provision in the UK Code that the roles of chairman and CEO should be kept separate, some companies have not complied. Instead they have appointed the same individual to both roles and chosen to explain their non-compliance. Although this happens, it should normally be considered bad corporate governance practice.

The UK Code states that: 'if exceptionally a board decides that a chief executive should become chairman, the board should consult major shareholders in advance and set out its reasons to shareholders at the time of the appointment and in the next annual report.'

 CASE EXAMPLE 4.2

In the UK, Mr Luc Vandevelde was appointed as chairman and CEO of Marks & Spencer some years ago, at a time when its business operations were in difficulty and the share price was falling sharply. This appointment attracted some criticism but appears to have been a successful short-term measure. By 2002, the company's fortunes had improved to the point where he relinquished the position of CEO and announced his intention to become part-time chairman. However, in 2008 Marks & Spencer's CEO, Sir Stuart Rose, was also appointed as company chairman for a limited period until a successor to the role of CEO could be identified and appointed. This appointment, given the previous appointment of Vandevelde, attracted strong criticism from institutional investors. Institutional investor Legal & General publicly criticised the decision by Marks & Spencer to appoint Sir Stuart Rose as executive chairman, saying it was an arrangement that made it difficult to appoint a successor to Sir Stuart as CEO. However, shareholders could not prevent the appointment of the new chairman because this was a decision of the board. Shareholders were able, however, to vote on the re-election of Sir Stuart Rose as director at the AGM in 2008, and 22% of shareholders either opposed his re-election or abstained in the vote.

 CASE EXAMPLE 4.3

In 2007 the Association of British Insurers (ABI) stated that it would issue an 'amber top' warning to its members over plans by pharmaceuticals company Shire to appoint its CEO as non-executive chairman. The company also proposed to replace the CEO with the company's long-standing finance director. The director of investment affairs at the ABI was reported to have said: 'The chairman is supposed to oversee strategy and makes sure the board tests it and decision-making is robust (sic). If the chairman was the chief executive who developed the strategy, he is supervising himself. There are risks in that.'

CASE EXAMPLE 4.4

The potential risk of a company and board being subjected to a dominant personality can be illustrated by the case of the UK company Polly Peck International. Polly Peck, a FTSE 100 company during the 1980s, was effectively run by a single individual, Asil Nadir, who was both CEO and board chairman. The company collapsed without warning in October 1990. During the administration process, the system of internal controls at the company's London head office was found to be virtually non-existent. As a result, Nadir had been able to transfer large amounts of money from the company's UK bank accounts to personal accounts with a bank in Northern Cyprus, without any questions being asked. After the company collapsed, Nadir fled to Northern Cyprus. He returned to London in 2010 to face trial and was found guilty of 10 counts of theft totalling £29 million and in 2012 was sentenced to 10 years in prison. In 2016 he was transferred to a Turkish prison.

7.6 Holding more than one chairmanship of a major company: the chairman's other commitments

A problem with non-executive chairmen – as with NEDs generally – is that the individual may not have enough time to devote to the role of chairman because of a large number of other commitments. For example, the chairman of a large company may also be the chairman of other companies, not-for-profit entities and government-sponsored bodies, so that they do not have enough time to fulfil all these roles adequately.

Originally, the UK Code stated that an individual should not be the chairman of more than one FTSE 100 company. However, possibly because of a recognised shortage of individuals capable of acting as chairman of a major company, this provision in the Code was abolished in 2008.

Even so, chairmen need to be able to demonstrate that they have sufficient time to perform their role to the standards expected. The Walker Report on corporate governance in banks (2009) following the financial crisis of 2007–2009 suggested that the chairmen of large banks would need to spend about two-thirds of their time with the company.

The UK Corporate Governance Code is less specific on the amount of time that a chairman should commit to the company. However, a provision of the Code is that when a chairman is appointed, the **nomination committee** (see also Chapter 5) should prepare a job description, which should:

■ include an assessment of the amount of time commitment that should be expected; and
■ recognise the need for the chairman to make himself or herself available in a time of crisis.

The chairman's other commitments should be disclosed to the board before his or her appointment and included in the next annual report and accounts. If there are changes to the time commitment required from or provided by the chairman, these should be disclosed to the board and reported in the next annual report and accounts.

TEST YOUR KNOWLEDGE 4.6

a   What is the role of a company chairman? Why should this role not be combined with the role of CEO?
b   What are the requirements of the UK Code of Corporate Governance with regard to the independence of the company chairman?
c   In what circumstances is it acceptable for an individual to be the chairman of more than one FTSE 100 company at the same time?

CASE QUESTION

Refer back to Stenning Tull, the company featured in the case study at the beginning of Part Two. In your view, should a new chairman be appointed externally, or should the current chairman be allowed to remain in place as head of the board of directors? Give your reasons.

8 Executive directors

The role of the CEO was described earlier. The FRC Guidance on Board Effectiveness makes some further comments about the role of executive directors generally.

- All directors on a unitary board have the same duties. The duties or responsibilities of an executive director are not restricted to the area of their executive responsibilities.
- Executive directors should not think of themselves as a member of the CEO's executive team when they are engaged in board business.
- The chairman has a responsibility to ensure that their induction on appointment and subsequent training provide them with suitable guidance on how to carry out their board role.
- The understanding of executive directors about their responsibilities as a director may be improved if they are able (and allowed) to take a non-executive directorship position with another company.
- The CFO has particular responsibilities for providing the board with high-quality financial information.

The Guidance comments that executive directors 'should appreciate that constructive challenge from NEDs is an essential aspect of good governance, and should encourage their non-executive colleagues to test their proposals in the light of the non-executives' wider experience outside the company'.

9 Non-executive directors (NEDs)

A NED is a member of the board of directors without executive responsibilities in the company. NEDs should be able to bring judgement and experience to the deliberations of the board that the executive directors on their own would lack.

To be effective, a NED has to understand the company's business, but there appears to be general consensus that the experience and qualities required of a NED can be obtained from working in other industries or in other aspects of commercial and public life. NEDs may therefore include individuals who:

- are executive directors in other public companies;
- hold NED positions and chairmanship positions in other public companies;
- have professional qualifications (e.g. partners in firms of solicitors); and
- have experience in government, as politicians or former senior civil servants.

However, research has been carried out into identifying and recruiting suitable individuals as NEDs from a wider variety of sources and backgrounds (see below).

NEDs are expected not only to bring a wide range of skills and experience to the deliberations of the board, particularly in the area of strategy and business development, but also to ensure that there is a suitable balance of power on the board. A powerful chairman or CEO might be able to dominate other executive directors, but in theory at least, independent NEDs should be able to bring different views and independent thinking to board deliberations. Decisions taken by the board should therefore be better and more in keeping with the aims of good corporate governance.

There is a serious possibility that NEDs, either individually or as a group, will be treated with suspicion or dislike by their executive director colleagues who may wonder what 'part-time' directors are doing in the company, and what they can bring to the board that full-time executive directors cannot. In order to become effective contributors to the board, NEDs need to work at overcoming this hostile attitude. To do this, they should both support the executive directors in their management of the business, but also monitor their conduct within an atmosphere of 'mutual respect'. This is perhaps more easily stated than achieved in practice!

9.1 The UK Corporate Governance Code on NEDs

The UK Code sets out about the role of NEDs.

- A principle of the Code is that as part of their role, NEDs should 'constructively challenge and help develop proposals on strategy'.
- NEDs should also scrutinise the performance of management in meeting agreed goals and objectives, and they should monitor the reporting of performance (to ensure that this is honest and not misleading).
- NEDs should satisfy themselves about the integrity of the financial information produced by the company, and that the **financial controls** and systems of risk management are 'robust and defensible'.
- They should be responsible for deciding the remuneration of executive directors.
- They should have a prime role in the appointment (and where necessary removal) of executive directors and in succession planning.

The UK Code recognises there are matters that the NEDs should discuss without executive directors being present, and a provision of the UK Code is that:

- the chairman should hold meetings with the NEDs without executive directors being present; and
- without the chairman and led by the SID (see section 10 'Senior independent director (SID)'), the NEDs should meet at least once a year to appraise the performance of the chairman. They should also meet on other occasions if this is deemed appropriate.

9.2 FRC Guidance on the role of NEDs

The FRC Guidance on Board Effectiveness makes the following recommendations.

- On first appointment, a NED should devote time to a comprehensive, formal and tailored induction, and should subsequently devote time to developing and refreshing his or her knowledge and skills.
- NEDs should make sufficient time available so that they can carry out their responsibilities effectively.
- Their letter of appointment should specify the amount of time that the NED will be expected to spend on the company's business, and should indicate the possibility that additional time will be required at times of particular board activity, such as when a takeover is planned or when the company is facing a major problem in its operations.
- Because of the importance of decision-making as a board responsibility, NEDs should insist on receiving accurate, clear and comprehensive information sufficiently in advance of board meetings, so that they have time to read and study all the material. Papers should include an executive summary or should indicate what action is required from the NED on the particular issue (although the chairman, assisted by the company secretary, is responsible for providing timely, clear and comprehensive information, NEDs should make sure that they get it).

9.3 The role of NEDs in banks

The Walker Report, referred to earlier in this chapter, suggested that the role of NEDs is crucial to the effectiveness of a board in formulating and implementing business strategy. Although the report is concerned with banks and other financial institutions (such as insurance companies), it included some useful general comments about NEDs.

An up-to-date statement on the role of NEDs in banks is that of the Prudential Regulation Authority (PRA) issued in March 2016: Supervisory Statement | SS5/16 Corporate governance: Board responsibilities. The PRA is a UK financial services regulatory body, wholly owned by the Bank of England and is responsible for the prudential regulation and supervision of banks, building societies, credit unions, insurers and major investment firms. It sets standards and supervises financial institutions at the level of the individual firm.

The respective roles of executive and non-executive directors

Unitary boards comprise a combination of executive and non-executive directors. Executive directors have specific management responsibilities for which they are accountable to the board. It is their responsibility to manage the firm's business on behalf of the board and exercise judgement in the running of the business on a day-to-day basis. They should exercise that judgement within the strategy, risk appetite and other assessment and control frameworks set and overseen by their board. Non-executive directors' responsibilities require them to both support and oversee executive management. As board members, they all share in the wider board duty to promote the success of the company and to ensure that the regulated firm for which they are responsible continues to meet the Threshold Conditions.

In discharging their responsibilities boards should act in a co-operative and collegiate manner whereby the non-executives support and encourage executive management and vice versa. But this should not inhibit the non-executive directors from challenging executive management and holding them to account effectively. The PRA expects the chairman to play a pivotal role in facilitating this culture.

Executive management manage the firm's business on behalf of the board. Boards therefore delegate a wide range of duties and responsibilities to the chief executive or to executive management.

Accordingly the board and particularly the non-executive directors on the board should hold management to account against the matters delegated and be able to challenge the executive effectively and promptly.

Knowledge and experience of non-executive directors

Between them the non-executive directors need to have sufficient current and relevant knowledge and experience, including sector experience, to understand the key activities and risks involved in the business model and to provide effective challenge across the major business lines of the firm. The PRA expects to see evidence of effective challenge, particularly in relation to key strategic decisions. It is the role of the chairman to ensure that all views are heard and that the executives are not able to control the board discussion. However, board responsibility is collective and an effective board is not simply a collection of specialists. So just as the board should not delegate responsibility for major decisions to particular directors, the non-executives should not simply delegate responsibility for challenging the executives on particular issues to individuals among them who are considered specialist in the area.

Even a broadly constituted and well-experienced board cannot necessarily be expected to have expertise in every aspect of a broad and complex financial business. The point is to have the diversity of experience and capacity to provide effective challenge across the full range of the firm's business and the opportunity to explore key business issues rigorously. Sometimes that may require the board to understand and reach decisions on complex technical, legal, regulatory or other issues. It is the responsibility of the executives to explain such issues in clear and transparent terms that enable the board to exercise their collective judgement and, where necessary, non-executive directors should be able to call on appropriate professional advice, although the directors will always remain ultimately and collectively accountable for all the board's decisions.

The workload of NEDs

In a 2010 NEDs survey, PricewaterhouseCoopers (PwC) reported that NEDs spent on average 20% more time on their boardroom duties in 2010 than in 2009 and expected to commit even more time in 2011. The reasons were:

- having to deal with more regulatory requirements;
- helping their company through the economic downturn;
- more demanding committee work: for example, audit committee members were spending more time on matters relating to risk, including attending meetings of executive risk committees to find out more about the company's risk profile and risk exposures; and
- more time committed to board meetings, especially on the boards of global companies where board meetings are often held in different countries.

The PwC report commented that, in view of the growing demands on NEDs, it may be getting much harder now for executive directors to accept NED positions in other companies.

9.4 Independence of NEDs

The concept of independence can be confusing, since all directors of companies are required to exercise independent judgement. In spite of this, it is recognised that they may be inclined to take a particular point of view. For example, a director may be inclined to support the views of the CEO (especially if the director is an executive of the company). Occasionally a director may be appointed to represent the interests of a major shareholder, and the views of this individual will obviously be influenced by this role.

For the purpose of the UK Corporate Governance Code, NEDs are either independent or non-independent.

The UK Code does not suggest that all NEDs should be independent. Non-independent NEDs are permissible, although the majority of the total board should consist of independent NEDs. However, if there are NEDs on the board who are not considered to be independent, this could create problems with the size and composition of the board. It may be considered necessary to appoint independent NEDs to act as a counter-balance to the NEDs who are not independent.

Executive directors cannot be independent. Not only are they involved in the running of the company's operations and report (and are accountable) to the CEO for this aspect of their work, they also rely on the company for most (if not all) of their remuneration.

Independent NEDs are supposed to bring an independent view to the deliberations of the board. However, they are in a difficult position as they are legally liable in the same way as executive directors. For example, they have the same fiduciary duties to the company, and the duty of skill and care. As fellow directors, they might also be reluctant to blow the whistle on their executive colleagues. If they have been selected and appointed by the chairman or the CEO, they will be less likely to ask tough questions about the way the company is being run. This is sometimes known as the 'St Thomas à Becket' problem (the twelfth-century Archbishop of Canterbury Becket was appointed by Henry II, but then took a stand against him on issues concerning the roles of the King and the Church in the governance of the country).

When considering what is meant by 'independent', it is easier to specify what is 'not independent'. A NED is not independent if his or her opinions are likely to be influenced by someone else, in particular by the senior executive management or by a major shareholder.

If a NED is likely, for whatever reason, to side with the CEO, he or she is they are unlikely to bring the much-needed balance of power to the board. The independence of a NED could be challenged, for example, if the individual concerned:

- has a family connection with the CEO – a problem in some family-controlled public companies;
- until recently used to be an executive director in the company;
- until recently used to work for the company in a professional capacity (e.g. as its auditor or corporate lawyer); or
- receives payments from the company in addition to their fees as a NED.

A person cannot be independent if he or she personally stands to gain or otherwise benefit substantially from:

- income from the company, in addition to his or her fee as a NED; or
- the company's reported profitability and movements in the company's share price.

A NED cannot be properly independent, for example, if he or she accepts a fee from the company for consultancy work. Consultancy involves the individual in the operational aspects of the company, and by implication puts him or her on the side of the executives. Nor can an individual be independent if he or she has been awarded a large number of share options by the company. Holding share options gives the individual a direct interest in the share price of the company around the time the options can be exercised. The individual might therefore favour decisions that improve the reported profitability of the company at this time, because good financial results are likely to be good for the share price.

A former executive director might be appointed as a NED on his or her retirement. When this happens, his or her attitudes and judgements are likely to remain on the side of the executive management, and he or she unlikely to make criticisms of the executive management that might indirectly reflect adversely on his or her own performance as an executive manager prior to retirement.

Occasionally, NEDs are appointed to represent the opinions of a major shareholder. In such cases, the individual can be expected to voice the wishes of the shareholder, and so could not be regarded as independent.

To ensure that NEDs should not rely for their tenure in office on one or two individuals, the UK Code recommends that they should be selected through a formal process.

STOP AND THINK **4.5**

Directors may hold some shares in their company. Holding some shares may be encouraged, since it will help directors to identify themselves more closely with the company and its shareholders. However, if a director is a significant shareholder, he or she will not be considered independent, because of the size of his or her investment in the company and personal interest in it.

9.5 Criteria for judging independence: UK Code guidelines

The UK Corporate Governance Code requires the board to identify in the annual report each NED it considers to be independent. Although this is a matter for the board's judgement, the Code sets out circumstances in which independence would usually be questionable. The board would need to explain why it considers a NED to be independent in any of these circumstances:

- The director has been an employee of the company within the last five years.
- The director has a material business relationship with the company (or has had such a relationship within the last three years). This relationship might be as a partner, shareholder, director or employee in another organisation that has a material business relationship with the company.
- The director receives (or has received) additional remuneration from the company other than a director's fee, or is a member of the company's pension scheme, or participates in the company's share option scheme or a performance-related pay scheme.
- The director has close family ties with any of the company's advisers, directors or senior employees.
- The director has cross-directorships or has significant links with other directors through involvement in other companies or organisations. A cross-directorship exists when an individual is a NED on the board of Company X and an executive director on the board of Company Y, when another individual is an executive director of Company X and NED on the board of Company Y.
- The director represents a significant shareholder.
- The director has served on the board for more than nine years since the date of his or her first election.

These criteria of independence should be applied to the chairman (on appointment) as well as other NEDs.

- Circumstances may change, and the independence of NEDs should be kept under review.
- However, this provision does not apply to the chairman. Although the UK Code states that the chairman should be independent on first appointment, the test of independence is 'not appropriate' to the chairman thereafter.

9.6 The nine-year rule on independence

The provision in the UK Code that a NED should not be considered independent after serving on the board for over nine years arises from the general view that the independence of a NED is likely to diminish over time, as the NED becomes more familiar with the company and executive colleagues. The risk is that the NED will take more of the views of executive colleagues on trust and will be less rigorous in his questioning.

The King IV Code states that:

'A NED may continue to serve, in an independent capacity, for longer than nine years if, upon an assessment of the governing body conducted every year after nine years, it is concluded that the member exercises objective judgement and there is no interest, position, association or relationship which is likely to influence unduly or cause bias in decision-making.'

Larger quoted companies appear reluctant to lose NEDs after nine years of service, due largely to a perceived lack of potential candidates with the suitable qualifications to be an effective NED. It is therefore worth remembering that the UK Code is pragmatic in its approach to the nine-year rule. If the board considers that a director is still independent even after nine years' service, they may still be considered 'independent' for the purposes of the corporate governance provisions.

The 'nine-year rule' may also suggest that if a director has served for a long time on the board, but for less than nine years, his or her continuing independence should be subject to careful scrutiny. At some stage, perhaps after exactly nine years but possibly sooner, a NED may be asked to resign, so that the board can be refreshed with new directors bringing new ideas and experiences to the deliberations of the board.

The Pensions and Lifetime Savings Association (PLSA) in its Corporate Governance Policy and voting Guidelines (2015/16) recognises the connection between the 'nine-year rule' and refreshing the board membership.

'The value of the tenure guideline of nine years is to drive refreshment of the board overall rather than marking a limit on the value offered by an individual. With increasing tenures directors will be subject to increasing scrutiny as to their effectiveness and independence. Most importantly boards should set out their forward-looking succession and refreshment plans in detail when they propose the re-election of a long-serving non-executive director, especially when the director is chairing an important board committee.'

 STOP AND THINK 4.6

The guidelines on 'independence' in the UK Code are concerned with factors that may lead to a conclusion that an individual is not entirely independent, and may therefore be inclined to express views that represent an established interest.

However, if an individual 'passes the independence test' of the UK Code, this does not mean that he or she is necessarily independent-minded. The independence of a director should be judged by what they do and say, not just by conformity with guidelines for independence. The contribution of individual directors to the board's discussions, and the independence of mind displayed by the director, should be reviewed regularly – in an annual review of board performance.

9.7 Protecting the independence and effectiveness of board committees

As a way of protecting the independence and improving the effectiveness of board committees, the UK Corporate Governance Code includes the following supporting principles:

- When deciding the chairmanship and membership of board committees, consideration should be given to the benefits of ensuring that committee membership is refreshed (i.e. membership rotation) and that undue reliance is not placed on particular individuals.
- The only individuals who are entitled to attend meetings of the nomination, remuneration and audit committees are the chairman and members of the committee, although other individuals may attend at the invitation of the committee.

9.8 Comparison of executives and NEDs

Unlike NEDs, executive directors are full-time employees of the company, with executive management responsibilities in addition to their responsibilities as directors. For the executive directors, there is a tension between:

■ their role as members of the board, 'one step down from the shareholders'; and
■ their role as senior operational directors, 'one step up from management'.

Executive directors, led by their CEO, may often want to present a united front to the rest of the board, to justify what the management team has done and achieved, or what it would like to do. However, if the executive directors come together with a united opinion, this will question their ability to fulfil the role of all directors to provide effective challenge in discussions on strategy. In comparison, independent NEDs do not have this problem, which is why they should be more effective in providing effective challenge in board discussions, encouraged by the chairman.

The problems for executive directors are therefore that:

■ they may be inclined to support the views of the CEO on all matters, including strategy; and
■ they may mistrust the NEDs as 'outsiders' who do not know much about the company and its business.

In recognition of this problem, the guidance 'Improving Board Effectiveness' suggests that executive directors should see themselves as representatives of the shareholders rather than as executive managers who are responsible and accountable to the CEO. The chairman should encourage this attitude among the executive directors, partly through ensuring that they receive appropriate induction and training for their role as company director.

Executive directors should have a very detailed knowledge of the company and its business, and should apply this knowledge when making judgements about company strategy. However, they should also recognise that constructive challenge from NEDs is an essential part of good corporate governance, and they should welcome and encourage such challenges. For an effective board, the executive directors and NEDs must work constructively together.

TEST YOUR KNOWLEDGE 4.7

a What are the intended functions of independent NEDs?
b According to Higgs, what are the four broad roles of NEDs?
c According to the UK Code of Corporate Governance, what are the roles of NEDs?
d List six circumstances in which a NED would not normally be considered independent.
e To comply with UK corporate governance requirements, what measures should be taken if a company appoints a NED who is not considered independent?

---

10 Senior independent director (SID)

There could be occasions when institutional shareholders are in disagreement with the board of directors, but are unable to make their opinions heard due to the negative attitudes of the chairman and CEO. For this reason, a provision was included in the UK governance code that the board of directors of large companies should nominate an independent NED as the SID, whom shareholders could approach to discuss problems and issues when the normal communication route through the chairman has broken down.

In addition, if the chairman fails to pass on the views of the institutional shareholders to the NEDs, there should be another channel of communication that could be used instead.

The UK Corporate Governance Code states that the board should appoint one of the independent NEDs to be the SID.

■ The SID should provide a sounding board for the chairman, and as such may act as an intermediary through whom the other NEDs can express their views and concerns to the chairman.

■ The SID should also 'be available to shareholders if they have concerns which contact through the normal channels of chairman, chief executive or other executive directors has failed to resolve, or for which such contact is inappropriate'. The SID is therefore a channel of communication between the company and its shareholders when normal channels don't work – perhaps when the principles of good corporate governance are not being applied.

The FRC Guidance on Board Effectiveness makes a distinction between the role of the SID in 'normal times' and when the board is undergoing 'a period of stress'. At normal times, the role of the SID is to:

■ act as a sounding board for the chairman, to help the chairman formulate his or her ideas and opinions and provide support for the chairman; and
■ carry out the annual review of the performance of the chairman, in conjunction with the other NEDs (see Chapter 5).

The SID may also take responsibility for the orderly succession process of a new chairman, when the current chairman resigns and leaves the company. At times of stress for the board, the role of the SID should be to take the initiative to resolve the problem, working with the other directors and shareholders and/or the chairman, as appropriate. Examples of problems where intervention by the SID may be appropriate include situations where:

■ there is a dispute between the chairman and the CEO;
■ shareholders or the NEDs have expressed serious concerns that are not being addressed by the chairman or CEO;
■ the strategy pursued by the chairman or CEO is not supported by the rest of the board;
■ there is a very close relationship between the chairman and the CEO, and decisions are being taken without the approval of the board; or
■ succession planning is being ignored.

Issues where intervention may be required should be considered when defining the responsibilities of the SID and should be set out in writing.

The role of the SID is therefore likely to be more important at times when the board is under stress, such as when there are disagreements between the chairman and major shareholders, or between the NEDs and executive directors. Critics of the SID concept argue that the chairman should be able to resolve difficulties between a company and its shareholders, and the position of SID should therefore be superfluous. Opening up the possibility of an additional channel of communication for shareholders is perhaps more likely to undermine company–shareholder relationships than improve them.

STOP AND THINK 4.7

It may be tempting to think that the main role of the SID or lead independent director is to act as a check on the board chairman, for example by providing an alternative channel of communication for shareholders who are not satisfied with the responses they have received from the chairman and CEO.

However, good corporate governance requires a united board. Board members may have lively debates and occasional disagreements, but the role of the SID, who may also be the deputy chairman, is generally to support the board chairman, and not oppose him or her.

11 Board committees and NEDs

An aspect of best practice in corporate governance is that for some issues that the board should decide, the executive directors should be excluded from the decision-making or monitoring responsibilities. This is achieved by delegating certain governance responsibilities to committees of the board. A board committee might consist entirely or mostly of NEDs, and have the responsibility for dealing with particular issues and making recommendations to the full board. The full board is then usually expected to accept and endorse the recommendations of the relevant board committee.

In the UK, three committees are recommended by the UK Corporate Governance Code (and governance codes in several other countries):

1 A nomination committee.
2 An audit committee.
3 A remuneration committee.

In the UK, there is no statutory requirement for a nomination committee or a remuneration committee, but, following the implementation of the EU Statutory Audit Directive in 2008, quoted companies are required to have an audit committee.

Some boards might establish other committees. For example, a company might have an environment committee if its business activities are likely to have important consequences for the environment, involving government regulation, the law and public opinion. However, there is no requirement for these committees to consist wholly or mainly of NEDs.

Table 4.1 summarises the UK Code's recommendations about membership of board committees.

TABLE 4.1 Summary of the UK Code's recommendations regarding membership of board committees

Nominations committee	Audit committee	Remuneration committee
Composition: majority of members should be independent NEDs.	Composition: all independent NEDs – in large companies, at least three, in smaller companies two.	Composition: all independent NEDs – in large companies, at least three, in smaller companies two.
Chairman should be the chairman of the board or an independent NED.	In smaller companies, the chairman of the board may also be a member of the audit committee (but not chairman of the committee), in addition to the independent NEDs – but only if he or she was independent on appointment to the chairmanship.	The chairman of the board may also be a member of the remuneration committee (but not chairman of the committee), but only if he or she was independent on appointment to the chairmanship.
If the board chairman is the company chairman, he or she should not act as chair when the committee is considering a successor for the chairmanship.	At least one member of the committee should have 'recent and relevant financial experience'.	

11.1 The role of board committees

The roles of these committees are explained in detail in subsequent chapters. It is important, however, to understand the general nature of the responsibilities of board committees.

Board committees are established to improve the effectiveness of the board. Committees can give more time to particular issues, and the work done by committees can save a lot of time at board meetings, and help the board to make more effective use of its time.

A board committee is also able to consider issues that would be inappropriate for the full board to discuss.

■ The full board cannot discuss the remuneration of executive directors, because those directors would be involved in decision-making about their own pay, not just as the individual negotiating his or her remuneration package but also as a decision-maker awarding the package.
■ Similarly, it is difficult for the board to discuss the audit of the annual accounts when the finance director and CEO are present.

A board committee does not have responsibilities, however, that the board as a unit does have. In particular, board committees do not have any executive management responsibilities. They may receive reports from management and have discussions with management, but they cannot tell management how to do their work. Similarly, they cannot get involved in activities that are the responsibilities of management.

This may perhaps seem an obvious point, but it is a common source of misunderstanding.

12 Effectiveness of NEDs

There are differing views about the effectiveness of NEDs. The accepted view is that NEDs bring experience and judgement to the deliberations of the board that the executive directors on their own would lack. An alternative view is that the effectiveness of NEDs can be undermined by:

- a lack of knowledge about the business operations of the company;
- insufficient time spent with the company;
- the weight of opinion of the executive directors on the board; and
- delays in decision-making.

12.1 Insufficient knowledge

The quality of decision-making depends largely on the quality of information available to the decision-maker. The UK Code states that the board as a whole should be 'supplied in a timely manner with information in a form and of a quality appropriate to enable it to discharge its duties'. However, the senior executives in a company control the information systems, and so control the flow of information to the board. It is quite conceivable, for example, that the CEO and other executive directors might have access to management information that is withheld from the board as a whole, or that is presented to the board in a distorted manner. Lacking the 'insider knowledge' of executive managers about the business operations, and having to rely on the integrity of the information supplied to them by management and executive directors, restricts the scope for NEDs to make a meaningful contribution to board decisions.

12.2 Insufficient time

NEDs often have executive positions in other companies and organisations, where most of their working time is spent. As a general rule, NEDs do not have an office at the company headquarters and may spend at most one or two days a month on the company's business. A further criticism of NEDs is that some individuals hold too many NED positions, with the result that they cannot possibly give sufficient time to any of the companies concerned. It could be argued, for example, that an individual cannot be an effective NED of a company if they are also the CEO of another public company and hold four or five other NED positions in other companies.

The UK Code states that all directors should be able to allocate sufficient time to the company to discharge their responsibilities effectively. Although this principle of the Code applies to all directors, the main concern is with NEDs (since executive directors are usually full-time employees) and in particular the chairman. The UK Code requires that when a chairman is appointed, the nomination committee should prepare a job specification that includes an assessment of the expected time commitment and recognising the need for the chairman to be available to the company in times of crisis.

Similarly, when a NED is appointed (other than a chairman), the letter of appointment should set out the expected time commitment.

12.3 Overriding influence of executive directors

Yet another criticism of NEDs is that if a difference of opinion arises during a meeting of the board, the opinions of the executive directors are likely to carry greater weight, because they know more about the company. NEDs may be put under pressure to accept the views of their executive director colleagues. This potential problem provides an argument for the role of a strong SID, to ensure that the opinions of the independent NEDs are properly considered.

12.4 Delays in decision-making

It may be argued that NEDs delay decision-making within a company. Major decisions should be reserved for the board; therefore, to implement an important new strategy initiative it may be necessary to call a board meeting. The time required to hold the meeting, giving the NEDs sufficient time to reach a well-informed opinion about the matter, may delay the implementation of the proposed strategy. It has also been argued that NEDs may be conservative in outlook, whereas the board of directors needs to be 'entrepreneurial'.

One counter-argument is that when a major new strategy or initiative is proposed, it should be given full and careful consideration before a decision is made. NEDs, with their range of skills and experience, can contribute positively to this decision-making process.

12.5 Myners Report and criticisms of NEDs

Weaknesses in the system of appointing NEDs have been recognised for many years and criticisms made in 2002 are probably still valid today. In February 2002, Paul Myners (subsequently appointed as a government minister) issued a UK government-backed report into pension fund investment. He accused boards of directors of public companies of being a 'self-perpetuating oligarchy', which failed to stand up for shareholders' rights against over-powerful executives. He condemned NEDs as the 'missing link' in the chain of good corporate governance. In particular, he criticised the way NED appointments were made and the number of NED positions that some individuals held.

- Some individuals held too many NED positions in large public companies, more than they could possibly serve effectively.
- Non-executive directorships were frequently given to the executive directors of other listed companies, giving rise to the concerns about a 'I'll help you if you help me' favouritism culture. A NED might tacitly undertake not to ask awkward questions or take a stand against executives on the board, provided that the NEDs of his or her own company act in the same way.
- NEDs should help to make the board more accountable to the shareholders. However, shareholders have opportunities to discuss the company's affairs with the NEDs in a formal setting, at general meetings of the company only. Any other discussions between shareholders and NEDs must be informal, if they take place at all.
- The law makes no distinction between executives and NEDs. In principle, the NEDs could be equally liable with the executive directors for negligence and failure of duty. Arguably, this threat of criminal or civil liability could make NEDs more likely to support their executive colleagues.
- Faith in NEDs to bring sound corporate governance practice to public companies could therefore be misplaced – a view that has been expressed. Lord Young, outgoing president of the UK Institute of Directors (IoD), for example, argued in a speech to the IoD annual convention in the same year as the Myners Report (2002) that NEDs cannot hope to govern their company better than the executive directors, because they cannot know as much about the company as full-time executives:

'The biggest and most dangerous nonsense is the role we now expect NEDs to perform. Even if they spend one day a week in the company, can the non-execs ever know the business as well as the execs? No, they can't. So why bother with non-execs at all?'

13 Unitary and two-tier boards

Companies in most countries have **unitary boards**, consisting of both executive directors and NEDs under the leadership of the company chairman. A unitary board makes collective decisions and is accountable to the shareholders. It is commonly accepted governance practice that the NEDs in a listed company should be independent, although this is not a legal requirement.

13.1 Two-tier boards

Some countries, including Germany and Austria, have **two-tier boards**. With a two-tier structure, there is a **supervisory board** and a **management board**.

- The management board is responsible for managing the company. It is led by the chairman of the managing board, who is the CEO; its members are appointed by the supervisory board. It develops strategy for the company, in cooperation with the supervisory board, and is responsible for implementing the agreed strategy. It also has responsibility for risk management and the preparation of the annual financial statements (which are examined by the auditors and the supervisory board; see also Chapter 7).
- The supervisory board is responsible for general oversight of the company and of the management board. Its members are elected by the shareholders, except that in public companies with more than 500 employees, a minimum proportion of the supervisory board must consist of representatives of the employees. The supervisory board is led by the company chairman. It advises the management board and must be involved in decision-making on all fundamental matters affecting the company; these include 'decisions or measures which fundamentally change the asset, financial or earnings situations of the enterprise' (German Corporate Governance Code 2015). The audit committee consists entirely of supervisory board members.

In a two-tier structure, there has to be a functional relationship between the management board and the supervisory board, and the chairman of the supervisory board plays a key role. They are responsible for making sure that the two boards work well together, and the most powerful individuals in the company are the chairman of the supervisory board and the CEO who is in charge of the management board. The CEO reports to the supervisory board chairman. If the relationship between these two works well, the chairman will effectively speak for the management at meetings of the supervisory board.

The management board consists entirely of executive directors. The supervisory board consists entirely of NEDs. In Germany, supervisory board members include:

- representatives of trade unions and/or the company's employees;
- representatives of major shareholders; and
- former executives of the company.

The supervisory board NEDs are therefore not necessarily independent, particularly employee representatives. It can therefore be difficult to reconcile the differing views of employee representatives and representatives of major shareholders, without antagonising the executives on the management board. On the other hand, where there is a large number of former executives on the supervisory board, there is a risk that the supervisory board could take a lenient and easy-going view of what management are doing. In addition, some independent supervisory board directors might well be senior managers of other companies, where they are management board members. These individuals might therefore sympathise with the views of the management board.

The success of corporate governance depends on a good working relationship between the supervisory board and the management board, and in particular a good working relationship between the company chairman and the head of the management board. The German code states that 'the Management Board and Supervisory Board co-operate closely to the benefit of the enterprise' and the management board should discuss the implementation of strategy regularly with the supervisory board.

13.2 Criticisms of the two-tier board structure

There have been some criticisms of a two-tier board structure. The main concerns are as follows.

- Supervisory boards are too big, having up to 20 members. German supervisory boards include a large number of employee representatives, and large numbers can result in inefficient meetings.
- It has been common to appoint retired former managers of the company to the supervisory board, and these individuals might be tempted to retain some influence over the actions and operational decisions of their successors. This is not the purpose of a supervisory board. On the other hand, if former managers are appointed to the supervisory board, the supervisory board will benefit from their knowledge and experience of the business. A law introduced in Germany in 2009 prohibits former managers from 'moving upstairs' to the supervisory board for at least two years, unless the move receives the support of at least 25% of shareholders; the rationale for this law is that for the first two years after retiring, a former executive will not be sufficiently independent.

■ Companies with more than 500 employees are required to have workers' representatives or trade union representatives on the supervisory board. Companies with more than 2,000 employees are required to have an even greater percentage of employee representatives on the supervisory board. This requirement is an enforcement of the principle of 'co-determination', embodied in German law, that the workers as well as the management and owners should determine the future of their companies. Unfortunately, workers' representatives often lack the competence to consider strategic issues or are not independent from the company. In some instances, worker members of a supervisory board opposing planned initiatives by the company have been accused of leaking confidential information to the press.

Concerns about information leaks can damage communications between supervisory and management boards. Developments in some German companies in recent years suggest that the supervisory boards of large German companies are becoming more responsive to the interests of their shareholders.

CASE EXAMPLE 4.5

There was a bribery scandal at German engineering group Siemens in 2005, with allegations that senior managers had paid €1.3 billion in bribes worldwide to secure contracts. The supervisory board took legal action against the managers concerned, including the former CEO and chairman of the company. Its members believed that they had no choice other than to take legal action to obtain compensation, since shareholders would otherwise sue them. In December 2009 it was announced that settlements had been reached with nine former Siemens executives, who each agreed to pay compensation to the company.

13.3 Two-tier boards in the UK?

At about the time of the Cadbury Report (1992) there was much debate about whether governance in UK companies would be improved by a switch from a unitary board system to a two-tier system. This is no longer a serious consideration, for two reasons:

■ The unitary board system has been improved by the introduction of a system of board committees (audit committee, remuneration committee, nomination committee and possibly also a risk committee). Committees are able to consider some issues in more detail than the full board, and some issues can be dealt with successfully by a committee where involvement of the whole board might be inappropriate (e.g. decisions about senior executive remuneration).
■ The two-tier board structure has been criticised.

The Walker Report UK (2009) on corporate governance in banks considered whether unitary boards may have contributed to the scale of the financial crisis in 2007–2009, and whether a two-tier board structure might therefore be more suitable for large banks. Its conclusions were fairly critical:

'In practice, two-tier structures do not appear to assure members of the supervisory board of access to the quality and timeliness of management information flow that would generally be regarded as essential for non-executives on a unitary board. Moreover, since, in a two-tier structure, members of the supervisory and executive boards meet separately and do not share the same responsibilities, the two-tier model would not provide opportunity for the interactive exchange of views between executives and NEDs, drawing on and pooling their respective experience and capabilities in the way that takes place in a well-functioning unitary board. Directors and others whose experience is substantially that of the unitary model appear generally to conclude that such interaction is commonly value-adding in the context of decision-taking in the board. On this criterion, the two-tier model did not in general yield better outcomes than unitary boards in the period before the recent crisis phase and recent experience, in particular in Germany, Switzerland and the Benelux, makes no persuasive case for departing from the UK unitary model.'

TEST YOUR KNOWLEDGE 4.8

a   What are the respective roles of a management board and a supervisory board in a two-tier board structure in Germany?

b   What are the criticisms of a two-tier board structure?

CHAPTER SUMMARY

■ Every company should be headed by an effective board, which has the collective responsibility for the long-term success of the company. Various corporate governance codes have identified the responsibilities of the board.

■ There should be a schedule of matters reserved to the board for its own decision-making. ICSA has issued a guidance note 2013 indicating what these matters should be.

■ A board should not be so large that it is unwieldy nor so small that it lacks sufficient skills and experience. The UK Code recommends that at least 50% of the board (excluding the chairman) should be independent NEDs, except for smaller companies (listed companies outside the FTSE 350) where there should be at least two independent NEDs.

■ Directors, and not shareholders, may exercise all the powers of the company. These powers are defined in the company's constitution (articles of association) but are subject to some restraints in provisions of company law.

■ In UK common law, directors have a fiduciary duty and a duty of skill and care to the company. This duty is owed to the company, not the shareholders. The common law duties of directors have now effectively been included in UK statute law, with the inclusion of a number of statutory general duties of directors in CA2006. These statutory duties are the duties to act within their powers, promote the success of the company, exercise independent judgement, exercise responsible care, skill and diligence, avoid conflicts of interest, not accept benefits from third parties and declare any interest in a proposed transaction.

■ If a director is in breach of a duty, shareholders may bring a derivative claim against him or her for breach of duty, in the name of the company.

■ In the UK, listed companies are required by the DTR to announce to the stock market any proposed related party transaction above a certain size, and to obtain shareholder approval for the transaction.

■ The chairman is the leader of the board and the CEO is the leader of the executive management team.

■ The UK Code states that the chairman should be independent on first appointment. It is therefore inappropriate to appoint a former CEO as chairman.

■ The UK Code also states that the roles of chairman and CEO should not be combined and given to one individual, because this would create a position of 'unfettered power' on the board and would disturb the balance of the board and the ability of NEDs to challenge the executive management.

■ NEDs fulfil various roles: they contribute to discussions and decision-making by the board on strategy, they review the performance of executive management, they have a responsibility to ensure the integrity of financial information issued by the company and the effectiveness of risk management and internal control, and they are involved in the appointment of new directors and the remuneration of executive directors and other senior executives.

■ 'Independence' of a NED is defined by the UK Code in terms of circumstances where a NED would normally be considered 'not independent'.

■ The UK Code recommends that one of the independent NEDs should be nominated as the SID.

■ The UK Code (and other national corporate governance codes) calls for the establishment of board committees with governance responsibilities. The remuneration committee and the audit committee should consist entirely of independent NEDs and the nominations committee should have a majority of independent NEDs.

■ There have been criticisms of NEDs. These include the argument that they are ineffective because they devote insufficient time to the company or have insufficient knowledge of the company's business.

■ In most countries, there is a unitary board structure. In a few countries, notably Germany, there is a two-tier board structure with a supervisory board of NEDs led by the company chairman and a management board of executives led by the CEO. The two boards need to interact closely and constructively, even though one has a supervisory role over the other.

5 Governance and boardroom practice

■ CONTENTS

■ INTRODUCTION

This chapter deals with a variety of governance issues relating to the board of directors. There are important governance issues relating to the identification and appointment of new directors, including the issue of boardroom diversity, and the **induction** and continuing professional development of board directors. The chapter also considers boardroom ethics, the potential personal liability of directors and the need for directors to check that sufficient directors and officers (D&O) liability insurance is provided by the company to give adequate protection.

1 Good boardroom practice and board behaviours

1.1 Boardroom practice and behaviours

Boardroom practice refers to the way in which a board conducts its procedures and reaches its decisions. Boardroom behaviours refer to the way that a board conducts itself, and its culture and values, and ethics or code of conduct.

A board should have established methods of carrying on its business, but its effectiveness will depend largely on the character of its members.

1.2 Corporate culture

In the Foreword to the Financial Reporting Council (FRC) report 'Corporate Culture and the Role of Boards. Report of Observations' 2016 Sir Winfried Bischoff, Chairman of the FRC wrote:

'There needs to be a concerted effort to improve trust in the motivations and integrity of business. Rules and sanctions clearly have their place, but will not on their own deliver productive behaviours over the long-term. This report looks at the increasing importance which corporate culture plays in delivering long-term business and economic success.

A healthy culture both protects and generates value. It is therefore important to have a continuous focus on culture, rather than wait for a crisis. Poor behaviour can be exacerbated when companies come under pressure. A strong culture will endure in times of stress and mitigate the impact. This is essential in dealing effectively with risk and maintaining resilient performance.

Strong governance underpins a healthy culture, and boards should demonstrate good practice in the boardroom and promote good governance throughout the business. The company as a whole must demonstrate openness and accountability, and should engage constructively with shareholders and wider stakeholders about culture.

In taking action on culture, I should like all those involved to consider three important issues:

Connect purpose and strategy to culture. Establishing a company's overall purpose is crucial in supporting the values and driving the correct behaviours. The strategy to achieve a company's purpose should reflect the values and culture of the company and should not be developed in isolation. Boards should oversee both.

Align values and incentives. Recruitment, performance management and reward should support and encourage behaviours consistent with the company's purpose, values, strategy and business model. Financial and non-financial incentives should be appropriately balanced and linked to behavioural objectives.

Assess and measure. Boards should give careful thought to how culture is assessed and reported on. A wide range of potential indicators are available. Companies can choose and monitor those that are appropriate to the business and the outcomes they seek. Objectively assessing culture involves interpreting information sensitively to gain practical insight.

I also ask investors and other stakeholders to engage constructively to build respect and trust, and work with companies to achieve long-term value. Investors should consider carefully how their behaviour can affect company behaviour and understand how their motivations drive company incentives.

In its research for this project the FRC has seen abundant evidence that companies and boards are taking action to shape their culture in order to encourage investment. This will drive efficient capital allocation, improve productivity and deliver sustainable value. We commend these companies and encourage them to maintain this focus. We encourage those companies yet to take action, to consider the benefits of addressing this important issue.'

1.3 Frequency of board meetings

A basic requirement of an effective board is that there should be regular board meetings. The UK Corporate Governance Code states simply that the board should meet sufficiently regularly to discharge its duties effectively, and there should be a formal schedule of matters reserved for the board.

 STOP AND THINK 5.1

How often do you think that the board of a listed company should meet?

Answer: The frequency of meetings will depend on the circumstances of a company and events. A board may decide, for example, to meet regularly every three months but to hold unscheduled meetings whenever any particular matter arises unexpectedly that calls for a board decision.

Board committees will meet sufficiently frequently to fulfil their functions. The audit committee may meet fairly regularly, whereas the nomination committee may normally meet only once in the year, and the remuneration committee perhaps two or three times (with unscheduled meetings whenever a new senior executive appointment is made).

1.4 The agenda

The agenda for board meetings is a corporate governance issue in the sense that the chairman decides what the board will discuss when he or she sets the agenda. Although directors can raise matters as 'any other business', most of the time at board meetings is spent in discussion of the items listed by the chairman on the agenda.

It is therefore important that the agenda should include all matters reserved for board decision, whenever they arise. The company secretary can assist the chairman by providing advice and reminders.

1.5 Information

To enable them to contribute effectively to board discussions, directors must be provided with relevant information. They should receive relevant documents in advance of a board meeting, so that they have time to read them and think about the issues they deal with. The UK Code states that:

'The board should be supplied in a timely manner with information in a form and of a quality appropriate to enable it to discharge its duties.'

The chairman has the responsibility for ensuring that directors receive the information that they need in sufficient time. The Code states that management has an obligation to provide the required information, but that the directors should ask for clarification or additional information if required.

Information flows should be both formal and informal. Information is provided formally in documents or files, but this is supplemented by informal communication by email, telephone or face-to-face conversation. Whether providing information formally or informally, the company secretary should ensure that there are good information flows between the board and its committees, between committees, and between executive managers and non-executive directors (NEDs).

 STOP AND THINK 5.2

It is easy to ignore the importance of effective information. The board chairman, assisted by the company secretary, should try to ensure that the information provided to directors in advance of meetings is useful and comprehensible, and that it is a manageable quantity.

■ There may be a risk of information overload – providing directors with more information than they can absorb in the time they have for reading the board papers. Too much detail can be as unhelpful as too little.

■ Some information may be provided as a matter of routine, but have little or no value. Directors may get into the habit of ignoring these items altogether.

■ Information may be insufficient, especially when NEDs are not familiar with the operational detail contained in reports from management. Information should avoid jargon and should not make inappropriate assumptions about what the reader already knows.

■ Many issues for the board to consider are delegated to board committees, and much of the work of board committees should be reported back to the main board. Board members should want to know what the various board committees have been discussing and recommending or deciding. They can be kept informed by including minutes of meetings of board committees in the papers sent out before a main board meeting. As the company secretary, or someone senior in the company secretarial department, will act as secretary to board committees and take minutes of their meetings, distributing this information to board members should not be a problem.

1.6 Support

There may be occasions when directors, especially non-executives, are looking for information in addition to the board papers they are given. An important source of information should be the company secretary. In companies that have their own in-house legal department, NEDs may also be able to get information from an in-house lawyer.

In addition to receiving relevant and timely information, directors should be given access to independent professional advice, at the company's expense, when they consider this necessary in order to discharge their responsibilities as director (UK Code). For example, a director might ask to consult a lawyer for advice on a matter where the legal position is not clear.

NEDs and possibly executive directors may also need administrative support or advice on routine matters, and the UK Code includes provisions that:

- board committees should be provided with sufficient resources to carry out their duties; and
- all directors should have access to the advice and assistance of the company secretary.

2   Appointments to the board: nomination committee

2.1 Board appointments

The membership of a board of directors changes regularly, as some individuals resign or retire and new appointments are made. There are no regulations on the overall size of the board (unless a provision about the composition of the board is included in the company's constitution), so that:

- there are no restrictions on making new appointments; and
- with the exceptions of the positions of chairman and chief executive officer (CEO), there is no requirement to replace individuals stepping down from the board.

It is an accepted principle of good corporate governance that the power over board appointments should rest with the whole board. In the UK, new appointments are made to the board at any time during the year, but each newly appointed director must offer himself for re-election at the next annual general meeting (AGM). The chairman of the company and the chairmen of the board committees are appointed by the board, and chairmanship appointments are not subject to shareholder approval at the next AGM.

Recommendations about new appointments should not belong exclusively to the chairman and/or the CEO. Appointments should be made on merit and against objective criteria; however, in practice, criticism has been expressed about the way in which most appointments are made, particularly appointments of NEDs. This criticism centres on the fact that most NED appointments come from a fairly small circle of successful businessmen, many of whom know each other, whereas the net should be cast much wider and individuals from more diverse backgrounds should be chosen.

The UK Corporate Governance Code states that there should be 'a formal, rigorous and transparent procedure for the appointment of new directors to the board'.

- A formal procedure involves the nomination committee (see section 2.2 Nomination committee).
- The procedure of identifying candidates for a directorship should be rigorous, and candidates should be investigated thoroughly before the directorship is offered. The UK Code states that appointments should be made on 'merit' and 'against objective criteria'. However, it does not specify what these 'objective criteria' should be.
- The Code also states that appointments to the board should be made 'with due regard to the benefits of diversity on the board, including gender'. This reflects the widely expressed concern that the boards of major UK companies are dominated by middle-aged to older white males with a commercial or financial background, and that there are not enough directors with different attributes, talents and experience to provide boards with an appropriate balance. The relative shortage of female board directors has been well publicised. Diversity is discussed in more detail later.
- The procedure should be transparent so that shareholders and other stakeholders are able to see what is happening (what type of person the company is looking for and why a particular individual has been appointed).

2.2 Nomination committee

The detailed corporate governance guidelines on the role of the nomination committee vary between countries, but in many countries they are similar. In the UK, the recommended framework for making appointments is that:

- the search for new directors should be carried out by a nomination committee of the board, to which the full board delegates the responsibility;
- the nomination committee should make recommendations to the board; and
- the board should consider the recommendations of the committee, and in normal circumstances should be expected to accept the recommendation.

However, the board chairman also has responsibility for ensuring that the board is effective, and is of an appropriate size and with an appropriate mix of members. The board chairman therefore needs to work closely with the members of the nomination committee. For this reason, the chairman of the board may also be appointed as chairman of the nomination committee.

It is important to note that a nomination committee does not have the authority to make new appointments; it simply carries out the search and makes the recommendation. Appointing new directors is a matter for the board, and decisions should therefore be made by the whole board.

It is also important to note that the need for a new board appointment, or a replacement for an existing board member (succession planning), is not necessarily decided by the nomination committee. The chairman has responsibility for ensuring that the composition of the board is appropriate, and may discuss his or her ideas with the chairman of the nomination committee. The need for a new NED may also emerge from the annual review of board performance, if an existing NED has not been performing as well as expected, or if a gap is identified in the range of skills and experience that the board needs.

The chairman is also responsible for ensuring that there is succession planning for board positions, and may therefore ask the nomination committee to identify potential successors.

2.3 Composition of the nomination committee

The UK Corporate Governance Code recommends that a nomination committee should be established by the board, and this committee should 'lead the process for board appointments and make recommendations to the board'.

- The majority of members should be independent NEDs.
- The committee chairman should be either the board chairman or an independent NED.
- If the board chairman is the chairman of the nomination committee, they should not chair the committee when it is dealing with the succession to the chairmanship.
- Executive directors may be members of the nomination committee, provided they are not in a majority. This means, for example, that the CEO may be a committee member.

The existence of a majority of NEDs should ensure that the appointments process is not dominated by the chairman and CEO. When the chairman and/or CEO is a member of the committee, the other committee members have a responsibility for preventing these individuals from dominating the decision-making process about new board appointments.

On the other hand:

- Since both the chairman and the nomination committee have responsibilities for the size and composition of the board, it could make good sense to appoint the board chairman as chairman of the nomination committee. This is fairly common practice.
- When a board includes executive directors, there is value in having executive directors on the nomination committee, to provide direct input – rather than external advice – about new appointments of executive directors to the board.

The committee should consider new appointments to the board and make recommendations to the full board. The full board should then reach a decision about offering a position to the individual concerned so that final responsibility for board appointments remains with the board as a whole.

ICSA Guidance note terms of reference for the nomination committee 2013 recommends as a matter of good practice that the company secretary should act as secretary to the committee.

STOP AND THINK 5.3

The UK Code provision that allows the board chairman to be the chairman of the nomination committee may well seem good sense to you. The board chairman has overall responsibility for the effectiveness of the board and so has an interest in its size and the composition of its membership. The board chairman also has a responsibility to act on the results of the annual performance review of directors (described later), which is also a matter of interest to the nomination committee. Appointing the board chairman to the chairmanship of the nomination committee may be a useful way of bringing together their overlapping interests into a practical working arrangement.

The board chairman should not, however, be involved in succession planning for his or her successor and should not be in attendance at committee meetings where this matter is discussed.

2.4 The main duties of the nomination committee

The principal duties of the nomination committee are suggested in ICSA's guidance note, 'Terms of reference for the nomination committee' (2013), and they may include the following. The nomination committee should:

- regularly review the structure, size and composition (including the skills, knowledge, experience and diversity) of the board and make recommendations to the board with regard to any changes;
- give full consideration to succession planning for directors and other senior executives in the course of its work;
- keep under review the leadership needs of the organisation, both executive and non-executive, with a view to ensuring the continued ability of the organisation to compete effectively in the marketplace;
- keep up to date and fully informed about strategic issues and commercial changes affecting the company and the market in which it operates;
- be responsible for identifying and nominating for the approval of the board, candidates to fill board vacancies as and when they arise before any appointment is made by the board, evaluate the balance of skills, knowledge, experience and diversity on the board, and, in the light of this evaluation, prepare a description of the role and capabilities required for a particular appointment;
- for the appointment of a chairman, the committee should prepare a job specification, including the time commitment expected;
- prior to the appointment of a director, the proposed appointee should be required to disclose any other business interests that may result in a conflict of interest and be required to report any future business interests that could result in a conflict of interest;
- ensure that on appointment to the board, non-executive directors receive a formal letter of appointment setting out clearly what is expected of them in terms of time commitment, committee service and involvement outside board meetings;
- review the results of the board performance evaluation process that relate to the composition of the board;
- review annually the time required from non-executive directors. Performance evaluation should be used to assess whether the non-executive directors are spending enough time to fulfil their duties; and
- work and liaise as necessary with all other board committees.

Recommendations by the nomination committee to the board should include:

- plans for the succession of NEDs and executive directors;
- recommendations about the reappointment of NEDs at the end of their term of office;
- recommendations about candidates to be appointed as senior independent director (SID);
- recommendations of candidates for membership of board committees;
- recommendations about the submission of any director for re-election by the shareholders under the retirement by rotation rules in the company's constitution (articles of association);

- matters concerning the continuation in office of any director at any time; and
- recommendation for the appointment of any director to executive or other office.

It is also the responsibility of the chairman of the nomination committee to ensure that the UK Corporate Governance Code provisions relating to the composition of the board are complied with.

The UK Code requires that a separate section of the annual report should describe the work of the nomination committee, including the process it has used in relation to board appointments. This section should include a description of the board's policy on diversity, including gender, any measurable objectives that it has set for implementing the policy, and progress on achieving the objectives.

If advertising the vacancy or the services of a headhunter were not used, this would suggest that the appointment was made of a person that the nomination committee already knew or who was recommended privately: this would be contrary to the requirement for a formal, rigorous and transparent appointment procedure. Executive directors may be appointed from within the company, so the requirement applies only to the appointment of a chairman or NED.

2.5 UK Corporate Governance Code provisions on board nominations

The UK Code includes several provisions about appointments to the board.

- The committee 'should evaluate the balance of skills, experience, independence and knowledge on the board, and, in the light of this evaluation, prepare a description of the role and capabilities required for a particular appointment'.
- On initial appointment, the chairman should meet the criteria for independence.
- For the appointment of a chairman, the nomination committee should prepare a job specification, including an assessment of the time required and recognising the need for the chairman's availability in times of crisis.
- The departing chairman should not chair the nomination committee when it is meeting to consider the appointment of the successor to the chairmanship.
- A proposed new chairman's other significant commitments should be disclosed to the board before an appointment is made, and included in the annual report (subsequent changes should also be disclosed and reported).

Provisions relating to succession planning and the time commitment of NEDs are also included in the Code, and are explained later in this chapter.

2.6 Practical aspects of board appointments: time commitment

In practice, a nomination committee is likely to carry out its responsibilities by:

- using a firm of headhunters to find individuals outside the firm who might be suitable for appointment (as NED, CEO, finance director, and so on);
- vetting the candidates put forward by the headhunters; and
- making a selection and recommendation to the full board.

When an individual is appointed to the board, the appointment may be for a fixed term. This is usually the case with NEDs; in the UK, NEDs are typically appointed on a fixed three-year contract, which may then be renewed at the end of each three-year term. Executive directors are commonly appointed for an indeterminate length of time, subject to a minimum notice period (typically one year or even less).

'All directors should be able to allocate sufficient time to the company to discharge their responsibilities effectively' (UK Code).

Executive directors are full-time appointments, so the problem of time commitment is not usually significant for them (unless the executive is also appointed as a NED for another company). The main problem is ensuring that the chairman and NEDs give sufficient time to the company. More time will probably be required from the chairman than from a NED, and some NEDs (e.g. the chairman of the audit committee) will be expected to commit more time than other NEDs.

When the nomination committee prepares a job description for the position, this should include an estimate of the time commitment expected. A NED should undertake that they will have sufficient time to meet what is expected of them. This undertaking could be written into the NED's contract.

If an individual who is proposed to the board as chairman or NED has significant time commitments outside the company, this should be disclosed to the board before the appointment is made.

A company should also protect itself against the risk that an executive director is unable to commit sufficient time to the company because of NED appointments with other companies. The UK Code states that the board should not allow one of its own full-time executive directors to take on:

- more than one NED post in a FTSE 100 company; or
- the chairmanship of a FTSE 100 company.

3 Appointments to the board: diversity

There could be a tendency for directors, and NEDs in particular, to be recruited from a narrow circle of potential candidates. The Higgs Report (January 2003) found that the majority of NEDs were white, middle-aged males, many with previous experience as a plc board director.

- The need for boardroom diversity is now well recognised in the UK. The FRC Guidance on Board Effectiveness (2011) comments that: 'Diversity in boardroom composition is an important driver of a board's effectiveness, creating a breadth of perspective among directors and breaking down the tendency towards "group think".'
- A government-sponsored report by Lord Davies (the Davies Report) recommended that there should be a greater diversity in board membership and in particular that there should be more women on the boards of FTSE 350 companies. This recommendation led to a revision to the UK Corporate Governance Code in 2012 (this is explained later; see section 3.3).
- A report by the Association of British Insurers (ABI) (2011) on board effectiveness commented that achieving 'diversity of perspective' should be a key objective for board appointments and that companies should provide clear statements about what they are doing to achieve this. Companies should also recognise their role in developing women 'throughout the corporate pipeline' and should adopt measurable objectives for promoting diversity, and especially gender diversity, at senior management level.

3.1 The talent pool for new directors: Tyson Report

Following publication of the Higgs Report in 2003, the government set up a taskforce under the chairmanship of Laura Tyson, Dean of the London Business School, to look into the recruitment and development of NEDs. The Tyson Report on the Recruitment and Development of NEDs was published in June 2003. The report argued that a range of different experiences and backgrounds among board members could enhance the effectiveness of the board, and suggested how a broader range of NEDs could be identified and recruited.

The Report criticised the practice (current at that time) of appointing individuals without a formal interview. This method of recruitment tended to overlook a number of potentially rich sources of NEDs, such as those listed below.

- The 'marzipan layer' of corporate management, just below board level. The CEO of a company might be willing to allow managers to act as NEDs of companies that are not competitors, although they might be less willing if the demands on the individual's time increase. Another advantage of this source of NEDs is that the 'marzipan layer' includes a large number of women.
- Individuals in private sector companies.
- Individuals in the public sector/non-commercial sector.
- Individuals working for business consultancies or professional firms (lawyers, accountants) and retired professional accountants.

Although elements of the Tyson Report remain valid, the issue of diversity on boards of listed companies has developed, with the publication of the Davies Report in 2011 and subsequent FRC measures to amend the UK Corporate Governance Code.

3.2 The Davies Report: 'Women on Boards'

In 2011, a government-commissioned report by Lord Davies on 'Women on Boards' was published. The report (or 'review') made a strong case for greater diversity on boards, and recommended in particular that there should be a greater proportion of women on the boards of FTSE 350 companies. Its general argument in favour of greater diversity was that diverse and balanced boards 'are more likely to be effective boards, better able to understand their customers and stakeholders, and to benefit fresh perspectives, vigorous challenge and broad experience. These in turn lead to better decision-making.'

The report rejected the view, for example, that directors (and particularly NEDs) should have had experience of financial responsibilities before their appointment. 'Although there is a real need for financial literacy, financial responsibility ... can be taught and should not be a prerequisite for appointments.'

The report was concerned primarily with women on boards, and it presented several reasons in favour of greater boardroom representation for women.

- There is research to support the view that appointing women to the board leads to improvements in the company's performance. This is probably attributable to the different perspectives that women bring, and their willingness to ask awkward questions.
- In many countries, including the UK, women make up a large proportion of university graduates and people in employment. It is therefore logical to suppose that similar percentages should be found in senior positions in companies, including the boardroom.
- Women are responsible for a majority of purchasing decisions by households. Women on boards may therefore be more aware of customer needs, and more responsive to those needs. Responding to customer needs is a requirement for success for most companies.
- Evidence also shows that boards with more women are also more likely to follow best practice recommendations for corporate governance.

The report stated that in 2010 women made up only 12.5% of board members of FTSE 100 companies, and commented that:

'When women are so under-represented on corporate boards, companies are missing out, and they are unable to draw from the widest possible range of talent.'

There are two problems to be overcome in order to appoint substantially more women to boards.

- **Supply of suitable candidates.** The report commented that 'part of the challenge is around supply – the corporate pipeline'. Companies are not promoting enough women to senior positions, and women with senior executive experience should be suitable boardroom candidates.
- **Demand for women directors.** A second problem is that companies are not looking hard enough for women to appoint as directors. 'There are women in the UK more than capable of serving on boards who are not currently getting those roles.'

There are two 'populations' of women to consider for board appointments: those in the corporate sector and those outside the corporate mainstream (such as academics and government officials). The Davies Report made specific recommendations (early in 2011):

- FTSE 100 companies should aim to have a minimum of 25% female representation on their board by 2015.
- Quoted companies should be required to disclose each year the proportion of women on their board, in senior executive positions and in the whole organisation. The UK Corporate Governance Code should require listed companies to establish a policy for boardroom diversity, including measurable policy objectives. They should also disclose each year a summary of this policy and report on the progress towards achieving the policy objectives.

- The UK Code requires the nomination committee to report on its work in the annual report. In line with this requirement, companies should disclose 'meaningful information' about their appointment process and how they address the issue of diversity (including a description of the search and nominations process).

In addition:

- When searching for a new board appointee, companies should occasionally advertise the position, because this may result in greater diversity among applicants.
- Executive search consultants should draw up a voluntary code of conduct for their 'industry', which addresses gender diversity and best practice, with regard to search criteria and nomination processes for appointments to the boards of FTSE 350 companies.

STOP AND THINK 5.4

Progress is being made in the UK towards greater diversity of board membership, particularly in the appointment of women to positions on the boards of FTSE 350 companies and the UK government has announced a voluntary target for these companies of 33% women directors by 2020. Most current appointments of women, however, are to non-executive positions rather than to executive director positions.

The Professional Boards Forum BoardWatch reported in October 2016 that among the FTSE 100 companies, 26.8% of directors were women: 31.9% of NEDs were women and just 11.5% of executive directors). There were no all male boards within the FTSE 100.

Among the next largest listed companies (the FTSE 250), 21.3% of directors were women: 26.4% of NEDs were women and just 6.5% of executive directors). 12 companies (4.8%) still had all male boards.

Hampton-Alexander Review

In February 2016, Sir Philip Hampton, chairman of GlaxoSmithKline, and Dame Helen Alexander, chairman of UBM, were appointed to carry out a new board review to continue the work of Lord Davies. The review continues to champion work to improve the representation of women on FTSE 350 boards and considers options for building the talent pipeline, focusing on improving the representation of women in the executive layer of FTSE 350 companies.

The first Hampton-Alexander report was published in November 2016 (by FTSE Women Leaders) and set out a number of recommendations, including raising the target of women on FTSE 350 boards to 33% by 2020 and extending the scope to include FTSE 350 Executive Committees and direct reports to the Executive Committee.

The review also recommends that the FRC amends the UK Corporate Governance Code so that FTSE 350 companies are obliged to disclose the gender balance of their executive committees. This will be considered as part of the expected review of the Code in 2017.

3.3 The Parker Report into the Ethnic Diversity of UK Boards

The Parker Report into the Ethnic Diversity of UK Boards (November 2016) found that:

'As a general matter, the Boardrooms of Britain's leading public companies do not reflect the ethnic diversity of either the UK or the stakeholders that they seek to engage and represent. This Report highlights that ethnic minority representation in the Boardrooms across the FTSE 100 is disproportionately low, especially when looking at the number of UK citizen directors of colour. We believe that in order for corporate Britain to reflect the progress that is being made in diversity, equality and inclusion generally, changes are needed in the Boardrooms where leadership, stewardship and corporate ethics are of utmost importance. However, the recommendations we are making are underpinned by strong industrial logic and the need for UK companies to be competitive in the increasingly challenging and diverse marketplace.'

The Review made three recommendations:

1 Increase the ethnic diversity of UK boards.
2 Develop candidates for the pipeline and plan for succession.
3 Enhance transparency and disclosure.

EHRC inquiry into FTSE 350 appointments

In March 2016, the Equality and Human Rights Commission (EHRC) published *An inquiry into fairness, transparency and diversity in FTSE 350 board appointments.* This report set out the results of the inquiry launched by the EHRC in 2014 into how FTSE 350 companies and executive search firms recruit and select board directors.

The aim was to determine whether recruitment and selection practices are transparent, fair and result in selection on merit, and to identify areas where companies and search firms can make improvements to support more diverse appointments to company boards.

The report made a number of recommendations concerning board evaluations, diversity policies and targets, role descriptions, the search process, the selection of candidates, the role of the nomination committee and means of improving diversity in the talent pipeline and candidate pool. The EHRC also produced a six-step practical guide for companies to help them improve board diversity, both when making an appointment and in respect of ongoing action that can be taken to increase diversity across the entire workforce, particularly to ensure a pipeline of diverse talent for future board appointments.

3.4 The UK Corporate Governance Code on diversity

Since 2012, the UK Corporate Governance Code has addressed the issue of board diversity.

A supporting principle (to main principle B2) states that: 'The search for board candidates should be conducted, and appointments made, on merit, against objective criteria and with due regard for the benefits of diversity on the board, including gender.'

The nomination committee should inform shareholders about the approach that it has taken to making new board appointments, by providing a report on the work of the committee in the annual report and accounts. The provision of the Code (B2.4) dealing with the nomination committee's report on appointments to the board now states:

> 'A separate section of the annual report should describe the work of the nomination committee, including the process it has used in relation to board appointments. This section should include a description of the board's policy on diversity, including gender, any measurable objectives that it has set for implementing the policy, and progress on achieving the objectives.'

The issue of diversity on boards of directors is not simply a matter of progress towards gender equality. The Preface to the UK Code makes an interesting comment on the benefits of diversity generally:

> 'Essential to the effective functioning of any board is dialogue which is both constructive and challenging.... One of the ways in which constructive debate can be encouraged is through having sufficient diversity on the board. This includes, but is not limited to, gender and race. Diverse board composition in these respects is not on its own a guarantee. Diversity is as much about differences of approach and experience.'

 TEST YOUR KNOWLEDGE 5.1

a In the UK, what are the responsibilities or rights regarding new appointments to the board of the nominations committee, the board of directors and the company's shareholders?

b What are the responsibilities of a nomination committee?

c According to the UK Code, what should be the composition of a nominations committee in a FTSE 350 company and who may be its chairman?

d What were the recommendations of the 2011 Davies Report?

e What are the provisions in the UK Corporate Governance Code relating to nominations and appointments to the board?

4 Accepting an offer of appointment as a NED

The formal procedures for appointing a new NED are the same for the appointment of an executive director. However, a NED will be less familiar with the company than a senior executive manager and he or she should not accept an appointment without first being satisfied that there are no matters of concern. An individual should not be willing to accept an appointment as a NED if:

■ the company uses unethical business practices or has a bad reputation; or
■ the company is not a going concern and is in serious financial difficulties.

ICSA issued a guidance note on 'Joining the right board: due diligence for prospective directors' (2011). Before accepting an appointment, a prospective NED should carry out a 'due diligence' check or examination of the company, to obtain satisfaction that they have confidence in the company and that they will be well suited to working in it.

ICSA commented:

'By making the right enquiries, a prospective director can reduce the risk of unwelcome surprises and dramatically increase the likelihood of success.'

In its guidance, ICSA suggested an approach to carrying out due diligence.

■ Look at the company's annual report and also its website, to obtain information about:
  – the company's business model and its governance;
  – the market environment and market dynamics;
  – recent operational performance;
  – the company's strategy;
  – the main risks and uncertainty facing the company;
  – **sustainability** issues/sustainability policies; and
  – financial performance.
■ Check the company's website for regulatory or media announcements that have been issued since the company issued its most recent annual report.

ICSA guidance states that it is most unlikely that this search will reveal any wrongdoing by the company, but a 'lack of transparency' in the information may be a reason for proceeding with caution.

The individual should also arrange meetings with the CEO, chief financial officer (CFO), company secretary, and all members of the nomination committee (or possibly the entire board). These meetings may be with individuals, but it may be better to hold meetings with small groups of two or three, in order to obtain some understanding of the dynamics and interactions of individuals on the board.

If the individual is expecting to be appointed as the board chairman or a committee chairman, meetings may also be arranged, as appropriate, with the external auditors, chief internal auditor and remuneration advisers.

An individual needs to be satisfied that:

■ they can commit to the role in the time that the company expects;
■ they will be able to make a positive contribution to the effectiveness of the board;
■ if the company is not performing well at the moment, they have the time, desire and capability to make an impact and help to turn the company's fortunes around;
■ there is no risk that the directors of the company could be held liable for any breach of duty, and that there is sufficient D&O liability insurance as protection against this risk;
■ the fee that the company has offered is adequate;
■ there will be a suitable induction programme; and
■ there will be sufficient support from the company secretary and secretariat.

4.1 Terms of engagement

If a prospective NED decides to accept the offer of the appointment, terms of engagement should be agreed with the company. ICSA issued a guidance note (2011) 'sample non-executive director's appointment letter'. The terms of engagement in a formal letter of appointment should include:

- Details of the role that the NED will be required to perform (including initial membership of board committees).
- The expected time commitment. The company must indicate how much time the NED is expected to commit to the company, and the NED should make this commitment. This should be included in the formal letter of appointment. Typically, NEDs may be expected to commit between 15 and 30 days each year, and more for a committee chairman.
- The term of the appointment (typically for an initial term of three years unless terminated earlier by either party).
- The remuneration (and allowable expenses).
- If the individual is considered independent, a requirement that any changes in the individual's circumstances that may create conflicts of interest should be notified to the chairman and company secretary immediately.

The letter of engagement should also:

- specify that the NED should treat all information received as a director as confidential to the company;
- remind the individual of the rules against dealing in the company's shares when in possession of price-sensitive information;
- indicate the arrangements for induction;
- give details of the D&O liability insurance that will be available;
- state that the individual will have the right to obtain independent professional advice in circumstances where this is appropriate for performing the duties as NED; and
- state what company resources will be made available to the NED (e.g. desk, computer terminal and telephone).

 TEST YOUR KNOWLEDGE 5.2

a What issues should an individual consider before accepting the offer of an appointment as independent NED of a listed company?

b How much time should NEDs be required to commit to the company, and should this be a contractual commitment?

5 Succession planning

A supporting principle in the UK Corporate Governance Code states that:

'The board should satisfy itself that plans are in place for orderly succession for appointments to the board and to senior management, so as to maintain an appropriate balance of skills and experience within the company and on the board, and to ensure progressive refreshing of the board.'

5.1 Succession planning for chairman and CEO

The key positions on the board of directors are the chairman of the board and the CEO. The individuals holding these positions will retire or resign at some time, e.g. because the individual has reached retirement age or has come to the end of a fixed-term contract.

The board of directors should try to ensure a smooth succession, with a replacement lined up to take the place of the departing individual.

- In the case of a departing CEO, the successor might be an existing executive manager who has been groomed for the role. It may be an external appointment, but this may indicate to investors that the company has not prepared sufficiently for the eventual succession and an external appointment is made because there is no one 'good enough' within the existing senior executive ranks.

- In the case of a departing chairman, the successor might be an external appointment, but may be the current deputy chairman or SID, especially if they have been appointed with a view to eventual succession as chairman.

A smooth succession is desirable to avoid disruptions to the company's decision-making processes or changes in policy or direction. The succession can also be planned well in advance, so that the newly appointed individuals will have an opportunity to learn about their new role before the actual succession occurs.

The positions of chairman and CEO (and finance director or CFO) are important, and it is undesirable to have vacancies in these positions for more than a short time. Ideally, the successor should be in place for immediate appointment. This is why succession planning should be carried out in advance.

Succession planning should be delegated to the nomination committee. If the board intends to breach the governance code by appointing the current CEO as the next chairman, it would be advisable for a suitable representative of the board (e.g. the chairman of the nomination committee or the SID) to discuss the reasons for their choice with major shareholders and representative bodies of the institutional shareholders. These discussions should take place well in advance of any final decision about the appointment.

Institutional investors are unlikely to support the appointment of an individual as both chairman and CEO, except as a temporary measure when the CEO resigns unexpectedly. Exceptions do occur, but shareholders tend to be suspicious and unsupportive.

5.2 Succession planning for other board members

There should also be succession planning for NEDs and executive directors other than the CEO. As stated above, NEDs are typically appointed in the UK for a fixed period of three years, but a requirement of the UK Code is now that directors of FTSE 350 companies should stand for re-election annually. The three-year contract for a NED may be extended at the end of that time for another three years and so on. Over time, a NED may lose some of his or her independence. It was explained in the previous chapter that a NED is generally considered 'not independent' if they have been with the company for nine years or more. The UK Code also includes a provision that any term beyond six years for a NED should be subject to particularly rigorous review. The board should be continually refreshed, and this is achieved by:

- appointing a new NED when the three-year term of an existing NED reaches its end; or
- in cases where a NED of a FTSE 350 company has performed poorly, not supporting his or her annual re-election.

The nominations committee may recommend the re-appointment of a NED at the end of their first-year term, but should be more inclined to terminate the appointment after six years, when the second three-year term ends.

The UK Code states that there should be 'progressive refreshing of the board'. Refreshing the board calls for succession planning, and the nomination committee should be aware when a vacancy is expected to arise and should plan in advance to appoint the type of person it considers would improve the balance of skills and experience on the board.

To be able to perform this function properly, members of the nomination committee need to keep up-to-date with the strategic issues and commercial changes that are affecting the company, so that they are aware of changes that may be appropriate in the mix of skills and experience on the board. As a simple example, if a company is significantly expanding its foreign operations, it may be appropriate to appoint a NED with knowledge of those countries and markets.

They should also be aware of the requirements, described earlier, for a balanced board with sufficient diversity, especially female representation.

A nomination committee may therefore take the following measures to review the composition of the board and plan for board succession for positions other than chairman and CEO (and possibly finance director). Remember that the chairman of the committee will normally be the board chairman. The committee should:

- be aware which directors are intending to resign when their current contract expires;
- be aware which directors will be standing for re-election at the next AGM. In FTSE 350 companies, this should be the entire board;
- consider the performance of current directors, especially the NEDs, and their contribution to board and committee meetings and their time commitment to the company. This information should be available from the performance review of the directors;
- consider the current balance of the board and the balance of the board after planned departures have occurred; and compare this with the required spread of skills and experience required;
- consider the board balance and diversity of membership;
- reach decisions about the future succession to board membership, and prepare a description of the role and responsibilities for the anticipated vacancy; and
- prepare recommendations for the board.

If the board approves the recommendations of the nomination committee, the committee will be authorised to search for an individual to fill the anticipated vacancy.

A key feature of succession planning is that it should happen in advance. It should not be a reactive measure to board appointments when vacancies unexpectedly arise. Planning in advance, and identifying new appointees, will enable board changes to happen smoothly, with minimum disruption to the company and its business.

5.3 Current issues in succession planning

In May 2016, the FRC published a feedback statement summarising responses to its October 2015 discussion paper UK Board Succession Planning. This was an area of focus as board evaluations often highlight the quality of succession planning as an issue, and the FRC had been asked by the Parliamentary Committee on Banking Standards to investigate aspects of non-executive director appointments. The FRC wanted to promote good practice in this area to raise quality. The areas explored in the discussion paper and feedback statement were:

- How effective board succession planning is to business strategy and culture.
- The role of the nomination committee in succession planning.
- Board evaluation and its contribution to board succession.
- Identifying the internal and external 'pipeline' for executive and non-executive directors.
- Ensuring diversity on the board.
- The role of institutional investors in succession planning.

As part of the continuation of the FRC review of culture, and in light of the responses to the discussion paper on succession planning, the FRC will consider guidance to nomination committees as part of a consultation on the Code and associated guidance in 2017.

In the meantime, the Feedback Statement prompted companies to focus on the need to have an active nomination committee that considers the alignment of board composition with company strategy, both current and future. There is also a need to ensure the board, and the company as a whole, has the necessary skills, to secure its long-term success.

ICSA and EY also issued a report on this subject, 'The Nomination Committee – Coming Out of the Shadows', published in May 2016. The report followed a series of discussions with mostly FTSE 350 board chairs, nomination committee chairs and members as well as company secretaries. The role of the nomination committee, its membership and reporting were examined. Questions for boards and nomination committees to consider were provided, along with the following three key points:

- Look deeper into the company to identify and help to develop future leaders by considering executive succession and the talent pipeline, as well as executive development.
- Cast the net wider to identify potential non-executive directors by determining the specific skill sets required, as well as personal attributes.
- Think further ahead than the immediate replacement of a retiring board member as this will help the company prepare for future challenges.

6 Re-election of directors: refreshing the board membership

6.1 Re-election of directors

The re-election of directors by the shareholders at AGMs is primarily a matter for the company's constitution (articles of association). However, it is widely accepted that directors should be subject to re-election by the shareholders at regular intervals. The UK Code states as a main principle that: 'All directors should be submitted for re-election at regular intervals, subject to continued satisfactory performance.'

The provisions that are included in the 2016 UK Code are now as follows:

FTSE 350 companies	Listed companies outside the FTSE 350
All directors should be subject to annual re-election by the shareholders at the AGM.	All directors should be subject to election by the shareholders at the AGM following their appointment, and should be subject to re-election at least every three years after that.
	Non-executive directors who have been on the board for more than nine years should be subject to annual re-election.

The UK Code also requires that when the board proposes a NED for election at an AGM, they should present reasons why the directors believe that the individual should be appointed. When a director is proposed for re-election, the chairman should confirm to the shareholders that following a formal performance evaluation of the individual, he or she has concluded that the individual's performance continues to be effective and the individual remains committed to the role.

 STOP AND THINK 5.5

The election or re-election of directors is put forward as a resolution at the AGM, and there is a separate resolution for each director seeking election/re-election. The resolution has the support of the rest of the board. As a result, shareholders will normally be expected to vote to elect or re-elect the individual without question.

Occasionally, however, shareholders may wish to express their opposition to the re-election of a particular director. For example, they may oppose the re-election of the chairman of the remuneration committee if they are angry about an issue elating to senior executive remuneration.

When a board proposes the re-election of a NED, it should have considered the advice of the nomination committee, and should be aware of the plans for the eventual replacement of the director, as part of succession planning to keep the board refreshed.

6.2 Refreshing the board membership

The requirement for the board to ensure planned and progressive refreshing means that re-election of current directors, particularly NEDs, should not be an automatic process. As indicated earlier, plans to refresh the board with new NEDs should be a part of succession planning.

The nomination committee and the board chairman together have a responsibility to consider how the composition of the board needs to change, as the circumstances of the company change. There are several factors to consider when planning board succession and changes to the board size and composition.

- NEDs should be appointed because they will bring particular skills and experiences to the board, but they are appointed for a fixed term, typically for three years which may then be renewable at the end of each three-year period. However, they are not employees of the company, and they should not necessarily expect a renewal of their contract at the end of its term.

It should be explained to them that their appointment may well be terminated in order to bring new ideas and new experiences to the board, with new appointments.

■ The skills and experience required from board members may change as the company grows. For example, if a UK-based company expands overseas, it might be appropriate for the board to consider new appointments of non-executive directors (or possibly an additional executive director) with knowledge of the overseas business and its environment.

■ The requirement to increase the proportion of women on the board should also be taken into consideration in succession planning.

■ Some directors, particularly non-executive directors, may fail to make the contribution to the board that is required from them. Poor performance can be discussed during the annual performance review of the board, and individuals may be asked to step down from the board, or may be told that their appointment will not be renewed when the current contract comes to an end.

However, plans for the continual refreshing of a board of directors should be seen more as a process of maintaining an effective board by bringing in new skills and experience, rather than getting rid of ineffective board members. It should be a natural process of change and development.

TEST YOUR KNOWLEDGE 5.3

a   Why is it desirable to plan for board succession?
b   What are the requirements in the UK Corporate Governance Code regarding the re-election of directors?

---

7   Induction and training of directors

7.1 Induction of new directors

The induction of directors is a process by which new directors familiarise themselves with the business, its products or services and how it operates. New directors need induction in order to become effective contributors to the board decision-making process. ICSA's guidance note, 'Induction of directors' (2012), comments that: 'The objective of induction is to provide a new director with the information he or she will need to become as effective as possible in their role within the shortest practicable time.'

The need for induction is more important for NEDs than for internally appointed executive directors, who should be familiar with much of the business before their appointment to the board. However, newly appointed executive directors may not be familiar with all the responsibilities and duties of being a director, and may need induction to make them more aware of what will be expected of them in their new role.

The UK Code of Corporate Governance states that all directors should receive induction on joining the board and that 'to function effectively all directors need appropriate knowledge of the company and access to its operations and staff'.

The chairman is responsible for ensuring that new directors receive 'full, formal and tailored' induction. Although there is no specific reference to the company secretary, the chairman will probably ask the company secretary to arrange for each director to receive a personalised induction programme. The aim should be to make the director an effective member of the board as quickly as possible, and an induction programme may therefore focus initially on providing essential information and familiarity with the company. Over time, further induction may then be provided.

The programme should avoid overloading the new director with too much information all at once. This means that induction should be planned and may be carried out over a period of time.

A programme of induction may include:

- providing copies of minutes of previous board meetings and copies of any current strategy documents that the board has approved;
- visits to key company sites;
- product presentations;
- meetings with senior management and staff;
- meetings with external advisers of the company, such as the auditors or company's solicitors; and
- meetings with major shareholders (should any such shareholders want one). The UK Code states that as part of the induction process, directors should be offered the opportunity to meet with the company's major shareholders.

Reading is an effective way for an individual to absorb new information quickly, and the company secretary might therefore wish to give a new director a selection of documents as an induction pack. However, induction should be much more extensive than this. The FRC Guidance on Board Effectiveness 2011 states that on appointment, NEDs should devote time to a 'comprehensive, formal and tailored induction, which should extend beyond the boardroom'. A new NED should expect to visit and talk with senior and middle managers in the main areas of the company's business activities.

ICSA's guidance on induction of directors recommends that there should be variety in the methods used in an induction programme for a new director: 'Vary the delivery of information, and limit the amount of data presented just as reading material ....' As indicated above, induction should be a planned mixture of reading material, meetings with executives and company advisors, external training courses, organised site visits and meetings with other important stakeholders.

7.2 Induction of an executive manager as an executive director

The induction process described above is much more relevant to an individual joining as a director from outside the company. For an individual who is already an executive manager of the company and now appointed as an executive director, the induction process needs a different focus. A senior executive of the company should already be familiar with many aspects of the company's operations (although their induction might include visits to parts of the company they have not worked with before).

An executive manager 'promoted' to the board is much more likely to lack knowledge and experience about being a director and corporate governance. However, some large companies try to give their senior executives experience as a director, by allowing them to take a position as a NED in another company.

An induction programme for such an individual may therefore need to focus on matters such as:

- the role of the board, including matters reserved for the board and oversight of management;
- the powers and duties of directors, and the rights of shareholders (the new director should be given a copy of the company's constitution (articles of association));
- the role of board committees;
- the role of the board in monitoring risk and internal control (see also Chapter 10);
- membership of the board and its committees, how the board operates and the role of the company secretary;
- frequency of board meetings;
- what the new director will be expected to contribute;
- who the major shareholders are and their relationship with the company;
- compliance with corporate governance requirements;
- the law relating to inside information, insider lists and share dealing by directors;
- the potential liabilities of directors;
- directors' liability insurance;
- company policy on corporate secretarial responsibility (CSR); and
- arrangements for monitoring the performance of board members.

This list is not exhaustive. However, in some cases it might be considered too long. The main point is that an executive manager appointed as a director needs to learn about the differences in the roles of manager and director, and that he or she has not been appointed as a director simply to be a 'high level' executive of the company.

7.3 Training and professional development

Directors should keep their knowledge and skills up to date, so that they can continue to perform effectively, and the company should ensure that this is provided. The appropriate training and personal development for each individual director will depend on the director's personal situation.

- All directors may need training or updating when there is a change in an important aspect of the law or when new regulations are introduced that affect the company's operations or its governance.
- Members of board committees may need to be updated or may need to acquire greater in-depth knowledge of matters affecting the work of their committee.
- Directors may need to be informed about an important new product or an important new acquisition for the company.

The UK Code states that:

'The chairman should ensure that the directors continually update their skills and the knowledge and familiarity with the company required to fulfil their role both on the board and on board committees. The company should provide the necessary resources for developing and updating its directors' knowledge and capabilities.'

 STOP AND THINK 5.6

Students often confuse 'induction' and 'training', and assume that they are different words for the same thing. This is not the case.

Induction is a process of 'leading someone in'. In the case of a new director, it involves providing information and assistance to the director to become familiar with the requirements of his or her new role. For a non-executive director, an important aspect of induction is helping the director to become familiar with the company, its business, its operations and its key personnel. For a new executive director, induction may focus more on the responsibilities of a board director. All new directors need to be made familiar with recent discussions and decisions of the board; and they should be given copies of minutes of the most recent board meetings. The company secretary may also be able to give them useful information about board activities.

Training (and development) is an ongoing requirement for all directors throughout their time on the board. Training is needed to make sure that directors remain up-to-date and fully informed about matters that are relevant to their role. It may involve technical training, such as training in new financial accounting standards or tax rules for members of the audit committee and the finance director, or updating in the risks relating to cybercrime.

The particular training and development needs for each individual director should be assessed by the chairman, but each director should be able to make suggestions about the type of training or development that might be suitable for him personally. The UK Code includes a provision that the chairman should agree a personalised approach to training and development with each director. This should be reviewed regularly. The obvious time to do this is during the annual performance review of the director. Performance reviews are described throughout section 8 below.

TEST YOUR KNOWLEDGE 5.4

a What should the induction of a new director consist of?
b What is the difference between induction and training?

8 Performance evaluation of the board

8.1 Requirement for annual evaluation

A possibly contentious issue in corporate governance is the extent to which the performance of directors should be monitored and assessed, and what form such assessments should take. In the UK, a requirement for directors to undergo formal performance appraisals each year was introduced into the corporate governance code in 2003.

The UK Code states as a main principle that the board should undertake a 'formal and rigorous annual evaluation of its own performance and that of its committees and individual directors'. Evaluation of individual directors should aim to show whether each director:

- continues to contribute effectively; and
- continues to demonstrate commitment to the role (e.g. in terms of time spent in carrying out the director's duties, attendance at board and committee meetings, and on other duties).

The evaluation of performance is probably particularly important for NEDs. Executive directors commit all or most of their time to the company and should be fully familiar with the business and the company's operations. In contrast, NEDs spend only part of their time with the company, even though they make up the membership of key board committees – the audit and remuneration committees in particular (see also Chapter 6). There is a possibility that NEDs will lose some of their enthusiasm for the company, and may get into a habit of missing meetings and not spending as much time with the company as expected. In some cases, a director may fail to keep up to date with an important area of their supposed expertise.

The FRC Guidance on Board Effectiveness 2011 states that 'evaluation should be bespoke in its formulation and delivery'.

The requirement for regular performance evaluation of directors varies between countries, but is not restricted to the UK. For example, it is included as a recommendation in the King IV Code.

Originally, the UK governance code did not recommend how the performance evaluation of the board, its committees and individual directors should be carried out, or who should do it. It became established practice, however, that except for the performance review of the chairman himself or herself, the chairman should organise the performance review process and should be closely involved in it. The FRC Guidance suggests that the chairman has overall responsibility for the process and should:

- select an appropriate approach or method for the performance appraisal; and
- act on its outcome.

One approach is for the chairman to carry out the reviews personally, possibly with advice and assistance from the company secretary. Alternatively, the chairman may be responsible for deciding on the process that should be used for the performance review, and should act on the findings of the review, but may hand the responsibility for conducting the review to another board member, such as the SID. Companies may also use the services of specialist external consultants.

The UK Code requires that the board should state in the company's annual report how the performance evaluation of the board, its committees and individual directors has been carried out.

STOP AND THINK 5.7

It may be supposed that the nomination committee should be given responsibility for the annual performance review of the board, its committees and individual directors, but this arrangement would have problems.

■ The committee would have responsibility for the review of its own performance.
■ The members of the committee would be responsible for the review of their performance as individuals.

On the other hand, the board chairman may not have sufficient expertise to carry out the performance review (except for his or her own review) without suitable advice and support.
    For this reason, the benefit of assistance from external independent consultants is recognised as something that can make the annual review process more useful.

8.2 Evaluation of the board

In the UK, the potential value of external consultants has been recognised, and the UK Code states that for the evaluation of the board as a whole:

■ the evaluation of the board of FTSE companies should be 'externally facilitated' at least every three years; in other words, the company should use specialist external consultants at least once every three years; and
■ where the company uses external consultants, the company should make a statement of whether the consultants have any other connection with the company (independent consultants are more likely to provide better advice).

A FTSE 350 company might therefore use external consultants in one year, and then the chairman might use the lessons obtained from the consultants to carry out an internal performance evaluation for the next two years. In year four, external consultants might be used again as a way of learning new lessons or checking the quality of the internal evaluation process. The FRC Guidance on Board Effectiveness suggests that the use of external consultants may also be appropriate when:

■ a new chairman has been appointed, who is not yet fully familiar with the company and its board members;
■ there is a known problem with one or more board members that needs tactful handling around the board table; or
■ there is an external perception that the board is or has been ineffective.

The possible reasons for an ineffective board may be any of the following.

■ Insufficient information provided to the directors to enable them to make properly considered decisions.
■ Directors not given sufficient time before a board meeting to read relevant papers, and so arrive at the meeting not properly briefed.
■ Directors not bothering to take time before a board meeting to read relevant papers, and so arrive at the meeting not properly briefed.
■ Individual directors failing to attend meetings of the board or meetings of board committees.
■ Individual directors not being given enough opportunity to contribute to discussions in board meetings (this would arguably be a failing of the chairman rather than an indication of an ineffective board).
■ The board failing to carry out its responsibilities in full.
■ The board failing to take its annual performance evaluation seriously enough.
■ The board making ill-considered (bad) strategic decisions.

FRC Guidance on Board Effectiveness identifies issues that should be considered in a performance review include the following.

- The mix of skills, experience, knowledge and diversity on the board in the context of the challenges facing the company (see below).
- Succession and development plans.
- How the board works as a unit, and the tone set by the chairman and the CEO.
- The effectiveness of key board relationships, and in particular chairman/CEO, chairman/SID, chairman/company secretary and executive directors/NEDs.
- The clarity of the SID's role.
- The effectiveness of individual directors.
- The effectiveness of the board committees.
- The quality of the information provided to the board about the company and its performance.
- The quality of board papers and presentations.
- The quality of discussions at board meetings on proposals for decision by the board.
- The process used by the chairman to ensure that sufficient debate is allowed for issues at board meetings.
- The clarity of the board's decision-making process.
- The process used by the board (and relevant committees) for identifying and reviewing risk.
- How the board communicates with and listens to the views of shareholders and other stakeholders, and how it responds to those views.

The Code principle B.6, which deals with board evaluation, includes a specific reference to reviewing the composition of the board and its diversity, including gender:

> 'Evaluation of the board should consider the balance of skills, experience, independence and knowledge of the company on the board, its diversity, including gender, how the board works together as a unit, and other factors relevant to its effectiveness.'

8.3 Evaluation of board committees

Board committees should be evaluated in a similar way to the board as a whole. For each committee, there should be a comparison between what the committee is responsible for doing and what it has actually done.

- Has the nomination committee been successful in identifying suitable individuals for board appointments?
- Have any individuals been appointed to the board who, in retrospect, were not as good as originally thought?
- Has the nomination committee done any succession planning and if so, how good have its plans been?
- Has the committee made clear recommendations to the board, and has the board acted on its recommendations?
- Is the committee an appropriate size and is the mix of members suitable? Are changes needed?
- Have there been enough committee meetings during the past year?

Similar questions can be asked about the remuneration committee and audit committee, whose work is described in later chapters. The FRC Guidance on Board Effectiveness suggests that the chairman of the board committee should be involved in the performance evaluation of the committee.

8.4 Evaluation of individual board members

The performance of individual executive directors as executive managers is not dealt with by a corporate governance code, because individual executive performance is not a governance issue. For governance purposes, the evaluation of performance relates to performance as a director.

For an independent NED, key questions for evaluation include the following.

- How many board meetings has the director attended, and how many times have they been absent?
- How well prepared has the individual been for meetings, e.g. have they read the relevant papers in advance?

- What has been the quality of contributions of the individual to board meetings, e.g. on strategic development and risk management?
- Has the individual shown independence of character, or have they tended to go along with the opinions of certain other board members?
- How many board committee meetings has the director attended and how many have they missed?
- What has the individual contributed to committee meetings? Has the time commitment of the director been sufficient? Has the time commitment been as much as expected, or as much as stated in the director terms of appointment?
- Does the NED continue to show interest in and enthusiasm for the company?
- Are there reasons why the director may no longer be considered independent?
- Does the director communicate well with the other directors and with senior executives of the company?

The UK Code states that: 'Individual evaluation should aim to show whether each director continues to contribute effectively and to demonstrate commitment to the role (including commitment of time for board and committee meetings and any other duties).'

 STOP AND THINK 5.8

The evaluation of the board members is an evaluation of their performance as directors of the company. This applies to executive directors as well as to non-executive directors.

Executive directors will also have an annual performance review for their performance as executives of the company. This review is the responsibility of the chief executive officer, and is entirely separate from the annual review of board performance.

8.5 Evaluation of the chairman

The UK Code states that the NEDs, led by the SID, should be responsible for the performance evaluation of the chairman, 'taking into account the views of executive directors'. However, the actual performance review of the chairman may be conducted for the NEDs by external consultants.

The chairman's performance should be assessed by comparing their responsibilities with their achievements, and asking whether they have been successful in providing the board leadership that should be expected of them.

The non-executive directors should consider whether the chairman is effective in providing leadership to the board, and the performance of the chairman is therefore closely associated with the effectiveness of the board as a decision-making unit.

8.6 Using the results of a performance review

To obtain practical value from an annual evaluation of the board, its committees and its individual directors, the board should be prepared to act on its findings whenever performance is not considered to be as good as it should be. The chairman has the responsibility for acting to deal with poor performance.

The **UK Corporate Governance Code** makes the following provisions for how the performance review should be used:

'The chairman should act on the results of the performance evaluation by recognising the strengths and addressing the weaknesses of the board and, where appropriate, proposing new members be appointed to the board or seeking the resignation of directors.'

In the preface to the 2016 UK Code, the chairman of the FRC stated: 'Chairmen are encouraged to report personally in their annual statements how the principles relating to the role and effectiveness of the board have been applied.' The recommendation is that the chairman of a company should recognise his or her personal responsibility for performance and effectiveness of the board, and a company should not simply disclose its procedures for assessing performance in a 'boilerplate' fashion.

The chairman may also consider the need for changes to the composition of board committees and may ask for the resignation of a committee chairman. Some improvements may be achieved by changing board procedures (e.g. holding meetings more frequently, or changing the dates of meetings to give management more time to prepare the information required).

Although the chairman has the primary responsibility for acting on the results of the annual performance review, the FRC Guidance on Board Effectiveness states that the outcome of a board evaluation should be shared with the board as a whole and fed back, as appropriate, into the board's work on composition, and the design of induction and development programmes.

8.7 Problems with performance reviews

The performance evaluation of the board and its directors is recognised in the UK as a valuable tool for the assessment of the effectiveness of the board, and institutional investors have shown an interest in obtaining information about the evaluation process.

- They want to know that an evaluation has taken place, but they also need assurance that the evaluation process is of a suitable quality standard and rigour. This is a reason why the UK Code introduced a requirement for external consultants to be used at least every three years.
- Investors would also like to know more about the action that has been taken following an annual performance review, because they want assurance that the review is being used to improve the effectiveness of the board. However, it may be difficult to provide as much information about the performance review, especially the review of individual directors, without compromising the confidentiality of the exercise.

In its report on Board Effectiveness (2011), the ABI recommended that:

- Companies should explain the methodology they have used for the performance evaluation of the board and its directors.
- Companies should report more openly on the key outcomes of their evaluations and the steps that are being taken to deal with the issues that have arisen.
- Companies should report in their next year's annual report on the outcomes of the action they have taken to remedy problems that were revealed by their board evaluation the previous year.
- External evaluations should be carried out by independent consultants; therefore, evaluations should not be carried out by firms that are used by the company as recruitment consultants or remuneration consultants.

TEST YOUR KNOWLEDGE 5.5

a   What are the requirements in the UK Code for the performance evaluation of the board, its committees and its individual directors?

b   What is the purpose of an annual performance evaluation of the board and its directors?

c   What factors should be considered when reviewing the performance of a NED?

d   How might a chairman arrange for the evaluation of the performance of the board and its directors?

---

9   Boardroom ethics

It was explained in Chapter 1 that ethical business practice is an important aspect of good corporate governance. Ethics are discussed in more detail in Chapters 1 and 11. The ethical culture of a company and its employees is established by the board of directors and senior executives. The following paragraphs deal with ways in which some unethical practices by directors are regulated, and how directors may be liable for failure to perform their duties adequately, e.g. their duty of skill and care – even if their failure of duty is unintentional.

9.1 Disqualification of directors

In UK law, the Company Directors Disqualification Act 1986 identifies certain categories of misconduct that could lead to the disqualification of a person from acting as a company director of any company for a number of years. Often, the misconduct is an offence in connection with the formation or insolvency of a company.

9.2 Dealings by directors in shares of their company

Restrictions on dealings in shares by directors

Directors usually own some shares in their company. Even if an executive director is not a long-term holder of the company's shares, they are likely to acquire shares at some time or another, through the grant of shares or exercising share options that have been awarded as part of their remuneration package.

A governance issue that arises with share dealing by directors is that the directors of a public company are likely to know more about the financial position of the company than other investors. They are also likely to hear about any takeover bid involving the company before it is announced to the stock market.

It is therefore conceivable that some directors might take advantage of their inside knowledge to buy or sell shares in the company before information affecting the share price is released to the stock market. For example, a director might buy shares in the company if they know that financial results shortly to be announced to the market will be very good, and likely to give a boost to the share price. Similarly, the directors might sell shares when they know the company is in trouble, and before the bad news is announced, in order to sell at a higher price than they would otherwise be able to obtain. If an individual buys or sells shares in a company with the knowledge that the share price will soon rise or fall, and with the intention of making a personal profit from the share dealing, this would in effect be making a gain at the expense of other investors. Not surprisingly, it is considered illegal.

There are two separate but related regulations relating to share dealings by directors (and their connected persons):

- The law, which makes insider dealing a criminal offence for any person who is an 'insider'.
- The Market Abuse Regulation 2016 (MAR) which applies to share dealings by directors at any time, even if they are not in possession of inside information.

9.3 Insider dealing by directors

In the UK, Part V of the Criminal Justice Act 1993 makes it a criminal offence for anyone to make use of 'inside information' to buy or sell shares in a company in a regulated stock market. Other countries have similar legislation. Inside information has the following characteristics.

- It has not yet been made public and released to the stock market.
- It is specific or precise. For example, it may be information that the company will announce an increase in annual profits of about 50% or that the company is about to become the target for a takeover bid by Company X. Information that a company has had a good year financially and will be announcing higher profits is not specific enough to be 'inside information'.
- The information must also be price-sensitive. This means that if the information were to be made public, it would have a significant effect on the price of the company's shares.

An 'insider' is someone in possession of inside information. In UK law it is illegal for any insider to make use of **price-sensitive information** to deal in shares of a company or to encourage anyone else to deal in shares of the company.

Directors are insiders and are subject to these prohibitions against insider dealing. This is hardly surprising. If a director made a personal profit from dealing in the company's shares by making use of inside information, the profit would be obtained at the expense of other investors – shareholders or former shareholders in the company. However, insiders may be other employees of a company or advisers to a company, such as accountants or investment bankers giving advice on a proposed takeover bid that has not yet been announced to the stock market. If an insider passes on price-sensitive information to someone else, the recipient of the information also becomes an insider, and must not deal in shares of the company until the information becomes public knowledge.

Insider dealing is a criminal offence, with offenders liable to a fine, imprisonment or both. However, in practice there have been relatively few successful prosecutions of individuals for insider dealing in the UK, because the guilt of an alleged insider dealer has been difficult to prove in specific cases.

 CASE EXAMPLE 5.1

Company X is a listed company in the UK. In July the company was at an advanced stage of negotiations for the friendly takeover of another listed company, Company Y. Documents relating to the proposed takeover bid were distributed to the directors of Company X, in advance of a board meeting at the end of July when the decision to approve the bid and announce it to the stock market would be made. The takeover went ahead in August and the cash purchase price for Company Y was 30% above its market value just before the takeover was announced.

It was subsequently reported that the wife of one of the NEDs of Company X had purchased a large quantity of shares in Company Y at the end of July and had sold them at a profit in August. The NED was asked if he had told his wife about the takeover or shown her the relevant documents; he said no, that the documents had been in his close possession at all times except for one day when he had left them in the garden of his house when he went in for lunch for about an hour. When challenged, the wife of the NED denied all knowledge of the documents and confirmed that she had not spoken to her husband about the takeover.

The other directors of Company X did not believe the assurances of the NED, but had no evidence to prove insider dealing. They had to accept that the NED had not acted unethically.

The chairman of the board subsequently discussed with the chairman of the nomination committee the need to refresh the board, although the NED in question was not due to retire for another 18 months.

Market abuse

In the UK, activity that could be classified as insider dealing would also be classified as **market abuse** under the provisions of the Financial Services and Markets Act 2000 (FSMA). This Act gives the financial markets regulator the power to fine any individuals for market abuse, which is easier to prove than insider dealing under the Criminal Justice Act.

 CASE EXAMPLE 5.2

In 2010, the Financial Services Authority (FSA) (then the UK financial markets regulator) imposed a fine of nearly £1 million on the chief executive of Genel Enerji, a Turkish exploration company. This individual had dealt in the shares of Heritage Oil, a UK listed company and partner of Genel Enerji in a business venture, on the basis of inside information. Two other executives in the company were also fined for a similar offence. The inside information related to the results of tests by Heritage at the Miran oil field: the individuals concerned bought shares in Heritage on the basis of the test results before these were disclosed to the stock market. When the test results were announced publicly, the shares in Heritage Oil rose in price by 25%. In his defence, the CEO of Genel Enerji said that he was unaware of UK law prohibiting dealing in shares under these circumstances.

9.4 The Market Abuse Regulation and directors' share dealings

Prior to July 2016, in the UK, the law on dealing in shares by directors was supplemented, in the case of stock market companies, by the Listing Rules which included a Model Code for share dealing by directors and 'relevant employees'. With effect from 3 July 2016, the MAR came into effect across the EU containing prohibitions on insider dealing and market manipulation, and provisions to prevent and detect these. The FCA is the designated competent authority in the UK for MAR.

MAR makes insider dealing and market manipulation civil offences and gives the FCA powers and responsibilities for preventing and detecting market abuse. Criminal insider dealing is an offence under Part V of the Criminal Justice Act 1993, and criminal market manipulation is an offence under ss. 89–91 of the Financial Services Act 2012.

It may be very difficult in practice to bring a successful criminal prosecution against a director for insider dealing; but the confidence of investors in a company may be undermined by rumours or suspicions of insider dealing at board level. MAR therefore contains stringent rules on share dealings by directors (and connected persons), as a means of ensuring that directors do not deal in shares of their company at the expense of other shareholders.

Listed companies are required to have rules for share dealings by their directors that are no less stringent than the rules in MAR. The purpose of the restrictions is to try to ensure that directors 'do not abuse, and do not place themselves under suspicion of abusing, inside information that they may have or be thought to have, especially in periods leading up to an announcement of the company's results'. MAR stipulates that directors (and connected persons) are not permitted to deal in their company's shares during any 'closed period', being 30 calendar days before the announcement of an interim financial report or a year-end report.

Insider lists

MAR obliges listed companies, or any person acting on their behalf, to draw up a list of all persons who have access to inside information and who are working for them under a contract of employment, or otherwise performing tasks through which they have access to inside information, including accountants and other advisers. Such a list is referred to as an 'insider list'.

An insider list must be promptly updated as required. The FCA may request that a company's insider list be provided to it.

Companies must take all reasonable steps to ensure that any person on an insider list acknowledges, in writing, the legal and regulatory duties entailed and is aware of the sanctions applicable to insider dealing and unlawful disclosure of inside information.

An insider list should include at least:

- the identity of any person having access to inside information;
- the reason for including that person on the insider list;
- the date and time at which that person obtained access to inside information; and
- the date on which the insider list was drawn up.

Updates to an insider list must be made:

- where there is a change in the reason for including a person already on the insider list;
- where there is a new person who has access to inside information and needs to be added to the insider list; and
- where a person ceases to have access to inside information.

Each update must specify the date and time when the change triggering the update occurred.

Companies must retain an insider list for a period of at least five years after it is drawn up or updated.

MAR also places requirements on regulators and companies to be able to receive whistle-blowing notifications.

Compliance with MAR should ensure that directors (and other individuals with access to key unpublished financial information about the company) do not breach the rules against insider dealing and do not give investors any grounds for suspecting insider dealing or unethical dealing in the company's shares.

The main provisions of a company's rules on share dealings by directors would be likely to include:

- Directors must not deal in shares of their company during a closed period.
- A director must not deal at any time that they are privy to price-sensitive information. Information is price-sensitive if its publication could have a significant effect on the share price.
- A director must seek clearance from the chairman (or another designated director) prior to dealing in the company's shares. Clearance must not be given during a closed period. The chairman must seek clearance to deal from the CEO, and the CEO must seek clearance from the chairman.
- In exceptional circumstances, clearance to deal can be given during a closed period where the director has a pressing financial commitment or would suffer financial hardship if unable to deal.
- A director must ensure that none of his connected persons deals without clearance. Connected persons include spouse and infant children, and companies in which the director controls over 20% of the equity.

Reporting requirements

Under MAR, firms and individuals must make the following notifications to the FCA:

- Suspicious transaction and order reports (STORs).
- Persons discharging managerial responsibilities (PDMRs) notifications.
- Delaying disclosure of inside information.

Buy-back transactions and stabilisation activity notifications

The ICSA issued a guidance note Market Abuse Regulation (MAR) Dealing Code and policy document (2016) in conjunction with GC100 and the Quoted Companies Alliance. It includes a specimen:

- group wide dealing policy;
- dealing code; and
- dealing procedures manual.

9.5 Notification to the stock market of dealings in shares by directors

For stock market companies in the UK, there are requirements for disclosure of dealings by directors in shares in their company.

Under MAR Article 10, 'persons discharging managerial responsibilities (PDMRs)' must notify details of dealings by themselves and 'connected persons' in shares of the company, including details of the quantity of shares and price. This applies to transactions once the total amount of EUR 5,000 has been reached in a calendar year. The notification must be made promptly and no later than three business days after the transaction date. The company is required to disseminate this information to the stock market through a Regulated Information Service (RIS).

TEST YOUR KNOWLEDGE 5.6

a What are the requirements of the MAR in respect of director share dealings for listed companies in the UK?
b What provisions would normally be included in a company's rules on share dealings by directors?

9.6 Material personal interest in a transaction with the company

Directors are required by UK law to avoid conflicts of interest with their company. However, a situation may arise in which a director has a material (significant) personal interest in a transaction with the company and will stand to gain if the transaction goes ahead. If the transaction is considered to be in the interests of the company, there would be no conflict of interest for the director.

Companies Act 2006 (CA2006) makes it a duty of the director in these circumstances to disclose their interest in the transaction to the board of directors. If the rest of the board give their consent, the director is permitted to retain his or her interest in the transaction at the board meeting where the transaction is considered by the board, and they will not be required to account to the company for any profit or benefit that they make from the transaction.

Failure by a director to disclose an interest in a contract with the company makes the contract voidable. This means that the company can choose to declare the contract void, but it is not automatically void. The company can also seek to hold the individual director to account for any profit that he or she has made on the contract.

10 Liability of directors

10.1 Potential personal liability of directors

There is some personal financial risk in becoming a company director or acting in an official capacity on behalf of a company (see also Chapter 10). If an individual commits a 'wrongful act' as a director, he or she could become liable (personally or together with other directors) and could become the target of a civil legal action. A director who is sued individually is exposed to certain costs, such as:

- the costs of legal advice and paying for defence against the legal action; and
- a compensation payment in the event that the legal action is decided in favour of the claimant and against the director.

'Wrongful acts' have been explained as 'actual or alleged breach of duty, breach of trust, mis-statement, misrepresentation, omission or breach of warranty of authority, libel or slander'. For example, a director may be sued for an alleged mis-statement in a document issued to shareholders by the board. There may be a legal action against a director for an alleged breach of duty, and even if the allegation is found to be unjustified, the director may find that he or she has incurred some costs that cannot be recovered from the person who made the allegation.

10.2 Directors' and officers' liability insurance

Directors should expect their company to provide insurance against some of these liabilities. The insurance that a company may pay for, to provide protection for its directors (and other officers), is called D&O liability insurance.

D&O liability insurance is relevant to corporate governance because without it, directors could be dangerously exposed to the risk of legal action for 'wrongful acts'. If this risk is seen to be excessive, individuals should refuse to accept the offer of an appointment as director (or company secretary), and it could be extremely difficult for companies to appoint anyone to their boards.

D&O liability insurance contracts vary in some important ways.

- They may differ in the nature of the 'wrongful acts' that are covered by the policy; some policies provide wider protection than others.
- They may differ in the financial amount or value of protection that they provide.

A company cannot insure a director against personal liability for illegal or fraudulent acts by a director. However, directors can be insured against legal costs incurred in defending an action (civil or criminal) for alleged negligence, default, breach of duty or breach of trust in relation to the company. If a director is found guilty of a criminal action, there is no insurance cover for any fine or penalty that the court decides to impose. However, insurance cover can be provided for the costs of a settlement in a civil action.

A provision of the UK Corporate Governance Code is that the company has a responsibility for providing D&O liability insurance: 'The company should arrange appropriate insurance cover in respect of legal action against its directors.'

Before accepting an appointment as director, an individual should look carefully into the nature of the D&O liability insurance cover that will be provided. If necessary, he or she should take legal advice to decide whether or not the cover is adequate.

10.3 Personal risk review

- NEDs might be well advised to keep their potential liabilities under continual review, possibly by carrying out a personal risk review regularly throughout the term of their office. It might be useful to go through a 'tick' list of items for review, as below.
- Has the NED spent enough time on his or her duties? If not, is it likely that the NED has been negligent in some way?
- Have they kept their skills and knowledge refreshed?
- Have there been any concerns with financial reporting, narrative reporting or any other information issued by the company?
- Is the NED satisfied that the company remains a going concern?
- Does the company appear to have sound systems in place for monitoring and controlling risks?
- Are there any regulatory issues involving the company that might expose the NED to legal liability?
- Is the NED satisfied that the company has complied with the provisions of the UK Corporate Governance Code, or that reasons for any non-compliance are justified?

 TEST YOUR KNOWLEDGE 5.7

What is D&O liability insurance?

 CASE QUESTION

1 What do the original owners of Stenning Tull (Don Stenning and Rebecca Tull) need to be aware of when working with a new team of directors as the board of a new listed company?

2 What recommendations would you make to ensure that the new and existing directors work effectively, both individually and together as a team?

11 Corporate governance and unlisted companies

The UK Corporate Governance Code can be adopted by any company, but in practice it is directed at companies in the UK with a premium listing, where there is a significant separation of ownership from control and consequently a need to ensure that the directors and management behave in a responsible way and are suitably accountable to the shareholders.

In smaller companies, especially family businesses, the owners of the company are often also its managers and there is little or no separation of ownership from control.

Listed companies are required to comply with the UK Code, or explain their non-compliance, by the requirements of the Listing Rules. For unlisted companies, compliance with established principles of corporate governance, or a corporate governance code, is voluntary. In addition, regulation of unlisted companies is less extensive and burdensome than regulation of public companies.

It is argued, however, that even in small companies there is a need to maintain certain standards of corporate governance. The Institute of Directors (IoD) in the UK, together with the European Confederation of Directors Associations (ecoDa), published 'Corporate Governance Guidance and Principles for Unlisted Companies' in the UK in 2010. This is a voluntary code for corporate governance, but is recommended as a way of helping to ensure the long-term survival and sustainability of the company as it develops and 'gets older'. The IoD code also provides a very good basis for a study of corporate governance issues for unlisted companies.

In November 2016 the UK Government issued a Green Paper: Corporate Governance Reform in response to various concerns about corporate governance, including in unlisted companies seeking views on 'whether some of the features of corporate governance that have served us well in our listed companies should be extended to the largest privately-held companies at a time in which different types of ownership are more common'.

11.1 Differences in corporate governance between listed and unlisted companies

An important difference between listed and unlisted companies is ownership, and the relationship between the board of directors and the shareholders. The executive summary to the IoD guidance states:

> 'Many unlisted enterprises are owned and controlled by single individuals or families. Good corporate governance in this context is not primarily concerned with the relationships between boards and shareholders (as in listed companies). Nor with a focus on compliance with formal rules and regulations. Rather, it is about establishing a framework of company processes and attitudes that add value to the business, help build its reputation and ensure its long-term continuity and success.'

Good governance is particularly important for **minority shareholders** in unlisted companies.

Shareholders in listed companies are able to sell their shares at any time, whereas small shareholders in unlisted companies cannot. Their shares are illiquid.

Because they cannot easily sell their shares, they are tied in as investors in the company. Their capital investment may be described as 'patient capital' because they have to invest long term.

Good governance in unlisted companies is important to small shareholders because it provides assurance that their investment will be safeguarded and their interests respected by the board of directors. Good governance should help to ensure that small private companies are not treated as an extension of their personal property by the majority shareholder, who may be the entrepreneurial founder of the company.

Good governance is also important for unlisted companies that are seeking to grow and develop. During the early years of its existence, an unlisted company may rely on the entrepreneur's own capital (or family capital) and retained profits as the main sources of finance. As it grows, the company will eventually need new sources of finance from external investors or lenders. Some new capital may be provided by external investors in new share capital. New investors will expect the company to safeguard their investment and interests, and they are more likely to invest their money if they believe that the company has a good corporate governance framework and complies with an established governance code.

11.2 IoD corporate governance guidance and principles for unlisted companies

The IoD corporate governance guidance is presented as 14 principles of governance, divided into two phases. The guidance recognises that the requirements for good corporate governance will evolve as the company grows and becomes more established.

It also recognises that in the earlier years of its existence, an unlisted company may be led by its entrepreneurial founder, who may be both chairman and chief executive. Eventually, the entrepreneur will reduce his or her input to the company, and at some stage will retire. The entrepreneur may retire gradually by giving up his role as chief executive officer and becoming a non-executive chairman.

For a company to survive, it will have to make the transition from entrepreneurial leadership to a more professionally governed organisation. This is recognised by the IoD's two phases of principles.

■ Phase 1 principles are universal principles that should apply to all unlisted companies.
■ Phase 2 principles apply to large and/or more complex companies, including those that may have plans for eventually progressing to public company and listed company status.

The principles are set out briefly below. Note how many of them apply to the board of directors. Other governance issues, insofar as they apply to listed companies, will be described in the chapters that follow.

IoD Phase 1 principles

There are nine Phase 1 principles.

1   Shareholders should establish an appropriate constitutional framework and governance structure for the company. For example, the governance framework should establish what matters should be decided by shareholders and which should be matters for the board.
2   Every company should try to establish an effective board, which should be collectively responsible for the long-term success of the company, including its strategy. An interim step for small owner-managed companies may be to set up an advisory board.
3   The size and composition of the board should reflect the scale and complexity of the company's business operations.
4   The board should meet sufficiently regularly to discharge its duties and it should be supplied in a timely manner with appropriate information.
5   Levels of remuneration should be sufficient to attract, retain and motivate executives and non-executives of the quality required to run the company successfully.
6   The board is responsible for the oversight of risk and should maintain a sound system of internal control to safeguard the shareholders' investment and the company's assets.
7   There should be dialogue between the company's board and the shareholders based on a mutual understanding of objectives. Directors need to understand that shareholders should be treated equally.
8   All directors should receive induction on joining the board and should keep up-to-date and regularly refresh their skills.
9   Family-controlled companies should establish a system for family governance that promotes understanding and coordination between the family members and establishes a suitable relationship between family governance and corporate governance.

IoD Phase 2 principles

There are five Phase 2 principles.

1   There should be a clear division of responsibilities at the head of the company between running the board and running the company's business operations. No individual should have 'unfettered powers of decision'.
2   All boards of directors should have a suitable mix of competencies and experience. No one individual (or group) should dominate decision-making by the board.
3   The board should establish appropriate committees to discharge its duties more effectively.
4   There should be periodic appraisal by the board of its performance and the performance of individual directors.
5   The board should present a balanced and understandable assessment for the shareholders of its position and prospects, and there should be a suitable programme for engagement with stakeholders.

These principles may suggest to you that although the reasons for having standards of corporate governance may differ between listed and unlisted companies, many of the core principles are the same or similar.

The same applies to governance in central and local government, and in voluntary organisations. The reasons for needing high standards of governance may differ, but many of the principles are the same or similar, and many of these relate to the requirement for a well-constituted and effective board at the head of the organisation.

11.3 Green Paper Corporate Governance Reform

This Green Paper seeks views on three areas where we want to consider options for updating our corporate governance framework including whether some of the features of corporate governance that have served us well in our listed companies should be extended to the largest privately-held companies at a time in which different types of ownership are more common.

The Green Paper discusses:

'The problem

The UK's strongest corporate governance and reporting standards are focused on public companies where the owners or shareholders are distant from the executives running the company. These standards provide independent shareholders with reassurance that the company is being run in their interests and that they have the information needed to hold the executive to account.

The UK, however, is home to a significant number of large, private companies and limited liability partnerships (LLPs). There are, for example, approximately 2,500 private companies and 90 LLPs with more than 1,000 employees. These businesses are not expected or required to meet the same formal corporate governance and reporting standards as publicly listed companies, yet the consequences when things go wrong can be equally severe for other stakeholders.

The main rationale for the different treatment lies in the ownership structure. The owners of privately-held businesses do not need the same levels of reassurance and information as owners of public companies because ownership and control are usually closely intertwined. There are, nevertheless a number of reasons for exploring whether similar standards should apply to at least some of these businesses.

- First, good governance is about more than the relationship between the owners and the managers of a business. There are other stakeholders with a strong interest in whether a business is well run, including employees, customers, supply chains and pension fund beneficiaries. They all suffer when a private company fails as the recent failure of BHS has demonstrated.

- Second, society has a legitimate expectation that companies will be run responsibly in return for the privilege of limited liability, a privilege that is enjoyed by all companies and LLPs, irrespective of their size and status. High standards of corporate governance can help provide the necessary assurance that limited liability will not be abused. The majority of businesses already meet these expectations and standards.

- Third, since 1999, there has been a steady decline in the number of public companies whilst in the same period there has been an increase in privately-held businesses. There are a range of reasons suggested for this trend, including the diminishing importance of public equity markets as a source of capital. Irrespective of the reasons, increasing numbers of large businesses are choosing to operate as private businesses. In doing so, they are excluded from the higher levels of public scrutiny and formal corporate governance discipline associated with being traded on a public market.

- Finally, it is in the interests of businesses themselves to have good corporate governance. It provides confidence not just to shareholders but to other key stakeholders that a company is being well-run. In particular, it can help build and sustain the confidence of banks, investors and suppliers giving businesses better access to external finance at a lower cost and on a longer-term basis than would otherwise be the case. It can help build a company's reputation and ensure its long-term success.

Context

Corporate governance is the system of common rules, practices and processes under which companies can operate effectively. It is generally focused on the composition and workings of company boards and the engagement with shareholders, but also looks at the relationships companies have with other stakeholders. It covers factors such as having appropriate internal controls in place to mitigate and manage risks and making use of independent non-executive directors with different perspectives to challenge and develop company strategy. Effective corporate governance frameworks also include reporting standards because transparency is a key tool in providing information about key aspects of how the business is being run.'

CHAPTER SUMMARY

- There are certain fundamental requirements for an effective and efficient board. These include: having directors of appropriate character, sufficiently frequent board meetings, and appropriate agendas for board meetings; providing timely and sufficient information to all directors (but particularly NEDs); providing administrative support and advice to directors; and, when required, access to professional advice for directors. The provision of administrative support and advice to NEDs is usually the responsibility of the company secretary.

■ ICSA has issued a report on boardroom behaviours, identifying the characteristics of best practice in boardroom behaviour and suggesting guidelines for best practice.

■ The board of directors may delegate to a nomination committee the task of recommending new appointees to the board. In the UK, the UK Corporate Governance Code recommends that a majority of the nominations committee should be independent NEDs and that its chairman should be either the chairman of the board or an independent director.

■ The nomination committee should also be responsible for making recommendations for board succession and changes in the size and composition of the board. The committee should also consider the need to refresh the board with new NEDs, and should therefore also make recommendations about the re-appointment of NEDs who are reaching the end of their contract. In 2003, the Tyson Report in the UK recommended that companies should search more widely for candidates to act as independent NEDs. Appointments to the board are made by the board as a whole, on the recommendation of the nomination committee, but directors who have been appointed must (in the UK) stand for election by the shareholders at the following AGM.

■ In making appointments to the board, the need for diversity of board membership should be considered; in particular, the need for a greater proportion of women on boards is considered important. This was recommended for FTSE 350 companies in the Davies Report, and the recommendations have been accepted by the FRC, which intends to alter the UK Corporate Governance Code in 2012.

■ Before accepting the offer of appointment as NED, an individual should consider a range of issues. A NED is typically appointed with a three-year contract and is paid a fixed annual fee. Contracts may be renewed at the end of each three-year period, although the independence of a NED may be brought into question if he or she has held the position for nine years or more. ICSA has issued a guidance note on the due diligence that prospective NEDs should undertake before accepting the appointment. In the past it has been usual practice in the UK for directors to stand for re-election every three years, at the AGM. A new requirement was introduced by the UK Corporate Governance Code in 2010. All directors of FTSE 350 companies and NEDs who have been board members for more than nine years should stand for re-election annually.

■ There should also be suitable induction for new directors. This is the responsibility of the chairman, who may delegate the task to the company secretary.

■ Directors should also receive further training throughout their term in office. The chairman is responsible for ensuring that appropriate training is provided.

■ The UK Code states that there should be an annual performance review of the entire board, its committees and individual directors. This is the responsibility of the chairman, but at least every three years the performance evaluation process should be 'externally facilitated' by specialist consultants.

■ The NEDs, led by the SID, should carry out the performance review of the chairman.

■ The performance review of the board should assess its effectiveness. Guidelines have been issued about how the performance of the board, its committees and its individual directors (particularly the NEDs) may be assessed.

■ Directors should act ethically and provide ethical leadership. There are legal provisions for the disqualification of individuals who have been in serious breach of their duties as a director. A disqualified individual cannot hold any company directorship for the period of disqualification.

■ The MAR contains prohibitions on insider dealing and market manipulation, and provisions to prevent and detect these.

■ Insider dealing, by directors and others, is a criminal offence. In addition, directors of listed companies in the UK are required to comply with the rules of their company about the periods of time during which they cannot deal in shares in their company ('closed periods'). These rules must be no less stringent than those set out in the MAR.

■ Directors may be taken to court for alleged breaches of duty and could be personally liable for expenses resulting from this. Companies should provide D&O liability insurance as cover for this risk. An individual should not accept an appointment as director without being satisfied that the D&O liability insurance is sufficient.

■ The corporate governance principles and provisions in the UK Code are designed primarily for large quoted companies, and not all of them may be appropriate for unlisted companies. Recognising this, the IoD has issued corporate governance principles and guidance for unlisted companies.

6 Remuneration of directors and senior executives

■ CONTENTS

■ INTRODUCTION

The remuneration of executive directors and other senior executives has been a contentious issue, partly because of the amounts paid to top executives in some companies and partly because remuneration for senior executives has risen by a much bigger percentage than increases in pay for other employees. Remuneration packages should be sufficient to attract and retain executives of a suitable calibre, but should not be excessive. Remuneration packages should also reward executives for successful performance, in both the short term and the longer term, because pay incentives are expected to encourage executives to perform better. Contracts of employment for senior executives should also try to minimise the risk of paying large 'rewards for failure' when a senior director fails to perform to a satisfactory standard and is dismissed. This chapter looks at the role of the remuneration committee, the problems with negotiating a satisfactory remuneration package for senior executives, and what the elements of that package should be. Shareholders cannot decide the remuneration packages of individual directors and cannot vote to reject contracts of employment that have already been agreed. However, in the UK shareholders in quoted companies have some legal rights over remuneration policy and payments. These were strengthened by changes in the law which became effective from October 2013.

1 Remuneration as a corporate governance issue

Until the 1990s in the UK and early 2000s in the US, the remuneration of executive directors and senior executives was not seen as a major problem of corporate governance. A sense that something might be wrong began when:

- the general public, alerted by the media, criticised some top executives for being paid far more money than they were worth; and
- investment institutions criticised directors for receiving ever-increasing rewards even when their company performed badly.

In the UK, the problem was further aggravated by the fact that in many listed companies during the 1980s and early 1990s, the chief executive officers (CEOs) and executive chairmen of many companies were involved in deciding their own remuneration package. Concern about remuneration has grown in other countries, particularly with regard to the banking crisis in 2007–2009 and the high rewards earned by senior bankers in spite of the large amounts of public funds provided to prevent banks from financial collapse.

In the UK, the remuneration of top executives has increased rapidly regardless of company performance and even through the global recession (and at a faster annual rate than the remuneration of other company employees), whereas a principle of good corporate governance is that remuneration should be linked to some extent to company performance, so that a director will earn more if the company does well, but less if it does badly.

1.1 Public attitudes

A general belief that directors pay themselves far too much can have a damaging effect on the stock market. Private investors may be reluctant to invest in companies that reward their leaders far more than they deserve. It can be particularly damaging to the capital markets when public anger is stirred against directors who continue to pay themselves more when their companies are performing badly.

The problem emerged in the UK during the 1990s, largely as a result of the privatisation of state-owned industries such as water and electricity supply companies. The same individuals who had run the former state-owned enterprises were appointed as directors of newly established listed companies, with a much improved remuneration package. The popular press led a campaign against 'fat cat' directors, such as the leaders of British Gas and United Utilities.

Similar concerns were expressed in the US in the early 2000s, following a number of corporate scandals. Alan Greenspan (at the time, chairman of the US Federal Reserve), commenting in 2002 on the collapse in the stock markets, accused senior executives of 'infectious greed' during the period of the stock market boom in the late 1990s, when the size of reported corporate profits and rapidly increasing value of shares provided an 'outsized increase in opportunities for avarice'.

In 2002, the President of the Federal Reserve, Bill McDonough, attacked the high levels of remuneration for CEOs as 'morally dubious'. He commented that the average CEO now earned more than 400 times the average employee's income, compared with 42 times more than the national average 20 years before, but their performance was not ten times better.

In the UK, during 2002–2003, there was institutional investor concern, supported by widespread media coverage, about large remuneration packages for senior directors where the size of the reward did not seem sufficiently linked to performance, and large **severance payments** (payments on dismissal) to outgoing senior executives who had been ousted from their job following poor company performance. High severance payments to unsuccessful directors were seen as 'rewards for failure'.

Following the global banking crisis of 2007–2009, there was also widespread criticism of remuneration in banks, whereby top executives and traders received large bonuses even though their bank may have been close to collapse or in need of government financial support to remain in business.

The problem of inappropriate remuneration policies for senior executives is now well recognised, but a satisfactory solution has not necessarily been found. However, a distinction should be made between:

- the unethical 'corporate greed' of some senior executives; and
- a reasonable desire by senior executives to be well remunerated for what they do.

Similarly, it is important to make the distinction between:

- high rewards that are justified by performance; and
- high rewards that are earned in spite of poor performance.

CASE EXAMPLE 6.1

Agencies that advise institutional investors how to vote are influential. The Association of British Insurers (ABI) voting service issues red, amber, blue and green 'tops' to alert members about governance issues in company reports. RiskMetrics is another influential service, especially for cross-border voting. In the Shell case in 2009, the ABI issued an 'amber top', which indicates potentially serious issues of which shareholders should be aware before they vote.

In December 2009, shareholders of Punch Taverns (a UK pub-leasing and managing company) voted against the remuneration report with a 55% majority. Shareholders were angered by the large pay awards given to executives in a year when the group suspended dividend payments after its annual loss quintupled to over £400 million. The ABI had issued a **red top alert**.

From your general reading or awareness of the business news, can you name any other example of public anger or concern about remuneration for 'greedy' corporate leaders? Are you aware of any opposition by institutional investors to a director's remuneration package, and what their reasons for opposing it were?

1.2 Why is remuneration a corporate governance issue?

Remuneration of senior executives is a corporate governance issue for several reasons.

- As indicated earlier, excessive remuneration for senior executives that is not clearly linked to good performance can undermine confidence in the stock markets. Executives should not be rewarded for failure.
- Any arrangement in which directors are in a position to decide their own remuneration cannot be good for governance. There would be a risk of excessive payments, and a risk that the company would be governed in the interests of the directors rather than the shareholders.
- Large companies need to attract and retain talented professional businessmen to provide them with effective leadership. Top executives are attracted and retained by the remuneration packages they are offered.
- Companies need effective boards and senior executive management. Remuneration incentives can be used to motivate executives to perform better and to achieve better results for the company.
- However, remuneration incentives should be designed carefully to align the interests of the shareholders and executives as much as possible, in both the short term and the longer term.
- The remuneration of senior executives may antagonise employees (and employee representatives) when it appears that senior executives are paid excessive amounts in comparison with their own pay. A sense that benefits or rewards are unfairly distributed could lead to industrial unrest within the company.
- Institutional investors have demanded greater transparency about senior executive remuneration, and several countries (including the UK) now have laws that require disclosure of directors' remuneration in the annual report and accounts.
- Shareholders may object to having little or no influence over the remuneration of directors and senior executives. High levels of remuneration can seriously affect profits and dividends.

Remuneration as a governance issue applies to senior executives below board level, as well as to directors. This is because in most companies the board includes only a small number of executive directors, and the use of remuneration packages as an incentive to management applies to other powerful individuals who are not on the board.

STOP AND THINK 6.1

What are the potential problems for good corporate governance when the annual remuneration of senior executives rises at a very much higher percentage rate than the salaries of other employees over a period of several years?

TEST YOUR KNOWLEDGE 6.1

For what reasons is the remuneration of senior executives considered a corporate governance issue in some countries?

2   Principles of senior executive remuneration

Principles of remuneration are now included in the corporate governance codes of many countries. In a system of good corporate governance:

- the remuneration of directors and key senior executives should be sufficient to attract and retain individuals of a suitable calibre; and
- there should be adequate disclosure of the remuneration package of individual directors, as well as the board's remuneration policy for the company's senior executives.

At the same time, the structure of a senior executive's remuneration package should motivate the individual towards the achievement of performance that is in the best interests of the company and its shareholders, as well as those of the individual.

The UK Corporate Governance Code 2016 states as a main principle that:

'Executive directors' remuneration should be designed to promote the long-term success of the company. Performance-related elements should be transparent, stretching and rigorously applied.'

It is widely accepted that senior executives should be able to earn a high level of remuneration in return for the work they do and the responsibilities they carry. If a company does not offer an attractive package, it will not attract individuals of the required calibre. It is also generally accepted that the level of remuneration should be linked in some way to satisfactory performance. If an executive performs well, they should receive more rewards than if they perform only reasonably well.

On the other hand, companies should be discouraged from paying their senior executives, including executive directors, too much. Excessive payments are against the interests of shareholders, because they reduce profits. They can also create resentment amongst other employees, who may see the gap between the pay of senior executives and their own pay increasing to a level they consider unfair. This can be damaging to morale as well as employee motivation.

The UK Code therefore has two supporting principles on remuneration:

- The remuneration committee should judge where to position the company and its senior executive pay levels relative to other companies. The committee should also make comparisons with caution, because of the risk of an 'upward ratchet' in pay levels. This may occur because of a wish to be seen as bigger or more important than other companies, so remuneration committees may seek to raise pay levels above those offered by the other companies they use for comparison purposes.
- The remuneration committee should also be sensitive to pay and employment conditions of other employees in the company, especially when deciding annual salary increases.

2.1 Senior executive pay and performance

The central issue for corporate governance is concerned with the link between pay and performance for senior executives, including executive directors.

- The remuneration package should include a performance-related element. If the director successfully achieves predetermined levels of performance, they should be rewarded accordingly. There could be some debate as to how much remuneration should be performance related, but there is a view that a substantial part of a director's total potential remuneration should be linked to performance.

- The purpose of performance-related remuneration is to give a director an incentive to achieve the performance targets. This is why potential performance-related pay should be substantial.
- It is clearly in the interest of good corporate governance that directors should be motivated to perform, but it is equally important that the performance targets set for each individual director are: (1) sufficiently challenging; and (2) related to objectives that are in the interests of the company and its shareholders. Performance targets should therefore be challenging, and large rewards should not be paid for average performance.

Linking remuneration, wholly or in part, to performance is not an easy task, however, as the following shows.

- Unsuitable measures of performance may be selected, so that although the individual executive succeeds in achieving targets that earn high rewards, the company itself and its shareholders do not obtain a comparable benefit.
- Many performance measures are based on the short term, possibly linked to annual results. This may not be in the interests of the company's longer-term development and performance.
- Remuneration systems are normally designed to provide the reward after the performance has been made. This time delay means that if the company has poor results in the current year after having done well in the previous year, an executive may be paid high remuneration (for the previous year) at a time the company is doing badly.

The best remuneration packages align the interests of the individual directors with those of the company and its shareholders. However, some shareholders may focus on short-term performance with the intention of selling their shares if the share price rises. Other shareholders may intend to invest for the longer term, but could be persuaded to sell by a large rise in the share price. The interests of shareholders are therefore both short term and longer term.

A supporting principle states that the performance-related elements of a remuneration package for a senior executive should be 'stretching' and should also be designed in a way that:

- aligns the interests of the executive with the interests of the shareholders; and
- promotes the long-term success of the company.

The view of the UK Code is therefore that the interests of shareholders in the longer term should not be subordinated to short-term considerations.

 CASE EXAMPLE 6.2

Problems with setting suitable remuneration packages for executives are well illustrated by the 2002 case of Vodafone and its CEO Sir Christopher Gent. The company consulted widely with institutional investors about a new remuneration package for the CEO, and obtained their approval for the principles of the package. However, when the company eventually applied the principles to devise a detailed package, many shareholders were dissatisfied. Three particular controversies were reported in the run-up to the company's 2002 annual general meeting (AGM).

Sir Christopher was awarded a special payment of £10 million for his role in the acquisition of the German company Mannesmann. The problem with payments based on successful takeovers is that there is often no way of knowing for some time whether a takeover has been a success or not. In the case of Vodafone and Mannesmann, the takeover occurred at a time when the telecommunications industry appeared to be growing rapidly and share prices in telecommunications companies were rocketing. Two years or so later, after the worldwide share price collapse in 2001, the wisdom of the Mannesmann deal was called into question.

A second problem was that Sir Christopher received large bonus payments for the year to 31 March 2002, when the company reported a loss of £13.5 billion, the largest in UK corporate history. Here, the problem is one of trying to ensure, as far as possible, that bonus payments are linked to the achievement of satisfactory performance targets, although these could include longer-term targets and non-financial targets.

 **CASE EXAMPLE** **6.2** *continued*

A third problem was the announcement of a new remuneration policy, in response to investor criticisms of the old policy. The company consulted with City institutions when formulating the new policy, with the intention of winning their approval. However, investment institutions might be willing to support the principle of a remuneration policy, yet still be angered by the details. Regardless of the general aims of a remuneration policy, the problem is in getting the details right. In particular, there could be general approval of which performance measures should be used, but disagreement about how challenging the performance targets should be, and what limits, if any, should be placed on the size of bonus payments. When the shareholders voted on the remuneration package at the company's AGM in July 2002, the package was approved, but there was a fairly large vote against.

 STOP AND THINK **6.2**

In response to the threat of measures by the UK government to levy a higher rate of tax on bonuses for bank executives, a UK bank was reported in 2009 to have increased the basic salaries of many of its executives by about 25% to 30%. Was this an example of poor government policy, bad corporate governance by the bank, or both?

In 2014 the EU introduced a new rule to limit bonuses for bankers to no more than 200% of their basic salary. Banks appear to have responded to this by increasing basic salaries (and so also increasing the bonus cap), or by paying bankers role-based allowances – payments that the banks claimed were not bonuses and so not subject to the EU rule.

3 Elements of remuneration for executive directors and other senior executives

3.1 The component elements of executive directors' remuneration

The remuneration package for a senior executive is likely to consist of a combination of:

- a basic salary;
- a payment by the company into a pension scheme arrangement for the individual;
- an annual bonus, tied perhaps to the annual financial performance of the company; and
- long-term incentives, usually in the form of share option awards or the granting of fully paid company shares (sometimes called 'restricted stock awards').

In addition, executives might enjoy a number of other perks such as free private medical insurance, a company car and the use of a company aeroplane or apartment. Remuneration can be divided into two elements, a **fixed pay** element and a variable pay element.

- The fixed element is the remuneration received by the director regardless of performance, such as fixed salary and salary-related pension.
- The variable element consists of the performance-related incentives (cash bonuses, awards of share options or shares depending on performance, etc.). The size of the remuneration depends on the performance achieved.

A problem in negotiating a remuneration package with an executive is to decide on the balance between the fixed and the variable elements, and to agree on measures of performance as the basis for deciding on how much the performance-related payments should be. The variable element can also be divided into:

- short-term incentives, often in the form of cash bonuses or possibly bonuses in the form of grants of company shares; and
- long-term incentives, in the form of share options or share grants.

Short-term incentives are based on annual performance targets. Long-term incentives may be awarded each year, but are linked to performance over a longer period of time, typically three years (or longer). Another problem in deciding a remuneration package is to find a suitable balance between short-term and longer-term incentives.

3.2 Short-term performance-based incentives

Performance-based incentives reward executives, usually with one or more cash bonus payments, if actual performance during a review period reaches or exceeds certain predetermined targets.

A performance target may be for an annual period, with the executive rewarded according to the financial performance of the company in a financial year. However, there are different ways of measuring financial performance. Here are just a few possible measures:

- annual profit after taxation;
- annual profit before interest and taxation (PBIT);
- annual earnings before interest, taxation, depreciation and amortisation (EBITDA); and
- the annual increase in profit, PBIT or EBITDA, compared with the previous year.

There are several problems with using profit measures as a basis for a reward system.

Annual profitability can often be manipulated within the accounting rules, so that executives seeking a high current annual bonus might be able to make the profit more than the profit that would be reported if more conservative accounting policies and judgements were applied.

Achieving profit targets does not necessarily mean that the shareholders benefit. Higher annual profits do not guarantee higher dividends and higher share prices. However, an ideal bonus system is one that links rewards to executives with the benefits accruing to shareholders, so that the interests of directors and shareholders are in alignment.

Other types of remuneration scheme are to reward executives on the basis of achieving:

- a number of different performance targets, some of them non-financial; or
- longer-term strategic objectives.

A CEO might have two or more annual cash bonus schemes, with one bonus payment linked to short-term financial results and another linked to longer-term strategic achievements. A problem with rewarding executives for long-term performance, however, is that an incoming CEO inherits the long-term results of the efforts of his predecessor. The CEO might also move on to another position before the full impact of his own efforts is fully appreciated.

It is important to recognise that there are different ways of arranging a bonus payments scheme for executives, but none are perfect because it is difficult to devise a scheme for individuals that ties bonus payments in a satisfactory way to performance that benefits shareholders in the long term.

 **CASE EXAMPLE** **6.3**

In September 2002, the finance director of Anite plc (a UK IT software and services company) resigned in the face of strong criticism from investors who were angry at the company's remuneration policy and acquisition strategy.

The individual concerned was one of the highest paid finance directors among UK technology companies, and his remuneration for the year to 30 April 2002 had risen 10%, despite a collapse in the company's performance compared with the previous year.

Bonuses for the CEO and the finance director were based on the profits before tax, exceptional items and goodwill, rather than earnings (profits after exceptional items, writing off goodwill and tax).

The company had a policy of growth through acquisitions, and had made 17 acquisitions since April 2000. These resulted in large amounts of purchased goodwill, and writing off this goodwill reduced earnings, but not profits before goodwill.

CASE EXAMPLE 6.3 *continued*

The acquisitions were made with an open-ended purchase price. The final purchase price depended on the performance of the purchased assets, with an 'earn-out' for the sellers of the acquired companies. All the purchases were paid for with new Anite shares.

The Anite share price fell by about 80% in the year to 30 April 2002, which meant that more shares had to be issued to pay for new acquisitions. The result was a big dilution in earnings per share.

The dilution in earnings per share had no effect, however, on the bonuses of the CEO and finance director. On the contrary, the new acquisitions added to profits before tax, exceptional items and goodwill, even though profits after exceptional items and goodwill fell.

The finance director, who was closely associated with the funding of the acquisitions, was therefore put under pressure to resign by shareholders. However, questions remained about the responsibility of the whole board for both the directors' remuneration policy and the acquisition funding policy.

Although the finance director was not removed from office by a vote of the shareholders at an AGM, the threat that shareholders would exercise this right was sufficient in this case to achieve the desired result.

3.3 Long-term incentives: share options

Long-term incentive plans usually take the form of an award of either share options or fully paid shares in the company. The award of share options or the grant of shares should be conditional on the director or senior executive meeting certain performance targets.

Share options may be given to an executive director or manager. Each option gives its holder the right to buy new shares in the company at a fixed price, on or after a specified date in the future (typically three years after the options are issued), provided that the individual still works for the company at that time.

The fixed purchase price for the new shares (the exercise price of the options) may be the current market price of the shares when the options are issued. In the UK, the exercise price for options must not be less than the current market price for the company's shares on the date that the options are granted. This means that if the market price of the company's shares goes up in the period between the issue of the options and the date they can be exercised, the option holder will be able to make an immediate profit by exercising the options and selling the shares that they receive.

When options can be exercised, usually three years after they have been granted, they do not have to be exercised immediately. The executive can hold on to the share options and exercise them later, when the share price may have risen even further (however, options must be exercised within a maximum period after they have been granted, typically nine years, after which they lapse).

3.4 Long-term incentives: grants of shares ('performance shares')

An alternative to a share option scheme is a share grant scheme. This may be referred to as awarding performance shares. Directors or senior executives are rewarded by the grant of existing shares in the company (which the company has bought back from other shareholders), provided that they are still in their job after a specified period of time, typically three years. The granting of shares may also be conditional on the achievement of certain financial targets by the company during that time. For example, a scheme might award shares to a director provided that the company achieves targets for total shareholder return (TSR) over a three-year period relative to comparator companies. The individual might receive 30% of the available shares, say, if the company matches the TSR of comparator companies and 100% of the available shares if the company's TSR is comparable with the top quartile (25%) of comparator companies. When the recipient of the shares acquires ownership, the shares are said to 'vest'.

With share options, the executive gets no benefit if the share price remains below their exercise price (and the options are 'under water'). With share grant schemes, however, the executive benefits even if the share price falls, because the shares (unlike under water options at the exercise date) have a value.

A company might also offer a **deferred annual bonus scheme** whereby participating executive directors and other senior managers are entitled to use some or all of their annual cash bonus to buy shares in the company. These shares might then be held in trust for three years, after which the individual is entitled to the award of additional free matching shares from the company, subject to a requirement that the company should have met a target growth objective for the three-year period.

3.5 Share-based remuneration: holding on to some of the shares

Schedule A to the UK Code deals with various aspects of designing performance-related remuneration for executive directors.

- It includes a recommendation that with share option schemes in normal circumstances, options should not be exercisable in less than three years from the date of their grant, and the remuneration committee should consider requiring directors to hold a minimum number of the shares for a further period after the options have been exercised.
- Similarly with share grant schemes in normal circumstances, shares should not 'vest' in less than three years from the date of their grant, and the remuneration committee should consider requiring directors to hold a minimum number of the shares for a further period after vesting.

3.6 Use of remuneration consultants

Companies often use remuneration consultants, who give advice to the remuneration committee on remuneration packages, including basic salary levels for senior executives. Consultants should not be given responsibility for deciding remuneration; this responsibility should remain with the remuneration committee of the boards.

Consultants may use competitive pay data to recommend a basic package for senior executives. Competitive pay data is simply information about the rewards that are being paid to senior executives in other top companies. At first sight, this might seem a sensible way of setting a total value for a remuneration package. Unfortunately, over-reliance on competitive pay data is likely to result in a sharp upward spiral in executive remuneration. Suppose, for example, that one of the top 100 companies in the stock market is looking for a new CEO; in order to decide on the remuneration package it should offer, it hires a firm of remuneration consultants. The remuneration consultants are likely to suggest that since the company is one of the top 100 companies in the country, it should be looking for a top-quality individual, and to get the man or woman it needs, the company should be prepared to pay above-average remuneration. Even a company that is at the bottom of the 100 companies might be encouraged to offer above-average remuneration. If every top company believes it must do the same, remuneration packages will inevitably rise rapidly.

If a UK listed company does use the services of remuneration consultants, it should make available a statement of whether they have any other connection with the company. This statement may help to indicate whether the consultants are independent and provide objective advice.

3.7 UK Voluntary Code of Conduct for remuneration consultants

Remuneration consultants who provide advice on the remuneration of directors and other senior executives are usually hired by the remuneration committee, and the committee is their client. However, there has been criticism of their role and doubts have been expressed about the objectivity of the advice they give.

- There can be a conflict of interests between the remuneration committee, representing the interests of the company and its shareholders, and the self-interest of the company's executive directors and other senior executives. In carrying out their work, it will usually be necessary for consultants to discuss aspects of remuneration with executives of the company.

There is a possible risk that consultants will 'take the side of' executives, and will not necessarily provide advice that is in the best interests of the company.

- Consultants may be inclined to recommend complex remuneration schemes, because this will make it more difficult for the remuneration committee to dispense with their services in future years.
- Consultants may try to persuade a remuneration committee to take their advice, when the responsibility for remuneration decisions should remain with the remuneration committee, not its advisers. Advice therefore needs to be objective, and the basis for the advice that has been given should be clear ('transparent') to the remuneration committee and the executives concerned.

In the UK, the Remuneration Consultants Group was established in 2009, as a representative body for most firms of remuneration consultants. Its purpose was to publish a voluntary code of practice for firms and individual consultants in the industry. This Code, first published in 2009 (and reviewed biannually thereafter) is entitled 'Voluntary Code of Conduct in Relation to Executive Remuneration Consulting in the United Kingdom'.

The Code consists of a number of fundamental principles that consultants should apply in their work, particularly in giving advice to FTSE 350 companies. These principles are transparency; integrity; management of conflicts to ensure objectivity; competence and due care; and confidentiality. The Code also provides some guidelines on how these fundamental principles should be applied in practice.

3.8 Problems with linking rewards to performance

The purpose of incentive schemes is to provide an incentive to an executive director or senior manager to improve the company's performance by linking rewards to performance. However, experience has shown that there are a number of severe practical problems in devising a satisfactory scheme.

- There may be disagreement about what the performance targets should be, and at what level they should be set. For example, should short-term incentives be based exclusively on one or more financial targets, or should there be rewards for the achievement of non-financial targets?
- Executives are usually rewarded with a cash bonus for achieving a short-term (annual) financial target, such as a target for growth in earnings per share. Short-term profit-based incentives are often set without any consideration being given to the potential long-term consequences for the company.
- Executives might develop an expectation that they should receive annual rewards regardless of the actual performance of the company.
- Newly appointed executives might benefit from a 'legacy effect' from their predecessor in the job. The bonuses paid to a new director, for example, might arise because of the effort and work of his or her predecessor in the job.
- Occasionally, rewards are paid to incentivise directors for doing something that should be a part of their normal responsibilities, such as rewarding a CEO for helping the nominations committee to find a successor to replace them when they retire.

3.9 Drawbacks to rewarding executives with options

There are several drawbacks to using share options in a long-term incentive scheme. Rewarding executives with share options is intended to align the interests of shareholders and directors (and other senior executives rewarded with options). However, an excessive use of options can result in a serious misalignment of interests.

- They reward the option holder for increases in the share price. Although shareholders also benefit from a rising share price, many might prefer higher dividends. For example, given the choice between a 10% increase in dividends and no increase in dividends but a 1% increase in the share price, many shareholders might prefer the higher dividends. Option holders do not benefit from dividend payouts, and executive directors holding share options may have a personal interest in a low dividend payout policy, in order to reinvest the company's profits to achieve further growth.

■ Share price movements are unpredictable over the short to medium term. When the stock markets have a bull run, as they did for much of the 1990s, share prices tend to rise regardless of the underlying long-term strength of the company's business. In these circumstances, option holders can make profits on their options without having to do much to earn them. On the other hand, when the stock markets go into decline (a **bear phase**), options lose value, and might even become worthless. In 2001 and 2002, when the major stock markets went from a bull phase to a bear phase, many senior executives were able to cash in their profits on share options whilst share prices were still high, and then see the value of the company's shares tumble.

■ Share options lose all their value when their exercise price falls below the current market price of the shares. Options that are **out-of-the-money** or **under water** lose their ability to act as incentives to executives. When this happens, the remuneration committee of a company's board might decide to re-price the options, or to re-issue new options at a lower exercise price. The problem with re-pricing options, or issuing new options at a lower exercise price, is that executives are protected from the **downside risk** (see also Chapter 9) of a falling share price, whereas their shareholders have no such protection. The option scheme therefore fails to align the interests of executives and shareholders.

■ For this reason, executive directors may prefer a long-term incentive scheme involving the grant of shares, since the shares will always have some market value once they have vested.

TEST YOUR KNOWLEDGE 6.2

a   What are the main component elements of the remuneration package of a senior executive director?

b   What does the UK Corporate Governance Code state about the general level of senior executive remuneration?

c   What company performance targets might be used as a basis for fixing annual bonus payments to a CEO?

d   What are the problems with linking rewards to performance for senior executives?

e   What are the advantages and problems with the remuneration committee using the services of remuneration consultants?

f   What company performance targets might be used as a basis for deciding how many shares should be granted to a senior executive as a long-term incentive arrangement?

g   What are the drawbacks to using share options for long-term incentive schemes?

International Financial Reporting Standard 2 (IFRS2) Share-based Payment requires companies to recognise the award of share options as an expense, chargeable against the company's profits, from the time that the share options are granted. The potential effect of share option awards on reported profits may have discouraged some companies from using options as an incentive.

4   The design of performance-related remuneration

The UK Corporate Governance Code requires that the responsibility for setting the remuneration of executive directors (and possibly other senior executives) should be delegated by the board to a remuneration committee. The remuneration committee is explained in more detail later; however, an Appendix to the UK Code sets out provisions for the design of the performance-related elements of a remuneration package that the remuneration committee should apply. Some of these provisions offer a useful insight into how incentive schemes may be structured and approved.

4.1 The UK Code and general provisions for the design of remuneration packages

Schedule A to the UK Code includes some general provisions about performance-related remuneration.

- The remuneration committee should decide on an appropriate balance between fixed pay (basic salary and pension rights) and performance-related pay (short-term and long-term incentives).
- Performance conditions should be 'relevant, stretching and designed to promote the long-term success of the company'.
- There should be upper limits on incentives, which should also be compatible with the company's risk policies. In other words, executives should not be incentivised to take excessive risks in order to earn high rewards.

The Schedule also states that:

- in general only the basic salary of the director (a fixed element of remuneration) should be pensionable;
- grants of share options or shares in a long-term incentive scheme should normally be phased over several years, and not awarded in a single large block. This is to reduce the risk that executives will seek measures to boost the share price, even if temporarily, at the date when the options can be exercised or the share vest.

4.2 Clawback of bonuses

Concern has been expressed that executives may deliberately provide misleading information about the performance of their company in order to increase their entitlement to bonuses. For example, the CEO and finance director may be tempted to 'window dress' the accounts of the company in order to boost profits (see also Chapter 7), or to 'hide losses' so that reported profits are higher than they should be. The true situation may become apparent later, but the executives by that time may have received their bonuses.

There may also be occasions when it is found that the profits or performance of the company have been over-stated, without any deliberate attempt by senior executives to window dress the figures.

The UK Code therefore states that incentive schemes 'should include provisions that would enable the company to recover sums paid, or withhold the payment of any sum, and specify the circumstances in which it would be appropriate to do so'. This is known as 'clawback' of bonuses.

The clawback of a bonus that has been paid but subsequently found to be excessive may be achieved in one of two ways:

- There may be a clause in the contract or remuneration agreement of the individual that provides for clawback in the event that a bonus has been over-paid.
- The chairman may discuss the matter with the individual and try to persuade him to repay voluntarily some or all of the excess bonus. If the individual refuses, he or she runs the risk of a shareholder vote against their re-election at a subsequent AGM.

Even so, unless there is a contractual entitlement for the company to reclaim an over-paid bonus, the company cannot force an individual to make the repayment, and has to rely on persuasion.

4.3 The UK Code and longer-term incentives

Schedule A to the UK Code states that the remuneration committee should consider whether the directors should be eligible for benefits under long-term incentive schemes.

- Traditional share option schemes should be weighed against other types of long-term incentive scheme.
- Executive share options should not be offered at a discount to the current market price of the shares (except in certain cases permitted by the UK Listing Rules).

- Any proposed new long-term incentive scheme should be approved by the shareholders.
- The total rewards available in any long-term incentive scheme 'should not be excessive'.

Directors should be encouraged to hold their shares for a further period after they have been granted or after the share options have been exercised (subject to the need to finance any costs of purchase or any associated tax liabilities). For example, suppose that a director is able to exercise options on 10,000 shares at an exercise price of £3 per share, when the share price is £5. The director would need £30,000 to buy the shares. Ignoring the tax that may be payable on the profit that the director has made, the provision in the Code suggests that the director should be encouraged to hold up to 4,000 shares for a period after exercising the options. The director could pay for the 10,000 shares he has bought at £3 by selling 6,000 of the shares at £5, leaving him with 4,000 shares.

The provisions in the Code also suggest that awards of share options and grants of shares should normally be phased over time rather than granted in a single large block. This is to avoid a situation in which the size of the rewards for a director relies excessively on the share price at a particular date. For example, suppose that a director receives a grant of 30,000 shares that 'vest' after three years on 1 January Year 4, and that he has no other long-term incentives from the company. Contrast this with a situation where a director is granted 10,000 shares each year, for three years, that 'vest' on 1 January in Year 4, Year 5 and Year 6. The director whose shares all vest on 1 January Year 4 will have an incentive to maximise the value of the company's shares at 1 January Year 4, whereas the director who receives shares each year will have a much longer-term interest in the share price.

 TEST YOUR KNOWLEDGE 6.3

a What are the general provisions in the UK Corporate Governance Code on the design of remuneration packages?

b What are the provisions in the UK Corporate Governance Code on short-term and long-term incentive schemes?

c Why, in the interests of good corporate governance, should non-executive directors (NEDs) be paid a basic annual fee and no incentive?

---

5 The remuneration committee

It is a well-established principle of 'best practice' in corporate governance that:

- there should be a formal procedure for deciding on remuneration for directors and senior executives; and
- no individual should be involved in setting their own remuneration.

This means that executive directors should not be involved in setting their remuneration packages (although they can negotiate with the individuals who make the decision) and NEDs should not decide their fees.

In the past, it has been quite common for the top executives in a company, notably the CEO and the executive chairman, to be involved in setting their own remuneration. Such a system, however, is open to abuse. Without controls and restraints, there is a risk that executives will pay themselves excessively.

The remuneration of executive directors was recognised as an important governance issue in the UK in the 1990s with the work of the Greenbury Committee, whose recommendations were subsequently incorporated into the UK governance code in 1998.

5.1 UK Corporate Governance Code requirements for a remuneration committee

The UK Corporate Governance Code states that:

'There should be a formal and transparent procedure for developing policy on executive remuneration and for fixing the remuneration packages of individual directors. No director should be involved in deciding his or her own remuneration.'

It goes on to make a provision that:

'[T]he board should establish a remuneration committee ... [which] should make available its terms of reference, explaining its role and the authority delegated to it by the board.'

The remuneration committee is responsible for both developing remuneration policy and for negotiating the remuneration of individual directors. Although these two matters are related, they are different.

- The remuneration committee should consist entirely of independent NEDs. In larger companies, the committee should consist of at least three members, and in smaller companies (i.e. companies below the FTSE 350) at least two members.
- The company chairman may be a member of the committee, but not its chairman, provided that he or she was considered to be independent on appointment as company chairman.
- The remuneration committee should have delegated responsibility for setting the remuneration for all executive directors and the chairman (including pension rights and any compensation payments or severance payments).
- The remuneration committee should also recommend and monitor the level and structure of remuneration for senior management. The definition of 'senior management' is a matter for the board to decide, but it will normally include the first level of management below board level.
- However, shareholders should be invited specifically to approve all new long-term incentive schemes (and changes to existing schemes) that are recommended by the remuneration committee and the board.

An ICSA guidance note, 'Terms of reference for the remuneration committee' (2013), suggests that it is good practice for the company secretary to be secretary of the committee, and also that appointments to membership of the committee should be made on the recommendation of the nomination committee in consultation with the remuneration committee chairman.

5.2 Consultation with the chairman or CEO about executive remuneration

A remuneration committee does not make decisions about remuneration packages in isolation and it will usually seek the advice and opinions of the CEO or other executive directors or senior executives. The committee may also decide to use the services of a firm of remuneration consultants to assist them.

The remuneration committee is responsible for deciding whether to appoint remuneration consultants to advise it.

If executives or senior managers are involved in giving advice to the remuneration committee, the committee should take care to recognise and avoid any conflicts of interest.

- The remuneration committee should keep the board chairman informed about its decisions on remuneration policy and the remuneration of individual directors. The UK Code states that 'the chairman of the board should ensure that the (remuneration) committee chairman maintains contact as required with its principal shareholders about remuneration'.

5.3 The principal duties of the remuneration committee

A list of duties of the remuneration committee were at one time included as an annex to the UK Combined Code, and they are now indicated in ICSA's guidance note on the terms of reference for a remuneration committee. Typically, the duties of a remuneration committee are as follows.

- The committee should determine and agree with the main board the remuneration policy for the CEO, the board chairman, and any other designated executive managers. This policy should provide for executive managers to be given appropriate incentives for enhanced performance.
- To maintain and assure his independence, the committee should also decide the remuneration of the company secretary.
- The committee should decide the targets for performance for any performance-related pay schemes operated by the company.
- It should decide the policy for and scope of pension arrangements for each executive director.
- It should ensure that the contractual terms for severance payments on termination of office are fair to both the individual and the company, that failure is not rewarded and that the director's duty to mitigate losses is fully recognised.
- Within the framework of the agreed remuneration policy, it should determine the remuneration package of each individual executive director, including bonuses, incentive payments and share options.
- It should be aware of and advise on any major changes in employee benefit structures throughout the company and group.
- It should agree the policy for authorising expense claims from the chairman and CEO.
- It should ensure compliance by the company with the requirements for disclosure of directors' remuneration in the annual report and accounts.
- It should be responsible for appointing any remuneration consultants to advise the committee.
- In the company's annual report, it should report the frequency of committee meetings and the attendance by members.
- It should make available to the public its terms of reference, setting out the committee's delegated responsibilities. Where necessary, these should be reviewed and updated each year.

The company secretary (or someone from the company secretary's department) should act as secretary to the remuneration committee, because it is the company secretary's responsibility to ensure that the board and its committees are properly constituted and advised. The company secretary can also play a role as intermediary and coordinator between the committee and the main board.

 TEST YOUR KNOWLEDGE 6.4

a   What are the principal responsibilities of a remuneration committee?
b   According to the UK Code, what should be the composition of a remuneration committee for a company in the FTSE 350 and who may be its chairman?
c   Is it appropriate for a remuneration committee to consult the company chairman or CEO on remuneration packages for individual executive directors?

In order to decide what a suitable remuneration arrangement should be for executive directors and senior executives, the remuneration committee needs to be aware of the remuneration arrangements and levels of similar companies. External remuneration consultants may be able to assist by providing this information.

5.4 Criticisms of remuneration committees

The remuneration of senior executives has become a major political issue in some countries, including the UK. The criticism has been that the remuneration of senior executives has risen at a much higher percentage rate than the remuneration of other employees, and there is no justification for this.

One of the criticisms has been that remuneration committees consist of executive directors of other companies, or former executives of other companies, who have no incentive to restrain the increase in executive remuneration. This has led to suggestions that remuneration committees should include employee representatives, or that members of the committee should not be executives in other companies.

Another suggestion has been that shareholders should be given the right to vote against the company's remuneration policies in a binding vote.

It is important to recognise, however, that remuneration is a corporate governance issue and should be considered from the perspective of the company, its shareholders and its other stakeholders. It is probably unhelpful to think of the topic as an emotive political issue.

 STOP AND THINK 6.3

The remuneration committee has the difficult task of discussing remuneration packages with individual directors. In many cases, the individual directors will have an exalted view of their own worth. Discussions can be difficult when individuals are demanding more than the remuneration committee members are prepared to allow them. The task of the remuneration committee may therefore be very tough.

Measures introduced in the UK from October 2013 for quoted companies may give some support to the remuneration committee, because shareholders will have the right to a binding vote on their company's remuneration policy and most payments to directors must comply with the policy that the shareholders have approved (this is explained in more detail later).

---

6 The remuneration of NEDs

NEDs are not company employees. They receive a fee for their services, not a salary. In the UK, it is usual for a NED to receive a fixed annual fee, typically in the region of £30,000 to £80,000 (or possibly more), for attending board meetings, some committee meetings and general meetings of the company – chairmen are usually paid slightly higher fees.

The principle that individuals should not decide their own remuneration applies to NEDs as well as to executive directors. This means that a remuneration committee should not decide the fees of the NEDs. Deciding the remuneration of the NEDs should be the responsibility of the chairman and the executive directors (or the shareholders if required by the articles of association). Where permitted by the articles, the board may delegate this responsibility to a committee which might include the CEO.

A provision in the UK Corporate Governance Code is that the level of remuneration for NEDs should reflect the time commitment and responsibilities of the role.

A company may permit an executive director to serve as NED on the board of another company. When this happens in the UK, the company must disclose in its annual remuneration report (a part of the annual report and accounts) a statement about:

- whether or not the individual is allowed to retain his earnings as NED, instead of handing them to the company; and
- if the director does retain his earnings as NED for the other company, the amount of the earnings must be disclosed in the remuneration report.

6.1 Additional fees

NEDs may receive other forms of remuneration or reward from the company, in addition to a basic fee, but this could raise questions about their independence.

For example, a NED might be paid additionally as a 'consultant' to the company. No matter how genuine and useful these consultancy services are, they put his independence at risk because the size of a consultancy fee is decided by executive management. Management also has the decision about extending or renewing a consultancy agreement.

- If a NED creates trouble for executive management in board meetings or at board committee meetings, there is always the chance that the consultancy agreement will be axed. If he or she is supportive, the fee may be raised.
- A consultancy agreement could also bring a NED and the executive management into a close working relationship, such that the independence of the NED is compromised, possibly through friendship or learning to look at problems from a management perspective.

6.2 The UK Code on performance-related rewards for NEDs

The UK Corporate Governance Code makes specific provisions about performance-related rewards for NEDs, including the award of share options to NEDs.

- As a general rule, the remuneration of NEDs should not include share options or any other performance-related reward, since this might compromise their independence.
- In exceptional cases, share options may be granted. However, the approval of the shareholders should be obtained in advance, and if the NED subsequently exercises options to acquire shares in the company, these shares should be held until at least one year after the NED leaves the board.

 CASE EXAMPLE 6.4

In 2006, Coca-Cola in the US attracted considerable attention for a remuneration initiative for its NEDs. In April, Coca-Cola announced major changes in the remuneration structure for its NEDs. Previously, NEDs had been paid a fixed annual fee of $125,000 ($50,000 in cash, and the rest in Coca-Cola stock), with extra fees for chairing board committees and attending board meetings and committee meetings. Under the new 'all-or-nothing' arrangement, directors would receive no remuneration unless earnings per share grew by at least 8% compound over three years, and there would be no payments to the NEDs during that time. The aim was to achieve greater alignment of the interests of the NEDs with those of the shareholders.

Critics of the new scheme argued that linking NED pay to company performance could threaten the independence of the directors from executive management, rather than align the interests of NEDs and shareholders. In addition, it was argued that by delaying payment of non-executive remuneration for three years, it would be more difficult for the company to recruit directors from less affluent socio-economic backgrounds (on the assumption that this is a desirable objective).

 STOP AND THINK 6.4

Some NEDs, particularly company chairmen, have substantial shareholdings in their company. Would you consider that paying NEDs in shares rather than cash would be likely to compromise their independence?

7 Compensation for loss of office: severance payments

7.1 Dismissal of directors and severance payments

Most executive directors have employment contracts with their company that provide for an annual review of their remuneration and a minimum period of notice in the event of dismissal. When a company decides to dismiss a director, it is bound by the terms of the employment contract.

There are various reasons why an individual might leave the company.

■ They might be regarded as having failed to do a good job, and someone else should do the job instead. A high severance payment would be seen as 'rewarding failure'.
■ There could be a disagreement or falling out between directors, resulting in one or more directors being asked to leave.

The service contract of a director might provide for the payment of compensation for loss of office. Alternatively, a company might be required to give the individual a minimum period of notice, typically one year or six months in the UK. If an individual is asked to leave, he or she might be paid for the notice period, without having to work out the notice. In addition, the individual may be entitled to further bonus payments under the terms of their remuneration package – in spite of being considered a failure in the job.

Shareholder concerns with compensation for loss of office arise in cases where an individual is dismissed for having performed badly. In the past, severance payments have been high for executives who are seen to have failed, having led their company to setbacks in business strategy or even financial catastrophe. A large compensation payment can seem annoying, because it seems that the individual is being rewarded for failure.

When a director is first appointed, it may seem inappropriate to negotiate terms in the contract that deal with dismissal; however, a failure to negotiate satisfactory terms could expose the company to very large payments if and when a decision is taken at a later date to get rid of the individual for poor performance. Measures that restrict severance payments must be taken when the individual is appointed and the employment contract is agreed.

7.2 Severance payments and payments on retirement

UK Code provisions about payments to directors on leaving office

The UK Code contains two provisions about service contracts and compensation for termination of office, or payments to a director who is retiring.

■ When negotiating the terms of appointment of a new director, the remuneration committee should consider what compensation commitments the company would have in the event of early termination of office. More specifically, the aim should be to avoid rewarding poor performance. The committee should 'take a robust line' on reducing the amount of compensation to reflect a departing director's obligation to mitigate losses.
■ Notice periods in the employment contract of an executive director should be set at one year or less. If it is necessary to offer a longer notice period to a director coming into the company from outside, the notice period should subsequently be reduced to one year or less 'after the initial period'. This is to avoid a situation in which a director is dismissed for poor performance, but is entitled under the terms of his or her employment contract to several years of basic pay in lieu of notice.

The reference to taking a robust line on a director's duty to mitigate losses is a suggestion that a director's contract should provide for a payment of compensation in stages, which would be halted in the event of the director finding employment elsewhere.

Joint ABI/PLSA statement on severance pay

In the UK, the ABI and PLSA (formerly NAPF) produced a joint statement (2008) on severance pay. The statement is aimed at the boards and remuneration committees of companies, and is intended to assist them in negotiating contracts with senior executives, and to make them aware that shareholders (institutional investors) want companies to avoid situations in which departing executives are rewarded for failure.

The joint statement sets out certain principles on executive contracts and severance pay, including the following:

■ Employment contracts for senior executives should not provide for additional financial protection for any director in the event that the company performs badly. The level of remuneration that senior executives receive provides adequate compensation for the risk associated with their role.

- Severance payments arising from poor corporate performance should not extend beyond basic salary.
- Companies should provide full disclosure in their remuneration report of the constituent elements in a severance payment, and should justify the total amount and each of the elements paid.

The joint statement goes on to specify certain guidelines about severance payments:

- Remuneration committees must understand clearly their responsibility to negotiate suitable contracts and must be able to justify severance payments to shareholders.
- A 12-month notice period in the employment contracts of directors should be a maximum.
- The board of directors must establish a policy that non-contractual payments should be linked to performance. No director should be entitled to a discretionary payment from the company in the event of termination of their contract for poor corporate performance.
- Remuneration committees should consider whether the company should retain an entitlement to reclaim bonuses if performance achievements are subsequently found to have been materially mis-stated.
- Contracts of employment should not provide for compensation payments to senior executives in the event of a change of control over the company (a takeover).
- Remuneration committees should ensure that the benefits of mitigation are obtained when an individual is dismissed. This should include a contractual obligation of the dismissed individual to mitigate the loss incurred through severance by looking for other employment. The contract should provide for the severance payment to be reduced in circumstances where the individual finds alternative employment.
- Phased payments are more appropriate than a severance payment as a single lump sum.
- Pension arrangements that guarantee pensions, with limited or no abatement in the event of dismissal or early retirement, 'are no longer regarded as acceptable' (unless they are available to all employees, which is unlikely).

If companies choose to ignore the ABI/PLSA guidelines on severance pay, they face the risk that these organisations will advise their members to vote at the next company AGM against the company's remuneration report and against any remuneration committee member who is standing for re-election.

 CASE EXAMPLE **6.5**

In August 2006, the ABI sent a letter to the FTSE 350 companies, asking them to review their pension arrangements for senior executives, and warning that some major shareholders would be concerned about the pensions aspect of excessive severance packages. The specific matter of concern was that executives might have employment contracts that entitle them to a large increase in their pension fund, as part of any severance package. The letter asked the remuneration committees to look at the pension arrangements in executives' contracts, to make sure that they were in line with best practice.

The reason for the letter was a payout to four former directors of Scottish Power, who had all retired with large increases in their pension funds. The former CEO had benefited from a doubling of his pension fund arrangements. The company admitted that the cost of the retirement of the four directors had been £11 million, but justified its action by stating that it was contractually obliged to make the pension increases, but was now reviewing its pension arrangements for senior executives.

The ABI expressed its concern that other companies might have similar arrangements that the shareholders were unaware of. Although the ABI has expressed its strong disapproval of any such arrangements that might exist, it would not necessarily be easy for companies (even if they wanted to do so) to persuade executives to agree to changes in the pension arrangements in their contracts.

TEST YOUR KNOWLEDGE 6.5

a What are the principles or provisions of the UK Code with regard to severance payments for senior executives?

b What principles on severance pay were recommended in the joint ABI/PLSA statement?

8 Directors' remuneration and the directors' remuneration report

The main arguments about directors' remuneration can be summarised as follows. Top executives have to be paid well in order to attract and retain them. A remuneration package for a senior executive should offer incentives for achieving performance targets, and incentive-based payments should be a substantial element in the total package. However, it is very difficult to devise an incentive-based system that properly aligns the interests of top executives with those of the shareholders. Top executives should not be allowed to decide their own remuneration packages. The responsibility for executive remuneration decisions can be given to a remuneration committee of NEDs. This committee should try to find the elusive balance between rewarding their top executives sufficiently, while structuring the reward package so as to bring the interests of shareholders and executives into alignment.

It is noticeable that within these arguments, the interests of shareholders are mentioned, but there is no suggestion that shareholders should get involved in making remuneration decisions themselves. Shareholder involvement, however, is desirable, and there are two ways in which this might happen: (1) disclosure, and (2) shareholder voting on remuneration.

8.1 Directors' remuneration report

In the UK, quoted companies are required by the Companies Act 2006 (CA2006) to include a directors' remuneration report for each financial year. This report must be approved by the board and signed on its behalf. A copy must be circulated to shareholders in the same way as the annual report and accounts, and it is normal for the remuneration report to be included in the same document.

The law relating to the directors' remuneration report changed from October 2013.

Before the change in the law, shareholders of quoted companies voted on the remuneration report at the annual general meeting. The report consisted mainly of details of the actual remuneration of directors in the previous financial year and also some information on the company's remuneration policy.

Shareholders voted at the AGM on a resolution (ordinary resolution) to approve the report, but this was an advisory vote only. The shareholders could not, for example, vote against the remuneration package awarded to any individual director. Any vote against the remuneration policy of the board, being advisory only, could be ignored by the board. However, a vote against the remuneration report was a way for shareholders to express their strong disapproval of the company's remuneration policies and practices.

Shareholder votes against the directors' remuneration report also attracted strong attention from the financial media.

- UK law on the directors' remuneration report for quoted companies changed from 1 October 2013. 'Quoted companies' are defined by the legislation as UK-registered companies which are listed companies in the UK or whose shares are listed on the main market of any country in the European Economic Area, New York or NASDAQ in the US. The rules do not apply to Alternative Investment Market (AIM listed) companies.
- The new rules are explained below.

Contents of the directors' remuneration report

A directors' remuneration report should contain:

- a statement by the chairman of the remuneration committee;
- the company's policy on directors' remuneration; and
- an implementation report, containing information about how the remuneration policy was implemented during the financial year.

The remuneration policy should set out how the company proposes to pay directors, including every element of remuneration that a director will be entitled to. The policy should also provide details on remuneration for newly-appointed directors, and on 'loss of office payments'. The policy should also cover remuneration for NEDs as well as executive directors, since UK law makes no distinction between the two types of director.

The report on the company's remuneration policy, in a year when the shareholders have a binding vote, should be contained in a separate section of the directors' remuneration report. In a year when there is a binding vote on remuneration policy, shareholders will be asked to vote at the AGM on:

- the remuneration policy (binding vote); and
- the rest of the remuneration report (advisory, non-binding vote).

Voting on remuneration policy

The shareholders of quoted companies have the following voting rights on remuneration policy.

- The shareholders have a binding vote on a resolution to approve the remuneration policy. It is an ordinary resolution, requiring a simple policy for approval or rejection.
- If the shareholders reject the remuneration policy, the board of directors may amend the policy and present the revised policy to the shareholders for approval at another general meeting. Alternatively, they may continue with the most recent remuneration policy to have received shareholder approval.
- If the company wants to make changes to the remuneration policy, it must put the new policy to the shareholders for approval at a general meeting.
- The company must put the remuneration policy to the shareholders for a binding vote at least every three years. However, since even small changes to remuneration policy require formal shareholder approval, companies may decide to hold a binding vote on remuneration policy at every AGM.

Once a remuneration policy has been approved, a company will only be allowed to make remuneration payments to directors that are consistent with the approved remuneration policy, which should include the company's policy for and payments for loss of office. If the company wishes to make a remuneration payment that does not comply with the approved policy, any non-compliant payment must be approved by a separate resolution of the shareholders in a general meeting.

Voting on the annual implementation report

The shareholders also vote on the implementation report annually, at the AGM.

The implementation report contains information about how the company has implemented the remuneration policy in the previous year. This will include a single figure for the total amount of remuneration for directors in the year. This total figure will allow shareholders to compare total remuneration payments from year to year.

The shareholder vote on the implementation report is an advisory vote only, not a binding vote. However if the shareholders vote against an implementation report, the board will be required to put the remuneration policy to the shareholders in a binding vote at the next AGM.

In addition, whenever a director leaves office, the company is required to publish a statement, as soon as reasonably practicable, stating what the payments to the director have been, and what the (ex-) director may receive in the future.

'Grandfather' provisions

The new regulations on payments to directors came into force from the beginning of the second financial year following 1 October 2013 (so from 1 January 2015 for companies with a 31 December year-end). Before this dates, payments that are not consistent with the company's remuneration policy are not unlawful.

The regulations also allow payments to directors that are not compliant with the company's remuneration policy, provided that these payments are required under a legal obligation made to the individual director before 27 June 2012 which has not been amended or renewed since.

Unauthorised payments

If a payment is made to a director or ex-director which is inconsistent with the company's remuneration policy, and which has not been separately approved by the shareholders, the director holds the payment on trust. The company can bring a legal action to recover the payment.

Action by the company to recover a payment may be initiated by the directors, on behalf of the company.

If the directors do not bring an action to recover an unauthorised payment, shareholders can apply to the court for permission to bring a derivative action in the name of the company, for the recovery of the payment.

The directors who authorised the payment may be liable for any losses arising as a result of the payment – for example, if the director or ex-director is unable to return the money.

 STOP AND THINK 6.5

The government's objective in bringing in the new voting regime for directors' remuneration was 'to enable shareholders to promote a stronger, clearer link between pay and performance in order to prevent rewards for mediocrity or failure, while still allowing for exceptional performance to be rewarded'. How far do you think this objective has been met?

8.2 Effect of the 2013 UK rules on directors' remuneration

The 2013 UK rules on directors' remuneration give more power to shareholders than they had under the previous regulations.

- Under the 'old' rules, shareholders were informed about remuneration policy in the directors' remuneration report, and could vote on it, but the vote was advisory only, not binding on the company.
- Under the 2013 rules, shareholders have a binding vote on remuneration policy at least every three years, and must be informed annually about the implementation of remuneration policy.

The impact of the 2013 rules on directors' remuneration, including payments for loss of office, may not be fully apparent for some time. They do, however, appear to give substantial extra rights to shareholders over directors' remuneration, which is possibly one of the most contentious issues in corporate governance.

GC100 and Investor Group's revised directors' remuneration reporting guidance

In August 2016, the GC100 and Investor Group published a revised version of its directors' remuneration reporting guidance, which replaced the 2013 version and provides guidance on the Directors' Remuneration Reporting Regulations 2013.

This second edition reflects changes in response to a review that was carried out over the 2014 to 2016 AGM seasons. The aim of the guidance is to assist companies in seeking to satisfy the reporting requirements prescribed by the Regulations. Key changes to the guidance in 2016 included:

- Clarifying the remuneration committee's use of discretion in determining remuneration outcomes, including the situations in which investors generally expect the committee to consider exercising discretion to moderate formulaic remuneration outcomes.
- Expanding the guidance on companies' use of commercial sensitivity as a reason not to disclose performance measures or targets in the remuneration report including setting out general investor expectations on the prospective and retrospective disclosure of performance targets and measures related to short-term and long-term incentives.
- If a company chooses a comparator group of employees when reporting on the percentage change in the chief executive's remuneration, clarifying that investors (and other stakeholders) generally expect a meaningful comparator group and not a narrow group consisting of senior managers.
- Reinforcing that in the future policy table the maximum amount that may be paid for each component of remuneration, including salary, must be specified.

In May 2009, shareholders of UK engineering company Kentz voted against the remuneration policy of the board. They also voted against the remuneration report, but this was not a binding vote. 51% of shareholders voted against the remuneration policy and a further 6% abstained from the vote. The company was obliged to develop a new remuneration policy, taking the concerns of the shareholders into consideration.

At the height of the banking crisis in 2009, 80.1% of Royal Bank of Scotland (RBS) shareholders voted against the remuneration report. In 2012, 59% of shareholders voted against the £6.8 million pay deal for Sir Martin Sorrell at his advertising company WPP. Other shareholder revolts on remuneration include 57.1% of Royal Dutch Shell investors in 2009 and 54% of Aviva shareholders in 2012.

 CASE EXAMPLE 6.6

In July 2014, before the introduction of the new rules on shareholder approval of remuneration policy, UK company Burberry faced a revolt over pay at its AGM, with over 52% of shareholders voting against the company's remuneration report. This was just an advisory vote, but shareholders were angry at a one-off award of shares worth about £15 million to the company's new CEO.

 CASE EXAMPLE 6.7

In April 2016, after the introduction of the new rules on shareholder approval of remuneration policy, 59.29% of shareholders voted against a £14 million pay package for the chief executive of BP (Bob Dudley), in a year in which the company had reported record losses, cut thousands of jobs and froze its employees' pay.

According to data compiled by the shareholder advisory group Manifest, this vote was the second biggest rebellion of its kind at a large company (after the RBS vote in 2009).

On the same day as the BP AGM, more than 50% of investors voted against pay deals at the medical equipment group Smith & Nephew following a decision to allow a long-term incentive plan to pay out £2.1 million to 60 senior executives even though the performance criteria had not been reached.

The Institute of Directors' (IoD) director general, Simon Walker, said: 'British boards are now in the last chance saloon. If the will of shareholders in cases like this is ignored, it will only be a matter of time before the government introduces tougher regulations on executive pay.'

Stefan Stern, director of the High Pay Centre, said: 'We are reaching a point where the largest CEO packages represent a material issue for shareholders that is big enough to require serious consideration. We could be reaching a point where more shareholders will argue that it is too damaging to businesses' own interests to allow top pay to rise this high.'

TEST YOUR KNOWLEDGE 6.6

a What are the rules in the UK for the disclosure of details of directors' remuneration by listed companies?

b Why might it be appropriate for shareholders to be allowed to vote on remuneration policy for directors, but not on the remuneration package of individual directors?

9 Institutional shareholder views on directors' remuneration

In the UK, the associations of institutional investors have developed strong views on directors' remuneration. The ABI and the PLSA have issued guidelines on executive remuneration, and issue occasional 'red top' notices to their members recommending that they vote against the boards of companies on resolutions relating to pay. Guidance from these bodies may influence shareholder voting on remuneration policy.

9.1 Investment Association Principles of Remuneration

The Investment Association is the trade body that represents UK investment managers. It has issued principles and guidance for its members on executive remuneration: 'The Investment Association Principles of Remuneration' October 2016.

Most of the principles are consistent with those in the UK Corporate Governance Code, but some principles provide an interesting viewpoint from the perspective of institutional investors. On the structure of remuneration packages, the Principles state that:

- Remuneration Committee should select a remuneration structure which is appropriate for the specific business, and efficient and cost-effective in delivering its longer-term strategy. These Principles do not seek to prescribe or recommend any particular remuneration structure.
- Complexity is discouraged. Shareholders prefer simple and understandable remuneration structures.
- Executives and shareholders can have divergent interests, particularly in relation to time horizons and the consequences of failure or corporate underperformance. Therefore, remuneration structures should be designed to reward sustainable business performance and therefore deliver long-term value to shareholders.
- Given the range of business models across industry sectors, remuneration committees are encouraged to adopt the structure which is most appropriate for the implementation of their business strategy.

Structures should also include provisions that allow the company, in specified circumstances, to:

- forfeit all or part of a bonus or long-term incentive award before it has vested and been paid ('performance adjustment' or 'malus'); and/or
- recover sums already paid ('clawback'). Executives should build up a high level of personal shareholding to ensure alignment of interests with shareholders. The shareholding should be maintained for a period after they have left the company.

Dilution of shareholders through the issuing of shares to employees can represent a significant transfer of value. Dilution limits are an important shareholder protection and should be respected.

9.2 PLSA Corporate Governance Policy and Voting Guidelines 2015/16

The PLSA (formerly NAPF) has issued guidelines on corporate governance and shareholder voting by its members. The guidelines include suggestions about the circumstances in which a vote against a company's remuneration policy may be warranted.

- When there seems to an insufficient alignment between the interests of executive directors and those of the shareholders. The guidelines suggest that insufficient alignment may exist when the requirement for executive directors to hold shares in the company is limited to less than twice their annual salary.
- The targets for receiving bonuses or awards under long-term incentive schemes are not sufficiently stretching.
- There are no provisions for clawback of rewards already paid.
- A recruitment policy which is vague
- If there are guaranteed pensionable, discretionary or 'one-off' annual bonuses, or termination payments.
- If there is any provision for re-testing of performance conditions
- The policy providing for the addition of a new share award scheme on top of an existing scheme.

9.3 Green Paper on Corporate Governance Reform

As noted in Chapter 1, the UK Government issued a Green Paper on Corporate Governance Reform in November 2016. The Green Paper seeks views on three areas where we want to consider options for updating our corporate governance framework including on shareholder influence on executive pay, which has grown much faster over the last two decades than pay generally and than typical corporate performance.

The Green Paper explores options for strengthening shareholder influence over directors' remuneration, increasing transparency and simplifying and strengthening long-term incentive plans. It discusses:

'The problem
- It is right that our major companies should be able to attract and retain top management talent, recognising that many of the leaders of our most successful companies are recruited from outside the UK. However, there is a widespread perception that executive pay has become increasingly disconnected from both the pay of ordinary working people and the underlying long-term performance of companies. Executive pay is an area of significant public concern, with surveys consistently showing it to be a key factor in public dissatisfaction with large businesses. A growing number of institutional investors have also been speaking out, particularly since executive pay reforms in 2013 which gave shareholders a stronger role in executive pay.

    For example, Opinium research for PWC's "Time to Listen" paper published in June 2016 found that two-thirds of respondents believe executive pay is too high; and in a YouGov poll for CIPD in Sept 2015, only 14% of respondents agreed that CEO pay is good value for investors.
- Total pay for the CEOs of FTSE 100 companies has increased very significantly over the last 18 years, up from an average of c. £1m in 1998 to c. £4.3m in 2015 (although that is slightly down on a peak of c. £4.75m in 2011). This quadrupling of CEO pay is largely accounted for by the growth in annual bonus payments and long-term pay incentives. It has far outstripped growth in average pay in the UK. In 1998 the ratio of average FTSE 100 CEO pay to the average pay of full-time employees in the UK was 47:1. This ratio increased to 132:1 in 2010 and stood at 128:1 in 2015.
- A number of shareholders and other stakeholders have queried whether this very significant increase in FTSE 100 CEOs' pay has been matched by increases in the long-term value of the companies they manage. For example, the recent report of the investor-led Executive Remuneration Working Group observed that "rising levels of executive pay over the last 15 years have not been in line with the performance of the FTSE over the same period, feeding the increasingly negative perception of listed companies by the public".

- It is difficult to assert with confidence the link between executive pay and long-term company performance at individual companies. Some UK, US and other international evidence does suggest a correlation between the pay of CEOs and company performance, but it is harder to establish a strong causal link.
- Establishing such a link has arguably been made more challenging by the growing complexity of executive pay packages in recent years. The Executive Remuneration Working Group's report states that:

    "Executive pay is opaque to the outsider and difficult even for some participants, remuneration committees and shareholders to understand. Growing complexity has contributed to poor alignment between executives, shareholders and the company, sometimes leading to levels of remuneration which are very difficult to justify."

... Options for reform

- The Green Paper is inviting views on the case for changes to the UK's executive pay framework for quoted companies in five areas: (A) shareholder voting and other rights; (B) shareholder engagement on pay; (C) the role of remuneration committees; (D) pay disclosure; and (E) long-term pay incentives.'

 END OF CHAPTER QUESTIONS

---

1 Referring to the case study at the beginning of Part Two, what changes – if any – would be appropriate in the remuneration packages and employments of Don Stenning and Rebecca Tull?

2 What measures should be taken by the remuneration committee and the board to introduce incentive schemes for senior executives?

CHAPTER SUMMARY

- Public hostility to excessive remuneration for directors can affect investor confidence in companies and the stock markets. Senior executives should be well rewarded, but not excessively so.
- An attractive basic salary should be offered to directors to attract and keep capable and talented individuals. A large part of an executive's remuneration package, however, should be in the form of incentives.
- A remuneration package consists of fixed pay elements (salary, pension contributions) and variable pay elements (annual bonuses, long-term incentives).
- Incentives could be bonus payments linked to short-term performance (e.g. growth in earnings per share) or possibly long-term performance. Unless appropriate incentives are selected, executives could earn a high bonus even when the company performance is disappointing.
- The UK Corporate Governance Code includes provisions and guidelines on remuneration.
- A major concern with corporate governance is that incentive schemes do not achieve their intended purpose, which is to attract and retain talented executives, and then to motivate them to achieve performance targets that are in the best interests of the company's shareholders.
- A problem is to find a suitable balance between fixed base pay (and pension entitlements) and variable rewards, and also to find a suitable balance between short-term cash bonuses and longer-term share-based incentives.
- NEDs should be paid a flat fee and in normal circumstances should not be given incentive-linked rewards.
- Individuals should not be allowed to fix their own remuneration. Remuneration for executive directors and other senior executives should be decided by a remuneration committee consisting entirely of independent NEDs, although this committee may consult the chairman and CEO. The requirement for a remuneration committee is included in the UK Corporate Governance Code. Shareholders should have the right to approve all new and amended long-term incentive schemes.
- The UK Code includes provisions relating to severance payments when a director or senior executive leaves the company. The aim should be, as much as possible, to avoid rewarding departing executives for 'failure'. A joint statement on this subject has been issued by the ABI and PLSA.

■ In the UK, rules introduced from 1 October 2013 require listed companies to include the remuneration policy of the company and an implementation report in the directors' remuneration report. The remuneration policy includes policy on payments for loss of office.

■ Shareholders in these companies have a binding vote on remuneration policy at least every three years and an advisory vote on the implementation report each year.

■ Directors or ex-directors hold the money in trust if they receive a payment that is not permitted by remuneration policy and which has not been separately approved by the shareholders. The company can bring a legal action to recover the payment from the individual concerned.

■ In the UK, institutional shareholders have indicated their concerns about the details of directors' remuneration packages, and the ABI and PLSA have issued guidelines on the subject. The ABI guidelines are quite extensive.

■ In the UK concerns about corporate governance, including excessive remuneration led to the government issuing a Green Paper on Corporate Governance Reform in 2016.

Reporting to shareholders and external audit

■ **CONTENTS**

■ **INTRODUCTION**

This chapter considers the relevance to good corporate governance of financial reporting and other statutory reporting, and the importance of having reliable reports for shareholders. It then goes on to look at the role and responsibilities of the external auditors, the issue of auditor independence and the responsibilities of the directors for financial reporting. Although the financial statements are an important source of information for shareholders and other stakeholders, listed companies are also required to provide extensive information of a non-financial nature, much of it in narrative form. This chapter discusses some of the aspects of narrative reporting, and current initiatives to improve the quality and scope of narrative reporting. Disclosure requirements about directors' remuneration were explained in Chapter 6. This chapter introduces **integrated reporting**, but social and environmental reporting and **sustainability reporting** are described in more detail in Chapter 12.

   The annual report and accounts should be seen as the single most important communication between a company and its shareholders. Although much of the content of the report and accounts is determined by law and regulation, there is considerable scope for companies to communicate in some detail their governance arrangements, including board oversight of strategy and the key risks associated with strategy implementation.

1   Financial reporting and corporate governance

The annual report and accounts of a company (and the interim financial statements of a listed company) are the principal way in which the directors make themselves accountable to the shareholders.

■ The financial statements present a report on the financial performance of the company over the previous financial year and the financial position of the company as at the end of that year.
■ The directors' report, the strategic report and other statements published in the same document provide supporting information, much of it in narrative rather than numerical form.
■ For larger companies, the annual financial statements and elements of the annual report are audited by a firm of independent external auditors.

Shareholders and other investors use the information in the annual report and accounts to assess the stewardship of the directors and the financial health of the company.

The annual report and accounts is an important document for corporate governance because it is a means by which the directors are made accountable to the shareholders, and provides a channel of communication from directors to shareholders. The report and accounts enable the shareholders to assess how well the company has been governed and managed. It should therefore be:

- clear and understandable to a reader with reasonable financial awareness; and
- reliable and 'believable'.

There are two widely expressed concerns about the annual report and accounts of companies.

- Whether the accounts are reliable, and can be 'trusted' when it comes to making decisions about the company; for example, whether to sell, hold or buy shares in the company.
- Whether the annual report is clear and helps the reader to understand the performance, position and future prospects of the company. A big problem with the annual reports of major companies has been their length: reports often contain a large amount of standard 'boiler-plate' disclosures, which makes it difficult to spot the more interesting and useful information in the report.

The reliability of the annual report and accounts depends on several factors, including those that follow.

- The honesty of the company in preparing them: if allowed to do so by accounting regulations, companies might indulge in **window dressing** their financial performance or financial position through the use of accounting policies (methods) that hide the true position of the company.
- The care used by directors to satisfy themselves that the financial statements do give a 'true and fair view' and that everything of relevance has been properly reported.
- The opinion of the external auditors, which the shareholders should be able to rely on as an objective and professional opinion.

If financial statements are produced in a way that is intended deliberately to mislead shareholders, the persons responsible would be guilty of fraud, which is a crime. Misleading financial statements, however, could only be issued if the:

- audit committee is satisfied with their preparation;
- external auditors provide a 'clean' audit report; and
- the board of directors approves the financial statements.

In most companies, this would require deception by a small group of executives, such as the CEO and finance director.

Although fraudulent financial reporting is a crime, so-called **aggressive accounting** policies may be permissible within existing accountancy regulations and standards, and accepted by the company's external auditors. The effect of aggressive accounting may be to make the financial performance and position of the company seem better than they really are, and to have the effect of hiding information from shareholders, at least in the short term. The financial performance of a company for the current financial year might be flattered by using certain accounting policies, but in the longer term (say, in one or two years' time) the 'bad news' will eventually emerge.

Significantly, many corporate governance 'scandals' resulting in the collapse or near-collapse of a company have involved fraudulent or aggressive financial reporting.

Trustworthy financial reporting and auditing is probably the most significant issue for corporate governance. Good corporate governance should ensure that financial reporting is reliable and honest, and that the opinion of the external auditors is objective and unbiased.

1.1 Financial reporting and investor confidence

In the UK, the Cadbury Code on corporate governance in 1992 happened as a direct consequence of concerns about the quality of financial reporting in the UK and the ability of the auditing profession to provide sufficient assurances to the investment community about the reliability of company financial statements. Similar concerns were expressed in the US during the stock market depression of 2002. If investors have doubts about the honesty or transparency of financial reporting, they will hold back from investing, and share values will suffer as a result.

The problem extends to the corporate bond markets. Many companies have borrowed heavily by issuing bonds to investors. Bond investors rely on **bond credit ratings** in making their investment decisions. Investors are unlikely to purchase a company's bonds unless they have been rated for creditworthiness by at least one, and more usually two, top ratings agencies. In the US, the top three agencies are Moody's, Standard & Poor's and Fitch, which have the status of nationally recognised statistical ratings organisations (NRSROs).

The US crisis of investor confidence about financial reporting in mid-2002 brought the role of the credit rating agencies into question. The agencies defended themselves publicly against allegations that they failed to identify the financial problems in companies such as Enron (see Chapter 1), when they should have been much more alert and in a position to forewarn investors about companies that were getting into financial difficulties. The reliability of credit ratings was also brought into question by the financial crisis in banking in 2007–2008, when many highly rated collaterised debt obligations (CDOs) were found to be more or less worthless even though they were valued at substantial amounts in the accounts of the banks that owned them.

When a company proposes to issue new bonds, a ratings agency carries out an investigation and then gives a rating to the bonds. The interest rate the company has to offer on the bonds will depend on the rating awarded. After the bonds have been issued, the ratings agencies review the rating continually and adjust it if the financial condition of the company improves or worsens.

Bond investors therefore use the ratings agencies as 'gatekeepers to the financial markets'. Their decisions whether or not to invest in bonds, and the rate of interest they require for doing so, depend on the judgement of the agencies.

As mentioned earlier, the collapse of Enron is described in Chapter 1; however, it is useful to consider some of the financial reporting and auditing features of the Enron scandal.

 CASE EXAMPLE 7.1

Enron used accounting and financial transactions to increase reported income and asset values, and to take liabilities off its balance sheet. One technique was to record up to $200 million costs of projects as assets, even though the projects had been cancelled. This was justified on the grounds that the projects had not been officially cancelled. Capitalising expenses meant that the costs were not charged against reported profits. Another technique was to set up special purpose entities in order to take liabilities and losses off the balance sheet. In 2001, a whistleblower reported her concerns about the company's accounting practices to the chairman/CEO, but her allegations were rejected. Soon afterwards, the company was obliged to re-state its financial statements for the previous four years, which resulted in a reduction in the company's equity by over 10% ($1.2 billion). Investors complained that the Enron accounts lacked transparency, and were so complex they were impossible to understand.

Enron's auditors were the Houston office of Arthur Andersen, one of the five largest audit firms in the world. However, the Houston office relied on Enron for much of its income for both audit and **non-audit work**. In 2000, the firm earned $25 million from the audit and $27 million from non-audit work for Enron – more than 25% of the total annual income of the Houston office. It appears that Arthur Andersen, and the Houston office in particular, may have gone along with the financial reporting practices of Enron in order to retain the work, and their independence was compromised. When the Securities and Exchange Commission (SEC) announced an investigation into Enron after its collapse in late 2001, Andersen tried to cover up evidence of inadequate audit work by shredding several tons of documents and deleting about 30,000 emails and computer files.

The Enron story is an excellent example of the importance of good corporate governance of transparent and honest financial reporting and independent **external audits**.

STOP AND THINK 7.1

A report was published in the US in March 2010 into the collapse of the bank Lehman Brothers in September 2008, the biggest bankruptcy in US history. The report stated that in late 2007 and 2008, Lehman Brothers had used sale and repurchase transactions at the end of each financial quarter in order to reduce the leverage (gearing) in its reported balance sheet. Normally, sale and repurchase transactions, or repos, are accounted for as short-term loans and the liability to repay the loan is included in debts in the balance sheet. The special transactions used by Lehman, known to the bank as repo 105 transactions, were treated as sales of securities. The cash received from these 'sales' (rather than 'loans') was used to pay off other debts. The result was that Lehman's reported balance sheet showed fewer assets and fewer liabilities than was the actual case in reality. Soon after the end of the financial quarter, Lehman had to borrow more money to pay back the cash received from the repo transactions, with interest. The bank did not disclose its use of these transactions, or its method of accounting for them, in its published accounts.

Critics of Lehman Brothers argued that the bank had deliberately manipulated its financial statements to mislead investors about its actual financial condition. In response, lawyers for former Lehman executives argued that the financial reporting was within the rules. The bank's accounts had been audited by Ernst & Young, who saw no problem with what the bank was showing in its accounts, and who stated that the bank's accounting methods were consistent with generally accepted accounting principles. The bank had also obtained a letter from UK law firm Linklaters stating that its scheme was 'legal' under British law.

Critics were therefore arguing that the accounting practices of the bank were intended to deceive investors and that the directors of the bank and the bank's auditors were culpable. The counterargument was that everything the bank did was within the rules, and no one should be made liable.

1.2 Accountability and transparency

Producing the annual report and accounts is the main way in which a company's directors are held accountable to shareholders and other stakeholders. The information in the report and accounts is used to assess the success of the company and the effectiveness of its board.

It is therefore essential that the report and accounts should give a clear presentation of the position and performance of the company. In other words, there should be transparency in reporting by companies, so that the recipients of the reports can see what the company has achieved and assess what is likely to happen in the future.

The UK Corporate Governance Code states as a main principle that: 'The board should present a fair, balanced and understandable assessment of the company's position and prospects' in its report and accounts and in its interim reports and other public statements. This principle applies to narrative reporting in the annual report as well as to the financial statements.

Unfortunately, annual reports and accounts have acquired a reputation, in many cases, for lack of transparency and clarity. Reports have increased substantially in length over recent years, and increased length has often been associated with increased obscurity.

1.3 Misleading financial statements

There are several ways, however, in which published financial statements could be misleading.

■ There could be a fraudulent misrepresentation of the affairs of the company, where the company's management deliberately presents a false picture of the financial position and performance.

■ The company might use accounting policies whereby it presents its reported position and profits more favourably than would be the case if more conservative accounting policies were used.

■ The financial statements could be complex and difficult for investors to understand. It is a relatively easy matter for accountants, particularly in companies whose business is itself quite complex, to present financial statements in a way that readers will find difficult to comprehend properly.

Occasionally, some companies may want to report strong growth in revenues and profits, or even to improve the look of the balance sheet (statement of financial position) by 'hiding' debts or other liabilities. The company could probably succeed in presenting an excessively favourable picture of its performance for a number of years, particularly when the economy is strong and business is growing. Eventually, however, it becomes impossible to 'massage' the figures any further. Unless the business can sustain a strong 'real' growth in its operations, it cannot achieve strong profits growth indefinitely. Eventually, a company that uses 'creative accounting' methods will have to report declining profits or re-state the accounts for previous financial years and disclose hitherto hidden losses.

Improving the reported financial position, at least in the short term, shows the board of directors in a favourable light and helps to boost the share price. Individual directors could therefore stand to benefit from higher annual bonuses and more valuable share options.

1.4 Ways of window dressing financial reports

There are several ways in which a company might improve its reported financial position or reported performance and so window dress its financial statements. The methods used may sometimes be deliberately incorrect. More often, a company may use accounting policies that are acceptable to the auditors, but succeed in giving a flattering picture of the company's position.

■ A company may claim to earn revenue and profits earlier than it probably should. For example, a company that enters into a three-year contract that will earn £12 million in total might try to claim all the revenue of £12 million in the first year instead of spreading the revenue over the three-year life of the contract.
■ A company may try to take debts off its balance sheet. This can sometimes be achieved by setting up separate companies known as 'special purpose vehicles'.
■ A company may try to disguise money from loans as operating income, to increase its reported cash flow from operating activities.
■ A company may over-value assets that it owns, either to increase its reported balance sheet reserves or avoid writing off a fall in value as a loss in its income statement.

The following examples of investor concerns about financial statements and company announcements are from the period of stock market turmoil in the US during mid-2002. In each of these examples, concerns about the accuracy of financial reporting helped to undermine investor confidence in companies, because the financial report and accounts remain the principal method of communication between a public company and the investment community. If the report and accounts can't be trusted, what can?

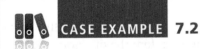 **CASE EXAMPLE** 7.2

In June 2002, US telecommunications company WorldCom announced a huge $3.8 billion accounting fraud. The Justice Department launched a criminal investigation. The nature of the fraud was apparently quite simple. WorldCom had incurred running costs of $3.8 billion that had been accounted for as capital expenditure. Instead of charging the expenses against profits, the cost had therefore been capitalised and reported as assets in the balance sheet, even though no assets existed.

Another consequence of this fraud was that the company's reported cash flows looked much better than they actually were. Investment analysts judged the strength of the cash flows of telecommunications companies according to the cash generated by their business operations, and disregarded cash spent on capital expenditure, which was seen as necessary for growing capital-intensive businesses such as WorldCom. By reporting running costs as capital expenditure, the company therefore improved the look of its cash flows by $3.8 billion.

CASE EXAMPLE 7.2 *continued*

When WorldCom announced its accounting fraud, its auditors Arthur Andersen tried to lay the blame on the company's chief financial officer (CFO) who, Andersen claimed, had withheld important information from them, preventing them from carrying out their audit properly. The fraud had been discovered by an internal auditor of the company in a routine audit check, and not by a member of the external audit team. Questions were raised, however, about the quality of the external audit: for a transaction of such a large size, it should be expected that the auditors would want to know what it was for and satisfy themselves that it had been accounted for properly.

1.5 FRC review of corporate reporting and audit, 2011

In 2011, the Financial Reporting Council (FRC) produced a report: 'Effective Company Stewardship: Enhancing Corporate Reporting and Audit'. This report was the outcome of a review by the FRC into the lessons that could be learned for financial reporting and audit from the global financial crisis in banking in 2007–2009. The FRC made several recommendations, stating that its aim was to increase transparency in the way that directors report their company's activities, including their management of risk.

The report referred to several studies that had been published, criticising the quality of company reporting.

- A 2011 report by Deloitte stated that company reports and accounts for listed companies were 41% longer than in 2005 and on average were over 100 pages long.
- While a different report in 2009 by Black Sun found that 40% of companies failed to report any non-financial key performance indicators, and although the quantity of reporting on corporate social responsibility had increased, the quality of the material was generally poor since it did not explain how corporate social responsibility (CSR) was an integral part of the company's business.
- Black Sun also found that most narrative reporting on risk was a list of 'boilerplate disclosures' that did not provide meaningful information about the potential impact of risks or what the company was doing to mitigate them.
- Narrative reporting on corporate governance was also mainly a 'box-ticking exercise'.

The stated aims of the FRC were set out in 'Effective Company Stewardship'. The stated aims of the FRC were as follows.

- There should be higher quality narrative reporting, particularly on business strategy and risk management.
- The annual report should communicate high-quality and relevant narrative and financial information to the market.
- Directors should take full responsibility for ensuring that an annual report, viewed as a whole, provides a fair and balanced report on their stewardship of the business.
- Directors should describe in more detail the steps that they take to ensure the reliability of the information on which the management of a company, and therefore the directors' stewardship, is based, and transparency about the activities of the business and any associated risks.

The FRC also wanted to enhance the profile of the audit committee, whose role is described later in this chapter. Its aims for the audit committee were:

- More widespread recognition of the importance of audit committees, and greater emphasis on their contribution to the integrity of financial reporting.
- Greater transparency in the way that audit committees discharge their responsibilities in relation to the integrity of the annual report, including oversight of the external auditors.

TEST YOUR KNOWLEDGE 7.1

In what ways might financial statements be misleading to shareholders and other investors?

2 Financial reporting: directors' duties and responsibilities

2.1 Legal duties of directors for financial reporting: UK law

The company's directors are responsible for the preparation and content of the financial statements.

The directors of a company have certain legal duties with regard to financial reporting. The duties set out below relate to UK law.

- Companies must prepare an annual report and accounts and, in the case of a parent company, consolidated accounts for the group (Companies Act 2006 (CA2006)). The accounts must be approved by the board and signed on behalf of the board by a director.
- Directors have a duty to prepare a directors' report, which must also be approved by the board and signed on its behalf by a director or the company secretary. Unless the company is subject to the small companies' regime, the directors' report must contain a strategic report. The strategic report is described in more detail later in this chapter.
- The directors of a quoted company have a duty to prepare a directors' remuneration report, which must be approved by the board and signed on its behalf by a director or the company secretary. This report is explained in Chapter 6.
- These accounts and reports of a public company must be laid before the shareholders in a general meeting and the shareholders of a quoted company must be invited to approve the company's remuneration policy (in a binding vote) and approve the directors' remuneration report or implementation report (in an advisory vote).
- In respect of each financial year, the directors must file with the Registrar of Companies a copy of the annual accounts, the directors' report, the auditors' report and, in the case of quoted companies, the directors' remuneration report.

2.2 Responsibilities of the directors for financial reporting

There is sometimes confusion and misunderstanding about responsibilities for financial reporting, and a mistaken belief that the external auditors are responsible for the 'true and fair view' in the financial statements. If misleading and incorrect financial statements are produced, it may therefore be supposed that the auditors have been negligent and must be to blame. This view is incorrect. The directors are responsible for the financial statements: they prepare the financial statements and have the primary responsibility for the reliability of the information they provide.

- Management and the directors are therefore responsible for identifying and correcting any errors or misrepresentations in the financial statements.
- The responsibility of the external auditors is to obtain reasonable assurance, in their professional opinion, that the financial statements are free from material error or misstatement. They present a professional opinion to the shareholders, not to the directors of the company, and the directors should not rely on the opinion of the external auditors in reaching their own view.

In UK law the directors are also potentially liable for any errors or misleading information in the annual report and accounts. Any person (for example, an investor) suffering a loss as a consequence of an error or mis-statement in a company's report and accounts may sue the company, and the company may then take legal action against the directors to recover any losses it has incurred from the legal action.

2.3 Directors' responsibilities for financial reporting: UK Corporate Governance Code requirements

As stated earlier, a main principle in the UK Code is that the directors should present a fair, balanced and understandable assessment of the company's position and prospects.

A supporting principle is that the board should establish arrangements that will enable it to ensure that the information presented is fair, balanced and understandable. An associated UK Code provision states that the directors should explain in the annual report their responsibility for preparing the annual report and financial statements. They should also state that they consider the annual report and accounts, taken as a whole:

- to be fair, balanced and understandable; and
- to provide the information necessary for shareholders to assess the company's performance, business model and strategy.

There should also be a supporting statement by the auditors (in their report) about their reporting responsibilities.

The UK Code refers to the requirement to provide information to shareholders, rather than to all users of reports and accounts. This is to be consistent with the Companies Act, and is also based on the assumption that the information required by shareholders is also appropriate for other users of reports and accounts.

The UK Code also requires that the directors should include in their annual report an explanation of the:

- basis on which the company generates or preserves value over the longer term (its 'business model'); and
- strategy for delivering the objectives of the company.

The directors should also report, in both the half-yearly and the annual financial statements:

- whether they consider it appropriate for the company to adopt the going concern basis of accounting, when preparing the financial statements; and also
- identify any material uncertainties about the company's ability to do so over a period of at least 12 months from the date of their approval of the financial statements.

The meaning of these 'going concern' provisions is explained later.

 STOP AND THINK 7.2

Do you know what 'business model' means?

There isn't an exact definition, but a business model provides a description or explanation of how a company seeks to create value from its business. A business models should therefore include an explanation of how a company makes and distributes its products (or delivers its services), and how it prices them and markets them, It may also include a description of how the company distinguishes itself from competitors. Business models therefore provide an insight into a company's business strategy.

 STOP AND THINK 7.3

The responsibility of the board for providing a fair assessment of the company's financial position and prospects may seem obvious, but in practice there may be difficulties in fulfilling this responsibility adequately. This is because of the nature of the report and accounts.

The FRC report 'Effective Company Stewardship' commented that financial reporting has moved substantially away from reporting assets and liabilities at their historical cost.

Some assets and liabilities are reported at their market value, rather than at cost. Although this change has improved the value of accounts – historical numbers are easy to obtain but often meaningless – it has increased their complexity and requires companies and auditors to exercise significantly greater judgement. As a result, the reliability of financial statements is now more dependent on:

- the approach that the company takes to establishing the current values of assets and liabilities; and
- the quality of the external audit.

2.4 Going concern statement

A key accounting concept is the 'going concern' concept. This is the view that the company will continue to trade for the foreseeable future (at least the next 12 months). The financial statements are therefore prepared on this basis, and assets are valued differently from what their value might be on a break-up basis (in a fire sale, if the company went into liquidation).

There are several rules or guidelines that require the directors to make a **going concern statement** in the annual report. This is a statement that in their opinion the company is a going concern and will continue to be so for at least the next year.

- The UK Listing Rules (refer back to Chapter 2) require the directors of listed companies to make a statement in the report and accounts that the company is a going concern, together with supporting assumptions and qualifications as necessary.
- For other companies, there are requirements in both international and UK accounting standards that the directors should satisfy themselves that it is reasonable for them to conclude that the company is a going concern, so that the financial statements can be prepared on a going concern basis.
- The UK Corporate Governance Code includes a similar provision that the directors should state in the company's annual and half-yearly financial statements whether they consider it appropriate to adopt the going concern basis for accounting.

A typical going concern statement within a corporate report might be as follows:

'The directors, on the basis of current financial projections and facilities available, have a reasonable expectation that the company and group have adequate resources to continue in operational existence for the foreseeable future. The directors accordingly continue to adopt the going concern basis in the preparation of the group's financial statements.'

It may seem that if a company is unlikely to survive for the next 12 months, it should not adopt the going concern basis for accounting; and if it can be expected to survive for at least 12 months, it should use the going concern basis. However, the accounting rules are not quite so straightforward. As a result, in addition to the provision about the going concern basis of accounting, the UK Code contains another provision (which is part of the Risk Management and Internal control section of the Code) which focuses more specifically on the risks that may threaten the company's future.

This provision states that: 'Taking account of the company's current position and principal risks, the directors should explain in the annual report how they have assessed the prospects of the company, over what period they have done so and why they consider that period to be appropriate. The directors should state whether they have a reasonable expectation that the company will be able to continue in operation and meet its liabilities as they fall due over the period of their assessment, drawing attention to any qualifications or assumptions as necessary.'

TEST YOUR KNOWLEDGE 7.2

What is a going concern statement?

3 The role of the external auditors: the audit report

Investors, creditors and other stakeholders in a company rely on the information contained in the annual report and accounts, which are audited each year by a firm of independent auditors. The purpose of an independent audit is to make sure, as far as reasonably possible, that the financial statements are objective and can be relied on.

After completing their annual audit, the auditors are required to prepare a report to the shareholders of the company, which is included in the published report and accounts of public companies. The audit report has two main purposes:

- to give an expert and independent opinion on whether the financial statements give a true and fair view of the financial position of the company as at the end of the financial year covered by the report, and of its financial performance during the year; and
- to give an expert and independent opinion on whether the financial statements comply with the relevant laws.

In the UK, auditors of listed companies are also required to review the company's compliance with the UK Corporate Governance Code, and to obtain evidence to support the company's statement (in the annual report and accounts) of its compliance with the Code.

3.1 The purpose of the external audit

The audit report is contained in the company's annual report and accounts, and is addressed by the auditors to the shareholders of the company. The main purpose of the audit report is to give the users of a company's financial statements (and in particular the shareholders) some reassurance that the information in the statements is believable and that the financial statements present a 'true and fair view' of the company's financial position and performance. The opinion of the auditors should be the opinion of independent professional experts, based on an investigation of the company's control systems, accounting systems and financial/business transactions.

3.2 Responsibility for detecting errors and fraud

Shareholders would probably like to assume that if the auditors provide a favourable audit report, the financial statements must be 'correct', and there has not been any fraud or error that has resulted in:

- incorrect use of accounting policies;
- omissions of fact; or
- misinterpretation of fact.

'Fraud' is intentional; 'error' is unintentional: both lead to incorrect figures in the financial statements, if they have not been discovered.

This view is based on the belief that if professional accountants have checked the figures, they must be correct – unless the accountants have been negligent and have failed to do their job properly. However, it is a popular misconception that the auditor is responsible for detecting fraud or error in a company's financial statements. This is not the case.

- The board of directors is responsible for preventing fraud in their company, or detecting fraud if it occurs. The company's system of internal control, described in Chapter 10, should be designed to limit the risk of fraud and error, and the board is responsible for monitoring the effectiveness of the internal control system. The responsibility of the board (with delegated responsibility of management) for the prevention and detection of fraud and error is a core principle of corporate governance. The directors are fully accountable to the shareholders and so are fully responsible for the information presented in the annual report and accounts.
- It is not the primary responsibility of the external auditors to detect fraud. The auditors will assess the risk or possibility that fraud or error might have caused the financial statements to be materially misleading. The auditors should therefore design audit procedures that will provide reasonable reassurance that material fraud or error has not occurred, and that the financial statements give a true and fair view of the company's financial position and performance. The external audit might also act as a deterrent to fraud, because the auditors will carry out checks of control procedures, documents and transactions in the course of their audit work. They might discover fraud during the course of their audit work, in which case it would be their responsibility to report the matter to the directors (unless the fraud is carried out by the directors themselves).

No matter how well an audit is planned and carried out, there will always be some risk that fraud or error has occurred but not been detected. Given the nature of auditing, for which there is only a limited amount of time and resources, and which is carried out through a process of sampling and testing, it would be impossible to ensure that all errors are detected. Accounting systems and internal control procedures are also vulnerable to fraud and error, arising for example from:

■ criminal collusion between employees; and
■ decisions by management to override the system of controls.

An area for dispute, however, is whether the auditors ought to be able to identify fraud or a significant error during the course of their audit work, whenever a fraud or error occurs. Although they are not responsible for the financial statements, it can be argued that a failure by the auditors to discover a major fraud or material error might be the result of professional negligence. If they are negligent, they should be held liable to the company and its shareholders. Uncertainty about the extent to which auditors might be held liable for professional negligence has led to new rules in the UK CA2006 that enable companies to limit auditor liability.

3.3 Criminal liability of auditors for recklessness

Although CA2006 provides the possibility of some protection for auditors against liability for negligence or breach of duty (with so-called limited liability agreements) it also introduced two new criminal offences for auditors in connection with the auditors' report. It is a criminal offence, punishable by a fine, to:

■ knowingly or recklessly cause an audit report to 'include any matter that is misleading, false or deceptive in any material particular'; or
■ knowingly or recklessly cause an audit report to omit a statement that is required by certain specified sections of the act.

3.4 Auditors' liability to third parties (other stakeholders)

The auditors have a legal duty of care to the company and its shareholders. There is some doubt as to whether they might also have a duty of care to other parties. In the UK, the extent of auditor liability to external parties was tested in two legal cases. In response to the outcome of the Bannerman case, PricewaterhouseCoopers decided to include a disclaimer of liability to third parties using its audit reports. In January 2003, the Institute of Chartered Accountants in England and Wales recommended the inclusion of a disclaimer in audit reports.

A disclaimer within the audit report might be worded as follows:

'This report, including the opinions, has been prepared for and only for the company's members as a body in accordance with ... the Companies Act 2006 and for no other purpose. We do not, in giving this opinion, accept or assume responsibility for any other purpose or to any other person to whom this report is shown or into whose hands it may come save where expressly agreed by our prior consent in writing.'

3.5 Unmodified and modified audit reports

Auditors' reports may be unmodified or modified. Nearly all of them in practice are unmodified.

 SAMPLE WORDING 7.1

Unmodified audit report

An unmodified audit report states that in the opinion of the auditors, the company's financial statements present a true and fair view of the financial performance of the company during the reporting year, and its financial position as at the end of the year. The wording of an unmodified audit report is usually fairly standard, although reports are longer for public companies (where the auditors might also report on some corporate governance statements) and differ between countries.

SAMPLE WORDING **7.1** *continued*

An unmodified audit report may include an 'emphasis of matter' paragraph. Although the audit report is not modified, and the auditors consider that the financial statements present a true and fair view, there is an item that the auditor wants to bring to the attention of users because it is of some importance for an understanding of the statements. Even so, the financial statements present a 'true and fair view'.

Here is a simplified example of a typical unmodified audit report.

Report on the financial statements

We have audited the accompanying financial statements of XYZ Company, which comprise the statement of financial position as at 31 December 20XX, and the statement of comprehensive income, statement of changes in equity, and cash flows for the year then ended, and a summary of significant accounting policies and other explanatory notes.

Management's responsibility for the financial statements

Management is responsible for the preparation and fair presentation of these financial statements in accordance with IFRS. This responsibility includes: designing, implementing and maintaining internal control relevant to the preparation and fair presentation of financial statements that are free from material mis-statement, whether due to fraud or error; selecting and applying appropriate accounting policies; and making accounting estimates that are reasonable in the circumstances.

Auditor's responsibility

Our responsibility is to express an opinion on these financial statements based on our audit. We conducted our audit in accordance with International Standards on Auditing. Those standards require that we comply with ethical requirements and plan and perform the audit to obtain reasonable assurance whether the financial statements are free from material mis-statement.

An audit involves performing procedures to obtain audit evidence about the amounts and disclosures in the financial statements. The procedures selected depend on the auditor's judgement, including the assessment of the risks of material mis-statement of the financial statements, whether due to fraud or error. In making those risk assessments, the auditor considers internal control relevant to the entity's preparation and fair presentation of the financial statements in order to design audit procedures that are appropriate in the circumstances, but not for the purpose of expressing an opinion on the effectiveness of the entity's internal control. An audit also includes evaluating the appropriateness of accounting policies used and the reasonableness of accounting estimates made by management, as well as evaluating the overall presentation of the financial statements.

We believe that the audit evidence that we have obtained is sufficient and appropriate to provide a basis for our audit opinion.

Opinion

In our opinion, the financial statements give a true and fair view (or present fairly, in all material respects) of the financial position of XYZ Company as at 31 December 20XX, and of its financial performance and its cash flows for the year then ended in accordance with IFRS.

Report on other legal and regulatory requirements

(Form and content of this section of the report will vary depending on the nature of the auditor's other reporting responsibilities.) Signed: (Auditor)

3.6 The significance of a modified audit report

An audit report may be modified. It is unusual for auditors to present a **modified audit report**. When this happens, there is a potentially serious problem with the financial statements and, by implication, the financial condition of the company. It also means that the auditors have been unable to agree with the directors of the company about what information the financial statements should contain. Because the directors and the auditors cannot agree, the auditors have considered it necessary to give a statement to shareholders to this effect. There are three types of modified audit opinion:

- a qualified opinion;
- an adverse opinion; and
- a disclaimer of opinion.

A qualified audit opinion is sometimes called an 'except for' opinion. It is given when, in the opinion of the auditor, the financial statements would give a true and fair view except for a particular matter, which the auditor explains.

An adverse opinion is given when the auditor considers that there are material mis-statements in the accounts and that these are 'pervasive'. In effect, the auditor is stating that the figures in the accounts are seriously wrong.

A disclaimer of opinion is given in cases where the auditor has been unable to obtain the information that they need to give an audit opinion. The lack of information means that the auditor is unable to state that the financial statements give a true and fair view, and that there may possibly be serious mis-statements that the auditor has been unable to check.

In the rare circumstances that the auditors give a modified audit report to the shareholders, a situation has arisen where professional accountants have given an opinion that the shareholders cannot trust the information that has been given to them by the directors. If the shareholders cannot trust the directors, the quality of corporate governance could hardly be lower.

A criticism that could be made of external audits is that they rarely result in a modified report. When companies continue successfully in business, this should normally be expected. Unfortunately, there have been occasional instances where a company has revealed serious financial difficulties after having issued an annual report with an unmodified audit opinion. Incidents such as this raise questions about the effectiveness of the audit.

TEST YOUR KNOWLEDGE 7.3

a What is the purpose of the external audit?

b Who is responsible for detecting fraud or errors in financial statements?

c Who is responsible for detecting fraudulent activity within the company, by some of its employees or others?

d What are the responsibilities of the external auditors with regard to the financial statements of a company?

e What types of audit opinion might be given in an audit report? What is the significance of a modified audit opinion?

4 Independence of the external auditors

The external auditor should be independent of the client company, so that the audit opinion will not be influenced by the relationship between the auditor and the company. The auditors are expected to give an unbiased and honest professional opinion to the shareholders about the financial statements. An unmodified audit report is often seen by investors as a 'clean bill of health' for the company. However, doubts are sometimes expressed about the independence of the external auditors. It could be argued that unless suitable corporate governance measures are in place, a firm of auditors may reach audit opinions and judgements that are heavily influenced by their wish to maintain good relations with the management of a client company. If this happens, the auditors are no longer independent and the shareholders cannot rely on their opinion.

For example, an official 2010 report on the collapse of Lehman Brothers (in the US in 2008) criticised the external auditors Ernst & Young for allowing the company to account for certain transactions (repo 105 transactions) in a way that misleadingly improved the look of the end-of-quarter balance sheets during 2007 and 2008, in the months before the bank eventually collapsed.

 **CASE EXAMPLE 7.3**

The energy corporation Enron, which had been one of the largest corporations in the world by stock market value, collapsed towards the end of 2001. In January 2002, the company's auditor, Arthur Andersen, announced that its employees had shredded documents relating to Enron after it had received a subpoena from the SEC in November 2001. This announcement was part of a chain of events that led to Arthur Andersen being prosecuted for its role in the Enron affair.

In June 2002, Arthur Andersen was found guilty by a US court of obstructing justice during investigations into the collapse of Enron. The Enron scandal and the alleged role of Arthur Andersen prompted moves in both the US and the UK to review accounting and auditing standards. Arthur Andersen subsequently lost major clients quickly and the firm collapsed. It was subsequently alleged that the Houston office of the firm, which conducted the annual audit of Enron, was not independent of its client and relied on Enron for a large proportion of its annual fee income.

4.1 Ethics and the accounting profession

Auditors provide an independent professional opinion about whether the financial statements of a company provide a true and fair view, and users of the financial statements, including shareholders, rely on that opinion. The annual report and accounts are the main document through which the directors are accountable to the shareholders. It is therefore extremely important for corporate governance that the opinion of the auditors should be trusted – which means that the auditors must be independent, and must be seen to be independent of the companies whose accounts they audit.

Like other professionals, qualified accountants are expected by their professional body to act with integrity and honesty, and to follow a code of ethics in the work they do. However, there can be pressure on accountants to ignore ethical considerations and to allow their judgement to be affected by other considerations. These pressures might apply both to accountants in industry as well as those in the profession acting as auditors.

4.2 Threats to auditor independence

Perhaps the most significant threat to auditor independence is that the audit firm relies on the company's management to secure its appointment and reappointment as the company's auditor. Although companies may give their audit committee responsibility for recommending the appointment of the auditors, the opinions of senior management are often decisive in the matter of auditor selection. The auditor is therefore reliant for future audit work from the company on the views of the management whose financial statements it is their job to audit. In addition, the audit firm has to rely extensively on management for the information and explanations needed to enable them to carry out their audit work.

The accounting profession has to be aware of its integrity and reputation, and there are strong codes of ethical behaviour and professional conduct that accounting firms and individual members of the accounting profession are required to comply with.

Professional guidelines are given to auditors by national and international accountancy bodies, notably the International Federation of Accountants (IFAC). The IFAC Code of Ethics for Professional Accountants 2006 identifies certain ways in which the integrity, objectivity and independence of the auditors might be put at risk.

An audit firm should not have to rely on a single company for a large proportion of its total fee income, because undue dependence on a single audit client could impair objectivity. IFAC does not specify what amounts to 'undue dependence' on a single client.

- A risk to objectivity and independence arises when the audit firm or anyone closely associated with it (such as an audit partner) has a mutual business interest with the company or any of its officers. Similarly, objectivity could be threatened when there is a close personal relationship between a member of the audit firm and an employee of the company.
- The audit firm should not have a client company in which a partner holds a significant number of shares.
- The IFAC Code does not have any objection in principle to an audit firm providing non-audit services (such as consultancy services) to a client, although the auditor should not perform any management functions in a company nor take any management decisions.

The audit profession has identified potential threats to auditor independence. Auditors are required to be aware of these threats, and to take measures to eliminate them or reduce them to an insignificant level. However, it is appropriate for companies (and audit committees) to be aware that these threats exist.

- **Self-interest threat**. This is the threat that an auditor or audit firm is earning such a large amount of fee income from the audit and non-audit work that its judgement will be affected by a desire to protect this income stream. For example, if the audit firm earns a large proportion of its revenue from a client company, it may be unwilling to annoy that client by challenging the figures and assumptions used by management to prepare the company's financial statements.
- **Self-review threat**. This can arise when the audit firm does non-audit work for the company, and the annual audit involves checking the work done by the firm's own employees. The auditors may not be as critical of the work, or prepared to challenge it, because this would raise questions about the professional competence of the audit firm. For this reason, the accountancy profession has an ethical rule that firms must not take on non-audit work that may be the subject of future audit by its staff.
- **Advocacy threat**. This can arise if the audit firm is asked to give its formal support to the company by providing public statements on particular issues (such as promoting a new issue of shares by the company) or supporting the company in a legal case. Acting as advocate for a company means taking sides, and this implies a loss of independence. The **accountancy** profession therefore has an ethical rule that firms should not take on any non-audit work in which they may be required to act as 'advocate' for the client.
- **Familiarity threat**. A threat to independence occurs when an auditor is familiar with a company or one of its directors or senior managers, or becomes familiar with them through a working association over time. Familiarity leads to trust and a willingness to believe what the other person says, without carrying out an investigation into its accuracy or honesty. The auditor will also be unwilling to think that the other person is capable of making a serious error or committing fraud. A familiarity threat may also arise through personal association (for example, family connections) and through long association with the company and its management.
- **Intimidation threat**. An auditor may feel threatened by the directors or senior management of a company. For example, a company CEO or finance director may act aggressively and in a bullying manner towards audit staff, so that the auditors are browbeaten into accepting what the 'bully' is telling them. Both real and imagined threats can affect the auditor's independence. A company may also threaten to take away the audit or stop giving the firm non-audit work unless the auditor accepts the opinions of management.

In practice, the threats to auditor independence are most likely to be self-interest threats, familiarity threats and, possibly, intimidation threats.

Threats to auditor independence must be identified, and measures should be taken to limit the threat to an acceptable level of risk. This is a professional requirement for audit firms, but companies should also be aware of the need to ensure the independence of their auditors and take appropriate measures. Three areas of debate about how to ensure auditor independence have been:

- whether auditors should be prevented from carrying out non-audit work for clients, or whether the amount of non-audit work they do should be restricted;
- whether there should be a regular rotation of either the audit firm or the audit partner and other senior members of the audit team; and
- whether companies should put their audit out to tender on a regular basis.

4.3 Non-audit work for a client by an audit firm

The codes of conduct of national professional accountancy bodies are similar to the IFAC Code and lack any clear restrictions on the performance of non-audit work for an audit client. Suggestions for regulatory measures to ensure auditor independence have included proposals to restrict the amount of non-audit work, or the type of non-audit work, that the firm of auditors is permitted to carry out for a client company. Non-audit work might include:

- consultancy on taxation issues; for example, helping a group of companies to minimise tax;
- liabilities by setting up subsidiaries in countries with a low-tax regime;
- investigating targets for a potential takeover bid;
- helping a company to construct a bid for a major government contract;
- providing advice and expert assistance on IT systems;
- internal audit services;
- valuation and actuarial services;
- services relating to litigation; and
- services relating to recruitment and remuneration.

The main problem with auditors doing non-audit work is that when the firm audits transactions recommended by its consultancy arm, it is unlikely to take an independent view.

The risk to auditor objectivity and independence from carrying out non-audit work became apparent in the wake of the Enron collapse, which has been described previously. Arthur Andersen was the auditor of Enron, and in the financial year prior to the company's collapse in 2001, they earned more fee income from Enron for non-audit work than from audit work. The audit firm was suspected of failing to carry out a proper audit of the company, with two main reasons being suggested.

1 It was claimed that the audit firm would have been reluctant to question the accounts of Enron because it would risk losing not just the audit work but also the substantial non-audit fee income.
2 In addition, it was suggested that since the information in the company's financial statements reflected the non-audit consultancy advice given by the audit firm, the firm's auditors would be unlikely to challenge the fairness and accuracy of the statements. In other words, Andersen's auditors would not challenge the opinions of Andersen's consultants.

Audit firms have denied that fees from non-audit work will affect their independence, arguing that the individuals who work as consultants for a client company (e.g. on IT projects) are not the same individuals who work on the company audit. Even so, activist shareholder groups continue to challenge this assertion. In the UK, a well-reported attempt was made several years ago (2002) by some institutional shareholders to vote against the reappointment of Deloitte as auditors to Vodafone at the AGM of the company. The 'dissidents' argued their case on the grounds that the audit firm did too much non-audit work for the company and so could not be considered sufficiently independent.

4.4 Approaches to the regulation of non-audit work

There are three broad approaches to the regulation of non-audit work by audit firms.

1 There should be no restrictions at all on non-audit work by the audit firm.
2 There should be a total prohibition on non-audit work for a corporate client by the audit firm.
3 There should be a partial prohibition on non-audit work for a corporate client by the audit firm. This could take either of two forms. There could be a prohibition on audit firms from taking on certain types of consultancy work where their independence as auditors could be put at risk; for example, tax planning advice work. However, audit firms would be free to carry out other types of non-audit work. The second approach to restricting non-audit work would be to set a limit on the amount of fees an audit firm could earn from non-audit work, expressed perhaps as a proportion of the fees it earns from the audit. For example, a limit might be imposed restricting non-audit fees to, say, 50% of the fees from the audit work.

The difficulty with a partial restriction on non-audit work is that rules have to be devised and agreed as to what permissible and non-permissible non-audit work should be, or what the maximum amount of non-audit fee income should be.

In the UK, the audit profession is governed by ethical principles rather than rules and regulations about non-audit work for audit clients. The Institute of Chartered Accountants in England and Wales (ICAEW) has made the following statements about non-audit work.

'The most effective way to ensure the reality of independence is to provide guidance centred around a framework of principles rather than a detailed set of rules that can be complied with to the letter but circumvented in substance.'

'A blanket prohibition on the provision of non-audit services to audit clients can be inefficient for the client and is neither necessary to ensure independence, nor helpful in contributing to the knowledge necessary to ensure the quality of the audit.'

The need for auditor independence when the audit firm does non-audit work is recognised in the UK Corporate Governance Code. The Code includes a provision that:

'if the external auditor provides non-audit services an explanation of how auditor objectivity and independence are safeguarded.'

In the US, the Sarbanes-Oxley Act 2002 (SOX 2002) introduced restrictions on the types of non-audit work that can be carried out by the audit firm for a client company (ss. 201 and 202). Prohibited services include book-keeping services and other services related to the accounting records or financial statements of the company, the design and implementation of financial information systems, actuarial services, valuation services, internal auditing services (out-sourced to external accountants), legal services, management functions, and broker/dealer or investment advice services. Tax services are specifically permitted by the Act, unless they come within a prohibited category of non-audit services.

4.5 EU regulations on non-audit work

In 2014, the EU introduced new regulations about non-audit work by audit firms, in an EU Audit Directive and Regulation. This applies to 'EU public interest entity audit clients' (mainly listed companies in the EU).

The regulation, which came into force from 17 June 2016:

- restricts the amount of non-audit work that audit firms can undertake from these clients to no more than 70% of the average fees from audit work over the previous three financial years; and
- imposes a ban by audit firms on certain types of non-audit work, including: tax advice; services involving management/decision-making for the client; book-keeping; and designing or implementing internal controls relating to financial information.

At the time of updating this text, it is not yet clear what impact this regulation will have on auditor–client relationships in the EU.

4.6 Directorships for former auditors

Yet another potential threat to auditor independence is the practice whereby public companies appoint a former auditor to their board as CFO/finance director. It could be reasoned that if an auditor sees the possibility of a lucrative promotion to the board of a major public company, they will do nothing to threaten the relationship built up with the management of the company.

ICAEW requirements in this respect are that the acceptance by a key audit partner of a key management position in his or her audit client would be considered to cause an unacceptable threat to the appearance of independence unless a period of at least two years has elapsed since the conclusion of the relevant audit. Thus, if a key audit partner were to join their own client within two years of fulfilling a key partner role on that audit, the audit firm would have to resign from the engagement after the individual concerned has left the audit firm.

The UK Corporate Governance Code also suggests that if a former audit partner is appointed to the board of a company, the individual is unlikely to be considered independent. Independence must be called into question where the director within the previous three years has been a partner or senior employee in any entity that has (or has had) a material business relationship with the company. This includes the company's auditors.

4.7 Rotation of audit partner or audit firm

Another suggestion for protecting auditor independence is that there should be 'rotation' of auditors. After a maximum period of a stated number of years, there should be a change in the auditors. There is an important distinction, however, between the following:

- rotation of audit personnel, whereby the audit engagement partner and other key individuals involved in the annual audit should be removed from the audit after a certain number of years, and new individuals assigned to the work; and
- rotation of an audit firm, whereby a firm is required to give up the audit for a company after a maximum number of years, and the company must appoint different auditors.

Audit partner rotation

An argument put forward by the major accountancy firms is that the requirement for rotation should apply, not to the firm of auditors, but to the individual partner of a firm in charge of the audit. For example, it might be acceptable for ABC Corporation to retain the services of Ernst & Young indefinitely, provided that the partner in charge of the company audit is replaced every, say, five or seven years. Supporters of this argument claim that the independence of the audit is threatened by the personal relationship an audit partner builds up with the client company, not the length of association of the audit firm with the company.

In the case of large companies, there is also an argument for a regular rotation of other senior audit managers, as well as the lead partner.

A counter-argument, however, is that audit partner rotation would not have prevented the problem that arose between Andersen and its clients Enron and WorldCom. Although Andersen as a whole was not over-dependent on Enron, the company was a vital client for the firm's Houston office, which carried out the audit. Similarly, the Andersen office in Jackson, Mississippi was heavily dependent on the work that it did for WorldCom. To prevent loss of audit independence, audit partner rotation would almost certainly have been ineffective, whereas audit firm rotation might have been much more effective.

Current requirements in the UK for audit partner rotation are contained in Ethical Standard 3 Long Association with the Audit Engagement 2009, issued by the Auditing Practices Board (a part of the FRC). This states that the lead audit partner (the 'audit engagement partner') should be rotated at least every five years (or up to seven years in circumstances where the audit committee believes this is necessary to maintain audit quality and the extension is disclosed to shareholders). Other audit partners involved in the audit of a company should be rotated at least every seven years.

Currently, regulations in most countries favour audit partner rotation rather than audit firm rotation.

Rotation of audit firm

Rotation of the audit firm would be a requirement to change the audit form after a given number of years. It has been argued that audit firm rotation would enhance auditor independence because a firm of auditors would have little to gain by going along with the wishes of the client company, and carrying out a less than rigorous audit, if it knows that it will soon lose the audit work anyway. The work of outgoing auditors would also be subject to review – and criticism – by the firm of auditors taking their place.

A disadvantage of **audit firm rotation** is that the incoming firm of auditors might need one or two years to get to know the business of the client company, and might be unable to conduct an audit to the same standard as their predecessor.

The EU in 2014 introduced an Audit Directive and Regulation. The Directive requires the rotation of audit firms for 'EU public interest entities' (European companies). The new rules are explained later.

4.8 Tendering for the annual audit

In the UK, the current requirement is for FTSE 350 companies to put their audit out to tender periodically. Under the UK Corporate Governance Code, since 2012 FTSE 350 companies should retender their audits every ten years. This concept was then taken forward in a Competition and Markets Authority (CMA) Order.

CASE EXAMPLE 7.4

Schroders announced in 2013 that it would be replacing PwC as its auditor with KPMG. PwC had been the company's auditor for 50 years. The audit work is valuable: in 2011 PwC earned £2.7 million for its annual audit work and £1.8 million for other services to the company during the year.

There are other examples of companies changing auditors. For example in August 2014, the banking corporation HSBC announced a change of auditors to PwC from KPMG, which had been the bank's auditors for over 20 years. In April 2014, the London Stock Exchange announced a change of auditors from PwC to EY, the first time it had changed its auditors since it became a public company in 2011.

4.9 EU Audit Directive on mandatory audit firm rotation

In 2014 the EU introduced an Audit Directive, requiring 'EU public interest entities' (which it is easy to think of as large European listed companies) to change their audit firm at least every ten years. The rule will apply from 2016.

There is an option, however, that mandatory rotation is necessary only every 20 years provided that there are rules for annual tendering of the audit every ten years. The UK implementation of the EU statutory audit directive and regulation in 2016 requires a ten-year retendering period for Public Interest Entities (PIEs) and for the first time introduces mandatory rotation of auditors, after a maximum term of 20 years.

TEST YOUR KNOWLEDGE 7.4

a   Give examples of non-audit work for a company by a firm of auditors.
b   What are the five categories of threats to auditor independence?
c   What is the difference between audit firm rotation and audit partner rotation?

5   The audit committee

The UK Corporate Governance Code requires that a board of directors should establish formal and transparent arrangements for:

- considering how they should apply the corporate reporting and risk management and internal control principles; and
- maintaining an appropriate relationship with the company's auditors.

These arrangements should be met by establishing an audit committee, which should be given certain responsibilities by the board.

The role of the audit committee in applying the principles of risk management and **internal audit** is described in Chapters 9 and 10; this chapter concentrates on the role of the audit committee as applying corporate reporting principles and maintaining an appropriate relationship with the external auditors.

5.1 Role and responsibilities of the audit committee

The UK Code lists the role and responsibilities of an audit committee. Excluding those concerned with risk management and internal control, they are as follows:

- To monitor the integrity of the company's financial statements and any formal announcements relating to the company's financial performance. In doing so, it should review 'significant financial judgements' that these statements and announcements contain.

- To make recommendations to the board in relation to the appointment, reappointment or removal of the company's external auditors, to put to the shareholders for approval in a general meeting of the company.
- To approve the remuneration and terms of engagement of the external auditors (after they have been negotiated with the auditors by management).
- To review and monitor the independence of the external auditors, and also the objectivity and effectiveness of the audit process, taking into account relevant UK professional and regulatory requirements.
- To develop and implement the company's policy on using the external auditors to provide non-audit services. This should take into account any relevant external ethical guidance on the subject. The committee should report to the board, identifying actions or improvements that are needed and recommending the steps to be taken.
- To report to the board on how it has discharged its responsibilities.

The terms of reference of the audit committee, including its role and the authority delegated to it by the board, should be 'made available'.

The UK Code also requires the board of directors to provide a fair, balanced and understandable assessment of the company's position and prospects. The board can ask for the audit committee to provide advice on this matter. The UK Code states:

'Where requested by the board, the audit committee should provide advice on whether the annual report and accounts taken as a whole is fair, balanced and understandable and provides the information necessary for shareholders to assess the company's position and performance, business model and strategy.'

The FRC Guidance on Audit Committees 2016 adds that the advice/report from the audit committee to the board 'will inform the board's statement on these matters'. To assist the board to make that statement, any review would need to assess whether other information presented in the annual report is consistent with the financial statements.

5.2 Composition of the audit committee

The UK Code states that an audit committee should consist of at least three members (or at least two members in the case of smaller companies, outside the FTSE 350). All members of the audit committee should be independent non-executive directors (NEDs).

- In FTSE 350 companies, the company chairman should not be a member of the committee.
- In companies outside the FTSE 350, the chairman may be a member of the audit committee (but not chairman of the committee) provided that he was considered independent on appointment as chairman.

The FRC Guidance on Audit Committees states that appointments to the committee should be made by the board on the recommendation of the nomination committee, in consultation with the audit committee chairman.

The UK Corporate Governance Code also states that the board should satisfy itself that at least one member of the committee has 'recent and relevant financial experience'. This individual should ideally have a professional qualification from one of the accountancy bodies, and the degree of financial literacy required from the other committee members will vary according to the nature of the company.

ICSA Guidance note Terms of reference for the audit committee 2013 states that as a matter of good practice, the company secretary should act as secretary to the audit committee.

5.3 Legal requirement for an audit committee: UK law

UK listed companies are required to have an audit committee, following the implementation in 2008 of the requirements of the EU Statutory Audit Directive. This statutory requirement is applied through the FSA's DTR, which also specify the responsibilities of an audit committee. The rules are less onerous and less detailed than the requirements of the UK Corporate Governance Code. However, they are significant because they are an enforceable regulatory requirement implementing an EU Directive.

It is important to note that national laws vary, and not all countries have a legal requirement for listed or quoted companies to have an audit committee. However, a legal requirement exists throughout the EU and also in some other countries, including the US where – under the provisions of the SOX – national securities exchanges are prohibited from listing the securities of any company unless it has an audit committee and complies with certain audit committee requirements – such as the requirement that all committee members must be independent.

5.4 The FRC Guidance on audit committees

In the UK, the FRC's Guidance on Audit Committees 2016 is not obligatory, and boards of directors are not required to comply with it. However, it is intended to assist boards with the implementation of the requirements on audit committees of the UK Code.

The introduction to the Guidance makes the following comments.

- Best practice requires that every board should consider in detail what audit committee arrangements are best suited for its particular circumstances. Audit committee arrangements need to be proportionate to the task, and will vary according to the size, complexity and risk profile of the company.
- While all directors have a duty to act in the interests of the company the audit committee has a particular role, acting independently from the executive, to ensure that the interests of shareholders are properly protected in relation to financial reporting and internal control. However, the board has overall responsibility for an organisation's approach to risk management and internal control and nothing in the guidance should be interpreted as a departure from the principle of the unitary board. Any disagreement within the board, including disagreement between the audit committee's members and the rest of the board, should be resolved at board level.
- The guidance contains recommendations about the conduct of the audit committee's relationship with the board, with the executive management and with internal and external auditors. The essential features of these interactions are a frank, open working relationship and a high level of mutual respect. The audit committee must be prepared to take a robust stand, and all parties must be prepared to make information freely available to the committee, to listen to their views and to talk through the issues openly.
- In particular, the management is under an obligation to ensure the audit committee is kept properly informed, and should take the initiative in supplying information rather than waiting to be asked. The board should make it clear to all directors and staff that they must co-operate with the audit committee and provide it with any information it requires.
- In addition, executive board members will have regard to their duty to provide all directors, including those on the audit committee, with all the information they need to discharge their responsibilities as directors of the company.
- Many of the core functions of audit committees set out in this guidance are expressed in terms of 'oversight', 'assessment' and 'review' of a particular function. It is not the duty of audit committees to carry out functions that properly belong to others, such as the company's management in the preparation of the financial statements or the auditors in the planning or conducting of audits. To do so could undermine the responsibility of management and auditors. However, the audit committee should consider key matters of their own initiative and the oversight function may well lead to detailed work. The audit committee must intervene if there are signs that something may be seriously amiss.
- For groups, it will usually be necessary for the audit committee of the parent company to review issues that relate to particular subsidiaries or activities carried on by the group.
- Consequently, the board of a UK-listed parent company with a Premium listing of equity shares in the UK should ensure that there is adequate cooperation within the group (and with internal and external auditors of individual companies within the group) to enable the parent company audit committee to discharge its responsibilities effectively.

The board should decide just what the role of the audit committee should be, and the terms of reference should be tailored to the company's particular circumstances. However, the audit committee should review its terms of reference and effectiveness annually, and recommend any necessary changes to the board. The board should also review the effectiveness of the audit committee annually. See Chapter 5 for a description of performance evaluation.

5.5 Remuneration, induction and training of committee members

The FRC Guidance comments that the audit committees have wide-ranging, time-consuming work and sometimes intensive to do, and companies should make the necessary resources available. This includes making suitable payments to the members of the audit committee, in view of the responsibilities they have and the time they must commit to the work. The amount of remuneration paid to the audit committee members should take account of the remuneration paid to other members of the board. The committee chairman's responsibilities and time commitments will normally be greater than those of the other committee members, and this should be reflected in his or her remuneration.

The committee should have the support of the company secretary and should have access to the services of the company's secretariat.

Audit committee members must also be given suitable induction and training. Ongoing training should include keeping the committee members up to date on developments in financial reporting and related company law. It may, for example, include understanding financial statements, the application of particular accounting standards, the regulatory framework for the company's business, the role of internal and external auditing, and risk management.

5.6 Audit committee meetings

The audit committee chairman should decide the timing and frequency of committee meetings, in consultation with the company secretary, and there should be as many meetings as the role and responsibilities of the committee require. The FRC Guidance suggests the following:

- There should be no fewer than three committee meetings each year, timed to coincide with key dates in the financial reporting and audit calendar. For example, meetings might be held when the audit plans are available for review and when interim statements, preliminary announcements and the full annual report are near completion. Most audit committee chairmen will probably want to call meetings more.
- Sufficient time should be allowed between audit committee meetings and meetings of the main board to allow any work arising out of the committee meeting to be carried out and reported to the board as appropriate.
- Only the audit committee chairman and members are entitled to attend meetings of the committee. It is for the committee to decide whether other individuals should be invited to attend for a particular meeting or a particular agenda item. It is expected that the audit lead partner and the company's finance director will be invited regularly to attend meetings.
- At least once a year, the audit committee should meet the external and internal auditors, without management being present, to discuss matters relating to its responsibilities and issues arising from the audit.

Formal meetings are at the heart of the work of the audit committee, but meetings alone will rarely be sufficient for the committee chairman (and to a lesser extent, the other committee members). The committee chairman should expect to keep in touch with key people, such as the board chairman, CEO, finance director (CFO), external audit lead partner and the head of internal audit.

5.7 Relationship between the audit committee and the board

The board decides the role of the audit committee and the extent to which they should undertake tasks on behalf of the board, and the committee should report on its activities to the board. The FRC Guidance states that the audit committee should report to the board on how it has discharged its responsibilities including:

- the significant issues that it considers in relation to the financial statements, and how these were addressed;
- its assessment of the effectiveness of the external audit process and its recommendation on the appointment or reappointment of the external auditor; and
- other issues where the board has asked for the audit committee's opinion.

5.8 Financial reporting and the role of the audit committee

The FRC Guidance states that it is the responsibility of management, not the audit committee, to prepare complete and accurate financial statements. It is the responsibility of the audit committee to review the significant financial reporting issues and judgements that are made in connection with these statements, having regard to any matters communicated to the committee by the auditors.

- The audit committee should consider significant accounting policies used to prepare the statements, any changes to them, and any significant estimates or judgements on which the statements have been based.
- Management should inform the committee about the methods they have used to account for significant or unusual transactions, where the accounting treatment is open to different approaches.
- Taking the external auditors' views into consideration, the committee should consider whether the company has adopted appropriate accounting policies and made appropriate estimates and judgements.
- The committee should also consider the clarity and completeness of the disclosures in the financial statements.

If the committee is not satisfied with any aspect of the proposed financial reporting by the company, it should report its views to the board (FRC Guidance). The committee should also review related information presented with the financial statements, including the business review and the corporate governance statements relating to audit and risk management.

5.9 Appointment and removal of external auditors

Under the UK Code, the audit committee is the body responsible for maintaining the company's relations with its external auditors. The Code states that the audit committee has the primary responsibility for making a recommendation to the board on the appointment, reappointment or removal of the external auditors. The assessment should be carried out annually. If the board does not accept this recommendation, it should:

- include in the annual report, and in any papers recommending the appointment or reappointment of the auditors, a statement from the audit committee explaining its recommendation; and
- give reasons why the board has taken a different position.

If the audit committee recommends to the board that new external auditors should be selected, the committee should 'oversee' the selection process (FRC Guidance). The committee's recommendation should be based on the following assessments:

- the qualification and expertise of the auditors;
- the resources of the auditors.

If the external auditors resign, the audit committee should investigate the issues that gave rise to the resignation, and consider whether any action is needed (FRC Guidance).

Terms and remuneration of the auditors

The audit committee should approve the terms of engagement of the external auditors and the remuneration to be paid to the auditors for their audit services (the committee should approve the terms and remuneration, but is not required to negotiate them itself). It should satisfy itself that the amount of the fee payable for the audit services is appropriate, and that an effective audit can be carried out for such a fee. The fee should not be too large, but neither should it be too low. A low audit fee creates a risk that the audit might be of an inadequate scope or quality.

The committee should review and agree the engagement letter issued by the external auditors at the start of each audit, to make sure that it has been updated to reflect any changes in circumstances since the previous year.

The committee should also review the scope of the audit with the auditor. If it is not satisfied that the proposed scope is adequate, the committee should arrange for additional audit work to be undertaken (FRC Guidance).

5.10 Audit committee responsibilities and auditor independence

The UK Corporate Governance Code gives the audit committee the responsibility for monitoring and ensuring the independence of the external auditors. If the external auditors provide non-audit services to the company, the annual report should explain how auditor independence and objectivity are safeguarded.

The audit committee should have procedures for ensuring the independence and objectivity of the external auditors and the effectiveness of the audit process. The FRC Guidance suggests various measures for the committee to take.

- The audit committee should assess the independence and objectivity of the external auditor annually, taking into consideration relevant UK law, regulation, the Ethical Standard and other professional requirements. The audit committee should consider the annual disclosure from the statutory auditor and discuss with the auditor the threats to their independence and the safeguards applied to mitigate those threats. This assessment should involve a consideration of all relationships between the company and the audit firm, including throughout the group and with the audit firm's network firms, and any safeguards established by the external auditor. The audit committee should consider whether, taken as a whole and having regard to the views, as appropriate, of the external auditor, management and internal audit, those relationships appear to impair the auditor's independence and objectivity.
- The audit committee should monitor the external audit firm's compliance with the Ethical Standard, the level of fees that the company pays in proportion to the overall fee income of the firm, or relevant part of it, and other related regulatory requirements.
- The audit committee should seek annually from the audit firm information about policies and processes for maintaining independence and monitoring compliance with relevant requirements, including those regarding the rotation of audit partners and staff.
- The audit committee should agree with the board the company's policy for the employment of former employees of the external auditor, taking into account the Ethical Standard and legal requirements and paying particular attention to the policy regarding former employees of the audit firm who were part of the audit team and moved directly to the company. The audit committee should monitor application of the policy, including the number of former employees of the external auditor currently employed in senior positions in the company, and consider whether in the light of this there has been any impairment, or appearance of impairment, of the auditor's independence and objectivity in respect of the audit and consider the committee's own safeguards around independence in its review of effectiveness.

5.11 Provision of non-audit services

The FRC Guidance states that the audit committee is responsible for approving non-audit services. The objective of the audit committee should be to ensure that the provision of non-audit services by the company's audit firm would not impair the objectivity and independence of the auditors.

The committee should consider:

- whether the skills and experience of the audit firm make it a suitable supplier of the non-audit services;
- whether there are safeguards in place for ensuring that there would be no threat to the objectivity and independence of the auditors arising from the provision of these services;
- the nature of the non-audit services and the fees for these services;
- the level of fees for individual non-audit services and the fees in aggregate for these services, relative to the size of the audit fee; and
- the criteria governing the compensation of the individuals who perform the audit.

The audit committee should set and apply a formal policy specifying the types of non-audit service for which use of the external auditor is pre-approved. Such approval should only be in place for matters that are clearly trivial. Reporting of the use of non-audit services should include those subject to pre-approval.

The audit committee needs to set a policy for how it will assess whether non-audit services have a direct or material effect on the audited financial statements, how it will assess and explain the estimation of the effect on the financial statements and how it will consider the external auditors' independence. If the external auditors do provide non-financial services, the annual report should explain to shareholders how auditor independence and objectivity is safeguarded (UK Corporate Governance Code).

5.12 The audit committee and the annual audit cycle

The FRC Guidance goes into some detail on the annual audit cycle, and the relationship between the audit committee and the external auditors during this process.

- At the start of each annual audit, the audit committee should ensure that appropriate plans are in place for the audit.
- The committee should consider whether the auditors' overall work plan (including the planned levels of materiality and the proposed resources to carry out the audit) seems consistent with the scope of the audit engagement. This assessment should have regard to the seniority, expertise and experience of the audit team.
- The audit committee should review, with the external auditors, the findings of their work. As a part of this review, the committee should:
  - discuss with the external auditor major issues that arose during the course of the audit and have subsequently been resolved and those issues that have been left unresolved;
  - ask the auditor to explain how they addressed the risks to audit quality;
  - weigh the evidence they have received in relation to each of the areas of significant judgement and review key accounting and audit judgements;
  - ask the auditor for their perception of their interactions with senior management and other members of the finance team; and
  - review levels of errors identified during the audit, obtaining explanations from management and, where necessary, the external auditors as to why certain errors might remain unadjusted.

The FRC Guidance states that the audit committee should review the following:

- The audit representation letters from management, before they are signed, and consider whether the information provided is complete and appropriate, based on the knowledge the committee has.
- The management letter from the auditors, and the responsiveness of the company's management to the auditors' findings and recommendations.

Management representations

Representation letters from the company's management are a part of the audit evidence collected and considered by the auditors. They contain information from management to the auditors. These deal with matters for which other audit evidence does not exist; therefore, the auditors are relying on what management tell them. Representations are required:

- from the directors, acknowledging their collective responsibility for the financial statements and confirming that they have approved them; and
- with regard to matters where knowledge of the facts is confined to management (e.g. management's intention to sell off a division of the business) or where there is a matter of judgement and opinion (for example, with regard to the trading position of a major customer and debtor, or the likely outcome of litigation in progress).

The audit committee should review these representations from management and assess whether (on the basis of the knowledge of the committee members) the information provided seems complete and appropriate.

Audit review by the audit committee

The FRC Guidance states that at the end of the audit cycle, the audit committee should assess the effectiveness of the audit process. As a part of this assessment, the committee should:

- review whether the auditors have met the agreed audit plan and consider the reasons for any changes;

- consider the 'robustness and perceptiveness' of the auditors, in their handling of key accounting and audit judgements, and in their commentary on the appropriateness of the company's internal controls;
- obtain feedback about the conduct of the auditors from key people within the company, such as the finance director and the head of internal audit;
- review the auditors' management letter, to assess whether it is based on a good understanding of the business and to establish whether the auditors' recommendations have been acted on (and if not, why not); and
- report to the board on the effectiveness of the external audit process.

5.13 Annual report by the audit committee to shareholders

The UK Code requires that a separate section of the annual report should describe the work of the audit committee in discharging its responsibilities. This report should include:

- The significant issues that the committee considered in relation to the financial statements, and how these issues were addressed (having regard to matters communicated by the external auditors).
- An explanation of how it has assessed the effectiveness of the external audit process.
- An explanation of the approach it has taken to the appointment or reappointment of the external auditor, and information on the length of tenure of the current audit firm and when the tender process was last conducted (so that shareholders can understand why the committee reached its decision about a reappointment or change of auditors) and advance notice of any retendering plans..
- If the external auditor provides non-audit services, an explanation of how auditor objectivity and independence is safeguarded.

The FRC Guidance on Audit Committees adds that the committee will need to use judgement when deciding which significant issues to include in its report to shareholders. However, the committee would not be expected to disclose information that would be prejudicial to the interests of the company (for example, because it relates to impending developments or matters that are in a process of negotiation).

The chairman of the audit committee should be present at the AGM to answer questions on the separate section of the annual report describing the audit committee's activities and matters within the scope of the audit committee's responsibilities.

 TEST YOUR KNOWLEDGE 7.5

a   Who should be the members of an audit committee?
b   According to the FRC Guidance on Audit Committees, what should be the responsibilities of an audit committee in connection with:
  – audit committee meetings;
  – financial reporting;
  – the provision of non-audit services by the firm of external auditors; and
  – review of the annual audit?
c   What are the provisions of the UK Code with regard to the appointment, reappointment or removal of the external auditors?
d   What is the legal requirement for audit committees in the UK?
e   What induction or training might be provided for members of an audit committee?
f   What does the FRC Guidance say about the frequency of audit committee meetings?
g   What measures might an audit committee take to monitor the independence of the external auditors on a regular basis?

6 Disclosures of governance arrangements

The UK Code 2016 Schedule B states that corporate governance disclosure requirements are set out in three places:

- FCA Disclosure and Transparency Rules (DTR) which set out certain mandatory disclosures;
- FCA Listing Rules (LR) which includes the 'comply or explain' requirement; and
- the UK Corporate Governance Code – in addition to providing an explanation where they choose not to comply with a provision, companies must disclose specified information in order to comply with certain provisions.

The UK Code states that:

'There is some overlap between the mandatory disclosures required under the DTR and those expected under the Code. Areas of overlap are summarised in the Appendix to this Schedule. In respect of disclosures relating to the audit committee and the composition and operation of the board and its committees, compliance with the relevant provisions of the Code will result in compliance with the relevant Rules.'

The Appendix in the UK Code is summarised in Table 7.1.

7 Reporting non-financial information: narrative reporting

7.1 Additional financial reporting by listed companies

Listed companies are required to make various announcements about their financial performance or prospects to the stock market, in addition to publishing their annual report and accounts.

- They are required to issue an interim financial statement for the first six months of the financial year. This is not audited.
- They are also required to announce to the stock market relevant information affecting their business (e.g. a profits warning). This information must be issued to the stock market through a Regulated Information Service (RIS).
- The Transparency Directive requires listed companies that do not publish quarterly reports to issue two interim management statements, one during the first half and the other during the second half of the financial year. These should include information on trading performance, financial position and any major transactions or events that have occurred during the relevant period.

Other disclosure provisions in the UK Code, which are described in other chapters, are quite extensive. They include:

- A statement of how the board operates, and a high level statement of which types of decisions are taken by the board and which are taken by management.
- The number of board meetings and committee meetings held during the year, and attendances at those meetings by individual directors.
- A statement of how the performance evaluation of the board, its committees and individual directors was conducted.
- An explanation by the directors about how the company generates or preserves value over the longer term (the company's business model) and the strategy for delivering the objectives of the company.
- A description of the principal risks facing the company and an explanation of how these are managed or mitigated.
- A statement by the directors about their assessment of the prospects of the company and whether they reasonably expect the company to continue in operation over the period of their assessment.
- A report on the board's review of the effectiveness of the company's internal control and risk management systems.
- Steps that have been taken by the board to ensure that its members, especially the NEDs, develop an understanding of the views of the company's major shareholders.

TABLE 7.1 Overlap between the Disclosure and Transparency Rules and the UK Corporate Governance Code

Disclosure and Transparency Rules	UK Corporate Governance Code
Sets out minimum requirements on composition of the audit committee or equivalent body.	**Provision C.3.1** Sets out the recommended composition of the audit committee.
Sets out minimum functions of the audit committee or equivalent body.	**Provision C.3.2** Sets out the recommended minimum terms of reference for the audit committee.
The composition and function of the audit committee or equivalent body/bodies must be disclosed in the annual report.	This requirement overlaps with a number of different Code provisions: **A.1.2**: The annual report should identify members of the board and board committees. **C.3.1**: Sets out the recommended composition of the audit committee. **C.3.2**: Sets out the recommended minimum terms of reference for the audit committee. **C.3.3**: The terms of reference of the audit committee, including its role and the authority delegated to it by the board, should be made available. **C.3.8**: The annual report should describe the work of the audit committee.
The corporate governance statement must contain a description of the main features of the issuer's internal control and risk management systems in relation to the financial reporting process. *While this requirement differs from the requirement in the Code, it is envisaged that both could be met by a single internal control statement.*	**Provision C.2.1**: The directors should confirm that they have carried out a robust assessment of the principal risks facing the company – including those that would threaten its business model, future performance, solvency or liquidity. The directors should describe those risks and explain how they are being managed or mitigated. **Provision C.2.3**: The board should monitor the company's risk management and internal control systems and, at least annually, carry out a review of their effectiveness, and report on that review in the annual report. The monitoring and review should cover all material controls, including financial, operational and compliance controls.
The corporate governance statement must contain a description of the composition and operation of the issuer's administrative, management and supervisory bodies and their committees.	This requirement overlaps with a number of different Code provisions: **A.1.1**: The annual report should include a statement of how the board operates. **A.1.2**: The annual report should identify members of the board and board committees. **B.2.4**: The annual report should describe the work of the nomination committee. **C.3.3**: The terms of reference of the audit committee, including its role and the authority delegated to it by the board, should be made available. **C.3.8**: The annual report should describe the work of the audit committee. **D.2.1**: A description of the work of the remuneration committee should be made available.

7.2 The nature of narrative reporting by companies

Published financial statements are historical in outlook and contain very little non-financial information. Although they can help users to understand the prospects for the company, it has been argued that more information should be provided to improve users' understanding.

In addition, it has been argued that International Financial Reporting Standards (IFRS) have possibly made financial statements more difficult for many investors to read and understand. In the attempt to make financial statements more informative and relevant to investors, the accounting standards bodies may have gone the other way and made them more obscure (this is a matter of argument and debate).

The result of this debate, however, has been a general agreement that companies should present information about their company's performance, and possibly also about its future prospects, in a way that is clear and transparent, and which covers non-financial as well as financial aspects of performance and the company's position.

Transparency is a core principle of good governance, and by providing non-financial information and forward-looking information, in addition to historical financial statements, companies make their situation much more apparent and easier to comprehend.

Requirements have been introduced for additional reporting by companies to improve the quality of communications with their shareholders. These combine financial and non-financial information, and should improve corporate governance by enhancing the quality and content of the information provided to shareholders and other stakeholders.

7.3 Disclosures about greenhouse gas emissions

Quoted companies are required to include in the annual directors' report information about greenhouse gas emissions, specifically the actual quantity of emissions, in tonnes, of 'carbon dioxide equivalent' from activities for which it is responsible, including the combustion of fuel and operation of any facility resulting from the purchase of electricity, heat, steam or cooling by the company for its own use.

The directors' report must also state at least one ratio which expresses the company's greenhouse gas emissions in relation to a quantifiable factor associated with the company's activities.

Much of the reporting of environmental (and social) matters has been provided by companies on a voluntary basis (see Chapter 12), but this amendment to UK law in 2013 has introduced compulsory reporting of emissions by quoted companies.

8 Strategic report

The Companies Act 2006 (Strategic Report and Directors' Report) Regulations 2013 has introduced a requirement for all companies (excluding small companies) to include a strategic report in their annual report and accounts. This report replaced the business review. It is presented as a separate section of the annual report, and not as part of the directors' report. The purpose of the strategic report is to provide a company's shareholders with a holistic and meaningful picture of a company's business model, strategy, development, performance, position and future prospects. The purpose of the strategic report is to provide a company's shareholders with a holistic and meaningful picture of a company's business model, strategy, development, performance, position and future prospects.

A strategic report must contain:

■ a fair review of the company's business; and
■ a description of the principal risks and uncertainties facing the company.

The review should provide an analysis of the development and performance of the company's business during the financial year and the position of the company as at the end of the year.

To the extent necessary for an understanding of the company's business, the review should also include:

■ analysis using KPIs; and
■ where appropriate analysis using non-financial KPIs, information relating to environmental matters and employee matters (however, medium-sized companies are not required to comply with this requirement about non-financial KPIs).

In addition, the strategic report of a quoted company must also include the following, to the extent necessary for an understanding of the company's business:

- The main trends and factors likely to affect the future development, performance and position of the company's business.
- Information, including information about the company's policies and the effectiveness of those policies, on:
  - environmental matters, including the company' s impact on the environment;
  - the company's employees; and
  - social, community and human rights issues.

For quoted companies, the strategic report should also contain:

- a description of the company's strategy;
- a description of the company's business model; and
- a gender breakdown: the number of persons of each sex at the end of the financial year who were directors of the company, senior managers of the company and employees of the company.

It is a criminal offence for a director to approve the strategic report knowing that it does not comply with the requirements of the Act.

The FRC Guidance 2014 on the Strategic Report is for directors and is intended to serve as best practice for all entities preparing strategic reports.

8.1 Directors' 'safe harbour provisions'

The CA2006 includes **'safe harbour provisions'** for directors.

When the requirement for a business review was first introduced into UK law, concerns were expressed about the potential liability of directors for statements they would be required to make in the review, especially statements that are forward-looking and so impossible to make with certainty. To meet general concerns about the potential liability of directors for the contents of reports, the 2006 Act included so-called safe harbour provisions.

These provisions state that a director can be liable for untrue or misleading statements only if he knew them to be untrue or misleading, or was 'reckless' as to whether they were untrue or misleading. Similarly a director can only be responsible for an omission if he knew the omission to be a 'dishonest' concealment of a material fact.

The safe harbour provisions remain and apply to the strategic report (as well as to the directors' report and directors' remuneration report), to give directors confidence to make forward-looking statements without fear of criminal prosecution or other legal action.

8.2 The value of a strategic report for investors

The strategic report, particularly the strategic report of a quoted company, provides information to shareholders (and other users of the annual report and accounts) that supplements the information in the financial statements. Investors may find this information useful for making investment decisions.

- It assists the analysis of the company's financial performance during the year by analysing financial KPIs, as well as any significant non-financial KPIs.
- Much of the report is forward-looking and includes information about the company's objectives, business model and strategy for achieving objectives; and also about the main trends and factors that are likely to affect the company's development in future.
- It provides information about the main risks facing the company: investors should be interested in risks as well as potential returns when making investment decisions.
- For investors with concerns about social and environmental issues, the strategic report of quoted companies will usually include information about environmental issues the company's employees, and social, community and human rights issues.

9   Introduction to integrated reporting

Another initiative on reporting has come from the International Integrated Reporting Council (IIRC). This is a global body established to promote the worldwide adoption of integrated reporting as the main annual report by companies.

The objective of the IIRC is to encourage integrated reporting by companies. The IIRC aims to 'promote a more cohesive and efficient approach to corporate reporting that draws on different reporting strands and communicates the full range of factors that materially affect the ability of the organisation to create value over time' (IIRC International Framework 2013).

The IIRC has been working to achieve consensus among governments, listing authorities, standard setters, companies and investors about the use of integrated reporting by listed companies.

As its name suggests, an integrated report should bring together into a single report different aspects of a company's activities which contribute to the creation of (or destruction of) value.

Value is accumulated in the form of six different types of capital: financial capital, manufactured capital, human capital, intellectual capital, natural capital and social capital. It is therefore argued that an integrated report should provide information about the company's policies and performance with regard to each of these aspects of capital.

Integrated reporting is explained in more detail in Chapter 12. It is sufficient at this stage to note that 'capital', as defined for the purpose of integrated reporting, includes aspects of the company's policies and performance with regard to employees, the environment and society. These are issues that quoted companies may be expected to include in their strategic report.

The IIRC's International Framework states that an integrated report should contain eight elements:

1   Overview of the organisation and its external environment.
2   Governance and how the governance structure supports the company's ability to create value.
3   Business model: a description of the company's business model.
4   Risks and opportunities that affect the organisation's ability to create value, and how the organisation is dealing with them.
5   Strategy and resource allocation. What are the company's strategies and strategic objectives, and how does it intend to get there?
6   Performance. To what extent has the company achieved its strategic objectives for the period, in terms of effects on the 'six capitals'?
7   Outlook: challenges and uncertainties.
8   Basis of presentation. How does the organisation decide what to include in the integrated report and how are these matters quantified/measured?

Reporting on social and environmental issues, sustainability reporting and integrated reporting are described more fully in Chapter 12.

TEST YOUR KNOWLEDGE **7.6**

a   In UK law, which companies must publish an annual strategic report?
b   What should be the contents of a strategic report for a quoted company?

END OF CHAPTER QUESTIONS

Refer to the case study at the beginning of Part Two and answer these questions.

1   What changes will be required in the reporting arrangements of the company, to comply with legal, regulatory and corporate governance requirements?

2   Should the company make changes to its arrangements for the annual external audit, and if so, what might those changes be?

CHAPTER SUMMARY

- Financial reporting is an important aspect of corporate governance because it is a means by which the directors of a company are made accountable to the shareholders.

- Shareholders and other investors depend on the reliability of the financial statements when making their investment decisions. Reliable financial reporting helps to maintain investor confidence.

- Concerns of investors about misleading financial statements have been a major factor in the development of corporate governance codes and statutory provisions in recent years. Financial statements can be misleading, due to the selection of inappropriate accounting policies.

- The directors, not the external auditors, are responsible for the financial statements.

- The external auditors provide an opinion on whether the financial accounts appear to provide a true and fair view of the company's performance and financial position.

- Similarly, the board of directors, who have a responsibility to safeguard the assets of the company, are responsible for the prevention or detection of fraud within the company. Fraud may take the form of criminal activity by employees or others (such as theft) or deliberate misrepresentation in published financial statements. Measures to prevent or detect fraud should be a part of the internal control system in the company.

- The external auditors do not have a direct responsibility for detecting fraud, but may discover fraud in the course of their annual audit work which should then be reported to senior management (or the authorities, if senior management appear to be responsible themselves for the fraud). However, if the auditors fail to detect fraud when they should reasonably have been expected to do so, they may be liable for negligence.

- To perform their role, the external auditors must be independent from the company.

- Threats to independence include self-interest threats, self-review threats, advocacy threats, familiarity threats and intimidation threats. Carrying out non-audit work for an audit client may create self-interest threats (concerns about losing the work and the fees). Familiarity threats can be reduced by audit firm rotation (not common) or audit partner rotation.

- For large quoted EU companies, the EU has introduced a regulation, effective from June 2016, which puts a cap on the value of non-audit work that the auditors can perform for its audit client, and the regulation also bans audit firms from doing certain types of non-audit work for their clients.

- In the UK, the largest listed companies will be required to put their audit out to tender at least every ten years.

- The EU's Audit Directive, effective from June 2016, requires large quoted EU companies to change their auditors at least every ten years, although this may be extended to every 20 years in EU countries that have audit tendering every ten years.

- Doubts have been expressed about the independence of auditors from the companies to which they provide an audit service. The audit firm (through the ethical codes of the profession) and the company's board of directors both have a responsibility to protect the independence of the auditors.

- Control over the audit profession is therefore a corporate governance issue.

- An audit committee, properly constituted, could provide a valuable role in improving the relationship between a company and its auditors and helping to ensure that the external audit process is satisfactory and that the external auditors remain independent. In Europe, there is now a statutory requirement for quoted companies to have an audit committee.

- An audit committee should consist entirely of independent NEDs. The UK Corporate Governance Code specifies that at least one member should have recent and relevant financial experience.

- The responsibilities of an audit committee in the UK are set out in detail in the FRC's guidance on the responsibilities of the audit committee.

- Companies are required to include certain information in their annual report to shareholders. In the UK, this includes a requirement for a strategic report (with the exception of small companies). Quoted companies must include more than medium-sized companies in their strategic report.

- The strategic report, which is largely in narrative form, should include non-financial information as well as financial information, and should be forward-looking as well as commenting on historical performance. In this way it provides more information to shareholders, and improves both accountability and transparency.

- Changes in the required contents of the annual report from October 2013 may be a first step towards integrated reporting by UK quoted companies.

Relations with shareholders

■ **CONTENTS**

■ **INTRODUCTION**

This chapter explores the various aspects of the relationship between a company and its shareholders. Regular and constructive dialogue between a company and its shareholders can help investors understand what the board of directors is planning and how the company intends to set about achieving its objectives. Open communications also help shareholders to better understand the performance and financial position of the company. At the same time, the board of directors should try to learn more about shareholders' expectations and concerns. It is the responsibility of both the board and institutional investors to improve the relationship between them, with a view to improving corporate governance. In the UK, company responsibilities for this relationship are included in the UK Corporate Governance Code, and the responsibilities of institutional investors are set out in the UK Stewardship Code. There has been some development towards greater activism by institutional shareholders, and electronic communications may encourage more shareholders to vote at company general meetings. There is also recognition in the UK of the need for better engagement between companies and their shareholders, especially institutional investors who are shareholders in the company. Guidance on better engagement has been issued by ICSA.

1 Governance responsibilities of the board and the shareholders

In listed public companies, management is separate from ownership, and the shareholders rely on management to run the company in their interests. Management in return should be able to rely on the support of the shareholders, particularly where new initiatives, such as a proposed takeover, have to be put to a vote at a general meeting. In practice, however, the relationship between shareholders and management can be difficult. Shareholders may suspect management of putting their own interests first or of being incompetent. Management in turn may suspect shareholders of not understanding the business, or not showing enough interest.

In the story *The Forsyte Saga*, the novelist John Galsworthy gave a sharp illustration of the difficult relationship that can exist between a company board and its shareholders. Although set in the late nineteenth century, the insights remain relevant today. Describing an annual general meeting (AGM) of a company where Old Jolyon Forsyte was the chairman, and his nephew Soames was in attendance, he wrote:

'And now old Jolyon rose, to present the report and accounts.

Veiling under a Jove-like serenity that perpetual antagonism deep-seated in the bosom of a director towards his shareholders, he faced them calmly ...

"If any shareholder has any question to put, I shall be glad to answer it." A soft thump. Old Jolyon had let the report and accounts fall, and stood twisting tortoise-shell glasses between thumb and forefinger.

The ghost of a smile appeared on Soames' face. They had better hurry up with their questions! He well knew his uncle's method (the ideal one) of at once saying, "I propose, then, that the report and accounts be adopted!" Never let them get their wind – shareholders were notoriously wasteful of time!'

The impression given here is that a chairman, representing the board, regards the shareholders as an irritation whose views are irrelevant, and who can be kept quiet through careful but firm handling. This attitude is perhaps not as old-fashioned or unrealistic as might be supposed.

At the same time, shareholders can be indifferent to their company boards, often failing to attend general meetings or even submit **proxy votes** and seeming to show little interest in the company's affairs, apart from the immediate share price and dividend prospects, until something goes wrong. However, relations between the company's board and its shareholders are an important aspect of corporate governance and both boards of directors and shareholders have responsibilities for improving corporate governance through active engagement with each other.

1.1 Responsibilities of the board for relations with shareholders

From the company's perspective, the directors should recognise that although their legal duties are to the company, the shareholders of the company are its owners. The board should therefore keep the shareholders well informed about what the company is doing and should seek to engage with them and understand what their expectations are. The responsibilities of the board for promoting relations with shareholders should be included in codes of corporate governance. The UK Corporate Governance Code identifies two ways in which relations with shareholders should be developed:

1 through dialogue with shareholders; and
2 through constructive use of the AGM and other general meetings of the company.

1.2 Responsibilities of shareholders for engagement with companies in which they invest

From the shareholders' perspective, only institutional shareholders normally have the time, as well as the understanding, to monitor the performance of companies and the activities of their boards. Traditionally, institutional investors have taken the view that if they disapprove of a particular company or its management, they can always sell their shares and invest somewhere else. Another view is that many investments by institutional shareholders may be of a long-term nature. Activist shareholders would argue that, over the long term, companies that are better governed will create more value than those that are badly governed. It is therefore in the interest of institutional investors, and the clients or beneficiaries they represent, to encourage companies to adopt best practices in corporate governance.

1.3 Categories of shareholders

Shareholders in listed companies consist of different types of investor. There are institutional shareholders, small private shareholders, large private shareholders and corporate shareholders. Shareholders may invest for only a short time: speculators, for example, may buy shares in companies in the expectation of being able to make a quick profit from movements in the share price. On the other hand, some shareholders may expect to hold shares as a longer-term investment; although they always have the option of selling their shareholding at any time.

Some shareholders might choose to 'play the stock market', and buy and sell shares regularly. Although they might be long-term investors in some companies, they might treat other shareholdings as short-term investments. If shareholders come and go regularly, a company's board of directors cannot possibly get to know them or develop a relationship with them. Directors should consider the longer-term interest of the company, and their engagement with shareholders should be directed principally to longer-term investors.

1.4 Institutional investors

Institutional shareholders are organisations that have large amounts of funds to invest, and put much of these funds into company shares. In the UK, the institutional investors include pension funds, insurance companies and collective investment institutions such as unit trust funds and open-ended investment companies.

- These operate in the interests of beneficiaries, such as members of pension schemes and holders of life assurance policies.
- They may appoint agents to manage their investments. These investment management firms will be given responsibility for buying and selling investments for their client institution within the framework of investment fund mandates that indicate how the money should be invested and how the shares should be voted.
- Institutional investors may also use the services of proxy voting agencies, which offer research and voting services to institutional clients, and voting advisory services.

All of these different organisations can be classified as 'institutional investors'. There are national associations of institutional investors, such as the ABI and the PLSA in the UK, but in many countries (including the UK) a large proportion of shares in listed companies are owned by foreign investment institutions. Although there are international organisations such as the ICGN, it is difficult for institutional investors to monitor the governance of all the companies in which they invest in every country. The international nature of investment therefore adds to the difficulties of establishing a good relationship between a company and its shareholders.

 STOP AND THINK 8.1

In 2010, US group Kraft Foods succeeded with a hostile takeover bid for UK confectioner Cadbury in a deal valued at nearly £12 billion. The board of directors opposed the bid until it became inevitable that it would succeed. In the days before a shareholder vote on accepting the terms of the offer, it was reported that about a quarter of Cadbury shares were in the hands of speculators hoping to make a quick profit from the deal. It was also reported that Warren Buffet (the 'Sage of Omaha'), head of investment group Berkshire Hathaway and owner at the time of 10% of Kraft shares, opposed the bid because it was a bad deal for Kraft shareholders. In this situation, should the Cadbury board have given more consideration to the objectives of its short-term speculative shareholders? Should the Kraft board have given greater consideration to the opposition from its major shareholder? Was this a takeover battle in which the boards of the respective companies did not give sufficient consideration to shareholder interests?

STOP AND THINK 8.2

In the UK, institutional investment organisations that obtain funds for investment include pension funds, life assurance companies and investment trust organisations. These organisations might appoint investment management companies to invest the funds on their behalf ('manage the funds'). The investment managers decide how the money should be invested, possibly with some policy guidance from their client, what investments to buy and whether to sell. The legal owners of the investments are the investment managers, and it is the investment managers (not their clients, the pension funds or life assurance companies) who have the equity voting rights in the companies. Investment managers effectively hold the investments of their clients in a stewardship capacity, on behalf and in the interests of their clients. Pension funds and other investment organisations may be answerable to their own beneficiaries for the way in which the funds are invested, but to be properly accountable to their beneficiaries, they need to monitor the activities of their investment managers. Investment managers, more so than the pension funds and insurance companies, have the task as shareholders of trying to ensure that best practice in corporate governance is followed by the companies in which they invest.

TEST YOUR KNOWLEDGE 8.1

According to the UK Corporate Governance Code, in what ways should a listed company try to improve relations with its shareholders?

2   Rights and powers of shareholders

Shareholders do not get involved directly in the management of quoted companies, although they may occasionally express their views about corporate strategy to the chairman or other members of the board. The board of directors and management of the company make the strategic and operational decisions. However, as owners of the company, the shareholders should expect their views to be heard by the board of directors, in cases where a substantial proportion of them hold similar opinions.

Shareholders have certain rights in law and under the constitution (articles of association) of their company. For example, they should have a right to receive the annual report and accounts, the right to vote at general meetings and the right to a share of the profits of the company. The powers of shareholders to exercise their rights are limited, and are mainly restricted to:

- voting powers at general meetings; and
- taking legal action in cases where the directors have acted illegally.

2.1 Pre-emption rights and right to approve long-term incentive schemes

In some countries, including the UK, shareholders have pre-emption rights. When a company issues new shares for cash, existing shareholders have the first right of refusal, and should be offered the right to buy new shares in proportion to their existing shareholding. They may agree to waive these rights, e.g. in order to allow a share option scheme to be implemented for employees of senior executives of the company.

In addition to pre-emption rights, shareholders may be given the right to approve any new or amended long-term incentive scheme for the company (this is a provision of the UK Corporate Governance Code). Institutional shareholders will normally approve long-term incentive schemes provided the terms are reasonable and the new shares issued as a consequence of the scheme would not result in an increase in share capital by more than a maximum percentage limit.

These rights give shareholders some influence over remuneration schemes for directors and senior executives.

2.2 Election and re-election of directors and auditors

Shareholders could hold individual directors (or the board as a whole) to account for their actions by voting against their re-election. The articles of association of a public company should provide for the directors to retire by rotation, and if they wish to submit themselves for re-election at the AGM of the company. In the UK, the articles of most public companies provide for directors to stand for re-election at the AGM following their initial appointment and subsequently every three years. A simple majority is required for the re-election of a director, which means that a simple majority is required to successfully oppose a re-election.

The UK Corporate Governance Code includes a provision that *all* directors of FTSE 350 companies should submit themselves for annual re-election at the company's AGM.

The requirement for directors to stand for periodic re-election offers the shareholders an opportunity to vote a director out of office, or to reject a new director recently appointed by the board. Some activist shareholder groups have occasionally encouraged investment institutions to vote against particular directors. However, most shareholders tend to vote in support of the directors, and it is still difficult for active shareholders to vote successfully against the re-election of any director. Even so, **shareholder activism** (see section 6.2 later in this chapter) means that shareholder leverage over changes to the board of directors is greater now than it has been in the past.

The shareholders also have the right to approve (or reject) the appointment of the auditors each year.

2.3 Approval of remuneration policy

As explained in Chapter 6, the shareholders of quoted companies have the right to a binding vote at least every three years on the company's remuneration policy, which should be set out in the directors' remuneration report. They are also entitled to an advisory vote on an annual implementation report, also included within the directors' remuneration report, which explains how the remuneration policy has been implemented in the previous year.

Taken together, these votes should give shareholders some influence over the remuneration of directors (both executive and non-executive). Influence over the remuneration of executive directors should also be expected to have a knock-on effect, to influence over the remuneration of senior executives in the company generally.

2.4 Other voting rights

In UK law, shareholders have a right to:

- call a general meeting of the company, and call for a vote on a resolution that they put to the meeting; or
- propose a resolution to be voted on at the AGM.

Shareholders can require the directors to call a general meeting if together they hold at least 5% of the voting share capital.

Shareholders have a statutory right to include a matter in the business of the AGM of the company provided they hold at least 5% of the voting share capital. The request to include the item in the AGM must be received not later than six weeks before the date of the AGM, and if the request is received before the end of the company's financial year preceding the AGM, the company must bear the costs of circulating the details of the matter to the other shareholders. Shareholders will only seek to call a general meeting of the company in extreme circumstances, and possibly as a means of shaking the board of directors into re-thinking its attitude to the matter that is causing the shareholders extreme concern.

In UK law, if the shareholders are dissatisfied with a director, they have the right under s. 168 of the Companies Act 2006 (CA2006) to remove a director by an ordinary resolution in a general meeting, before the end of his or her term of office. In principle, shareholders holding at least 5% of the share capital of their company may therefore call for the removal of the entire board from office, at the AGM or at a general meeting called for the purpose.

However, it is important to understand that attempts by shareholders to call a general meeting or to put an additional resolution to the AGM are not common. To do so, the shareholders must agree collectively what they want to happen, so that they can formulate a proposal to put to the general meeting for a vote.

2.5 Regulatory requirements for shareholder involvement

To a limited extent, the UK Disclosure and Transparency Rules (DTR) give shareholders some rights by obliging a company to keep shareholders informed of certain developments and to obtain shareholder approval for certain transactions. UK listed companies are required to provide certain information to the stock market, such as profit warnings, changes in major shareholdings, changes in directors' shareholdings, and so on. In addition, listed companies must obtain prior approval from the shareholders, by vote in a general meeting, for:

- transactions above a certain size, relative to the size of the company; and
- transactions with related parties.

Large transactions for which prior shareholder approval is required are known as **Class 1 transactions**; these include major takeovers or the disposal of a large part of the company's business operations. Transactions with related parties are outside the normal commercial business operations of the company between the company and a major shareholder or a director, or someone closely associated with a major shareholder or director (e.g. a relative or business partner). One example of a transaction with a related party is the sale of a company property to one of its directors.

When major transactions or transactions with related parties are planned, the board will have to send out a circular to its shareholders, explaining the reason for the transaction and justifying it, in order to win shareholder approval. In some sense, the company is therefore obliged in these situations to communicate with its shareholders and seek their support. Legal requirements relating to shareholders' rights to notice of general meetings and to vote at general meetings are described later in this chapter.

2.6 Limitations of shareholder powers

The powers of shareholders are limited, and for shareholders to exert positive influence on a board of directors, there has to be a positive relationship between them, with constructive dialogue. When there is strong disagreement between the board and some shareholders, it is usually the directors who 'win' and get their way.

 **CASE EXAMPLE** 8.1

After successfully ousting the chairman of the board of directors, the shareholders of listed UK company SkyePharma requisitioned an EGM at which a proposal would be made for the installation of the nominee of a shareholder group as new chairman. The shareholders requisitioning the EGM also asked for the suspension of any attempts to break up the company before the new chairman was appointed. The shareholder initiative was led by an activist group, North Atlantic Value (NAV), which claimed the support of 37% of the shareholders.

The board of directors defied the shareholders and their demands. In February 2006, it appointed a chairman of its own choice and announced the sale of a US-based subsidiary. NAV accused the directors of 'astonishing arrogance' and stated that it was 'surprised that a board that contains a number of seasoned operators should behave in such a cavalier way towards shareholders. We as shareholders are owners of the company, it is not their company'.

STOP AND THINK 8.3

There has been an increase in shareholder dissent against policies of the board of directors, especially on matters related to remuneration. A large minority vote against a resolution at a general meeting of the company is seen as a 'warning' to the company, but it does not prevent the board from succeeding in getting their resolutions accepted. For example, in 2010, 32% of shareholders voted against the remuneration report at the AGM of retailer Tesco and three large shareholders voted against the remuneration report at the AGM of insurance company Prudential (following a failed takeover bid for the AIA insurance group in Asia); and about 20% of shareholders voted against a proposed new pay scheme at advertising group WPP. At the 2010 AGM of HSBC, nearly 25% of shareholders voted against the remuneration report or abstained; following this protest vote, the HSBC chairman announced that the company would review its remuneration policies.

TEST YOUR KNOWLEDGE 8.2

a   What rights do shareholders have in UK law to approve remuneration arrangements or schemes for executives?
b   What issues do shareholders have a right to vote on at general meetings of the company?
c   In the UK, how soon after his or her appointment and then how frequently may shareholders of a listed company vote to elect or re-elect the company chairman?
d   In the UK, how could shareholders dismiss the chairman or chief executive of their company?
e   In UK law, what is the minimum percentage of voting shares that must be held by a group of shareholders to requisition an EGM?
f   In UK law, what is the minimum percentage of voting shares that must be held by a group of shareholders to add a resolution to the agenda for the AGM?

3   Dialogue between the board and shareholders

Achieving good relations between a company and its shareholders is desirable on a regular and established basis. This calls for measures by both the board and by the shareholders. The UK has developed these ideas a long way, and current thinking on the subject provides a useful framework for study and analysis. Responsibilities of the board of directors are included in the UK Corporate Governance Code; responsibilities for institutional shareholders are set out in the UK Stewardship Code.

3.1 Board responsibility to maintain a dialogue with institutional shareholders

A main principle of the UK Code of Corporate Governance is that:

'There should be a dialogue with shareholders based on the mutual understanding of objectives. The board as a whole has responsibility for ensuring that a satisfactory dialogue with shareholders takes place.'

Dialogue with institutional shareholders calls not just for regular formal announcements by a company to the stock market generally, but also for regular, informal contact with the larger shareholders in the company. In practice, the main point of contact between shareholders and the board is the chairman, the chief executive officer (CEO) or the finance director. However, the UK Code states as supporting principles that:

- the chairman should ensure that all the directors are made aware of the issues and concerns of the company's major shareholders; and
- the board should keep in touch with shareholder opinion in the most practical and efficient ways, whatever these may be.

The UK Code states a number of practical requirements for maintaining dialogue.

- The chairman should ensure that the views of the shareholders are communicated to the board as a whole.
- The chairman should discuss strategy and governance with the major shareholders.
- Non-executive directors (NEDs) should be given the opportunity to attend existing meetings with major shareholders.
- If requested to attend meetings with major shareholders, NEDs should expect to attend them.
- The senior independent director (SID) should attend enough meetings with a range of major shareholders to listen to their views, in order to develop a 'balanced understanding' of their concerns and views.

In the annual report, the board should report on the steps that have been taken to ensure that members of the board, especially the NEDs, develop an understanding of the views of the shareholders, e.g. through face-to-face meetings, analysts' or brokers' briefings or surveys of shareholder opinion.

Guidance on better shareholder engagement is discussed in more detail later.

3.2 Institutional shareholder responsibility for dialogue with companies

In 2009, the International Shareholders Committee (ISC) published a Code on the Responsibilities of Institutional Investors. These were then adopted by the FRC and included (with some minor amendments) in the UK Stewardship Code for institutional investors, for which the FRC is responsible.

The Stewardship Code is described in more detail later in this chapter.

TEST YOUR KNOWLEDGE 8.3

According to the UK Code, what practical requirements are needed for a board of directors to maintain a dialogue with major shareholders?

4 Constructive use of the AGM and other general meetings

4.1 General meetings; principles and provisions in the UK Code

The UK Corporate Governance Code states as a main principle that: 'The board should use general meetings to communicate with investors and to encourage their participation.' The provisions in this part of the UK Code are concerned mainly with:

- encouraging attendance by shareholders at the AGM and other general meetings;
- giving shareholders an opportunity to ask questions and to hear about the company during the meeting; and
- giving shareholders the opportunity to use their vote and greater openness in voting procedures at general meetings.

The Code provisions are as follows.

- **Encouraging attendance.** The company should arrange for the notice of the AGM and the related papers to be sent to the shareholders at least 20 working days before the meeting. The minimum notice of an AGM required by CA2006 (s. 369) is just 21 calendar days.

- **Giving shareholders an opportunity to ask questions.** The board chairman should arrange for the chairmen of the audit, nomination and remuneration committees to be available to answer questions at the AGM, and for all directors to attend the meeting.
- **Voting procedures.** At the AGM, there should be a separate resolution for each substantially separate issue. This requirement is intended to prevent the practice of combining two or more issues, one 'popular' and the other more controversial, into a single resolution. Each issue will then be voted on separately.
- **Proxy voting forms should include a 'vote withheld' box.** This is in addition to the 'for' and 'against' boxes for each resolution. The **'vote withheld'** box allows shareholders to indicate their displeasure about a company's proposals without actually voting against the resolution in question. However, a vote withheld is not a vote in law and so does not count towards the proportion of votes cast in favour of or against a resolution (for the purpose of deciding whether a resolution has been passed or rejected).
- **Disclosure of information about proxy votes.** After a resolution has been dealt with on a show of hands, the company should indicate the level of votes lodged for and against the resolution, including proxy votes, and the number of shares in respect of which there was a specific instruction to withhold a vote. This information should be given at the meeting itself and made available as soon as practicable afterwards on the company's website. By announcing the number of votes including proxy votes, companies will give some recognition to the views of shareholders unable to attend the meeting, and will not be able to pass controversial resolutions simply on a show of hands of shareholders present and attending the meeting, when a vote on a show of hands differs significantly from what the results of a poll vote would have been.

4.2 Voting rights of proxies

Under the provisions of CA2006 (s. 324), all registered shareholders have the right to nominate one or more proxies, with each proxy having the right to attend and speak at general meetings, demand a poll and vote on any resolution (in both a vote by show of hands and a poll vote).

The right to appoint more than one proxy, with each proxy representing a different part of the shareholder's total shareholdings, might make it easier than in the past for proxies to demand a poll vote on a resolution after the chairman has taken a vote by show of hands. This would be consistent with the view of many institutional shareholders, including the Shareholder Voting Working Group, that chairmen of companies should use poll votes rather than voting by show of hands for all resolutions at company meetings.

The CA2006 also requires quoted companies to make available on their website details of polls taken at their general meetings, showing the number of votes cast in favour for and against the resolution.

 STOP AND THINK 8.4

The AGM may be seen as a legal requirement for companies, where shareholders have an opportunity to show their opposition to the board's policies, for example by voting against the remuneration report or the re-election of certain directors.

While it is true that shareholder opposition to the board's policies or actions can be expressed through votes at the AGM, it is also useful to think of the AGM as an opportunity for the board to engage in constructive dialogue with its shareholders. The chairman should be able to explain the company's strategies and objectives, and governance arrangements; and should allow a suitable amount of time for questions and answers.

Other board members, including the CEO and the chairmen of the board's committees, should be required to attend in order to answer questions relating to their area of responsibility.

Questions and answers, if given honestly and transparently, should help to foster a better understanding between the company and its shareholders.

4.3 Limitations of AGMs

Unfortunately, there are some fairly obvious limitations of AGMs as a vehicle for dialogue between shareholders and the board of directors.

■ They are held only once a year.
■ It may be difficult for shareholders to attend. Foreign shareholders in particular may have difficulty in sending representatives. Attendance levels need to be high to make dialogue and communication effective.
■ AGMs are of limited time duration. The chairman should try to allow a suitable amount of time for questions and discussion, but the time available may not be sufficient.

This is why other methods of encouraging better engagement between a company and its shareholders are also needed.

5   Electronic communications and electronic voting

5.1 Benefits of electronic communications with shareholders

■ Companies and shareholders may communicate electronically.
■ Companies may send out documents and other information to shareholders, either by email to individual shareholders or by posting information on their website.
■ Shareholders may be able to communicate with their companies on some matters, such as appointing proxies for a general meeting (or possibly casting votes in advance of a general meeting).

Some of the benefits of electronic communications for companies should be apparent.

■ It should be much cheaper to produce documents in electronic form, and use emails or a website for communicating with shareholders, than it is to print documents and send them out by post.
■ There may also be environmental benefits, for large companies with many shareholders (less wastage of natural resources such as paper).

There are also potential benefits for shareholders.

■ For some shareholders, particularly foreign shareholders, communication should be much faster and possibly more reliable.
■ Companies should also be able to provide more communication, such as posting the results of polls at general meetings on their website, so that shareholders are better informed.
■ Large institutional investors may also benefit, because information sent or notified electronically is more likely to be seen by the key decision makers within large investor institutions: printed copies of annual reports and accounts are more likely to be handled by junior staff.
■ The ability to appoint proxies electronically (or vote electronically, in some countries) may also improve the probability that shareholders will participate in decision-making by submitting proxy votes.

5.2 UK law on electronic communications

In the UK, companies may provide in their articles of association for the company's website to be used for communication with shareholders, and documents (e.g. the annual report and accounts, summary financial statements and notices of meetings) can be sent to shareholders in electronic form, although individual shareholders may opt out of receiving communications from a company through the company website and ask for communications to be sent in written form. However, if a company adopts a system of electronic communications, it is required to notify the shareholders whenever a message has been posted on the website. Companies whose shares are traded on a regular stock market in the UK are also subject to the FCA's DTR, which permit electronic communications.

Shareholders are also permitted to appoint proxies electronically, to vote on their behalf at general meetings, and companies must provide an electronic address for the receipt of any message or instruction relating to proxies at a forthcoming general meeting.

The results of poll votes at general meetings should also be posted on the website of 'traded' companies (most quoted companies), showing the total number of votes cast, the proportion of the issued share capital that the votes represent, and the number of votes for and against the resolution and the number of votes withheld.

In the UK it has been decided that the appointment of proxies electronically is sufficient, but other countries may provide for shareholders to cast their votes electronically in advance of a general meeting, without the need to appoint proxies.

5.3 ICSA guidance on electronic communications

ICSA has issued a guidance note on 'Electronic communications with shareholders' (2013), which includes practical guidelines for best practice in communication in electronic form. These recommendations are largely a matter of common sense, and include the following suggestions.

- The facility to communicate in electronic form should be offered to all shareholders on equal terms.
- Shareholders should be able to retain a copy of any document or information sent to them in electronic form.
- Any electronic communication sent by a company giving notice of a general meeting and proxy voting should not include any electronic address unless the company intends that this address may be used by shareholders to respond to their communication.
- When information or notifications of availability (of information on the website) are sent to shareholders, the company should use a system for producing a list of recipients or a total number of messages sent, as 'proof of sending'.
- Shareholders opting to communicate electronically should be warned that if they file an electronic proxy voting form containing a virus, the company will not accept it.
- The company should alert shareholders to the fact that the company's obligation to communicate electronically ends with the transmission of the message, and the company cannot be responsible for failed transmissions that are outside their control. However, in the case of failed transmissions, the company should send a written communication to the shareholder within 48 hours of the failure.

STOP AND THINK 8.5

In what ways do you think that a public company might use its website to improve relations with its shareholders and other investors?

TEST YOUR KNOWLEDGE 8.4

a What are the provisions in the UK Code for making constructive use of the AGM?
b What are the benefits of electronic communications between a company and its shareholders?

6 Institutional shareholder responsibilities

6.1 Expecting companies to comply with best corporate governance practice

Developing good relations between a company and its shareholders is as much a task for the shareholders as for the board. Institutional investors, as 'professional' shareholders with large investments in public companies, should be particularly responsible for improving the dialogue and conveying the concerns of shareholders to the board. Institutional shareholders, particularly in the US and UK, express active concern about corporate governance in the companies in which they invest. In the UK, this has been demonstrated largely through the various representative bodies of the institutional investor organisations, particularly the ISC, ABI and PLSA, although in 2010 the FRC took on responsibility for a Stewardship Code for institutional investors. The interests of institutional investors in good corporate governance can be explained as follows.

■ Investors expect a return on their investment. Most evidence suggests that well-governed companies deliver reasonable returns over the long term, and shareholders in these companies are less exposed to downside risk than shareholders in companies that are not so well governed.

■ Institutional investors also have legal responsibilities (fiduciary duties) to the individuals on whose behalf they invest. For pension funds, these individuals are the beneficiaries of the funds. In fulfilling their responsibilities, institutions should try to ensure that they make a decent return on investment, and promoting good corporate governance is one way of trying to do this.

6.2 Shareholder activism

In response to a suggestion that shareholders should be given more extensive rights under company law, a frequent counter-argument is that shareholders already have sufficient rights, but do not use them constructively enough. Corporate governance would be improved if shareholders were more active in making their views known to their company, and using their votes against the board of directors if the company failed to respond in a satisfactory way to their concerns.

The term 'shareholder activism' refers to activities by institutional investors to influence governance and strategy decisions in companies in which they invest. In most cases, activism is constructive, involving dialogue and discussion, and it is only when a board of directors fails to respond in an acceptable and appropriate way to shareholder concerns that more aggressive action may be considered. This further action will often involve withholding a vote at an AGM, or voting against a resolution at a general meeting, including votes against the re-election of certain directors.

Shareholder activism attracts publicity. Its potential strength is that it brings pressure to bear on companies from the negative publicity that shareholder opposition to the board can create.

A problem for effective shareholder activism is that powers over a company are held by the board of directors, and not by the shareholders. In the face of a continuing refusal by the board to listen to their concerns, shareholders can only make their opposition felt by voting against the board's proposals at general meetings. To do this successfully, they need a majority of the votes. Since most shareholders in large public companies hold a relatively small percentage of the total number of shares, organising a group of dissident shareholders into a voting majority is difficult, although voting guidelines on some issues are occasionally issued by institutional investor organisations or voting advisory firms, and such guidelines (such as 'red top' notices) may have the effect of persuading shareholders how to vote.

 **CASE EXAMPLE** **8.2**

There have been cases where activist shareholders with only a fairly small shareholding in a company have attempted, sometimes successfully, to influence the decisions of company management.

In March 2007, the confectionery and drinks group Cadbury-Schweppes announced its intention to split the drinks division from the confectionery division, with a view to a possible demerger or a sale of the drinks division. This followed an announcement by the company in February that it had no such plans to split the group.

Some City observers believed that the company management had been pushed into a change of mind by the acquisition of 3% of the company's shares by an activist hedge fund that wanted the company to be split up (although the company denied that it had given way to any pressure).

A leading UK fund manager commented in the *Financial Times* in June 2007 that the suspicion that Cadbury-Schweppes had given way to activist pressure 'could represent a come-on to every corporate raider and activist investor'.

In 2010, Cadbury's was subsequently taken over by US food company Kraft.

CASE EXAMPLE 8.3

In December 2011, Mr Harvey McGrath, chairman of the Prudential group, announced that he would retire from the chairmanship in 2012 once a successor had been found. The announcement followed pressure for him to leave the job. At the company's 2011 AGM, more than a fifth of the shareholders voted against his re-appointment. This was in protest over a costly failure by the company to take over AIA, a major insurance company in Asia. The failed bid cost the company £377 million in fees and other expenses.

Prudential had abandoned its bid for AIA when investors signalled that they would not back the deal. Mr McGrath was criticised for his role in the failed bid, particularly because he had failed to control the ambitions of the company's new chief executive (who escaped investor criticism). Even after the vote at the AGM, pressure for Mr McGrath to resign remained strong and some observers regarded his eventual retirement as an inevitable consequence of investor pressure.

 CASE EXAMPLE 8.4

The following episode probably illustrates the problems that occur when shareholders and board cannot get into constructive dialogue with each other more than it shows the benefits of shareholder activism.

A bitter dispute developed between the board of UK listed company Mitchells & Butlers (M&B) and some of its largest shareholders following a failed hedging transaction in January 2008 when the company lost hundreds of millions of pounds. Investor Joe Lewis acquired a substantial equity shareholding through an investment company, Piedmont, and succeeded in getting some of his representatives appointed as directors of the M&B board. Following continuing disagreements, the chairman of M&B managed to sack four NEDs, including two representatives of Piedmont, and reported Piedmont – unsuccessfully – to the Takeover Panel, alleging that it was plotting with other shareholders to seize control of the company. At an AGM in January 2010, the situation was reversed. By a majority of 66%, the chairman of M&B and two other NEDs who were standing for re-election failed to be re-appointed, and another NED stood down from the board. The meeting then appointed as directors three individuals proposed by Piedmont, including a new chairman. However, although there was a large majority in favour of removing the former chairman and two NEDs, most of the votes probably came from Piedmont and six or seven other shareholders, whereas the majority of shareholders by number (rather than size of shareholdings) had supported their re-appointment. A representative of the ABI subsequently commented that it was regrettable that a minority shareholder (Piedmont) had in effect been able to decide the composition of the majority of the M&B board.

7 The UK Stewardship Code

7.1 The Stewardship Code and the UK Corporate Governance Code

Both the UK Stewardship Code and the UK Corporate Governance Code are the responsibility of the FRC. The FRC agreed to take on responsibility for the Stewardship Code because it saw an opportunity to build a critical mass of institutional investors who would comply with the Stewardship Code, and in doing so commit themselves to high-quality dialogue with the companies in which they invest. The FRC has stated that it sees the Stewardship Code as 'complementary' to the UK Corporate Governance Code, in promoting dialogue between institutional investors and UK listed companies.

7.2 The meaning of stewardship

The Introduction to the 2012 version of the Stewardship Code comments that the aim of stewardship is to promote the long-term success of the company in such a way that the 'ultimate providers of capital' also prosper. The Code refers to 'investors' rather than 'shareholders', suggesting that long-term investors in debt capital have stewardship responsibilities as well as shareholders.

The Code goes on to state that responsibilities for stewardship are shared.

- The primary responsibility lies with the board of the company, which oversees the actions of management.
- Investors also have an important role, in holding the board to account for the fulfilment of its responsibilities.

For investors, stewardship involves voting at general meetings, and the way in which votes are used. However, stewardship for investors is more than just voting. 'Activities may include monitoring and engaging with companies on matters such as strategy, performance, risk, capital structure and corporate governance, including culture and remuneration. Engagement is purposeful dialogue with companies on these matters as well as on issues that are the immediate subject of votes at general meetings.'

7.3 Who should apply the Stewardship Code?

The Stewardship Code is intended for institutional investors who are either:

- asset owners; or
- asset managers.

Asset owners are institutions that own company securities (shares and bonds) such as pension funds, insurance companies, investment trusts and other collective investment organisations (such as unit trusts).

Asset managers are organisations that have day-to-day responsibility for managing investment funds: these are commonly known as 'fund managers'. Providers of services to institutional investors, such as investment consultants and proxy advisers (advisers on voting), are also included.

7.4 Objectives of the UK Stewardship Code

The UK Stewardship Code 2012 aims to enhance the quality of engagement between investors and companies to help improve long-term risk-adjusted returns to shareholders.

The UK Stewardship Code sets out the principles of effective stewardship by investors. In so doing, the Code assists institutional investors better to exercise their stewardship responsibilities, which in turn gives force to the 'comply or explain' system.

7.5 Comply or explain

Not all investment institutions will want to engage directly with companies, e.g. it might not be consistent with the investment strategy of some investment firms. Not all parts of the Code are relevant to smaller investment institutions, and some foreign investment institutions may prefer to follow the requirements of a different code in their own country.

The UK Stewardship Code as with the UK Corporate Governance Code, is therefore applied on a 'comply or explain' basis. Organisations that adopt the Stewardship Code should provide a statement on their website containing:

- a description of how the principles of the Stewardship Code have been applied;
- disclosure of specific information that is required by the Stewardship Code; and
- an explanation of any non-compliance with the Code.

7.6 The seven principles of the UK Stewardship Code

The Code consists of seven principles, with some guidance for each principle.

Principle 1: Institutional investors should publicly disclose their policy on how they will discharge their stewardship responsibilities.
Discharging responsibilities means monitoring and engaging with companies, as explained previously.

Public disclosure should be in a policy statement (or **'stewardship statement'**) by the institutional investor, which should indicate how the institution applies stewardship with the intention of enhancing and protecting value for their ultimate beneficiaries or clients (such as pension fund beneficiaries and investors in unit trusts).

The policy statement should reflect the institution's position within the 'investment chain', as asset owners or asset managers.

Principle 2: Institutional investors should have a robust policy on managing conflicts of interest in relation to stewardship, which should be publicly disclosed.
Institutional investors should have a 'robust policy' on managing conflicts of interest in relationship to stewardship, and they should make public disclosure of this policy.

Guidance on this principle comments that institutional investors should act in the interests of their clients or beneficiaries, but conflicts of interest between beneficiaries or clients will inevitably arise from time to time.

Principle 3: Institutional investors should monitor their investee companies.
Institutional investors should monitor the companies in which they invest, in order to decide when it is necessary to enter into an active dialogue with their board of directors. They should try to identify problems in a company at an early stage, to minimise the potential loss of shareholder value, and they should make their concerns known to appropriate members of the company's board.

Principle 3 encourages investment institutions to:

- keep abreast of the company's performance and developments that affect the company's value and risks;
- satisfy themselves that the company has effective leadership;
- satisfy themselves that the board and its committees adhere to the spirit of the UK Corporate Governance Code: they can do this through meetings with the board chairman and other board members;
- consider the quality of the company's reporting; and
- attend general meetings of companies in which they have a 'major' holding, where this is possible and appropriate.

The Code suggests that investors should consider any non-compliance by a company with the provisions of the UK Code. If they do not agree with the company's position, they should:

- give a timely explanation to the company, in writing where appropriate; and
- be prepared if necessary to enter into a dialogue with the company.

Institutional investors should also try to identify at an early stage issues that may result in significant loss in investment value. They should make sure that members of the company's board or its management are made aware of any concerns that they have.

There is a problem, however, that by engaging in dialogue with a company, an institutional investor may become an insider, and so unable to buy or sell shares. Guidance to the Code suggests:

'Institutional shareholders may not wish to be made insiders. An institutional investor who may be willing to become an insider should indicate in its stewardship statement the willingness to do so and the mechanism by which this should be done.'

Principle 4: Institutional investors should establish clear guidelines on when and how they will escalate their stewardship activities (escalating shareholder activism).

Institutional investors should set out the circumstances when they will intervene actively, e.g. when they have concerns about the company's strategy, performance, corporate governance, remuneration or its approach to risks arising from environmental or social matters.

Initial discussions with the company should be on a confidential basis, but if the company's board does not respond constructively, the institutional investor should consider whether to escalate their action, for example by:

- holding additional meetings with management to express their concern;
- expressing their concern through the company's advisers, e.g. the company's investment bank and sponsor;
- meeting with the chairman, or other board members;
- intervening jointly with other investment institutions on a particular issue;
- making a public statement in advance of an AGM or EGM;
- submitting resolutions to general meetings of the company (if sufficient support can be obtained from other shareholders, to get the 5% required) or speaking at an AGM or EGM; and
- requisitioning an EGM, possibly to propose changes to board membership.

Principle 5: Institutional shareholders should be willing to act collectively with other investors where appropriate.

Institutional investors should be willing to act collectively with other investors where appropriate. 'At times collaboration with other investors may be the most effective manner in which to engage.'

Collaborative engagement may be particularly appropriate at times when the company is under severe stress, or when risks threaten to 'destroy significant value'.

Principle 6: Institutional investors should have a clear policy on voting and disclosure of voting activity.

Institutional investors should seek to vote all the shares that they hold. They should not automatically support the board of directors. Where they have been unable to reach a satisfactory outcome through dialogue, they should consider withholding their vote on resolutions at a general meeting, or voting against. It is good practice to notify the company of an intention to vote against a resolution or withhold a vote.

Institutional investors should make public disclosure of their voting records.

Principle 7: Institutional investors should report periodically on their stewardship and voting activities.

Institutional investors should report periodically on stewardship and voting activities. Investment managers should report to their clients, and institutions that represent the interests of an end-investor or act as principals should report at least annually to those people to whom they are accountable.

The information that is reported may include both qualitative and quantitative information, but the particular information reported (including details of voting) are a matter for agreement between the agent and their client.

7.7 Monitoring and review of the UK Stewardship Code

The FRC is responsible for monitoring and review of the UK Stewardship Code. Since 2011, the FRC has published an annual report on the implementation of the UK Corporate Governance and Stewardship Codes and related developments. The annual reports are available on their website.

- Separately, the Investment Association also undertakes an annual monitoring exercise of how investors are implementing the Code. The reports since 2011 are available on their website.

TEST YOUR KNOWLEDGE 8.5

What are the seven principles of the Stewardship Code?

8 Engagement with shareholders

Constructive dialogue between a board of directors and its shareholders calls for:

- a desire on the part of the board to engage with its shareholders;
- shareholders who want to engage with the board and who see themselves as long-term investors in the company, and so who are concerned about the company's future and objectives; and
- practical arrangements for engaging with each other.

Engagement takes the form mainly of:

- meetings between members of the board (for example the chairman and CEO) and the larger shareholders: the larger shareholders of European and US listed companies are mostly institutional investors; and
- feedback following meetings, typically in the form of a letter from the shareholder to the board members they met.

The UK Code has a provision that when, in the opinion of the board, a significant proportion of votes have been cast against a resolution at any general meeting, the company should explain when announcing the results of voting what actions it intends to take to understand the reasons behind the vote result.

8.1 Meetings between the company and institutional shareholders

The ABI in its report on Improving Corporate Governance and Shareholder Engagement 2013 identified the following types of meeting, or reasons for meeting, between a company and institutional shareholders.

TABLE 8.1 ABI guidelines identifying types of meeting between a company and institutional shareholders

Type of meeting	
Ongoing meetings	These are regular meetings between senior members of the board (such as the chairman and CEO) for regular updates and discussions about strategy, financing, company performance and governance issues. Meetings are normally arranged by the company, which invites its largest shareholders to the meeting. These regular meetings give the shareholders an opportunity to express their concerns about any issues.
Specific meetings	These are meetings between the company and its larger shareholders, usually initiated by the company to consult the shareholders on a specific issue that has arisen or a specific proposal that the board intends to put to a general meeting of the company. The board is seeking shareholder views before it makes a final decision about the issue in question. The specific issue may for example relate to remuneration policy, or a proposed change in the company strategy, or a major new appointment to the board. Although specific meetings are usually called by the company, they may be requested by a shareholder with a concern about a specific issue that it wishes to discuss with the company.

Type of meeting	
Reactive meetings	These are meetings relating to Issues that have emerged unexpectedly, such as an issue relating to the remuneration of a director, the announcement of poor financial results, an unexpected change in the board, and so on. The company may call such a meeting with its larger shareholders to ask for their views and to try to ensure that the company responds to the issue in a way that shareholders will find acceptable.
Proactive meetings	These are meetings initiated by a shareholder (institutional investor) when it has concerns about a deteriorating trend or change that appears to be happening. For example a shareholder may have concerns about the company's environmental performance, or its lack of progress in appointing women to senior positions. The shareholder seeks to persuade the company to deal with the issue, before matters get worse.
Systematic meetings	These are similar to proactive meetings, in that they are initiated by the shareholder. However, the shareholder has a system for reviewing its investments and identifying companies where it considers that closer engagement is needed.

8.2 Escalation of action by concerned shareholders

The ABI Report found if shareholders become concerned by the decisions taken by a board, there are various options they may wish to pursue, some or all of which may be appropriate, depending on the circumstances:

- **Voice:** In the normal course, shareholders may wish to attempt to exert influence over the board and encourage them to reconsider the course being adopted. Given the likely sensitivity of the topics and the need to build mutual trust, it is generally appropriate for this dialogue to be private.
- **Escalate:** By the same token, depending on the nature of the problem, it may be appropriate to escalate engagement activities, for example by co-ordinating with a wider group of shareholders.
- **Vote:** Depending on the result of these activities, shareholders may wish to express disagreement with the board by voting against resolutions at a general meeting. They may also wish to propose their own resolutions.
- **Exit:** Having reviewed changes to a strategy or governance model that they consider detrimental to shareholders' interests, they may choose to sell shares.

8.3 Collective engagement

Collective engagement means joint action by several shareholders to engage with their company on a particular issue. The ABI Report states that most members do not contemplate collective engagement unless they have first raised the issue individually with the company and concluded that insufficient or no progress is being made.

However, often there are no clear and agreed objectives within collective engagement, particularly when a larger number of shareholders are involved. Equally, if efforts are made to reach a single view, the concern arises that members' individual views may be diluted or lost. Members are particularly concerned if they feel pushed towards solutions that they individually consider counter-productive.

8.4 Engagement and the law on insider dealing

Engagement between a company and its shareholders through private meetings carries the risk that the shareholders will become 'insiders' and so at risk of being prosecuted for insider dealing if they buy or sell shares in the company until the information becomes public knowledge or is no longer correct.

Some institutional investors have 'Chinese wall' procedures to prevent communications between its traders in shares and the corporate finance or corporate governance teams that meet with the company. These procedures may be sufficient to enable the institutional investor to deal in the company's shares without restriction.

Where this is not possible, the shareholder should be asked by the company whether it is willing to become an insider. The shareholder may agree to this, depending on the size of its shareholding and the length of time for which it would be expected to remain an inside. For example, a shareholder may agree to become an insider for a week, but if the expected time is longer than this, it may refuse to meet with the company and receive the inside information.

8.5 ICSA guidance on engagement

In 2013, ICSA published guidance 'Enhancing Stewardship Dialogue' which provides guidance on the relationship between companies and their investors. The aim of the guidance is to improve the process of engagement, with the focus of conversations on 'the things that really matter in creating and destroying value, that is on strategy, risk and long-term comparative performance'.

It recognises that companies may have difficulty in identifying which investors it should engage with (since the share register may continually change) and which individuals within large institutional investor organisations it should be speaking with.

There are four main elements to the ICSA guidance.

1   Develop an engagement strategy. Companies should develop an investor engagement strategy and review it annually. This annual review should be referred to in the corporate governance section of the company's annual report. The strategy should consist of a combination of one-to-one meetings with the largest shareholders and group meetings for a number of smaller investors. Meetings should be ongoing – regular, and not driven by events or specific issues. The ICSA guidance also suggests that there may occasionally be merit in organising collective engagement for a number of the largest shareholders.

2   Get the housekeeping right. The company should ensure that it invites the 'right people' to meetings. These will be mainly large shareholders and investors with a strong track record of engagement. The company should also ensure that individuals within the company attend who are best placed to speak on the issues that will be discussed at the meeting. From the investors' point of view, voting at the next annual general meeting should reflect the outcome of discussions at the meetings held as part of the engagement process. If shareholders intend to vote differently at the AGM, they should tell the company in advance, to give the board of directors time to work further on the engagement process.

3   Strengthen the conversation. Meetings should discuss matters that are of direct relevance to the company's value. There should be at least one engagement meeting a year that focuses on the company's strategy and performance. Remuneration should not be allowed to dominate discussions and should be discussed within the context of creating value. The ICSA guidance suggests that although executive directors may be invited to the strategy and performance meeting, they may be asked at some stage to leave the meeting, so that the shareholders can discuss the issues with the chairman and other non-executive directors.

4   Provide feedback. There should be feedback in both directions. The procedures for providing feedback should be agreed, and should relate to the matters discussed at meetings and the engagement process overall. From the company's perspective, feedback may consist of a series of questions from the company, such as:
    – Did you meet the right people?
    – Did the meeting cover all the topics that you expected?
    – Were there any aspects of the discussions that surprised you?
    – Have you learned anything from the meeting that might influence your view of the company as an investment?

9   Institutional investors: using their votes

Institutional shareholders will support the board of directors unless they have a good reason not to. When a shareholder thinks that it should vote against the board, it should first make representations to the board in time for the problem to be considered, with a view to reaching a satisfactory solution.

Company law requires some proposals to be approved by the shareholders voting in a general meeting, and specifies the size of majority needed for a resolution to be passed. In the UK, most votes by shareholders require a simple majority (an 'ordinary resolution'), but a 75% majority vote is required for a 'special resolution'. For example, in the UK the shareholders have the right to appoint or re-appoint the company's auditors at the AGM and to approve the directors' remuneration report. The most significant voting rights for shareholders are probably the binding vote on remuneration policy (quoted companies) and the right to re-elect directors, in accordance with the company's articles of association and the UK Corporate Governance Code.

An example of how institutional investors may use their votes to indicate displeasure with the decisions of the board of directors are shown in Table 8.2.

TABLE 8.2 Examples of voting guidelines illustrating how shareholders might vote on governance issues

Governance issue	Possible vote to indicate disapproval
There are not enough independent NEDs on the board.	Vote against the re-election of the chairman of the nomination committee, or a member of the committee.
The company chairman sits on the audit committee.	Given the broader consequence of voting against the re-election of the chairman, consider abstaining on a vote to re-elect him or her.
The company chairman was not independent when appointed.	Voting against the election of a company chairman has broad implications for a company; therefore, it may be appropriate to consider an 'actively withheld vote' or a vote against the re-election of the chairman of the nomination committee.
The newly appointed chairman was previously the company CEO.	Consider an 'actively withheld vote' or a vote against the re-election of the chairman of the nomination committee. In exceptional circumstances, vote against the incoming company chairman.
A NED has a poor record of attendance at board meetings, or there is evidence of poor performance.	In the absence of a sufficient explanation, vote against the re-election of the NED.
There are shortcomings in the annual performance evaluation process for the board and its directors.	Abstain or vote against the re-election of the company chairman or the SID.
The company's remuneration policy contains features that are unacceptable.	Vote against approval of the annual remuneration policy (quoted companies) and possibly also the implementation report.
The annual report fails to provide information about non-audit fees paid to the auditors.	Vote against the re-election of the chairman of the audit committee or any other member of the audit committee.

The key point to understand is that shareholder votes against board proposals (or abstention from voting) will only be considered when the company is somehow in breach of the UK Corporate Governance Code.

Companies have a responsibility to give a full explanation of any non-compliance with the Code, and should not use 'boilerplate' explanations. Institutional shareholders should evaluate explanations of non-compliance and should not take a 'mechanistic' approach in responding to them. An effective 'comply or explain' regime 'must be based on regular and open dialogue between companies and shareholders, which should extend beyond the voting season'.

Non-compliance issues that would be of particular concern to institutional shareholders should include failure to separate the roles of chairman and CEO, failure to appoint a SID, the independence of NEDs and the company's policy for refreshing the board, particularly with regard to gender and ethnic diversity.

10 PLSA Corporate Governance Policy and Voting Guidelines

The PLSA state that: 'Members of the PLSA have a clear interest in promoting the success of the companies in which they invest. As a consequence of this, we have long considered that one of our prime functions is to support members in engaging with investee companies. Our efforts are directed towards maximising the long-term returns of pension schemes' assets, irrespective of the potential for short-term discomfort.

Our 'Corporate Governance Policy and Voting Guidelines' provide our members with examples of good stewardship practice and recommendations for key votes at the Annual General Meetings of their investee companies, on subjects such as executive pay, the re-election of directors and the approval of the annual report. The recommendations, which are agreed in consultation with the PLSA membership, are based on our members' interest in ensuring that companies are run in a sustainable, accountable fashion that generates returns for investors over the long term while also behaving in a responsible manner and supporting the interests of wider society.

Our wider work on corporate governance and stewardship informs our annual review of the guidelines. For example, our 2016 AGM report highlighted continuing controversy around excessive executive pay awards and also found much higher levels of dissent on shareholder votes over executive pay practices than for votes against the re-election of the directors responsible for those practices. As such, our 2017 iteration of the guidelines suggests that our members take a much stronger line against the re-election of remuneration committee chairs at companies with problematic remuneration practices, recommending that shareholders voting against a remuneration policy should also vote against the re-election of the remuneration committee chair.

The 2017 guidelines also incorporate the recommendations of our stewardship toolkit on the reporting of corporate cultures and working practices and emphasises the importance of boardroom diversity, with particular reference to the targets on gender and ethnic diversity identified in the Davies and Parker reports respectively.'

TEST YOUR KNOWLEDGE 8.6

a   What is **responsible voting**? Why is responsible voting recommended by associations of institutional investors (such as the PLSA) to their members?

b   For what reasons might the PLSA recommend to its members that they should vote against the re-election of the company chairman as a director of the company?

CHAPTER SUMMARY

- Relations between a company and its shareholders can be poor, particularly when there is a lack of meaningful communication and dialogue.
- However, the UK Corporate Governance Code calls for the creation of good relations between a company and its shareholders through dialogue with institutional investors and constructive use of the AGM.
- A company might have a majority shareholder, and/or a mix of institutional shareholders and other shareholders. Other shareholders might be corporates or private individuals, and large or small

shareholders. The interests and concerns of each type of shareholder, and their relations with the company, will differ.

■ The powers of shareholders are limited mainly to voting at general meetings and, in extreme cases, taking a company's directors to court. Voting rights include the right to vote on waiving pre-emption rights when new shares are issued for cash, approval of new long-term incentive schemes for executives, the election or re-election of directors and approval of the remuneration report (which is only an advisory vote). The UK government is proposing to give shareholders a binding vote on pay policy every three years.

■ Shareholders could propose resolutions at general meetings, such as a resolution to dismiss one or more directors (provided the resolution is permitted by the company's articles of association). However, shareholders with at least 5% of the company's shares are required to call an EGM or include a resolution to be voted on at the AGM, and a majority of votes at the meeting will be required to pass the resolution. In practice, this is a difficult task for shareholders to achieve, unless the situation has become very serious and contentious.

■ Companies should make efforts to improve communications with shareholders. The UK Corporate Governance Code encourages companies to enter into constructive dialogue with its institutional shareholders.

■ The ISC Code and the Stewardship Code also encourage institutional investors to enter into constructive dialogue with the companies in which they invest.

■ The UK Code also requires companies to make constructive use of the AGM to communicate with smaller shareholders and encourage their participation.

■ Participation by shareholders can be improved by offering a 'vote withheld' option on proxy forms, the legal entitlement of proxies to vote when a vote is taken by a show of hands, and requirements for a company to report on its website the results of poll votes at general meetings.

■ Communications with shareholders are improved by electronic communications. Benefits include faster and more reliable delivery of messages, particularly for foreign shareholders; lower costs due to savings in print and postage costs; a better chance that key decision makers in institutional investor organisations will see messages from a company and act on them; and the likelihood of greater participation by shareholders in the company's affairs due to the convenience of appointing proxies electronically.

■ Shareholder activism might be encouraged to bring pressure to bear on companies to pay greater attention to the wishes and concerns of their shareholders. Activism might involve voting against resolutions at general meetings, such as resolutions for the re-election of directors retiring by rotation.

■ In the UK, the ISC issued a code of practice for UK institutional investors (and inviting foreign shareholders in UK companies to adopt the Code too). This contains seven principles of engagement by investors in companies. This Code was adopted by the FRC in 2010 and issued as a Stewardship Code for institutional investors. It was reviewed and its guidance was revised in 2012.

■ In 2013, ICSA and the ABI separately issued guidance on better engagement between companies and their shareholders. The ICSA recommendations include a suggestion that companies should develop an engagement strategy and review it annually.

■ Associations of institutional investors encourage their members to use responsible voting, generally giving support to the board of directors. Voting guidelines, in the event that shareholders disagree with aspects of a company's performance or decisions, are set out for its members in the PLSA/NAPF's Corporate Governance Policy and Voting Guidelines.

■ In the UK, the DTR require listed companies to report changes in shareholdings of significant shareholders. This should help a company to monitor the identity of its main shareholders.

Risk management and internal control

■ LIST OF CHAPTERS

■ OVERVIEW

The third part of this study text considers risk and risk management as issues in corporate governance. The leaders of companies (and other organisations) are responsible for deciding risk strategies and risk policies, and for ensuring that the internal control system is effective. The responsibilities of the board of directors for risk management and internal control are specified in some corporate governance codes, including the UK Corporate Governance Code and King IV Code.

Chapter 9 explains the nature of business risk and the responsibility of the board for deciding how much risk the company should be prepared to accept in order to achieve hoped-for financial returns, and also how much risk the company should be able to tolerate. The main focus of this chapter is on **strategic risks** and the management of these risks.

Exposures to business risk should not exceed the levels determined by the board, and the risk management system should be effective in ensuring that board strategies and policies are implemented and also reviewed. The chapter describes the elements that may be found in a risk management system, including the role of a risk committee of the board (or the audit committee) and the measures that may be taken by executive management to implement and monitor risk strategies. The chapter concludes with a brief consideration of how executive remuneration packages might be arranged so that incentive schemes make suitable allowance for risk and risk exposures.

Chapter 10 examines internal control systems. Whereas strategic risk is an unavoidable aspect of engaging in business activities and is external to a company, internal control is concerned with risks that are mostly internal to a company and so within management control. The chapter describes the nature of operational, financial and **compliance risks** and internal controls that are applied to prevent adverse risk events from happening, or identifying them and taking corrective measures when they do happen. A board of directors is responsible for ensuring that the system of internal control is effective, and achieves its purpose. The chapter describes the guidance given to UK listed companies on internal control systems. It then goes on to describe several elements of internal control in more detail: the role of internal audit in internal control (and whether companies should have an internal audit function); the benefits of **disaster recovery planning**; and whistleblowing procedures that enable employees to report suspicions of wrongdoing outside normal lines of reporting through the management hierarchy. The chapter concludes with a description of the statutory measures implemented in the US by the Sarbanes-Oxley Act (SOX) to ensure more effective internal control within companies.

■ LEARNING OUTCOMES

Part Three should enable you to:

■ apply the principles of risk management;

■ appraise the significance of risk management for good governance;

■ advise on the appropriate arrangements for an effective risk management system;

■ advise on the board's responsibility for internal control to meet good governance guidelines;

■ appraise the effectiveness of an internal control system;

■ understand and apply the UK principles and guidance in relation to internal audit; and

■ develop appropriate policies and procedures to mitigate the impact of operational disaster and devise a whistleblowing procedure.

 PART 3 CASE STUDY

Hunnerware plc is a successful UK listed company whose revenues and profits have been growing at over 20% per year for the past ten years and the company could soon be included in the FTSE 350 list of companies. It operates a large fleet of small aircraft that carry passengers (mainly business passengers) and freight between locations not serviced by larger airlines.

The board of directors is keen to continue with strategies for growth, and a decision has recently been taken to establish a specialised subsidiary company for the maintenance of small aircraft. This maintenance service will be offered to other airline companies as well as Hunnerware's own fleet of planes. Hunnerware is sponsored by the investment banking division of a large bank, which informed the company chairman that some shareholders were becoming concerned about the risk exposures of the company. They considered that the company is becoming over-exposed to high risks in its pursuit of growth. Some concerns had also been expressed about the company's disputes with government. Twelve months ago, the company had been fined by the authorities for allegedly price-fixing on one of its routes: the other company in the price-fixing arrangement had confessed what it had done to the authorities and its evidence had been used against Hunnerware. Hunnerware was still disputing the fine. The company has also been fined for four breaches of health and safety regulations in the past five years. It has also been accused of tax evasion by the tax

authorities, but has denied the charge, claiming that its tax arrangements were entirely tax avoidance measures and within the law.

The chairman discussed the matter of the company's poor reputation for risk management with the chairman of the nomination committee, who agreed that the board probably gave insufficient attention to risk strategy and lacked board members with experience and knowledge of risk management. Sometime later, the nomination committee reported to the board that they were recommending changes to the composition of the board. One of the independent non-executive directors (NEDs) would not be invited to remain on the board for a further three years when his contract expired soon, and a new appointment to the board was recommended. This was an individual with extensive experience in risk management, at one time as a partner in a risk management consultancy firm. The change in the board was made, in accordance with the nomination committee recommendations. The new director raised the subject of risk at the first board meeting he attended. The board meeting was held soon after an unusual event had affected the airline industry in Europe generally: a large cloud of volcanic ash from an erupting volcano in Iceland had resulted in the closure of much European air space for several days. As a result, the company had lost a substantial amount of business and revenue. At the meeting, the new director told the other board members that

PART 3 CASE STUDY *continued*

having met and spoken with senior executives in the company, as well as the executive directors, he was unaware of any disaster recovery plan for the company or of any stress testing to assess risk exposures. He recommended that the board should give serious consideration to the development of a risk strategy and the introduction of a risk awareness culture into the company's management and other employees. He also recommended that the company should introduce a system for scenario-based risk identification as an immediate urgent measure.

9 Risk management and corporate governance

■ CONTENTS

1   Risk management and governance
2   The nature of risk
3   Business risk: strategic risk and operating risks
4   Risk committees and risk managers
5   The UK Corporate Governance Code on risk management
6   FRC Guidance on risk management
7   Elements in an effective risk management system
8   Senior executive remuneration: bonuses and risk adjustment

■ INTRODUCTION

The responsibility of the board for effective risk management came under close scrutiny following the banking crisis in 2007–2009. Many banks were criticised for getting into financial difficulty because of reckless business strategies and failing to recognise the business risks that they were taking. Business risks are risks to profitability and financial security that arise from factors in the business environment, including competition, over which management has no direct control. A business must take risks to make profits; but how much risk should it be prepared to tolerate, and would it be able to withstand 'shocks' in the business environment if an unexpected event or development were to occur? The board has the responsibility for strategic decisions on risk, and an important aspect of corporate governance is for the board to recognise its responsibilities and ensure that the risk management system in the company is effective. Risk management is a very important element of corporate governance.

---

1   Risk management and governance

1.1 The relevance of business risk for corporate governance

The board of directors has a responsibility to govern the company in the interests of the share-holders and other stakeholders. A part of this responsibility is to decide the objectives and strategic direction for the company, to approve detailed strategic plans put forward by management, and to monitor and review the implementation of those plans. An important objective of a commercial company is to make a profit, and the company's strategies should be directed towards this. However, any business strategy involves taking risks and actual profits may be higher or lower than expected. When very big risks are taken, a company might even become insolvent and go out of business if actual events turn out much worse than anticipated.

Bad corporate governance can result in the insolvency and collapse of a company, and excessive risk-taking is one aspect of poor governance. The board of directors should take risk into consideration when it makes strategic business decisions. It should choose policies that are expected to be profitable, but should limit the risks to a level that it considers acceptable. For example, when the board takes major investment decisions itself or decides on corporate strategy, risks as well as expected returns are properly assessed.

The board should also be satisfied that in their decision-making, managers take risk as well as expected returns into account. The Cadbury Report (1992) described risk management as 'the process by which executive management, under board supervision, identifies the risk arising from business ... and establishes the priorities for control and particular objectives'.

The significance of risk management for corporate governance was demonstrated forcibly by the global banking crisis in 2007–2009. In the UK, the government initiated a review into the failures in the banking industry and the resulting Walker Report was published in 2009. It commented that although there were failures in the regulation of the banking industry, much of the blame for the crisis was attributable to poor governance, and in particular inadequate attention to risk management. 'Serious deficiencies in prudential oversight and financial regulation in the period before the crisis were accompanied by major governance failures within banks. These contributed materially to excessive risk-taking and the breadth and depth of the crisis.'

1.2 Definitions of risk and risk management

Risks are defined by the international standard ISO31000 as 'the effect of uncertainty on objectives, whether positive or negative'.

Risk management is concerned with:

- the identification, assessment and prioritisation of risks; and
- measures to minimise, control and monitor the probability or impact of adverse risk events or to maximise benefits from opportunities.

1.3 Responsibilities for risk management

The board has overall responsibility for risk management.

Responsibility for the management of risk is delegated to executive management, but the board:

- decides the **risk appetite** of the company;
- requires management to manage risks within the board guidelines for risk appetite;
- monitors the performance of management, to ensure that the business is being managed within the risk guidelines set by the board; and
- monitors the risk management system to ensure that it is effective, and achieves its purpose.

The principles and provisions of the UK Corporate Governance Code, and supporting Financial Reporting Council (FRC) Guidance, are described later in this chapter.

1.4 Risk appetite and risk tolerance

Companies should not avoid risk, because risks have to be taken in order to make profits. However, the level of exposure to risk that a company takes should be justified by the expected returns, and in addition, the risks should not be so great that the losses would be unacceptably high if events turn out in an unfavourable way. The board of directors has the responsibility for deciding the company's risk appetite.

Risk appetite is the level of risk that a company (or any other organisation) is willing to take in the pursuit of its objectives. Risk appetite can be defined as the combination of the desire to take on risk in order to obtain a financial return and its risk capacity.

The 'desire to take on risk' refers to the amount and type of risk that the board of directors would like the company to have exposure to.

- Risk capacity is the amount of risk that the company could accept without a serious threat to its financial stability.
- **Risk tolerance** is the amount of risk that the company is prepared to accept in order to achieve its financial objectives, expressed as a quantitative measure, such as a permitted range of deviation from a specified target, or a maximum limit. Risk tolerance is therefore a quantified expression of the amount of risk that a company's board of directors allows the company to accept.

Risk appetite should be reviewed regularly by the board, and decisions should be taken about the scale of risk that is desired or acceptable. For major organisations such as large banks, risk appetite should be reviewed regularly (at least annually) and included in the policy objectives of the board.

Risk tolerance could be expressed in numerical terms, such as the maximum loss that the board would be willing to accept on a particular venture if events turn out adversely. This type of risk management is found in banking, for example, where loss limits may be set by a bank for each aspect of its trading activities in the financial markets, and risk measures such as Value at Risk (VaR) are used. Alternatively, risk tolerance could be expressed in terms of a total ban on certain types of business activity or behaviour.

1.5 Institute of Risk Management: Risk appetite and risk tolerance

The Institute of Risk Management (IRM) issued guidelines in 2011 on 'Risk Appetite and Tolerance', which provide some useful insights.

■ Risk appetite should be formulated within the context of the company's risk management capability. There are two aspects to risk management: one is taking on risks and the other is exercising control over them. A company should not have a high risk appetite if its ability to control risk is weak.

■ The UK Corporate Governance Code focuses on risk at a strategic level, whereas in practice there has to be coordination at strategic, tactical and operational levels for risk management to make sense.

■ Risk appetite should be measurable; otherwise, statements about risk appetite may be 'empty and vacuous'.

The risk appetite decided by the board should be within the company's risk tolerance. For example, a company may be able to pursue business strategies where possible outcomes may range between a profit of £100 million and a loss of £40 million over the next five years. This would be the risk tolerance of the company. The board may decide that its risk appetite over the same period should be within a range of £50 million profit and £10 million loss. In other words, its preferred risk appetite would be less than the company's risk tolerance, and management would be expected to implement strategies that are appropriate for the risk appetite rather than the risk tolerance of the company (taking on risk that goes outside the company's risk tolerance may offer the possibility of higher profits, but might also risk losses that would threaten the company with insolvency).

The IRM guidelines suggest five tests that directors should use when reviewing the company's risk appetite framework.

■ Do managers, when they make decisions, understand the degree to which they individually are permitted to expose the company to the consequences of an adverse risk event or situation?

■ Do managers understand their aggregate interlinked level of risk, so that they can decide whether the company's exposure to risk is acceptable or not?

■ Does the board (and top executives) understand the aggregated risk for the company as a whole?

■ Do managers understand that risk appetite is not constant and that the board may change its risk appetite as the business environment and business conditions change?

■ Are risk decisions made with full consideration of the potential rewards or returns?

TEST YOUR KNOWLEDGE 9.1

a What is the responsibility of a board of directors for risk?
b What is risk appetite and risk tolerance?

2   The nature of risk

Risk refers to the possibility that something unexpected or not planned for will happen. In many cases, risk is seen as the possibility that something bad might happen. In everyday life, there is a risk of becoming seriously ill, being involved in a road accident, having a house burgled or flooded, having a motorcar breakdown, and so on. This can be described as downside risk, because it is a risk that something will happen that would not normally be expected.

There is **upside risk** too. This is the possibility that actual events might turn out better than expected. In a business context, an example is the possibility that sales volumes will be higher than planned or that working days lost through industrial action will be lower than anticipated.

Risk management involves making decisions about upside risks as well as downside risks. For example, businesses make investment decisions. Every investment is risky. Actual returns could be lower or higher than expected. In deciding whether or not to undertake an investment, the risks as well as the potential returns should be taken into consideration. Shareholders would like to see their company earning high returns, but might be unwilling to see the management taking excessive investment risks in trying to achieve those returns.

Some risks are easy to recognise, because they are always present and a company may have had many years of experience in dealing with them. For example, financial risks include the risk that customers will not pay what they owe (credit risk), or that interest costs of borrowing will increase or (in the case of an exporting company) that foreign exchange rates will move adversely. Other risks, however, are more difficult to identify and anticipate. The Walker Report commented:

'While a clear continuing responsibility of the board is to ensure that [recognisable financial] risks are indeed appropriately managed and controlled, different and potentially much more difficult issues arise in the identification and measurement of risks where past experience is an uncertain or potentially misleading guide. When risk materialises, it may do so as a risk previously thought to be understood and managed that turns out to be very different indeed. ...'

TEST YOUR KNOWLEDGE 9.2

a   What may be the consequences of failing to consider business risk strategy or establish an effective risk management system?

b   What is business risk and how could it be measured?

3   Business risk: strategic risk and operating risks

A distinction can be made between strategic risk and internal operating risks (sometimes called governance risk).

- Strategic risks are risks that occur and arise in the external business environment in which a company operates. The risks faced by a company are determined by the strategies that the company pursues.
- Operating risks are risks of losses that arise through ineffective controls within the processes and systems of a company's business operations. Operating risk is risk within an organisation; strategic risk is risk in the external environment. Operating risk can be classified into three types of risk: operational risk, financial risk (especially reporting risk), and compliance risk.

This chapter is concerned mainly with the management of strategic risk. Chapter 10 describes **internal control systems** and the management of operational, financial and compliance risks.

3.1 Categories of strategic risk

The nature and severity of strategic risks vary from one company to another. Risks also change over time: some become less significant, and new risks emerge.

Strategic risks are risks that the actual performance of the business could be much worse (or better) than expected, due to unexpected developments in the business environment. For example, when a company develops a new product or service, it will have an expectation of the likely sales demand. Actual demand could be higher or lower than expected. With some new products, the risk that sales demand will differ from expectation could be much more severe than with other new products. There are various reasons why sales demand and profits may be less than expected, or may fall unexpectedly. Competitors may take away some of the company's market share; a company may suffer from bad publicity and so lose customer loyalty; there may be new regulations making the sale of a particular product or service more difficult.

CASE EXAMPLE 9.1

In the early 2000s, there was rapid growth in investment in IT and third generation (3G) telecommunications services. The investments in IT were high risk because huge amounts of money had to be invested to create the service, and there was no certainty that sales demand would achieve the expected levels. Actual demand for the services fell far short of expectation, with the result that many dot.com companies and telecommunications companies collapsed in 2002, resulting in a stock market crash (mainly in the US).

CASE EXAMPLE 9.2

In some cases, companies may experience a big fall in sales as a result of bad publicity or acquiring a poor reputation for something. This is reputation risk. In 2010, it was reported that sales of some models of car produced by Toyota had fallen sharply, following the recall of millions of vehicles to rectify a design fault that caused unintended acceleration. There were also suspicions that the company had tried to cover up the scale of the problems. Sales of the cars had been affected by the damage to the company's reputation.

Risks can be categorised or identified in different ways, but it may help to understand the variety of risks by considering the following sources of risk.

- **Reputation risk.** The risk of loss in customer loyalty or customer support following an event that damages the company's reputation. Reputation risk is often associated with risks arising from unethical behaviour by a company, including policies and practices that damage the environment or affect human rights. This is considered in more detail in the chapter on corporate social responsibility (Chapter 11).
- **Competition risk.** The risk that business performance will differ from expected performance because of actions taken (or not taken) by business rivals.
- **Business environment risks.** These are risks of significant changes in the business environment from political and regulatory factors, economic factors, social and environmental factors and technology factors (the so-called 'PEST' factors). For example, business performance may be affected by the introduction of new regulations, political upheaval in a country, economic decline or growth, environmental issues, unexpected changes in social habits, or technological change.
- **Risks from external events**. These are risks that financial conditions may change, with adverse changes in interest rates or exchange rates, higher losses from bad debts or changes in prices in financial markets (such as changes in share prices).
- **Liquidity risk**. This is the risk that the company will have insufficient cash to settle all its liabilities on time, and so may be forced out of business. The board of directors should

monitor this risk at least annually when they prepare their going concern statement for the annual report and accounts.

 **CASE EXAMPLE 9.3**

In 2005, the banking group Citigroup Inc took a strategic decision, based partly on advice from outside consultants, to invest more heavily in its 'fixed income' business, which included collateralised debt obligations (CDOs). The bank believed that this new strategic direction offered opportunities for long-term growth. The global banking crisis from 2007 resulted in a collapse in the market value of CDOs. At a hearing of the Financial Crisis Inquiry Commission in Washington in April 2010, former chief executive officer (CEO) Mr 'Chuck' Prince and former head of the bank's executive committee Mr Robert Rubin said that they did not become aware of the scale of the problem – and its losses – until September 2007. They had been unaware of the scale of the bank's positions in CDOs and the risks surrounding them. Citigroup eventually received a $45 billion bail-out from the Federal government in 2008 to prevent its collapse.

In making the decision to invest more heavily in CDOs, the bank took a strategic risk without being fully aware of the size of the risk it was taking. Risk management systems may also have been ineffective in alerting management to the problems until it was too late to avoid a rescue by the government.

Each industry and each company within an industry faces different risks. The questions that management should ask are as follows.

- What risks does this company face?
- How can these risks be measured? It may be possible to assess the risk in a business in terms of unpredictable variations in key factors such as sales demand or market prices. High volatility is associated with high business risk.
- For each of these risks, how would the company be affected if the worst outcome came about, or if a fairly bad outcome happened?
- What is the likelihood of a bad outcome for that risk item?
- What is the company's risk appetite or risk tolerance?
- What should the company be doing to manage the risk, either by avoiding it altogether or planning to deal with the problems that will arise in the event of a bad outcome?

 TEST YOUR KNOWLEDGE 9.3

a   How might risks be categorised?
b   What is the difference between strategic risk and operating risk?

---

4   Risk committees and risk managers

4.1 Risk committees

Responsibilities for risk management vary between companies. An important distinction should be made between the arrangements whereby responsibilities for risk management are fulfilled by:

- the board; and
- executive management.

At board level, responsibility for reviewing the effectiveness of the risk management system may be delegated by the board to the audit committee, which is also likely to have responsibility for reviewing the internal control system.

Alternatively, the board may prefer to establish a separate **risk committee** of the board. Some large listed UK companies, particularly banks, have done so. The advantages of having a separate risk committee are as follows.

- It can focus on risk issues and reviewing the company's risk management system, without having to concern itself with other issues (such as the external auditors). It can give advice to the board on matters such as risk appetite and risk strategy.
- The composition of the board is not restricted by requirements of the corporate governance code. A risk committee should ideally consist mainly of non-executive directors (NEDs) but should also have the finance director as a member. If the audit committee had responsibility for the oversight of risk management, the finance director could not be a committee member (although he or she could be invited to meetings of the audit committee to give their views).

A separate risk committee for the board is probably much more useful for a bank or other large financial institution than for other public companies, although some large non-bank companies (for example, oil companies) may also establish a board risk committee because of the complexity of their risk exposures. In general, however, non-bank companies are unlikely to have a risk committee as a sub-committee of the board.

At executive management level, however, there may be a risk committee consisting of senior executives, chaired by the CEO. This committee would be responsible for risk management at an operational level and should report (through the CEO) to the board on risk matters.

4.2 ICSA guidance on the terms of reference of a risk committee

ICSA has issued a guidance note on the 'Terms of reference for the risk committee' (2013), emphasising that these are relevant mainly for banks and other financial institutions (such as insurance companies).

The terms of reference make the following suggestions:

- A risk committee should consist of a majority of NEDs and the chairman should be a NED.
- The finance director (chief financial officer (CFO)) should either be a member of the committee or should be in attendance regularly at committee meetings.
- The chief risk officer (CRO) should also attend the committee meetings.
- The CEO may be asked to attend meetings.
- There has to be good communication between the risk committee and the audit committee, since there will be some overlap in their roles. It may therefore be appropriate for the chairman of the audit committee to be a member of the risk committee.

4.3 Role of a risk committee

Where a risk committee is established, it will be given a role and responsibilities. These should not overlap with the responsibilities of the audit committee. To promote co-operation between the two committees, it may be appropriate for the chairman of each committee to also be a member of the other committee. The audit committee has responsibilities for audit and financial reporting, and even when a separate risk committee is established, the audit committee should therefore retain responsibility for monitoring financial risks and the effectiveness of internal controls relating to financial reporting (this is explained in the next chapter).

A risk committee will rely on information provided to it by risk managers possibly also by internal auditors in the company. The role of a risk committee may include the following responsibilities:

- Providing assurance to the board that risk management and processes for control over risk are effective.
- Where risk areas seem to require particular attention, making recommendations to the board.
- Providing information to the board to help with strategy formulation, for example with regard to risk appetite in the company's strategy. This is achieved by helping the board to understand the key risks facing the company, its risk tolerances and its defences against those risks.

4.4 Risk officers

Some large companies, such as banks and major oil companies, may appoint specialist executive managers with responsibility for risk. The risk management team would be headed by a CRO. The Walker Report recommended that the CRO should:

■ report directly to the finance director or CEO; but also
■ have direct access to the board and provide advice to the board on all risk issues affecting the company.

'Alongside an internal reporting line to the CEO or CFO, the CRO should report to the board risk committee, with explicit, and what is clearly understood to be, direct access to the chairman of the committee in the event of need, for example, if there is a difference of view with the CEO or CFO.'

The Report emphasises the need to protect the independence of the CRO from the influence of the CEO or finance director, and it also recommends that (like the company secretary) only the board should be able to appoint or dismiss the CRO, and the remuneration of the CRO should be decided by the company chairman or the remuneration committee.

TEST YOUR KNOWLEDGE 9.4

a   What is the difference between a risk committee of the board and a **risk management committee**?
b   What are the responsibilities of the audit committee for business risk and the business risk management system?

4.5 Risk management policies, systems and procedures

To enable the board of directors to carry out its responsibilities for risk management effectively, there are two essential requirements.

1   Board members should have an understanding of risks and risk management.
2   There should be a risk management system in place that the board as a whole or the appropriate board committee can review.

Training in risk management should be particularly important for members of the board committee (audit committee or risk committee) with responsibility for reviewing the risk management system.

The collapse of Enron has been referred to previously in this text (see, for example, Chapter 1). One of the weaknesses in governance that became apparent after the collapse was the lack of understanding of the risks in the business by the members of the Enron board. Before its collapse, Enron had a good reputation for financial risk management. Because of volatility in prices and supply in the energy industry, Enron used derivative instruments to hedge its long-term exposures to price risk. However, it hedged these risks with special purpose entities (specially created companies) that it owned itself and, as a result, effectively retained the risks itself. These practices were reported to the board, but the board did nothing to stop them or question them, and actually approved resolutions that made some of these dubious 'off balance sheet' hedging transactions possible. After the collapse of the company at the end of 2001, it became apparent that although the members of the Enron board had been given information about risk management, they did not know enough about derivatives and 'off balance sheet' accounting to understand and assess the risks.

5   The UK Corporate Governance Code on risk management

The UK Corporate Governance Code contains some brief but important principles on the corporate governance aspects of risk management.

- The board is responsible for determining the nature and extent of the principal risks it is willing to take to achieve its strategic objectives. In other words, the board is responsible for deciding the company's risk appetite.
- The board should maintain a sound system of risk management and internal control. Risk management is considered in this chapter: internal control is explained in Chapter 10.

The board should therefore satisfy itself that appropriate systems are in place to identify, evaluate and manage the significant risks faced by the company. The UK Code therefore includes requirements for:

- a system of risk management, which includes a strong element of **risk assessment**; and
- regular reviews of the system (at least annually) by the board.

With regard to the board's responsibility for determining the level and extent of tolerable risks, the UK Code contains the following provisions:

- The directors should carry out a 'robust assessment' of the principal risks facing the company, and confirm in the annual report that they have done so. Principal risks include risks that threaten the company's business model, future performance, solvency or liquidity.
- The directors should also explain in the annual report how they have assessed the prospects of the company and its ability to continue in operation over a future assessment period. This provision has already been described previously in Chapter 7, in relation to going concern.

TEST YOUR KNOWLEDGE 9.5

With regard to the responsibility of the board for maintaining a sound system of risk management and internal control, the UK Code states that: 'The board should monitor the company's risk management and internal control systems and, at least annually, carry out a review of their effectiveness, and report on that review in the annual report.'

What are the principles and provisions of the UK Corporate Governance Code with regard to business risk management?

---

6   FRC Guidance on risk management

In September 2014, the FRC published a guidance document called 'FRC Guidance on Risk Management, Internal Control and Related Financial and Business Reporting'. This provides guidance on how the provisions of the UK Code should be applied.

The Guidance makes an introductory comment that the board should not restrict sensible risk-taking that is critical to achieving growth. However, it is important to assess risks as part of the normal business planning process, and:

- respond promptly to risks when they arise; and
- ensure that shareholders and other stakeholders are kept well-informed about the main risks facing the company and how they might affect the company's prospects.

The Guidance sets out the responsibilities of the board for risk management and internal control (which are discussed jointly). The board should:

- ensure that there are 'appropriate' systems for identifying the risks facing the company and enabling the board to make a 'robust assessment' of those risks;
- determine the nature and extent of the principal risks facing the company and those risks that the company is willing to take to achieve its strategic objectives (i.e. it should determine its risk appetite);

- ensure that the appropriate culture and reward systems are embedded throughout the company;
- agree how the principal risks should be managed or mitigated to reduce the probability that they will occur and/or their impact if they do occur;
- review the effectiveness of the risk management and internal control systems and take corrective action where necessary; and
- ensure that there are sound processes for internal and external communications on risk management and internal control.

The Guidance states that it is the responsibility of management to take day-to-day responsibility for the board's policies on risk management and internal control, but the board needs to ensure that management:

- understands the risks;
- implements appropriate policies and controls;
- monitors the controls; and
- provides the board with timely information so that it can fulfil its own responsibilities.

7 Elements in an effective risk management system

There are several 'models' for a risk management system. One of these models, known as the Enterprise Risk Management model, was formulated in the US by an organisation called COSO (Committee of Sponsoring Organisations of the Treadway Commission). The ERM model applies to all categories of risk: strategic, operational, financial reporting and compliance risks.

The model has eight components or elements. All eight components must function effectively for an effective risk management system.

Component		
1	**Internal environment**	There must be a culture within the company that recognises the importance of risk management and also ethical behaviour.
2	**Objective setting**	There must be a process for setting objectives for the company that are consistent with the organisation's aims and the board's risk appetite.
3	**Risk identification**	There must be processes for identifying potential threats and opportunities in the business environment (strategic risks) and within the company's operating processes.
4	**Risk assessment**	There must be processes for assessing the significance of each risk, and prioritising them for management action. The significance of risks may be assessed according to their potential severity and also the probability that a 'risk event' will happen.
5	**Risk response**	For strategic risk, there should be a process for deciding how to respond to each risk and 'manage' the risk.
6	**Control activities**	For operational risks, financial reporting risks and compliance risks, suitable internal controls should be designed and implemented. The FRC Guidance states that risk management and internal control systems should be embedded in the company's operations, and should not be seen as an occasional compliance exercise. When controls are embedded in operations, it means that they are part of normal procedures, and are put into effect as part of those normal procedures. However, the cost and effectiveness of controls should be assessed relative to the benefits they provide.
7	**Information and communication**	Relevant information relating to risks and controls should be identified, captured and communicated to the people who need it.

Component		
8	**Monitoring**	There should be regular monitoring of the effectiveness of risk management and the internal control system. At management level, systems should be established to monitor risks and controls. There should be a system for identifying situations that are getting out of control or where significant events have developed or are developing. At board level, the board should carry out regular reviews of the effectiveness of the risk management system. The UK Code states that reviews should take place at least annually.

7.1 Risk identification

A company should have a procedure in place for reviewing and identifying the risks it faces. Risks change over time, and risk reviews should therefore be undertaken regularly.

Strategic risk can be divided into three broad categories:

■ Risks that arise from changes in the general business environment (such as economic recession, or significant technological changes).
■ Risks that arise in the industry in which the company operates (such as a risk of decline in the industry and falling customer demand).
■ Risks from unexpected actions by major competitors.

After the terrorist attack on the World Trade Center and other US targets on 11 September 2001, the need for a reassessment of the risk from terrorist attacks was all too obvious. The US banks Morgan Stanley and Goldman Sachs, for example, quickly developed new plans to move significant operations out of the lower Manhattan financial district. The terrorist attack had exposed flaws in their contingency plans, because too many of their operations had been located in a 'campus' area, sharing the same telecommunications and power grids. Morgan Stanley moved some operations to the suburbs north of New York City and Goldman Sachs moved its equities business across to New Jersey.

7.2 Risk assessment

The assessment of risks calls for procedures to assess the potential size of the risk. The expected losses that could occur from adverse events or developments depend on the:

■ probability that an adverse outcome will occur; and
■ size of the loss in the event of an adverse outcome.

Where a risk is unlikely to materialise into an adverse outcome, and the loss would in any case be small, no management action might be necessary. Where the risk is higher, measures should be taken to protect the organisation so that the remaining exposure to risk is within the company's tolerance level and consistent with its risk appetite.

7.3 Risk responses

Risk responses are the measure taken to deal with strategic risks that have been identified and assessed.

The measures taken to deal with each risk are decided by management, which is accountable to the board for the measures they take. In broad terms, strategic risks can be dealt with by avoiding them or by taking steps to limit the exposure.

■ Some risks can be avoided. For example, a car manufacturer might be concerned about the risk of losses at a subsidiary specialising in car repairs, due to the strength of competition in the car repair industry. It could decide to avoid the risk by selling the subsidiary.
■ Many risks have to be accepted as an inevitable feature of business. For significant risks, a company should decide what measures might be necessary to reduce the risk to acceptable proportions. Strategic risks may be reduced through any of the following measures (sometimes called the '4 Ts').

For strategic risks, the possible responses are to:

- **Tolerate.** Accept the risk, because it is not a significant threat, or because they are external risks (such as regulatory risks and market risks) over which the company has no control.
- **Transfer.** Move some or all of the risk to someone else, for example by entering joint ventures to share risk or by purchasing insurance against risk events.
- **Trim.** Take suitable measures to reduce the risks – by reducing the probability of an adverse risk event or by reducing the impact if a risk event occurs.
- **Terminate.** Avoid the risk entirely, by withdrawing from the area of business operations where the risk exists.

Measures to manage risk may reduce the risk without eliminating the risk entirely. When this happens, there is some residual risk, but this should be within the level or limit that the board is prepared to tolerate.

From a corporate governance perspective, it should be a responsibility of the board to make sure that risks are reviewed regularly and that management take suitable measures to deal with them.

7.4 Risk registers and other risk management processes

A company might use risk registers for:

- recording risks that have been identified;
- actions taken to investigate the risk;
- the outcome of the investigation and assessment of the risks;
- identifying the person with management responsibility for the risk;
- recording measures that have been taken to deal with the risks;
- recording the effects of control measures, to assess whether control is effective or whether new measures are required; and
- recording regular reviews of the risk, to determine whether it is becoming more significant or less significant.

Risk registers are maintained by executive management, but at a corporate level, a risk register can be used by the risk committee of the board (or the audit committee) as a way of reviewing the effectiveness of the risk management system.

The King IV Code in South Africa has a Principle that 'The governing body should govern risk in a way that supports the organisation in setting and achieving its strategic objectives'.

7.5 Stress testing

Stress testing is widely used by major companies to assess their ability to withstand extreme 'shocks' or unexpected events in the business environment. This can be done by taking the normal business planning or forecasting model used by the company, and altering a key variable, such as the rate of growth (or decline) in economic growth, a very large increase in a major resource such as the cost of oil, loss of access to a key market for purchases or sales, and so on. The purpose of stress testing is to assess whether the company could survive the shock. If there are doubts about this ability, the company should consider measures to reduce the risk, perhaps by developing contingency plans, or taking measures to improve their capital or liquidity.

 TEST YOUR KNOWLEDGE 9.5

a What are the provisions of the UK Corporate Governance Code with regard to risk management?

b What are the main elements of a business risk management system?

c What is a risk register?

d What is the purpose of stress testing?

8 Senior executive remuneration: bonuses and risk adjustment

The UK Corporate Governance Code states that remuneration policies should be compatible with risk policies and systems. The purpose of this provision is to reduce the likelihood that executives will be paid large annual bonuses for achieving high levels of performance in the short term, but by taking risks that result in a decline in performance in the following years.

A method of adjusting bonus payments for risk is therefore to defer the incentive payments over a number of years, say three to five years. If an executive director is entitled to an annual bonus of £900,000, the incentive scheme could provide for this to be paid over a three-year period. If performance in subsequent years declines, as a consequence of the risks that the company has been exposed to, the amount of the bonus payments could then be reduced in the second and/or third years.

TEST YOUR KNOWLEDGE 9.6

How might executive rewards be adjusted for business risk?

END OF CHAPTER QUESTIONS

Refer to the case study at the beginning of Part Three.

1 What significant exposures to business risk are apparent in the case study?
2 Suggest what the newly appointed NED should do to alert his board colleagues to the risk management problems within the company, and try to initiate improvements.

3 In the past, Hunnerware has not given as much attention to business risks as it should have done. Outline the areas that the board should consider in developing a better approach to risk management.
4 Explain the nature of scenario-based risk assessment, and suggest how this might be incorporated into the system of risk management within the company.

CHAPTER SUMMARY

■ Companies can get into financial difficulty by taking too much risk. The board of directors has a responsibility for making sure that risks to which the company is exposed, or might be exposed in the future, are considered acceptable.

■ Business risks may be classified as strategic risks, operational risks, financial risks and compliance risks.

■ All businesses must accept strategic risks in order to make a profit. As a general rule, higher risks must be taken to obtain higher returns. The board should decide how much strategic risk the company wants to accept in order to achieve its financial objectives.

■ Risk appetite is the amount of exposure to risk the board wants to take, so that targets for financial performance can be achieved.

■ Risk tolerance is the amount of risk that the board is willing to accept. Risk tolerance may be measured quantitatively, so that actual exposures to risk can be compared with a target or tolerance limit.

■ The board should review risk appetite and risk tolerance regularly.

■ Strategic risks are risks that arise from unexpected changes or developments in the business environment that are outside the control of management. These include unexpected initiatives by competitors, unexpected changes in customer demand patterns and changes in the political, regulatory, economic, social and technological environment. Unexpected changes can be positive as well as negative.

- A measure of high risk is unpredictable variability in key factors such as sales demand or market prices. High volatility is associated with high strategic risk.
- Business risk should be distinguished from internal control risk. Internal control risk arises from factors within the company (or other organisation) that are within the ability of management to control. Business risks are external and cannot be controlled. However, they should be managed.
- Examples of risk are reputation risk, competition risk, business environment risk, financial risks in the business environment (such as interest rate risk and foreign exchange rate risk) and liquidity risk.
- The UK Corporate Governance Code includes a requirement for companies to have an effective system of risk management, with regular reviews (at least annually) of the effectiveness of the system.
- There may be a separate risk committee of the board, with special responsibility for monitoring the risk management system.
- In addition, companies may establish a risk management committee of senior executives, chaired perhaps by the CEO and also including specialist risk officers (or the head of internal audit).
- There are several models of a risk management system. One of these is the COSO ERM model. The basic elements of a risk management system are procedures for identifying risks, assessing the risks that have been identified and assessing their significance, taking measures to manage the risks that are consistent with board policy on risk appetite and risk tolerance, control of the system and regular monitoring of the effectiveness of the system.
- The UK Corporate Governance Code states that remuneration policies should be compatible with risk policies and systems. One way of doing this is to defer the payment of annual bonuses or spread the payment over several years. Payments can then be reduced or cancelled if it is subsequently found that short-term performance measures were misleading, or that performance levels on which the bonuses were calculated are unsustainable beyond the short term.

10 Internal control systems

■ INTRODUCTION

A company may fail to achieve its objectives because of failures or weaknesses within its systems and operating procedures, or due to human error. These failures and weaknesses could be avoided, or the consequences of failures could be restricted, by means of controls. Internal control risks are the risks of failures in systems and procedures to achieve their intended purpose. Internal controls are measures or arrangements that are intended to prevent failures from happening, limiting their potential effect, or identifying when a failure has occurred so that corrective measures can be taken. This chapter explains the nature of internal control and the internal control system, and the responsibilities for internal control within an organisation. Internal control is an aspect of corporate governance, because the board of directors has a responsibility to ensure that the assets of the company are not threatened, and the interests of the shareholders (and other stakeholders) are not damaged, by making sure that an effective system of internal control is in place.

1 Elements of an internal control system

Strategic risks are risks that arise in the business environment and markets in which a company operates. Operating risks are risks that arise within an organisation because of weaknesses in its systems, procedures, management or personnel. Unless there are controls to deal with them, operating risks can lead to losses because of operational failures, errors or fraud. The controls for these risks are 'internal controls' and internal controls are applied within an internal control system.

It is the responsibility of the board of directors of a company to ensure that the internal control system (and the internal controls within this system) is effective in preventing losses from risk events, or identifying risk events and taking corrective action when they occur.

CASE EXAMPLE 10.1

A small company operated from four separate locations in the same city. At one of these locations, a considerable amount of revenue was received in cash, which was kept in a safe in the manager's office. One day, two uniformed individuals came to the building and said that they had instructions to take the safe to the company's head office, which was in a different building. They were allowed to take the safe and the security guard actually helped them to put it into their vehicle, parked outside the front door of the building. The two individuals drove off with the safe, containing over £100,000, and were not seen again.

It should be apparent that the company lost £100,000 because of basic mistakes, which point to weaknesses in internal controls.

Why was there was a lot of money in the safe? Why had most of it not been taken to the bank? Why were the two individuals allowed to take the safe without checking their authorisation to take it? How did they gain access to the building so easily?

There were weaknesses in the procedures for banking cash, building security and authorisation of actions. If suitable internal controls had been in place, the loss of the money should not have occurred.

1.1 Definitions of internal control and an internal control system

Internal control systems are concerned with the management of business risks other than strategic risks. These are risks which can be controlled by measures taken internally by the organisation.

A useful definition of internal control has been suggested by COSO: 'Internal control is broadly defined as a process, effected by an entity's board of directors, management and other personnel, designed to provide reasonable assurance regarding the achievement of objectives in the following categories:

1 Effectiveness and efficiency of operations.
2 Reliability of financial reporting.
3 Compliance with applicable laws and regulations.'

Internal controls are part of an internal control system. An internal control system has been defined as follows: 'An internal control system consists of all the procedures, methods and measures (control measures) instituted by the Board of Directors and executive management to ensure that operational activities progress in a proper fashion. Organisational measures for internal control are integrated into operations, which means that they are performed simultaneously with working processes or performed directly before or after work is carried out' (PwC).

 STOP AND THINK 10.1

As the name 'internal control' might suggest, the focus is on controls that can be established internally, within the organisation. Many of the risks that an internal control system seeks to manage are risks from errors, fraud, breakdowns and other internal failures. Other internal control measures may relate to the risks of external events, such as a natural disaster (fire or flood): disaster recovery measures are essentially internal controls, because they are subject to management planning and control.

1.2 Categories of risks

The risks that are managed by an internal control system can be categorised into three broad types.

1 **Financial risks**. These are risks of errors or fraud in accounting systems, and in accounting and finance activities. Errors or fraud could lead to losses for the organisation, or to incorrect financial statements. Weak controls may also mean that financial assets are not properly protected. Examples of financial risks include the risk of:
   - failure to record financial transactions in the book-keeping system;
   - failure to collect money owed by customers;
   - failure to protect cash;
   - financial transactions (such as payments) occurring without proper authorisation; and
   - mis-reporting (deliberate or unintentional) in the financial statements.

2 **Operational risks**. A helpful definition of 'operational risk' is given by the Basel Committee for banking supervision. Although this definition applies to risks in the banking industry, it has a wider application. Operational risk is 'the risk of losses resulting from inadequate or failed internal processes, people and systems, or external events'. Operational risks include:
   - the risk of a breakdown in a system due to machine failures or software errors;
   - the risk of losing information from computer files or having confidential information stolen;
   - the risk of a terrorist attack;
   - losses arising from mistakes or omissions by staff; and
   - inefficient or ineffective use of resources.

3 **Compliance risks**. These are risks that important laws or regulations will not be complied with properly. Failure to comply with the law could result in legal action against the company and/or fines.

Many companies rely extensively on IT systems, which are exposed to operational risks that include software viruses, hacking of files (including cyber-attacks), cybercrime, corruption or loss of data, system breakdowns or malfunctions, and so on.

The potential scale and significance of IT risks means that in some countries (such as South Africa with the King IV report), IT risks and IT controls are regarded as a separate classification of risks and internal controls.

1.3 The purpose of an internal control system and internal controls

An internal control system is the system that an organisation has for identifying operational, financial and compliance risks, applying controls to reduce the risk of losses from these risks and taking corrective action when losses occur.

- There should be controls to ensure that the organisation, its systems and procedures operate in the way that is intended, without disruption or disturbance.
- There should be controls to ensure that assets are safeguarded. For example, there should be controls to ensure that money received is banked and is not stolen, and that operating assets such as items of equipment and computers are not damaged or lost.
- Controls should include measures to reduce the risk of fraud.
- Financial controls should ensure the completeness and accuracy of accounting records, and the timely preparation of financial information.

Controls should be in place to ensure compliance with key regulations, such as health and safety regulations or, in the case of banks, anti-money laundering regulations.

Internal controls can be classified into three main types:

- **Preventive controls.** These are controls that are intended to prevent an adverse risk event from occurring; for example to prevent opportunities for fraud by employees.
- **Detective controls.** These are controls for detecting risk events when they occur, so that the appropriate person is alerted and corrective measures taken.
- **Corrective controls.** These are measures for dealing with risk events that have occurred, and their consequences.

1.4 Internal controls: financial, operational and compliance controls

There should be financial, operational and compliance controls for dealing with financial, operational and compliance risks – preventing losses or adverse events from happening, or detecting and correcting the problem when losses or adverse events do occur.

Financial controls

Financial controls are internal accounting controls that are sufficient to provide reasonable assurance that:

- transactions are made only in accordance with the general or specific authorisation of management;
- transactions are recorded so that financial statements can be prepared in accordance with accounting standards and generally accepted accounting principles;
- transactions are recorded so that assets can be accounted for;
- access to assets is only allowed in accordance with the general or specific authorisation of management;
- the accounting records for assets are compared with actual assets at reasonable intervals of time; and
- appropriate action is taken whenever there are found to be differences.

The maintenance of proper accounting records is an important element of internal control. Effective financial controls should ensure:

- the quality of external and internal financial reporting, so that there are no material errors in the accounting records and financial statements;
- that no fraud is committed (or that fraud is detected when it occurs); and
- that the financial assets of the company are not stolen, lost or needlessly damaged, or that these risks are reduced.

Operational controls

Operational controls are controls that help to reduce operational risks, or identify failures in operational systems when these occur. They are designed to prevent failures in operational procedures, or to detect and correct operational failures if they do occur. Operational failures may be caused by:

- machine breakdowns;
- human error;
- failures in IT systems;
- failures in the performance of systems (possibly due to human error);
- weaknesses in procedures; and
- poor management.

Operational controls are measures designed to prevent these failures from happening, or identifying and correcting problems that do occur. Regular equipment maintenance, better training of staff, automation of standard procedures, and reporting systems that make managers accountable for their actions are all examples of operational controls.

Compliance controls

Compliance controls are concerned with making sure that an entity complies with all the requirements of relevant legislation and regulations.

The potential consequences of failure to comply with laws and regulations vary according to the nature of the industry and the regulations. For a manufacturer of food products, for example, food hygiene regulations are important. For a bank, regulations to protect consumers against mis-selling and regulations for detecting and reporting suspicions of money laundering are important.

It can be difficult to understand the nature of internal control risks and internal controls to deal with them. There are many different risks and many controls that are applied. The following are simple examples.

CASE EXAMPLE 10.2

The owners of a farm located near a major international airport turn some of their land into a car park in the holiday months, and customers can park their cars at the farm and take a taxi service from there to the airport. Customers pay in cash, and the owners of the farm use part-time employees to operate the car park, which remains open for 18 hours each day, and seven days a week. One financial risk is that if fees for parking are charged by the day, customers may pay for the wrong number of days. Another risk is that customers may pay in cash, and employees may keep the cash for themselves, and not report the income to the owners of the farm. Without going into the detail of suitable controls, it may be apparent that to reduce the risk of losses from these risks, there should be a ticketing system based on sequentially numbered tickets for the car park, with the date of the arrival in the car park recorded on each ticket. Other controls would also be necessary to protect the cash from theft. These would be internal financial controls.

CASE EXAMPLE 10.3

A manufacturing company may use large items of machinery that have moving parts, and there is a risk that employees getting too close to the machinery may be injured by a moving part. This is an operational risk. An operational control for this risk would be to surround the machinery with guards or safety rails, with warning signs not to enter inside them.

CASE EXAMPLE 10.4

Another example of operational risk is the risk of a failure in health and safety systems and system controls. A well-publicised example was the series of apparent safety failures (and failures in safety controls) that led to an explosion at the Texas oil refinery of oil company BP in 2005, where 15 people were killed and about 500 injured. In addition to the direct losses suffered by BP, the incident also led to over 1,000 civil legal actions against the company and a federal grand jury investigation into whether criminal charges should be brought against the company.

1.5 Internal control risks

'Internal control risks' are risks that internal controls will fail to achieve their intended purpose, and will fail to prevent, detect or correct adverse risk events.

These risks can occur because:

- they are badly designed, and so not capable of achieving their purpose as a control; or
- they are well-designed, but are not applied properly, due to human error or oversight, or deliberately ignoring or circumvention of the control (a form of operational risk event).

An internal control system needs to have procedures for identifying weak or ineffective internal controls. This is one of the functions of monitoring the effectiveness of the internal control system.

1.6 Elements of an internal control system

Internal controls are an essential part of an internal control system, but an internal control system should also have other elements in order to be effective and achieve its objectives.

The COSO Framework for an internal control system

The COSO Framework for an internal control system (which is consistent with COSO's Enterprise Risk Management (ERM) system) identifies five elements to a system of internal control.

1 **A control environment**. A control environment describes the awareness of (and attitude to) internal controls in the organisation, shown by the directors, management and employees generally. It therefore encompasses corporate culture, management style and employee attitudes to control procedures. The control environment is determined by the example given by the company's leaders to control and their expectations that employees should also be risk-conscious. Factors in the control environment include:
    – integrity and ethical values within the organisation, such as the existence of a code of ethics;
    – a commitment to competence in performance;
    – the commitment of the board of directors and the audit committee to monitoring management, and their independence from management; and
    – human resources policies and practices, such as the company's policies on performance evaluation and rewarding employees for performance.
2 **Risk identification and assessment**. There should be a system or procedures for identifying the risks facing the company (and how these are changing) and assessing their significance. Controls or management initiatives should be devised to deal with significant risks. Internal control risks can be categorised as financial risks, operational risks and compliance risks.
3 **Internal controls**. Controls should be devised and implemented to eliminate, reduce or control risks. Internal controls can be categorised as financial controls, operational controls and compliance controls, to deal respectively with financial risks, operational risks and compliance risks.
4 **Information and communication**. All employees who are responsible for the management of risks should receive information that enables them to fulfil this task. More generally, there should be a system of information provision and communication within the organisation so that individuals are aware of what is expected of them. It can be described as providing the right people in sufficient detail and on time with information to let them do their job well. Communication within an internal control system also includes the existence and use of a whistleblowing procedure.
5 **Monitoring**. The effectiveness of the internal control system should be monitored regularly. Internal audit is one method of monitoring the internal control system. Internal controls are also monitored by executive management and (as part of their annual audit) by the external auditors. The board of directors also has a responsibility to review the effectiveness of the system.

 STOP AND THINK 10.2

Compare the elements in COSO's internal control system model with the elements in COSO's ERM model, which was described in the previous chapter. Note the similarities between them.

The nature and extent of the internal controls an organisation has in place will depend to a large extent on its size, what controls it can afford and whether the benefits obtained from any particular control measure are sufficient to justify its cost. The internal control system should, however, be sufficiently robust and effective to minimise the risk of serious losses through error or fraud.

■ In a large company, we should expect thousands of different financial operational and compliance controls, each designed to prevent particular financial, operational or compliance failures, or to detect them if they occur.
■ An important aspect of corporate governance is to ensure that the system of internal control (and the internal controls within that system) is adequate and effective in preventing or detecting failures in the system. For example, if the system is ineffective, a company may be exposed to a high risk of fraud and also to a high risk that its annual financial statements will not be accurate or reliable.

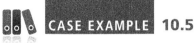 **CASE EXAMPLE 10.5**

In 1995, Barings Bank collapsed as a result of losses incurred in trading in Asia by a 'rogue trader', Nick Leeson. Leeson was sent to the Singapore office of the bank in 1992 as a general manager. He then took an examination that qualified him to trade on the Singapore exchange SIMEX. He acquired a position of considerable authority in the Singapore office, where he became its head trader and the effective head of the 'back office operations' (including settlement of trading transactions), as well as general manager.

There should have been controls within the bank to prevent speculative trades by the bank's traders that would expose the bank to excessive risks. For example, there should have been effective limits on the exposures to risk that Leeson was allowed to take. Because of his powerful position in the office, Leeson was able to ignore and override the controls. He took unauthorised speculative positions by trading on the SIMEX exchange and Japan's Osaka exchange. He had hoped to make large profits on his deals, but he made losses. However, by hiding the losses in an unused error account, number 88888, he was able to present figures that made it seem that he was making large profits. The losses hidden in this account rose from £2 million at the end of 1992 to £23 million at the end of 1993 and £208 million at the end of 2004. Leeson was able to fund the losses by borrowing money from other parts of the bank and from client accounts (by falsifying documentation and account records). Senior managers of the bank in London were not aware of what was happening.

Although the losses on his trades were building up, Leeson was able to report profits, partly by cross-trading with account 88888, so that the profits were actually achieved by adding to the losses in account 88888. Leeson and his staff in the Singapore office were paid bonuses on the basis of these reported profits.

The situation could not remain hidden forever, and in February 1995 Leeson fled Singapore, leaving behind losses of £827 million. The bank could not afford losses of this size, and it collapsed soon after.

The collapse of Barings can be explained by severe weaknesses in the internal control system.

- The control environment was poor and the control culture was not strong enough.
- Bonuses were paid for reported profits on trading, regardless of the risks in the trades.
- Internal controls were inadequate. Leeson was general manager, trader and in charge of the settlement of trading transactions in the Singapore office, and there was no segregation of duties whereby one person could act as a check on the activities of someone else. Leeson was inadequately supervised and reporting to management was inaccurate (falsified). Systems of authorisation and approval were inadequate; Leeson was able to borrow large amounts of money from other offices of the bank, which he could use to pay for his losses, and no one had oversight to stop him from doing this.
- Monitoring of the internal control system was also inadequate, and the weaknesses in the system were not identified until it was too late.

It might have been thought that the collapse of Barings Bank would provide a lesson about internal control to all other banks, but an even larger scandal rocked the French Bank Société Générale (SocGen) in 2008. The bank's independent directors identified 'weaknesses' in the bank's controls that led to the biggest fraud in banking history. The losses of nearly €5 billion were triggered by junior trader Jérome Kerviel. The independent directors identified 75 'warning signals' on Kerviel's trading that the bank failed to follow up. Kerviel's supervisor accepted explanations that he gave without verifying them, and in spite of warnings about Kerviel from derivatives exchange Eurex. There were also no controls on cancelled or modified trades, which Kerviel used extensively. Within the bank, there may have been a culture of deference by risk managers to successful traders. Subsequent investigations by internal and external auditors for the bank found that traders and their superiors at SocGen frequently flouted the rules, giving Kerviel an opportunity to take €50 billion in unauthorised trades. There was a low appreciation of the risk of fraud, a strong entrepreneurial culture and the emergence of unauthorised practices with trading limits regularly exceeded.

CASE EXAMPLE 10.6

In April 2010, the UK Financial Services Authority (FSA) fined the former deputy CEO of Northern Rock bank (Mr DB) over £500,000 and banned him from the industry. It also fined the former managing credit director of Northern Rock (Mr RB) and banned him from holding a senior position. The action against DB arose from a conference call in January 2007, in which he told investors that arrears and repossession levels for Northern Rock mortgages were exceptionally low compared with those of other mortgage lenders, even though he knew that 1,917 loans had been excluded from this total. These loans had been classified into a separate category (loans for which a possession order had been obtained but not yet enforced) that was excluded from the reported total of arrears and repossessions. If they had been included, Northern Rock's reported proportion of overdue loans would have been 50% higher.

DB did not report the correct figures to his CEO in the bank. There was no evidence that he had gained personally from his action. He claimed that his action had been taken in an effort to protect RB, whose wife was seriously ill, and whom he had given another six months to sort out the problem of overdue loans.

The FSA action against Mr RB arose from his failure to take action when he learned of the problems in the process of reporting overdue loans and repossessions by the bank.

The FSA commented that the misreporting of the figures reflected 'pressure' on staff in the bank to keep the reported number of loan arrears below those of competitors in the mortgage market, and also failure to put in place suitable internal controls to prevent this misreporting from happening.

The action by DB explained the surprising apparent success of Northern Rock in the mortgage market at the time. Northern Rock had pursued an aggressive strategy of winning market share by offering large mortgage loans in relation to borrowers' income. Analysts had not been able to understand how Northern Rock could have pursued such an aggressive strategy without suffering from higher mortgage arrears. The answer was that the bank had deceived or misled the market.

This case illustrates how issues in corporate governance and business ethics are interconnected. DB said that the action he took was to protect a colleague who was going through anxieties in his personal life, but to do this DB had lied to investors. The need to lie resulted from the pressure on staff within the bank and the culture that this pursuit of growth and market share created. Even so, with suitable internal controls, the deception with the reporting of the figures should not have been allowed to happen.

 CASE EXAMPLE 10.7

In 2010, the US National Highway Traffic Safety Administration imposed a fine of $16.4 million on car-maker Toyota, the heaviest fine permitted by law, for failing to notify the US authorities promptly about defective accelerator pedals in about 2 million of its cars. The company had delayed the recall of 2.3 million cars by almost four months after becoming aware of the problem with the accelerator pedals. Toyota agreed to pay the fine to avoid a protracted dispute, but denied that it had breached the US Safety Act or vehicle safety regulations.

Whatever the reasons, Toyota had not reported the problem to the authorities promptly. The issue raises questions about whether compliance controls within the company were sufficiently robust. Could the problem have been that the company did not have internal controls in place to recognise the need to report to the authorities? Or did internal controls succeed in recognising the problem, but management then decided to ignore it? No doubt Toyota's management looked at the problem in hindsight and took measures to prevent anything similar from happening again. On the same day that the fine was imposed, Toyota announced that it was recalling the 2010 version of another of its models from North America and Europe, to deal with a different safety problem.

TEST YOUR KNOWLEDGE 10.1

a What are the main elements of a system of internal control? Give six examples of financial risk within a company.

b What might be the main operational risk or compliance risk concerns for a company that operates a chain of family holiday centres and sports centres?

c For what reason are procedures for the authorisation of expenditures and approval of payments for expenditures an internal control?

d For what reason are procedures for the selection of appropriate applicants to fill job vacancies a part of an internal control system?

e Identify two or more examples of significant internal control failings in major companies in the past.

2 The UK corporate governance framework for internal control

In the UK, the connection between good corporate governance and risk management has been recognised for some years, with the inclusion of provisions in the original Combined Code on corporate governance in 1998.

2.1 UK Corporate Governance Code requirements: internal control and risk management systems, and internal audit

A main principle of the UK Code is that: ' The board is responsible for determining the nature and extent of the significant risks it is willing to take in achieving its strategic objectives. The board should maintain sound risk management and internal control systems.' The board has overall responsibility for the system of internal control, but the responsibility for designing and implementing the system, and for operating it, is delegated to management (responsibility for risk management was explained in Chapter 9).

■ The UK Code has a provision that the board should, at least annually, conduct a review of the effectiveness of the company's risk management and internal control systems and should report to the shareholders on the review in the annual report. '**The monitoring and review should cover all material controls, including financial, operational and compliance controls.**' In other words, the board's responsibility for reviewing internal controls (and risk management) extends beyond financial matters to the business operations (operational controls) and regulatory compliance (compliance controls).

Role of the audit committee

Another main principle of the UK Code is that 'the board should establish formal and transparent arrangements for considering how they should apply the corporate reporting and risk management and internal control principles and for maintaining an appropriate relationship with the company's auditors'. An audit committee should have responsibility for corporate governance matters relating to corporate reporting and the company's relationship with its external auditors (as explained in Chapter 7).

The board may delegate responsibility for the governance aspects of risk management and internal control to the audit committee (or, some companies, to a risk committee of the board). The board may set up a risk committee to deal with risk management matters and give the responsibilities for review of the internal control system to the audit committee. However, delegated responsibilities to board committees may differ between companies.

The UK Code states that the responsibilities of the audit committee should include:

- review the company's internal financial controls;
- review the internal control system and risk management system, unless this responsibility is given to a separate risk committee of the board composed of independent directors or by the board itself; and
- monitoring and review of the effectiveness of the company's internal audit function.

Internal audit arrangements are described later in this chapter.

The responsibility for reviewing the effectiveness of financial controls is closely linked to the audit committee's responsibility for reviewing financial reporting issues and the integrity of the company's financial reporting. Failures in financial controls can lead to mis-reporting of the company's financial performance or position.

TEST YOUR KNOWLEDGE 10.2

a What are the provisions of the UK Corporate Governance Code relating to internal control?

b What are the responsibilities of an audit committee with respect to internal control and internal audit, as stated in the UK Code?

---

3 FRC Guidance on internal control

When principles and provisions relating to internal control and risk management were first introduced into the UK governance code in 1998, a working party, known as the Turnbull Committee, published guidelines to listed companies on how to apply them. These became known as the Turnbull Guidance, and became the responsibility of the FRC.

The current FRC Guidance on 'Risk Management, Internal Control and Related Financial and Business Reporting' was issued in 2014 and is outlined below.

3.1 Board responsibilities for risk management and internal control

The board has responsibility for an organisation's overall approach to risk management and internal control. The board's responsibilities are:

- ensuring the design and implementation of appropriate risk management and internal control systems that identify the risks facing the company and enable the board to make a robust assessment of the principal risks;
- determining the nature and extent of the principal risks faced and those risks which the organisation is willing to take in achieving its strategic objectives (determining its 'risk appetite');
- ensuring that appropriate culture and reward systems have been embedded throughout the organisation;
- agreeing how the principal risks should be managed or mitigated to reduce the likelihood of their incidence or their impact;
- monitoring and reviewing the risk management and internal control systems, and the management's process of monitoring and reviewing, and satisfying itself that they are functioning effectively and that corrective action is being taken where necessary; and
- ensuring sound internal and external information and communication processes and taking responsibility for external communication on risk management and internal control.

It is the role of management to implement and take day-to-day responsibility for board policies on risk management and internal control. But the board needs to satisfy itself that management has understood the risks, implemented and monitored appropriate policies and controls, and are providing the board with timely information so that it can discharge its own responsibilities. In turn, management should ensure internal responsibilities and accountabilities are clearly established, understood and embedded at all levels of the organisation. Employees should understand their responsibility for behaving according to the culture.

3.2 Establishing the risk management and internal control systems

The risk management and internal control systems encompass the policies, culture, organisation, behaviours, processes, systems and other aspects of a company that, taken together:

- facilitate its effective and efficient operation by enabling it to assess current and emerging risks, respond appropriately to risks and significant control failures and to safeguard its assets;
- help to reduce the likelihood and impact of poor judgement in decision-making; risk-taking that exceeds the levels agreed by the board; human error; or control processes being deliberately circumvented;
- help ensure the quality of internal and external reporting; and
- help ensure compliance with applicable laws and regulations, and also with internal policies with respect to the conduct of business.

A company's systems of risk management and internal control will include: risk assessment; management or mitigation of risks, including the use of control processes; information and communication systems; and processes for monitoring and reviewing their continuing effectiveness.

The risk management and internal control systems should be embedded in the operations of the company and be capable of responding quickly to evolving business risks, whether they arise from factors within the company or from changes in the business environment. These systems should not be seen as a periodic compliance exercise, but instead as an integral part of the company's day-to-day business processes.

The board should ensure that sound risk management and internal control systems are in place to identify the risks facing the company and to consider their likelihood and impact if they were to materialise.

3.3 Monitoring and review of risk management and internal control systems

The UK Corporate Governance Code states that the board of directors (or the audit committee) should carry out, at least annually, a review of the effectiveness of the system of internal control (and risk management). In order to review the effectiveness of the system of internal control, there must be procedures for monitoring and review. The FRC Guidance says the annual review of effectiveness should, in particular, consider:

- the company's willingness to take on risk (its 'risk appetite'), the desired culture within the company and whether this culture has been embedded;
- the operation of the risk management and internal control systems, covering the design, implementation, monitoring and review and identification of risks and determination of those which are principal to the company;
- the integration of risk management and internal controls with considerations of strategy and business model, and with business planning processes;
- the changes in the nature, likelihood and impact of principal risks, and the company's ability to respond to changes in its business and the external environment;
- the extent, frequency and quality of the communication of the results of management's monitoring to the board which enables it to build up a cumulative assessment of the state of control in the company and the effectiveness with which risk is being managed or mitigated;
- issues dealt with in reports reviewed by the board during the year, in particular the incidence of significant control failings or weaknesses that have been identified at any time during the period and the extent to which they have, or could have, resulted in unforeseen impact; and
- the effectiveness of the company's public reporting processes.

3.4 The board's statement on risk management and internal control

The UK Corporate Governance Code states that the board should report to shareholders each year that it has conducted the annual review of the effectiveness of the systems of internal control and risk management. The Disclosure and Transparency Rules (DTR) for listed companies also requires companies to report on the main features of their internal control and risk management systems in relation to financial reporting. This information is provided within the annual report as a section on internal control.

Although the review of the effectiveness of internal control may be delegated to the audit committee, the board as a whole is responsible for the statement on internal control in the company's annual report and accounts.

The FRC Guidance states that in its statement the board should, as a minimum, acknowledge: that it is responsible for those systems and for reviewing their effectiveness and disclose that:

- there is an ongoing process for identifying, evaluating and managing the principal risks faced by the company;
- the systems have been in place for the year under review and up to the date of approval of the annual report and accounts; and
- they are regularly reviewed by the board; and the extent to which the systems accord with the guidance in this document.

The board should summarise the process it has applied in reviewing the effectiveness of the system of risk management and internal control. The board should explain what actions have been or are being taken to remedy any significant failings or weaknesses.

In reporting on these actions, the board would not be expected to disclose information which, in its opinion, would be prejudicial to its interests.

3.5 Carrying out an annual evaluation: questions to ask

The FRC Guidance includes in an Appendix a list of questions that the board should consider when conducting its annual review of the effectiveness of risk management and internal control systems. There should be satisfactory answers to each question. The list of questions is not reproduced in full here, but several questions are shown to demonstrate the approach to evaluation that the directors should take.

Risk management and internal control systems

- To what extent do the risk management and internal control systems underpin and relate to the company's business model?
- How are authority, responsibility and accountability for risk management and internal control defined, co-ordinated and documented throughout the organisation? How does the board determine whether this is clear, appropriate and effective?
- How effectively is the company able to withstand risks, and risk combinations, which do materialise? How effective is the board's approach to risks with 'low probability' but a very severe impact if they materialise?
- What are the channels of communication that enable individuals, including third parties, to report concerns, suspected breaches of law or regulations, other improprieties or challenging perspectives?
- How does the board satisfy itself that the information it receives is timely, of good quality, reflects numerous information sources and is fit for purpose?
- How does the board ensure it understands the company's exposure to each principal risk before and after the application of mitigations and controls, what those mitigations and controls are and whether they are operating as expected?

Monitoring and review

- What are the processes by which senior management monitor the effective application of the systems of risk management and internal control?
- In what way do the monitoring and review processes take into account the company's ability to re-evaluate the risks and adjust controls effectively in response to changes in its objectives, its business, and its external environment?
- How are processes or controls adjusted to reflect new or changing risks, or operational deficiencies? To what extent does the board engage in horizon scanning for emerging risks accord with the FRC guidance?

3.6 Disclosure of internal control weaknesses

The UK Corporate Governance Code and FRC Guidance do not call for disclosures of specific failures in internal controls or the measures that have been taken to deal with them. The DTR are restricted to a requirement that (listed) companies should include in their corporate governance statement (in the annual report) a description of the main features of the company's internal control and risk management systems relating to the financial reporting process. In this respect, UK governance practice is more limited than reporting requirements in the US. However, a board of directors may consider its obligations under the DTR to report significant internal control weaknesses, when they occur, if the company's financial performance or position will be badly affected as a result.

 CASE EXAMPLE 10.8

In February 2007, following an internal investigation, accounting irregularities were discovered at a subsidiary company of Alfred McAlpine, a UK support services group. Over a period of about three years, the management of the subsidiary had been deliberately supplying false reports of production volumes and sales. The board was informed, and made an immediate announcement to the stock market information services, reporting the discovery of the accounting irregularities and 'the possibility of fraud'. The statement to the stock market suggested that as a result of the problem, the net assets of the group had been over-stated by about £11 million in the financial statements for the previous financial year and the company would be substantially reducing its profit forecast for the current year. It was also announced that the managers suspected of falsifying the reports had been suspended, and that independent forensic accountants would be appointed to investigate the problem in detail. This would delay publication of the annual report and accounts for 2006.

Following the announcement, the company's share price immediately fell by over 20%. However, the prompt reporting of the problem by the board of directors was a necessary part of good governance – even though the failure to detect the accounting irregularities for three years was a clear indication of skilful fraud or, perhaps more likely, severe weaknesses in internal control.

 TEST YOUR KNOWLEDGE 10.3

a What are the main recommendations in the FRC Guidance on Risk Management, Internal Control and Related Financial and Business Reporting?
b How might an audit committee review the effectiveness of the company's system of internal control?

4 Internal audit

The UK Corporate Governance Code states that the audit committee should monitor and review the effectiveness of the activities of the company's internal audit activities.

If the company does not have an internal audit function:

■ the committee should consider annually whether there is a need for an internal audit function, and make a recommendation to the board; and
■ the reasons why there is no internal audit function should be explained in the 'relevant section' of the annual report.

STOP AND THINK 10.3

It may be useful to stop and think about the nature of audit. Audit is a checking process. Auditors are used to investigate an activity or operation or procedure, in order to assess whether it has functioned (or is functioning) in the way that is expected.

To do this, auditors need a standard procedure, established rules or a benchmark that they can use for comparison and making the assessment.

An internal audit investigation of a procedure or activity may therefore involve an investigation into an operation, to assess whether it has functioned as it should, whether the established control procedures (for example, procedures for identifying risks, or internal controls to prevent or detect risk events) have worked as they should have done. The auditors should then report back to the body or individual that commissioned the work, for example the audit committee.

4.1 Function and scope of internal audit

The Chartered Institute of Internal Auditors state that 'The role of internal audit is to provide independent assurance that an organisation's risk management, governance and internal control processes are operating effectively'.

An organisation might have an internal audit unit or section, which carries out investigative work.

- An internal audit function should act independently of executive managers, but normally reports to a senior executive manager such as the finance director.
- Additionally, internal auditors may report to the board itself or the audit committee. The FRC Guidance on Audit Committees suggests that the audit committee should ensure that the internal auditor has direct access to the board chairman and the audit committee, and is also responsible to the audit committee.
- This means that the internal auditors may be in an unusual position within the company.
- For operational reasons, they may have a line-reporting responsibility to a senior executive manager such as the finance director. Executive managers may also ask the internal auditors to carry out audits or reviews of the systems or procedures (and internal controls) for which they are responsible. However, the senior internal auditor should have some control over deciding what aspects of the company's systems should be investigated or audited, and also has a responsibility for reporting to the audit committee and the chairman of the board.

The work done by any internal audit unit is not prescribed by regulation, but is decided by management or by the board (or audit committee). The possible tasks of internal audit include the following.

- **Reviewing the internal control system.** Traditionally, an internal audit department has carried out independent checks on the financial controls in an organisation, or in a particular process or system. The checks would be to establish whether suitable financial controls exist, and if so, whether they are applied properly and are effective. It is not the function of internal auditors to manage risks, only to monitor and report them, and to check that risk controls are efficient and cost-effective.
- **Special investigations.** Internal auditors might conduct special investigations into particular aspects of the organisation's operations (systems and procedures), to check the effectiveness of operational controls.
- **Examination of financial and operating information.** Internal auditors might be asked to investigate the timeliness of reporting and the accuracy of the information in reports.
- **Value for money (VFM) audits.** This is an investigation into an operation or activity to establish whether it is economical, efficient and effective.
- **Reviewing compliance by the organisation with particular laws or regulations.** This is an investigation into the effectiveness of compliance controls.
- **Risk assessment.** Internal auditors might be asked to investigate aspects of risk management, and in particular the adequacy of the mechanisms for identifying, assessing and controlling significant risks to the organisation, from both internal and external sources.

4.2 Investigation of internal financial controls

Internal auditors are commonly required to check the soundness of internal financial controls. In assessing the effectiveness of individual controls, and of an internal control system generally, the following factors should be considered.

- **Whether the controls are manual or automated.** Automated controls are by no means error-proof or fraud-proof, but may be more reliable than similar manual controls.
- **Whether controls are discretionary or non-discretionary.** Non-discretionary controls are checks and procedures that must be carried out. Discretionary controls are those that do not have to be applied, either because they are voluntary or because an individual can choose to disapply them. Risks can infiltrate a system, for example, when senior management chooses to disapply controls and allow unauthorised or unchecked procedures to occur.
- **Whether the control can be circumvented easily**, because an activity can be carried out in a different way where similar controls do not apply.
- **Whether the controls are effective in achieving their purpose.** Are they extensive enough or carried out frequently enough? Are the controls applied rigorously? For example, is a supervisor doing their job properly?

Reports by internal auditors can provide reassurance that internal controls are sound and effective, or might recommend changes and improvements where weaknesses are uncovered.

4.3 The objectivity and independence of internal auditors

The manager of an operation or department should monitor the internal controls within the operation and try to identify and correct weaknesses. He or she should also report on reviews of the effectiveness of internal control. However, a line manager cannot be properly objective, because they could face 'blame' for control failures in the system or operation for which they are responsible.

In contrast, internal auditors ought to be objective, because they investigate the control systems of other departments and operations. However, they are also employees within the organisation and report to someone on the organisation structure. If the internal auditors report to the finance director, they will find it difficult to be critical of the finance director himself. Similarly, if the internal auditors report to the CEO, they will be reluctant to criticise him or her. In this respect, their independence could be compromised.

TEST YOUR KNOWLEDGE 10.4

a   What is the purpose of an internal audit function?
b   What tasks might be carried out by an internal audit department?
c   What should UK listed companies include in their annual report on internal control?
d   How can the independence of the head of internal audit be protected?

To protect the independence of the internal audit function, the FRC's Guidance on Audit Committees 2016 states that the audit committee should approve the appointment or termination of appointment of the head of internal audit. Internal audit should have access to the audit committee and board chairman where necessary and the audit committee should ensure internal audit has a reporting line which enables it to be independent of the executive and so able to exercise independent judgement.

4.4 Review of the effectiveness of the internal audit function

The board or audit committee should review the effectiveness of the internal audit function each year. As part of this review, the FRC Guidance on Audit committees states that the committee should:

- meet with the head of internal audit without the presence of management to discuss the effectiveness of the function;
- review and assess the annual internal audit work plan;
- receive a report on the results of the internal auditors' work; and
- monitor and assess the role and effectiveness of the internal audit function in the overall context of the company's risk management system.

5 The need for an internal audit function

The UK Corporate Governance Code requires the audit committee to monitor and review the effectiveness of the internal audit function. Where there is no internal audit function, the audit committee should consider annually whether there is a need for one, and make a recommendation to the board.

The FRC's Guidance on Audit Committees suggested that the need for an internal audit function depends on factors such as company size, diversity and complexity of activities and number of employees, as well as cost–benefit considerations. The Guidance comments:

'In the absence of an internal audit function, other processes may need to be applied to provide assurance to management, the audit committee and the board that the system of internal control is functioning as intended. In these circumstances, the audit committee will need to assess whether such processes provide sufficient and objective assurance.'

6 Disaster recovery plans

As its name suggests, a disaster recovery plan is a plan of what to do in the event of a disaster that is unconnected with the company's business and outside the control of management. Disaster recovery planning goes beyond procedures that should be taken in an emergency, such as a fire or explosion in a building. It is intended to establish what should be done in the event of an extreme disaster that threatens the ability of the company to maintain its operations. Examples of disasters are natural disasters, such as major fires or flooding or storm damage to key installations or offices, and major terrorist attacks.

Disaster recovery plans are most needed in industries where a lengthy or widespread shutdown of operations could be catastrophic, such as in the banking industry, energy supply industry and airline industry. However, all companies should have such plans, which need to be kept under continual review and about which employees need to be kept fully aware and, where appropriate, trained.

Typically, a disaster recovery plan should do these things.

- Specify which operations are essential, and must be kept going.
- Where operations rely on IT systems, identify the computers or networks to which the system can be transferred in the event of damage to the main system.
- Specify where operations should be transferred to, if they cannot continue in their normal location.
- Identify key personnel who are needed to maintain the system in operation.
- Identify who should be responsible for keeping the public informed about the impact of the disaster and the recovery measures that are being taken.

A review of disaster recovery plans may therefore be a part of the annual review of the effectiveness of internal control by the board or audit committee.

TEST YOUR KNOWLEDGE 10.5

Why should disaster recovery planning be a part of the internal control system of a large company?

7   Whistleblowing procedures

The UK Corporate Governance Code states that the audit committee should 'review arrangements by which staff of the company may, in confidence, raise concerns about possible improprieties in matters of financial reporting or other matters'. In other words, the audit committee should be responsible for review of the provisions and procedures for whistleblowing within the company.

The objective of the audit committee should be to ensure that there are satisfactory arrangements in place for the 'proportionate and independent investigation' of allegations by whistleblowers and appropriate follow-up action.

7.1 The nature of whistleblowing

A whistleblower is an employee who provides information about his or her company that he or she reasonably believes provides evidence of:

- fraud;
- a serious violation of a law or regulation by the company or by directors, managers or employees within the company;
- a miscarriage of justice;
- offering or taking bribes;
- price-fixing;
- a danger to public health or safety, such as dumping toxic waste in the environment or supplying food that is unfit for consumption;
- neglect of people in care; or
- in the public sector, gross waste or misuse of public funds.

The British Standards Institution's (BSI's) 'Whistleblowing Arrangements: Code of Practice' 2008 provides the following definition:

> 'Whistleblowing is the popular term used when someone who works in or for an organisation … raises a concern about a possible fraud, crime, danger or other serious risk that could threaten customers, colleagues, shareholders, the public or the organisation's own reputation.'

It can act as an early warning system to the employer about improper or illegal behaviour within the organisation.

A feature of whistleblowing is that the individual concerned has been unable to get a response from the company's management through normal lines of reporting, which has forced the individual to go to someone else with the information. The whistleblower presumably hopes that this person will take action to deal with the misdemeanour. Whistleblowing can arise in different situations and for different reasons.

- There have been instances in the past where an employee of a company manufacturing defence equipment has passed information to the press about an illegal arms sale. Presumably, the whistleblower in each case disapproved of the transaction and believed that the company was aware that it was in breach of the law, but intended to go through with the sale.
- An employee may have evidence that his or her superiors are in breach of company regulations and so reports the facts to someone else in a position of seniority within the company, such as a managing director. In these cases, the individual believes the company's senior management is unaware of the problem, but will take action if alerted. This situation arose, for example, with the whistleblowing at Enron in 2001 (see also Chapter 1).

7.2 Whistleblowing and internal control

There is a strong connection between corporate governance and whistleblowing. An employee may honestly believe that there is (or has been or could soon be) serious malpractice by someone within the company, but feels unable to report their concerns in the normal way. This could be because the individual to whom they normally report is involved in the suspected malpractice. Serious malpractice or a misdemeanour could be damaging to the company.

- It might suffer financial loss if some employees are acting fraudulently.
- It might incur severe penalties as a consequence of employees breaking the law or regulations.
- There could be damage to the company's reputation if the misdemeanour is made public.

The need for whistleblowing arises when normal procedures and internal controls will not reveal the illicit activity, because the individuals responsible for the activity are somehow able to ignore or get round the normal controls.

However, although whistleblowing procedures are an internal control, they are not an embedded control within the company's regular procedures, and their effectiveness relies on the willingness of genuine whistleblowers to come forward with their allegations. The incidence of illicit or illegal behaviour should be uncommon; therefore whistleblowing should be an occasional event.

7.3 Potential problems with whistleblowing systems

Concerns about whistleblowing have grown in recent years, for the following reasons.

- A huge amount of information about a company is held on computer files, which are accessible to many employees. Individual employees prepared to spend the time to look closely into a matter are likely to discover a large amount of information that they might not 'officially' be supposed to know, or information that no one else has yet become aware of. Companies are now aware, for example, that they could become liable for information held as email messages in the files of employees.
- In many companies, there is a strong culture of loyalty to the company. Employees who question or criticise the actions of management might be considered to be 'traitors'. Despite laws designed to protect them, whistleblowers run the risk of retaliatory action. When they report their suspicions, they may be sacked on the grounds of making false and malicious allegations. It would certainly appear to be the case that whistleblowers are more likely to be dismissed than rewarded. This is particularly the case when the whistleblower passes the information to someone outside the company, such as the media.
- Individual whistleblowers played an important part in uncovering information about financial and accounting mismanagement and corruption at Enron (2001) and WorldCom (2002), and in criticising the handling of security information by the FBI before the September 11 2001 terrorist attacks in New York. The public became aware not only that companies were being mismanaged, but also that honest attempts to reveal the problems were being disregarded by senior management.

As these case examples show, whistleblowers may put their job at risk. An employer taking retaliatory action may claim that sacking the employee had nothing to do with the revelations the employee had made, or claim that the employee was sacked because his or her statements were vindictive and untrue.

7.4 Whistleblowing: best practice

If an employee has a genuine, honest concern about something happening within the company, which he or she believes to be dishonest or improper, there should be a way for the employee's concerns to be brought to the attention of management and dealt with in a constructive way. Having a system for listening to employees' concerns should be a part of an effective risk management system within the organisation, because diligent employees can act as an early warning system of problems. However, there are several problems with whistleblowing procedures and policies.

As stated earlier, experience in many organisations appears to show that an individual who reports concerns about illegal or unethical conduct is often victimised by colleagues and management. If the allegations by the whistleblower are rejected, they might not receive the same salary increases as colleagues, or they may be overlooked for promotion. The attitude of colleagues and managers might also be hostile, making it difficult for the individual to continue in the job.

On the other hand, employees may deliberately make false claims about their colleagues or bosses, out of spite or a desire for revenge for some actual or perceived 'wrong'. It would be inappropriate to provide protection for individuals making malicious and intentionally false allegations.

Companies therefore need to establish a whistleblowing system that:

- encourages employees to report illegal or unethical behaviour; but
- discourages malicious and unfounded allegations.

A company might state its policy on whistleblowing in the following terms.

- An employee is acting correctly if, in good faith, he or she seeks advice about improper behaviour or reports improper behaviour, where it is not possible to resolve the individual's concerns through discussions with colleagues or line management. Whistleblowing is appropriate if the employee does it in good faith and is not being malicious, and there is no other way to resolve the problem.
- The company will not tolerate any discrimination by employees or management in the company against an individual who has reported in good faith their concerns about illegal or unethical behaviour. This is a policy statement that whistleblowers will be protected if they have made their report in good faith.
- Disciplinary action will be taken against any employee who knowingly makes a false report of illegal or improper behaviour by someone else (malicious reporting should not be tolerated).

In practice, employees may feel obliged to take their concerns (possibly anonymously) to someone outside the company, risking the anger of the employer for breach of proper procedures if they are identified. An employee can be disciplined for making groundless complaints and allegations in bad faith about their employer. On the other hand, there are some 'official' whistleblowing channels that provide a way of reporting concerns to someone outside the employer organisation. An example in the UK is the Whistleblowing Line operated by the Financial Conduct Authority (FCA) for the financial services industry.

7.5 Internal procedures for whistleblowers' allegations

A company should have a fair system for dealing internally with accusations from whistleblowers, so that an honest individual does not feel under threat. Employees ought to know what those procedures are. Since whistleblowing is not a regular event, a company may simply try to deal with each case on its merits when it arises, without any formal procedures or channels of complaint being established. The employee will therefore not know whom to complain to, and will probably go to the most senior manager available – possibly the CEO.

A problem with dealing with whistleblowing incidents on an ad hoc basis is that the accusations may relate to the senior executive directors themselves. An employee who believes the CEO or finance director to be guilty of wrongdoing will have no option other than to resign or take the complaint to an external authority, such as the press or the police.

It may therefore be more appropriate to establish a formal internal channel for dealing with whistleblowers.

- If the company has a culture of ethical conduct, it should be prepared to encourage whistleblowing, and should provide a channel for reporting complaints and allegations by employees about their bosses. At the same time, it should make clear its policy about disciplining employees found to have been malicious in making allegations.
- Although it will often be necessary to involve senior executives in the investigation of allegations, the channel for complaints should not be to senior executive management or the board. One possible arrangement would be for allegations to be made to the company secretary, who would then arrange for the senior independent director (SID) to be notified. The SID, or a committee of NEDs, could then decide how the allegation should be investigated.
- An allegation might be investigated on behalf of a company by a firm of solicitors, because of the possibility of criminal activity or a misdemeanour that could expose the company to a large civil liability. If so, the solicitors asked to do the work should not have a close relationship with the company, so that their investigation can be independent. For example, the company should not be a large client of the solicitors for other legal work.

However, until every company has adopted an enlightened approach to dealing with employee allegations, and every employee can feel that he or she is not risking job security by making accusations, many will not trust internal procedures and will prefer to go to an external authority. Anyone making allegations about their company and its management to an external authority could be putting their job at risk. In recognition of the risks taken by honest whistleblowers, the law should offer some protection.

7.6 Establishing whistleblowing procedures

In the UK, the most authoritative guide to whistleblowing procedures is probably now: 'Whistleblowing Arrangements Code of Practice', which was issued by the BSI in 2008 (it is also referred to as 'PAS 1998: 2008': PAS stands for Publicly Available Specification).

The Code of Practice states that an internal whistleblowing procedure will be effective only if it has the confidence of the employees, who are its intended users. Confidence in the system will be obtained only if the employer is genuinely committed to the procedure. The Code also recommends that employees' representatives should be involved in establishing the procedure and monitoring its implementation.

The company secretary will often be given an important role in establishing an internal whistleblowing policy and procedures. They need to ensure that there are trained people in the organisation to operate the procedure so that any matters raised under the internal procedure are dealt with effectively. The Code adds that if someone does report a genuine concern in good faith, these individuals must be supported. Providing support might be a role for the company secretary.

The Code of Practice suggests that features of an internal whistleblowing policy and procedure should include the following provisions.

- The internal whistleblowing procedures should be documented and a copy should be given to every employee.
- It should set out the key aspects of the procedure, such as the person to whom employees should report their suspicions or concerns. This might be the company secretary or internal audit.
- It should contain a statement that the employer takes malpractice or misconduct seriously, and is committed to a culture of openness in which employees can report legitimate concerns without fear of penalty or punishment.
- It should give examples of the type of misconduct for which employees should use the procedure and set out the level of proof that there should be in an allegation (although positive proof might not be required, a whistleblower should be able to provide good reasons for their concern).
- The document should set out the procedures by which an allegation will be investigated.
- It should make clear that false or malicious allegations will result in disciplinary action against the individual making them.
- It should make clear that no employee will be victimised for raising a genuine concern. Victimisation for raising a qualified disclosure should be a disciplinary offence.
- An external whistleblowing route should be offered, as well as an internal reporting procedure.
- There should be an undertaking that, as far as possible, whistleblowers will be informed about the outcome of their allegations and the action that has been taken.
- Whistleblowers should be promised confidentiality, as far as this is possible.

8 The Bribery Act and its implications for internal control

In the UK, the Bribery Act 2010 has made bribery a criminal offence. It has created three offences:

- Offering bribes (active bribery) and receiving bribes (passive bribery).
- Bribery of foreign public officials for business benefit.
- Failure to prevent a bribe being paid on the organisation's behalf.

The Act therefore makes bribery by businesses for commercial benefit (commercial bribery) a criminal offence, and it applies to UK businesses regardless of whether the act of bribery occurs inside or outside the UK.

A consequence of the Bribery Act is that UK companies must ensure that they have internal controls sufficient to prevent bribery by any of its employees or agents, or detecting bribery when it occurs. However, the Act recognises that it is impossible to prevent bribery at all times, and a valid defence against a charge of failing to prevent a bribe being paid on its behalf will be evidence that procedures were in place to prevent bribery.

The Ministry of Justice has issued guidance on the Bribery Act, which in its introduction states: 'At stake is the principle of free and fair competition, which stands diminished by each bribe offered and accepted.' This guidance promotes six principles:

1   **Proportionate procedures.** The procedures of a commercial organisation to prevent bribery by people associated with it should be proportionate to the risk of bribery that it faces and the nature and scale of its commercial activities.
2   **Top-level commitment.** Top-level management should be committed to preventing bribery and should foster a culture in their organisation in which bribery is considered unacceptable.
3   **Risk assessment.** There should be periodic, informed and regular assessment by organisations of the nature and extent of potential bribery by people associated with it.
4   **Due diligence.** There should be due diligence of third party intermediaries and local agents who will act on behalf of the organisation, with a view to identifying and mitigating bribery risk.
5   **Communication (including training).** Commercial organisations should seek to ensure that policies against bribery are embedded and understood, by means of communication and training that is proportionate to the bribery risk that the organisation faces.
6   **Monitoring and review.** There should be monitoring and review of the procedures designed to prevent bribery, and improvements should be made when weaknesses are detected.

8.1 Whistleblowing procedures and the Bribery Act 2010

A company could avoid conviction of failing to prevent bribery if it can show that, although bribery may have occurred, it has in place 'adequate processes' to prevent bribery. Having suitable whistleblowing procedures could be a sufficient defence against a criminal charge, provided that the company can demonstrate that the procedures work well in practice. It should not be sufficient simply to have a whistleblowing policy in existence, but which no one uses.

 END OF CHAPTER QUESTIONS

1 What internal control risks are evident from the case study and who should be responsible for internal control within the company?	**3** What are the potential risks to Hunnerware from ineffective systems of internal control and risk management? What might be the implications for Hunnerware if the board does not respond positively to the concerns expressed by the new NED?
2 How might disaster recovery planning be of value to the company? Use information in the case study to illustrate your argument.	

CHAPTER SUMMARY

■ Risks that are managed within an internal control system are the risks of losses due to failures or weaknesses in the systems, operating procedures and personnel within an organisation.
■ These risks can be categorised into financial risks, operational risks and compliance risks.
■ An internal control system should prevent risk events, reduce the potential impact of risk events, or identify failures when they occur and ensure that corrective measures are taken to deal with them.
■ An internal control system includes internal controls, which may be categorised as financial controls, operational controls or compliance controls, according to the type of risk they are intended to control.
■ An internal control system is not just a larger number of internal controls. There should be an appropriate control environment within the organisation, with leadership from the board. There should also be procedures for identifying and assessing internal control risks, designing and implementing

suitable internal controls, and communication of control information about monitoring of the effectiveness of controls and the control system as a whole.

- The board of directors is responsible for ensuring that there is an effective system of internal control. The UK Corporate Governance Code requires the board to review at least annually the effectiveness of the systems of internal control and risk management, and report to the shareholders that they have done so.

- The board may delegate the task of carrying out the review of the effectiveness of internal control and the risk management system to the audit committee. Occasionally, a company's board may give the task of monitoring the risk management systems, but not financial risk controls, to a risk committee of the board.

- The UK Corporate Governance Code requires listed companies to include in their annual report and accounts a statement on internal control from the board. The board's responsibility for internal control extends to all types of internal control risk, not just financial risks.

- In the UK, following publication of the 1998 Combined Code, the Turnbull Committee issued guidelines on how to establish and maintain a sound system of internal controls. The Turnbull Guidance became the responsibility of the FRC, which issued revised guidance in 2005 and again in 2014.

- Internal controls should be embedded within operations and procedures, and many are automated. However, some controls are initiated from 'outside' such as internal audit investigations and whistleblowing.

- The review of the effectiveness of the internal control system by the audit committee or the board relies mainly on regular risk reports to the committee (or the board) from management, possibly with occasional additional reports from the internal auditors or external auditors (for example, in their end-of-audit report on any weaknesses in internal controls).

- The UK Code requires the board to state that it is responsible for internal control and has reviewed the effectiveness of the internal control system, but does not require weaknesses that have been identified in the system to be disclosed. The DTR require listed companies to report on the main features of the internal control system for financial reporting (but not operational or compliance controls).

- A company may have an internal audit department or function. Internal audit is audit work carried out at the request of management, for which there is no statutory requirement. The tasks of internal auditors can vary, but can include investigations into aspects of financial, operational or compliance controls in the company's systems and procedures. Internal audit investigations may be carried out at the request of operational management, senior financial management or the audit committee (or board).

- Internal audit can therefore be used to test the effectiveness of internal controls within a company's systems and operations, and report to management or the audit committee on their findings and recommendations.

- Internal auditors must be as objective and independent as possible. This is difficult for employees of the company. Although the head of internal audit may have a line-reporting responsibility to the finance director, they should also have direct access if required to the audit committee.

- The UK Code requires companies to review each year the effectiveness of the internal audit function, and if the company does not have an internal audit function, to consider the need for one and make a recommendation to the board.

- Companies may have disaster recovery planning as part of their internal control system.

- The UK Code requires the board to assess its whistleblowing procedures.

- There are extensive guidelines on whistleblowing within companies, but whistleblowing procedures are often ineffective.

- In the UK, the Bribery Act (2010) makes it an offence to give or receive bribes or to bribe a foreign public official for business benefit. It is also a criminal offence (commercial bribery) for an organisation to fail to prevent an employee or agent from paying a bribe on its behalf. Companies must therefore have internal controls in place to prevent bribery by its employees or agents or to detect bribery if it occurs.

Corporate social responsibility and sustainability

■ LIST OF CHAPTERS

■ OVERVIEW

The fourth part of this study text looks at corporate social responsibility (CSR) and sustainability as features of corporate governance and ways in which companies might report their plans, targets and actual performance to stakeholders on a range of CSR and sustainability issues. It also considers the significance of CSR issues for companies themselves, for shareholders and for other stakeholders (including the general public).

Chapter 11 explains the nature of CSR and corporate citizenship, and why CSR is an issue for corporate governance. It also explains sustainability in the context of the 'six capitals' model, and compares sustainability with CSR. It describes the views of different stakeholder groups, including the government and investors (who might include **socially responsible investment (SRI)** within their own organisational objectives). The chapter also explains how companies might benefit from the pursuit of CSR and sustainability policies, and how these might be implemented.

Chapter 12 discusses the reporting of CSR and sustainability issues by companies to shareholders and other stakeholders. Companies should not only pursue CSR and sustainability policies; they should also report their intentions and achievements to stakeholders, including the general public. Much of this reporting is on a voluntary basis; however, many quoted companies recognise its importance, and the requirement for strategic reports may be moving corporate reporting towards an integrated reporting framework, in which sustainability issues feature prominently. The chapter explains the nature of social and environmental reporting, and the problems with producing meaningful reports in the absence of standardisation and benchmarking.

■ LEARNING OUTCOMES

Part Four should enable you to:

■ compare the responsibilities of organisations to different stakeholder groups, and advise on the application of principles of corporate responsibility or corporate citizenship;

■ analyse the benefits of CSR policies to companies;

■ give advice on developing and implementing a CSR strategy appropriate to your organisation;

■ apply the principles and guidelines concerning CSR reporting; and

■ explain the significance and advise on the use of sustainability reporting.

 PART 4 CASE STUDY

MGX Industrial is a large global company with industrial and manufacturing operations in many countries of the world. It has a listing in the UK. Four years ago, the board made its operations director responsible for reporting to the board on social and environmental issues. The company announced that this appointment demonstrated its commitment to acting as a corporate citizen in all parts of the world where it had operations.

The company is subject to various items of environmental legislation and regulation in the countries where it operates. In addition, local site managers are continually under pressure from national governments, local government authorities, regulatory authorities, pressure groups and local communities to improve their social and environmental performance, and to give greater consideration to social and

	Target	Actual performance	Trend	Target date for achievement of target performance
Zero harm	Zero fatalities at operating sites	5 fatalities	Worse than the previous year (3 fatalities)	Ongoing. Target established 4 years ago.
	Zero major environment incidents	No incidents	Better than previous year (1 incident)	Ongoing. Target established 2 years ago.
Health	25% reduction in the incidence of occupational disease over a 7-year period	21% reduction in the 5 years since the target was established	On track for achievement	2 years' time
Safety	50% reduction in the incidence of recordable injuries at operating sites over a 10-year period	10% reduction in the 3 years since the target was established	Below expectation in achieving improvements	7 years' time
Environment	10% reduction in greenhouse gas emissions per unit produced	8% reduction in the 3 years since the target was established	On target for achievement	2 years' time
	15% reduction in carbon-based energy use per unit produced	6% reduction in the 3 years since the target was established	Target unlikely to be achieved	2 years' time
	12% improvement in ratio of water recycled/re-used to high-quality water consumed	9% reduction in the 3 years since the target was established	On target for achievement	2 years' time
Community	1.5% of pre-tax profits to be invested in community projects	1.5% of pre-tax profits were invested	Target achieved	Ongoing

PART 4 CASE STUDY *continued*

environmental issues. There has been an increase in the past two years of requests by institutional shareholders to discuss environmental issues with the company's board.

The company publishes a social and environmental (SE) report each year, which is produced at the same time as its annual report and accounts. The SE report is produced as a separate document and is also accessible on the company's website. The main part of the report begins with a list of social and environmental targets, and actual performance to date. Most of the report is a narrative description of these targets, and the reasons for failure to achieve any of them or a description of

how a target has been achieved or should be achieved by the target date. An extract from the list of social and environmental reports in the company's most recent SE performance data is shown above.

The director responsible for social and environmental matters is disappointed by the lack of widespread interest in the company's policies or its SE reports. He believes that the problem may be the negative publicity the company received for major environmental contamination at two of its operating sites two or three years ago, and the company's slow response in clearing the pollution and compensating the victims of the accidents.

11

Corporate social responsibility and sustainability

■ CONTENTS

■ INTRODUCTION

Advocates of an integrated approach or pluralist approach to corporate governance would argue that the board of directors has a responsibility for the formulation of policies on ethical behaviour, employee welfare, social issues and environmental issues. The board should also monitor the effectiveness of these strategies. There is some recognition of the responsibility of the board for **corporate social responsibility (CSR)** issues, although concern for CSR issues varies between countries. This chapter considers the nature of CSR and also sustainability. The following chapter discusses ways in which companies should report to shareholders and other stakeholders on these issues.

1 The nature of corporate social responsibility (CSR)

Business for Social Responsibility has defined CSR as:

> 'While there is no single, commonly accepted definition of CSR, it generally refers to business decision-making linked to ethical values, compliance with legal requirements, and respect for people, communities and the environment.'

It is also known as **corporate citizenship**. Companies should see themselves as citizens within society, and as such they should be expected to behave as 'good citizens' towards all their neighbours; for example, companies should:

■ treat employees fairly and with respect;
■ operate in an ethical way and with integrity;
■ respect basic human rights;
■ sustain the environment for future generations; and
■ be a responsible neighbour in their communities.

CSR is therefore consistent with a stakeholder approach to corporate governance by companies (or at the very least an enhanced form of 'enlightened shareholder approach' to governance). Several issues come together in a CSR approach to conducting business:

■ an ethical approach to conducting business;
■ concern for all stakeholders;
■ concern for social and environmental issues; but also
■ a recognition that a company must be profitable to survive and succeed in the long term.

Although CSR is commonly associated with ethical values and social and environmental issues, it is important to recognise that companies must carry on business in a way that is financially viable and profitable. CSR recognises social, environmental and economic (financial) issues (sometimes known as SEE), and is concerned with how companies can integrate the requirements of each into their business strategies and activities. The EU has stated: 'Through CSR, enterprises of all sizes, in co-operation with their stakeholders, can help to reconcile economic, social and environmental ambitions.'

The ethical element of CSR should not be forgotten either. A socially responsible company should be expected to act in an ethical way, and should not condone the use of unethical practices such as bribery to win contracts.

2   Sustainability and sustainable development

The concept of 'sustainability', also called 'sustainable development' or 'sustainable business', is linked to CSR, although its rationale is different. Its focus is on the long-term sustainability of the business, rather than on responsibilities to society. Even so, CSR and sustainability have much in common.

2.1 Definition of sustainability

Sustainability is emerging as an objective for major companies; however, there is no generally accepted definition of what it actually means. The Brundtland Report (for the World Commission on Environment and Development, 1987) defined sustainable development as 'development that meets the needs of the present without compromising the ability of future generations to meet their own needs'.

However, there are difficulties with what this definition means in practice.

- There can be disagreement about the meaning of 'needs of the present'. Presumably these are more than the bare minimum needs for survival, because in much of the world consumption is well above survival level and affluent societies do not accept the need to reduce consumption to levels in other countries of the world.
- Similarly, it is not clear what the needs of future generations are. If they are just survival needs, there must be an inherent assumption that at some time in the future economic wealth must decline in the more affluent societies.
- It is not clear over what period of time the needs of future generations should be considered and measured. In theory, society's long-term needs should be recognised. However, governments and companies are likely to plan over much shorter timescales. Since companies plan for the future and report their performance within fairly short time frames, reporting for sustainable development by companies is likely to focus on relatively short-term measures of sustainability.
- Should sustainability be measured collectively for all people in all societies of the world, or should it be measured in terms of individual countries or regions?

In general terms, however, sustainability is concerned with conducting business operations in a way that can be continued into the foreseeable future, without using natural resources at such a rate or creating such environmental damage that the continuation of the business will eventually become impossible.

The definition of sustainable development in the Brundtland Report is also unsatisfactory because it has an environmental focus, whereas for businesses sustainability involves a broader range of factors.

For a company, sustainability might be defined as the ability to keep a business in operation over the long term, adding or preserving value. To do this a business needs to be profitable and it may also need to grow. It also needs to operate in a business environment, as well as a natural environment, where it is able to carry on its business operations.

It may therefore be useful to think of sustainability for businesses in the context of the 'six capitals model'.

2.2 Six capitals model

The basic idea of the six capitals model is that an organisation creates or destroys value over time, by using and affecting six types of capital. The value that is created or destroyed is reflected in changes to the values of these six types of capital.

All organisations depend, in differing ways, on various forms of capital for their success. This includes capital that they do not own.

The six capitals are:

- financial capital;
- manufactured capital;
- human capital;
- intellectual capital;
- natural capital; and
- social capital.

A sustainable organisation is one that can continue to exist over the longer term. Where possible it will enhance these stocks of capital assets, rather than deplete or downgrade them.

Financial capital

Financial capital consists of items that enable other types of asset to be owned and traded. It includes shares (and the value of shares) and money. Companies increase their financial value by increasing the financial value of its shares and bonds, and by accumulating cash.

Financial measurements have traditionally been used to measure changes in the reported capital of companies, such as increases in capital due to profits and asset revaluations.

In order to maintain or accumulate cash over the long term, a company needs to be profitable (or at worst, break even).

Manufactured capital

Manufactured capital is any physical means of production and infrastructure that contribute to provision of products or services by the organisation. It may help to think of manufactured capital as 'fixed assets', such as tools, technology, machines, buildings and all forms of infrastructure, such as transport and communications networks and waste disposal systems.

A sustainable business is often one that is able to increase the value of its manufactured capital, as well as its financial capital, and to operate in countries where efficient and modern infrastructures are in place.

Human capital

Human capital consists of the people who work for the organisation, and their collective skills and experience. A healthy, motivated and skilled workforce creates more value than a workforce that is unhealthy and unskilled, and lacks motivation.

Sustainable businesses should seek to enhance the value of their workforce through policies for motivation, training and health care.

Intellectual capital

Intellectual capital is linked to human capital. It represents the value of the accumulated intellectual property of the organisation. This may take the form of:

- legal rights and protection, such a patents and copyrights;
- brand values; and
- accumulated knowledge – the 'knowledge capital' of the organisation.

Organisations may need to sustain their intellectual capital, perhaps by creating new intellectual capital, in order to be a sustainable business over the long term.

Natural capital

Natural capital is the environment. It consists of the stock of natural raw materials and energy that are used to make products and provide services, and the flows of these materials and energy. It includes natural resources, which may be either renewable but potentially in scarce supply (such as water, timber and fish) or non-renewable (such as oil and other fossil fuels). Natural capital also includes:

- 'sinks' which are parts of the environment (such as oceans and forests) that absorb or recycle waste and pollution; and
- processes such as climate change, the carbon cycle and the ecological food chain.

Companies may not 'own' natural capital, but they use it and rely on it, to different degrees and in differing ways, depending on the nature of their business operations. For long-term sustainability of the business, however, companies may need to consider environmental protection measures such as measures for:

- renewing renewable natural resources and energy;
- substituting materials in abundant supply in place of materials in short supply; and
- using smaller amounts of scarce resources, such as using water more efficiently and recycling more waste.

Social capital

This is perhaps the most difficult of the six capitals to understand. Social capital can be defined as any value added to an organisation by social relationships and institutions, such as human relationships, co-operation, networks, communication channels, families, communities and schools. Organisations rely on social relationships to achieve their objectives. They also need social acceptance to support their survival over time.

Sustainability and maintenance of the six capitals

To be a sustainable business, a company must consider all six aspects of its capital. To add to its business value, a company should add to its total capital, recognising capital that there is risk of destroying aspects of capital in the policies that it pursues.

A company that seeks to be a sustainable business should develop policies for all six aspects of capital. In developing policies for human capital, natural capital and social capital, sustainability has close similarities with CSR.

3 Social, economic and environmental issues

CSR policies and sustainability policies integrate social, economic and environmental objectives.

- **Economic objectives** are well understood, and are common to most commercial companies. Economic objectives should be to achieve profitability over the longer term, protect and develop the assets of shareholders and provide shareholders with a satisfactory return on their investment. Objectives can be set in terms of targets for profitability, earnings per share (EPS), EPS growth, share price growth, cash flow targets, and so on.
- Social and environmental policies are more difficult to define, because these vary between companies and differ according to the industrial sector and the countries in which they operate.
  - **Social policies** may relate to the company's employees, the employees of major suppliers to the company, local communities or the concerns of wider society, and also concern for customers.
  - **Environmental objectives** often relate to issues such as reducing pollution levels, reducing waste and reducing the consumption of non-renewable natural resources, but specific objectives vary between industries because each industry has its own particular forms of pollution and resource consumption.

3.1 King IV Code and CSR

The concepts of sustainability and corporate citizenship are key elements in the King IV Report (2016) on corporate governance for companies in South Africa the Report states that: 'Sustainable development ... is a primary ethical and economic imperative. It is a fitting response to the organisation being an integral part of society, its status as a corporate citizen and its stakeholders' needs Interests and expectations'.

The Report emphasises the concept of corporate citizenship. The report has a principle that 'The governing body should ensure that the organisation is and is seen to be a responsible corporate citizen'. This is the idea that companies are a 'person' in law and as such are members of the society in which they operate. Like all other members of society, they should be expected to acknowledge the needs and concerns of other citizens, and to act like a good citizen.

3.2 The voluntary aspect of CSR

To some extent, companies are required by law and regulation to act in socially responsible ways. For example, there are laws and regulations to protect health and safety, prevent contamination of the environment and protect employees. An important feature of CSR is that CSR policies are largely voluntary and driven by companies themselves, not by external regulation.

CSR relates to the idea that companies, in addition to their responsibilities to shareholders, also have responsibilities to other stakeholders and to society at large. These responsibilities can be divided into two distinct elements:

- generally accepted responsibilities that the company must fulfil in order to succeed in business or comply with legislation or regulations; and
- functions considered by some groups, including investors, to be responsibilities that go beyond compliance with the law and regulations, and beyond the measures necessary for achieving commercial success.

Whereas it would be widely accepted by directors that companies should comply with the law and should give serious attention to the company's reputation risk, there are probably differences of opinion about the extent to which companies need to go beyond legal, regulatory and commercial requirements in pursuing CSR policies.

3.3 Reasons for developing interest in CSR

The development of concern for CSR by companies has come from several sources, but in particular:

- government;
- investors; and
- companies themselves.

The interests of government, investors and companies in CSR are explained in the following paragraphs.

TEST YOUR KNOWLEDGE 11.1

a Define CSR and outline some examples of how companies might act in accordance with an awareness of social responsibility.
b What is a corporate citizen?
c Define sustainability.
d What are the six capitals whose value companies should seek to maintain or enhance?

4   CSR and government

Many governments are interested in CSR because they want to improve the quality of life of their citizens and to protect the environment, while encouraging the successful development of business.

4.1 UK company law and CSR

In the UK, the Companies Act 2006 (CA2006) does not refer specifically to CSR, but it includes as a statutory duty of directors a requirement to promote the success of the company. In fulfilling this duty, directors are required to have regard, among other matters, to:

- the interests of the company's employees;
- the need to foster relationships with suppliers and customers;
- the impact of the company's actions on the community and the environment; and
- the desirability of maintaining a reputation for high standards of conduct.

This in effect is a requirement that directors should have some regard for CSR issues, and should take an enlightened shareholder approach to governance. See also Chapter 12 concerning the CA2006 and the strategy report.

4.2 The OECD and CSR

In 2001, the OECD issued Guidelines for Multinational Enterprises (these Guidelines were reviewed in 2011). The Guidelines were issued by the governments of subscribing countries to multinationals with the aim of encouraging 'the positive contributions that multinational enterprises can make to economic, environmental and social progress and to minimise the difficulties to which their various operations may give rise'. The objective of the governments was to encourage multinationals to operate in ways that would improve the welfare and living standards of their peoples, by taking into consideration the stakeholders in the countries where they operate. Although the Guidelines are directed at multinational companies, similar guidelines should apply to local companies. Some of the Guidelines are listed below, to provide an indication of the nature of CSR issues that may affect companies and in which governments may have an interest.

General policies

The OECD Guidelines suggest several general policies that multinationals should adopt. These include having policies that:

- contribute to economic, social and environmental development with a view to achieving sustainable development;
- respect the human rights of those people affected by their activities;
- encourage the development of local business through cooperation with local communities;
- encourage the development of human capital in those communities, by creating employment and providing training;
- refrain from seeking or accepting exemptions from local laws on the environment or health;
- support and promote good corporate governance practice; and
- avoid improper involvement in local politics.

Employment policies

The OECD Guidelines include more specific policy guidelines on employment and industrial relations. These include requirements for multinationals to:

- respect the right of employees to be represented by trade unions;
- contribute to the abolition of child labour;
- contribute to the abolition of forced labour;
- avoid discrimination on the grounds of race, gender, religion or political opinion;
- observe standards of employment that are not less favourable than those provided by comparable employers in the host country;
- take adequate steps to ensure occupational health and safety;
- as much as possible, use local labour and provide them with skills training; and
- in negotiations with trade union representatives, avoid using the threat of moving all or part of the company's operations to another country or region.

Environment policies

The OECD Guidelines on the environment include requirements for multinationals to:

- establish and maintain a system of environmental management that includes the collection of adequate information about the environmental and health and safety effects of their activities, targets for improvements in environmental performance and regular monitoring of actual performance in comparison with the established targets;

- provide the public with adequate information about environmental and health and safety matters, and engage with communities that are directly affected by the environmental and health and safety policies of the company;
- consider the long-term environmental, health and safety-related consequences when making decisions;
- continually seek to improve environmental performance through encouraging environmentally friendly technologies and developing environmentally friendly products; and
- maintain contingency plans for dealing with unforeseen environmental, health and safety damage arising from their operations, including accidents and emergencies.

There are other policies in the Guidelines, such as the requirement that multinationals should avoid the use of bribery of officials to obtain contracts and revenue.

 TEST YOUR KNOWLEDGE 11.2

a   What are the general OECD Guidelines for multinational companies, and why were these considered necessary?

b   What are the OECD Guidelines to multinational companies on employment policies?

---

5   Investors: responsible investing and socially responsible investing (SRI)

Investors may have strong views about social and environmental issues, and their investment decisions may be strongly influenced by the way in which company managements address their social, environmental and also governance issues.

5.1 Responsible investment

Guidance on **responsible investment** has been issued for its members by the Pensions and Lifetime Savings Association (PLSA) (formerly NAPF) in the Responsible Investment Guide 2013.

This guidance comments that: 'There is robust evidence that extra-financial factors – often referred to as **Environmental, Social or Governance (ESG)** factors ... – can significantly impact a company's long-term value, reputation, brand, growth rate, margins, market share and borrowing costs.' It recommends that investors should therefore take these factors into account when making investment decisions, and consider whether the policies and actions of the company are consistent with value protection and enhancement.

The guidance identifies the following areas of ESG issues and company policy that may be of particular concern to investors.

- Environmental risks
  - climate change;
  - energy use;
  - natural resources;
  - water.
- Governance risks
  - board independence;
  - succession planning;
  - board diversity;
  - auditor independence.
- Social risks
  - human rights;
  - employment;
  - health and safety;
  - supply chain.

Responsible investment is closely connected to sustainability. The PLSA defines responsible investment as: 'an investment approach in which investors recognise the importance of the long-term health and stability of the market as a whole; seeking to incorporate material extra-financial factors alongside other financial performance and strategic assessments within investment decisions; and utilise ownership rights and responsibilities attached to assets to protect and enhance shareholder value over the long term – primarily through voting and engagement.'

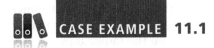

CASE EXAMPLE 11.1

Social and environmental risk often arises directly from the actions of companies, but there may also be indirect risks too. The following comment about social and environmental risks came from the website of Barclays Bank:

'Barclays has a strong and longstanding commitment to managing the environmental and social risks associated with commercial lending. We recognise that a bank's major environmental impacts tend to be indirect, arising from the provision of financial services to business customers operating in sensitive sectors. We also believe that taking due account of our environmental and social impacts is not only the right thing to do, but also makes good business sense.'

5.2 Socially responsible investing (SRI)

The PLSA guidance makes a distinction between responsible investing and socially responsible investing or SRI. It recommends that investors should consider ESG issues as a fundamental part of investment decision-making. However, it states specifically that its guidance does not cover SRI, which is something different.

A distinction can be made between ethical investing and SRI.

- Ethical investing means refusing to invest in 'unethical' companies and 'sin stocks', because the activities of the company are inconsistent with the investor's ethical, moral or religious beliefs.
- SRI investing goes further. It includes refusing to invest in 'unethical' companies, but SRI investors also encourage companies to develop CSR policies and objectives, in addition to pursuing financial objectives. SRI investors may be involved in shareholder activism when companies have social or environmental policies with which they disagree.

SRI (also known as ethical investment and sustainable investment) can be defined as an approach to investment management that takes into account a proper analysis of the CSR responsibilities of companies to society as a whole and particular stakeholder groups.

It is a process whereby the principles of the investor, and ethical views of the investor, affect their choice of which companies to invest in and how they should exercise their rights as shareholders.

It involves both the screening and selection process for investment decision-making and the process of engagement between shareholders and companies.

5.3 PLSA policy on CSR and SRI

In a 2005 paper on CSR/SRI, the PLSA explained that it had given some consideration to whether it should be active in promoting good CSR practices in companies, in the same way that it had been active in promoting good corporate governance. Its conclusion was that, unlike corporate governance, CSR should be seen as 'a fundamental part of the normal running of the business'.

- CSR is a management responsibility, and management should be allowed to get on with their task without interference from institutional investors.
- Boards should be accountable to shareholders for the way they run the business, including their CSR policies.

■ Boards should develop CSR policies as part of their normal business agenda, which they should disclose to shareholders and other stakeholders in the normal process of disclosure by companies.

The PLSA therefore recognised the potential importance of CSR issues, but stated that it did not intend to issue specific guidelines. One of its statements of underlying principles summarised its position:

'At all times the board and Management should be mindful of the wider role of the Company in society, bearing in mind that maximisation of short-term gain in a manner which is deemed unacceptable by society as a whole can seriously damage the longer term prospects of a Company and lead to real financial losses for shareholders. Such losses may come about as a result of either changing consumer preferences or legislation putting additional cost on the Company, or both.'

5.4 Pursuing an SRI strategy

There are several different ways in which institutional investors may pursue an SRI strategy:

■ engagement;
■ investment preference; and
■ screening.

With an engagement strategy, the institutional investor acquires shares in which it wants to invest (for financial reasons) but then engages with the board of directors and tries to persuade the company to adopt policies that are socially responsible, or to make improvements in its CSR policies. Engagement may therefore involve expressing the views of the investor about telling what the CSR policies of the company should be and persuading it to change its policies in some areas (through regular meetings with its senior directors). If the company indicates its willingness to make changes, the investor may also offer to help with the formulation of new policies.

With an investment preference strategy, the investor develops a set of guidelines that companies should meet. The investor will then invest only in the shares (or other securities) of companies that meet the guidelines, some of which will be social, ethical or environmental in nature. With this strategy, its investment decisions need not be based entirely on SRI considerations. The investor can also consider the expected financial returns from an investment, and the selected investment portfolio can be a suitable balance of investments that are ethically sound and those that are not as ethical (or are 'more risky' in social or environmental terms) but should provide better financial returns.

With a screening strategy, investments are restricted to companies that pass a 'screen test' for ethical behaviour. Screening may be positive or negative. Positive screening means that companies must meet certain criteria for ethical and socially responsible behaviour; otherwise, the investor will not buy its shares. Negative screening means that an investor will identify companies that fail to meet certain minimum criteria for socially responsible behaviour, and will refuse to buy shares in those companies. The screening process could make use of a published **CSR index** (see also Chapter 12), such as the Dow Jones Sustainability Indices or the FTSE 4 Good indices, or (in the UK) the Business in the Community Corporate Responsibility Index. These are described in Chapter 12.

Investors that have an SRI strategy need information about the CSR performance of companies in order to assess the success of their investment strategies. Methods of reporting CSR performance are described in Chapter 12.

 TEST YOUR KNOWLEDGE 11.3

a Define SRI and explain three different approaches to implementing an SRI strategy.
b For what reasons might an institutional investor adopt an SRI strategy?

6 CSR, sustainability and corporate strategy

Government and investor pressure on companies to develop voluntary policies on ESG issues would probably have relatively little effect unless companies themselves saw benefits in the adoption of suitable policies. Perceptions about the benefits of ESG policies may vary, but over the past ten years or so it would appear that there has been a growing understanding of how CSR or sustainability policies can benefit companies commercially – and possibly financially – to the point where some listed companies now have an ethics and CSR sub-committee of the board.

6.1 The potential benefits of CSR for companies

There are differing views about the extent to which companies benefit commercially from CSR policies. In 2004, the ABI published a research report on CSR and its impact on company performance and investor relations. The key findings of the report were as follows.

- Some studies had found that companies with active CSR policies benefited financially. The evidence was not conclusive but suggested that companies may benefit in areas such as corporate reputation, consumer acceptance, employee loyalty and environmental management.
- The benefits of CSR for companies were not uniform across all companies or sectors.
- The strategic risk aspects of CSR were as important as the effect on short-term profitability. Companies should recognise CSR risks in their strategic planning and management, because they can have important implications for brand value and market acceptability. There was now a greater awareness of the importance of risk as well as returns, including risk to reputation. Social, cultural, demographic and technological changes meant that social and environmental risks were now more significant than in the past.

The potential benefits of CSR policies for companies may be divided broadly into these categories:

- reduction in **reputational risk**;
- business probity risk;
- public relations and marketing benefits; and
- commercial and financial benefits.

It must be stressed that these benefits may vary between companies, industries and countries.

6.2 CSR policies and reputational risk

Reputation risk is difficult to measure (quantify). It is the risk that a company's reputation with the general public (and customers), or the reputation of its product (brand), will suffer damage. Damage to reputation can arise in many different ways: incidents that damage reputation are often reported by the media.

There appears to be a link between public attitudes towards a company and the way in which the company presents itself as an organisation concerned with social, ethical and environmental issues. There is a risk to a company's reputation, depending on the CSR policies it adopts. A company's reputation can be damaged by adverse publicity and public comment from incidents such as a serious environmental spillage or a serious accident. Reputational risk exists for many large companies, not just the obvious examples of companies in mining and extracting, pharmaceuticals and food.

- In the UK, the rail system operator Railtrack failed to recover from the damage to its reputation from the safety concerns of the public following the Hatfield rail crash in 2001, and the company collapsed the following year.
- Some years ago, a company selling a global brand of leisure footwear suffered damage to its reputation following a report that that one of its footwear suppliers in the Far East used child labour and slave labour. On publication of this news, the company's sales and profits (temporarily) fell. Many Western companies that source their supplies from developing countries have now become alert to the reputational risks of using suppliers whose employment practices are below the standards that their customers would consider morally acceptable.
- In 2012, commercial banks were the focus of widespread media criticism, following incidents of mis-selling of insurance and manipulating a key money market interest rate. It was

reported that a substantial number of customers had switched their current accounts from a bank to a building society.

Managing reputational risk and protecting a company's name or brands against reputational damage is now regarded as a key policy objective for companies with well-known brands. The potential significance of CSR from a financial rather than an ethical perspective is therefore:

- cost of fines and other legal penalties, payments to victims of environmental damage, cost of defending legal claims;
- cost of rectifying environmental damage or improving environmental and safety features;
- loss of future contracts as a result of damaged reputation; and
- loss of consumer sales.

There are also benefits to be obtained from having a strong reputation for business ethics and CSR policies.

- Employees may prefer working for ethical organisations.
- Customers may prefer buying from them and suppliers may prefer dealing with them.
- Perhaps even more significantly, as discussed previously, investors may prefer holding the shares of ethical companies (and companies with good governance practices).

Reputation risk may be affected by a company's choice of suppliers, the activities of those suppliers, or its ability to coordinate information and management.

- BP suffered a damaging loss of reputation following the oil spill in the Gulf of Mexico at its Macondo Well. A significant contributory cause of the disaster was the failure of management at BP and its sub-contractors, Transocean and Halliburton, to exchange information which, if seen together, would have indicated the probability of a blow-out at the well.
- In the early 2000s, British Airways outsourced its in-flight food services to an external service provider, Gate Gourmet. Catering staff at the company went on strike, attracting widespread publicity and disrupting BA's in-flight meals service. The strike was a problem for Gate Gourmet, but the reputational damage affected BA much more.

6.3 Business probity risk

Business probity risk is the risk to a company from a failure to act in an honest or ethical way. Dishonest activity can expose a company not only to reputational risk, but also the risk of regulatory or legal action for breaching rules and laws. Bribery is a well-recognised but seemingly widespread dishonest practice.

In order to win sales in some countries, companies might pay bribes (or 'commissions') to individuals. They might take the view that unless they pay bribes, they will not win major contracts. However, by paying bribes, companies act dishonestly, and could be exposed to regulatory action or criminal action by the authorities if evidence of bribery is uncovered. This problem has been reported, for example, in the markets for the sale of military equipment, where the US government authorities in particular have been active in identifying and punishing companies.

Companies should be aware of the risk of unethical practices to their reputation and business. This should extend to avoiding the use of suppliers who make use of child labour or slave labour, and avoiding trading with countries where there are human rights concerns.

 **CASE EXAMPLE 11.2**

In 2006, the British Jewellers' Association took an ethical stance against the sourcing of diamonds from countries such as the Congo and Sierra Leone, where fighting over diamonds has led to civil war and widespread slaughter. It called these diamonds 'blood diamonds' and attempted to eliminate the trade in the UK.

6.4 Reputation and public relations

Companies that might suffer losses from damage to their reputation need to be vigilant and alert for any incident that could create adverse publicity. CSR policies may therefore be used to create favourable publicity, and public relations (PR) consultants may be used to publicise ethical or socially responsible activities by companies, including sponsorship of charity events or involvement in community activities.

It may therefore be argued that some CSR policies that companies attempt to publicise are little more than attempts to promote the company and so are similar in many ways to advertising, except at a lower cost.

 CASE EXAMPLE 11.3

In 2003, the reputation of the banking group Citigroup was damaged by its associations with companies such as Enron, WorldCom, Adelphia and Parmalat, as a provider of both on-balance sheet and off-balance sheet finance.

The newly appointed chief executive officer (CEO) Chuck Prince wanted to improve the image and reputation of the bank. He believed that this meant improving its cultural and ethical outlook. He therefore introduced a code of conduct, which stated that the bank should aspire to be a company with the highest standards of ethical conduct and an organisation that people could trust. The bank's executives worldwide were asked to adhere to this code and promote the ethical status of the group.

In 2004, a problem occurred in London on the bank's trading desk for European government bonds. The desk was under pressure to increase its profits, and the management spotted an opportunity to exploit a weakness in MTS, an Italian-based electronic trading system for government bonds. They planned and executed a trade that came to be known as 'Doctor Evil'. They sold a large quantity of bonds early one morning, sufficient to send bond prices falling sharply, then bought the bonds back at much lower prices later the same morning. The trade earned a profit of over £18 million for Citigroup at the expense of other participant banks in the bond market.

The aftermath was that some banks refused to honour their commitment to make a market in government bonds on MTS, and in the next three months, daily trading volumes on MTS fell by 30%. Some European governments expressed concerns about whether they would be able to continue issuing bonds (to raise new finance) at a reasonable rate of interest. Some governments withdrew business from Citigroup as an expression of their anger. In the UK, the Financial Services Authority (FSA) fined the bank £14 million for failing to exercise due skill, care and diligence.

The traders responsible for 'Doctor Evil' were suspended. There had been a serious breach of the bank's new code of conduct. Moreover, the incident demonstrated that the change in culture that the code of conduct had intended to introduce had not reached the heart of cultural attitudes within the bank. After a brief suspension, the traders returned to work. The bank admitted to bad ethical behaviour and poor professionalism, but no one within the bank was held responsible.

 CASE EXAMPLE 11.4

In the past, oil company BP has promoted itself as a company whose policies and strategies give due regard to its CSR and it publicised its 'green credentials'. In spite of some environmental incidents, the company was successful in promoting its reputation as a supporter of CSR. However, in 2010 there was a major oil leak in a BP deep water well in the Gulf of Mexico, causing the biggest environmental damage in US history. In May 2010, President Obama ordered all 33 deep-water rigs in the Gulf of Mexico to stop drilling, and extended by six months an existing moratorium on new deep water wells. He also put on hold planned new drilling off the coast of Alaska and the Virginia coast. As public anger against BP mounted in the US, the President also stated that the company

CASE EXAMPLE **11.4** *continued*

or companies responsible would be made to pay for 'every cent' of the damage caused. With this incident, the reputation of BP as a CSR company was shattered. It also raised questions about the sincerity of all companies claiming CSR credentials. In an article in the *Financial Times* (28 May 2010), David Scheffer, Professor at Northwestern University School of Law in the US, wrote: 'BP's catastrophic gusher shows how corporate hype can peddle an illusion at the expense of the oceans.'

6.5 Commercial and financial benefits of CSR policies

Many companies, however, can see commercial and financial benefits from CSR policies. As environmental and social regulations are extended, and governments introduce stricter laws on environmental protection and health and safety, new commercial opportunities for environmentally friendly technologies and environmentally friendly products will emerge. Developing new technologies and new products can take a long time, and require substantial investment, but companies might need to make these investments in order to survive in the long term. The development of renewable energy technology and environmentally friendly cars are perhaps well-known examples.

Many companies have also improved their technology for reducing waste or toxic emissions, in order to avoid fines and penalties.

Although companies may be prepared to develop environmentally friendly products and technologies, they are unlikely to do so unless required by law or regulation, or if a commercial benefit can be obtained by selling more products to earn more profit. Although some consumers may buy Fairtrade products, for example, they are unlikely to do so if these products are a lot more expensive than similar products without a Fairtrade label. Similarly companies may voluntarily take measures to reduce waste and pollution, but only if the spending is kept within acceptable limits or, even better, savings can be obtained.

CSR issues vary between companies and industries, but it may be helpful to consider a number of CSR initiatives by major companies in recent years, and the commercial benefits that have been obtained by their actions. These include measures to protect or sustain supplies of key raw materials for the longer term.

- In 2008, Walmart told 1,000 Chinese suppliers that it would hold them to strict environmental and social standards. It has encouraged companies to cut down on packaging – if suppliers do this, more can be fitted into delivery trucks, and carbon emissions and spending on petrol are reduced. If producers make concentrated laundry detergent, this saves on both packaging and shelf space.
- In 2009, Mars announced that by 2020 its entire cocoa supply will be 'produced in a sustainable manner'. Mars said it would be working with the Rainforest Alliance to encourage farmers in the cocoa-growing regions to preserve their environment.
- Cadbury (prior to its takeover by Kraft in 2010) announced its concern about the sustainability of cocoa supplies, and reported that few children were willing to follow their parents into cocoa farming. It also announced that all the cocoa in Dairy Milk, its biggest-selling brand, would be certified by Fairtrade (which works to ensure a minimum price for farmers). Cadbury was hoping that Fairtrade would encourage the next generation into cocoa production, and sustain supplies into the longer-term future.
- In developing a fuel-efficient propulsion system, Norwegian shipping company Wilh. Wilhelmsen found opportunities for using a catalytic converter that injects ammonia to neutralise nitrogen dioxide, a technology for 'sulphur scrubbing' to reduce emissions, a switch to water-based cleaning products instead of chemical-based ones, a better air conditioning system and a cleaning system for ballast water on its ships that reduced the spread of bacteria around the world. The savings in energy costs and the reduced risk of penalties for pollution that the company achieved from these changes justified the new propulsion system financially.
- GSK, the pharmaceuticals group, announced in 2009 that it had set a target to cut the waste generated by medicines production at its factories worldwide by two-thirds by 2015. The target was to cut from 100kg to 30kg of waste for each 1kg of 'active pharmaceutical

ingredient' (API). The need to cut waste was recognised both for cost-cutting and environmental reasons. The vice president of GSK responsible for the environment is reported to have said: 'It was the idea of sustainability that drove the idea. You make an improvement to the environment and you achieve a reduction in costs.' Another pharmaceuticals company, AstraZeneca, said that it had succeeded in cutting waste in production by over 50% between 2006 and 2009.

 CASE EXAMPLE 11.5

In 2010, retailer Marks & Spencer announced a new list of ethical and environmental commitments up to 2020, and its intention to become one of the world's most environmentally friendly retailers by 2015. An initial list of 100 five-year ethical and environmental targets had been announced in 2007, including the aim of becoming carbon neutral and eliminating landfill waste, and the company expected to achieve its targets. It had also expected to commit £40 million in expenditure each year to this initiative, but in 2009 it had saved over £50 million. For example, it had achieved a 20% reduction in fuel costs by using aerodynamic lorries for its deliveries. Its new targets for 2020 included sourcing all food, clothing and home items from sustainable or ethical sources such as the Fairtrade scheme and trying to persuade its clothing suppliers, especially in India, to pay a living wage to its employees, but without adding to costs for the consumer.

 TEST YOUR KNOWLEDGE 11.4

a   Give three examples of companies that have reduced costs by implementing environmentally friendly business initiatives.
b   How might companies be affected by a bad reputation for concerns about social and environmental issues?

■ InterfaceFlor produces floor products. It found that its products were 'over-engineered' and designed to last much longer than customers actually used them before throwing them away and replacing them. This led it to develop a new design of flooring that used much less oil-based yarn without significantly affecting durability and performance. It also found that it was able to cut waste in production through process re-design, such as introducing a new cutting machine that reduced wastage in cutting materials for floor tiles by 80%. The company has also been re-designing its processes so that it is able to allow old products to be recycled into the production of new ones.

Developing innovative products

There is a demand for environmentally friendly products, and companies that can innovate by producing environmentally friendly products have opportunities for commercial growth. For example, it has been reported that Unilever, the Anglo-Dutch consumer products group, has developed a laundry product that reduces the amount of rinsing required. This could result in huge savings in water requirements, which may attract users in countries such as India where water is a scarce resource.

Compliance with environmental or health regulations

Laws and regulations can also have implications for the use of natural resources in products. For example, legislation in the EU controls the use of toxic chemicals or chemicals that are damaging to the environment. Although these laws do not directly affect companies outside the EU, they do affect all companies wanting to sell their chemical products in the EU, which is a major market. Indirectly, the law therefore affects all global companies producing chemical products.

Other possible commercial benefits: employee talent

There are other possible commercial benefits from pursuing CSR policies. One is that companies that are seen to act in a socially or environmentally aware manner may well attract talented employees. In the longer term, employing talented individuals is likely to result in better corporate performance.

An interesting example is the pharmaceuticals company Merck, which in 1987 produced a new drug that cures river blindness. River blindness has been a particular problem in parts of West Africa, but there was no market for the drug because the countries in this region of Africa could not afford them. The company therefore decided to give away the drug free, and even established a distribution system to deliver the drug to areas where it was needed.

The CEO of Merck at the time explained that the decision to give away the drug free:

- was consistent with Merck's general philosophy of 'doing well by doing good';
- made Merck a place where people were proud and excited to work because they wanted to make lives better around the world; and
- benefited shareholders, because through corporate generosity and by making Merck a better place to work, it attracted the best talent, which in time would lead to higher profits.

The CEO's claims have not necessarily been proved, but Merck's policy towards its drug to cure river blindness is still in place today.

7   Formulating CSR or sustainability policies

The significance of CSR or sustainability policies varies between companies in different industries, and companies finding themselves subject to the closest scrutiny – and with the biggest potential to benefit commercially – include those:

- with a dominant market position, such as former state-owned utility companies;
- dealing directly with consumers, such as retailers and commercial banks;
- producing essentials, such as food and drugs;
- exploiting natural resources; and
- depending on supply chains in developing countries, such as clothing manufacturers.

Companies face different ESG risks, according to the nature of their business. Consequently they will develop different policies with differing objectives.

The responsibility for developing and implementing CSR or sustainability policies may be split. The company secretary or compliance managers may have responsibility for ensuring compliance with regulations and the application of the company's code of ethics. The PR department may have responsibility for protecting the company against reputation risk and for promoting publicity about the company's CSR policies. Operational managers may have the responsibility for developing environmentally friendly processes and products, and the marketing department may have responsibility for advertising and selling the environmentally friendly products that the company makes. Ideally, there should be someone at board level who has overall responsibility for CSR policies. Companies may therefore appoint a director with specific responsibilities for ethics and CSR policies, or it may establish an ethics and CSR sub-committee of the board. A company formulating a CSR policy should:

- decide on its CSR values (and possibly publish a code of ethics);
- establish the company's current position on these values, and identify the gap between 'where we are' and 'where we want to be';
- obtain board support for the policy and identify responsibilities: nominate board leaders and local 'champions';
- develop realistic strategies and targets;
- implement these on a local and global (company-wide) basis;
- identify key stakeholders whose views the company wishes to influence (employees, pressure groups, customers);
- communicate the company's targets, policies and activities to its stakeholders, including the general public; and
- monitor achievements.

7.1 CSR and executive remuneration

Companies are more likely to pursue CSR initiatives if senior managers are rewarded for achieving CSR objectives. It is usual for bonus schemes and incentive schemes to be based on the achievement of financial objectives, and possibly also non-financial operational objectives. There has been some progress, however, towards the use of CSR targets in bonus schemes and long-term incentive schemes. This progress is most noticeable in the Netherlands.

- DSM, a life sciences company that sells chemicals, plastics and nutritional products, announced proposals in 2010 that 50% of bonuses and long-term incentives for its senior executives would be linked to targets such as a reduction in greenhouse gas emissions and energy use, introducing new environmentally friendly products and raising employee morale and satisfaction. The other 50% of bonuses and incentives would be linked to financial targets.
- Akzo Nobel, a paints company, has based 50% of the awards under its long-term incentive scheme on the position that the company achieves in the Dow Jones Sustainability Index, an index that ranks comparable companies according to their success in achieving sustainable development.
- Royal Dutch Shell uses safety targets and the same index as the basis for calculating some bonuses for senior executives.

7.2 Ethical leadership and corporate citizenship: recommendations of King IV

The King IV Code of governance principles emphasise the ethical and CSR aspects of governance. Its first two principles are that 'The governing body should lead ethically and effectively' and that 'The governing body should govern the ethics of the organisation in a way that supports the establishment of an ethical culture'. It states that: 'Ethical leadership is exemplified by integrity, competence, responsibility, accountability, fairness and transparency. It involves the anticipation and prevention, or otherwise amelioration, of the negative consequences of the organisation's activities and outputs of the economy, society and the environment and the capitals is uses and effects.'

The King IV Code also requires listed South African companies to issue an integrated report at least annually that includes both financial reports and information about sustainability performance (integrated reports are explained in Chapter 7).

 END OF CHAPTER QUESTIONS

Refer to the case study at the beginning of Part Four.

1 Has the company taken sufficient appropriate measures to restore its reputation on CSR issues? From the information available, does the company seem committed to acting as a corporate citizen?

2 What should be the role of the director who has been given responsibility for SEE issues and what should he be doing to perform this role effectively?

3 What are the risks to the company of failing to address concerns about its social and environmental policies?

CHAPTER SUMMARY

- CSR is a concept whereby companies integrate social and environmental concerns into their business strategies, to complement financial concerns.
- CSR policies are ethical policies, which may be based on the principles of treating employees fairly, behaving ethically, respecting human rights, sustaining the environment for future generations and being a responsible neighbour in the communities where the company operates.
- Sustainability or sustainable development means is conducting a business in a way that sustains the environment for future environments and protects environmental resources in a way that will enable

the business to continue operating into the foreseeable future. However, sustainability also recognises the need for companies to be profitable and financially secure in order to survive.

- Sustainability is concerned with the maintenance and growth of business value, and the ability of an organisation to survive and prosper over the long term.
- The concept of sustainability is linked to the view that companies need to enhance, or at least maintain, six different types of capital.
- Sustainability policies should consider all six capitals, even though the company does not have ownership of all of them.
- Sustainability may be very similar to CSR in matters such as the environment and social issues, including employment policies.
- The board of directors is responsible for developing CSR/sustainability strategies and monitoring the effectiveness of their implementation by management.
- CSR policies are usually seen as voluntary measures, in addition to statutory and regulatory requirements imposed by government.
- CSR as a concept is consistent with a stakeholder/pluralist approach to corporate governance, or an enlightened shareholder/integrated approach.
- From the perspective of investors in company shares, a distinction can be made between responsible investment, which focuses on value and sustainability, and SRI, which has a more ethical emphasis and therefore focuses on CSR objectives.
- In South Africa, the King IV Report recognises both sustainability and corporate citizenship as key governance objectives.
- There are several reasons for the development of concerns about and interest in CSR issues. Governments have increased social and environmental regulation, and companies have responded by improving their policies to exceed minimum regulatory requirements. Some major institutional investors have SRI policies. Some companies have seen commercial benefits in the adoption of CSR policies.
- The OECD has issued Guidelines for multinational enterprises, encouraging them to pursue CSR policies in the developing countries in which they operate.
- Companies may recognise the need to be seen to adopt CSR policies in order to avoid reputational risk. Some companies use CSR initiatives for PR and marketing purposes. In addition, some companies have identified ways in which environmentally beneficial initiatives can reduce costs or secure long-term supplies of key natural resources. It is recognised that consumers will not pay much extra for environmentally friendly goods; therefore there should also be commercial/financial reasons for CSR initiatives.
- In some countries, some large companies use CSR performance measures as a basis for calculating a large part of bonuses or long-term incentive rewards for senior executives.

Reporting corporate social responsibility and sustainability

12

■ **INTRODUCTION**

The previous chapter explained the nature of corporate social responsibility (CSR) and sustainable development, and developing CSR or sustainability policies. Shareholders and other stakeholders have an interest in what a company has been doing and what it plans to do in the future to implement sustainability or CSR measures. They expect to receive information on these matters, or to have access to information. Reporting by companies on these issues is a combination of regulatory requirement and voluntary disclosures, but to a large extent companies have a large amount of discretion about what they report. This chapter explains the nature and content of such reports.

1 Reporting corporate social responsibility (CSR) issues to stakeholders

The previous chapter dealt with the formulation of policies for sustainability or CSR. Having formulated and implemented policies, companies should be expected to report on performance and future intentions to their stakeholders.

■ The government may wish to encourage companies to provide information on environmental, social and governance issues to shareholders. In the UK there is a requirement for quoted companies to provide some information about social and environmental issues in their strategy report.

■ Investors may wish to know about a company's ESG policies, in order to make their investment decisions.

■ Other stakeholders, including employees and the general public, may have an interest in the social (including employment) and environmental policies, plans and performance of companies.

■ Companies with sustainability or CSR policies should report internally to management on actual performance.

■ The board of directors may believe that it is good governance practice to provide much of this information to stakeholders. In other words, the impetus to report on social and environmental issues may come from companies themselves, as well as investors, the public and government.

1.1 Company reporting on social and environmental issues

In the UK, the Companies Act 2006 (CA2006) includes requirements for quoted companies to report on social and environmental issues in their strategy report. The Act states that, to the extent necessary for understanding the development, performance or position of the company's business, the business review should include information about:

- environmental matters (including the impact of the company's business on the environment);
- the company's employees; and
- social, community and human rights issues.

To the extent necessary for understanding the development, performance or position of the company's business, a strategy report should also, where appropriate, include non-financial key performance indicators, including information relating to environmental matters and employee matters.

Although the Act makes it a statutory duty for quoted companies to report on these matters, the decision about what should be reported, and how much should be reported, about social and environmental issues is left largely for the companies themselves to decide.

 STOP AND THINK **12.1**

The previous chapter explained the nature of CSR policies or sustainability policies. This chapter is concerned with disclosures about social and environmental issues.

As most disclosures about social and environmental matters by companies are voluntary, a problem is knowing to what extent a company is reporting on its policies (and their effect) honestly, or whether they are reporting only the 'good news' and not the less impressive aspects of performance.

It is therefore necessary to keep a distinction in your mind between what a company does and what it claims to have done. To what extent can published disclosures be trusted? Standardised reporting and independent auditing of social and environmental reports may be part of the answer.

1.2 ABI guidelines to companies on CSR/ESG disclosures

The Association of British Insurers (ABI) has issued guidelines (revised in 2007) on the 'responsible investment disclosures' about environmental, social and governance issues that they expect companies to provide to their shareholders. These are broad guidelines to all companies about the types of disclosure that institutional investors will expect companies to make about social, ethical and environmental issues.

The guidelines, which are consistent with the UK company law requirements for coverage of ESG issues in the annual strategic report, state that shareholders place great value on 'narrative reporting which (1) sets environmental, social and governance (ESG) risks in the context of the whole range of risks and opportunities facing a company; (2) contains a forward-looking perspective; and (3) describes the actions of boards in mitigating these risks'.

The ABI guidelines take the form of disclosures, which investment institutions should expect to see included in the annual report of listed companies. There are three areas of ESG reporting where companies should make disclosures.

- ESG risk assessment by the board: whether the board takes account of the significance of ESG matters; whether it has identified and assessed the significant ESG risks; and whether it has ensured that the company has in place effective systems for managing and mitigating significant risks.
- ESG risk: policies and procedures. The annual report should include information about significant ESG risks that could affect value and how they might impact on the company, together with a description of the policies and procedures for managing these risks (or a statement that there are no such policies or procedures). The report should also include information about the extent to which the company has complied with its policies and procedures for managing material risks (with key performance indicators (KPIs) where appropriate) and the role of the board in providing oversight.

- Remuneration and ESG issues. In the directors' remuneration report, the company should state whether the remuneration committee is able to consider ESG issues when setting the remuneration of executive directors, and whether the committee has ensured that the incentive structure for senior management does not raise ESG risks by 'inadvertently motivating irresponsible behaviour'.

The ABI commented that if companies provide these disclosures, this should help them to develop appropriate ESG policies and provide a constructive basis for 'engagement' between shareholders and their companies.

TEST YOUR KNOWLEDGE 12.1

a What are the UK statutory requirements for companies to report on social and environmental issues in their annual report and accounts?

b What are the main ABI guidelines to companies about ESG reporting?

2 Voluntary reporting on social and environmental (SE) issues

There are no legal requirements for companies to report on social and environmental issues, other than the requirements for the strategic report and for quoted companies to report on their greenhouse gas emissions (see Chapter 7). However, many listed companies voluntarily publish a report each year, as a means of communicating with a wider group of stakeholders, including not only shareholders but also employees, investors and the community in general. These may be called SE reports, CSR reports, ESG reports or possibly sustainability reports. ESG reports include disclosures about governance issues as well as SE issues.

These reports are commonly prepared as a separate booklet at the same time as the company's annual report and accounts.

2.1 The reason for SE reports

There are various reasons why companies might want to report voluntarily on SE issues.

- They might have a genuine concern for SE issues, and consider that they are fulfilling their responsibilities to stakeholders by reporting on these matters.
- The company might recognise that its reputation with the public may be at risk because of the nature of their business activities. Mining companies and oil and gas extraction companies are examples, since the public is aware that they deplete the world's natural resources and pollute the environment. Reporting on social and environmental issues allows the company to demonstrate that it understands the concerns of society and explain how it is addressing them with its SE policies.
- A company might see an opportunity to gain a competitive advantage over rival companies by reporting on its SE policies. A company whose policies are 'greener' and more environmentally friendly than its competitors may hope to build their reputation and attract more customers.
- There might be pressure on companies to report more extensively on ESG issues from major shareholders or bodies representing investment institutions (e.g. the ABI or PLSA).
- Companies might recognise that the general public has lost trust in the ethical behaviour of companies, and reporting on ESG issues is a way of trying to rebuild such trust.

CASE EXAMPLE 12.1

The mining group Xstrata once explained its reasons for publishing annual sustainability reports as follows:

'Our commitment to the principles of sustainable development is based on our belief that operating responsibly and to the highest international standards . . . mitigates risk, creates opportunities and enhances our reputation and competitive position. In particular, a strong reputation for operational and environmental excellence and industry-leading community engagement enables us to gain access to new resources, maintain a social licence to operate from the communities associated with our operations, attract and retain the best people and access diverse and low-cost sources of capital.'

2.2 Reasons against voluntary SE reporting

Although many listed companies do publish SE reports, they can control the content of their reports. There might be an inclination to include 'good news' and exclude aspects of the company's SE performance that would attract stakeholder disapproval. For example, a chemical manufacturing company might include a section on health and safety measures at its processing plants without reporting the actual number of accidents and injuries sustained by employees during the year.

There are various reasons why companies might not report SE issues voluntarily.

- The company's directors and senior management might be insufficiently aware of SE issues.
- Companies might be deterred by the cost of obtaining relevant information for reporting, or the difficulty in collecting reliable and useful SE information.
- The company might be reluctant to disclose any information that it is under no legal requirement to provide, possibly to avoid giving sensitive data to competitors or regulators.
- The company might want to avoid the risk of damage to its reputation if it were to present unfavourable information about itself.

CASE EXAMPLE 12.2

Companies in industries whose operations affect the environment are often very conscious of their responsibilities, but also subject to much more pressure from ethical investors and environmental groups. In 2010, oil group BP was shortlisted for the UK's annual Corporate Responsibility Reporting Awards. At the same time, a group of dissident shareholders proposed a resolution at the company's annual general meeting (AGM) in relation to the company's proposed investment in Canada's oil sands. Oil sands extraction produces more carbon dioxide than 'traditional' oil extraction, and is also damaging to the local environment.

The shareholder resolution proposed that the company should commission a report setting out the assumptions that it has used when deciding on investment in the oil sands, including factors such as the market price of oil, the cost of greenhouse gas emissions and legal and reputation risks arising from environmental damage. BP had already released much of this information, but it opposed the shareholder resolution because it called for commitment (in time and cost) to producing a special report to satisfy a particular shareholder interest group. The company believed that this would be interfering with the right of management to manage the company. At the same time, the company acknowledged the environmental concerns and its chief executive officer (CEO) stated his belief that the company would be able to cut emissions more than expected through applications of new technology.

CASE EXAMPLE   12.2 *continued*

At the AGM there was a vote of only 5.6% in favour of the shareholder resolution and 85.2% against. However, environmental campaigners claimed success in bringing the matter to the attention of the public, and believed that the company would not now be able to ignore their views. The company chairman is reported to have said at the AGM: 'This does not mean that we think the resolution is wrong. It only means that we think the concerns raised are in hand.'

This case raises an interesting question about the extent to which special interest groups of shareholders should be able to influence the actions of management. Was it right that the shareholder group tried to force the company to produce a special report, because it should be their right as owners of the company to bring this sort of pressure to bear on management? Or should management be left to manage the company? And if management is given a free hand to manage the company, to what extent should they take SE concerns of shareholders into consideration when making their decisions?

The case of BP is also interesting because shortly after the matter of the Canada oil sands was dealt with, the company faced an even bigger environmental problem in the Gulf of Mexico, referred to in Chapter 11. In April 2010, a deep-sea oilrig exploded, killing 11 men and causing a major oil leak from the deep water well. The oil leak threatened the ecosystems of the Gulf of Mexico, including the shores of Louisiana, Alabama and Florida, and BP became liable for clean-up and legal costs amounting to billions of dollars. It was reported that a shareholder had sued the company, accusing it of putting profits before oil safety and asking for court-enforced changes to BP's corporate governance. The company responded quickly to the disaster, but could not escape accusations that its risk management and safety measures were not as good as company management had supposed.

2.3 Risk society theory of SE reporting

In spite of reasons against SE reporting, it seems probable that voluntary CSR/ESG reporting will increase, because stakeholders in companies want to be given the information that these reports contain.

In her book *Corporate Governance and Accountability*, Jill Solomon made an interesting reference to risk society theory as a possible explanation of the big changes in society's attitudes to social, ethical and environmental issues. Risk society theory was developed in the early 1990s by Ulrich Beck, a German sociologist. He argued that in today's society there has been an increase in 'high consequence risks' such as global warming and the risk of a major nuclear accident or incident. The whole of society is affected by these risks, at a global level, and although human and corporate behaviour has contributed to these problems, they are largely unmanageable and the blame cannot be placed entirely on specific causes and specific companies. A clear connection between cause and effect does not exist.

As a result, people have lost trust in leaders and institutions. They do not believe that companies have genuine ethical, social or environmental concerns, and do believe that companies act unethically and damage society and the environment through their self-centred activities.

Risk society theory can be used to suggest that companies see voluntary SE reporting as an attempt to rebuild public trust in the company. Communicating with stakeholders on these issues is a necessary step towards re-establishing trust.

2.4 The content of SE reports

There are no rules about what SE reports should contain, or how SE information should be presented. Some companies produce a separate SE report. Others give information about social, ethical and environmental issues in the chairman's report or report of the CEO in the published annual report and accounts, as well as in the strategy report. Many SE reports have consisted largely of a narrative report with some quantitative measures of targets and performance levels achieved.

Reporting on environmental performance: 'environmental footprints'

A company might report its environmental performance in terms of selected quantitative measures, which are sometimes referred to as its 'environmental footprint'. The measurements for each individual company might vary according to the nature of its business, but it is generally accepted that a company's impact on the environment can be measured in terms of impact on the air, water or land, or 'noise pollution'. Reported environmental performance targets and measurements of actual performance may be:

- the company's use of key resources such as land, and also its consumption of materials subject to depletion (such as quantities of livestock, wild fish or forest timber) and non-renewable resources (such as coal, oil and natural gas, reported perhaps in terms of total energy use for lighting and heating, total fuel use for transport, total water usage);
- pollution caused by the company's activities, measured (for example) in terms of carbon dioxide emissions, chemical waste or spillages of oil; and
- an assessment in either qualitative or quantitative terms of the broader effect of the company's resource consumption and pollution on the environment.

TEST YOUR KNOWLEDGE 12.2

a   Why might companies decide to produce voluntary SE reports?
b   What might be the arguments against voluntary SE reporting by companies?

3   Sustainability reporting: triple bottom line reporting

Chapter 11 describes sustainable development as an approach to developing and growing a business that does not put at risk the ability of the business to continue into the foreseeable future. To do this, companies must be profitable, but they must also consider a range of issues, including SE issues. Companies that have a policy of sustainable development may produce an annual sustainability report. This is similar to a CSR report or SE report, but with more quantitative performance measures. Sustainability reports also emphasise the importance of financial objectives as well as SE targets, and so are possibly targeted more at shareholders and other investors rather than the general public.

Sustainability reports are also known as **triple bottom line reporting**. The term 'triple bottom line' was coined in 1994 by John Elkington. Its aim is to encourage companies to recognise SE issues in their business reporting systems, as well as financial issues. Its use is encouraged by the **Global Reporting Initiative (GRI)**, an internationally recognised body that promotes sustainability reporting. The term 'triple bottom line' comes from the fact that sustainability reports should provide key measurements for three aspects of performance:

1   Economic indicators.
2   Social indicators.
3   Environmental indicators.

Triple bottom line reporting is therefore providing a quantitative summary of a company's economic, environmental and social performance over the previous year.

3.1 Economic indicators

Economic indicators in sustainability reports are measures typically associated with financial reporting, such as measurements relating to:

- sales revenue;
- profits, earnings and earnings per share;
- dividends per share;

- global market share (the percentage share of the global market captured by the company's products or services);
- in industries manufacturing standard products, such as car production, units of sale worldwide.

3.2 Social indicators

Social indicators might include measures relating to employment and employees, and measurements relating to society and the community, such as:

- employee diversity (e.g. the percentage of its employees who are female and the percentage who come from minority groups);
- the recordable injury rate per 1,000 employees; and
- work done by the company in communities of developing countries to provide better standards of education and health.

3.3 Environmental indicators

Environmental indicators might include measurements relating to targets for:

- reducing the consumption of materials in products and services;
- reducing energy use;
- minimising the release of toxic materials/pollutants;
- improving the recycling of materials;
- maximising the use of renewable resources; and
- extending the life of a product.

3.4 Limitations of triple bottom line reporting

There are several limitations to triple bottom line reporting.

- There are no widely established standards for triple bottom line reporting, and no standard methods for measuring SE impacts. It is therefore difficult to compare the sustainability of one company with the sustainability of another.
- The GRI is attempting to standardise measurements for the triple bottom line and has published Sustainability Reporting Guidelines since 1999 (see later in this chapter).
- If the SE measures are not subject to independent audit, there might be doubts about the reliability of the data presented in a company's report. Companies have a vested interest in presenting 'good news' but withholding 'bad news' in any form of voluntary reporting.

3.5 Sustainability reporting and integrated reporting

The issues that are covered by sustainability reports are consistent with the issues that are recommended for inclusion in an integrated report.

For example, the King IV Code in South Africa requires listed companies to produce an integrated report at least annually, which reports on:

- financial results, and how the company made its money; and
- ESG issues.

Integrated reporting is described in more detail in Chapter 7.

 STOP AND THINK 12.2

Use an internet search engine to locate examples of CSR reports (or SE reports) by large listed companies, and make an assessment of the nature and value of the information that they provide.

4   The GRI reporting framework: sustainability reporting

A problem with sustainability reports is the absence of standardisation. Financial reports are produced in accordance with accepted accounting standards, but sustainability reporting can be in any format and contain whatever narrative items and performance measures that the company chooses. There is also no requirement for sustainability reports by the same company to be in the same format each year.

The GRI framework is a voluntary framework that is intended to introduce some standardisation into sustainability reporting. Companies worldwide are invited to adopt the GRI framework for reporting.

The GRI is an organisation that has developed a framework for sustainability reporting. It sets out the principles and indicators that companies can use to report on their economic, social and environmental performance. The GRI reporting framework is based on a number of general guidelines for all companies, together with unique indicators for industry sectors. Reports produced using the GRI framework are similar in format and use similar performance measures (standardised disclosures) calculated on a similar basis.

The current version of the GRI Framework is known as G4. This was issued in 2013, replacing the previous G3 guidelines. The G4 Guidelines have been superseded by the GRI Sustainability Reporting Standards (GRI Standards). The GRI Standards will be required for all reports or other materials published on or after 1 July 2018 – the G4 Guidelines remain available until this date.

The GRI has commented that its Sustainability Reporting Framework is:

'[A]pplicable to organisations of any size or type, and from any sector or geographic region, and has been used by thousands of organisations worldwide as the basis for their sustainability reporting. It facilitates transparency and accountability by organisations, and provides stakeholders a universally applicable, comparable framework from which to understand disclosed information.'

4.1 Preparing a sustainability report that follows the GRI G4 guidelines

A GRI G4 report should specify aspects that it covers and boundaries for each of these aspects.

■ **Aspects** are simply the aspects of economic, environmental and social issues that are covered by the report, because they are materially significant for the company.
■ **Boundaries** indicate whether the consequences for each of these aspects affect the company internally or are felt outside the company's boundaries. Material aspects whose impact is inside and outside the organisation should both be reported.

There should be two types of disclosure in a report:

■ **General standard disclosures.** These disclosures set the context for the sustainability report and are common to all types of organisation. There are seven types of disclosures, including the organisation's strategic perspective on sustainability issues and its approach to engaging with stakeholders about them.
■ **Specific standard disclosures.** These are divided into two types of disclosure, disclosures on the management approach to sustainability issues; and quantified indicators of performance.
■ **Disclosures on management approach**. These are disclosures on how management has approached the material aspects covered by the report. It should explain:

- why each of the selected material aspects is material for the organisation;
  - how its impacts are being managed; and
  - how the management approach to the aspect and its impacts is evaluated.
- **Indicators**. These are quantitative measures of performance for each of the aspects of sustainability selected by the organisation for inclusion in the report as a material issue. Only material aspects should be reported. The GRI G4 framework contains indicators for a wide range of sustainability issues (aspects). For example, a company's indicators might include measures for water usage, health and safety, human rights or the company's impact on local communities. By providing a range of measures/indicators for a wide range of aspects of sustainability, the GRI framework encourages companies to use similar measures of performance for similar aspects of sustainability.

4.2 Aspects of sustainability that may be reported

GRI groups its standard disclosures, including performance indicators, into the three 'triple bottom line' areas: economic, environmental and social. It sub-divides social disclosures into:

- labour practices and decent work;
- human rights;
- society; and
- product responsibility.

Each sub-division is further sub-divided into the following areas:

TABLE 12.1 Sub-divisions of GRI standard disclosures

Social disclosures	
Labour practices and decent work	**Human rights**
Employment	Investment
Labour/management relations	Non-discrimination
Occupational health and safety	Freedom of association and collective bargaining
Training and education	Child labour
Diversity and equal opportunity	Forced or compulsory labour
Equal remuneration for men and women	Indigenous rights
Supplier assessment: labour practices	Assessment of human rights practices
Labour practice grievance procedures	Supplier assessment: human rights
Society	**Product responsibility**
Local communities	Customer health and safety
Anti-corruption	Product and service labelling
Public policy	Marketing communications
Anti-competitive behaviour	Customer privacy
Compliance	Compliance (with laws and regulations)
Supplier assessment: Impacts on society	

Environmental disclosures are sub-divided into 12 areas:

1 Materials.
2 Energy.
3 Water.
4 Biodiversity.
5 Emissions.
6 Effluents and waste.
7 Products and services.
8 Compliance.
9 Transport.
10 Overall (total environmental expenditures).
11 Suppliers: environmental assessment.
12 Environmental grievance mechanisms.

A company should use only those standard disclosures that are relevant to its circumstances, but where it chooses to report on an item, it should do so using the standard method of disclosure and standard performance measures (metrics).

An indication of the types of performance indicators that GRI includes as standard disclosures/indicators is shown in the following table.

TABLE 12.2 Types of performance indicators that GRI includes as standard disclosures/indicators

Economic performance indicators include:	Environmental performance indicators include:
■ Direct economic value generated and distributed, including: 　– revenues 　– operating costs 　– employee compensation 　– donations and other community investments 　– retained earnings, and 　– payments to capital providers and governments. ■ Coverage of the organisation's defined benefit plan obligations. ■ Range of ratios of standard entry level wage by gender compared to local minimum wage at significant locations of operation. ■ Policy, practices, and proportion of spending on local suppliers at significant locations of operation. ■ Development and impact of infrastructure investments and services provided primarily for public benefit.	***Aspect: Water*** ■ Total water withdrawal by source. ■ Water sources significantly affected by withdrawal of water. ■ Percentage and total volume of water recycled and reused. ***Aspect: Emissions, effluents and waste*** ■ Total direct and indirect greenhouse gas emissions by weight. ■ Other relevant indirect greenhouse gas emissions by weight. ■ Initiatives to reduce greenhouse gas emissions and reductions achieved. ■ Emissions of ozone-depleting substances by weight. ■ Ozone-depleting substances and other significant air emissions by type and weight. ■ Total water discharge by quality and destination. ■ Total weight of waste by type and disposal method. ■ Total number and volume of significant spills.
Labour practices and decent work performance indicators include:	**Human rights performance indicators include:**
■ Total workforce by employment type, employment contract and region, broken down by gender. ■ Total number and rate of new employee hires and employee turnover by age group, gender and region. ■ Return to work and retention rates after parental leave, by gender. ■ Percentage of employees covered by collective bargaining agreements. ■ Rates of injury, occupational diseases, lost days, absenteeism ■ Total number of work-related fatalities, by region and by gender. ■ Education, training, counselling, prevention and risk-control programmes in place to assist workforce members, their families, or community members regarding serious diseases. ■ Average hours of training per year per employee by gender and by employee category.	■ Percentage of significant suppliers, contractors and other business partners that have undergone human rights screening and actions taken. ■ Total number of incidents of discrimination and corrective actions taken. ■ Operations and significant suppliers identified in which the right to exercise freedom of association and collective bargaining may be violated or at significant risk and actions taken to support these rights. ■ Operations and significant suppliers identified as having significant risk for incidents of child labour and measures taken to contribute to the effective abolition of child labour. ■ Operations and significant suppliers identified as having significant risk for incidents of forced or compulsory labour and measures to contribute to the elimination of all forms of forced or compulsory labour. ■ Number of grievances related to human rights filed, addressed and resolved through formal grievance mechanisms.

Society performance indicators include:	Product responsibility performance indicators include:
■ Percentage of operations with implemented local community engagement, impact assessments and development programmes. ■ Operations with significant potential or actual negative impacts on local communities. ■ Prevention and mitigation measures implemented in operations with significant potential or actual negative impacts on local communities. ■ Percentage and total number of business units analysed for risks related to corruption. ■ Actions taken in response to incidents of corruption. ■ Monetary value of significant fines and total number of non-monetary sanctions for non-compliance with laws and regulations.	■ Life cycle stages in which health and safety impacts of products and services are assessed for improvement. ■ Total number of incidents of non-compliance with regulations and voluntary codes concerning product and service information and labelling. ■ Total number of incidents of non-compliance with regulations and voluntary codes concerning marketing communications, including advertising, promotion and sponsorship. ■ Total number of substantiated complaints regarding breaches of customer privacy and losses of customer data. ■ Monetary value of significant fines for non-compliance with laws and regulations concerning the provision and use of products and services.

This list may suggest that meaningful sustainability reporting can be a detailed and complex challenge.

4.3 Comparison of sustainability reports and integrated reports

Sustainability reporting communicates the organisation's economic, environmental, social and governance performance, both positive and negative. Sustainability reporting is driven by the aspects of sustainability that the organisation considers material to its own circumstances. Reports are targeted at the organisation's stakeholders generally, not just the shareholders.

In contrast, integrated reports, as an emerging trend in corporate reporting, are targeted mainly at the company's shareholders and other providers of capital, and focuses on the key factors that are material to value creation.

Integrated reports can build on the foundations provided by sustainability reporting but sustainability reports and integrated reports are not the same thing.

5 Benchmarking and CSR reporting

A major problem with ESG reporting is the diversity of environmental and social issues, and the varying importance of these issues for different companies. Users of reports may want to compare the performance of different companies, but without standards for the content and format of reports, it is difficult to make such comparisons.

Developments in CSR reporting have been assisted by co-operation between companies willing to have their policies and practices assessed and compared with those of other companies, in all industrial sectors. Comparisons provide benchmarks for comparison and standards for attainment. Given suitable data, they can also be used to establish an index for CSR performance measurement.

5.1 CSR indices

There are now several indices that measure and rate companies in terms of their CSR performance. These include the Dow Jones Sustainability Indices and the FTSE4Good Index Series.

■ The Dow Jones Sustainability Indices, first published in 1999, are indices that track the financial performance of the leading sustainability-driven companies worldwide. The advantage for companies of inclusion in an index is that a number of investment funds base their investment policy on holding a portfolio of shares of companies within a Dow Jones

Sustainability Index. Companies must apply to qualify for inclusion in an index, and the selection of companies for inclusion in each index is based on a corporate sustainability assessment. Much of the information for an assessment is supplied by the companies themselves, which complete a questionnaire. External assurance is provided to ensure that the corporate sustainability assessments are completed in accordance with the defined rules.

- The FTSE4Good Index Series is similar in purpose to the Dow Jones Sustainability Indices. It is intended to appeal to investors who wish to invest only in companies with good standards in CSR, or who want to minimise the SE risks in their investment portfolios. The criteria for selecting companies for inclusion in the Index Series 'have been designed to identify companies that meet globally recognised and accepted responsible investment criteria'. Companies are not accepted for inclusion unless they meet certain criteria, and companies that fall below the standards required are deleted from their index. To be included in an index, companies need to demonstrate that they are working towards environmental management, climate change mitigation and adaptation, countering bribery and upholding human and labour rights.

5.2 BiTC Corporate Responsibility (CR) Index

Another interesting development in the UK has been the CR Index published annually by Business in the Community (BiTC). Developed in consultation with business leaders the first CR Index survey was launched in 2002. In addition to it being a public exercise in transparency the Index is a robust tool to help companies systematically measure, manage and integrate responsible business practice.

It takes the form of an online survey and companies follow a self-assessment process intended to help them identify both the strengths in their management and performance and gaps, where future progress can be made. Business in the Community believes that self-assessment is the starting point for action and improvement.

All submissions must be signed off at main board level to ensure director-level commitment to the veracity of the responses to the survey. The team at Business in the Community reviews submissions to ensure consistency and reliability, both between and within company submissions.

CR Index Framework

The CR Index follows a systematic approach to managing, measuring and reporting on business responsible business practices, companies are assessed using the framework below.

- **Corporate strategy** looks at the main corporate responsibility risks and opportunities to the business and how these are being identified and then addressed through strategy, policies and responsibilities held at a senior level in the company.
- **Integration** is about how companies organise, manage and embed corporate responsibility into their operations through KPIs, performance management, effective stakeholder engagement and reporting.
- **Management** builds on the Integration section looking at how companies are managing their risks and opportunities in the areas of community, environment, marketplace and workplace.
- **Performance and impact** asks companies to report performance in a range of SE impacts areas. Participants complete three environmental and three social areas based on the relevance to their business.

5.3 Conversion factors to standardise measurements and provide comparability

Comparability between companies on environmental performance can be improved by government guidance. In the UK, the government has issued guidelines on the use of conversion factors for environmental reporting. Conversion factors can be used to convert measures of resource consumption, or activities that create emissions or waste, into a small number of standard environmental performance measures. Reporting environmental performance in terms of a limited number of measures (such as carbon dioxide emissions, landfill quantities, water consumption and so on, which are all measured using the same conversion factors) provides comparability that would not otherwise be possible.

For example, a company may wish to report on the quantity of greenhouse gases it has emitted during the year.

■ One source of emissions is boilers. Companies can measure their yearly energy consumption from the use of boilers by measuring the kilowatt hours (kWh) and converting this into tonnes of CO_2 emitted using conversion factors provided by the Department for Environment, Food and Rural Affairs (Defra).
■ Another source of emissions is the consumption of fuel by motor vehicles used by a company's employees and vehicle fleets. The distance travelled by vehicles during the year can be measured from employees' expenses claims and annual servicing records of fleet vehicles. The total mileage can be converted into tonnes of CO_2 emitted using conversion factors provided by Defra.

Another measure of environmental performance is the quantity of landfill waste produced. The volume of waste produced by a company can be measured by the number of bins or skips removed for recycling, and this can be converted into landfill quantities using a Defra conversion factor.

Other standard measures of environmental performance are also produced by UK companies using Defra conversion factors.

TEST YOUR KNOWLEDGE 12.4

a What is the purpose of conversion factors for measuring waste, pollution and the consumption of non-renewable natural resources?
b What is the GRI Sustainability Reporting Framework?

END OF CHAPTER QUESTIONS

1 Why might there be limited interest in the company's SE reports?
2 What weaknesses are evident in the company's SE reporting, and what measures could be taken to improve the standard and quality of reporting?

CHAPTER SUMMARY

■ Companies provide information on CSR issues to shareholders and other stakeholders, partly because of statutory requirements, partly in response to investor expectations and partly as a result of wanting to publicise the company's SE performance and policies (possibly for public relations purposes).
■ In the UK, quoted companies are required by the CA2006 to include information about environmental, employee and social/community issues in their annual strategic report.
■ Companies may produce voluntary reports on SE (and governance) issues for all stakeholders. These reports are generally produced annually at the same time as the annual report and accounts, and published as a separate document. The report may be called a CSR report, an SE report, a SEE report, or an ESG report.
■ Sustainability reports are an alternative to SE reports. They are reports that focus on three aspects of performance: economic (financial), social and environmental. They include quantitative measures of performance for all three aspects. Unlike SE reports, they do not focus exclusively on social and environmental issues, and they recognise that economic performance is important. Producing sustainability reports based on these three aspects of performance is called triple bottom line reporting.
■ A problem with SE reports and sustainability reports is that they do not have a standard format or content, and the directors choose what information to put in and what to keep out.

■ The GRI G4 Reporting Framework is a framework for producing standardised sustainability reports on material sustainability issues affecting the organisation.

■ The King IV Report in South Africa calls for listed companies to produce integrated annual reports that combine reporting on financial matters with reporting on CSR issues.

■ Comparability may also be provided to some extent for investors by specialist indices such as the Dow Jones Sustainability Indices and the FTSE4Good Index Series. Companies apply for inclusion in the index but to do so must meet certain requirements. Investors can then make investment decisions based on whether the company is in one of these indices and their position within it.

■ Comparability on CSR performance between companies in the same industrial sector is provided in the UK by the BiTC Corporate Responsibility Index. Inclusion in an index for companies is voluntary.

■ There are also conversion factors whereby companies can convert measures of pollution or waste creation, or measures of the consumption of non-renewable natural resources, into standard measures of pollution or resource consumption. This improves the comparability of environmental performance reports of companies that use the same conversion factors. In the UK, conversion factors have been provided by the government.

Other governance issues

■ **OVERVIEW**

Most of this study text has explained corporate governance from the perspective of UK listed companies. General principles of good governance should also be applied to other organisations. These are similar in many ways to good governance in UK listed companies. However, there are also some differences.

Chapter 13 explains aspects of governance that apply to organisations other than UK listed companies. It considers some international aspects of governance and governance for non-listed companies. It then goes on to describe governance issues for government organisations and not-for-profit organisations. Again, much of the focus is on the UK, but the general principles have much wider application.

■ **LEARNING OUTCOMES**

Part Five should enable you to advise on governance issues across all sectors.

13 Other governance issues

INTRODUCTION

Principles of good governance apply internationally, to companies in all countries, to unlisted companies, and to government departments and agencies, and other not-for-profit organisations. The governance principles that apply to different organisations vary according to their ownership and objectives, but there is close similarity with the principles of good governance that apply to large companies. This chapter considers the nature of governance in these different types of organisation.

1 Corporate governance outside the UK

Most countries with developed or developing financial markets have a corporate governance framework, often with a corporate governance code for companies whose shares are listed on the country's main stock market.

Some governance codes are based on the UK model, but others are different. The European Corporate Governance Institute (ECGI) through its website makes available the full text of corporate governance codes, principles of corporate governance and corporate governance reforms both in Europe and elsewhere in the world. This chapter cannot go into the details of governance in every country, but the following governance frameworks are worth noting:

■ South Africa and King IV.
■ The US and the Sarbanes-Oxley Act.

2 The King Code (King IV)

Most codes of corporate governance are based on a 'shareholder' approach or 'enlightened shareholder' approach to corporate governance. The King IV Code (2016), which is the corporate governance code for South Africa, is distinctive because:

- it is a well-established governance code for a major developing economy;
- it adopts a 'stakeholder inclusive' approach to corporate governance; and
- it supports integrated reporting and reporting on sustainability issues.

It is called King IV because it is the fourth version of the code produced by the King Committee on Corporate Governance.

The Foreword to King IV states that 'Certain concepts [later described as 'underpinning philosophies'] form the foundation stones of King IV'. They are:

- ethical leadership;
- the organisation as an integral part of society;
- corporate citizenship – as the organisation is an integral part of society, it has corporate citizenship status. This status confers, rights, obligations and responsibilities on the organisation towards society and the natural environment on which society depends;
- sustainable development – understood as development that meets the needs of the present without compromising the ability of future generations to meet their needs is a primary ethical and economic imperative;
- stakeholder inclusivity – there is an interdependent relationship between the organisation and its stakeholders, and the organisation's ability to create value for itself depends on its ability to create value for others;
- integrated thinking – takes account of the connectivity and interdependence between the range of factors that affect an organisation's ability to create value over time; and
- integrated reporting.

The Foreword to King IV states that 'These concepts are relevant to three connected paradigm shifts in the corporate world':

- from financial capitalism to inclusive capitalism;
- from short-term capital markets to long-term, sustainable capital markets; and
- from siloed reporting to integrated reporting.

One of the main distinguishing features of King IV is the inclusion of 'Sector Supplements' to assist organisations in these different sectors to interpret and implement the Code, as appropriate to their particular circumstances.

2.1 Sections of the King IV Code

The Code itself has five parts, which incorporate 17 principles. The parts are:

1 Leadership, ethics and corporate citizenship.
2 Strategy, performance and reporting.
3 Governing structures and delegation.
4 Governance functional areas.
5 Stakeholder relationships.

TEST YOUR KNOWLEDGE 13.1

What are the concepts on which the King IV Code is based?

3 The Sarbanes-Oxley Act (SOX)

In the US, the largest companies have developed a voluntary framework for governance practice, but there is a stronger rules-based element to governance than in the UK.

Statutory measures relating to risk management and internal control were introduced by the SOX 2002 following the collapse of Enron and the other US corporate scandals, and a stock market collapse in 2002 with the bursting of the so-called 'dotcom bubble'.

Four sections of SOX have particular relevance to corporate governance:

- The Act created a central oversight board, the Public Company Accounting Oversight Board (PCAOB), to provide independent oversight of firms providing audit services for public companies.
- It set standards for independence of external auditors, for example by restricting the provision of non-audit services to audit clients.
- Senior executives are required to take individual responsibility for the accuracy and completeness of financial reporting by their company. The company's 'principal officers' (usually the chief executive officer (CEO) and chief financial officer (CFO)) must certify and approve the integrity of the company's published accounts.
- The Act also introduced rules relating to internal control.

3.1 SOX and internal control: section 404

Section 404 of the Act directed the Securities and Exchange Commission (SEC) to set rules requiring companies ('SEC registrants') to include an internal control report in their annual report. The Act specified that:

'The Commission shall prescribe rules requiring each annual report ... to contain an internal control report, which shall:

- state the responsibility of management for establishing and maintaining an adequate internal control structure and procedures for financial reporting; and
- contain an assessment, as of the end of the most recent fiscal year of the issuer, of the effectiveness of the internal control structure and procedures of the issuer for financial reporting.'

The SEC implemented s. 404 and introduced the following regulations.

- 'The management of each ... issuer ... must evaluate, with the participation of the issuer's principal executive and principal finance officers ... the effectiveness, as of the end of each fiscal year, of the issuer's internal control over financial reporting. The framework on which management's evaluation of the issuer's internal control over financial reporting is based must be a suitable, recognized control framework ...'
- 'The management of each issuer ... must evaluate, with the participation of the issuer's principal executive and principal finance officers ... any change in the issuer's internal control over financial reporting that has occurred during each of the issuer's fiscal quarters, or fiscal year in the case of a foreign private issuer, that has materially affected, or is likely to materially affect, the issuer's internal control over financial reporting.'
- Companies should also maintain evidence, including documentation, to provide reasonable support for management's assessment of the effectiveness of internal control over financial reporting.
- Management is required to disclose any material weaknesses in the company's internal control system for financial reporting, and is not permitted to conclude that the internal control is effective if one or more material weaknesses exist.

3.2 Annual statement on internal financial controls and auditors' attestation report

Section 404 requires companies to include in their annual report a report on 'internal control over financial reporting'. This should set out:

- a statement of management's responsibility for establishing and maintaining adequate internal controls over the company's financial reporting;
- a statement identifying the framework used by management for evaluating the efficiency and effectiveness of the internal control over financial reporting;
- an assessment by management of the effectiveness of the internal control over financial reporting, as at the end of the most recent fiscal year (and any 'material weakness' in internal control);

- disclosure of any material weakness in the company's internal control over financial reporting that management has identified; and
- a statement that the external auditors have issued an attestation report on management's assessment of the company's internal control over financial reporting. The auditors' attestation report should be filed as part of the company's annual report.

In order to prepare the report on internal control, management must:

- undertake a review of the effectiveness of internal controls over financial reporting (the 'review requirements'); and
- maintain evidence to provide reasonable support for management's assessment of the effectiveness of internal controls (the 'documentation requirements').

3.3 Review of the s. 404 requirements

Section 404 was criticised in the US, on the grounds that its requirements would take up much valuable management time and resources, and would add substantially to the costs paid to the external auditors for their attestation report. The heavy administrative burdens (and the potential liability that exists for the CEO and the CFO) were blamed for discouraging foreign companies from listing their shares in the US, and choosing alternative financial centres such as London, where the regulatory burden is much lower.

In December 2006, in response to the continuing criticisms, the SEC issued new guidance for management, allowing management more discretion in how the annual review of internal controls is carried out. It was also intended to free companies from a highly cautious box-ticking approach to compliance, to reduce reliance on advice from external auditors and to reduce the quantities of documentary evidence required. By easing the regulatory and compliance burden of s. 404, it was hoped that these changes would restore the attractiveness of New York as an international stock market.

TEST YOUR KNOWLEDGE **13.2**

What are the main requirements of s. 404 of the SOX in the US?

4   Guidance from international investor groups

Most institutional investors are members of national 'trade associations' that represent their interests on certain matters (such as discussions with government). In the UK, institutional investor organisations include the ABI, the PLSA and the Investment Management Association (IMA). These bodies collaborate on issues where they have a common interest.

However, many large institutions invest internationally, in stock markets around the world, and the membership of the UK's institutional investor trade associations is largely UK-based. International investors recognise that there is a risk of varying standards of governance in different countries. For example, a US institutional investor may want to invest in equities of Asian companies, but will want those companies to have governance standards that are comparable with those in the US. Unless they are satisfied with the standards in a particular country, they may be reluctant to invest in its stock market companies.

The International Corporate Governance Network (ICGN) is an investor-led organisation of governance professionals, with international membership. Its objective is to promote effective standards of corporate governance, in order to improve the efficiency of markets and economies world-wide.

4.1 ICGN Global Corporate Governance Principles

The ICGN was established in 1995 at the instigation of a group of major international institutional investors. It consists of investors, companies, financial intermediaries and academics; its aims are to promote international dialogue and best practice internationally in corporate governance. A significant feature of ICGN policy pronouncements arises from the fact that ICGN is an organisation of global investment institutions, and its policy guidelines apply to the activities of its members in all countries in which they invest.

The ICGN has published its own Global Governance Principles (revised in 2014), which its members are encouraged to promote in the countries in which they invest.

The Preamble to the Principles state that they: 'describe the responsibilities of boards of directors and investors respectively, and aim to enhance dialogue between the two parties. They embody ICGN's mission to inspire effective standards of governance and to advance efficient markets world-wide. The Principles are the ICGN's primary standard for well governed companies and set the framework for a global work programme focused around influencing public policy, connecting peers around the world and informing governance debate.'

The combination of responsibilities of boards of directors and investors in a single set of Principles emphasises a mutual interest in protecting and generating sustainable corporate value.

TEST YOUR KNOWLEDGE 13.3

Why should institutional investors want companies to comply with a code of corporate governance?

5 Corporate governance and unlisted companies

5.1 Quoted Companies Alliance (QCA) Corporate Governance Guidelines

The QCA is a body that represents smaller quoted companies, such as quoted companies whose shares are traded on the Alternative Investment Market (AIM), the London Stock Exchange's international market for smaller growing companies. It has issued Corporate Governance Guidelines for Small and Mid-Size Quoted Companies.

These guidelines are consistent with the UK Code for listed companies but are not as detailed or rigorous.

Any small or mid-size quoted company with ambitions to become a premium listed company will need to move towards standards of governance that comply with the provisions of the UK Code.

6 Governance in the public sector: Nolan principles

The initial impetus for improvements in corporate governance in the UK began with a series of scandals in listed companies. Investors demanded improvements in the way that companies were run and the way that they were treated by company management.

Developments in corporate governance led to a recognition that weaknesses in governance affected public sector bodies and not-for-profit bodies, as well as commercial companies. Several codes of governance have been developed for the public sector. The commercial pressure of accountability to shareholders, however, does not exist.

The public sector includes central government, state government (in some countries) and local government, state-run health and education services and many other regulatory and advisory bodies. Many of the principles of good corporate governance can be applied to the governing bodies of the public sector, but there are also significant differences. For example, public bodies are not profit-making and are not accountable to shareholders. Some governors of public sector bodies do their work for no remuneration. Public sector governance is also strongly influenced by:

- elected politicians, advised by senior administrators; and
- the general public and pressure groups: politicians are ultimately accountable to the electorate.

The public sector has therefore adapted principles of good governance to its own specific circumstances, and to some extent the definition of 'governance' for the public sector differs in some ways from 'governance' of companies.

6.1 Nolan principles

A key development for the governance of the UK public sector was the **Nolan Committee on Standards in Public Life**. The Committee was set up in 1995 in response to concerns that the conduct of some politicians was unethical and, in particular, allegations of MPs taking cash for putting parliamentary questions. While the Committee focused on MPs, its terms of reference also covered government departments and non-departmental public bodies (NDPBs). The Committee published a set of Principles of conduct. These Principles were originally intended as guidelines for individuals who were involved in public affairs and public bodies, whether as paid employees or as non-paid members of governing bodies. They are now considered to have much wider relevance and have formed the basis in the UK for developing governance guidelines for both the public sector and the voluntary sector.

Nolan's seven principles of public life

1   **Selflessness.** Holders of public office should take decisions solely in terms of the public interest. They should not do so to gain financial or other material benefits for themselves, their family or their friends.
2   **Integrity.** Holders of public office should not place themselves under any financial or other obligation to outside individuals or organisations that might influence them in the performance of their duties.
3   **Objectivity.** In carrying out public business, including making public appointments, awarding contracts or recommending individuals for rewards and benefits, holders of public office should make choices on merit.
4   **Accountability.** Holders of public office are accountable for their decisions and actions to the public and must submit themselves to whatever scrutiny is appropriate to their office.
5   **Openness.** Holders of public office should be as open as possible about the decisions and actions that they take. They should give reasons for their decisions and restrict information only when the wider public interest clearly demands.
6   **Honesty.** Holders of public office have a duty to declare any private interests relating to their public duties and to take steps to resolve any conflicts arising in a way that protects the public interest.
7   **Leadership.** Holders of public office should promote and support these principles by leadership and example.

7   Governance in central government

From a governance perspective, central government organisations differ from listed companies in two fundamental ways:

■   Government departments and stock market companies have different have different objectives. Whereas a company seeks to make profits, a government department does not.
■   The ownership structure is different. Listed companies are owned by their shareholders and led by a board of directors. Government departments are a part of the structure of government: they are 'owned' by the government (on behalf of the 'people') and in a democracy government is accountable to the electorate.

For central government in the UK, there is a code of good practice: 'Corporate governance in central government departments: Code of good practice 2011.' This Code sets out the composition and the role of the boards of central government departments.
  It states that:

'Government Departments are not the same as for-profit corporations, but they face many similar challenges. They need to be business-like. They can do this by tapping into the expertise of senior leaders with experience of managing complex organisations in the commercial private sector. These experts will provide challenge and support through their membership of Departmental Boards ...'

The challenges for governance in central government are to:

- have business-like decision-making from its leaders; but also
- retain ministerial accountability to Parliament and ensure that the department operates within its allocated budgetary allowance.

7.1 Governance structure: departmental boards

The governance structure set out in the Code is as follows.

- Each ministerial department has a departmental board, chaired by a senior government minister (in the UK, the senior minister is called a Secretary of State).
- The board should consist of roughly equal numbers of ministers (junior ministers), officials (civil servants) and non-executive members, drawn mainly from the commercial private sector.
- The role of the board is advisory and supervisory. It gives advice on matters relating to the department and monitors reporting from the department on its performance and its success in achieving objectives.
- The board has no policy-making responsibilities. Policy is decided at ministerial level, with advice from civil servants.
- Ministers are accountable to Parliament.

The reason for appointing individuals with a commercial background as non-executive members is to bring commercial experience to the discussions of the board.

The advice provided by the departmental board is concerned mainly with issues relating to:

- strategic clarity in the department's objectives and strategies;
- commercial sense in the department's aims and activities;
- the recruitment of talented individuals for the department;
- monitoring results and providing advice on performance; and
- management information within the department.

A Nominations and Governance Committee of the board advises on reward systems for senior civil servants in the department.

In its supervisory role, a departmental board scrutinises reports from officials about the performance of the department, and it can challenge the department on how well it is achieving its objectives. However, its views are advisory only. Control is exercised through the department's ministers and senior civil servants.

The government minister is accountable to Parliament for the exercise of the powers of the department. A head official (usually the departmental permanent secretary, who is also a member of the board) is the accounting officer (AO) for the department who must ensure that the department spends its budget in the way that Parliament intended.

Governance in central government is therefore complicated by the need for public accountability, and the potential conflict between politics and the need to have efficient civil service departments.

The success of a departmental board may depend crucially on the constructiveness of the relationship between the minister (board chairman) and the rest of the board. This is because the role of the board is advisory only, and it has no decision-making responsibilities. The key decisions are taken by ministers, not by the departmental board.

7.2 'Good Governance Standard for Public Service'

The Independent Commission on Good Governance in Public Service was established by the Office for Public Management (OPM) and the CIPFA, in partnership with the Joseph Rowntree Foundation. The role of the Commission was to develop a common code and set of principles for good corporate governance across all public services in the UK.

In 2004 it published 'Good Governance Standards for Public Service'. This is a guide for everyone concerned with governance in the public services, and applies to all organisations that work for the public using public money. Its application therefore extends from public sector bodies to all private sector organisations that use public money to work for the public.

In justifying the need for the application of good governance principles and practice in the public service sector, the Commission has commented that:

■ good governance encourages public trust and participation; whereas
■ bad governance fosters low morale and adversarial relationships.

The Commission's Good Governance Standard builds on Nolan's Principles. It consists of six main principles, each with supporting principles and guidelines on how they might be applied in practice. It is useful to look at these and compare them with the principles that apply to good corporate governance in the commercial (profit-making) sector. There are many similarities between these principles and those that should apply in corporate governance to companies.

The six main principles and their supporting principles are as follows.

1 Focusing on the organisation's purpose and on its outcome for citizens and users of the organisation's services.
 – Being clear about the purpose of the organisation and its intended outcomes for citizens and service users. It is suggested that the concept of 'public value' may be useful in helping organisations to identify their purpose and intended outcomes.
 – Making sure that users receive a high-quality service.
 – Making sure that taxpayers get value for money (VFM).
2 Performing effectively in clearly defined functions and roles.
 – Being clear about the functions of the organisation's governing body. It is recommended that the governing body should describe in a published document its approach to achieving each of its stated functions. This document can then be used as a basis for measuring actual performance and achievements by the governing body. Functions could include, for example, 'scrutinising the activities and performance of the executive management' and 'making sure that the voice of the public is heard in discussions and decision-making'.
 – Being clear about the responsibilities of the non-executive and the executive governors; these will differ. Many governing bodies consist of both executive and non-executive members (who may be unpaid for their services). However, they should have equal status in discussions on policy and strategy. The Framework recommends that the roles of chief executive and chairman of the governing body should not be held by the same individual. Making sure that these responsibilities are properly carried out.
 – Being clear about the relationship between the governors and the public, so that both sides in this relationship know what to expect from the other.
3 Promoting values for the whole organisation and demonstrating good governance through behaviour.
 – Putting the values of the organisation into practice. The governing body should take the lead in doing this.
 – Individual governors behaving in ways that uphold and exemplify effective governance.
4 Taking informed and transparent decisions and managing risk.
 – Being rigorous and transparent about how decisions are taken by the governing body. There should be clearly defined levels of delegation within the organisation. The governing body should not be concerned with matters that are more properly delegated to management. It should also be clear about what the objectives of its own decisions are.
 – Using good quality information, advice and support.
 – Making sure that an effective risk management system is in operation.
5 Developing the capacity and capability of the governing body to be effective.
 – Making sure that the governors have the skills, knowledge and experience to perform well.
 – Developing the capabilities of individuals with governance responsibilities.
 – Striking a balance in the membership of the governing body between continuity and renewal.

Best practice for the creation and refreshing of a governing body is similar in many respects to guidelines for corporate governance, except in the public sector, some governors may be elected representatives.

- Engaging stakeholders and making accountability real.
- Understanding formal and informal accountability relationships.
- Taking an active and planned approach to dialogue with and accountability to the public.
- Taking an effective and planned approach to accountability to staff.
- Engaging effectively with institutional stakeholders. Institutional stakeholders in the public sector are very different from institutional shareholders in the corporate world. In local government, for example, institutional stakeholders include bodies representing local people. Engagement with stakeholders should help to improve the accountability of the public sector body to the public.

These are general principles, and individual public sector bodies can develop their own codes of governance that are consistent with and based on these principles.

An important aspect of governance for public sector bodies, as with corporate governance, is risk management. When referring to 'risk management' in the public sector, the focus is likely to be mainly on 'internal control'. Public sector organisations have a long history of wasteful spending, inefficiency, errors and fraud. In England, for example, local government bodies are required by law to publish a statement of internal control each year.

8   Governance in local government

In the UK, the Chartered Institute of Public Finance and Accountancy (CIPFA) and Solace (the Society of Local Authority Chief Executives and Senior Managers) publish a governance framework aimed at local government bodies called 'Delivering Good Governance in Local Government: Framework'. The latest edition was published in 2016. This sets out principles of governance that local government bodies are encouraged to adopt and apply to their own particular circumstances. It is crucial that leaders and chief executives keep their governance arrangements up to date and relevant. To assist them, the Framework defines the principles that should underpin the governance of each local government organisation. It provides a structure to help individual authorities with their approach to governance.

This publication positions the attainment of sustainable economic, societal and environmental outcomes as a key focus of governance processes and structures. Outcomes are what give the role of local government its meaning and importance, and it is fitting that they have this central role in the sector's governance.

The focus on sustainability and the links between governance and public financial management are crucial – local authorities must recognise the need to focus on the long term. They have responsibilities to more than their current electors; they must take account of the impact of current decisions and actions on future generations.

To achieve good governance, each local authority should be able to demonstrate that its governance structures comply with the core and sub principles contained in this Framework. It should therefore develop and maintain a local code of governance/governance arrangements reflecting the principles set out. Whatever form of arrangements are in place, authorities should test their governance structures and partnerships against the Framework's principles.

Local authorities are required to prepare a governance statement in order to report publicly on the extent to which they comply with their own code of governance on an annual basis, including how they have monitored and evaluated the effectiveness of their governance arrangements in the year, and on any planned changes in the coming period. The process of preparing the governance statement should itself add value to the effectiveness of the governance and internal control framework.

The preparation and publication of an Annual Governance Statement in accordance with the Framework fulfils the statutory requirement in England, Scotland, Northern Ireland and Wales for a local authority to conduct a review at least once in each financial year of the effectiveness of its system of internal control and to include a statement reporting on the review with its Statement of Accounts.

9 Governance and the voluntary sector

The voluntary sector comprises a wide range of organisations, including charities and mutual self-help groups. Many UK charities are established as a trust, which is governed by a board of trustees. Large charities employ full-time managers and employees, whereas others rely entirely on voluntary and unpaid help.

Governance in the voluntary sector has been defined as:

'[T]he way that trustees work with chief executives and staff (where appointed), volunteers, service users, members and other stakeholders to ensure their organisation is effectively and properly run, and meets the needs for which the organisation was set up.' ('Good Governance: A Code for the Voluntary and Community Sector', revised 2010)

The development of codes and rules for corporate governance in the commercial sector and governance in the government sector has also reached the voluntary sector. For example, the National Council of Voluntary Organisations (NCVO) adapted Nolan's seven principles of public life into a Code of Conduct for Charity Trustees; and the Charity Commission's Statement of Recommended Practice requires larger charities to include a statement on risks in their annual report.

Awareness of the need for good governance has also developed in the voluntary sector's response to sector-specific issues, including:

- the increase in size and importance of the voluntary sector, particularly as a result of the contracting out of public service to voluntary organisations;
- a perception of a decline in public confidence in charities; charities and other bodies have tried to improve their standards of governance as a way of retaining public confidence in what they are doing;
- greater competition for funding; charities with better standards of governance may succeed better in attracting funds from government and the public;
- a lack of clarity about the duties of voluntary board members, and in particular concerns about the liabilities of charity trustees; these concerns are similar to those in corporate governance, about the responsibilities of the board, the duties of directors and the potential liability of directors;
- a growing demand for accountability to users and beneficiaries of the services provided by charities, and demands for greater transparency on how charities spend their donated income, in particular the proportion spent ('wasted') on administration.

A comment in 'Good Governance' suggests that the main responsibility for good governance in the voluntary sector lies with the board of directors or trustees: 'Trustees and board members carry an important responsibility to manage their organisations and deliver their objectives in a way that enhances public trust and support.'

9.1 'Good Governance: A Code for the Voluntary and Community Sector'

'Good Governance: A Code for the Voluntary and Community Sector' was published in the UK in 2005 and revised in 2010. A draft new code was issued in 2016 with the aim of publishing a revised code in 2017. This governance code was developed and endorsed by the Charity Commission and the NCVO, the Association of Chief Executives of Voluntary Associations (ACEVO), the Charity Trustee Networks (CTN) and ICSA. The Code is not mandatory, but organisations that comply with it are invited to say so in their annual report and other relevant published material. Smaller charities are invited to focus on complying with the general principles of the Code rather than the detailed guides on how to apply the principles in practice. The revised Code contains six high level principles. These are set out as ways in which the 'board' of the organisation should provide good governance and leadership.

1   **Understanding their role.** Members of the board should understand their role and respon- sibilities, both collectively and individually, with regard to matters such as their legal duties, their stewardship of the organisation's assets and its governing documents. For the trustees of a charity, understanding their role includes:
   - accepting responsibility for the way in which the organisation is managed and run to meet its purpose; and
   - ensuring the financial strength and solvency of the organisation.
2   **Ensuring delivery of organisational purpose.** The board should ensure that the organisation delivers its purposes or aims by ensuring that these remain relevant and valid, by developing and agreeing a long-term strategy, agreeing operational budgets, monitoring progress and assessing results and outcomes. The board should avoid 'mission drift'. Failure to ensure delivery of purpose would mean failing responsibilities to beneficiaries and the people who provide finance and support.
3   **Working effectively both as individuals and as a team.** The board's policies and procedures should include arrangements for finding and recruiting new board members to meet the organisation's changing needs, providing suitable induction for new board members, providing opportunities for training and development for all board members and reviewing the performance of the board, both as individual members and as a team.
4   **Exercising effective control.** As an accountable body, the board should ensure that the organisation understands and complies with all legal and regulatory requirements, continues to have good financial and management controls, identifies major risks facing the organisation and has a risk management system in place to deal with them. The board should also ensure that delegation of authority to committees, staff and volunteers works effectively and is properly supervised. 'Good Governance' comments: 'Boards should provide direction, leadership and oversight, but without inappropriate involvement in operational matters. Delegation needs to be effectively supervised and monitored.'
5   **Behaving with integrity.** The board should safeguard and promote the organisation's integrity, act according to high ethical standards, manage conflicts of interest and loyalty and maintain the independence of their decision-making. Unethical behaviour could cause serious reputational harm to the organisation.
6   **Being open and accountable.** The board should be open and accountable, both internally and externally. This requirement includes open communications (informing people about the organisation and its work), appropriate consultation on significant changes to the organ- isation's services or policies, listening and responding to the needs of its stakeholders and handling complaints constructively and impartially. In companies, accountability is associ- ated with management accountability to the board of directors and the board's account- ability to shareholders. In the voluntary sector, accountability also involves listening to stakeholders, and responding to their views and complaints.

For each of the six principles there is an explanation as to why it is needed and supporting material that suggests ways of applying it in practice.

9.2   Potential governance problems in the charities sector

Potential problems with governance in the charities sector may be:

- dominance by full-time senior officials over part-time elected politicians;
- 'mission drift' and losing sight of what the local government authority should be trying to achieve;
- excessive spending on administration and not enough on 'front-line' charitable activities; and
- reputational risk, which could seriously affect funding.

In not-for-profit organisations, as in government, there is no direct accountability of the board to owners of the organisation. In corporate governance (in contrast), an important element in good governance is accountability of the board to the shareholders. Arguably the problem of limited accountability may be greater in the charities sector than in government, because elected politicians are at least (eventually) answerable to the electorate.

TEST YOUR KNOWLEDGE 13.4

a How does governance in the public sector and not-for-profit sector differ from corporate governance?
b What are Nolan's seven principles of public life?
c What might be the consequences of bad governance practice in a police force?
d For what reasons have governance guidelines and codes of practice been developed for the not-for-profit sector?

10 Social responsibility in the public and voluntary sectors

Social responsibility in government and the public sector is more difficult to define and identify than in the corporate sector. This is because many aspects of government policy are directed towards the economic, social or environmental well-being of its citizens and, unlike companies, government does not have a profit objective in its policy objectives.

Within government, there may be particular responsibilities for social and environmental policy. In the UK, for example, the Department for the Environment, Food and Rural Affairs (Defra) is responsible for developing government policy on sustainable development and sustainable products. As a major buyer of goods and services from the private sector, the government is also able to pursue a procurement policy that awards supply contracts to companies that meet acceptable corporate social responsibility (CSR) standards.

Within the voluntary sector, many charities are established specifically for social or environmental objectives. In the UK, the Good Governance Code for the Voluntary and Community Sector does not specify any guidelines on environmental issues, although it does state that organisations should pursue equal opportunities for social policies with regard to:

- assessing needs to be met;
- allocating resources, providing services and making grants; and
- staff recruitment and training.

CHAPTER SUMMARY

- Many countries have developed corporate governance frameworks for major stock market companies. Most have a formal code of corporate governance for these companies, and companies must either apply the provisions of the code or explain any non-appliance.
- King IV in South Africa is notable because it takes a stakeholder-inclusive approach to governance, and promotes the concepts of integrated reports and sustainability.
- In most countries with a code of corporate governance, governance is largely principles-based (but with some aspects of governance a legal requirement). In the US, there is a more rules-based approach to corporate governance.
- The ICGN is an organisation that seeks to improve standards of corporate governance internationally, in the interests of global investment.
- Many principles of good corporate governance for major listed companies are relevant to unquoted companies and to quoted companies whose shares are traded on a junior stock market. However, the extent to which governance principles may sensibly be applied vary with the size of the company, its ownership structure and how close it might be to becoming a listed company.
- The Institute of Directors in the UK has issued guidance on governance for unlisted companies.
- Governance in the public sector has some similarities with corporate governance, but also significant differences.
- Leaders in government should be expected to uphold Nolan's seven Principles.

■ In the UK, central government departments have a board consisting of ministers, civil servants and non-executive members who are drawn mainly from a commercial background. The board is chaired by the senior department minister. The role of the board is advisory only: it has no decision-making responsibilities.

■ Governance in local government varies with the differing arrangements for providing local services.

■ In the voluntary sector, particularly charities, a major problem with governance may be the effectiveness of a board of part-time directors or trustees, and the influence of full-time executives.

■ There are codes of governance in the UK for central government departments, the local authority sector and the not-for-profit sector.

APPENDIX 1

The UK Corporate Governance Code

Financial Reporting Council, April 2016

Governance and the Code

1. The purpose of corporate governance is to facilitate effective, entrepreneurial and prudent management that can deliver the long-term success of the company.
2. The first version of the UK Corporate Governance Code (the Code) was produced in 1992 by the Cadbury Committee. Its paragraph 2.5 is still the classic definition of the context of the Code:

   Corporate governance is the system by which companies are directed and controlled. Boards of directors are responsible for the governance of their companies. The shareholders' role in governance is to appoint the directors and the auditors and to satisfy themselves that an appropriate governance structure is in place. The responsibilities of the board include setting the company's strategic aims, providing the leadership to put them into effect, supervising the management of the business and reporting to shareholders on their stewardship. The board's actions are subject to laws, regulations and the shareholders in general meeting.
3. Corporate governance is therefore about what the board of a company does and how it sets the values of the company. It is to be distinguished from the day to day operational management of the company by full-time executives.
4. The Code is a guide to a number of key components of effective board practice. It is based on the underlying principles of all good governance: accountability, transparency, probity and focus on the sustainable success of an entity over the longer term.
5. The Code has been enduring, but it is not immutable. Its fitness for purpose in a permanently changing economic and social business environment requires its evaluation at appropriate intervals.
6. The new Code applies to accounting periods beginning on or after 17 June 2016 and applies to all companies with a Premium listing of equity shares regardless of whether they are incorporated in the UK or elsewhere.

Preface

1. Over two decades of constructive usage of the Code have contributed to improved corporate governance in the UK. The Code is part of a framework of legislation, regulation and best practice standards which aims to deliver high quality corporate governance with in-built flexibility for companies to adapt their practices to take into account their particular circumstances. Similarly, investors must take the opportunity to consider carefully how companies have decided to implement the Code. There is always scope for improvement, both in terms of making sure that the Code remains relevant and improving the quality of reporting.
2. Boards must continue to think comprehensively about their overall tasks and the implications of these for the roles of their individual members. Absolutely key in these endeavours are the leadership of the chairman of a board, the support given to and by the CEO, and the frankness and openness of mind with which issues are discussed and tackled by all directors.
3. Essential to the effective functioning of any board is dialogue which is both constructive and challenging. The problems arising from "groupthink" have been exposed in particular as a result of the financial crisis. One of the ways in which constructive debate can be encouraged is through having sufficient diversity on the board. This includes, but is not limited to, gender and race. Diverse board composition in these respects is not on its own a guarantee. Diversity is as much about differences of approach and experience, and it is very important

in ensuring effective engagement with key stakeholders and in order to deliver the business strategy.

4. One of the key roles for the board includes establishing the culture, values and ethics of the company. It is important that the board sets the correct 'tone from the top'. The directors should lead by example and ensure that good standards of behaviour permeate throughout all levels of the organisation. This will help prevent misconduct, unethical practices and support the delivery of long-term success.

5. This update of the Code has been driven by the consequential changes required from the implementation of the European Union's Audit Regulation and Directive. Section C.3 on Audit Committees was reviewed to ensure it remained consistent and changes have only been made when necessary. It is important that companies view these changes alongside the revised Guidance on Audit Committees.

6. Following the 2014 Code amendments, which focussed on the provision by companies of information about the risks which affect longer term viability, the FRC will continue to monitor compliance with these changes. Companies should be presenting information to give a clearer and broader view of solvency, liquidity, risk management and viability. For their part, investors should assess these statements thoroughly and engage accordingly.

7. To run a corporate board successfully should not be underrated. Constraints on time and knowledge combine with the need to maintain mutual respect and openness between a cast of strong, able and busy directors dealing with each other across the different demands of executive and non-executive roles. To achieve good governance requires continuing and high quality effort.

8. Chairmen are encouraged to report personally in their annual statements how the principles relating to the role and effectiveness of the board (in Sections A and B of the Code) have been applied. Not only will this give investors a clearer picture of the steps taken by boards to operate effectively but also, by providing fuller context, it may make investors more willing to accept explanations when a company chooses to explain rather than to comply with one or more provisions.

9. While in law the company is primarily accountable to its shareholders, and the relationship between the company and its shareholders is also the main focus of the Code, companies are encouraged to recognise the contribution made by other providers of capital and to confirm the board's interest in listening to the views of such providers insofar as these are relevant to the company's overall approach to governance.

Financial Reporting Council
April 2016

Comply or Explain

1. The "comply or explain" approach is the trademark of corporate governance in the UK. It has been in operation since the Code's beginnings and is the foundation of its flexibility. It is strongly supported by both companies and shareholders and has been widely admired and imitated internationally.

2. The Code is not a rigid set of rules. It consists of principles (main and supporting) and provisions. The Listing Rules require companies to apply the Main Principles and report to shareholders on how they have done so. The principles are the core of the Code and the way in which they are applied should be the central question for a board as it determines how it is to operate according to the Code.

3. It is recognised that an alternative to following a provision may be justified in particular circumstances if good governance can be achieved by other means. A condition of doing so is that the reasons for it should be explained clearly and carefully to shareholders,[1] who may wish to discuss the position with the company and whose voting intentions may be influenced as a result. In providing an explanation, the company should aim to illustrate how its actual practices are consistent with the principle to which the particular provision relates, contribute to good governance and promote delivery of business objectives. It should set out the background, provide a clear rationale for the action it is taking, and describe any mitigating actions taken to address any additional risk and maintain conformity with the relevant

principle. Where deviation from a particular provision is intended to be limited in time, the explanation should indicate when the company expects to conform with the provision.

4. In their responses to explanations, shareholders should pay due regard to companies' individual circumstances and bear in mind in particular the size and complexity of the company and the nature of the risks and challenges it faces. Whilst shareholders have every right to challenge companies' explanations if they are unconvincing, they should not be evaluated in a mechanistic way and departures from the Code should not be automatically treated as breaches. Shareholders should be careful to respond to the statements from companies in a manner that supports the "comply or explain" process and bearing in mind the purpose of good corporate governance. They should put their views to the company and both parties should be prepared to discuss the position.

5. Smaller listed companies, in particular those new to listing, may judge that some of the provisions are disproportionate or less relevant in their case. Some of the provisions do not apply to companies below the FTSE 350. Such companies may nonetheless consider that it would be appropriate to adopt the approach in the Code and they are encouraged to do so. Externally managed investment companies typically have a different board structure which may affect the relevance of particular provisions; the Association of Investment Companies' Corporate Governance Code and Guide can assist them in meeting their obligations under the Code.

6. Satisfactory engagement between company boards and investors is crucial to the health of the UK's corporate governance regime. Companies and shareholders both have responsibility for ensuring that "comply or explain" remains an effective alternative to a rules-based system. There are practical and administrative obstacles to improved interaction between boards and shareholders. But certainly there is also scope for an increase in trust which could generate a virtuous upward spiral in attitudes to the Code and in its constructive use.

The Main Principles of the Code

Section A: Leadership

Every company should be headed by an effective board which is collectively responsible for the long-term success of the company.

There should be a clear division of responsibilities at the head of the company between the running of the board and the executive responsibility for the running of the company's business. No one individual should have unfettered powers of decision.

The chairman is responsible for leadership of the board and ensuring its effectiveness on all aspects of its role.

As part of their role as members of a unitary board, non-executive directors should constructively challenge and help develop proposals on strategy.

Section B: Effectiveness

The board and its committees should have the appropriate balance of skills, experience, independence and knowledge of the company to enable them to discharge their respective duties and responsibilities effectively.

There should be a formal, rigorous and transparent procedure for the appointment of new directors to the board.

All directors should be able to allocate sufficient time to the company to discharge their responsibilities effectively.

All directors should receive induction on joining the board and should regularly update and refresh their skills and knowledge.

The board should be supplied in a timely manner with information in a form and of a quality appropriate to enable it to discharge its duties.

The board should undertake a formal and rigorous annual evaluation of its own performance and that of its committees and individual directors.

All directors should be submitted for re-election at regular intervals, subject to continued satisfactory performance.

Section C: Accountability

The board should present a fair, balanced and understandable assessment of the company's position and prospects.

The board is responsible for determining the nature and extent of the principal risks it is willing to take in achieving its strategic objectives. The board should maintain sound risk management and internal control systems.

The board should establish formal and transparent arrangements for considering how they should apply the corporate reporting, risk management and internal control principles and for maintaining an appropriate relationship with the company's auditors.

Section D: Remuneration

Executive directors' remuneration should be designed to promote the long-term success of the company. Performance-related elements should be transparent, stretching and rigorously applied.

There should be a formal and transparent procedure for developing policy on executive remuneration and for fixing the remuneration packages of individual directors. No director should be involved in deciding his or her own remuneration.

Section E: Relations with shareholders

There should be a dialogue with shareholders based on the mutual understanding of objectives. The board as a whole has responsibility for ensuring that a satisfactory dialogue with shareholders takes place.

The board should use general meetings to communicate with investors and to encourage their participation.

Section A: Leadership

A.1: The Role of the Board

Main Principle

Every company should be headed by an effective board which is collectively responsible for the long-term success of the company.

Supporting Principles

The board's role is to provide entrepreneurial leadership of the company within a framework of prudent and effective controls which enables risk to be assessed and managed. The board should set the company's strategic aims, ensure that the necessary financial and human resources are in place for the company to meet its objectives and review management performance. The board should set the company's values and standards and ensure that its obligations to its shareholders and others are understood and met.

All directors must act in what they consider to be the best interests of the company, consistent with their statutory duties.[2]

Code Provisions

A.1.1. The board should meet sufficiently regularly to discharge its duties effectively. There should be a formal schedule of matters specifically reserved for its decision. The annual report should include a statement of how the board operates, including a high level statement of which types of decisions are to be taken by the board and which are to be delegated to management.

A.1.2. The annual report should identify the chairman, the deputy chairman (where there is one), the chief executive, the senior independent director and the chairmen and members of the board committees.[3] It should also set out the number of meetings of the board and those committees and individual attendance by directors.

A.1.3. The company should arrange appropriate insurance cover in respect of legal action against its directors.

A.2: Division of Responsibilities

Main Principle

There should be a clear division of responsibilities at the head of the company between the running of the board and the executive responsibility for the running of the company's business. No one individual should have unfettered powers of decision.

Code Provision

A.2.1 The roles of chairman and chief executive should not be exercised by the same individual. The division of responsibilities between the chairman and chief executive should be clearly established, set out in writing and agreed by the board.

A.3: The Chairman

Main Principle

The chairman is responsible for leadership of the board and ensuring its effectiveness on all aspects of its role.

Supporting Principles

The chairman is responsible for setting the board's agenda and ensuring that adequate time is available for discussion of all agenda items, in particular strategic issues. The chairman should also promote a culture of openness and debate by facilitating the effective contribution of non-executive directors in particular and ensuring constructive relations between executive and non-executive directors.

The chairman is responsible for ensuring that the directors receive accurate, timely and clear information. The chairman should ensure effective communication with shareholders.

Code Provision

A.3.1. The chairman should on appointment meet the independence criteria set out in B.1.1 below. A chief executive should not go on to be chairman of the same company. If exceptionally a board decides that a chief executive should become chairman, the board should consult major shareholders in advance and should set out its reasons to shareholders at the time of the appointment and in the next annual report.[4]

A.4: Non-Executive Directors

Main Principle

As part of their role as members of a unitary board, non-executive directors should constructively challenge and help develop proposals on strategy.

Supporting Principle

Non-executive directors should scrutinise the performance of management in meeting agreed goals and objectives and monitor the reporting of performance. They should satisfy themselves on the integrity of financial information and that financial controls and systems of risk management are robust and defensible. They are responsible for determining appropriate levels of remuneration of executive directors and have a prime role in appointing and, where necessary, removing executive directors, and in succession planning.

Code Provisions

A.4.1. The board should appoint one of the independent non-executive directors to be the senior independent director to provide a sounding board for the chairman and to serve as an intermediary for the other directors when necessary. The senior independent director should be available to shareholders if they have concerns which contact through the normal channels of chairman, chief executive or other executive directors has failed to resolve or for which such contact is inappropriate.

A.4.2. The chairman should hold meetings with the non-executive directors without the executives present. Led by the senior independent director, the non-executive directors should meet without the chairman present at least annually to appraise the chairman's performance and on such other occasions as are deemed appropriate.

A.4.3. Where directors have concerns which cannot be resolved about the running of the company or a proposed action, they should ensure that their concerns are recorded in the board minutes. On resignation, a non-executive director should provide a written statement to the chairman, for circulation to the board, if they have any such concerns.

Section B: Effectiveness

B.1: The Composition of the Board

Main Principle

The board and its committees should have the appropriate balance of skills, experience, independence and knowledge of the company to enable them to discharge their respective duties and responsibilities effectively.

Supporting Principles

The board should be of sufficient size that the requirements of the business can be met and that changes to the board's composition and that of its committees can be managed without undue disruption, and should not be so large as to be unwieldy.

The board should include an appropriate combination of executive and non-executive directors (and, in particular, independent non-executive directors) such that no individual or small group of individuals can dominate the board's decision taking.

The value of ensuring that committee membership is refreshed and that undue reliance is not placed on particular individuals should be taken into account in deciding chairmanship and membership of committees.

No one other than the committee chairman and members is entitled to be present at a meeting of the nomination, audit or remuneration committee, but others may attend at the invitation of the committee.

Code Provisions

B.1.1. The board should identify in the annual report each non-executive director it considers to be independent.[5] The board should determine whether the director is independent in character and judgement and whether there are relationships or circumstances which are likely to affect, or could appear to affect, the director's judgement. The board should state its reasons if it determines that a director is independent notwithstanding the existence of relationships or circumstances which may appear relevant to its determination, including if the director:
- has been an employee of the company or group within the last five years;
- has, or has had within the last three years, a material business relationship with the company either directly, or as a partner, shareholder, director or senior employee of a body that has such a relationship with the company;
- has received or receives additional remuneration from the company apart from a director's fee, participates in the company's share option or a performance related pay scheme, or is a member of the company's pension scheme;
- has close family ties with any of the company's advisers, directors or senior employees;

- holds cross-directorships or has significant links with other directors through involvement in other companies or bodies;
- represents a significant shareholder; or
- has served on the board for more than nine years from the date of their first election.

B.1.2. Except for smaller companies,[6] at least half the board, excluding the chairman, should comprise non-executive directors determined by the board to be independent. A smaller company should have at least two independent non-executive directors.

B.2: Appointments to the Board

Main Principle

There should be a formal, rigorous and transparent procedure for the appointment of new directors to the board.

Supporting Principles

The search for board candidates should be conducted, and appointments made, on merit, against objective criteria and with due regard for the benefits of diversity on the board, including gender.

The board should satisfy itself that plans are in place for orderly succession for appointments to the board and to senior management, so as to maintain an appropriate balance of skills and experience within the company and on the board and to ensure progressive refreshing of the board.

Code Provisions

B.2.1. There should be a nomination committee which should lead the process for board appointments and make recommendations to the board. A majority of members of the nomination committee should be independent non-executive directors. The chairman or an independent non-executive director should chair the committee, but the chairman should not chair the nomination committee when it is dealing with the appointment of a successor to the chairmanship. The nomination committee should make available its terms of reference, explaining its role and the authority delegated to it by the board.[7]

B.2.2. The nomination committee should evaluate the balance of skills, experience, independence and knowledge on the board and, in the light of this evaluation, prepare a description of the role and capabilities required for a particular appointment.

B.2.3. Non-executive directors should be appointed for specified terms subject to re-election and to statutory provisions relating to the removal of a director. Any term beyond six years for a non-executive director should be subject to particularly rigorous review, and should take into account the need for progressive refreshing of the board.

B.2.4. A separate section of the annual report should describe the work of the nomination committee,[8] including the process it has used in relation to board appointments. This section should include a description of the board's policy on diversity, including gender, any measurable objectives that it has set for implementing the policy, and progress on achieving the objectives. An explanation should be given if neither an external search consultancy nor open advertising has been used in the appointment of a chairman or a non-executive director. Where an external search consultancy has been used, it should be identified in the annual report and a statement made as to whether it has any other connection with the company.

B.3: Commitment

Main Principle

All directors should be able to allocate sufficient time to the company to discharge their responsibilities effectively.

Code Provisions

B.3.1. For the appointment of a chairman, the nomination committee should prepare a job specification, including an assessment of the time commitment expected, recognising the need for availability in the event of crises. A chairman's other significant commitments should be disclosed to the board before appointment and included in the annual report. Changes to such commitments should be reported to the board as they arise, and their impact explained in the next annual report.

B.3.2. The terms and conditions of appointment of non-executive directors should be made available for inspection.[9] The letter of appointment should set out the expected time commitment. Non-executive directors should undertake that they will have sufficient time to meet what is expected of them. Their other significant commitments should be disclosed to the board before appointment, with a broad indication of the time involved and the board should be informed of subsequent changes.

B.3.3. The board should not agree to a full time executive director taking on more than one non-executive directorship in a FTSE 100 company nor the chairmanship of such a company.

B.4: Development

Main Principle

All directors should receive induction on joining the board and should regularly update and refresh their skills and knowledge.

Supporting Principles

The chairman should ensure that the directors continually update their skills and the knowledge and familiarity with the company required to fulfil their role both on the board and on board committees. The company should provide the necessary resources for developing and updating its directors' knowledge and capabilities.

To function effectively all directors need appropriate knowledge of the company and access to its operations and staff.

Code Provisions

B.4.1. The chairman should ensure that new directors receive a full, formal and tailored induction on joining the board. As part of this, directors should avail themselves of opportunities to meet major shareholders.

B.4.2. The chairman should regularly review and agree with each director their training and development needs.

B.5: Information and Support

Main Principle

The board should be supplied in a timely manner with information in a form and of a quality appropriate to enable it to discharge its duties.

Supporting Principles

The chairman is responsible for ensuring that the directors receive accurate, timely and clear information. Management has an obligation to provide such information but directors should seek clarification or amplification where necessary.

Under the direction of the chairman, the company secretary's responsibilities include ensuring good information flows within the board and its committees and between senior management and non-executive directors, as well as facilitating induction and assisting with professional development as required.

The company secretary should be responsible for advising the board through the chairman on all governance matters.

Code Provisions

B.5.1. The board should ensure that directors, especially non-executive directors, have access to independent professional advice at the company's expense where they judge it necessary to discharge their responsibilities as directors. Committees should be provided with sufficient resources to undertake their duties.

B.5.2. All directors should have access to the advice and services of the company secretary, who is responsible to the board for ensuring that board procedures are complied with. Both the appointment and removal of the company secretary should be a matter for the board as a whole.

B.6: Evaluation

Main Principle

The board should undertake a formal and rigorous annual evaluation of its own performance and that of its committees and individual directors.

Supporting Principles

Evaluation of the board should consider the balance of skills, experience, independence and knowledge of the company on the board, its diversity, including gender, how the board works together as a unit, and other factors relevant to its effectiveness.

The chairman should act on the results of the performance evaluation by recognising the strengths and addressing the weaknesses of the board and, where appropriate, proposing new members be appointed to the board or seeking the resignation of directors.

Individual evaluation should aim to show whether each director continues to contribute effectively and to demonstrate commitment to the role (including commitment of time for board and committee meetings and any other duties).

Code Provisions

B.6.1. The board should state in the annual report how performance evaluation of the board, its committees and its individual directors has been conducted.

B.6.2. Evaluation of the board of FTSE 350 companies should be externally facilitated at least every three years. The external facilitator should be identified in the annual report and a statement made as to whether they have any other connection with the company.

B.6.3. The non-executive directors, led by the senior independent director, should be responsible for performance evaluation of the chairman, taking into account the views of executive directors.

B.7: Re-election

Main Principle

All directors should be submitted for re-election at regular intervals, subject to continued satisfactory performance.

Code Provisions

B.7.1. All directors of FTSE 350 companies should be subject to annual election by shareholders. All other directors should be subject to election by shareholders at the first annual general meeting after their appointment, and to re-election thereafter at intervals of no more than three years. Non-executive directors who have served longer than nine years should be subject to annual re-election. The names of directors submitted for election or re-election should be accompanied by sufficient biographical details and any other relevant information to enable shareholders to take an informed decision on their election.

B.7.2. The board should set out to shareholders in the papers accompanying a resolution to elect a non-executive director why they believe an individual should be elected. The chairman should confirm to shareholders when proposing re-election that, following formal performance evaluation, the individual's performance continues to be effective and to demonstrate commitment to the role.

Section C: Accountability

C.1: Financial and Business Reporting

Main Principle

The board should present a fair, balanced and understandable assessment of the company's position and prospects.

Supporting Principles

The board's responsibility to present a fair, balanced and understandable assessment extends to interim and other price-sensitive public reports and reports to regulators as well as to information required to be presented by statutory requirements.

The board should establish arrangements that will enable it to ensure that the information presented is fair, balanced and understandable.

Code Provisions

C.1.1. The directors should explain in the annual report their responsibility for preparing the annual report and accounts, and state that they consider the annual report and accounts, taken as a whole, is fair, balanced and understandable and provides the information necessary for shareholders to assess the company's position and performance, business model and strategy. There should be a statement by the auditor about their reporting responsibilities.[10]

C.1.2. The directors should include in the annual report an explanation of the basis on which the company generates or preserves value over the longer term (the business model) and the strategy for delivering the objectives of the company.[11]

C.1.3. In annual and half-yearly financial statements, the directors should state whether they considered it appropriate to adopt the going concern basis of accounting in preparing them, and identify any material uncertainties to the company's ability to continue to do so over a period of at least twelve months from the date of approval of the financial statements.[12]

C.2: Risk Management and Internal Control

Main Principle

The board is responsible for determining the nature and extent of the principal risks it is willing to take in achieving its strategic objectives. The board should maintain sound risk management and internal control systems.

Code Provisions

C.2.1. The directors should confirm in the annual report that they have carried out a robust assessment of the principal risks facing the company, including those that would threaten its business model, future performance, solvency or liquidity. The directors should describe those risks and explain how they are being managed or mitigated.

C.2.2. Taking account of the company's current position and principal risks, the directors should explain in the annual report how they have assessed the prospects of the company, over what period they have done so and why they consider that period to be appropriate. The directors should state whether they have a reasonable expectation that the company will be able to continue in operation and meet its liabilities as they fall due over the period of their assessment, drawing attention to any qualifications or assumptions as necessary.[13]

C.2.3. The board should monitor the company's risk management and internal control systems and, at least annually, carry out a review of their effectiveness, and report on that review in the annual report.[14] The monitoring and review should cover all material controls, including financial, operational and compliance controls.

C.3: Audit Committee and Auditors[15]

Main Principle

The board should establish formal and transparent arrangements for considering how they should apply the corporate reporting and risk management and internal control principles and for maintaining an appropriate relationship with the company's auditors.

Code Provisions

C.3.1. The board should establish an audit committee of at least three, or in the case of smaller companies[16] two, independent non-executive directors. In smaller companies the company chairman may be a member of, but not chair, the committee in addition to the independent non-executive directors, provided he or she was considered independent on appointment as chairman. The board should satisfy itself that at least one member of the audit committee has recent and relevant financial experience. The audit committee as a whole shall have competence relevant to the sector in which the company operates.[17]

C.3.2. The main role and responsibilities of the audit committee should be set out in written terms of reference[18] and should include:
- to monitor the integrity of the financial statements of the company and any formal announcements relating to the company's financial performance, reviewing significant financial reporting judgements contained in them;
- to review the company's internal financial controls and, unless expressly addressed by a separate board risk committee composed of independent directors, or by the board itself, to review the company's internal control and risk management systems;
- to monitor and review the effectiveness of the company's internal audit function;
- to make recommendations to the board, for it to put to the shareholders for their approval in general meeting, in relation to the appointment, re-appointment and removal of the external auditor and to approve the remuneration and terms of engagement of the external auditor;
- to review and monitor the external auditor's independence and objectivity and the effectiveness of the audit process, taking into consideration relevant UK professional and regulatory requirements;
- to develop and implement policy on the engagement of the external auditor to supply non-audit services, taking into account relevant ethical guidance regarding the provision of non-audit services by the external audit firm; and to report to the board, identifying any matters in respect of which it considers that action or improvement is needed and making recommendations as to the steps to be taken; and
- to report to the board on how it has discharged its responsibilities.

C.3.3. The terms of reference of the audit committee, including its role and the authority delegated to it by the board, should be made available.[19]

C.3.4. Where requested by the board, the audit committee should provide advice on whether the annual report and accounts, taken as a whole, is fair, balanced and understandable and provides the information necessary for shareholders to assess the company's position and performance, business model and strategy.

C.3.5. The audit committee should review arrangements by which staff of the company may, in confidence, raise concerns about possible improprieties in matters of financial reporting or other matters. The audit committee's objective should be to ensure that arrangements are in place for the proportionate and independent investigation of such matters and for appropriate follow-up action.

C.3.6. The audit committee should monitor and review the effectiveness of the internal audit activities. Where there is no internal audit function, the audit committee should consider annually whether there is a need for an internal audit function and make a recommendation to the board, and the reasons for the absence of such a function should be explained in the relevant section of the annual report.

C.3.7. The audit committee should have primary responsibility for making a recommendation on the appointment, reappointment and removal of the external auditors.[20] If the board does not accept the audit committee's recommendation, it should include in the annual report, and in any papers recommending appointment or re-appointment, a statement from the audit committee explaining the recommendation and should set out reasons why the board has taken a different position.

C.3.8. A separate section of the annual report should describe the work of the committee in discharging its responsibilities.[21] The report should include:

- the significant issues that the committee considered in relation to the financial statements, and how these issues were addressed;
- an explanation of how it has assessed the effectiveness of the external audit process and the approach taken to the appointment or reappointment of the external auditor, information on the length of tenure of the current audit firm, when a tender was last conducted and advance notice of any retendering plans;[22] and
- if the external auditor provides non-audit services, an explanation of how auditor objectivity and independence are safeguarded.

Section D: Remuneration

D.1: The Level and Components of Remuneration

Main Principle

Executive directors' remuneration should be designed to promote the long-term success of the company. Performance-related elements should be transparent, stretching and rigorously applied.

Supporting Principles

The remuneration committee should judge where to position their company relative to other companies. But they should use such comparisons with caution, in view of the risk of an upward ratchet of remuneration levels with no corresponding improvement in corporate and individual performance, and should avoid paying more than is necessary.

They should also be sensitive to pay and employment conditions elsewhere in the group, especially when determining annual salary increases.

Code Provisions

D.1.1. In designing schemes of performance-related remuneration for executive directors, the remuneration committee should follow the provisions in Schedule A to this Code.
Schemes should include provisions that would enable the company to recover sums paid or withhold the payment of any sum, and specify the circumstances in which it would be appropriate to do so.

D.1.2. Where a company releases an executive director to serve as a non-executive director elsewhere, the remuneration report[23] should include a statement as to whether or not the director will retain such earnings and, if so, what the remuneration is.

D.1.3. Levels of remuneration for non-executive directors should reflect the time commitment and responsibilities of the role. Remuneration for non-executive directors should not include share options or other performance-related elements. If, exceptionally, options are granted, shareholder approval should be sought in advance and any shares acquired by exercise of the options should be held until at least one year after the non-executive director leaves the board. Holding of share options could be relevant to the determination of a non-executive director's independence (as set out in provision B.1.1).

D.1.4. The remuneration committee should carefully consider what compensation commitments (including pension contributions and all other elements) their directors' terms of appointment would entail in the event of early termination. The aim should be to avoid rewarding poor performance. They should take a robust line on reducing compensation to reflect departing directors' obligations to mitigate loss.

D.1.5. Notice or contract periods should be set at one year or less. If it is necessary to offer longer notice or contract periods to new directors recruited from outside, such periods should reduce to one year or less after the initial period.

D.2: Procedure

Main Principle

There should be a formal and transparent procedure for developing policy on executive remuneration and for fixing the remuneration packages of individual directors. No director should be involved in deciding his or her own remuneration.

Supporting Principles

The remuneration committee should take care to recognise and manage conflicts of interest when receiving views from executive directors or senior management, or consulting the chief executive about its proposals. The remuneration committee should also be responsible for appointing any consultants in respect of executive director remuneration.

The chairman of the board should ensure that the committee chairman maintains contact as required with its principal shareholders about remuneration.

Code Provisions

D.2.1. The board should establish a remuneration committee of at least three, or in the case of smaller companies[24] two, independent non-executive directors. In addition the company chairman may also be a member of, but not chair, the committee if he or she was considered independent on appointment as chairman. The remuneration committee should make available its terms of reference, explaining its role and the authority delegated to it by the board.[25] Where remuneration consultants are appointed, they should be identified in the annual report and a statement made as to whether they have any other connection with the company.

D.2.2. The remuneration committee should have delegated responsibility for setting remuneration for all executive directors and the chairman, including pension rights and any compensation payments. The committee should also recommend and monitor the level and structure of remuneration for senior management. The definition of 'senior management' for this purpose should be determined by the board but should normally include the first layer of management below board level.

D.2.3. The board itself or, where required by the Articles of Association, the shareholders should determine the remuneration of the non-executive directors within the limits set in the Articles of Association. Where permitted by the Articles, the board may however delegate this responsibility to a committee, which might include the chief executive.

D.2.4. Shareholders should be invited specifically to approve all new long-term incentive schemes (as defined in the Listing Rules[26]) and significant changes to existing schemes, save in the circumstances permitted by the Listing Rules.

Section E: Relations with shareholders

E.1: Dialogue with Shareholders

Main Principle

There should be a dialogue with shareholders based on the mutual understanding of objectives. The board as a whole has responsibility for ensuring that a satisfactory dialogue with shareholders takes place.[27]

Supporting Principles

Whilst recognising that most shareholder contact is with the chief executive and finance director, the chairman should ensure that all directors are made aware of their major shareholders' issues and concerns.

The board should keep in touch with shareholder opinion in whatever ways are most practical and efficient.

Code Provisions

E.1.1. The chairman should ensure that the views of shareholders are communicated to the board as a whole. The chairman should discuss governance and strategy with major shareholders. Non-executive directors should be offered the opportunity to attend scheduled meetings with major shareholders and should expect to attend meetings if requested by major shareholders. The senior independent director should attend sufficient meetings with a range of major shareholders to listen to their views in order to help develop a balanced understanding of the issues and concerns of major shareholders.

E.1.2. The board should state in the annual report the steps they have taken to ensure that the members of the board, and in particular the non-executive directors, develop an understanding of the views of major shareholders about the company, for example through direct face-to-face contact, analysts' or brokers' briefings and surveys of shareholder opinion.

E.2: Constructive Use of General Meetings

Main Principle

The board should use general meetings to communicate with investors and to encourage their participation.

Code Provisions

E.2.1. At any general meeting, the company should propose a separate resolution on each substantially separate issue, and should in particular propose a resolution at the AGM relating to the report and accounts. For each resolution, proxy appointment forms should provide shareholders with the option to direct their proxy to vote either for or against the resolution or to withhold their vote. The proxy form and any announcement of the results of a vote should make it clear that a 'vote withheld' is not a vote in law and will not be counted in the calculation of the proportion of the votes for and against the resolution.

E.2.2. The company should ensure that all valid proxy appointments received for general meetings are properly recorded and counted. For each resolution, where a vote has been taken on a show of hands, the company should ensure that the following information is given at the meeting and made available as soon as reasonably practicable on a website which is maintained by or on behalf of the company:

- the number of shares in respect of which proxy appointments have been validly made;
- the number of votes for the resolution;
- the number of votes against the resolution; and
- the number of shares in respect of which the vote was directed to be withheld.

When, in the opinion of the board, a significant proportion of votes have been cast against a resolution at any general meeting, the company should explain when announcing the results of voting what actions it intends to take to understand the reasons behind the vote result.

E.2.3. The chairman should arrange for the chairmen of the audit, remuneration and nomination committees to be available to answer questions at the AGM and for all directors to attend.

E.2.4. The company should arrange for the Notice of the AGM and related papers to be sent to shareholders at least 20 working days before the meeting. For other general meetings this should be at least 14 working days in advance.

Schedule A: The design of performance-related remuneration for executive directors

Balance

The remuneration committee should determine an appropriate balance between fixed and performance-related, immediate and deferred remuneration. Performance conditions, including non-financial metrics where appropriate, should be relevant, stretching and designed to promote the long-term success of the company. Remuneration incentives should be compatible with risk policies and systems. Upper limits should be set and disclosed.

The remuneration committee should consider whether the directors should be eligible for annual bonuses and/or benefits under long-term incentive schemes.

Share-based remuneration

Traditional share option schemes should be weighed against other kinds of long-term incentive scheme. Executive share options should not be offered at a discount save as permitted by the relevant provisions of the Listing Rules.

Any new long-term incentive schemes which are proposed should be approved by shareholders and should preferably replace any existing schemes or, at least, form part of a well-considered overall plan incorporating existing schemes. The total rewards potentially available should not be excessive.

For share-based remuneration the remuneration committee should consider requiring directors to hold a minimum number of shares and to hold shares for a further period after vesting or exercise, including for a period after leaving the company, subject to the need to finance any costs of acquisition and associated tax liabilities. In normal circumstances, shares granted or other forms of deferred remuneration should not vest or be paid, and options should not be exercisable, in less than three years. Longer periods may be appropriate. Grants under executive share option and other long-term incentive schemes should normally be phased rather than awarded in one large block.

Pensions

In general, only basic salary should be pensionable. The remuneration committee should consider the pension consequences and associated costs to the company of basic salary increases and any other changes in pensionable remuneration, especially for directors close to retirement.

Schedule B: Disclosure of corporate governance arrangements

Corporate governance disclosure requirements are set out in three places:

- FCA Disclosure and Transparency Rules (DTR) sub-chapters 7.1 and 7.2, which set out certain mandatory disclosures;
- FCA Listing Rules (LR) 9.8.6 R, 9.8.7 R, and 9.8.7A R, which includes the "comply or explain" requirement; and
- The UK Corporate Governance Code (the Code) – in addition to providing an explanation where they choose not to comply with a provision, companies must disclose specified information in order to comply with certain provisions.

These requirements are summarised below, with the full text contained in the relevant chapters of the FCA Handbook.

The DTR sub-chapters 7.1 and 7.2 apply to issuers whose securities are admitted to trading on a regulated market (this includes all issuers with a Premium or Standard listing). The LR 9.8.6 R, 9.8.7 R and 9.8.7A R and the Code apply to issuers of Premium listed equity shares only.

There is some overlap between the mandatory disclosures required under the DTR and those expected under the Code. Areas of overlap are summarised in the Appendix to this Schedule.

In respect of disclosures relating to the audit committee and the composition and operation of the board and its committees, compliance with the relevant provisions of the Code will result in compliance with the relevant Rules.

Disclosure and Transparency Rules

DTR sub-chapter 7.1 concerns audit committees or bodies carrying out equivalent functions. DTR 7.1.1 R, 7.1.1A R and 7.1.3 R set out requirements relating to the composition and functions of the committee or equivalent body:

- DTR 7.1.1 R states that an issuer must have a body or bodies responsible for performing the functions set out in DTR 7.1.3 R.
- DTR 7.1.1A R requires that a majority of the members of the relevant body must be independent, at least one member must have competence in accounting or auditing, or both, and that members of the relevant body as a whole must have competence relevant to the sector in which the issuer is operating.
- DTR 7.1.2 G states that the requirements for independence and competence in accounting and/or auditing may be satisfied by the same members or by different members of the relevant body.
- DTR 7.1.3 R states that an issuer must ensure that, as a minimum, the relevant body must:
  1. monitor the financial reporting process and submit recommendations or proposal to ensure its integrity;
  2. monitor the effectiveness of the issuer's internal quality control and risk management systems and, where applicable, its internal audit, regarding the financial reporting of the issuer, without breaching its independence;
  3. monitor the statutory audit of the annual and consolidated financial statements, in particular, its performance, taking into account any findings and conclusions by the competent authority under article 26(6) of the Audit Regulation;
  4. review and monitor the independence of the statutory auditor, in accordance with articles 22, 22a, 22b, 24a and 24b of the Audit Directive and article 6 of the Audit Regulation, and in particular the appropriateness of the provision of non-audit services to the issuer in accordance with article 5 of the Audit Regulation;
  5. inform the administrative or supervisory body of the issuer of the outcome of the statutory audit and explain how the statutory audit contributed to the integrity of financial reporting and what the role of the relevant body was in that process;
  6. except when article 16(8) of the Audit Regulation is applied, be responsible for the procedure for the selection of statutory auditor(s) and recommend the statutory auditor(s) to be appointed in accordance with article 16 of the Audit Regulation.

DTR 7.1.5 R sets out what disclosure is required. Specifically:

- DTR 7.1.5 R states that the issuer must make a statement available to the public disclosing which body carries out the functions required by DTR 7.1.3 R and how it is composed.
- DTR 7.1.6 G states that this can be included in the corporate governance statement required under sub-chapter DTR 7.2 (see below).
- DTR 7.1.7 G states that compliance with the relevant provisions of the Code (as set out in the Appendix to this Schedule) will result in compliance with DTR 7.1.1 R to 7.1.5 R.

Sub-chapter 7.2 concerns corporate governance statements. Issuers are required to produce a corporate governance statement that must be either included in the directors' report (DTR 7.2.1 R); or set out in a separate report published together with the annual report; or set out in a document on the issuer's website, in which case there must be a cross-reference in the directors' report (DTR 7.2.9 R).

DTR 7.2.2 R requires that the corporate governance statement must contain a reference to the corporate governance code to which the company is subject (for companies with a Premium listing this is the Code). DTR 7.2.3 R requires that, where that it departs from that code, the company must explain which parts of the code it departs from and the reasons for doing so. DTR 7.2.4 G states that compliance with LR 9.8.6 R (6) (the "comply or explain" rule in relation to the Code) will also satisfy these requirements.

DTR 7.2.5 R, DTR 7.2.6 R, DTR 7.2.7 R and DTR 7.2.10 R set out certain information that must be disclosed in the corporate governance statement:

- DTR 7.2.5 R states that the corporate governance statement must contain a description of the main features of the company's internal control and risk management systems in relation to the financial reporting process. DTR 7.2.10 R states that an issuer which is required to prepare a group directors' report within the meaning of Section 415(2) of the Companies Act 2006 must include in that report a description of the main features of the group's internal control and risk management systems in relation to the financial reporting process for the undertakings included in the consolidation, taken as a whole.
- DTR 7.2.6 R states that the corporate governance statement must contain the information required by paragraph 13(2)(c), (d), (f), (h) and (i) of Schedule 7 to the Large and Medium-sized Companies and Groups (Accounts and Reports) Regulations 2008 (SI 2008/410) where the issuer is subject to the requirements of that paragraph.
- DTR 7.2.7 R states that the corporate governance statement must contain a description of the composition and operation of the issuer's administrative, management and supervisory bodies and their committees. DTR 7.2.8 G states that compliance with the relevant provisions of the Code (as set out in the Appendix to this Schedule) will satisfy these requirements.

Listing Rules

LR 9.8.6 R (for UK incorporated companies) and LR 9.8.7 R (for overseas incorporated companies) state that in the case of a company that has a Premium listing of equity shares, the following items must be included in its annual report and accounts:

- a statement of how the listed company has applied the Main Principles set out in the Code, in a manner that would enable shareholders to evaluate how the principles have been applied;
- a statement as to whether the listed company has:
  - complied throughout the accounting period with all relevant provisions set out in the Code; or
  - not complied throughout the accounting period with all relevant provisions set out in the Code, and if so, setting out:
    i   those provisions, if any, it has not complied with;
    ii   in the case of provisions whose requirements are of a continuing nature, the period within which, if any, it did not comply with some or all of those provisions; and
    iii the company's reasons for non-compliance.

LR 9.8.6 R (3) requires statements by the directors on:

a   the appropriateness of adopting the going concern basis of accounting (containing the information set out in provision C.1.3 of the Code); and
b   their assessment of the prospects of the company (containing the information set out in provision C.2.2 of the Code); prepared in accordance with the 'Guidance on Risk Management, Internal Control and Related Financial and Business Reporting' published by the Financial Reporting Council in September 2014;

The UK Corporate Governance Code

In addition to the "comply or explain" requirement in the LR, the Code includes specific requirements for disclosure which must be provided in order to comply. These are summarised below. The annual report should include:

- a statement of how the board operates, including a high level statement of which types of decisions are to be taken by the board and which are to be delegated to management (A.1.1);
- the names of the chairman, the deputy chairman (where there is one), the chief executive, the senior independent director and the chairmen and members of the board committees (A.1.2);
- the number of meetings of the board and those committees and individual attendance by directors (A.1.2);
- where a chief executive is appointed chairman, the reasons for their appointment (this only needs to be done in the annual report following the appointment) (A.3.1);
- the names of the non-executive directors whom the board determines to be independent, with reasons where necessary (B.1.1);

- a separate section describing the work of the nomination committee, including the process it has used in relation to board appointments; a description of the board's policy on diversity, including gender; any measurable objectives that it has set for implementing the policy, and progress on achieving the objectives. An explanation should be given if neither external search consultancy nor open advertising has been used in the appointment of a chairman or a non-executive director. Where an external search consultancy has been used it should be identified and a statement made as to whether it has any other connection with the company (B.2.4);
- the impact of any changes to the other significant commitments of the chairman during the year should explained (B.3.1);
- a statement of how performance evaluation of the board, its committees and its directors has been conducted (B.6.1). Where an external facilitator has been used, they should be identified and a statement made as to whether they have any other connection to the company (B.6.2);
- an explanation from the directors of their responsibility for preparing the accounts and a statement that they consider that the annual report and accounts, taken as a whole, is fair, balanced and understandable and provides the information necessary for shareholders to assess the company's position and performance, business model and strategy. There should also be a statement by the auditor about their reporting responsibilities (C.1.1);
- an explanation from the directors of the basis on which the company generates or preserves value over the longer term (the business model) and the strategy for delivering the objectives of the company (C.1.2);
- a statement from the directors whether they considered it appropriate to adopt the going concern basis of accounting in preparing them, and identify any material uncertainties to the company's ability to continue to do so over a period of at least twelve months from the date of approval of the financial statements (C.1.3);
- confirmation by the directors that they have carried out a robust assessment of the principal risks facing the company, including those that would threaten its business model, future performance, solvency or liquidity. The directors should describe the risks and explain how they are being managed or mitigated (C.2.1);
- a statement from the directors explaining how they have assessed the prospects of the company (taking account of the company's current position and principal risks), over what period they have done so and why they consider that period to be appropriate. The directors should state whether they have a reasonable expectation that the company will be able to continue in operation and meet its liabilities as they fall due over the period of their assessment, drawing attention to any qualifications or assumptions as necessary (C.2.2);
- a report on the board's review of the effectiveness of the company's risk management and internal controls systems (C.2.3);
- where there is no internal audit function, the reasons for the absence of such a function (C.3.6);
- where the board does not accept the audit committee's recommendation on the appointment, reappointment or removal of an external auditor, a statement from the audit committee explaining the recommendation and the reasons why the board has taken a different position (C.3.7);
- a separate section describing the work of the audit committee in discharging its responsibilities, including: the significant issues that it considered in relation to the financial statements, and how these issues were addressed; an explanation of how it has assessed the effectiveness of the external audit process and the approach taken to the appointment or reappointment of the external auditor, including the length of tenure of the current audit firm, when a tender was last conducted and advance notice of any retendering plans; and, if the external auditor provides non-audit services, an explanation of how auditor objectivity and independence is safeguarded (C.3.8);
- a description of the work of the remuneration committee as required under the Large and Medium-Sized Companies and Groups (Accounts and Reports) Regulations 2013, including, where an executive director serves as a nonexecutive director elsewhere, whether or not the director will retain such earnings and, if so, what the remuneration is (D.1.2);
- where remuneration consultants are appointed they should be identified and a statement made as to whether they have any other connection with the company (D.2.1); and
- the steps the board has taken to ensure that members of the board, and in particular the non-executive directors, develop an understanding of the views of major shareholders about their company (E.1.2).

The following information should be made available (which may be met by placing the information on a website that is maintained by or on behalf of the company):

- the terms of reference of the nomination, audit and remuneration committees, explaining their role and the authority delegated to them by the board (B.2.1, C.3.3 and D.2.1); and
- the terms and conditions of appointment of non-executive directors (B.3.2) (see footnote 9).

The board should set out to shareholders in the papers accompanying a resolution to elect or re-elect directors:

- sufficient biographical details to enable shareholders to take an informed decision on their election or re-election (B.7.1);
- why they believe an individual should be elected to a non-executive role (B.7.2); and
- on re-election of a non-executive director, confirmation from the chairman that, following formal performance evaluation, the individual's performance continues to be effective and to demonstrate commitment to the role (B.7.2).

The board should set out to shareholders in the papers recommending appointment or reappointment of an external auditor:

- if the board does not accept the audit committee's recommendation, a statement from the audit committee explaining the recommendation and from the board setting out reasons why they have taken a different position (C.3.7).

Additional guidance

The FRC publishes guidance on the strategic report, risk management, internal control, business and financial reporting and audit committees, which relate to Section C of the Code. These guidance notes are available on the FRC website.

Notes

1   References to shareholders in this section also apply to intermediaries and agents employed to assist shareholders in scrutinising governance arrangements.
2   For directors of UK incorporated companies, these duties are set out in the Sections 170 to 177 of the Companies Act 2006.
3   Provisions A.1.1 and A.1.2 overlap with FCA Rule DTR 7.2.7 R; Provision A.1.2 also overlaps with DTR 7.1.5 R (see Schedule B).
4   Compliance or otherwise with this provision need only be reported for the year in which the appointment is made
5   A.3.1 states that the chairman should, on appointment, meet the independence criteria set out in this provision, but thereafter the test of independence is not appropriate in relation to the chairman.
6   A smaller company is one that is below the FTSE 350 throughout the year immediately prior to the reporting year.
7   The requirement to make the information available would be met by including the information on a website that is maintained by or on behalf of the company.
8   This provision overlaps with FCA Rule DTR 7.2.7 R (see Schedule B).
9   The terms and conditions of appointment of non-executive directors should be made available for inspection by any person at the company's registered office during normal business hours and at the AGM (for 15 minutes prior to the meeting and during the meeting).
10   This requirement may be met by the disclosures about the audit scope and responsibilities of the auditor included, or referred to, in the auditor's report pursuant to the requirements of ISA (UK) 700 'Forming an Opinion and Reporting on Financial Statements' – Paragraphs 38-40. Copies are available from the FRC website.
11   Section 414C(8) (a) and (b) of the Companies Act 2006 requires a description of a company's business model and strategy as part of the Strategic Report that forms part of the annual report. Guidance as to the matters that should be considered in an explanation of the business model and strategy is provided in the FRC's "Guidance on the Strategic Report". Copies are available from the FRC website.
12   This provision overlaps with FCA Rules LR 9.8.6 R (3) (see Schedule B). Additional information relating to C.1.3 and C.2 can be found in "Guidance on Risk Management, Internal Control and Related Financial and Business Reporting". Copies are available from the FRC website.
13   This provision overlaps with FCA Rules LR 9.8.6 (3) R (see Schedule B).
14   In addition FCA Rule DTR 7.2.5 R requires companies to describe the main features of the internal control and risk management systems in relation to the financial reporting process.
15   "Guidance on Audit Committees" suggests means of applying this part of the Code. Copies are available from the FRC website.
16   See footnote 6.
17   This provision overlaps with FCA Rule DTR 7.1.1A R (see Schedule B).
18   This provision overlaps with FCA Rules DTR 7.1.3 R (see Schedule B).

19 See footnote 7.
20 This overlaps with Part 3 of The Statutory Audit Services for Large Companies Market Investigation (Mandatory Use of Competitive Tender Processes and Audit Committee Responsibilities) Order 2014 and the requirements of Chapter 2 of Part 16 of the Companies Act 2006 as inserted by the Statutory Auditors and Third Country Auditors Regulations 2016 on the appointment of auditors to public companies that are Public Interest Entities.
21 This provision overlaps with FCA Rules DTR 7.1.5 R and 7.2.7 R (see Schedule B).
22 This overlaps with Part 4 of The Statutory Audit Services for Large Companies Market Investigation (Mandatory Use of Competitive Tender Processes and Audit Committee Responsibilities) Order 2014.
23 As required for UK incorporated companies under the Large and Medium-Sized Companies and Groups (Accounts and Reports) Regulations 2013.
24 See footnote 6.
25 This provision overlaps with FCA Rule DTR 7.2.7 R (see Schedule B).
26 Listing Rules LR 9.4. Copies are available from the FCA website.
27 Nothing in these principles or provisions should be taken to override the general requirements of law to treat shareholders equally in access to information.

APPENDIX 2

G20/OECD Principles of Corporate Governance 2015

I. Ensuring the basis for an effective corporate governance framework

The corporate governance framework should promote transparent and fair markets, and the efficient allocation of resources. It should be consistent with the rule of law and support effective supervision and enforcement.

A. The corporate governance framework should be developed with a view to its impact on overall economic performance, market integrity and the incentives it creates for market participants and the promotion of transparent and well-functioning markets.

B. The legal and regulatory requirements that affect corporate governance practices should be consistent with the rule of law, transparent and enforceable.

C. The division of responsibilities among different authorities should be clearly articulated and designed to serve the public interest.

D. Stock market regulation should support effective corporate governance.

E. Supervisory, regulatory and enforcement authorities should have the authority, integrity and resources to fulfil their duties in a professional and objective manner. Moreover, their rulings should be timely, transparent and fully explained.

F. Cross-border co-operation should be enhanced, including through bilateral and multilateral arrangements for exchange of information.

II. The rights and equitable treatment of shareholders and key ownership functions

The corporate governance framework should protect and facilitate the exercise of shareholders' rights and ensure the equitable treatment of all shareholders, including minority and foreign shareholders. All shareholders should have the opportunity to obtain effective redress for violation of their rights.

A. Basic shareholder rights should include the right to: 1) secure methods of ownership registration; 2) convey or transfer shares; 3) obtain relevant and material information on the corporation on a timely and regular basis; 4) participate and vote in general shareholder meetings; 5) elect and remove members of the board; and 6) share in the profits of the corporation.

B. Shareholders should be sufficiently informed about, and have the right to approve or participate in, decisions concerning fundamental corporate changes such as: 1) amendments to the statutes, or articles of incorporation or similar governing documents of the company; 2) the authorisation of additional shares; and 3) extraordinary transactions, including the transfer of all or substantially all assets, that in effect result in the sale of the company..

C. Shareholders should have the opportunity to participate effectively and vote in general shareholder meetings and should be informed of the rules, including voting procedures that govern general shareholder meetings:

1. Shareholders should be furnished with sufficient and timely information concerning the date, location and agenda of general meetings, as well as full and timely information regarding the issues to be decided at the meeting.

2. Processes and procedures for general shareholder meetings should allow for equitable treatment of all shareholders. Company procedures should not make it unduly difficult or expensive to cast votes.

3. Shareholders should have the opportunity to ask questions to the board, including questions relating to the annual external audit, to place items on the agenda of general meetings, and to propose resolutions, subject to reasonable limitations.

4. Effective shareholder participation in key corporate governance decisions, such as the nomination and election of board members, should be facilitated. Shareholders should be able to make their views known, including through votes at shareholder meetings, on the remuneration of board members and/or key executives, as applicable. The equity component of compensation schemes for board members and employees should be subject to shareholder approval.

5. Shareholders should be able to vote in person or in absentia, and equal effect should be given to votes whether cast in person or in absentia.

6. Impediments to cross border voting should be eliminated.

D. Shareholders, including institutional shareholders, should be allowed to consult with each other on issues concerning their basic shareholder rights as defined in the Principles, subject to exceptions to prevent abuse.

E. All shareholders of the same series of a class should be treated equally. Capital structures and arrangements that enable certain shareholders to obtain a degree of influence or control disproportionate to their equity ownership should be disclosed.

1. Within any series of a class, all shares should carry the same rights. All investors should be able to obtain information about the rights attached to all series and classes of shares before they purchase. Any changes in economic or voting rights should be subject to approval by those classes of shares which are negatively affected.

2. The disclosure of capital structures and control arrangements should be required.

F. Related-party transactions should be approved and conducted in a manner that ensures proper management of conflict of interest and protects the interest of the company and its shareholders.

1. Conflicts of interest inherent in related-party transactions should be addressed.

2. Members of the board and key executives should be required to disclose to the board whether they, directly, indirectly or on behalf of third parties, have a material interest in any transaction or matter directly affecting the corporation.

G. Minority shareholders should be protected from abusive actions by, or in the interest of, controlling shareholders acting either directly or indirectly, and should have effective means of redress. Abusive self-dealing should be prohibited.

H. Markets for corporate control should be allowed to function in an efficient and transparent manner.

1. The rules and procedures governing the acquisition of corporate control in the capital markets, and extraordinary transactions such as mergers, and sales of substantial portions of corporate assets, should be clearly articulated and disclosed so that investors understand their rights and recourse. Transactions should occur at transparent prices and under fair conditions that protect the rights of all shareholders according to their class.

2. Anti-take-over devices should not be used to shield management and the board from accountability.

III. Institutional investors, stock markets, and other intermediaries

The corporate governance framework should provide sound incentives throughout the investment chain and provide for stock markets to function in a way that contributes to good corporate governance.

A. Institutional investors acting in a fiduciary capacity should disclose their corporate governance and voting policies with respect to their investments, including the procedures that they have in place for deciding on the use of their voting rights.

B. Votes should be cast by custodians or nominees in line with the directions of the beneficial owner of the shares.

C. Institutional investors acting in a fiduciary capacity should disclose how they manage material conflicts of interest that may affect the exercise of key ownership rights regarding their investments.

D. The corporate governance framework should require that proxy advisors, analysts, brokers, rating agencies and others that provide analysis or advice relevant to decisions by investors, disclose and minimise conflicts of interest that might compromise the integrity of their analysis or advice.

E. Insider trading and market manipulation should be prohibited and the applicable rules enforced.

F. For companies who are listed in a jurisdiction other than their jurisdiction of incorporation, the applicable corporate governance laws and regulations should be clearly disclosed. In the case of cross listings, the criteria and procedure for recognising the listing requirements of the primary listing should be transparent and documented.

G. Stock markets should provide fair and efficient price discovery as a means to help promote effective corporate governance.

IV. The role of stakeholders in corporate governance

The corporate governance framework should recognise the rights of stakeholders established by law or through mutual agreements and encourage active co-operation between corporations and stakeholders in creating wealth, jobs, and the sustainability of financially sound enterprises.

A. The rights of stakeholders that are established by law or through mutual agreements are to be respected.

B. Where stakeholder interests are protected by law, stakeholders should have the opportunity to obtain effective redress for violation of their rights.

C. Mechanisms for employee participation should be permitted to develop.

D. Where stakeholders participate in the corporate governance process, they should have access to relevant, sufficient and reliable information on a timely and regular basis.

E. Stakeholders, including individual employees and their representative bodies, should be able to freely communicate their concerns about illegal or unethical practices to the board and to the competent public authorities and their rights should not be compromised for doing this.

F. The corporate governance framework should be complemented by an effective, efficient insolvency framework and by effective enforcement of creditor rights.

V. Disclosure and Transparency

The corporate governance framework should ensure that timely and accurate disclosure is made on all material matters regarding the corporation, including the financial situation, performance, ownership, and governance of the company.

A. Disclosure should include, but not be limited to, material information on:
   1. The financial and operating results of the company.
   2. Company objectives and non-financial information.
   3. Major share ownership, including beneficial owners, and voting rights.
   4. Remuneration of members of the board and key executives.
   5. Information about board members, including their qualifications, the selection process, other company directorships and whether they are regarded as independent by the board.
   6. Related party transactions.
   7. Foreseeable risk factors.
   8. Issues regarding employees and other stakeholders.
   9. Governance structures and policies, including the content of any corporate governance code or policy and the process by which it is implemented.

B. Information should be prepared and disclosed in accordance with high quality standards of accounting and financial and non-financial reporting.

C. An annual audit should be conducted by an independent, competent and qualified, auditor in accordance with high-quality auditing standards in order to provide an external and objective assurance to the board and shareholders that the financial statements fairly represent the financial position and performance of the company in all material respects.

D. External auditors should be accountable to the shareholders and owe a duty to the company to exercise due professional care in the conduct of the audit.

E. Channels for disseminating information should provide for equal, timely and cost-efficient access to relevant information by users.

VI. The responsibilities of the board

The corporate governance framework should ensure the strategic guidance of the company, the effective monitoring of management by the board, and the board's accountability to the company and the shareholders.

A. Board members should act on a fully informed basis, in good faith, with due diligence and care, and in the best interest of the company and the shareholders.

B. Where board decisions may affect different shareholder groups differently, the board should treat all shareholders fairly.

C. The board should apply high ethical standards. It should take into account the interests of stakeholders.

D. The board should fulfil certain key functions, including:
1. Reviewing and guiding corporate strategy, major plans of action, risk management policies and procedures, annual budgets and business plans; setting performance objectives; monitoring implementation and corporate performance; and overseeing major capital expenditures, acquisitions and divestitures.
2. Monitoring the effectiveness of the company's governance practices and making changes as needed.
3. Selecting, compensating, monitoring and, when necessary, replacing key executives and overseeing succession planning.
4. Aligning key executive and board remuneration with the longer term interests of the company and its shareholders.
5. Ensuring a formal and transparent board nomination and election process.
6. Monitoring and managing potential conflicts of interest of management, board members and shareholders, including misuse of corporate assets and abuse in related party transactions.
7. Ensuring the integrity of the corporation's accounting and financial reporting systems, including the independent audit, and that appropriate systems of control are in place, in particular, systems for risk management, financial and operational control, and compliance with the law and relevant standards.
8. Overseeing the process of disclosure and communications.

E. The board should be able to exercise objective independent judgement on corporate affairs.
1. Boards should consider assigning a sufficient number of non-executive board members capable of exercising independent judgement to tasks where there is a potential for conflict of interest. Examples of such key responsibilities are ensuring the integrity of financial and non-financial reporting, the review of related party transactions, nomination of board members and key executives, and board remuneration.
2. Boards should consider setting up specialised committees to support the full board in performing its functions, particularly in respect to audit, and, depending upon the company's size and risk profile, also in respect to risk management and remuneration. When committees of the board are established, their mandate, composition and working procedures should be well defined and disclosed by the board.
3. Board members should be able to commit themselves effectively to their responsibilities.
4. Boards should regularly carry out evaluations to appraise their performance and assess whether they possess the right mix of background and competences.

F. In order to fulfil their responsibilities, board members should have access to accurate, relevant and timely information.

G. When employee representation on the board is mandated, mechanisms should be developed to facilitate access to information and training for employee representatives, so that this representation is exercised effectively and best contributes to the enhancement of board skills, information and independence.

APPENDIX 3
FRC Codes and Guidance and Other Sources of Information

FRC Guidance for boards and board committees

The FRC issues guidance and other publications to assist boards and board committees in considering how to apply the UK Corporate Governance Code to their particular circumstances. These publications cover:

1. Board effectiveness 2011
2. Audit committees 2016
3. Risk management, internal control and related financial and business reporting 2014

Other FRC Corporate Governance & Stewardship publications
The UK Stewardship Code 2012 sets out good practice for institutional investors on engaging with the companies in which they invest

Corporate Culture and the Role of Boards 2016

This report seeks to address how boards and executive management can steer corporate behaviour to create a culture that will deliver sustainable good performance. This report looks at the increasing importance which corporate culture plays in delivering long-term business and economic success. In doing so it focuses on the role of the board in shaping, monitoring and overseeing culture.

These FRC documents can be downloaded from the FRC website. Printed copies of the guidance notes can be obtained free of charge from FRC publications at www.frcpublications.com.

Directors' Duties

The legal duties of directors of UK Companies are set out in sections 170 to 177 of the Companies Act 2006. The Act can be found at:

www.legislation.gov.uk/ukpga/2006/46/contents

Other Sources of Information

Note: this is not a comprehensive list. Other sources of information and advice are available.
ICSA provides guidance on a wide range of board-related matters; for example, specimen terms of reference for board committees. This guidance can be found at:

www.icsa.org.uk/policy-guidance?c=1

The Institute of Directors (IoD) provides a wide range of guidance notes for directors, which are available at:

www.iod.com/Home/Business-Information-and-Advice/Being-a-Director/

Smaller listed companies may find the guidance produced by the Quoted Companies Alliance (QCA) useful. This can be found at:

www.theqca.com/shop/guides/

APPENDIX 4

FRC Guidance on Board Effectiveness 2011

March 2011

Contents

Preface Paragraph Numbers

Preface

The Guidance on Board Effectiveness is one of a suite of guidance notes issued by the Financial Reporting Council (FRC) to assist companies in applying the principles of the UK Corporate Governance Code. It replaces 'Good Practice Suggestions from the Higgs Report' (known as 'the Higgs Guidance'), which was last issued in 2006.

This guidance relates primarily to Sections A and B of the Code on the leadership and effectiveness of the board. As with the separate guidance notes on audit committees and internal control, the new guidance is not intended to be prescriptive. It does not set out 'the right way' to apply the Code. Rather it is intended to stimulate boards' thinking on how they can carry out their role most effectively. Ultimately it is for individual boards to decide on the governance arrangements most appropriate to their circumstances, and interpret the Code and guidance accordingly.

The guidance does not seek to address all the issues covered in Sections A and B of the Code, but only those where consultation with companies, individual board members and investors suggested that further guidance might be helpful. Nor does it include all of the material contained in the Higgs Guidance; for example, draft letters of appointment and terms of reference for board committees.

The UK Corporate Governance Code has evolved since it was first introduced in 1992. It has always placed great importance on clarity of roles and responsibilities, and on accountability and transparency. It has become increasingly clear in the intervening period that, while these are necessary for good governance, they are not sufficient on their own. Boards need to think deeply about the way in which they carry out their role and the behaviours that they display, not just about the structures and processes that they put in place.

This change of emphasis is reflected in the most recent edition of the UK Corporate Governance Code, published in 2010, and also in this guidance. For example, boards are encouraged to consider how the way in which decisions are taken might affect the quality of those decisions, and the factors to be taken into account when constructing the board and reviewing its performance. The FRC hopes that this guidance will assist in those considerations.

The FRC would like to express its gratitude to the Institute of Chartered Secretaries and Administrators and the Steering Group it established under the chairmanship of Sir John Egan for consulting on and developing this guidance on the FRC's behalf.

BARONESS HOGG
Chairman, Financial Reporting Council

1. The Role of the Board and Directors

An Effective Board

1.1. The board's role is to provide entrepreneurial leadership of the company within a framework of prudent and effective controls which enables risk to be assessed and managed.

1.2. An effective board develops and promotes its collective vision of the company's purpose, its culture, its values and the behaviours it wishes to promote in conducting its business. In particular it:

- provides direction for management;
- demonstrates ethical leadership, displaying – and promoting throughout the company – behaviours consistent with the culture and values it has defined for the organisation;
- creates a performance culture that drives value creation without exposing the company to excessive risk of value destruction;
- makes well-informed and high-quality decisions based on a clear line of sight into the business;
- creates the right framework for helping directors meet their statutory duties under the Companies Act 2006, and/or other relevant statutory and regulatory regimes;
- is accountable, particularly to those that provide the company's capital; and
- thinks carefully about its governance arrangements and embraces evaluation of their effectiveness.

1.3. An effective board should not necessarily be a comfortable place. Challenge, as well as teamwork, is an essential feature. Diversity in board composition is an important driver of a board's effectiveness – creating a breadth of perspective among directors, and breaking down a tendency towards 'group think'.

The Role of the Chairman

1.4. Good boards are created by good chairmen. The chairman creates the conditions for overall board and individual director effectiveness.

1.5. The chairman should demonstrate the highest standards of integrity and probity, and set clear expectations concerning the company's culture, values and behaviours, and the style and tone of board discussions.

1.6. The chairman, with the help of the executive directors and the company secretary, sets the agenda for the board's deliberations.

1.7. The chairman's role includes:

- demonstrating ethical leadership;
- setting a board agenda which is primarily focused on strategy, performance, value creation and accountability, and ensuring that issues relevant to these areas are reserved for board decision;
- ensuring a timely flow of high-quality supporting information;
- making certain that the board determines the nature, and extent, of the significant risks the company is willing to embrace in the implementation of its strategy, and that there are no 'no go' areas which prevent directors from operating effective oversight in this area;
- regularly considering succession planning and the composition of the board;

- making certain that the board has effective decision-making processes and applies sufficient challenge to major proposals;
- ensuring the board's committees are properly structured with appropriate terms of reference;
- encouraging all board members to engage in board and committee meetings by drawing on their skills, experience, knowledge and, where appropriate, independence;
- fostering relationships founded on mutual respect and open communication – both in and outside the boardroom – between the non-executive directors and the executive team;
- developing productive working relationships with all executive directors, and the CEO in particular, providing support and advice while respecting executive responsibility;
- consulting the senior independent director on board matters in accordance with the Code;
- taking the lead on issues of director development, including through induction programmes for new directors and regular reviews with all directors;
- acting on the results of board evaluation;
- being aware of, and responding to, his or her own development needs, including people and other skills, especially when taking on the role for the first time; and
- ensuring effective communication with shareholders and other stakeholders and, in particular, that all directors are made aware of the views of those who provide the company's capital.

1.8. The chairman of each board committee fulfils an important leadership role similar to that of the chairman of the board, particularly in creating the conditions for overall committee and individual director effectiveness.

The Role of the Senior Independent Director

1.9. In normal times, the senior independent director should act as a sounding board for the chairman, providing support for the chairman in the delivery of his or her objectives, and leading the evaluation of the chairman on behalf of the other directors, as set out in the Code. The senior independent director might also take responsibility for an orderly succession process for the chairman.

1.10. When the board is undergoing a period of stress, however, the senior independent director's role becomes critically important. He or she is expected to work with the chairman and other directors, and/or shareholders, to resolve significant issues. Boards should ensure they have a clear understanding of when the senior independent director might intervene in order to maintain board and company stability. Examples might include where:

- there is a dispute between the chairman and CEO;
- shareholders or non-executive directors have expressed concerns that are not being addressed by the chairman or CEO;
- the strategy being followed by the chairman and CEO is not supported by the entire board;
- the relationship between the chairman and CEO is particularly close, and decisions are being made without the approval of the full board; or
- succession planning is being ignored.

1.11. These issues should be considered when defining the role of the senior independent director, which should be set out in writing.

The Role of Executive Directors

1.12. Executive directors have the same duties as other members of a unitary board. These duties extend to the whole of the business, and not just that part of it covered by their individual executive roles. Nor should executive directors see themselves only as members of the CEO's executive team when engaged in board business. Taking the wider view can help achieve the advantage of a unitary system: greater knowledge, involvement and commitment at the point of decision. The chairman should make certain that executives are aware of their wider responsibilities when joining the board, and ensure they receive appropriate induction, and regular training, to enable them to fulfil the role. Executive directors are also likely to be able to broaden their understanding of their board responsibilities if they take up a non-executive director position on another board.

1.13. The CEO is the most senior executive director on the board with responsibility for proposing strategy to the board, and for delivering the strategy as agreed. The CEO's relationship with the chairman is a key relationship that can help the board be more effective. The Code states that the differing responsibilities of the chairman and the CEO should be set out in writing and agreed by the board. Particular attention should be paid to areas of potential overlap.

1.14. The CEO has, with the support of the executive team, primary responsibility for setting an example to the company's employees, and communicating to them the expectations of the board in relation to the company's culture, values and behaviours. The CEO is responsible for supporting the chairman to make certain that appropriate standards of governance permeate through all parts of the organisation. The CEO will make certain that the board is made aware, when appropriate, of the views of employees on issues of relevance to the business.

1.15. The CEO will ensure the board knows the executive directors' views on business issues in order to improve the standard of discussion in the boardroom and, prior to final decision on an issue, explain in a balanced way any divergence of view in the executive team.

1.16. The CFO has a particular responsibility to deliver high-quality information to the board on the financial position of the company.

1.17. Executive directors have the most intimate knowledge of the company and its capabilities when developing and presenting proposals, and when exercising judgement, particularly on matters of strategy. They should appreciate that constructive challenge from non-executive directors is an essential aspect of good governance, and should encourage their non-executive colleagues to test their proposals in the light of the non-executives' wider experience outside the company. The chairman and the CEO should ensure that this process is properly followed.

The Role of Non-Executive Directors

1.18. A non-executive director should, on appointment, devote time to a comprehensive, formal and tailored induction which should extend beyond the boardroom. Initiatives such as partnering a non-executive director with an executive board member may speed up the process of him or her acquiring an understanding of the main areas of business activity, especially areas involving significant risk. The director should expect to visit, and talk with, senior and middle managers in these areas.

1.19. Non-executive directors should devote time to developing and refreshing their knowledge and skills, including those of communication, to ensure that they continue to make a positive contribution to the board. Being well informed about the company, and having a strong command of the issues relevant to the business, will generate the respect of the other directors.

1.20. Non-executive directors need to make sufficient time available to discharge their responsibilities effectively. The letter of appointment should state the minimum time that the non-executive director will be required to spend on the company's business, and seek the individual's confirmation that he or she can devote that amount of time to the role, consistent with other commitments. The letter should also indicate the possibility of additional time commitment when the company is undergoing a period of particularly increased activity, such as an acquisition or takeover, or as a result of some major difficulty with one or more of its operations.

1.21. Non-executive directors have a responsibility to uphold high standards of integrity and probity. They should support the chairman and executive directors in instilling the appropriate culture, values and behaviours in the boardroom and beyond.

1.22. Non-executive directors should insist on receiving high-quality information sufficiently in advance so that there can be thorough consideration of the issues prior to, and informed debate and challenge at, board meetings. High-quality information is that which is appropriate for making decisions on the issue at hand – it should be accurate, clear, comprehensive, up-to-date and timely; contain a summary of the contents of any paper; and inform the director of what is expected of him or her on that issue.

1.23. Non-executive directors should take into account the views of shareholders and other stakeholders, because these views may provide different perspectives on the company and its performance.

2. Board Support and the Role of the Company Secretary

2.1. The requirement for a company secretary of a public company is specified in section 271 of the Companies Act 2006. The obligations and responsibilities of the company secretary outlined in the Act, and also in the Code, necessitate him or her playing a leading role in the good governance of the company by supporting the chairman and helping the board and its committees to function efficiently.

2.2. The company secretary should report to the chairman on all board governance matters. This does not preclude the company secretary also reporting to the CEO in relation to his or her other executive management responsibilities. The appointment and removal of the company secretary should be a matter for the board as a whole, and the remuneration of the company secretary might be determined by the remuneration committee.

2.3. The company secretary should ensure the presentation of high-quality information to the board and its committees. The company secretary can also add value by fulfilling, or procuring the fulfilment of, other requirements of the Code on behalf of the chairman, in particular director induction and development. This should be in a manner that is appropriate to the particular director, and which has the objective of enhancing that director's effectiveness in the board or board committees, consistent with the results of the board's evaluation processes. The chairman and the company secretary should periodically review whether the board and the company's other governance processes, for example board and committee evaluation, are fit for purpose, and consider any improvements or initiatives that could strengthen the governance of the company.

2.4. The company secretary's effectiveness can be enhanced by his or her ability to build relationships of mutual trust with the chairman, the senior independent director and the non-executive directors, while maintaining the confidence of executive director colleagues.

3. Decision Making

3.1. Well-informed and high-quality decision making is a critical requirement for a board to be effective and does not happen by accident. Flawed decisions can be made with the best of intentions, with competent individuals believing passionately that they are making a sound judgement, when they are not. Many of the factors which lead to poor decision making are predictable and preventable. Boards can minimise the risk of poor decisions by investing time in the design of their decision-making policies and processes, including the contribution of committees.

3.2. Good decision-making capability can be facilitated by:
- high-quality board documentation;
- obtaining expert opinions when necessary;
- allowing time for debate and challenge, especially for complex, contentious or business-critical issues;
- achieving timely closure; and
- providing clarity on the actions required, and timescales and responsibilities.

3.3. Boards should be aware of factors which can limit effective decision making, such as:
- a dominant personality or group of directors on the board, which can inhibit contribution from other directors;
- insufficient attention to risk, and treating risk as a compliance issue rather than as part of the decision-making process – especially cases where the level of risk involved in a project could endanger the stability and sustainability of the business itself;
- failure to recognise the value implications of running the business on the basis of self-interest and other poor ethical standards;

- a reluctance to involve non-executive directors, or of matters being brought to the board for sign-off rather than debate;
- complacent or intransigent attitudes;
- a weak organisational culture; or
- inadequate information or analysis.

3.4.   Most complex decisions depend on judgement, but the judgement of even the most well-intentioned and experienced leaders can, in certain circumstances, be distorted. Some factors known to distort judgement in decision making are conflicts of interest, emotional attachments, and inappropriate reliance on previous experience and previous decisions. For significant decisions, therefore, a board may wish to consider extra steps, for example:

- describing in board papers the process that has been used to arrive at and challenge the proposal prior to presenting it to the board, thereby allowing directors not involved in the project to assess the appropriateness of the process as a precursor to assessing the merits of the project itself; or
- where appropriate, putting in place additional safeguards to reduce the risk of distorted judgements by, for example, commissioning an independent report, seeking advice from an expert, introducing a devil's advocate to provide challenge, establishing a sole purpose sub-committee, or convening additional meetings. Some chairmen favour separate discussions for important decisions; for example, concept, proposal for discussion, proposal for decision. This gives executive directors more opportunity to put the case at the earlier stages, and all directors the opportunity to share concerns or challenge assumptions well in advance of the point of decision.

3.5.   Boards can benefit from reviewing past decisions, particularly ones with poor outcomes. A review should not focus just on the merits of the decision itself but also on the decision-making process.

4. Board Composition and Succession Planning

4.1.   Appointing directors who are able to make a positive contribution is one of the key elements of board effectiveness. Directors will be more likely to make good decisions and maximise the opportunities for the company's success in the longer term if the right skill sets are present in the boardroom. This includes the appropriate range and balance of skills, experience, knowledge and independence. Non-executive directors should possess critical skills of value to the board and relevant to the challenges facing the company.

4.2.   The nomination committee, usually led by the chairman, should be responsible for board recruitment. The process should be continuous and proactive, and should take into account the company's agreed strategic priorities. The aim should be to secure a boardroom which achieves the right balance between challenge and teamwork, and fresh input and thinking, while maintaining a cohesive board.

4.3.   It is important to consider a diversity of personal attributes among board candidates, including: intellect, critical assessment and judgement, courage, openness, honesty and tact; and the ability to listen, forge relationships and develop trust. Diversity of psychological type, background and gender is important to ensure that a board is not composed solely of like-minded individuals. A board requires directors who have the intellectual capability to suggest change to a proposed strategy, and to promulgate alternatives.

4.4.   Given the importance of committees in many companies' decision-making structures, it will be important to recruit non-executives with the necessary technical skills and knowledge relating to the committees' subject matter, as well as the potential to assume the role of committee chairman.

4.5.   The chairman's vision for achieving the optimal board composition will help the nomination committee review the skills required, identify the gaps, develop transparent appointment criteria and inform succession planning. The nomination committee should periodically assess whether the desired outcome has been achieved, and propose changes to the process as necessary.

4.6.   Executive directors may be recruited from external sources, but companies should also develop internal talent and capability. Initiatives might include middle management development programmes, facilitating engagement from time to time with non-executive directors, and partnering and mentoring schemes.

4.7. Good board appointments do not depend only on the nomination committee. A prospective director should carry out sufficient due diligence to understand the company, appreciate the time commitment involved, and assess the likelihood that he or she will be able to make a positive contribution.

5. Evaluating the Performance of the Board and Directors

5.1. Boards continually need to monitor and improve their performance. This can be achieved through board evaluation, which provides a powerful and valuable feedback mechanism for improving board effectiveness, maximising strengths and highlighting areas for further development. The evaluation process should aim to be objective and rigorous.

5.2. Like induction and board development, evaluation should be bespoke in its formulation and delivery. The chairman has overall responsibility for the process, and should select an appropriate approach and act on its outcome. The senior independent director should lead the process which evaluates the performance of the chairman. Chairs of board committees should also be responsible for the evaluation of their committees.

5.3. The outcome of a board evaluation should be shared with the whole board and fed back, as appropriate, into the board's work on composition, the design of induction and development programmes, and other relevant areas. It may be useful for a company to have a review loop to consider how effective the board evaluation process has been.

5.4. The Code recommends that FTSE 350 companies have externally facilitated board evaluations at least every three years. External facilitation can add value by introducing a fresh perspective and new ways of thinking. It may also be useful in particular circumstances, such as when there has been a change of chairman, there is a known problem around the board table requiring tactful handling, or there is an external perception that the board is, or has been, ineffective.

5.5. Whether facilitated externally or internally, evaluations should explore how effective the board is as a unit, as well as the effectiveness of the contributions made by individual directors. Some areas which may be considered, although they are neither prescriptive nor exhaustive, include:

- the mix of skills, experience, knowledge and diversity on the board, in the context of the challenges facing the company;
- clarity of, and leadership given to, the purpose, direction and values of the company;
- succession and development plans;
- how the board works together as a unit, and the tone set by the chairman and the CEO;
- key board relationships, particularly chairman/CEO, chairman/senior independent director, chairman/company secretary and executive/non-executive;
- effectiveness of individual non-executive and executive directors;
- clarity of the senior independent director's role;
- effectiveness of board committees, and how they are connected with the main board;
- quality of the general information provided on the company and its performance;
- quality of papers and presentations to the board;
- quality of discussions around individual proposals;
- process the chairman uses to ensure sufficient debate for major decisions or contentious issues;
- effectiveness of the secretariat;
- clarity of the decision processes and authorities;
- processes for identifying and reviewing risks; and

- how the board communicates with, and listens and responds to, shareholders and other stakeholders.

6. Audit, Risk and Remuneration

6.1.   While the board may make use of committees to assist its consideration of audit, risk and remuneration, it retains responsibility for, and makes the final decisions on, all of these areas. The chairman should ensure that sufficient time is allowed at the board for discussion of these issues. All directors should familiarise themselves with the associated provisions of the UK Corporate Governance Code and its related guidance, and any relevant regulatory requirements.

6.2.   Sufficient time should be allowed after committee meetings for them to report to the board on the nature and content of discussion, on recommendations, and on actions to be taken. The minutes of committee meetings should be circulated to all board members, unless it would be inappropriate to do so, and to the company secretary (if he or she is not secretary to the committee). The remit of each committee, and the processes of interaction between committees and between each committee and the board, should be reviewed regularly.

7. Relations with Shareholders

7.1.   Communication of a company's governance presents an opportunity for the company to improve the quality of the dialogue with its shareholders and other stakeholders, generating greater levels of trust and confidence.

7.2.   The annual report is an important means of communicating with shareholders. It can also be used to provide well-thought-out disclosures on the company's governance arrangements and the board evaluation exercise. Thinking about such disclosures can prompt the board to reflect on the quality of its governance, and what actions it might take to improve its structures, processes and systems.

7.3.   The Code emphasises the importance of continual communication with major shareholders, and of the AGM, as two aspects of a company's wider communications strategy. The chairman has a key role to play in representing the company to its principal audiences, and is encouraged to report personally about board leadership and effectiveness in the corporate governance statement in the annual report.

APPENDIX 5

FRC Guidance on Audit Committees

April 2016

Section 1: Introduction

1. This guidance is designed to assist company boards in making suitable arrangements for their audit committees, and to assist directors serving on audit committees in carrying out their role. While boards are not required to follow this guidance, it is intended to assist them when implementing the relevant provisions of the UK Corporate Governance Code and should, in particular, be read in conjunction with section C.3 of the Code.

2. Best practice requires that every board should consider in detail what audit committee arrangements are best suited for its particular circumstances. Audit committee arrangements need to be proportionate to the task, and will vary according to the size, complexity and risk profile of the company.

3. While all directors have a duty to act in the interests of the company the audit committee has a particular role, acting independently from the executive, to ensure that the interests of shareholders are properly protected in relation to financial reporting and internal control. However, the board has overall responsibility for an organisation's approach to risk management and internal control and nothing in the guidance should be interpreted as a departure from the principle of the unitary board. Any disagreement within the board, including disagreement between the audit committee's members and the rest of the board, should be resolved at board level.

4. The guidance contains recommendations about the conduct of the audit committee's relationship with the board, with the executive management and with internal and external auditors. The essential features of these interactions are a frank, open working relationship and a high level of mutual respect. The audit committee must be prepared to take a robust stand, and all parties must be prepared to make information freely available to the committee, to listen to their views and to talk through the issues openly.

5. In particular, the management is under an obligation to ensure the audit committee is kept properly informed, and should take the initiative in supplying information rather than waiting to be asked. The board should make it clear to all directors and staff that they must cooperate with the audit committee and provide it with any information it requires. In addition, executive board members will have regard to their duty to provide all directors, including those on the audit committee, with all the information they need to discharge their responsibilities as directors of the company.

6. Many of the core functions of audit committees set out in this guidance are expressed in terms of 'oversight', 'assessment' and 'review' of a particular function. It is not the duty of audit committees to carry out functions that properly belong to others, such as the company's management in the preparation of the financial statements or the auditors in the planning or conducting of audits. To do so could undermine the responsibility of management and auditors. However, the audit committee should consider key matters of their own initiative and the oversight function may well lead to detailed work. The audit committee must intervene if there are signs that something may be seriously amiss.

7. For groups, it will usually be necessary for the audit committee of the parent company to review issues that relate to particular subsidiaries or activities carried on by the group. Consequently, the board of a UK-listed parent company with a Premium listing of equity shares in the UK should ensure that there is adequate cooperation within the group (and with internal and external auditors of individual companies within the group) to enable the parent company audit committee to discharge its responsibilities effectively.

8. This guidance is set out over three sections. Section 2 addresses the establishment and effectiveness of the audit committee. Section 3 summarises the committee's roles and responsibilities and Section 4 provides an overview of communications with shareholders.

Section 2: Establishment and Effectiveness of the Audit Committee

Establishment and terms of reference

9. The board should establish an audit committee of at least three, or in the case of smaller companies[1] two, members. These should be independent non-executive directors.
10. The main role and responsibilities of the audit committee should be set out in written terms of reference tailored to the particular circumstances of the company.[2]
11. The audit committee and board should review annually the effectiveness of the audit committee.

Membership and appointment

12. Each audit committee will function differently depending on the composition of the board and committee and the business in which the company is involved.
13. Appointments to the audit committee should be made by the board on the recommendation of the nomination committee, in consultation with the audit committee chairman.

Skills, experience and training

14. The committee members should bring an independent mind-set to their role. Independent thinking is crucial in assessing the work of management and the assurance provided by the internal and external audit functions.
15. In considering the composition of the audit committee, the nominations committee and board should have regard to ensuring a range of skills, experience, knowledge and professional qualifications to meet the requirements of the Code. The committee as a whole should have competence relevant to the sector in which the company operates. The board should also satisfy itself that at least one member of the audit committee has recent and relevant financial experience.[3] The need for a degree of financial literacy among the other members will vary according to the nature of the company, but experience of corporate financial matters will normally be required. The availability of appropriate financial expertise will be particularly important where the company's activities involve specialised financial activities.
16. The company should provide an induction programme for new audit committee members. This should cover the role of the audit committee, including its terms of reference and expected time commitment by members; and an overview of the company's business model and strategy, identifying the main business and financial dynamics and risks. It could also include meeting some of the company staff.
17. Training should also be provided to members of the audit committee on an ongoing and timely basis and should include an understanding of the principles of and developments in corporate reporting and regulation. In appropriate cases, it may also include, for example, understanding financial statements, applicable accounting standards and recommended practice; the legal and regulatory framework for the company's business; the role of internal and external auditing; and risk management.

Meetings of the audit committee

18. It is for the audit committee chairman, in consultation with the company secretary, to decide the frequency and timing of its meetings. There should be as many meetings as the audit committee's role and responsibilities require. It is recommended there should be no fewer than three meetings during the year, held to coincide with key dates within the financial reporting and audit cycle.[4]

19. A sufficient interval should be allowed between audit committee meetings and main board meetings to allow any work arising from the audit committee meeting to be carried out and reported to the board as appropriate.

20. No one other than the audit committee's chairman and members is entitled to be present at a meeting of the audit committee. It is for the audit committee to decide if nonmembers should attend for a particular meeting or a particular agenda item. It is to be expected that the finance director, head of internal audit and external audit lead partner will be invited regularly to attend meetings.

21. The audit committee should, at least annually, meet the external and internal auditors, without management, to discuss matters relating to its remit and any issues arising from the audits.

22. Formal meetings of the audit committee are the heart of its work. However, they will rarely be sufficient. It is expected that the audit committee chairman, and to a lesser extent the other members, will wish to keep in touch on a continuing basis with the key people involved in the company's governance, including the board chairman, the chief executive, the finance director, the external audit lead partner and the head of internal audit.

Resources

23. The audit committee should be provided with sufficient resources to undertake its duties.

24. The audit committee should have access to the services of the company secretariat on all audit committee matters including: assisting the chairman in planning the audit committee's work, drawing up meeting agendas, taking minutes, drafting of material about its activities for the annual report, collection and distribution of information and provision of any necessary practical support.

25. The company secretary should ensure that the audit committee receives information and papers in a timely manner to enable full and proper consideration to be given to the issues.

26. The board should make funds available to the audit committee to enable it to take independent legal, accounting or other advice when the audit committee reasonably believes it necessary to do so.

Remuneration

27. Audit committees have wide-ranging, time-consuming and sometimes intensive work to do. Committee members – and particularly the audit committee chairman – bear a significant responsibility and they need to commit a significant extra amount of time to the job.

28. The level of remuneration paid to the members of the audit committee should take into account the level of fees paid to other members of the board. The chairman's responsibilities and time demands will generally be heavier than the other members of the audit committee and this should be reflected in his or her remuneration.

Section 3: Role and Responsibilities

Relationship with the Board

29. The audit committee should report to the board on how it has discharged its responsibilities, including:
    - the significant issues that it considered in relation to the financial statements and how these issues were addressed;
    - its assessment of the effectiveness of the external audit process and its recommendation on the appointment or reappointment of the external auditor;[5] and
    - any other issues on which the board has requested the committee's opinion. In doing so it should identify any matters in respect of which it considers that action or improvement is needed, whether the subject of a specific request by the board or not, and make recommendations as to the steps to be taken.

30. Where there is disagreement between the audit committee and the board, adequate time should be made available for discussion of the issue with a view to resolving the disagreement. Where any such disagreement cannot be resolved, the audit committee should have

the right to report the issue to the shareholders as part of the report on its activities in the annual report.

31. The audit committee should consider key matters of their own initiative rather than relying solely on the work of the external auditor. The audit committee should discuss what information and assurance it requires in order to properly carry out its roles to review, monitor and provide assurance or recommendations to the board and, where there are gaps, how these should be addressed. The audit committee should satisfy itself that these sources of assurance and information are sufficient and objective.

Annual reports and other periodic reports

32. The audit committee should review, and report to the board on, significant financial reporting issues and judgements made in connection with the preparation of the company's financial statements (having regard to matters communicated to it by the auditor)[6], interim reports, preliminary announcements and related formal statements.

33. It is the responsibility of management, not the audit committee, to prepare complete and accurate financial statements and disclosures in accordance with accounting standards and other regulations. The management should inform the audit committee of the methods used to account for significant or unusual transactions where the accounting treatment is open to different approaches. The audit committee should consider significant accounting policies and any changes to them.

34. Taking into account the external auditor's view on the financial statements, the audit committee should consider whether the company has adopted appropriate accounting policies and, where necessary, made appropriate estimates and judgements. The audit committee should review the clarity and completeness of disclosures in the financial statements and consider whether the disclosures made are set properly in context.

35. Where, following its review, the audit committee is not satisfied with any aspect of the proposed financial reporting by the company, it shall report its views to the board.

36. The audit committee should review related information presented with the financial statements, including the strategic report, and corporate governance statements relating to the audit and to risk management.

37. Where requested by the board, the audit committee should review the content of the annual report and accounts and advise the board on whether, taken as a whole, it is fair, balanced and understandable to inform the board's statement on these matters required under Section C.1.1 of the UK Corporate Governance Code.[7] To assist the board to make that statement, any review would need to assess whether other information presented in the annual report is consistent with the financial statements.

38. Where board approval is required for other statements containing financial information (for example significant financial returns to regulators and release of price sensitive information), whenever practicable the audit committee should review such statements first (without being inconsistent with any requirement for prompt reporting under the Listing Rules or Disclosure and Transparency Rules).

Internal control and risk management systems

39. The board has ultimate responsibility for an organisation's risk management and internal control systems, but the board may delegate to the audit committee some functions to assist the board in meeting this responsibility.

40. The audit committee should review the company's internal financial controls, that is, the systems established to identify, assess, manage and monitor financial risks, as part of their expected roles and responsibilities in the Code.[8]

41. The company's management has day-to-day responsibility for the risk management and internal control systems, including the financial controls, and these should form an integral part of the company's day-to-day business processes. If oversight of the function is so delegated, the audit committee should consider what role it can play in promoting sound risk management and internal control systems, including operational and compliance controls, and review these systems. If the function has been delegated to the audit committee it should receive reports from management on the effectiveness of the systems they have established and the conclusions of any testing carried out by internal or external auditors.

42. The audit committee should consider the level of assurance it is getting on the risk management and internal control systems, including internal financial controls, and whether this is enough to help the board in satisfying itself that they are operating effectively.

43. If risk management and internal control responsibilities are delegated to different committees the board should consider the impact of splitting those responsibilities.

44. Except to the extent that this is expressly dealt with by the board or risk committee, the audit committee should review and recommend to the board the disclosures included in the annual report in relation to internal control, risk management and the viability statement.

The internal audit process

45. The need for an internal audit function will vary depending on company specific factors including the scale, diversity and complexity of the company's activities and the number of employees, as well as cost-benefit considerations. Senior management and the board may desire objective assurance and advice on risk and control. An adequately resourced internal audit function (or its equivalent where, for example, a third party is contracted to perform some or all of the work concerned) may provide such assurance and advice.

46. The audit committee should regularly review the need for establishing an internal audit function. When undertaking its assessment of the need for an internal audit function, the audit committee should also consider whether there are any trends or current factors relevant to the company's activities, markets or other aspects of its external environment that have increased, or are expected to increase, the risks faced by the company. Such an increase in risk may also arise from internal factors such as organisational restructuring or from changes in reporting processes or underlying information systems. Other matters to be taken into account may include adverse trends evident from the monitoring of internal control systems or an increased incidence of unexpected occurrences.

47. In the absence of an internal audit function, other processes may need to be applied to provide assurance to management, the audit committee and the board that the system of internal control is functioning as intended. In these circumstances, the audit committee will need to assess whether such processes provide sufficient and objective assurance.

48. Where there is an internal audit function, the audit committee should review and approve its role and mandate; approve the annual internal audit plan; and monitor and review the effectiveness of its work. The audit committee should review and annually approve the internal audit charter to ensure that it is appropriate to the current needs of the organisation.

49. The audit committee should ensure that the internal audit plan is aligned to the key risks of the business. The audit committee should pay particular attention to the areas in which work of the risk, compliance, finance, internal audit and external audit functions may be aligned or overlapping and oversee these relationships to ensure they are coordinated and operating effectively to avoid duplication.

50. The audit committee should ensure that there is open communication between the different functions and that the internal audit function evaluates the effectiveness of the risk, compliance and finance functions as part of its internal audit plan.

51. The audit committee should ensure that the function has unrestricted scope, the necessary resources and access to information to enable it to fulfil its mandate, and is equipped to perform in accordance with appropriate professional standards for internal auditors.[9]

52. The audit committee should approve the appointment or termination of appointment of the head of internal audit. Internal audit should have access to the audit committee and board chairman where necessary and the audit committee should ensure internal audit has a reporting line which enables it to be independent of the executive and so able to exercise independent judgement.

53. In undertaking a review of effectiveness of the internal audit function the audit committee should confirm that it is satisfied that the quality, experience and expertise of the function is appropriate for the business. The audit committee should also consider the actions management has taken to implement the recommendations of the function and whether these properly support the effective working of the internal audit function.

54. In its annual assessment of the effectiveness of the internal audit function the audit committee should:
    - meet with the head of internal audit without the presence of management to discuss the effectiveness of the function;
    - review and assess the annual internal audit work plan;
    - receive a report on the results of the internal auditors' work; and
    - monitor and assess the role and effectiveness of the internal audit function in the overall context of the company's risk management system.

55. The audit committee may also wish to consider whether an independent, third party review of internal audit effectiveness and processes is appropriate.

56. If the external auditor is being considered to undertake aspects of the internal audit function,[10] the audit committee should consider the effect this may have on the effectiveness of the company's overall arrangements for internal control, the effect on the objectivity and independence of the external auditor and the internal audit function and investor perceptions in this regard. Investor perceptions are likely to be influenced by:
    - the reporting in the annual report on the nature and extent of the work being performed by the external auditor; and
    - whether, in the absence of internal audit work, the audit committee is wholly reliant on the views of the external auditor about the effectiveness of its system of controls

The external audit process[11]

57. The audit committee is the body responsible for overseeing the company's relations with the external auditor.

Appointment and tendering

58. The audit committee should have primary responsibility for the appointment of the auditor. This includes negotiating the fee and scope of the audit, initiating a tender process, influencing the appointment of an engagement partner and making formal recommendations to the board on the appointment, reappointment and removal of the external auditors.

59. The audit committee should be responsible for the selection procedure for the appointment of audit firms. When considering the selection of possible new appointees as external auditors, it should oversee the selection process, and ensure that all tendering firms have such access as is necessary to information and individuals during the duration of the tendering process.

60. The audit committee should annually assess, and report to the board on, the qualification, expertise and resources, and independence of the external auditors and the effectiveness of the audit process, with a recommendation on whether to propose to the shareholders that the external auditor be reappointed.[12] The assessment should cover all aspects of the audit service provided by the audit firm, and include obtaining a report on the audit firm's own internal quality control procedures and consideration of audit firms' annual transparency reports.

61. If the external auditor resigns, the audit committee should investigate the issues giving rise to such resignation and consider whether any action is required.

62. The audit committee should evaluate the risks to the quality and effectiveness of the financial reporting process, especially in light of the auditor's communications with the audit committee.

Terms and Remuneration

63. The audit committee should approve the terms of engagement and the remuneration to be paid to the external auditor in respect of audit services provided.

64. The audit committee should review and agree the engagement letter issued by the external auditor at the start of each audit, ensuring that it has been updated to reflect changes in circumstances arising since the previous year. The scope of the external audit should be reviewed by the audit committee with the auditor. If the audit committee is not satisfied as to its adequacy it should arrange for additional work to be undertaken.

65. The audit committee should satisfy itself that the level of fee payable in respect of the audit services provided is appropriate and that an effective, high quality, audit can be conducted for such a fee.

Independence, including the provision of non-audit services

66. The audit committee should assess the independence and objectivity of the external auditor annually, taking into consideration relevant UK law, regulation, the Ethical Standard and other professional requirements. The audit committee should consider the annual disclosure from the statutory auditor and discuss with the auditor the threats to their independence and the safeguards applied to mitigate those threats. This assessment should involve a consideration of all relationships between the company and the audit firm, including throughout the group and with the audit firm's network firms, and any safeguards established by the external auditor. The audit committee should consider whether, taken as a whole and having regard to the views, as appropriate, of the external auditor, management and internal audit, those relationships appear to impair the auditor's independence and objectivity.

67. The audit committee should monitor the external audit firm's compliance with the Ethical Standard, the level of fees that the company pays in proportion to the overall fee income of the firm, or relevant part of it,[13] and other related regulatory requirements.[14]

68. The audit committee should seek annually from the audit firm information about policies and processes for maintaining independence and monitoring compliance with relevant requirements, including those regarding the rotation of audit partners and staff.[15]

69. The audit committee should agree with the board the company's policy for the employment of former employees of the external auditor, taking into account the Ethical Standard and legal requirements and paying particular attention to the policy regarding former employees of the audit firm who were part of the audit team and moved directly to the company. The audit committee should monitor application of the policy, including the number of former employees of the external auditor currently employed in senior positions in the company, and consider whether in the light of this there has been any impairment, or appearance of impairment, of the auditor's independence and objectivity in respect of the audit and consider the committee's own safeguards around independence in its review of effectiveness.

70. The normal rotation period for the audit engagement partner and key audit partners is five years, but a degree of flexibility over the timing of rotation is possible for instance: where the audit committee decides that it is necessary to safeguard the quality of the audit without compromising the independence and objectivity of the external auditor. In such circumstances, the audit engagement partner may continue in this position for an additional period of up to two years, so that no longer than seven years in total is spent in this position.[16] The audit committee should disclose this fact and the reasons for it to the shareholders as early as practicable.

71. The audit committee should develop and recommend to the board the company's policy in relation to the provision of non-audit services[17] by the auditor,[18] taking into account the Ethical Standard and legal requirements, and keep the policy under review.

72. The audit committee is responsible for approving non-audit services. The committee's objective should be to ensure that the provision of such services does not impair the external auditor's independence or objectivity. In the context of non-audit services that are not prohibited by law, the audit committee should apply judgement concerning the provision of such services, including assessing:

   - threats to independence and objectivity resulting from the provision of such services and any safeguards in place to eliminate or reduce these threats to a level where they would not compromise the auditor's independence and objectivity;
   - the nature of the non-audit services;
   - whether the skills and experience of the audit firm make it the most suitable supplier of the non-audit service;
   - the fees incurred, or to be incurred, for non-audit services both for individual services and in aggregate, relative to the audit fee, including special terms and conditions (for example contingent fee arrangements); and
   - the criteria which govern the compensation of the individuals performing the audit.

73. The audit committee should set and apply a formal policy specifying the types of nonaudit service for which use of the external auditor is pre-approved. Such approval should only be in place for matters that are clearly trivial. Reporting of the use of non-audit services should include those subject to pre-approval.

74. The audit committee needs to set a policy for how it will assess whether non-audit services have a direct or material effect on the audited financial statements, how it will assess and explain the estimation of the effect on the financial statements and how it will consider the external auditors' independence.

Annual audit cycle

75. At the start of each annual audit cycle, the audit committee should ensure that appropriate plans are in place for the audit. The committee should consider whether the auditor's overall work plan, including planned levels of materiality and proposed resources to execute the audit plan, appears consistent with the scope of the audit engagement, having regard also to the seniority, expertise and experience of the audit team.[19]

76. The audit committee may also wish to hold an initial discussion without the auditor to consider factors that could affect audit quality and discuss these with the auditor. The audit committee should review with the external auditors, in a timely manner, the findings of their work and the auditor's report. In the course of its review, the audit committee should:
   - discuss with the external auditor major issues that arose during the course of the audit and have subsequently been resolved and those issues that have been left unresolved;
   - ask the auditor to explain how they addressed the risks to audit quality identified earlier;
   - weigh the evidence they have received in relation to each of the areas of significant judgment and review key accounting and audit judgements;
   - ask the auditor for their perception of their interactions with senior management and other members of the finance team; and
   - review levels of errors identified during the audit, obtaining explanations from management and, where necessary, the external auditors as to why certain errors might remain unadjusted.[20]

77. The audit committee should review and monitor management's responsiveness to the external auditor's findings and recommendations. The audit committee should also review the audit representation letters before signature and give particular consideration to matters where representation has been requested that relate to non-standard issues.[21] The audit committee should consider whether the information provided is complete and appropriate based on its own knowledge.

78. The audit committee should assess the effectiveness of the audit process. An assessment of external audit quality in the particular circumstances of the company requires consideration of mind-set and culture; skills, character and knowledge; quality control; and judgment, including the robustness and perceptiveness of the auditors in handling key judgements, responding to questions from the audit committee, and in their commentary where appropriate on the systems of internal control.[22]

79. In the course of its assessment of effectiveness, the audit committee should:
   - ask the auditor to explain the risks to audit quality that they identified and how these have been addressed;
   - discuss with the auditor the key audit firm and network level controls the auditor relied on to address the identified risks to audit quality and enquire about the findings from internal and external inspections of their audit and their audit firm;
   - review whether the auditor has met the agreed audit plan and understand the reasons for any changes, including changes in perceived audit risks and the work undertaken by the external auditors to address those risks;
   - obtain feedback about the conduct of the audit from key people involved, for example the finance director and the head of internal audit, including consideration of the external auditor's reliance on internal audit; and
   - review and monitor the content of the external auditor's management letter, and other communications with the audit committee, in order to assess whether it is based on a good understanding of the company's business and establish whether recommendations have been acted upon and, if not, the reasons why they have not been acted upon.

SECTION 4: Communication with Shareholders

80. The audit committee has a role in ensuring that shareholder interests are properly protected in relation to financial reporting and internal control. The committee should consider the clarity of its reporting and be prepared to meet investors. The annual report should include a separate section describing the work of the audit committee in discharging its responsibilities, signed by the chairman.

81. The audit committee section should include the following matters:
    - a summary of the role and work of the audit committee;
    - how the audit committee composition requirements have been addressed, and the names and qualifications of all members of the audit committee during the period, if not provided elsewhere;
    - the number of audit committee meetings;
    - how the audit committee's performance evaluation has been conducted;
    - an explanation of how the committee has assessed the effectiveness of the external audit process[23] and of the approach taken to the appointment or reappointment of the external auditor; the length of tenure of the current audit firm; the current audit partner name, and for how long the partner has held the role; when a tender was last conducted; and advance notice of any retendering plans[24];
    - if the external auditor provides non-audit services, the committee's policy for approval of non-audit services; how auditor objectivity and independence is safeguarded; the audit fees for the statutory audit of the company's consolidated financial statements paid to the auditor and its network firms for audit related services and other non-audit services, including the ratio of audit to non-audit work; and for each significant engagement, or category of engagements, explain what the services are and why the audit committee concluded that it was in the interests of the company to purchase them from the external auditor;
    - an explanation of how the committee has assessed the effectiveness of internal audit and satisfied itself that the quality, experience and expertise of the function is appropriate for the business; and
    - the significant issues that the committee considered, including:
        - issues in relation to the financial statements and how these were addressed, having regard to matters communicated to it by the auditors;[25]
        - the nature and extent of interaction (if any) with the FRC's Corporate Reporting Review team; and
        - where a company's audit has been reviewed by the FRC's Audit Quality Review team, the Committee should discuss the findings with their auditors and consider whether any of those findings are significant and, if so, make disclosures about the findings and the actions they and the auditors plan to take. This discussion should not include disclosure of the audit quality category.

82. The committee needs to exercise judgement in deciding which of the issues it considered in relation to the financial statements were significant. The audit committee should aim to describe the significant issues in a concise and understandable form whilst reporting on the specific circumstances of the company.

83. When reporting on the significant issues, the audit committee would not be expected to disclose information which, in its opinion, would be prejudicial to the interests of the company (for example, because it related to impending developments or matters in the course of negotiation).

84. The section need not repeat information disclosed elsewhere in the annual report and accounts, but could provide signposts to that information.

85. The chairman of the audit committee should be present at the AGM to answer questions on the separate section of the annual report describing the audit committee's activities and matters within the scope of the audit committee's responsibilities.

Notes:

1   Defined in the UK Corporate Governance Code as companies below the FTSE 350 index.

2   This overlaps with Financial Conduct Authority (FCA) Disclosure and Transparency Rule (DTR) 7.1.3 R.

3   This overlaps with FCA Rule DTR 7.1.1A R.

4   For example, when the audit plans (internal and external) are available for review and when interim statements, preliminary announcements and the full annual report are near completion.

5   Audit Quality: Practice aid for audit committees (May 2015) may help Audit Committees in undertaking their assessment of the effectiveness of the external auditor.

6   The auditor is required by auditing standards to communicate to the audit committee the information that the auditor believes will be relevant to the board and the audit committee (in the context of fulfilling their responsibilities under the Code) in order to understand the rationale and the evidence relied upon when making significant professional judgments in the course of the audit and reaching an opinion on the financial statements.

7   In addition, the auditor is required by auditing standards to report, in their report on the financial statements, if the board's statement in the annual report is inconsistent with the knowledge acquired by the auditor in the course of performing the audit.

8   Guidance on Risk Management, Internal Control and Related Financial and Business Reporting (September 2014) provides further guidance.

9   Guidance can be found in the Chartered Institute of Internal Auditors' Code of Ethics and the International Standards for the Professional Practice of Internal Auditing.

10   Public Interest Entities may not engage their external auditors to carry out internal audit work.

11   This section overlaps with Parts 3, 4 and 5 of The Statutory Audit Services for Large Companies Market Investigation (Mandatory Use of Competitive Tender Processes and Audit Committee responsibilities) Order 2014 and the requirements of Chapter 2 of Part 16 of the Companies Act 2006 as inserted by the Statutory Auditors and Third Country Auditors Regulations 2016 on the appointment of auditors to public companies that are Public Interest Entities. Audit Committees will be provided with information in accordance with the International Standards for Auditors that may overlap with topics covered in this section.

12   Audit Quality: Practice aid for audit committees (May 2015) may help in assessing effectiveness.

13   Where the audit firm's profits are not shared on a firm-wide basis, the relevant part of the firm is that by reference to which the audit engagement partner's profit share is calculated.

14   The Audit Committee should pay special attention to instances where the amount of work done for the entity by the auditor may impair its independence and objectivity as required by the Ethical Standard 4.42-4.43.

15   The International Standard on Auditing (UK) 260 (Revised June 2016) 'Communication with those charged with Governance' requires reporting on compliance with relevant ethical requirements regarding independence.

16   This overlaps with the Ethical Standard 3.15.

17   Non-audit services are any services other than statutory audit services. Section 5 of the Ethical Standard outlines those services which are considered prohibited non-audit services for public interest entities.

18   The audit committee should have regard to non-audit services provided by the audit firm and any of its network firms to any parents, subsidiaries or material affiliates to the company.

19   Further suggestions for the planning stage of the external audit are at Page 9 of the Audit Quality: Practice aid for audit committees (May 2015).

20   Audit Quality: Practice aid for audit committees (May 2015) may assist in assessing the external auditor.

21   Further guidance can be found in the International Standard on Auditing (UK) 580 'Written Representations'.

22   Audit Quality: Practice aid for audit committees (May 2015) provides further detail on assessment of external auditor quality.

23   Audit Quality: Practice aid for audit committees (May 2015) may assist in assessing effectiveness.

24   This overlaps with Part 4 of The Statutory Audit Services for Large Companies Market Investigation (Mandatory Use of Competitive Tender Processes and Audit Committee Responsibilities) Order 2014.

25   The auditor is required by auditing standards to report, in their report on the financial statements, if the section of the annual report describing the work of the audit committee does not appropriately address the matters communicated by the auditor to the audit committee.

APPENDIX 6

FRC Guidance on Risk Management, Internal Control and Related Financial and Business Reporting

September 2014

Section 1
Introduction

Applicability

1. This guidance revises, integrates and replaces the current editions of the Financial Reporting Council's ("FRC") 'Internal Control: Revised Guidance for Directors on the Combined Code' and 'Going Concern and Liquidity Risk: Guidance for Directors of UK Companies', and reflects changes made to the UK Corporate Governance Code ("the Code").

2. It aims to bring together elements of best practice for risk management; prompt boards to consider how to discharge their responsibilities in relation to the existing and emerging principal risks faced by the company; reflect sound business practice, whereby risk management and internal control are embedded in the business process by which a company pursues its objectives; and highlight related reporting responsibilities.

3. While it is hoped that this guidance will be useful to other entities, it is primarily directed to companies subject to the Code.[1] It applies to such companies for accounting periods beginning on or after 1 October 2014.

Background

4. The Code defines the role of the board as being "to provide entrepreneurial leadership of the company within a framework of prudent and effective controls which enables risk to be assessed and managed". Effective development and delivery of a company's strategic objectives, its ability to seize new opportunities and to ensure its longer term survival depend upon its identification, understanding of, and response to, the risks it faces.

5. Economic developments and some high profile failures of risk management in recent years have reminded boards of the need to ensure that the company's approach to risk has been properly considered in setting the company's strategy and managing its risks. There may be significant consequences if the company does not do so effectively.

6. Good stewardship by the board should not inhibit sensible risk taking that is critical to growth. However, the assessment of risks as part of the normal business planning process should support better decision-taking, ensure that the board and management respond promptly to risks when they arise, and ensure that shareholders and other stakeholders are well informed about the principal risks and prospects of the company.[2] The board's responsibility for the organisation's culture is essential to the way in which risk is considered and addressed within the organisation and with external stakeholders.

7. The Code was updated in 2010 to make it clear that, in addition to being responsible for ensuring sound risk management and internal control systems, boards should explain the company's business model and should determine the nature and extent of the principal risks they were willing to take to achieve the company's strategic objectives.

8. The Code was further updated in 2012 to improve financial and business reporting by making it clear that the board should:

- confirm that the annual report and accounts taken as a whole is fair, balanced and understandable and provides the information necessary for shareholders to assess the company's position and performance, business model and strategy; and
- establish arrangements that will enable it to make this assessment.

9. In 2011 the FRC published the 'Boards and Risk' report, which reflected the views of directors, investors and risk professionals and highlighted that the board's responsibilities for risk management and internal control are not limited to the oversight of the internal control system.

10. In 2012 the Sharman Inquiry into going concern and liquidity risk concluded that the board's declaration of whether the company remained a going concern should be more broadly based than is required to determine the accounting approach to be taken.

11. Taken together, the conclusions of the two reports can be summarised as:
    - the board must determine its willingness to take on risk, and the desired culture within the company;
    - risk management and internal control should be incorporated within the company's normal management and governance processes, not treated as a separate compliance exercise;
    - the board must make a robust assessment of the principal risks to the company's business model and ability to deliver its strategy, including solvency and liquidity risks. In making that assessment the board should consider the likelihood and impact of these risks materialising in the short and longer term;
    - once those risks have been identified, the board should agree how they will be managed and mitigated, and keep the company's risk profile under review. It should satisfy itself that management's systems include appropriate controls, and that it has adequate sources of assurance;the assessment and management of the principal risks, and monitoring and review of the associated systems, should be carried out as an ongoing process, not seen as an annual one-off exercise; and
    - this process should inform a number of different disclosures in the annual report: the description of the principal risks and uncertainties facing the company; the disclosures on the going concern basis of accounting and material uncertainties thereto; and the report on the review of the risk management and internal control systems.

12. In April 2014 the FRC also published its 'Guidance on the Strategic Report' as best practice[3]. It encourages companies to make the information in annual reports more relevant to shareholders. Recognising that an annual report comprises a number of components, it aims to promote cohesiveness amongst these components, with related information appropriately linked together.

Risk Management and Internal Control

13. The board has ultimate responsibility for risk management and internal control, including for the determination of the nature and extent of the principal risks it is willing to take to achieve its strategic objectives and for ensuring that an appropriate culture has been embedded throughout the organisation. This guidance provides a high-level overview of some of the factors boards should consider in relation to the design, implementation, monitoring and review of the risk management and internal control systems. Such systems cannot eliminate all risks, but it is the role of the board to ensure that they are robust and effective and take account of such risks.

14. Consistent with the amendment to Principle C.2 in the 2014 edition of the Code, this guidance asks boards to determine their "principal" risks, rather than "significant" risks as in earlier Code editions. This decision was taken to align the terminology with the new Strategic Report requirements. The term "principal risk" is defined in the FRC's 'Guidance on the Strategic Report'. The FRC considers that in this context the words "principal" and "significant" are interchangeable and that the amendment should not be seen as implying a change in the nature of the risks referred to in Principle C.2.

15. The guidance does not set out in detail the procedure by which a company designs and implements its risk management and internal control systems. Attempting to define a single approach to achieving best practice would be misguided if it led boards to underestimate the crucial importance to high quality risk management of the culture and behaviour they promote.

The Board's Statements on Longer Term Viability and on the Going Concern Basis of Accounting

16. The Sharman Inquiry concluded that the board's assessment as to whether a company remains a "going concern" should be more broadly based than is required to determine whether to adopt the going concern basis of accounting in the current financial statements and identify any material uncertainties about the company's ability to continue to do so in future.

17. The revised Code and this guidance use the term "going concern" only in the context of referring to the going concern basis of accounting for the preparation of financial statements, as defined in accounting standards. This usage is well-established but is different from the ordinary English usage of the term "going concern" to describe an entity that has a viable future.

18. In the 2014 edition of the Code, Provision C.1.3 has been revised to require an explicit statement in the financial statements about whether: the going concern basis of accounting has been adopted; and there are any material uncertainties about the company's ability to continue to do so in future. A new provision (C.2.2) requires a broader statement about the board's reasonable expectation as to the company's viability based on a robust assessment of the company's principal risks and the company's current position. This guidance addresses each of these statements.

How this Guidance is Structured

19. Sections 2 and 3 of this guidance summarise the board's responsibilities for risk management and internal control and identify some of the factors boards should consider in order to exercise those responsibilities effectively. Section 4 addresses the establishment of the risk management and internal control systems, Section 5 discusses the monitoring and review of those systems and Section 6 addresses the board's related financial and business reporting responsibilities.

20. Sections 4, 5 and 6 incorporate the core of the previous 'Internal Control: Guidance for Directors'. Sections 2 and 3 are new, and are intended to align the scope of the guidance with Principle C.2 on Risk Management and Internal Control and Provision C.1.3 on the going concern basis of accounting, by addressing the full range of the board's responsibilities for these matters and their inter-relationships.

21. Appendices A and B provide further guidance on adopting the going concern basis of accounting and related disclosures and on the longer term viability statement. In addition, the FRC has issued a separate Supplement for Banks on going concern, which addresses considerations specific to the banking sector, and which should be read in conjunction with this Guidance.

22. Appendix C contains questions that may assist boards in assessing how they are carrying out their responsibilities, the culture of the company, and the effectiveness of the risk management and internal control systems.

23. Appendix D contains an overview of a company's reporting requirements relating to risk and going concern.

Section 2
Board Responsibilities for Risk Management and Internal Control

24. The board has responsibility for an organisation's overall approach to risk management and internal control. The board's responsibilities are:
    - ensuring the design and implementation of appropriate risk management and internal control systems that identify the risks facing the company and enable the board to make a robust assessment of the principal risks;
    - determining the nature and extent of the principal risks faced and those risks which the organisation is willing to take in achieving its strategic objectives (determining its "risk appetite");

- ensuring that appropriate culture and reward systems have been embedded throughout the organisation;
- agreeing how the principal risks should be managed or mitigated to reduce the likelihood of their incidence or their impact;
- monitoring and reviewing the risk management and internal control systems, and the management's process of monitoring and reviewing, and satisfying itself that they are functioning effectively and that corrective action is being taken where necessary; and
- ensuring sound internal and external information and communication processes and taking responsibility for external communication on risk management and internal control.

25. The board's specific responsibility for determining whether to adopt the going concern basis of accounting and related disclosures of material uncertainties in the financial statements is a sub set of these broader responsibilities. A company that is able to adopt the going concern basis of accounting and does not have related material uncertainties to report, for the purposes of the financial statements, is not necessarily free of risks that would threaten the company's business model, future performance, solvency or liquidity were they to materialise. The board is responsible for ensuring this distinction is understood internally and communicated externally.

26. It is the role of management to implement and take day-to-day responsibility for board policies on risk management and internal control. But the board needs to satisfy itself that management has understood the risks, implemented and monitored appropriate policies and controls, and are providing the board with timely information so that it can discharge its own responsibilities. In turn, management should ensure internal responsibilities and accountabilities are clearly established, understood and embedded at all levels of the organisation. Employees should understand their responsibility for behaving according to the culture.

Section 3
Exercising Responsibilities

27. The board should establish the tone for risk management and internal control and put in place appropriate systems to enable it to meet its responsibilities effectively. These will depend upon factors such as the size and composition of the board; the scale, diversity and complexity of the company's operations; and the nature of the principal risks the company faces. But in deciding what arrangements are appropriate the board should consider, amongst other things:

- The culture it wishes to embed in the company, and whether this has been achieved.
- As with all aspects of good governance, the effectiveness of risk management and internal control ultimately depend on the individuals responsible for operating the systems that are put in place. In order to ensure the appropriate culture is in place it is not sufficient for the board simply to set the desired values. It also needs to ensure they are communicated by management, incentivise the desired behaviours and sanction inappropriate behaviour, and assess whether the desired values and behaviours have become embedded at all levels.

   This should include consideration of whether the company's leadership style and management structures, human resource policies and reward systems support or undermine the risk management and internal control systems.
- How to ensure there is adequate discussion at the board.
- The board should agree the frequency and scope of its discussions on strategy, business model and risk; how its assessment of risk is integrated with other matters considered by the board; and how to assess the impact on the company's risk profile of decisions on changes in strategy, major new projects and other significant commitments. The board needs to ensure that it engages in informed debate and constructive challenge and keeps under review the effectiveness of its decision-making processes.
- The skills, knowledge and experience of the board and management.

   The board should consider whether it, and any committee or management group to which it delegates activities, has the necessary skills, knowledge, experience, authority and support to enable it to assess the risks the company faces and exercise its responsibilities effectively. Boards should consider specifically assessing this as part of their regular evaluations of their effectiveness.

■ The flow of information to and from the board, and the quality of that information.

■ The board should specify the nature, source, format and frequency of the information that it requires. It should ensure that the assumptions and models underlying this information are clear so that they can be understood and if necessary challenged. Risks can crystallise quickly and the board should ensure that there are clear processes for bringing significant issues to its attention more rapidly when required, and agreed triggers for doing so.

The board should monitor the quality of the information it receives and ensure that it is of a sufficient quality to allow effective decision-making.

■ The use, if any, made of delegation.

■ The board should determine to what extent it wishes to delegate some activity to, or obtain advice from, committees or the management group and the appropriate division of responsibilities and accountabilities.

To the extent that designated committees or the management group carry out, on behalf of the board, activities that this guidance attributes to the board, the board should be satisfied that the arrangements for the work carried out, for the co-ordination of their work (if more than one is involved), and for reporting to the board are appropriate and operating effectively. The board retains ultimate responsibility for the risk management and internal control systems and should reach its own conclusions regarding the recommendations it receives.

The board should ensure that the remuneration committee takes appropriate account of risk when determining remuneration policies and awards, and whether the links between the remuneration committee and the risk and/or audit committee are operating effectively.

■ What assurance the board requires, and how this is to be obtained.

The board should identify what assurance it requires and, where there are gaps, how these should be addressed. In addition to the board, committee and management's own monitoring activities, sources of assurance might include reports on relevant matters from any compliance, risk management, internal control and internal audit functions within the company, the external auditor's communications to the audit committee about matters it considers relevant in fulfilling its responsibilities, and other internal and external sources of information or assurance.

The board should satisfy itself that these sources of assurance have sufficient authority, independence and expertise to enable them to provide objective advice and information to the board.

Section 4
Establishing the Risk Management and Internal Control Systems

28. The risk management and internal control systems encompass the policies, culture, organisation, behaviours, processes, systems and other aspects of a company that, taken together:
    ■ facilitate its effective and efficient operation by enabling it to assess current and emerging risks, respond appropriately to risks and significant control failures and to safeguard its assets;
    ■ help to reduce the likelihood and impact of poor judgement in decision-making; risk-taking that exceeds the levels agreed by the board; human error; or control processes being deliberately circumvented;
    ■ help ensure the quality of internal and external reporting; and
    ■ help ensure compliance with applicable laws and regulations, and also with internal policies with respect to the conduct of business.

29. A company's systems of risk management and internal control will include: risk assessment; management or mitigation of risks, including the use of control processes; information and communication systems; and processes for monitoring and reviewing their continuing effectiveness.

30. The risk management and internal control systems should be embedded in the operations of the company and be capable of responding quickly to evolving business risks, whether they arise from factors within the company or from changes in the business environment. These systems should not be seen as a periodic compliance exercise, but instead as an integral part of the company's day to day business processes.

31. The board should ensure that sound risk management and internal control systems are in place to identify the risks facing the company and to consider their likelihood and impact if they were to materialise.

32. When determining the principal risks, the board should focus on those risks that, given the company's current position, could threaten the company's business model, future performance, solvency or liquidity, irrespective of how they are classified or from where they arise. The board should treat such risks as principal risks and establish clearly the extent to which they are to be managed or mitigated.

33. Risks will differ between companies but may include financial, operational, reputational, behavioural, organisational, third party, or external risks, such as market or regulatory risk, over which the board may have little or no direct control.

34. The design of a robust assessment process to determine the principal risks and consider their implications for the company should be appropriate to the complexity, size and circumstances of the company and is a matter for the judgement of the board, with the support of management. Circumstances may vary over time with changes in the business model, performance, strategy, operational processes and the stage of development the company has reached in its own business cycles, as well as with changes in the external environment.

35. When considering risk the board should consider the following aspects:
    - the nature and extent of the risks, including principal risks, facing, or being taken by, the company which it regards as desirable or acceptable for the company to bear;
    - the likelihood of the risks concerned materialising, and the impact of related risks materialising as a result or at the same time;
    - the company's ability to reduce the likelihood of the risks materialising, and of the impact on the business of risks that do materialise;
    - the exposure to risks before and after risks are managed or mitigated, as appropriate;
    - the operation of the relevant controls and control processes;
    - the effectiveness and relative costs and benefits of particular controls; and
    - the impact of the values and culture of the company, and the way that teams and individuals are incentivised, on the effectiveness of the systems.

36. Training and communication assist in embedding the desired culture and behaviours in the company. To build a company culture that recognises and deals with risk, it is important that the risk management and internal control systems consider how the expectations of the board are to be communicated to staff and what training may be required. In considering communication systems, the board should also consider the company's whistle-blowing procedures.

37. Effective controls are an important element of the systems of risk management and internal control and can cover many aspects of a business, including strategic, financial, operational and compliance.

38. The board should agree how the principal risks will be managed or mitigated and which controls will be put in place. In agreeing the controls the board should determine what constitutes a significant control failing.

Section 5
Monitoring and Review of the Risk Management and Internal Control Systems

39. The existence of risk management and internal control systems does not, on its own, signal the effective management of risk. Effective and on-going monitoring and review are essential components of sound systems of risk management and internal control. The process of monitoring and review is intended to allow the board to conclude whether the systems are properly aligned with strategic objectives; and satisfy itself that the systems address the company's risks and are being developed, applied and maintained appropriately.

40. The board should define the processes to be adopted for its on-going monitoring and review, including specifying the requirements, scope and frequency for reporting and assurance. Regular reports to the board should provide a balanced assessment of the risks and the effectiveness of the systems of risk management and internal control in managing those risks. The board should form its own view on effectiveness, based on the evidence it obtains, exercising the standard of care generally applicable to directors in the exercise of their duties.

41. When reviewing reports during the year, the board should consider: how effectively the risks have been assessed and the principal risks determined; how they have been managed or mitigated; whether necessary actions are being taken promptly to remedy any significant failings or weaknesses; and whether the causes of the failing or weakness indicate poor decision-taking, a need for more extensive monitoring or a reassessment of the effectiveness of management's on-going processes.

42. In addition to its on-going monitoring and review, the board should undertake an annual review of the effectiveness of the systems to ensure that it has considered all significant aspects of risk management and internal control for the company for the year under review and up to the date of approval of the annual report and accounts. The board should define the processes to be adopted for this review, including drawing on the results of the board's on-going process such that it will obtain sound, appropriately documented, evidence to support its statement in the company's annual report and accounts.

43. The annual review of effectiveness should, in particular, consider:
    - the company's willingness to take on risk (its "risk appetite"), the desired culture within the company and whether this culture has been embedded;
    - the operation of the risk management and internal control systems, covering the design, implementation, monitoring and review and identification of risks and determination of those which are principal to the company;
    - the integration of risk management and internal controls with considerations of strategy and business model, and with business planning processes;
    - the changes in the nature, likelihood and impact of principal risks, and the company's ability to respond to changes in its business and the external environment;
    - the extent, frequency and quality of the communication of the results of management's monitoring to the board which enables it to build up a cumulative assessment of the state of control in the company and the effectiveness with which risk is being managed or mitigated;
    - issues dealt with in reports reviewed by the board during the year, in particular the incidence of significant control failings or weaknesses that have been identified at any time during the period and the extent to which they have, or could have, resulted in unforeseen impact; and
    - the effectiveness of the company's public reporting processes.

Section 6
Related Financial and Business Reporting

44. The assessment and processes set out in this guidance should be used coherently to inform a number of distinct but related disclosures in the annual report and accounts. These are:
    - reporting on the principal risks facing the company and how they are managed or mitigated (as required by the Companies Act 2006 (the "Companies Act") and the Code);
    - reporting on whether the directors have a reasonable expectation that the company will be able to continue in operation and meet its liabilities as they fall due (as required by the Code);
    - reporting on the going concern basis of accounting (as required by accounting standards and the Code); and
    - reporting on the review of the risk management and internal control system (as required by the Code), and the main features of the company's risk management and internal control system in relation to the financial reporting process (as required under the UK Listing Authority's Disclosure and Transparency Rules).

45. The purpose of such reporting is to provide information about the company's current position and prospects and the principal risks it faces. It helps to demonstrate the board's stewardship and governance, and encourages shareholders to perform their own stewardship role by engaging in appropriate dialogue with the board and holding the directors to account as necessary.

46. As with all parts of the annual report and accounts, the board should provide clear and concise information that is tailored to the specific circumstances material to the company, and should avoid using standardised language which may be long on detail but short on insight. In considering how to meet the different disclosures summarised below, the board should bear in mind the need for the annual report and accounts as a whole to be fair, balanced and understandable.

47. For groups of companies, all reporting should be from the perspective of the group as a whole. An explanation should be given of how the board assesses and manages the risks faced in relation to investments in material joint ventures and associates. Where the board does not have access to, and oversight of, detailed information concerning those entities' business planning, risk management and internal controls, this fact should also be disclosed.

Principal risks

48. The Companies Act requires companies to publish a Strategic Report that must include "a fair review of the company's business, and a description of the principal risks and uncertainties facing the company". The Code states that the board should confirm that it has carried out a robust assessment of the principal risks and that the board should describe those risks and explain how they are being managed or mitigated (Provision C.2.1).

49. A risk or uncertainty may be unique to the company, a matter that is relevant to the market in which it operates or something that applies to the business environment more generally. Where the risk or uncertainty is more generic, the description should make clear how it might affect the company specifically.

50. The descriptions of the principal risks and uncertainties should be sufficiently specific that a shareholder can understand why they are important to the company. The report might include a description of the likelihood of the risk, an indication of the circumstances under which the risk might be most relevant to the company and its possible impacts. Significant changes in principal risks such as a change in the likelihood or possible impact, or the inclusion of new risks, should be highlighted and explained. A high-level explanation of how the principal risks and uncertainties are being managed or mitigated should also be included.

Reasonable expectation that the company can continue in operation

51. Provision C.2.2 of the Code requires that the directors should explain in the annual report – taking account of the company's current position and principal risks – how they have assessed the prospects of the company, over what period they have done so and why they consider that period to be appropriate. They should also state whether they have a reasonable expectation that the company will be able to continue in operation and meet its liabilities as they fall due over the period of their assessment, drawing attention to any qualifications or assumptions as necessary. Further guidance is provided in Appendix B.

52. There is likely to be a degree of overlap with the disclosures on principal risks and any material uncertainties relating to the going concern basis of accounting, and companies should consider how best to link them.

Going concern basis of accounting and related disclosures

53. Accounting standards require companies to adopt the going concern basis of accounting, except in circumstances where management intends to liquidate the entity or to cease trading, or has no realistic alternative to liquidation or cessation of operations.

54. Provision C.1.3 of the Code states that the directors should make an explicit statement of whether they considered it appropriate to adopt the going concern basis of accounting in preparing the annual and half-yearly financial statements.

55. Accounting standards also require companies to make an assessment of their ability to continue to adopt the going concern basis of accounting and to disclose any material uncertainties identified. In performing this assessment, the directors should consider all available information about the future, the possible outcomes of events and changes in conditions and the realistically possible responses to such events and conditions that would be available to the directors.

56. The Code states that the directors should identify in the financial statements any such material uncertainties over a period of at least twelve months from the date of approval of those financial statements. Further guidance on adopting and reporting on the going concern basis of accounting and disclosures on material uncertainties to be included in the financial statements is provided in Appendix A.

Statement on risk management and internal control

57. Provision C.2.3 of the Code states that the board should report in the annual report and accounts on its review of the effectiveness of the company's risk management and internal control systems. In its statement the board should, as a minimum, acknowledge: that it is responsible for those systems and for reviewing their effectiveness and disclose:
    - that there is an on-going process for identifying, evaluating and managing the principal risks faced by the company;
    - that the systems have been in place for the year under review and up to the date of approval of the annual report and accounts;
    - that they are regularly reviewed by the board; and
    - the extent to which the systems accord with the guidance in this document.

58. The board should summarise the process it has applied in reviewing the effectiveness of the system of risk management and internal control. The board should explain what actions have been or are being taken to remedy any significant failings or weaknesses. Where this information has been disclosed elsewhere in the annual report and accounts, for example in the audit committee report, a cross-reference to where that information can be found would suffice. In reporting on these actions, the board would not be expected to disclose information which, in its opinion, would be prejudicial to its interests.

59. The statement should incorporate, or be linked to, a description of the main features of the company's risk management and internal control system in relation to the financial reporting process, as required under the Disclosure and Transparency Rules.

60. The report on the review of the risk management and internal control systems is normally included in the corporate governance section of the annual report and accounts, but this reflects common practice rather than any mandatory requirement and companies can choose where to position it in their report. In any event, companies should consider whether and how to link reporting on the review of the risk management and internal control systems to the information on principal risks in the Strategic Report and material uncertainties relating to the going concern basis of accounting in the financial statements.

Safe Harbour Provision in relation to the Strategic Report, Directors' Report and the Directors' Remuneration Report

61. In considering where and how to report, the board is likely to find it helpful to be mindful of its legal duties and the so-called safe harbour afforded it.

62. Section 463 of the Companies Act provides that directors are liable to compensate the company if the company suffers any loss as the result of any untrue or misleading statement in (or any omission from) the Strategic Report, the Directors' Remuneration Report or the Directors' Report. The extent of the liability is limited: directors are only liable to the company. Further, directors are only liable to the company if they knew that the statements were untrue or misleading or if they knew that the omission was a dishonest concealment of a material fact. This protection is sometimes known as 'safe harbour'.

63. Accordingly, provided directors do not issue a deliberately or recklessly untrue or misleading statement or dishonestly conceal a material fact by way of an omission, they will not be liable to compensate the company for any loss incurred by it in reliance on the report.

64. In order to benefit from this protection, it is generally accepted that directors should ensure that information required in one of the three specified reports is included in those reports, either directly or via a specific cross-reference.
65. The exact scope and extent of the protection (including whether it extends to information included in a report on a voluntary basis) has not been tested in court and hence the legal position in relation to the inclusion of such information remains uncertain.

Appendix A
Going Concern Basis of Accounting and Material Uncertainties

Determining whether to adopt the going concern basis of accounting

1. Companies are required to adopt the going concern basis of accounting, except in circumstances where management intends to liquidate the entity or to cease trading, or has no realistic alternative to liquidation or cessation of operations.
2. Accordingly, the threshold for departing from the going concern basis of accounting is a very high hurdle, as there are often realistic alternatives to liquidation or cessation of trading even when material uncertainties related to events or conditions that may cast significant doubt upon the entity's ability to continue as a going concern have been identified.
3. Provision C.1.3 of the Code requires that the directors make an explicit statement in annual and half-yearly financial statements whether they considered it appropriate to adopt the going concern basis of accounting in preparing the financial statements, and in identifying any material uncertainties to its ability to continue to do so.

Determining whether there are material uncertainties

4. Accounting standards also require an assessment to be made of the entity's ability to continue to adopt the going concern basis of accounting.[4] In performing this assessment, the directors should consider all available information about the future, the possible outcomes of events and changes in conditions and the realistically possible responses to such events and conditions that would be available to the directors.
5. Events or conditions might result in the use of the going concern basis of accounting being inappropriate in future reporting periods. As part of their assessment, the directors should determine if there are any material uncertainties relating to events or conditions that might cast significant doubt upon the continuing use of the going concern basis of accounting in future periods. Uncertainties relating to such events or conditions should be considered material, and therefore disclosed, if their disclosure could reasonably be expected to affect the economic decisions of shareholders and other users of the financial statements. This is a matter of judgement. In making this judgement, the directors should consider the uncertainties arising from their assessment, both individually and in combination with others.
6. In determining whether there are material uncertainties, the directors should consider:
   - the magnitude of the potential impacts of the uncertain future events or changes in conditions on the company and the likelihood of their occurrence;
   - the realistic availability and likely effectiveness of actions that the directors would consider undertaking to avoid, or reduce the impact or likelihood of occurrence, of the uncertain future events or changes in conditions; and
   - whether the uncertain future events or changes in conditions are unusual, rather than occurring with sufficient regularity to make predictions about them with a high degree of confidence.
7. Uncertainties should not usually be considered material if the likelihood that the company will not be able to continue to use the going concern basis of accounting is assessed to be remote, however significant the assessed potential impact.

Reporting on the going concern basis of accounting and material uncertainties

8. To be useful the disclosures of material uncertainties must explicitly identify that they are material uncertainties that may cast significant doubt upon the entity's ability to continue to apply the going concern basis of accounting.[5] Provision C.1.3 of the Code requires that the directors identify in the financial statements any such material uncertainties over a period of at least twelve months from the date of approval of the financial statements.[6]

9. In the annual financial statements, three reporting scenarios follow from the directors' assessment of whether to adopt the going concern basis of accounting and whether there are material uncertainties:
   - the going concern basis of accounting is appropriate and there are no material uncertainties. The directors should adopt the going concern basis of accounting as part of the company's financial statements, make an explicit statement that the adoption of the going concern basis of accounting is considered appropriate and make any disclosures necessary to give a true and fair view; or
   - the going concern basis of accounting is appropriate but there are material uncertainties. The directors should adopt the going concern basis of accounting in preparing the financial statements, make an explicit statement that the adoption of the going concern basis of accounting is considered appropriate, disclose and identify any material uncertainties and make any other disclosures necessary to give a true and fair view; or
   - the going concern basis of accounting is not appropriate. Such a conclusion is likely to be rare. The directors should make an explicit statement that the adoption of the going concern basis of accounting is not considered appropriate, disclose the basis of accounting adopted and make any other disclosures necessary to give a true and fair view.

Half-yearly financial statements

10. Where an entity is required to prepare half-yearly financial statements,[7] the same considerations should apply as for the annual financial statements in relation to disclosures about the going concern basis of accounting and material uncertainties.

    Directors should therefore build on their understanding of these matters since the completion of the last annual report, update their conclusions on the basis of accounting and the existence of material uncertainties and revise their disclosures as necessary.

Appendix B
Longer Term Viability Statement

1. Provision C.2.2 of the Code requires that the directors should explain in the annual report – taking account of the company's current position and principal risks – how they have assessed the prospects of the company, over what period they have done so and why they consider that period to be appropriate. They should also state whether they have a reasonable expectation that the company will be able to continue in operation and meet its liabilities as they fall due over the period of their assessment, drawing attention to any qualifications or assumptions as necessary. This statement is intended to express the directors' view about the longer term viability of the company over an appropriate period of time selected by them.

Reasonable expectation and period covered

2. Reasonable expectation does not mean certainty. It does mean that the assessment can be justified. The longer the period considered, the more the degree of certainty can be expected to reduce.

3. That does not mean that the period chosen should be short. Except in rare circumstance it should be significantly longer than 12 months from the approval of the financial statements. The length of the period should be determined, taking account of a number of

factors, including without limitation: the board's stewardship responsibilities; previous statements they have made, especially in raising capital; the nature of the business and its stage of development; and its investment and planning periods.

4. The statement should be based on a robust assessment of those risks that would threaten the business model, future performance, solvency or liquidity of the company, including its resilience to the threats to its viability posed by those risks in severe but plausible scenarios. Such an assessment should include sufficient qualitative and quantitative analysis, and be as thorough as is judged necessary to make a soundly based statement. Stress and sensitivity analysis will often assist the directors in making their statement. These simulation techniques may help in assessing both the company's overall resilience to stress and its adaptability and the significance of particular variables to the projected outcome.

5. The directors should consider the individual circumstances of the company in tailoring appropriate analysis best suited to its position and performance, business model, strategy and principal risks. These should be undertaken with an appropriate level of prudence, i.e. weighting downside risks more heavily than upside opportunities. This may include analysis of reverse stress, starting from a presumption of failure and seeking to identify the circumstances in which this could occur.

Ability to continue in operation and meet liabilities as they fall due

6. Directors are encouraged to think broadly as to relevant matters which may threaten the company's future performance and so its ability to continue in operation and remain viable. Directors should consider risks to solvency (the company's ability to meet its financial liabilities in full), as well as liquidity (the ability to meet such liabilities as they fall due) – which may be a timing issue even if the entity appears to be solvent over time – and other threats to the company's viability.

7. The board's consideration of whether a risk or combination of risks could lead to an inability to continue in operation should take full account of the availability and likely effectiveness of actions that they would consider undertaking to avoid or reduce the impact or occurrence of the underlying risks and that realistically would be open to them in the circumstances. In considering the likely effectiveness of such actions, the conclusions of the board's regular monitoring and review of risk and internal control systems should be taken into account.

Qualifications or assumptions

8. Any qualifications or assumptions to which the directors consider it necessary to draw attention in their statement should be specific to the company's circumstances, rather than so generic that they could apply to any predictions about the future. They should be relevant to an understanding of the directors' rationale for making the statement. They should only include matters that are significant to the company's prospects and should not include matters that are highly unlikely either to arise or to have a significant impact on the company. Where relevant, they should cross-refer to, rather than repeat, disclosures given elsewhere.

Appendix C
Questions for the Board to Consider

Questions which the board may wish to consider and discuss with management and others such as the risk or internal audit functions are set out below. If the answers to the questions pose concern for the board it may wish to consider whether action is needed to address possible failings. The questions are not intended to be exhaustive and not all will be appropriate in all circumstances, but should be tailored to the company.

This Appendix should be read in conjunction with the guidance set out in this document.

Risk appetite and culture

- How has the board agreed the company's risk appetite? With whom has it conferred?
- How has the board assessed the company's culture? In what way does the board satisfy itself that the company has a 'speak-up' culture and that it systematically learns from past mistakes?
- How do the company's culture, code of conduct, human resource policies and performance reward systems support the business objectives and risk management and internal control systems?
- How has the board considered whether senior management promotes and communicates the desired culture and demonstrates the necessary commitment to risk management and internal control?
- How is inappropriate behaviour dealt with? Does this present consequential risks?
- How does the board ensure that it has sufficient time to consider risk, and how is that integrated with discussion on other matters for which the board is responsible?

Risk management and internal control systems

- To what extent do the risk management and internal control systems underpin and relate to the company's business model?
- How are authority, responsibility and accountability for risk management and internal control defined, co-ordinated and documented throughout the organisation? How does the board determine whether this is clear, appropriate and effective?
- How effectively is the company able to withstand risks, and risk combinations, which do materialise? How effective is the board's approach to risks with 'low probability' but a very severe impact if they materialise?
- How has the board assessed whether employees have the knowledge, skills and tools to manage risks effectively?
- What are the channels of communication that enable individuals, including third parties, to report concerns, suspected breaches of law or regulations, other improprieties or challenging perspectives?
- How does the board satisfy itself that the information it receives is timely, of good quality, reflects numerous information sources and is fit for purpose?
- What are the responsibilities of the board and senior management for crisis management? How effectively have the company's crisis management planning and systems been tested?
- To what extent has the company identified risks from joint ventures, third parties and from the way the company's business is organised? How are these managed?
- How effectively does the company capture new and emerging risks and opportunities?
- How and when does the board consider risk when discussing changes in strategy or approving new transactions, projects, products or other significant commitments?
- To what extent has the board considered the cost-benefit aspects of different control options?
- How does the board ensure it understands the company's exposure to each principal risk before and after the application of mitigations and controls, what those mitigations and controls are and whether they are operating as expected?

Monitoring and Review

- What are the processes by which senior management monitor the effective application of the systems of risk management and internal control?
- In what way do the monitoring and review processes take into account the company's ability to re-evaluate the risks and adjust controls effectively in response to changes in its objectives, its business, and its external environment?
- How are processes or controls adjusted to reflect new or changing risks, or operational deficiencies? To what extent does the board engage in horizon scanning for emerging risks?

Public reporting

- How has the board satisfied itself that the disclosures on risk management and internal control contribute to the annual report being fair, balanced and understandable, and provide shareholders with the information they need?

- How has the board satisfied itself that its reporting on going concern and the longer term viability statement gives a fair, balanced and understandable overview of the company's position and prospects?

Appendix D
UK Corporate Governance Code and Other Regulatory Requirements

UK Corporate Governance Code (2014 edition)

Section C: Accountability

Principle C.1: Financial and Business Reporting: *The board should present a fair, balanced and understandable assessment of the company's position and prospects.*

Provision C.1.3: *In annual and half-yearly financial statements, the directors should state whether they considered it appropriate to adopt the going concern basis of accounting in preparing them, and identify any material uncertainties to the company's ability to continue to do so over a period of at least twelve months from the date of approval of the financial statements.*

Principle C.2: Risk Management and Internal Control: *The board is responsible for determining the nature and extent of the principal risks it is willing to take in achieving its strategic objectives. The board should maintain sound risk management and internal control systems.*

Provision C.2.1: *The directors should confirm in the annual report that they have carried out a robust assessment of the principal risks facing the company, including those that would threaten its business model, future performance, solvency or liquidity. The directors should describe those risks and explain how they are being managed or mitigated.*

Provision C.2.2: *Taking account of the company's current position and principal risks, the directors should explain in the annual report how they have assessed the prospects of the company, over what period they have done so and why they consider that period to be appropriate. The directors should state whether they have a reasonable expectation that the company will be able to continue in operation and meet its liabilities as they fall due over the period of their assessment, drawing attention to any qualifications or assumptions as necessary.*

Provision C.2.3: *The board should monitor the company's risk management and internal control systems and, at least annually, carry out a review of their effectiveness, and report on that review in the annual report. The monitoring and review should cover all material controls, including financial, operational and compliance controls.*

Provision C.3.2 states that it is the responsibility of the audit committee *"to review the company's internal financial controls and, unless expressly addressed by a separate board risk committee composed of independent directors, or by the board itself, to review the company's internal control and risk management systems"*. Further guidance on the audit committee's responsibilities is set out in the FRC's *Guidance on Audit Committees*.

Other Code provisions are also relevant to the board's consideration of, and reporting on, risk. For example, Provision C.1.1 states that the board must make a statement that "the annual report and accounts, taken as a whole, is fair, balanced and understandable and provides the information necessary for shareholders to assess the company's performance, business model and strategy". Provision C.1.2 states that "the directors should include in the annual report an explanation of the basis on which the company generates or preserves value over the longer term (the business model) and the strategy for delivering the objectives of the company".

Companies Act 2006

Section 414A of the Companies Act 2006 requires all UK incorporated companies that are not small to prepare a strategic report for each financial year of the company. This report must include, amongst other things, "a fair review of the company's business, and a description of the principal risks and uncertainties facing the company". The review should be a balanced and comprehensive analysis of "the development and performance of the company's business during the financial year, and the position of the company's business at the end of the year".

The purpose of the Strategic Report is to help "members of the company" (shareholders) assess how the board has performed its duty under Section 172 of the Companies Act, which requires that "a director of a company must act in the way he considers, in good faith, would be most likely to promote the success of the company for the benefit of its members as a whole".[8]

Disclosure and Transparency Rules

Section 7.2.5R of the UK Listing Authority's Disclosure and Transparency Rules states that companies whose securities are admitted to trading on a regulated market (which includes all companies with Premium or Standard listings in the UK) are required to include in the corporate governance statement contained in their annual report and accounts "a description of the main features of the company's internal control and risk management systems in relation to the financial reporting process".

Separately, the Disclosure and Transparency Rules also require companies to include in their half-yearly financial reports a description of the principal risks and uncertainties for the remaining six months of the year (DTR 4.2.7) and, where accounting policies are to be changed in the subsequent annual financial statements, to follow the new policies and disclose the changes and the reasons for the changes (DTR 4.2.6).

UK Listing Rules

Under the UK Listing Authority's Listing Rules all companies with a Premium listing of equity shares in the UK, irrespective of their country of incorporation, are required to include in the annual report and accounts a statement of how they have applied the Main Principles of the Code and whether they have complied with its provisions. Where they have not complied with a provision, they are required to explain the reason.

Under Listing Rule LR 9.8.6R (3), the annual report for a premium listed company must include "A statement made by the directors that the business is a going concern, together with supporting assumptions or qualifications as necessary, that has been prepared in accordance with Going Concern and Liquidity Risk: Guidance for Directors of UK Companies 2009, published by the Financial Reporting Council in October 2009". The FRC has contacted the Financial Conduct Authority and companies should use this guidance for reporting years starting on or after 1 October 2014 whilst the reference to out of date guidance is being updated.

Accounting Standards

Paragraph 25 of International Accounting Standard 1 (IAS 1)[9] states that: "When preparing financial statements, management shall make an assessment of an entity's ability to continue as a going concern. An entity shall prepare financial statements on a going concern basis unless management either intends to liquidate the entity or to cease trading, or has no realistic alternative but to do so. When management is aware, in making its assessment, of material uncertainties related to events or conditions that may cast significant doubt upon the entity's ability to continue as a going concern, the entity shall disclose those uncertainties. When an entity does not prepare financial statements on a going concern basis, it shall disclose that fact, together with the basis on which it prepared the financial statements and the reason why the entity is not regarded as a going concern".

Other regulatory requirements

Some companies may be subject to other relevant regulatory requirements, for example because they operate within a regulated sector or because they are registered or listed in more than one jurisdiction. Companies will need to bear any such requirements in mind when considering how to apply this guidance.

Notes

1   The UK Corporate Governance Code applies to all companies with a Premium listing of equity shares on the London Stock Exchange regardless of whether they are incorporated in the UK or elsewhere.

2   Principal risks are defined in the Guidance on the Strategic Report (2014) – see: https://www.frc.org.uk/Our-Work/Publications/Accounting-and-Reporting-Policy/Guidance-on-the-Strategic-Report.pdf. A principal risk is a risk or combination of risks that can seriously affect the performance, future prospects or reputation of the entity. These should include those risks that would threaten its business model, future performance, solvency or liquidity.

3   The Companies Act 2006 requires companies to provide a Strategic Report.

4   IAS 1 paragraphs 25 and 26.

5   IFRIC Update July 2010.

6   IAS 1 paragraph 26 requires that the minimum period considered be at least, but not limited to, twelve months from the reporting date. FRS 102 paragraph 3.8 requires that the minimum period considered be at least, but not limited to, twelve months from the date the financial statements are authorised for issue.

7   Companies listed on a regulated market are required under the Disclosure and Transparency Rules to produce half-yearly financial reports.

8   FRC Guidance on the Strategic Report: https://www.frc.org.uk/Our-Work/Publications/Accounting-and-Reporting-Policy/Guidance-on-the-Strategic-Report.pdf.

9   The equivalent requirement under UK GAAP is in paragraphs 3.8 – 3.9 of FRS 102.

APPENDIX 7

The UK Stewardship Code

Financial Reporting Council's September 2012

Stewardship and the Code

1. Stewardship aims to promote the long term success of companies in such a way that the ultimate providers of capital also prosper. Effective stewardship benefits companies, investors and the economy as a whole.
2. In publicly listed companies responsibility for stewardship is shared. The primary responsibility rests with the board of the company, which oversees the actions of its management. Investors in the company also play an important role in holding the board to account for the fulfilment of its responsibilities.
3. The UK Corporate Governance Code identifies the principles that underlie an effective board. The UK Stewardship Code sets out the principles of effective stewardship by investors. In so doing, the Code assists institutional investors better to exercise their stewardship responsibilities, which in turn gives force to the "comply or explain" system.
4. For investors, stewardship is more than just voting. Activities may include monitoring and engaging with companies on matters such as strategy, performance, risk, capital structure, and corporate governance, including culture and remuneration. Engagement is purposeful dialogue with companies on these matters as well as on issues that are the immediate subject of votes at general meetings.
5. Institutional investors' activities include decision-making on matters such as allocating assets, awarding investment mandates, designing investment strategies, and buying or selling specific securities. The division of duties within and between institutions may span a spectrum, such that some may be considered asset owners and others asset managers.
6. Broadly speaking, asset owners include pension funds, insurance companies, investment trusts and other collective investment vehicles. As the providers of capital, they set the tone for stewardship and may influence behavioural changes that lead to better stewardship by asset managers and companies. Asset managers, with day-to-day responsibility for managing investments, are well positioned to influence companies' long-term performance through stewardship.
7. Compliance with the Code does not constitute an invitation to manage the affairs of a company or preclude a decision to sell a holding, where this is considered in the best interest of clients or beneficiaries.

Application of the Code

1. The UK Stewardship Code traces its origins to 'The Responsibilities of Institutional Shareholders and Agents: Statement of Principles,' first published in 2002 by the Institutional Shareholders Committee (ISC), and which the ISC converted to a code in 2009. Following the 2009 Walker Review of governance in financial institutions, the FRC was invited to take responsibility for the Code. In 2010, the FRC published the first version of the UK Stewardship Code, which closely mirrored the ISC code. This edition of the Code does not change the spirit of the 2010 Code.
2. The Code is directed in the first instance to institutional investors, by which is meant asset owners and asset managers with equity holdings in UK listed companies. Institutional investors may choose to outsource to external service providers some of the activities associated with stewardship. However, they cannot delegate their responsibility for stewardship. They remain responsible for ensuring those activities are carried out in a manner consistent with their own approach to stewardship. Accordingly, the Code also applies, by extension, to service providers, such as proxy advisors and investment consultants.
3. The FRC expects signatories of the Code to publish on their website, or if they do not have a website in another accessible form, a statement that:

- describes how the signatory has applied each of the seven principles of the Code and discloses the specific information requested in the guidance to the principles; or
- if one or more of the principles have not been applied or the specific information requested in the guidance has not been disclosed, explains why the signatory has not complied with those elements of the Code.

4. Disclosures under the Code should improve the functioning of the market for investment mandates. Asset owners should be better equipped to evaluate asset managers, and asset managers should be better informed, enabling them to tailor their services to meet asset owners' requirements.

5. In particular the disclosures should, with respect to conflicts of interest, address the priority given to client interests in decision-making; with respect to collective engagement, describe the circumstances under which the signatory would join forces with other institutional investors to ensure that boards acknowledge and respond to their concerns on critical issues and at critical times; and, with respect to proxy voting agencies, how the signatory uses their advice.

6. The statement of how the Code has been applied should be aligned with the signatory's role in the investment chain.

7. Asset owners' commitment to the Code may include engaging directly with companies or indirectly through the mandates given to asset managers. They should clearly communicate their policies on stewardship to their managers. Since asset owners are the primary audience of asset managers' public statements as well as client reports on stewardship, asset owners should seek to hold their managers to account for their stewardship activities. In so doing, they better fulfil their duty to their beneficiaries to exercise stewardship over their assets.

8. An asset manager should disclose how it delivers stewardship responsibilities on behalf of its clients. Following the publication in 2011 of the Stewardship Supplement to Technical Release AAF 01/06, asset managers are encouraged to have the policies described in their stewardship statements independently verified. Where appropriate, asset owners should also consider having their policy statements independently verified.

9. Overseas investors who follow other national or international codes that have similar objectives should not feel the application of the Code duplicates or confuses their responsibilities. Disclosures made in respect of those standards can also be used to demonstrate the extent to which they have complied with the Code. In a similar spirit, UK institutions that apply the Code should use their best efforts to apply its principles to overseas equity holdings.

10. Institutional investors with several types of funds or products need to make only one statement, but are encouraged to explain which of their funds or products are covered by the approach described in their statements. Where institutions apply a stewardship approach to other asset classes, they are encouraged to disclose this.

11. The FRC encourages service providers to disclose how they carry out the wishes of their clients with respect to each principle of the Code that is relevant to their activities.

12. Signatories are encouraged to review their policy statements annually, and update them where necessary to reflect changes in actual practice.

13. This statement should be easy to find on the signatory's website, or if they do not have a website in another accessible form, and should indicate when the statement was last reviewed. It should include contact details of an individual who can be contacted for further information and by those interested in collective engagement. The FRC hosts on its website the statements of signatories without their own website.

14. The FRC retains on its website a list of asset owners, asset managers and service providers that have published a statement on their compliance or otherwise with the Code, and requests that signatories notify the FRC when they have done so, and when the statement is updated.

15. The FRC regularly monitors the take-up and application of the Code. It expects the content of the Code to evolve over time to reflect developments in good stewardship practice, the structure and operation of the market, and the broader regulatory framework. Unless circumstances change, the FRC does not envisage proposing further changes to the Code until 2014 at the earliest.

Financial Reporting Council
September 2012

Comply or Explain

1. As with the UK Corporate Governance Code, the UK Stewardship Code should be applied on a "comply or explain" basis.
2. The Code is not a rigid set of rules. It consists of principles and guidance. The principles are the core of the Code and the way in which they are applied should be the central question for the institutional investor as it determines how to operate according to the Code. The guidance recommends how the principle might be applied.
3. Those signatories that choose not to comply with one of the principles, or not to follow the guidance, should deliver meaningful explanations that enable the reader to understand their approach to stewardship. In providing an explanation, the signatory should aim to illustrate how its actual practices contribute to good stewardship and promote the delivery of the institution's or its clients' investment objectives. They should provide a clear rationale for their approach.
4. The Financial Services Authority requires any firm authorised to manage funds, which is not a venture capital firm, and which manages investments for professional clients that are not natural persons, to disclose "the nature of its commitment" to the Code or "where it does not commit to the Code, its alternative investment strategy" (under Conduct of Business Rule 2.2.3[1]).
5. The FRC recognises that not all parts of the Code are relevant to all signatories. For example, smaller institutions may judge that some of its principles and guidance are disproportionate in their case. In these circumstances, they should take advantage of the "comply or explain" approach and set out why this is the case.
6. In their responses to explanations, clients and beneficiaries should pay due regard to the signatory's individual circumstances and bear in mind in particular the size and complexity of the signatory, the nature of the risks and challenges it faces, and the investment objectives of the signatory or its clients.
7. Whilst clients and beneficiaries have every right to challenge a signatory's explanations if they are unconvincing, they should not evaluate explanations in a mechanistic way. Departures from the Code should not be automatically treated as breaches. A signatory's clients and beneficiaries should be careful to respond to the statements from the signatory in a manner that supports the "comply or explain" process and bears in mind the purpose of good stewardship. They should put their views to the signatory and both parties should be prepared to discuss the position.

The Principles of the Code

So as to protect and enhance the value that accrues to the ultimate beneficiary, institutional investors should:

1. publicly disclose their policy on how they will discharge their stewardship responsibilities.
2. have a robust policy on managing conflicts of interest in relation to stewardship which should be publicly disclosed.
3. monitor their investee companies.
4. establish clear guidelines on when and how they will escalate their stewardship activities.
5. be willing to act collectively with other investors where appropriate.
6. have a clear policy on voting and disclosure of voting activity.
7. report periodically on their stewardship and voting activities.

The UK Stewardship Code

Principle 1

Institutional investors should publicly disclose their policy on how they will discharge their stewardship responsibilities.

Guidance

Stewardship activities include monitoring and engaging with companies on matters such as strategy, performance, risk, capital structure, and corporate governance, including culture and remuneration. Engagement is purposeful dialogue with companies on those matters as well as on issues that are the immediate subject of votes at general meetings.

The policy should disclose how the institutional investor applies stewardship with the aim of enhancing and protecting the value for the ultimate beneficiary or client.

The statement should reflect the institutional investor's activities within the investment chain, as well as the responsibilities that arise from those activities. In particular, the stewardship responsibilities of those whose primary activities are related to asset ownership may be different from those whose primary activities are related to asset management or other investment-related services.

Where activities are outsourced, the statement should explain how this is compatible with the proper exercise of the institutional investor's stewardship responsibilities and what steps the investor has taken to ensure that they are carried out in a manner consistent with the approach to stewardship set out in the statement.

The disclosure should describe arrangements for integrating stewardship within the wider investment process.

Principle 2

Institutional investors should have a robust policy on managing conflicts of interest in relation to stewardship which should be publicly disclosed.

Guidance

An institutional investor's duty is to act in the interests of its clients and/or beneficiaries.

Conflicts of interest will inevitably arise from time to time, which may include when voting on matters affecting a parent company or client.

Institutional investors should put in place, maintain and publicly disclose a policy for identifying and managing conflicts of interest with the aim of taking all reasonable steps to put the interests of their client or beneficiary first. The policy should also address how matters are handled when the interests of clients or beneficiaries diverge from each other.

Principle 3

Institutional investors should monitor their investee companies.

Guidance

Effective monitoring is an essential component of stewardship. It should take place regularly and be checked periodically for effectiveness.

When monitoring companies, institutional investors should seek to:

- keep abreast of the company's performance;
- keep abreast of developments, both internal and external to the company, that drive the company's value and risks;
- satisfy themselves that the company's leadership is effective;
- satisfy themselves that the company's board and committees adhere to the spirit of the UK Corporate Governance Code, including through meetings with the chairman and other board members;
- consider the quality of the company's reporting; and
- attend the General Meetings of companies in which they have a major holding, where appropriate and practicable.

Institutional investors should consider carefully explanations given for departure from the UK Corporate Governance Code and make reasoned judgements in each case. They should give a timely explanation to the company, in writing where appropriate, and be prepared to enter a dialogue if they do not accept the company's position.

Institutional investors should endeavour to identify at an early stage issues that may result in a significant loss in investment value. If they have concerns, they should seek to ensure that the appropriate members of the investee company's board or management are made aware.

Institutional investors may or may not wish to be made insiders. An institutional investor who may be willing to become an insider should indicate in its stewardship statement the willingness to do so, and the mechanism by which this could be done.

Institutional investors will expect investee companies and their advisers to ensure that information that could affect their ability to deal in the shares of the company concerned is not conveyed to them without their prior agreement.

Principle 4

Institutional investors should establish clear guidelines on when and how they will escalate their stewardship activities.

Guidance

Institutional investors should set out the circumstances in which they will actively intervene and regularly assess the outcomes of doing so. Intervention should be considered regardless of whether an active or passive investment policy is followed. In addition, being underweight is not, of itself, a reason for not intervening. Instances when institutional investors may want to intervene include, but are not limited to, when they have concerns about the company's strategy, performance, governance, remuneration or approach to risks, including those that may arise from social and environmental matters.

Initial discussions should take place on a confidential basis. However, if companies do not respond constructively when institutional investors intervene, then institutional investors should consider whether to escalate their action, for example, by:

- holding additional meetings with management specifically to discuss concerns;
- expressing concerns through the company's advisers;
- meeting with the chairman or other board members;
- intervening jointly with other institutions on particular issues;
- making a public statement in advance of General Meetings;
- submitting resolutions and speaking at General Meetings; and
- requisitioning a General Meeting, in some cases proposing to change board membership.

Principle 5

Institutional investors should be willing to act collectively with other investors where appropriate.

Guidance

At times collaboration with other investors may be the most effective manner in which to engage.

Collective engagement may be most appropriate at times of significant corporate or wider economic stress, or when the risks posed threaten to destroy significant value.

Institutional investors should disclose their policy on collective engagement, which should indicate their readiness to work with other investors through formal and informal groups when this is necessary to achieve their objectives and ensure companies are aware of concerns. The disclosure should also indicate the kinds of circumstances in which the institutional investor would consider participating in collective engagement.

Principle 6

Institutional investors should have a clear policy on voting and disclosure of voting activity.

Guidance

Institutional investors should seek to vote all shares held. They should not automatically support the board.

If they have been unable to reach a satisfactory outcome through active dialogue then they should register an abstention or vote against the resolution. In both instances, it is good practice to inform the company in advance of their intention and the reasons why.

Institutional investors should disclose publicly voting records.

Institutional investors should disclose the use made, if any, of proxy voting or other voting advisory services. They should describe the scope of such services, identify the providers and disclose the extent to which they follow, rely upon or use recommendations made by such services.

Institutional investors should disclose their approach to stock lending and recalling lent stock.

Principle 7

Institutional investors should report periodically on their stewardship and voting activities.

Guidance

Institutional investors should maintain a clear record of their stewardship activities.

Asset managers should regularly account to their clients or beneficiaries as to how they have discharged their responsibilities. Such reports will be likely to comprise qualitative as well as quantitative information. The particular information reported and the format used, should be a matter for agreement between agents and their principals.

Asset owners should report at least annually to those to whom they are accountable on their stewardship policy and its execution.

Transparency is an important feature of effective stewardship. Institutional investors should not, however, be expected to make disclosures that might be counterproductive. Confidentiality in specific situations may well be crucial to achieving a positive outcome.

Asset managers that sign up to this Code should obtain an independent opinion on their engagement and voting processes having regard to an international standard or a UK framework such as AAF 01/06[2]. The existence of such assurance reporting should be publicly disclosed. If requested, clients should be provided access to such assurance reports.

Notes

1   http://fsahandbook.info/FSA/html/handbook/COBS/2/2
2   Assurance reports on internal controls of service organisations made available to third parties:
     http://www.icaew.com/en/technical/audit-and-assurance/assurance/technical-release-aaf-01-06

APPENDIX 8

FRC Corporate Culture and the Role of Boards: Report of Observations 2016

2016

The FRC Corporate Culture and the Role of Boards: Report of Observations 2016 can be downloaded here: https://frc.org.uk/Our-Work/Publications/Corporate-Governance/Corporate-Culture-and-the-Role-of-Boards-Report-o.pdf

APPENDIX 9

The King Code of Governance principles (King IV)

November 2016

The King Code of Governance principles (King IV) can be downloaded here: www.iodsa.co.za/page/KingIVReport

Glossary

Accountability The requirement for a person in a position of responsibility to justify, explain or account for the exercise of his/her authority and his/her performance or actions. Accountability is to the person or persons from whom the authority is derived.

Agency theory Theory based on the separation of ownership from control in a large organisation and the conflict of interests between the individuals who direct the organisation and the people who own it. In a company, the directors act as agents for the shareholders, and the conflict of interests between them should be controlled.

Aggressive accounting Accounting policies by a company that are just within accepted accounting practice, but which have the effect of making the company's performance seem better than it would if more conservative accounting policies were used. For example, accounting policies might be used that recognise income at an early stage in a transaction process, or defer the recognition of expenses.

Annual general meeting (AGM) An annual meeting of the equity shareholders of a company. Public companies are required to hold an annual general meeting.

'Apply or explain' rule Similar to the 'comply or explain' rule. Companies should apply the principles of a code or explain why they have not done so.

Audit committee Committee of the board, consisting entirely of independent non-executive directors, with responsibility (among other things) for monitoring the reliability of the financial statements, the quality of the external audit and the company's relationship with its external auditors.

Audit firm rotation Changing the firm of external auditors on a regular basis, say every seven years. Audit partner rotation Changing the lead partner (and possibly other partners) involved with a company audit on a regular basis, typically every five or seven years.

Audit report Report for shareholders produced by the external auditors on completion of the annual audit, and included in the company's published annual report and accounts. The report gives the opinion of the auditors on whether the financial statements present a true and fair view of the company's financial performance and position.

Balance of power A situation in which power is shared out more or less evenly between a number of different individuals or groups, so that no single individual or group is in a position to dominate.

Bear phase A period when a stock market goes into decline.

Board committee A committee established by the board of directors, with delegated responsibility for a particular aspect of the board's affairs. For example, audit committee, remuneration/compensation committee and nominations committee.

Board succession The replacement of a senior director (typically the chairman or CEO) when he or she retires or resigns.

Bond credit ratings Ratings given to issues of bonds by agencies such as Standard & Poor's and Moody's, which give an assessment of the credit risk for investors in the bonds, i.e. the risk of default by the credit issuer.

Box-ticking approach An approach to compliance based on following all the specific rules or provisions in a code, and not considering the principles that should be applied and circumstances where the principles are best applied by not following the detailed provisions.

Business risk Risks (and opportunities) facing the organisation. Consists of strategic risk, operational risk, financial (reporting) risk and compliance risk.

Cadbury Code A code of corporate governance, published by the Cadbury Committee in the UK in 1992 (and since superseded).

Chairman Leader of the board of directors. Often referred to as the 'company chairman' in companies and 'chair' in public bodies and voluntary organisations.

Chief executive officer (CEO) The executive director who is head of the executive management team in an organisation.

Class 1 transactions Large transactions for which prior shareholders approval is required, including major takeovers or the disposal of a large part of a company's business operations.

Close period A period of time during which directors should not (in normal circumstances) buy or sell shares in their company.

Combined Code The UK code on corporate governance for listed companies from 1998 to 2010. It was revised in 2010 and renamed the UK Corporate Governance Code.

Compliance controls Internal controls to prevent or detect errors resulting from compliance risks.

Compliance risk Risk of a failure to comply with laws or regulations, and the consequences of such a failure if discovered.

Compliance statement A statement by a listed company of whether it has complied with the requirements of the national code of corporate governance, and if not, in what ways has it failed to do so. In the UK, listed companies are required by the Listing Rules to include a compliance statement in their annual report and accounts.

Comply or explain rule Requirement (e.g. in the UK, a requirement of the Listing Rules) for a company to comply with a voluntary code of corporate governance (in the UK, the UK Corporate Governance Code) or explain any non-compliance.

Corporate citizen A company acting with due regard for its responsibilities as a member of the society in which it operates. Corporate citizenship is demonstrated through CSR policies.

Corporate ethics Standards of business behaviour, sometimes set out by companies in a code of corporate ethics.

Corporate governance The system by which a company is directed, so as to achieve its overall objectives. It is concerned with relationships, structures, processes, information flows, controls, decision-making and accountability at the highest level in a company.

Corporate social responsibility (CSR) Responsibility shown by a company (or other organisations) for matters of general concern to the society in which it operates, such as protection of the environment, health and safety, and social welfare.

CSR index An index that measures and rates companies in terms of their CSR performance. Produced by publishers of stock market indices (Dow Jones, FTSE). Used by institutional investors.

Deferred annual bonus scheme An element in a remuneration package for directors or senior executives whereby the individuals are allowed to use some or all of their annual cash bonus entitlement to acquire shares in the company, which are then matched after several years (typically three years) by the award of additional free shares.

Derivative action Legal action taken against a director by shareholders in the name of the company, alleging negligence or breach of duty.

Directors' report The 'report' in the annual report and accounts of a company. A report by the board of directors to the shareholders, contained in the annual report and accounts of the company and containing a variety of reports and information disclosures, such as the business review and remuneration report.

Disaster recovery plan Plans to be implemented, in the event of a disaster that puts normal operational systems out of action, to restore operational capability as quickly as possible. The need for many companies to have a disaster recovery plan was highlighted by the terrorist attack on the US on 11 September 2001.

Disclosure and Transparency Rules in the UK, rules on disclosures that listed companies are required to comply with. The rules (like the Listing Rules) are issued and enforced by the UK financial markets regulator.

Downside risk A risk that actual events will turn out worse than expected. Downside risk can be measure in terms of the amount by which profits could be worse than expected. The expected outcome is the forecast or budget expectation.

Duty of skill and care A duty owed by a director to the company. In the UK, this has been a common law duty, but became a statutory duty under the provisions of the Companies Act 2006. A question can be raised, however, about what level of skill and care should be expected from a director.

Enlightened shareholder approach Approach to corporate governance based on the view that the objective of its directors should be to meet the needs of shareholders, whilst also showing concern for other major stakeholders. Also called an inclusive approach to governance.

Environmental, social and governance (ESG) risks Environmental, social and governance risks. These are risks of adverse consequences to a company from circumstances or events relating to environmental, social or corporate governance issues.

EU Directive An instruction, devised by the European Commission and approved by the European Council and European Parliament. The contents of a Directive must be introduced into national law or regulations by all member states of the European Union. Some Directives, such as the Shareholder Rights Directive, deal wholly or partly with corporate governance issues.

European Commission The managing and administrative body of the European Union.

Executive director A director who also has executive responsibilities in the management structure. Usually a full-time employee with a contract of employment.

External audit Statutory annual audit of a company by independent external auditors.

Fairness Impartiality, a lack of bias. In a corporate governance context, the quality of fairness refers to things that are done or decided in a reasonable manner, and with a sense of justice, avoiding bias.

Fiduciary duty A duty of a trustee. The directors of a company are given their powers in trust by the company, and have fiduciary duties towards the company.

Financial controls Internal controls to prevent or detect errors resulting from financial risks.

Financial (reporting) risk A risk of a failure or error, deliberate (fraud) or otherwise, in the systems or procedures for recording financial transactions and reporting financial performance and position, or the risk of a failure to safeguard financial assets such as cash and accounts receivable.

Financial statement A statement containing financial information. The main financial statements by a company are the balance sheet and profit and loss account in the annual report and accounts. Other financial statements include a cash flow statement and the balance sheet and profit and loss account in a company's published interim or quarterly accounts.

Fixed pay The elements in a remuneration package that are a fixed amount each year, such as basic salary.

G20/OECD Principles of Corporate Governance General principles of corporate governance issued by the G20 and the Organisation for Economic Co-operation and Development, which all countries are encouraged to adopt.

General meeting A meeting of the equity shareholders of a company. Public companies are required to hold an annual general meeting (AGM).

Going concern statement A requirement of some corporate governance codes, such as the UK Corporate Governance Code. A statement by the board of directors that in their view the company will remain as a going concern for the next financial year.

Greenbury Report Report in the UK in 1995 by the Greenbury Committee, focusing mainly on corporate governance issues related to directors' remuneration.

GRI Sustainability Reporting Framework A voluntary framework for standardising the content of, and measurements in, sustainability reports.

Hampel Commitee Committee set up in the UK to continue the review of corporate governance practices in the UK, following the Cadbury and Greenbury Committee Reports. The Hampel Committee suggested that the recommendations of all three committees should be integrated into a single code of corporate governance, which was published in 1998 as the Combined Code.

Higgs Report The 2003 UK government-commissioned review into the role and effectiveness of non-executive directors.

Induction Process of introducing a newly appointed director into his or her role, by providing appropriate information, site visits, meetings with management and (where necessary) training.

Insider dealing Dealing in the shares of a company by an 'insider' (such as a company director or professional adviser) on the basis of knowledge of price-sensitive information that has not yet been made available to the public. A criminal activity.

Insider list A list of persons in a company who have access to inside information, which listed companies are required to prepare and maintain under the Market Abuse Regulation.

Institutional investor An organisation or institution that invests funds of clients, savers or depositors. The main institutional investors in the UK are pension funds, insurance/life assurance companies, investment trust companies and mutual organisations such as unit trusts and open-ended investment companies ('OEICs'). Institutional investors are the main investors in shares in the leading stock markets of the world. In the UK, most institutional investors are members of an 'industry association', such as the Association of British Insurers (ABI) and the Pensions and Lifetime Savings Association (PLSA).

Institutional Shareholders Committee (ISC) A collective body representing the associations of institutional investors in the UK, including the ABI and PLSA.

Integrated reporting Reporting on all aspects of a company's activities that have relevance to the creation or loss of value in six areas of capital: financial, manufactured, human, intellectual property, natural and social. Similar to sustainability reporting, but directed at the company's shareholders.

Internal audit Investigations and checks carried out by internal auditors of an organisation. Internal audit is a function rather than a specific activity. However, the programme of the internal audit team might reduce the amount of work the external auditors need to carry out in their annual audit, provided the internal and external auditors collaborate properly.

Internal control A procedure or arrangement that is implemented to prevent an internal control risk, reduce the potential impact of such a risk, or detect a failure of internal control when it occurs (and initiate remedial action).

Internal control report A statement by the board of directors of a listed company to the shareholders on internal control, and contained in the company's annual report and accounts. This statement is a requirement of the UK Corporate Governance Code and the Disclosure and Transparency Rules.

Internal control risk A risk of failure in a system or procedure due to causes that are within the control of management. They can be categorised as financial risks, operational risk and compliance risks.

Internal control system A system of internal controls within an organisation. The system should have a suitable control environment, and should provide for the identification and assessment of internal control risks, the design and implementation of internal controls, communication and information and monitoring. In the UK, the board of directors of a listed company has responsibility for the system of internal control.

International Corporate Governance Network (ICGN) A voluntary association of institutional investors which has the objective of raising standards of corporate governance globally, to meet the requirements and expectations of global investors.

King Code Also called the King Report and King IV (because it is the fourth version of the Code/Report, issued in 2016). The corporate governance code for listed companies in South Africa.

Majority shareholder A shareholder holding a majority of the equity shares in a company and so having a controlling interest in the company. A majority shareholder has the voting power to remove directors from the board, and so can control the board.

Management board A board of executive managers, chaired by the CEO, within a two-tier board structure. The chairman of the management board reports to the chairman of the supervisory board. The management board has responsibility for the operational performance of the business.

Market abuse Market abuse occurs when an individual distorts a market in investments, creates a false or misleading impression of the value or price of an investment, or misuses relevant information before it is published. Although it is similar to insider dealing, which is a criminal offence, this is a civil offence under the Financial Services and Markets Act.

Market Abuse Regulation (MAR) An EU regulation containing prohibitions of insider dealing and market manipulation, effective across the EU from 3rd July 2016.

Minority shareholders Shareholders holding a fairly small proportion of the total equity shares in a company who could be at risk of having their interests ignored in favour of a controlling shareholder or group of large shareholders.

Model articles of association In the context of UK company law, a company may adopt standard articles of association (company constitution) and amend these as necessary to meet the requirements and particular circumstances of the individual company. In practice, the articles of association of most UK companies formed under the Companies Act 1985 are based on the Table A Articles. Different model articles apply to companies formed under the Companies Act 2006.

Modified audit report Audit report in which the auditors express some reservations about the financial statements of the company, because of insufficient information to reach an opinion or disagreement with the figures in the statements.

Money laundering The process of transferring or using money obtained from criminal activity, so as to make it seem to have come from legitimate (non-criminal) sources. Companies are often used as a cover for money laundering.

Myners Report Produced in 1995 by a working group set up to look into the relationship between companies and institutional investors.

Nasdaq A stock market in the USA.

Nolan Committee on Standards in Public Life A committee set up in 1995 in response to concerns regarding governance of the UK public sector. The Committee published a set of Principles.

Nomination committee A committee of the board of directors, with responsibility for identifying potential new members for the board of directors. Suitable candidates are recommended to the main board, which then makes a decision about their appointment.

Non-audit work Work done by a firm of auditors for a client company, other than work on the annual audit, such as consultancy services and tax advice. In the context of corporate governance, the independence of the auditors might be questionable when they earn high fees for non-audit work.

Non-executive director A director who is not an employee of the company and who does not have any responsibilities for executive management in the company.

OECD Principles of Corporate Governance General principles of corporate governance issued by the G20 and the Organisation for Economic Co-operation and Development, which all countries are encouraged to adopt.

Operational controls Internal controls to prevent or detect errors resulting from operational risks.

Operational risk Risk of an error, deliberate or otherwise, in operating systems or procedures within an organisation; the risk of failure in equipment or system design; the risk of failures due to weak organisational structure; or risks due to human error including inefficient management. Includes health and safety risks, environmental risks.

Performance-based incentives Incentives to an individual, typically to an executive director and in the form of a cash bonus, that are payable if certain performance targets are achieved. Performance targets might be related to a rise in the share price, growth in sales or profits, growth in earnings per share, or to non-financial performance criteria.

Premium listing One of two categories of listing for companies in the UK. Companies with a premium listing are required to meet the highest standards of regulation and corporate governance.

Price-sensitive information Undisclosed information that, if generally known, would be likely to have an effect on the share price of the company concerned.

Principles-based code of governance A code based on general principles of best governance practice, rather than detailed rules and guidelines. A principles-based code may include some practical provisions or guidelines, but these are not comprehensive.

Proxy A person appointed by a shareholder to vote on the shareholder's behalf at a general meeting. In the UK, shareholders can appoint proxies electronically. They can either instruct a proxy how to vote on each resolution at a meeting, or can give the proxy freedom to decide how to vote on each resolution.

Proxy vote A vote delivered by an individual (a proxy) on behalf of a shareholder, in the shareholder's absence.

Red top warning A notice sent out by an institutional investor organisation to its members, advising the members who are shareholders to vote against a particular resolution at an approaching general meeting of a company.

Related party transaction A transaction by a company with a 'related party' such as a major shareholder, a director, a company in which a director has a major interest or a member of a director's family.

Remuneration committee A committee of the board of directors, with responsibility for deciding remuneration policy for top executives and the individual remuneration packages of certain senior executives, for example all the executive directors.

Reputation risk Risk to the reputation of a company or other organisation in the mind of the public (including customers and suppliers) when a particular matter becomes public knowledge.

Responsibility Having power and authority over something. A person in a position of responsibility should be held accountable for the exercise of that authority.

Responsible investing Investing with due consideration for environmental, social and governance issues, because these can affect the value of the business.

Responsible voting Voting by a shareholder in a way that fulfils the shareholder's responsibilities to another group, typically the shareholder's clients. The term is used in connection with voting by institutional shareholders. It is increasingly accepted that institutional shareholders should vote responsibly in the interests of their clients. Responsible voting is associated with upholding best practice in corporate governance.

Risk appetite The amount and type of business risk that the board of directors would like their company to have exposure to. Identifying risk appetite should be a part of strategic planning.

Risk assessment An assessment of risks faced by an organisation. Typically, risks are assessed according to how probable or how frequent an adverse outcome is likely to be in the planning period and the potential size of the losses if an adverse outcome occurs. The greatest risks are those with a high probability of an adverse outcome combined with the likelihood of a large loss if this were to happen.

Risk committee A committee of the board that a company may establish, with the responsibility of monitoring the risk management system within the company, instead of the audit committee. A risk committee may be established when the audit committee has too many other responsibilities to handle.

Risk management committee A committee of senior executive managers and risk managers, whose responsibility is to implement the risk management strategy of the board.

Risk tolerance The amount of business risk that the board is willing to let their company be exposed to.

Safe harbour provisions Provisions in the UK Companies Act whereby directors are not liable for incorrect or misleading statements (or omissions) in a report to shareholders, unless they knew the statements or omissions to be incorrect or misleading. These provisions reduced concern about directors' liability for the information provided by their company in its strategic report.

Sarbanes-Oxley Act Legislation, largely on corporate governance issues, introduced in the US in 2002 following a series of corporate scandals such as Enron and WorldCom.

Secret profit A profit that is not revealed. In the context of corporate governance, a director should not make a secret profit for his/her personal benefit and at the expense of the company.

Senior independent director (SID) A non-executive director who is the nominal head of all the non-executive directors on the board. The SID may act as a channel of communication between the NEDs and the chairman, or (in some situations) between major shareholders and the board.

Severance payment Payment to a director (or other employee) on being required to resign (or otherwise leave the company).

Share options Rights given to an individual giving him (or her) the right but not the obligation to buy new shares in the company at a fixed price (the exercise price), not earlier than a specified date and not later than a specified date in the future (typically not earlier than three years after the options are granted and not later than ten years respectively).

Shareholder activism A term that refers to (1) the considered use by institutional investors of their rights as shareholders, by voting against the board of directors at general meetings (or threatening to vote against the board); and (2) active dialogue with the boards of companies, to influence decisions by the board.

Shareholder engagement Similar in meaning to shareholder activism, except that the term is associated more with active and constructive dialogue rather than opposition to the board.

Shareholder value approach Approach to corporate governance based on the view that the objective of its directors should be to maximise benefits for shareholders.

Socially responsible investment (SRI) Investment by institutional investors that takes into consideration ethical issues and the CSR policies of companies when deciding which companies to invest in or whether to hold on to investments.

Stakeholder A stakeholder group is an identifiable group of individuals or organisations with a vested interest. Stakeholder groups in a company include the shareholders, the directors, senior executive management and other employees, customers, suppliers, the general public and (in the case of many companies) the government. Stakeholders may be categorised as financial or non-financial stakeholders, and as external or internal stakeholders (depending on whether they work in the company). The nature of their interests differs between stakeholder groups.

Stakeholder approach Approach to governance based on the view that the organisation should aim to satisfy the needs of all stakeholders. Also called a pluralist approach.

Stakeholder theory The view that the purpose of corporate governance should be to satisfy, as far as possible, the objectives of all key stakeholders.

Statutory duties Duties imposed by statute law.

Strategic risk Risk from unexpected events or developments in a business or in the business environment, which are outside the control of management. Business risks should be managed and kept within acceptable limits.

Stress testing Testing the ability of a business to withstand the effects of extreme adverse events or developments in the business environment.

Supervisory board A board of non-executive directors, found in a company with a two-tier board structure. The supervisory board reserves some responsibilities to itself. These include oversight of the management board.

Sustainability Conducting business operations in a way that can be continued into the foreseeable future, without using natural resources at such a rate or creating such environmental damage that the continuation of the business will eventually become impossible.

Sustainability report Report on the economic, social and environmental performance of a company.

Total shareholder return The total returns in a period earned by the company's shareholders, consisting normally of the dividends received and the gain (or minus the fall) in the share price during the period. The returns might be expressed as a percentage of the share value, e.g. the share price at the start of the period.

Transaction cost theory A theory about organisations that includes the view that management are opportunistic and may take opportunities that arise to pursue their personal interests.

Transparency Openness. Being clear about historical performance and future intentions, and not trying to hide information.

Triple bottom line reporting Reporting on the economic, social and environmental performance of a company.

Turnbull Guidance Initially a report of the Turnbull Committee in the UK, giving listed companies guidance on how the directors should carry out their responsibility for the internal control system, as required by the UK Corporate Governance Code. Now the responsibility of the FRC.

Two-tier board Board structure in which responsibilities are divided between a supervisory board of non-executive directors led by the chairman and a management board of executives led by the CEO.

UK Corporate Governance Code The code of corporate governance issued by the Financial Reporting Council in the UK, which is applied to UK listed companies. Formerly (until 2010) called the Combined Code.

UK Listing Rules Rules that apply to all listed companies in the UK. They include the 'comply or explain' rule on compliance with the UK Corporate Governance Code.

UK Stewardship Code A set of principles and guidelines for behaviour by institutional investors in their dealings with a company, issued by the FRC. This Code is based on a code previously issued by the ISC.

Unitary board Board structure in which decisions are taken by a single group of executive and non-executive directors, led by the company chairman.

Upside risk A risk that actual events will turn out better than expected and will provide unexpected profits. Some risks, such as the risk of a change in foreign exchange rates, a change in interest rates, or a change in consumer buying patterns could be 'two-way' with both upside and downside potential.

Voluntary code of governance A code of governance that is not enforced by law or regulation. However, as in the UK and South Africa, listed companies may be encouraged to adopt a voluntary code by means of a 'comply or explain' or 'apply or explain' regulation.

Vote withheld A voting option for shareholders who appoint a proxy, as an alternative to voting for or against a resolution, or not voting at all. The proxy may be instructed to abstain on a particular resolution at the general meeting. Votes withheld are 'positive abstentions' and the number of votes withheld should be counted and recorded.

Walker Report A report published in the UK in 2009 about corporate governance in banks and other financial services organisations, following the banking crisis of 2007–2008.

Window dressing of accounts Applying accounting policies that are just within the limits of permissible accounting practice, but which have the effect of making the company's performance or financial position seem better than it would if more conservative accounting policies were used. For example, accounting policies might be used that recognise income at an early stage in a transaction process, or defer the recognition of expenses.

Wrongful trading Wrongful trading occurs when a company continues to trade when the directors are aware that the company had gone into (or would soon go into) insolvent liquidation.

Directory

Further Reading

General

Barber, B., ICSA's *Corporate Governance Handbook*, 4th edition (ICSA Publishing, 2017)

Chambers, A., *Corporate Governance Handbook*, 4th edition (Bloomsbury Professional, 2008)

Charkham, J., *Keeping Better Company: Corporate Governance Ten Years on*, 2nd edition (Oxford University Press, 2008)

Clarke, T., *Theories of Corporate Governance* (Routledge, 2004)

Dattani, R., *The ICSA Directors' Handbook* (ICSA Publishing, 2009)

Herbert Smith LLP, *A Practical Guide to the UK Listing Regime*, 3rd edition (ICSA Publishing, 2014)

Keasey, K. (ed), *Corporate Governance: Accountability, Enterprise and International Comparisons* (John Wiley and Sons, 2005)

Mallin, C., *Corporate Governance*, 3rd edition (Oxford University Press, 2009)

Monks, A. G. and Minow, N. (eds), *Corporate Governance*, 3rd edition (Blackwell, 2007)

Solomon, J. F., *Corporate Governance and Accountability*, 3rd edition (John Wiley & Sons Inc, 2010)

Tricker, R. I., *Corporate Governance: Principles, Policies and Practices* (OUP, 2012)

Wearing, R., *Cases in Corporate Governance* (Sage, 2005)

Not-for-Profit/Public Sector

Carver, J. and Shrader, A., *Boards That Make a Difference: A New Design for Leadership in Nonprofit and Public Organizations*, 3rd edition (Jossey-Bass, 2006)

Charity Commission, *The Hallmarks of an Effective Charity* (2010)

CIPFA, *Approaches to Corporate Governance in the Public Sector* (2000)

Cornforth, C., *The Governance of Public and Non-Profit Organisations – What Do Boards Do?* (Routledge, 2005)

Dyer, P. and Ramrayka, L. (eds),*The Good Trustee Guide*, 5th edition (NCVO Publications, 2008)

National Housing Federation, *Competence and Accountability 2004 Code of Governance* (2004)

Priestley, Chris, *The ICSA Charity Trustee's Guide*, 3rd edition (ICSA Publishing, 2012)

Semple, K ed., *The ICSA Charities Handbook*, 3rd edition (ICSA Publishing, 2014)

Corporate Social Responsibility

Hoskins, T., *Corporate Social Responsibility Handbook: Making CSR Work for Your Business*, 3rd edition (ICSA Publishing, 2012)

OECD guidelines for multinational companies. See www.oecd.org

Directors, Boards and Committees

Executive remuneration: Guidelines on Policies and Practices (ABI, 2009). Available at www.ivis.co.uk

Bruce, M., *Rights and Duties of Directors*, 10th edition (Bloomsbury Professional, 2010)

Bruce, M., *The ICSA Director's Guide*, 5th edition (ICSA Publishing, 2013)

Cadbury, A., *Corporate Governance and Chairmanship: A Personal View* (Oxford University Press, 2002)

Charon, R., *Boards that Deliver* (Jossey-Bass, 2005)

Copnell, T., *The ICSA Audit Committee Guide*, 2nd edition (ICSA Publishing, 2010)

Coyle, Brian., *The Non-Executive Directors' Handbook*, 3rd edition (ICSA Publishing, 2013)

Dunne, P., *Running Board Meetings*, 3rd edition (Kogan Page, 2007)

Garrett, R., *Thin on Top* (Nicholas Brealey Publishing, 2006)

Leblanc, R. and Gillies, J., *Inside the Boardroom* (John Wiley and Sons, 2005)

Nadler, D.A., *Building Better Boards* (Pfeiffer Wiley, 2006)

Stiles, P. and Taylor, B., *Boards at Work* (Oxford University Press, 2002)

Shareholder relations

ABI/NAPF Statement on Responsible Voting (ABI/NAPF, 1999). Available at www.ivis.co.uk

Developments in Narrative Reporting: An ABI Position Paper (ABI, 2006)

Charkham, J. and Simpson, A., *Fair Shares: The Future of Shareholder Power and Responsibility* (Oxford University Press, 1999)

Copnell, T. and Ray, S., *ICSA Shareholder Questions and the AGM* (ICSA Publishing, 2007)

Hermes, *Hermes Statement on Corporate Governance and Voting Policy* (Hermes, 1998, updated 2001). Available at www.hermes.co.uk

Hermes, *The Hermes Responsible Ownership Principles* (Hermes, 2010). Available at www.hermes.co.uk

PIRC, *Shareholder Voting Guidelines* (PIRC, 2008)

PLSA, Corporate Governance Policy and Voting Guidelines (PLSA, 2015/16)

PLSA, Stewardship Policy. Available at www.plsa.co.uk

Reports, Codes of Practice and Guidelines

Boardroom Behaviours: A Report prepared for Sir David Walker by the Institute of Chartered Secretaries and Administrators, ICSA 2009

Directors' Remuneration: Report of a Study Group chaired by Sir Richard Greenbury (Greenbury Committee Report)

Executive Remuneration – ABI Guidelines on Policies and Practices (ABI 2009)

Investor Relations best practice guides, available from Investor Relations Society, www.irs.org.uk

Report of the Committee on the Financial Aspects of Corporate Governance: The Code of Best Practice (Cadbury Code)

Key Principles of Good Governance, 2010 Available from the Charity Commission www.charitycommission.gov.uk. Revises the principles first published in *Good Governance: A Code for the Voluntary and Community Sector* (2005) by the National Governance Hub (see below)

Myners, P., *Institutional Investment in the UK: A Review* (HM Treasury, 2001, updated 2007)

Sarbanes-Oxley Act of 2002, H.R. 3763

The European Commission's Action Plan for Company Law and Corporate Governance (2003)

The Stewardship Code (Financial Reporting Council (FRC) 2012)

The Tyson Report on the Recruitment and Development of Non-Executive Directors (2003)

The UK Corporate Governance Code Financial Reporting Council (FRC) 2016. The FRC also holds previous versions of the UK Combined Codes and related reviews and consultations. See also the FRC's Associated Guidance (*Turnbull and FRC Guidance on Audit Committees and Suggestions for Good Practice from the Higgs Report*). All available to download from www.frc.org.uk

Walker, Sir David, *A Review of Corporate Governance in UK Banks and Other Financial Industry Entities (Walker Review),* HM Treasury 2009, www.gov.uk/government/organisations/hm-treasury

ICSA Guidance Notes

The ICSA Policy Unit produces a range of Guidance Notes on Corporate Governance topics, including electronic communications and committee terms of reference. These are available for free for members and affiliates at www.icsa.org.uk/guidance

Magazines, journals and newsletters

Governance and Compliance
The ICSA monthly magazine carries regular updates and articles on a variety of corporate governance topics and issues. The magazine's companion website, www.icsa.org.uk/governance-and-compliance, has a searchable archive of recent features and daily news updates

The magazines published by ICSA Divisions in Malaysia, Singapore, Hong Kong and elsewhere also cover a broad range of corporate governance issues

Company Secretarial Practice (ICSA Publishing) An integrated resource, providing detailed explanation and commentary on all aspects of company law and corporate governance, and explaining how to put it into practice. There are precedents to help manage processes and procedures, together with specimen resolutions, checklists and proposed changes. Available online as CSPOnline at www.companysecretarialpracticeonline.co.uk

Corporate Governance: An International Review (Wiley-Blackwell Publishing) An academic research journal with particular emphasis on international issues

Global Proxy Watch
Monthly email or fax newsletter from Davis Global Advisors

Governance
An independent monthly newsletter, which is particularly strong on international developments. Available in print, electronically or both. Governance Publications www.governance.co.uk

Investor Relations (Cross-Border Publishing Ltd)
Monthly review with strong international coverage

Web resources

A regular review the key websites listed below will help to keep you up to date with current debates and issues

Accounting Standards Board: www.frc.org.uk/ASB.aspx
Asian Corporate Governance Association: www.acga-asia.org
Association of British Insurers: www.abi.org.uk
Association of British Insurers remuneration guidelines: www.ivis.co.uk
Business for Social Responsibility: www.bsr.org
Business in the Community: www.bitc.org.uk
Calpers www.calpers-governance.org
Charity Commission: www.charitycommission.gov.uk
Committee on Standards in Public Life, UK: www.public-standards.gov.uk
Corporate Social Responsibility: www.csr.gov.uk
Council of Institutional Investors, USA: www.cii.org
Department for Business, Innovation and Skills (BIS): www.gov.uk/government/organisations/department-for-business-innovation-skills
EIRIS (Ethical Investment Research Service): www.eiris.org
European Corporate Governance Institute: www.ecgi.org

The Financial Conduct Authority: http://www.fca.org.uk/ and the Prudential Regulation Authority: www.bankofengland.co.uk/pra
Financial Reporting Council: www.frc.org.uk: this website includes the UK Corporate Governance Code, the Stewardship Code and other FRC guidance.
G20/OECD Principles of Corporate Governance: www.oecd.org
Global Corporate Governance Forum: www.ifc.org/wps/wcm/connect/Topics_Ext_Content/IFC_External_Corporate_Site/Global+Corporate+Governance+Forum
Global Reporting Initiative: www.globalreporting.org
Hermes: www.hermes.co.uk
The Institute of Business Ethics: www.ibe.org.uk
The Institute of Chartered Secretaries and Administrators (ICSA): www.icsa.org.uk
The Institute of Directors: www.iod.com
Institutional Shareholder Services (ISS): www.issgovernance.com
International Corporate Governance Network: www.icgn.org
International Organization of Securities Commissions: www.iosco.org
Investor Relations Society: www.irs.org.uk
Investor Responsibility Research Institute: www.irrcinstitute.org
London Stock Exchange: www.londonstockexchange.com/home/homepage.htm
National Association of Corporate Directors, USA: www.nacdonline.org
National Council for Voluntary Organisations (NCVO): www.ncvo.org.uk
OECD Principles of Corporate Governance: www.oecd.org
Pensions & Investment Research Consultants Limited: www.pirc.co.uk
Pensions and Lifetime Savings Association (PLSA): www.plsa.co.uk
Public Concern at Work (Whistleblowing): www.pcaw.co.uk
Quoted Companies Alliance (QCA): www.theqca.com
Standard and Poor's (ratings): www.standardandpoors.com
SustainAbility: www.sustainability.com
GMI Ratings: www3.gmiratings.com
US Securities and Exchange Commission: www.sec.gov

Index